BLIAINIRIS ÉIREANNACH AN DLÍ IDIRNÁISIÚNTA
THE IRISH YEARBOOK OF INTERNATIONAL LAW

The Irish Yearbook of International Law is intended to stimulate further research into Ireland's practice in international affairs and foreign policy, filling a gap in existing legal scholarship and assisting in the dissemination of Irish thinking and practice on matters of international law. On an annual basis, the *Yearbook* will present peer-reviewed academic articles and book reviews on general issues of international law. Designated correspondents will provide reports on international law developments in Ireland, Irish practice in international fora and the European Union, and the practice of joint North-South implementation bodies in Ireland. In addition, the *Yearbook* will reproduce documents that reflect Irish practice on contemporary issues of international law.

Publication of *The Irish Yearbook of International Law* will make Irish practice and opinio juris more readily available to Governments, academics and international bodies when determining the content of international law. In providing a forum for the documentation and analysis of North-South relations the *Yearbook* will make an important contribution to post-conflict and transitional justice studies internationally.

As a matter of editorial policy, the *Yearbook* seeks to promote a multilateral approach to international affairs, reflecting and reinforcing Ireland's long-standing commitment to multilateralism as a core element of foreign relations.

Bliainiris Éireannach an Dlí Idirnáisiúnta

Imleabhar 1, 2006

Curtha in Eagar ag
Jean Allain agus Siobhán Ní Mhaolealaidh

·HART·
PUBLISHING

OXFORD AND PORTLAND, OREGON
2008

The Irish Yearbook of International Law

Volume 1, 2006

Edited by
Jean Allain and Siobhán Mullally

·HART·
PUBLISHING
OXFORD AND PORTLAND, OREGON
2008

Published in North America (US and Canada) by
Hart Publishing
c/o International Specialized Book Services
920 NE 58th Avenue, Suite 300
Portland, OR 97213-3786
USA
Tel: +1 503 287 3093 or toll-free: (1) 800 944 6190
Fax: +1 503 280 8832
E-mail: orders@isbs.com
Website: www.isbs.com

Hart Publishing, 16C Worcester Place, OX1 2JW
Telephone: +44 (0)1865 517530 Fax: +44 (0)1865 510710
E-mail: mail@hartpub.co.uk
Website: http://www.hartpub.co.uk

British Library Cataloguing in Publication Data
Data Available
ISBN: 978-1-84113-702-5

Typeset by Hope Services (Abingdon) Ltd
Printed and bound in Great Britain by
TJ International Ltd, Padstow, Cornwall

Editorial Board

Table of Contents

Editorial—Irish Yearbook of International Law

Jean Allain
Siobhán Mullally

The launching of the Irish Yearbook of International Law is, in many ways, long overdue.

Ireland's history since 1916, it has been noted, is the history of Irish foreign policy. Reflecting a commitment in White Paper on foreign policy, there is now an extensive body of research and scholarship exploring this history. A commitment to the peaceful settlement of disputes and to the general principles of international law is enshrined in the Constitution, *Bunreacht na hÉireann*. Irish foreign policy has always looked to international law, whether as a support for early claims to independence and more latterly to underpin its commitment to multilateralism. Membership of the United Nations has been a stalwart of Irish foreign policy, and more recently membership of the European Union. Both reflect a shift, in the words of one commentator from 'independence to internationalism'. Research and scholarship on Irish practice in international law remains, however, underdeveloped. In contrast to the rich body of literature on the history of Irish foreign policy, there is a dearth of research on international law in Ireland. The many gaps are reflected in the ambiguities surrounding the legal status of some of the bulwarks of Irish foreign policy, including membership of the United Nations and the commitment to neutrality.

For lawyers, recent publication such as of the *Documents in Irish Foreign Policy* series,—reviewed in this edition of the *Irish Yearbook*—ensure the increased accessibility of primary sources, and will facilitate further exploration of Irish practice, both domestically and in the international arena.

As a small state Ireland has played a significant role within the United Nations, notably in its contribution to peacekeeping and to international human rights law. It has often drawn on the support it can garner as a State that is situated between first and third worlds, a member of the European Union and a former colony. The specificity of this history has informed Irish practice in international law, and the idea, if not always the reality, of solidarity with poorer nations, has been a recurring theme. But there are, of course, many other influences that have shaped the direction of such practice. In earlier times, we can point to the close links with the Vatican, Ireland's concern to assert a distinct religious and cultural identity, and close links with the United States of America, both economically and culturally, built through a history of emigration. More recently, environmental concerns, and a concern, in particular, to protect the marine environment, has come to fore in Irish practice, leading to the initiation of the MOX proceedings, and ultimately to conflict with the European Commission as membership within the European Union has both shaped and constrained Irish practice. These diverse forces have often led to tensions in Irish practice, from being a State that has a policy, if not a legal commitment, to neutrality, to being a State that permits military transit of forces en route to theatres of conflict.

Internationally, Ireland has played an important role in the development of international human rights law, most recently in the lead role played to secure the adoption of the *Convention on the Rights of Persons with Disabilities.* And yet, international human rights law plays a limited role in domestic legal proceedings, as courts follow a strict dualist path, externalising international human rights obligations.

These tensions are explored in this Volume and it is hoped that the establishment of the *Irish Yearbook of International Law* will allow for ongoing reasoned debate on the complexities of Irish practice in international law.

The *Irish Yearbook of International Law* is intended to stimulate further research, filling a gap in existing legal scholarship and assisting in the dissemination of Irish thinking and practice on matters of international law. On an annual basis, the *Irish Yearbook of International Law* presents articles and book reviews on general issues of international law. Designated correspondents will provide reports on international law developments in Ireland, Irish practice in international fora and the European Union, and the practice of joint North-South implementation bodies. In addition, the *Irish Yearbook of International Law* reproduces documents that reflect Irish practice on contemporary issues of international law.

We hope that the publication of an *Irish Yearbook of International Law* will make Irish practice and *opinio juris* more readily available to other States and international bodies when determining the content of international law. As a matter of editorial policy, the *Yearbook* will seek to promote a multilateral approach to international affairs, reflecting and reinforcing Ireland's long-standing commitment to multilateralism as a core element of its foreign relations.

ARTICLES

International Environmental Law's 'Customary' Dilemma: Betwixt General Principles and Treaty Rules

David M Ong*

This article is an attempt to encapsulate the continuing difficulties faced by international environmental law as it matures into a viable field of public international law. International environmental law has now developed specific, and in many cases unique, substantive rules,[1] along with innovative procedural mechanisms to ensure compliance to these specific obligations and standards.[2] When coupled with the continuing evolution of general environmental principles, it is possible to envisage a relatively seamless international legal sub-system, consisting of over-arching general principles to guide State behaviour, together with individual treaty rules establishing specific legal obligations and standards, all of which constrain the effects of environmental damage caused by State activities. Unfortunately, this initially beguiling image of general environmental principles, suitably fleshed-out by treaty rules, and now increasingly buttressed by treaty-based non-compliance mechanisms, is undermined by continuing perceptions of a crisis engulfing international environmental law. In a nutshell, this sense of crisis arising from the apparent lack of success of international environmental law in tackling global environmental problems stems from at least two factors. First, a growing awareness within the *scientific* community of the enormity of the overall human impact on the environment that in turn generates continuing pressure for the international policy and law-making community to adopt more treaty rules and obligations to tackle these newly perceived environmental threats.[3] Second,

* Reader in International and Environmental Law, University of Essex, Wivenhoe Park, Colchester, Essex CO4 3SQ, UK. E-mail: daveo@essex.ac.uk

[1] Recent treaty regimes dealing with highly specific environmental pollution threats and wildlife species protection include the 2004 International Ballast Water Convention (Full title: the International Convention for the Control and Management of Ships Ballast Water and Sediments), adopted in London on 13 February 2004, accessible at: http://www.globallast.imo.org/index.asp; the 2001 Stockholm Convention on Persistent Organic Pollutants (POPs) Convention, adopted in Stockholm on 22 May 2001, entered into force: 17 May, 2004, accessible at: http://www.pops.int/; and the 1996 Agreement on the Conservation of Cetaceans in the Black Sea, Mediterranean Sea and Contiguous Atlantic Area (ACCOBAMS) adopted in Monaco on 24 November, 1996, accessible at: http://www.wdcs.org/; to name but a few examples of the immense variety of international environmental instruments to date.

[2] As discussed below (in Section V), the development of non-compliance mechanisms as an alternative means of ensuring the effective implementation of substantive treaty rules has occurred mainly within environmental treaty regimes. Foremost examples in this respect include the 1987 Montreal Protocol to the 1985 Vienna Convention on Substances that Deplete the Ozone Layer, the 1989 Basel Convention on the Transboundary Movement of Hazardous and Other Wastes, the 1997 Kyoto Protocol to the 1992 Framework Convention on Climate Change, and the 1998 Aarhus Convention on Access to Environmental Information, Citizen Participation in Environmental Decision-making, Access to Justice.

[3] This mainly scientific and environmental NGO-led campaign to address new and continuing environmental threats has resulted in a backlash against the need for new environmental policies and legislation. See Bjorn Lomborg, *The Skeptical Environmentalist*, Cambridge: Cambridge (2003) and Richard D North, *Life on a Modern Planet: A Manifesto for Progress* (Manchester: Manchester University Press, 1995).

a continuing *societal* perception of the relative lack of success of the now multitude of treaties addressing these environmental threats, both old and new.[4]

The following sections thus address what may been seen as the continuing *substantive* and *systemic* difficulties that undermine the development of international environmental law as a viable sub-discipline or branch of public international law. The *substantive* problems arise from the nature of the evolution of international environmental law and relate to the fact that the main principles of this still-developing body of law are to be found in either globally applicable but non-binding international environmental instruments, or individual treaties addressing specific environmental problems, or confined to a particular region; but not within a universally applicable treaty addressing global environmental threats. Whereas the *systemic* problems posed by international environmental law relate to the basic structure of public international law: as an autonomous legal system ostensibly applying to the entire international community, but which is nevertheless is reliant upon a bilateral system of dispute settlement, especially when these disputes come before judicial bodies, for the resolution of any *legal* differences within this international community.

Consideration thus turns to *substantive* and *systemic* types of problems posed by public international law to the continuing progressive development of international environmental law in the following manner. First, by examining the provenance of the most significant international environmental principles (Section I) and tracing the apparent difficulties encountered in both the articulation and application of these *substantive* environmental principles in relevant judgments of international tribunals (Sections II and IV). This reluctance on the part of various international tribunals to consider the specific application of these environmental principles to disputes brought before them is contrasted with their continuing implementation as specific treaty rules within an ever growing number of treaties (Section III). Throughout this exercise, expression will be given to the extent to which international law generally, and international environmental law specifically, fulfils what must be their ultimate combined goal: to protect the 'environment' in its entirety, including both its human and non-human or 'natural' elements, as well as those aspects of the 'environment' that are of equal concern to both of these, namely, the quality of air, water and soil within the 'environment'. Second, this study highlights the *systemic* discrepancies in the development of international environmental law in relevant international environmental instruments by noting the difficulties raised by the fact that specific treaty rules are unable to transcend their individual treaty status to become generally applicable rules of customary international law, unless suitably articulated as such by a globally codifying treaty exercise, or by virtue of confirming international court or tribunal judgments.

Having completed the diagnostic elements of the analysis, consideration then turns to the two main methods in which international environmental law has sought to improve its record of achievement of its objectives and implementation of its principles, namely, through the establishment of environmental treaty compliance mechanisms (in

[4] The most recent high profile report claiming to expose the lack of success of the environmental movement is Michael Shellenberger and Ted Nordhaus, *The Death of Environmentalism: Global Warming Politics in a Post-Environmental World*, released at an October 2004 meeting of the (US) Environmental Grantmakers Association. Accessible at: www.grist.org/news/. See also Adam Werbach's speech 'Is Environmentalism Dead?', which is at least partly in response to the above report, given at the Commonwealth Club of San Francisco (US) on 8 December 2004 and accessible at www.grist.org/news.

Section V) and efforts aimed at the development of a human right to a healthy environment (in Section VI). These two types of response to the dilemma facing international environmental law are assessed in terms of their potential to remedy the *substantive* and *systemic* problems identified earlier on in the study. Emanating from this is a consideration of the reasons for the continuing sense of uncertainty among international legal academics, practitioners, governments and even judicial bodies, both international and domestic, as to the legal status and application of the main principles of international environmental law.

This consideration of the underlying uncertainties afflicting international environmental law begins by observing that this field of public international law has developed on two main fronts. On the one hand, through the articulation of a set of general principles aimed at guiding States towards ensuring environmental protection; and on the other hand, through the adoption of specific treaty regimes addressing particular environmental problems, often through the establishment of detailed and technical international regulatory regimes aimed at controlling specific environmental threats. Both these trends are now well-established and can be seen as supporting each other through the development of an overall international legal framework providing for both specific treaty rules to address particular environmental problems and general environmental principles that serve as authoritative interpretive guidelines to fill the gaps and resolve any uncertainties that may remain both between and within these specific environmental treaty regimes. These environmental principles are also meant to govern State behaviour in their daily interaction with other States in the international arena, where these interactions can result in adverse environmental change.

The overall goal or objective of this general and specific interaction between environmental principles and specific environmental treaty rules and standards within the legal sub-discipline of international environmental law is the achievement of 'sustainable development'.[5] Among the most well-known and well-accepted (by States, if not necessarily well-implemented) of these environmental principles are as follows: 1) the environmental integration principle,[6] entailing the inclusion of environmental considerations within socio-economic development activities; 2) the preventive and precautionary principles,[7] providing that such activities do not cause environmental harm or damage; 3) the polluter-pays principle,[8] requiring that the polluter should pay

[5] 'Sustainable development' was first authoritatively defined as: 'development that satisfies the needs of present generations without compromising the ability of future generations to meet their own needs', by the World Commission on Environment and Development (WCED) led by Gro Harlem Brundtland, the former Norwegian Prime Minister. See WCED, *Our Common Future* (Oxford, OUP, 1987) at 43.

[6] Principle 4 of the 1992 Rio Inter-Governmental Declaration on Environment and Development, defines this principles as follows: 'In order to achieve sustainable development, environmental protection shall constitute an integral part of the development process and cannot be considered in isolation from it'.

[7] These two principles are increasingly taken together and constitute the single most important principle for environmental protection as they embody the imperative requirement of environmental law for *a priori* measures to prevent harm to the environment, rather than *ex post facto*, reactive responses providing for responsibility and liability to compensate for remedial measures to be taken for damaged environments. Principle 15 of the Rio Declaration provides that, '(I)n order to protect the environment, the precautionary approach shall be widely applied by States according to their capabilities. Where there are threats of serious and irreversible damage, lack of full scientific certainty shall not be used as a reason for postponing cost-effective measures to prevent environmental degradation'.

[8] There are different conceptions of this principle, ranging from a simple, but arguably simplistic, interpretation requiring the actual polluter to be liable for the environmental consequences of their activities, to the more sophisticated interpretation that envisages this principle as the application of a well-known concept within economics of requiring the internalisation of environmental costs incurred from polluting

for the environmentally damaging aspects of their activities; 4) the environmental impact assessment principle,[9] providing that the environmental impact of proposed socio-economic activities is fully accounted for; and 5) the principle of public participation on environmental issues in decision-making processes relating to such socio-economic development activities.[10]

These principles are now well-accepted by States both in terms of their legal status as applicable environmental 'principles' and their commonly accepted meanings. However, their specific implementation, both between and within States, as required of customary international environmental 'rules' remains in doubt. The continuing legal difficulties raised by these principles for the progressive development of international environmental 'rules' (as opposed to 'principles') of law are two-fold in nature. First, they are usually articulated in non-legally binding international instruments such as Declarations, Resolutions and Programmes of Action. Second, the question arises as to whether these environmental 'principles', currently articulated in 'general' terms within these international instruments, have developed into much more normatively significant 'rules' of customary international law, containing specific rights and duties for individual States in the environmental protection field.

Within this context, several eminent commentators have examined the still arguably 'soft' law status of these environmental principles with a view to determining their precise legal nature under international law. Boyle, for example, observes that they 'may lack the supposedly harder edge of a "rule" or an "obligation", but they are certainly not legally irrelevant. As such they constitute a very important form of law, which may be "soft", but which should not be confused with "non-binding" law'.[11] In a more recent study on normative hierarchy in international law, focusing inter alia on soft law, Shelton, too, notes the inherent paradox of such allegedly non-legally binding instruments in that they nevertheless allow conforming States to put political pressure on dissenting states into conforming to the soft law norms contained within these instruments. However, she cautions that generally, 'States cannot demand that others conform to legal norms the latter have not accepted'.[12] Shelton therefore concludes that 'nonbinding norms and informal social norms can be effective and offer a flexible and efficient way to order responses to common problems. They are not law and

activities that are usually left to society as a whole to absorb. Principle 16 of the 1992 Rio Declaration favours the latter approach: 'National authorities should endeavour to promote the internalisation of environmental costs and the use of economic instruments, taking into account the approach that the polluter should, in principle, bear the cost of pollution . . .'.

[9] This principle is now provided for in numerous multilateral, bilateral and domestic environmental instruments. In the 1992 Rio Declaration, Principle 17 provides that 'Environmental impact assessment, as a national instrument, shall be undertaken for proposed activities that are likely to have significant adverse impact on the environment . . .'.

[10] Principle 10 of the Rio Declaration provides as follows: 'Environmental issues are best handled with participation of all concerned citizens, at the relevant level. At the national level, each individual shall have appropriate access to environmental information concerning the environment that is held by public authorities, including information on hazardous materials and activities in their communities, and the opportunity to participate in decision-making processes. States shall facilitate and encourage public awareness and participation by making information widely available. Effective access to judicial and administrative proceedings, including redress and remedy, shall be provided'.

[11] Alan Boyle, 'Some Reflections on the Relationship of Treaties and Soft Law', *International and Comparative Law Quarterly*, Vol 48, Part 4 (October 1999) 901–913, at 907.

[12] Dinah Shelton, 'Normative Hierarchy in International Law', *American Journal of International Law*, Vol 100, No 2 (April 2006) 291–323, at 319.

they do not need to be in order to influence conduct in the desired manner'.[13] The flexibility of such environmental principles, due to the non-legally binding nature of their sources and their hortatory rather than imperative language, does however come at a price. This price is their uncertain legal status under international law: Are they general 'principles' or specific customary 'rules' of international environmental law?

Several of these environmental principles have now also been invoked by States in the context of legal claims against other States adjudicated before international tribunals. As Boyle observes in this respect, they 'may lay down parameters which affect the way courts decide cases or the way an international institution exercises its discretionary powers. They can set limits, or provide guidance, or determine how conflicts between other rules or principles will be resolved'.[14]

The continuing difficulty identified here is to translate these environmental principles in such a way as to be able to provide a clear delineation of their implications upon traditional international law concepts such as State sovereignty. In this respect, judicial pronouncements from international tribunals seized of these issues arguably leave much to be desired in terms of confirming the global application of these principles as rules of customary international law above and beyond the environmental treaty regimes where these principles are re-iterated as specific rules. Indeed, the analysis below, in Sections II and IV, of a number of significant cases before different international tribunals, namely, the International Court of Justice, the WTO Panels and Appellate Body and the International Tribunal for the Law of the Sea, suggests that there is a lack of confirming jurisprudence in favour of the application of significant environmental principles, such that there is arguably a lack of a certain 'animating spirit' within international environmental law. This lack of an 'animating spirit' does not allow these undoubtedly well-accepted, but generally-worded and in themselves non-binding, environmental principles to be applied in such a way that they can transcend their specific articulation within individual environmental treaties, and facilitate their transition to rules of customary international law providing for environmental protection. Such customary rules of international environmental law can then be employed or utilised by international tribunals to better decide so-called 'hard cases', entailing consideration of specific international legal limitations on State sovereignty and consequentially also over the autonomy and discretion usually afforded to States over potentially environmentally damaging activities within their territories, or subject to their jurisdiction or control.

Unfortunately, this is simply not the case at the present time. More worrying, it is suggested here, is that the reason why international tribunals are apparently reluctant to confirm the place of such well-known environmental 'principles' as applicable 'rules' within the customary international law between States is due to the reality that there is precious little evidence from domestic State practice alone that States abide by, and perhaps more important, actually implement, these general environmental principles fully, both as between themselves, and within their domestic legal regimes. This is so even where these principles are now articulated more specifically in individual treaty regimes, addressing particular environmental problems identified for concerted action by these very same States. Constant and uniform, if not universal, implementation of these environmental principles is still found to be wanting. This suggests that

[13] Shelton, above n 12, at 322.

[14] Boyle, above, n 11, at 907, and also his references in n 1, at 901.

States have actually accepted these principles merely as guidance for their domestic environmental policies, rather than implementation within their environmental laws.

Thus, a number of critical questions regarding the legal status and application of these general environmental principles remain unanswered. Have they transcended their status as environmental 'principles' to become 'rules', such that they should now be directly applicable to States as part of customary international law? Perhaps more importantly, where these environmental principles have been invoked in disputes between States, have they been confirmed as the applicable customary international rules by the international tribunals tasked with adjudicating between such disputing States? Or, do they remain only general environmental principles, and thereby act as mere guidelines for State behaviour in the environmental policy-making field, without the obligatory character inherent to rules of customary international law? To paraphrase de Sadeleer, have these general environmental principles made the successful transition from 'political slogans to legal rules'[15]? Moreover, if they have successfully become legal rules—what kind of international obligations do they entail? Do they convey the traditional, bilateral type of international obligation, owed only as between individual States? Or, as advocated by certain international environmental lawyers, do they form over-arching multilateral rules entailing *erga omnes* obligations on the basis that *all* States have an interest in global environmental protection.

This latter type of obligation is arguably still nascent in its development, even within general international law.[16] As Fitzmaurice notes, 'many aspects of the legal character of *erga omnes* obligations are still arguable', and furthermore, that it is 'unclear the extent to which States are responsible in relation to the environment towards the community of States generally'.[17] The precise legal implications of such *erga omnes* obligations have yet to be spelt out by any international tribunal. Since the development of international environmental principles, apart from the 'golden' or primary rule against transboundary environmental damage (considered below in Section I), are almost by definition meant to be *erga omnes* in their application, it is interesting to note that the International Court of Justice (ICJ) declined an opportunity to enunciate on this very issue in respect of the Australian application to intervene in the 1995 *Nuclear Tests* case, brought by New Zealand against France.[18] Moreover, the further question as to whether *erga omnes* obligations (even where they can be proved to apply to a particular situation) in turn give rise to the exercise of an *actio popularis* right by any State to enforce such obligations was also not addressed by the ICJ in the initial, 1974, *Nuclear Tests* cases.[19]

[15] See Nicolas de Sadeleer, *Environmental Principles: From Political Slogans to Legal Rules* (Oxford, Oxford University Press, 2002).

[16] See Maurizio Ragazzi, *Erga Omnes Obligations and International Law* (Oxford, Oxford University Press, 2000). More recently, see Christian Tams, *Enforcing Obligations Erga Omnes under International Law* (Cambridge, Cambridge University Press, 2005).

[17] Malgosia Fitzmaurice, 'International Responsibility and Liability', in Daniel Bodansky, Jutta Brunnée and Ellen Hey (eds), *The Oxford Handbook of International Environmental Law* (Oxford, Oxford University Press, 2007) 1010–1035, at 1011 and 1020–22.

[18] See Request for an Examination of the Situation in Accordance with para 63 of the Court's Judgment of 20 December 1974 in the Nuclear Tests (*New Zealand v France*) case, ICJ Reports (1995) 288. The Australian application to intervene was on the basis that the obligations allegedly owed by France to New Zealand were of an *erga omnes* character. A fuller consideration of the legal implications of this case is considered in Section IV below.

[19] *Nuclear Tests Cases* (*Australia v France, New Zealand v France*), *ICJ Rep* (1974) 253, at 387.

The dilemma that international environmental law now finds itself in as a result of the lack of authoritative judicial decisions and confirming State practice as to the binding legal status of important environmental principles is at least in part due to these *substantive* and *systemic* problems inherent to the discipline of public international law itself, which raise particular problems for the field of international environmental law. Chief among these is the *substantive* legal issue that the generally applicable environmental principles are contained within non-binding international instruments and therefore can only act as a guide and not an imperative of inter-State behaviour, whereas the specific rules and obligations are contained within treaty regimes and therefore struggle to transcend the bounds of the individual treaties and their parties to inform and bind all States as a matter of general or customary international law, alongside the general principles and specific treaty rules. As Sands notes, the 'international community has not adopted a binding international instrument of global application which purports to set out the general rights and obligations of the international community on environmental matters'.[20]

Unlike, for example, human rights law or trade law, environmental law does not have an all-encompassing global treaty regime that provides general rules for global protection. Both the above sub-disciplines of public international law are governed by rules articulated within globally applicable multilateral treaties: the 1966 Covenant on Civil and Political Rights in respect of the international protection of human rights and the 1994 World Trade Organization Agreement and 1947/1994 General Agreement on Tariffs and Trade in respect of world trade law. However, there is no equivalent, globally applicable, multilateral instrument codifying the general international legal principles for environmental protection, save perhaps for the 1992 Rio Declaration on Environment and Development, which is strictly speaking, a non-binding international instrument. Nor should this observation be taken to mean that efforts should be commenced in this regard. As Moltke warns, any 'attempt to develop a broader international agreement applicable to all international environmental regimes is necessarily fraught with risk: asked to codify current practice some countries are likely to seek to limit it'.[21]

Thus, the general environmental principles articulated within the Rio Declaration, which States re-affirmed their commitment to in the 2002 World Summit on Sustainable Development,[22] nevertheless have to be independently shown as binding upon States under customary international law. Such a requirement almost inevitably leaves the international environmental lawyer attempting to rely on these principles as authoritative under international law on the back foot, in the sense that they are then charged with the burden of proof to show that the specific environmental principle they are relying upon is both globally applicable and legally binding on the opposing

[20] Philippe Sands, *Principles of International Environmental Law*, 2nd edn (Cambridge, Cambridge University Press, 2003) at 234.

[21] Konrad von Moltke, 'Clustering International Environmental Agreements as an Alternative to a World Environment Organization', in Frank Biermann and Steffen Bauer (eds) *A World Environment Organization: Solution or Threat for Effective International Environmental Governance* (Aldershot, Ashgate, 2005) 175–204, at 196.

[22] See para 8 of the Johannesburg Declaration on Sustainable Development, adopted as an Annex to Resolution 1 (Political Declaration) at the 17th plenary meeting of the WSSD on 4 September 2002. For access to all documentation arising from this Summit, also known as Rio+10, or the Johannesburg Summit, see: *Report of the World Summit on Sustainable Development*, Johannesburg, South Africa, 26 August to 4 September 2002. Doc A/CONF.199/20 (re-issued) at: http://www.wssd.org.

State in the instant case before the international tribunal concerned. As Sands admits, any 'effort to identify general principles and rules of international environmental law must necessarily be based on a considered assessment of State practice, including the adoption and implementation of treaties and other international legal acts, as well as the growing number of decisions of international courts and tribunals'.[23] Fitzmaurice is even more explicit, noting that '. . ., the content of many of the fundamental primary environmental rules remains vague and subject to significant disagreement between States . . .',[24] citing sustainable development, inter-generational equity and the precautionary principle as examples of such disagreements.

This exercise in determining the actual *substantive* 'rules', as opposed to 'principles' of international environmental law is almost always a difficult task to perform in the absence of a globally-accepted treaty providing for their universal application; or consistent State practice, based on a common understanding of these 'principles', as being both applicable and binding 'rules' on the individual State(s) concerned. This is due to the paramount difficulty of discerning a cumulative and collective state of mind on the part of States for the fulfilment of the psychological aspect of customary international law, normally expressed as *opinio juris sive necessitates*. This in turn highlights the *systemic* problem inherent in public international law, namely that it is ultimately reliant upon a bilaterally-oriented judicial dispute settlement system for the resolution of differences between its principal actors—the States, whereas international environmental law has as its principal aim nothing less than the protection of the global environment in its entirety.

I. THE PAUCITY OF CUSTOMARY INTERNATIONAL LAW FOR GLOBAL ENVIRONMENTAL PROTECTION

The strictly speaking non-binding nature of many well-known environmental principles merely serves to highlight a deeper malaise afflicting the *corpus* of international environmental law. This more serious affliction is caused by the relative paucity of specifically-worded customary international 'rules', as opposed to more generally-worded 'principles', for ensuring environmental protection. Indeed, the reality of the sum total of customary international law on environmental protection is that it contains only one primary or 'golden' rule that is agreed and accepted as binding by all States, apparently without exception. This 'golden' rule was initially articulated and applied in the *Trail Smelter* arbitration (1938–41) between the United States and Canada, holds that under 'the principles of international law [. . .] no State has a right to use or permit the use of its territory in such a manner as to cause injury by fumes in or to the territory of another (State) of the properties or persons therein, when the case is of serious consequence and the injury is established by clear and convincing evidence'.[25] This golden rule has also been expressed in terms of the well known prin-

[23] Philippe Sands (2003), above n 20.

[24] Fizmaurice (2007), above, n 17, at 1017.

[25] *Trail Smelter* case (*United States v Canada*) Reports of the International Arbitration Awards (RIAA) Vol 3 (1941) at 1907. Also at 33 *American Journal of International Law (AJIL)* 182 (1939) and 35 *AJIL* 684 (1941). For an extended discussion of the implications of this case for international law generally, see the collection of essays in Rebecca M Bratspies and Russell A Miller (eds) *Transboundary Harm in International Law: Lessons from the Trail Smelter Arbitration* (Cambridge, Cambridge University Press, 2006).

ciple of Roman law, namely, *sic utero tuo alienum non laedas*—one must use his own so as not to damage that of another. Sands has little doubt as to the legal status of this rule as part of customary international law.[26] Benvenisti however exposes the fairly sparse legal authority on which this golden rule is built upon, noting that absent:

> clear pronouncements of this principle by other international tribunals, the tribunal followed 'by analogy' in the footsteps of three decisions handed down by the US Supreme Court. . . . Despite meagre evidence of State practice to support the decision, the norm prescribed was never questioned. It has since become a cornerstone of international environmental law.[27]

Moreover, while the golden rule under customary international law enunciated here is plainly applicable by analogy to any environmental damage in the territory of a State caused by activities within the territory of another State, it is instructive to note that in the actual *Trail Smelter* decision, Canada's international liability was limited to compensation in the form of property damage to cleared and un-cleared privately-owned land, used for crops and timber.[28] Indeed, further heads of claim in respect of damage to livestock and to 'business enterprise' by the US government were denied.[29] In other words, inter-State liability at the time was confined to the traditional heads for claims under tort law. This was limited to physical injury to persons and property damage, and did not even include so-called 'economic loss'. So-called 'pure' environmental damage, also known as ecological damage, to the natural (non-anthropocentric) elements of the environment, including loss or damage to wildlife and reduction of air, water and soil quality was neither claimed for,[30] nor indeed recognised as a viable head of claim under either tort law or international liability law at the time.

Redgwell neatly encapsulates the conceptual difficulties faced when attempting to expand the principle applied in the *Trail Smelter* decision to situations involving transboundary *environmental* damage, when she notes that traditional 'rules of State responsibility may also be criticised regarding their application in the environmental field, both in terms of the requirement for an "injured State" and in terms of the essentially incidental character of environmental protection to the primary complaint of damage to recognised economic (property) interests'.[31] More recently, Fitzmaurice observes presciently that the possible expansion of the 'injured State' concept to include third States wishing to redress breaches of *erga omnes* obligations under Article 48 of the 2001 International Legal Commission Articles on State Responsibility 'has not overcome the classical bilateralism of the redress of harm between States'.[32]

[26] Sands (2003), above n 20, at 241–2.

[27] Eyal Benvenisti, 'Customary International Law as a Judicial Tool for Promoting Efficiency', in Eyal Benvenisti and Moshe Hirsch (eds) *The Impact of International Law on International Co-operation: Theoretical Perspectives* (Cambridge, Cambridge University Press, 2004) at 94.

[28] *Trail Smelter Arbitration* (*US v Canada*), *RIAA* (1941), above, n 25, at 1907. The initial 1938 Tribunal decision allocated damages for the destruction of 'merchantable' timber only in relation to the impairment of the value of the land on which the trees had stood.

[29] *Trail Smelter*, above, n 25, at 1924–31.

[30] In fact, a claim for 'special damage' in respect of soil impairment through acidification, from sulphur dioxide (SO_2) either directly from fumes, or indirectly through various freshwater sources, was entertained but was held not to be proved, with one exception, involving a small farming property. Even here, 'the measure of damage was not the mere reduction in the value of the use of the land but the reduction in the value in the land itself'. See 1938 *Trail Smelter* Arbitral Tribunal Decision, above, n 28.

[31] Catherine Redgwell, *Intergenerational Trusts and Environmental Protection* (Manchester University Press, 1999) at 3, fn 11.

[32] Fitzmaurice (2007) above, n 17, at 1021, citing the Article 48 of the 2001 ILC Articles on Responsibility of States for Internationally Wrongful Acts (ILC Responsibility Articles)

This primary or golden rule against transboundary harm was re-iterated, albeit again in a non-environmental context involving damage and loss of life suffered on board British warships exercising their right of innocent passage in the *Corfu Channel case* (1949) between the UK and Albania, before the International Court of Justice. Here, it was enunciated as follows: Every State has an obligation 'not to allow its territory to be used for acts contrary to the rights of other States'.[33] This formulation of the golden rule has been affirmed by subsequent State practice in the form of international policy pronouncements, and its inclusion in treaties so that it is now in itself clearly accepted as part of customary international law. However, as Boyle notes, since 'then there has been only limited judicial elaboration at an international level, and the precise character of this elementary concept remains unsettled'.[34]

Thus, following these initial international judicial decisions that in themselves do not specify the primary international legal obligation for transboundary *environmental* (as opposed to personal injury and property) damage, the forum for the enunciation of this principle moved to that of the global international policy-making stage in the form of the 1972 Stockholm Conference on the Human Environment. Here, an expanded version of this principle was included as Principle 21 of the Stockholm Declaration adopted at the conclusion of the eponymous Conference, as follows: 'States have, [. . .] the sovereign right to exploit their own natural resources [. . .] and the responsibility to ensure that activities within their jurisdiction or control do not cause damage to the environment of other States or of areas beyond the limits of national jurisdiction'. The principle was re-iterated in Principle 2 of the 1992 Rio Declaration on Environment and Development, with further small but not insignificant additions to the enunciation of the Principle. As Tan notes, 'Principle 2 differs slightly in two respects: it provides for States to have the sovereign right to exploit their own *resources* (Principle 21 having referred to *natural resources*) pursuant to their own environmental *and developmental* policies (Principle 21 having referred only to environmental policies.) The reference to developmental policies was an explicit recognition of the growing importance attached to socio-economic development, especially by the developing countries, by the time of the 1992 UN Conference on Environment and Development (UNCED) was convened in Rio de Janeiro'.[35]

A further, slightly different version of the amended and expanded upon golden rule is also included under the chapeau 'Principle', within Article 3 of the Biodiversity Convention,[36] adopted at the very same Rio Conference in 1992. Here, the rule replicates the expansive change in wording from 'natural resources' (in Principle 21 of Stockholm) to 'resources' (in Principle 2 of Rio) but then retains the sovereign right of States to exploit such 'resources' in accordance with their 'environmental policies' (in Principle 21), rather than their 'environmental and developmental policies' (in Principle 2). Within the context of the negotiations to this Convention, the expansion of the scope of the sovereign rights of exploitation from 'natural resources' to 'resources' can be explained in terms of the attempts by developing countries to

[33] *Corfu Channel* case (*UK v Albania*) *ICJ Rep* (1949) 4, at 22.

[34] AE Boyle, 'Globalising Environmental Liability: The Interplay of National and International Law', *Journal of Environmental Law*, Vol 17, No 1 (2005) 3–26, at 3.

[35] Tan (1999) below, n 56, at 835.

[36] Full title: Convention on Biological Diversity, adopted in Rio de Janeiro, Brazil on 5 June, 1992; entered into force on 29 December, 1993. Source: 31 *ILM* 822 (1992) Accessible at: http://www.biodiv.org/

encompass intellectual property rights derived from the application of scientific techniques to the bio-genetic resources originating from their territories within the concept of 'resources'.[37] Notwithstanding the specific reasons why this slightly different, but possibly legally significant, wording was employed in the Biodiversity Convention, it should be noted that the legal status of the present principle is certainly enhanced by its inclusion in a globally applicable treaty, which presently numbers more than 180 States parties.[38] This is despite its arguably specific focus, *inter alia*, on the conservation and sustainable use of biological diversity, rather than general environmental protection.[39]

Apart from the small changes noted above, Principle 21/Principle 2 also clearly expands the scope of the previously obtaining golden rule under customary international law in at least three significant ways. These are as follows: first, the inclusion of the phrase 'jurisdiction or control' can be argued to considerably expand the potential scope of a State's obligation under international law beyond merely actions or omissions undertaken within its territorial jurisdiction. More far-reaching albeit controversial interpretations of this phrase would seek to include the activities of a State's flagship vessels, whether publicly or privately owned, on the basis that under the 1982 UN Law of the Sea Convention, for example, the flag State's civil and criminal law jurisdiction prevails over that vessel even in the (territorial sea and exclusive economic zone) waters of another State, save for internal waters. Indeed, the notion of activities within a State's 'control' can be argued to encompass even the damaging activities in one State of subsidiary companies of a parent company residing or registered in another State, assuming the home State can be implicated in the actions or omissions of the parent company concerned. Such arguments were raised in the context of the 1984 Bhopal (Union Carbide) disaster in India, for example.[40] On the other hand, it is important to note the apparent disjuncture between calls by the international community to further clarify the liability of States for transboundary damage and the reluctance of States to accept their individual responsibility and liability for such damage when it occurs. Boyle exposes this dichotomy when he notes that the re-commencement of the ILC work on this issue was almost surely due to a UN General Assembly request to this effect, but that at the same time State practice indicated a lack of acceptance of strict liability for transboundary harm.[41]

Second, the scope of the notion of harm from activities across international borders has been conceptually expanded to incorporate transboundary damage to the 'environment'. This paves the way for international recognition and acceptance by States of an extension of the golden or primary rule to damage inflicted upon the 'natural' or wildlife/ecosystem aspects of the 'environment'. This would be in addition to the traditional anthropocentric conceptions of environmental damage, which are in the main

[37] On this issue, see Jayan Nayar and David M Ong, 'Developing Countries, "Development" and the Conservation of Biological Diversity', in Michael Bowman and Catherine Redgwell (eds) *International Law and the Conservation of Biological Diversity* (London, Kluwer Law International), 235–53.

[38] As of 30 December 2006 there are 189 parties to this Convention, not including the United States, which remains only a signatory State to this Convention. See: http://www. cbd.int/

[39] At least according to Article 1 of this Convention. Cf however Sands, who notes that this provision was included within the text of the treaty (rather than merely within its Preamble) 'without express limitation to matters within the scope of the Convention'. See Sands (2003), above, n 20, at 244.

[40] See, for example, Upendra Baxi and Amita Dhanda, *Valiant Victims and Lethal Litigation. The Bhopal Case* (Bombay, NM Tripathi, 1990).

[41] Boyle (2005) above, n 34, at 5–6.

limited to human health and property concerns. As Fitzmaurice notes, '. . . the contemporary concept of harm arguably encompasses not only injury to persons and property, but also to the intrinsic value of the environment, including individual components and whole ecosystems'.[42] Allowance must however be made for the fact that in some respects these so-called 'human' and 'natural' environmental concerns are coincident, for example, in the context of concern over the deterioration of air, water, and soil quality standards. Thus, environmentalist attempts to distinguish between the so-called 'natural' and 'human' aspects of the 'environment' can be seen as artificial and arguably counter-productive to the overall cause of environmental protection. A further problem in this respect is the different thresholds for establishing a possible breach of this primary obligation within successive articulations of the 'golden' rule first in the international case law and then within the Stockholm and Rio Declarations. In this context, it will be recalled that the original *Trail Smelter* formulation laid down a threshold for transboundary injury of 'serious consequence' and further held that this injury must be 'established by clear and convincing evidence'. Whereas as Fitzmaurice notes, neither Principle 21 nor Principle 2 of the Stockholm and Rio Declarations, respectively, 'include any references to a threshold of harm'.[43]

On the other hand, the belated recognition of the possibility of damage to the 'natural' aspects of the 'environment' from human activities does not render the consequent task of valuing such damage any easier to undertake.[44] Shaw's comment on the relative success of efforts to expand the concept of transboundary harm in this respect is both succinct and quite apt: 'The type of harm that is relevant clearly now extends beyond damage to property, but problems do remain with regard to general environmental injury that cannot be defined in material form'.[45] Nevertheless, environmental law and economics are progressing well in arriving at a legally viable definition of 'pure' environmental or ecological damage and how this can be valued in strict monetary terms.[46] In this respect, the work of the United Nations Compensation Commission established in the aftermath of the 1991 Gulf War has made significant contributions to the definition and valuation of damage to natural resources and the

[42] Fitzmaurice (2007) above, n 17, at 1015, citing Boyle, 'Reparation for Environmental Damage in International Law: Some Preliminary Problems' in Michael Bowman and Alan Boyle (eds) *Environmental Damage in International and Comparative Law: Problems of Definition and Valuation*, (Oxford, Oxford University Press, 2002) at 17.

[43] Fitzmaurice (2007) above, n 17, at 1015.

[44] See David Ong, 'The Relationship between Pollution and Environmental Damage', in Bowman and Boyle (eds) (2002) above, n 42, at 191–212.

[45] Malcolm Shaw, *International Law*, 5th edn, (Cambridge, Cambridge University Press, 2003) at 767, citing both the successful Canadian claim for clean-up costs arising from the crash landing of a Soviet Union nuclear-powered satellite, Cosmos 954 in Canadian land territory (18 International Legal Materials (1979) at 902–30) which was settled on 2 April 1981, when the (then) USSR agreed to pay Canada $3 million Canadian Dollars in 'full and final' settlement of the Canadian claim, and UN Security Council Resolution 687 (1991) adopted in the aftermath of the Gulf War declaring that Iraq was liable under international law inter alia 'for any direct loss, damage, including environmental damage and the depletion of natural resources' as a result of the unlawful invasion, occupation and attempted annexation of Kuwait. (S/RES/687, adopted on 3 May 1991).

[46] See Louise Angelique de La Fayette, 'New Approaches for Addressing Damage to the Marine Environment', *International Journal of Marine and Coastal Law*, Vol 20, No 2 (September 2005) 167–224, as well as her previous work on the general aspects of this issue: de La Fayette, 'The Concept of Environmental Damage in International Liability Regimes' in Bowman and Boyle (eds) (2002), above, n 42, at 149–189.

environment,[47] including the costs of monitoring and assessing such environmental damage.[48]

Third, the golden or primary rule was expanded in terms of its geographical scope to 'areas beyond national jurisdiction'. Part XII of the 1982 UN Convention on the Law of the Sea on the Protection and Preservation of the Marine Environment contains yet another, even more extensive formulation of this rule, enunciated in Article 194(2) of the above instrument as follows:

> States shall take all measures necessary to ensure that activities under their jurisdiction or control are so conducted as not to cause damage by pollution to other States and their environment, and that pollution arising from incidents or activities under their jurisdiction or control does not spread beyond the areas where they exercise sovereign rights in accordance with this Convention.

This formulation of the expanded version of the 'golden' rule also appears to attach an *erga omnes* element to this primary obligation between States, at least in relation to marine pollution damage, in the sense that this obligation is apparently owed to all 'other States'. However, this arguably falls short of forming an adequate legal basis for *actio popularis* claims by any State, on behalf of natural environmental protection in areas of beyond national jurisdiction, against polluting activities. In this context, Fitzmaurice also notes the additional procedural requirements of consent for legal standing before international tribunals and the establishment of a well-defined legal interest, both of which render more difficult the possibility of claims for State responsibility over environmental damage to global commons areas such as the high seas.

The legal implications of all these conceptual innovations are significant for the progressive development of the international environmental law field but serious questions arise as to exactly how far these newer formulations of the so-called 'golden' rule have modified its original formulation as a purely inter-State rule designed to assign international tort liability under traditional headings of compensation such as personal injury and property damage. The immediate question posed here therefore is as to whether this undeniably expanded conception of the so-called 'golden' rule now provided for in Principle 21/Principle 2 commands the same level of binding authority under customary international law as the previous version most famously articulated and applied in the *Trail Smelter* and *Corfu Channel* decisions? In other words, the uncertainties arising from the scope and depth of the newer formulations of the so-called golden or primary rule that is apparently now encapsulated within Principle 21/Principle 2, strongly suggest that the original formulation of the 'golden' rule has been overshadowed to such an extent that it should not necessarily be presumed any longer that the Principle 21/Principle 2 formulation of this rule in fact constitutes the same 'golden' rule that was previously well-accepted as customary international law. Thus, Principle 21/Principle 2 should be considered to be a new, crystallising rule of customary international law governing transboundary harm, both to other national

[47] For an account of the UNCC's work in relation to environmental damage, see Mojtaba Katzazi, 'Environmental Damage in the Practice of the UNCC', in Bowman and Boyle (eds) (2002) above, n 42, at 111–131.

[48] Olufemi Elias, 'The UN Compensation Commission and Liability for the Costs of Monitoring and Assessment of Environmental Damage', Chapter 12 in Malgosia Fitzmaurice and Danesh Sarooshi (eds), *Issues of State Responsibility Before International Judicial Institutions: The Clifford Chance Lectures* (Oxford, Hart, 2004) 219–236.

jurisdictions and areas beyond all national jurisdictions. As such, it is suggested here that the Principle 21/Principle 2 formulation of this arguably crystallising, new customary rule requires the provision of further evidence of application by State practice and judicial support of the full extent of its implications (as discussed above) to establish its independent legal authority as the principal customary rule of international environmental law.

When considering the responses of various international judicial bodies that have pronounced on this issue, the answer is at best, mixed. For example, the 1996 Advisory Opinion of the ICJ on the *Legality of the Threat or Use by a State of Nuclear Weapons in Armed Conflict*, notes that the 'existence of the general obligation of States to ensure that activities within their jurisdiction and control respect the environment of other States or of areas beyond national control is now part of the *corpus* of international law relating to the environment'.[49] A number of points can be made in response to this judicial statement. First, it is important to note that this statement is contained within an Advisory Opinion of the ICJ.[50] As such, it is almost by definition *obiter dicta* and therefore arguably addressed only *in abstracto* to all States. Its legal status is clearly non-binding in respect of any individual State. Indeed, although the ICJ has asserted its discretion to provide an Advisory Opinion even where the Request for this Opinion relates to a legal question actually pending between certain States, it also clarified in the same paragraph that the 'Court's reply is only of an advisory character: as such it has no binding force'.[51] Moreover, within such an Advisory Opinion, the Court is only really concerned to lay down the applicable rule, rather than specify the actual standard of behaviour by an individual State, which if breached would raise issues of State responsibility and possible liability for any environmental damage incurred.

It would be interesting to see precisely how the ICJ would articulate the standard of behaviour that would need to be breached, or conversely the due diligence requirement that would need to be fulfilled, before international responsibility and consequent liability could be imputed upon an individual State in a true international dispute involving a legal claim brought by one State against another on the basis of environmental damage sustained within the claimant State, as a result of activities taking place within the territory (or jurisdiction or control) of the other State. In this respect, it should also be noted that when it was given an opportunity to do so in contentious proceedings between Hungary and Slovakia in the *Gabcikovo-Nagymaros* case a year later, the Court did not elaborate on the legal implications of the above finding of the general obligation enunciated above, preferring to content itself merely with repeating the statement it had made in the previous *Legality of Nuclear Weapons* Advisory Opinion.[52]

Second, it is noticeable that the Court did not actually specify that the Principle 21/Principle 2 re-formulation of the 'golden' rule is part of *customary* international

[49] *ICJ Rep* (1996) (I) 226, at 241–242, para 29. Emphasis added.

[50] Advisory Opinions are governed by Chapter IV of the Statute of the International Court of Justice, 1945 where it is provided *inter alia* that '(t)he Court may give an advisory opinion on any legal question at the request of whatever body may be authorized by or in accordance with the Charter of the United Nations to make such a request'. (Article 65.1 of the Statute.)

[51] Interpretation of Peace Treaties with Bulgaria, Hungary and Romania, (1950) ICJ Rep 65, at 71.

[52] *Case concerning the Gabcikovo-Nagymaros Project* (Hungary/Slovakia) *ICJ Rep* (1997) at para 53.

law.[53] Instead, the ICJ apparently contented itself with assigning this obligation as a part of the *corpus* (or body) of international law, without specifying whether it is to be regarded as only a general *principle* to guide State behaviour, or in fact as a legal requirement in the form of a customary *rule* of international law. It is certainly well-accepted by States as the former (general principle), but can it now also be considered to be the latter (customary rule of international law)? Third, there is arguably a significant difference in the normative magnitude of an obligation described by the phrase 'not to cause damage to the environment' (in Principle 21/2), as opposed to one using the phrase 'respect for the environment' (see *Legality of Nuclear Weapons* Advisory Opinion, above). Finally, the ICJ appears here to be limiting the application of this principle only to the body of international law 'relating to the environment', without defining or specifying the parameters of this concept and thereby implicitly negating the scope of this Principle 21/Principle 2 for transforming, or at least modifying, more general precepts of public international law, such as the territorial sovereignty of States.

Thus, and perhaps predictably, commentators have not been unanimous as to the actual meaning of this ICJ statement. As noted earlier, for Sands it is clear that the *Legality of Nuclear Weapons* opinion confirms this rule as customary international law.[54] McCaffrey too has little doubt that 'the principle now forms part of customary international law', noting significantly that in both this Advisory Opinion and the *Gabcikovo-Nagymaros* case Judgment, this statement was made without mentioning the first part of the 'golden' rule emphasising the sovereign rights of States over their natural resources, thus detaching it from the latter, obligatory aspect of this rule, requiring 'respect for the environment'.[55] The primary international obligation for environmental protection was therefore de-coupled from its hitherto balancing sovereign right of development.

On the other hand, according to Tan, this advisory opinion merely 'evidences the existence of the obligation to prevent transboundary environmental harm arising from hazardous activities',[56] without necessarily subscribing to it customary international law status. Bodansky too eschews describing what he calls the 'no harm' principle established in the *Trail Smelter* case, and expanded by Principle 21/2, as representing customary international law *per se*, preferring instead to ascribe it as a new source of international law, called 'declarative international law'.[57] Writing more recently, Victor focuses on the apparently contradictory juxtaposition of the two concepts of 'sovereignty' on the one hand and 'responsibility' on the other hand within Principle 21/2, rather trenchantly observing that nobody 'really knows what the sentence means. Advocates for sovereignty (especially in developing countries) claim that it endorses sovereign freedom of

[53] It is also noticeable that the International Court of Justice here apparently conjoins the twin requirements of 'jurisdiction and control', rather than 'jurisdiction or control', thereby arguably making it more difficult to prove any alleged breach of the primary or 'golden' rule, as these requirements must then be proven conjunctively, rather than disjunctively, on the part of the State concerned.

[54] Sands (2003) above, n 20, at 241.

[55] Stephen C McCaffrey, 'Of Paradoxes, Precedents, and Progeny: The Trail Smelter Arbitration 65 Years Later', in Bratspies and Miller (eds) (2006) above, n 25, at 34–45, at 42.

[56] Alan Khee-Jin Tan, 'Forest Fires of Indonesia; State Responsibility and International Liability', *International and Comparative Law Quarterly*, Vol 48, Part 4 (October 1999) 826–855, at 835.

[57] Daniel Bodansky, 'Customary (And Not So Customary) International Environmental Law', *Global Legal Studies Journal*, Vol 3 (1995) 105–119, at 116–119.

action, whereas advocates for environmental responsibility (notably NGOs from rich industrialised nations) claim that it establishes international duties'.[58] Fitzmaurice is one of the very few writers who has explicitly linked and then contrasted the specific normative strength of Principle 21/2 itself, with the generally weak role of customary international law in the evolution of international environmental law, when she concludes that, 'although customary law plays a secondary role (to) international treaties in the field of environmental protection, there has evolved certain norms the existence of which is beyond doubt. Of these, the most important is that contained in Principle 21 of the Stockholm Declaration and Principle 2 of the Rio Declaration'.[59]

Further international legal authority in support of the customary status of the expanded version of the golden rule enunciated in Principle 21/2, can be claimed by reference to the work of the International Law Commission in the form of its 2001 Draft Articles on Prevention of Transboundary Harm from Hazardous Activities.[60] Birnie and Boyle regard these Draft Articles as the 'codification of existing international law'.[61] More recently, however, Boyle has suggested that these 2001 Draft Articles 'codify only the legal framework for regulation and management of activities which pose a risk of transboundary harm. There is little in them of relevance to liability'.[62] Thus, the 2004 Draft Principles proposed by the ILC's Special Rapporteur on the Allocation of Loss in the Case of Transboundary Harm Arising Out of Hazardous Activities arguably represent a further attempt at the codification of the liability aspect of the expanded version of 'golden' rule.[63] These Principles are expressly stated to apply in relation to 'transboundary damage caused by activities not prohibited by international law which involve a risk of causing significant transboundary harm through their physical consequences'.[64] Principle 3 then provides that the 'Objective' of these Principles is to ensure 'prompt and adequate compensation to natural or legal persons, including States, that are victims of transboundary damage, including *damage to the environment*' (emphasis added). In this context, the 'environment' is defined as including 'natural resources, both abiotic and biotic, such as air, water, soil, fauna and flora and the interaction between the same factors; and the characteristic aspects of the landscape'.[65] Moreover, 'damage' here means '*significant* damage caused to persons, property or the environment;' (again, emphasis added) and includes 'loss or damage by impairment of the environment'.[66] The need for *significant* damage in order to fulfil the

[58] David G. Victor, 'Recovering Sustainable Development', *Foreign Affairs*, Vol 85, No 1 (January/February 2006) 91–103, at 93.

[59] Malgosia A Fitzmaurice, *International Protection of the Environment*, Recueil de Cours, Collected Courses of the Hague Academy of International Law, Vol 293 (2001) (The Hague, Martinus Nijhoff, 2002) at 205.

[60] See Official Records of the (UN) General Assembly, Fifty-sixth Session, Supplement No 10 (A/56/10), at para 97.

[61] Patricia Birnie and Alan Boyle, *International Law and the Environment*, 2nd. edn (Oxford, Oxford University Press, 2002) at 113.

[62] See Boyle (2005) above, n 34, at 5.

[63] See Report of the International Law Commission, Fifty-sixth session, (UN) General Assembly Fifty-ninth session, Supplement No 10 (A/59/10), adopted by the International Law Commission on first reading. Accessible at: http://www.un.org/ga/59/documentation/listo.html. Also reproduced in the *Journal of Environmental Law*, Vol 17, No 1 (2005) 155–157.

[64] See Principle 1, *ibid.*

[65] See Principle 3, *ibid.*

[66] See Principle 2(a), and especially 2(a)(iii), of these draft principles on the allocation of loss in the case of transboundary harm arising out of hazardous activities, *ibid.*, para 175, at 154.

definition of 'damage', and the fact that these Principles are directed only at such damage as arising from 'hazardous activity', which is in turn defined as 'an activity which involves a risk of causing *significant* harm through its physical consequences'.[67] suggests that a high threshold of proof is required for any alleged breach of this rule and consequent liability for such transboundary damage to the environment.

It should also be noted here that the alleged golden rule, as originally formulated in the *Trail Smelter* and *Corfu Channel* decisions, was confined to *transboundary* damage. Even if it were to be accepted that this rule has now been expanded in both its scope and definition to include transboundary *environmental* damage, it can still only be expected to apply to international incidents of a strictly *transboundary* nature. As such, this rule would not necessarily extend to cover diffuse sources of pollution into regional or global commons areas such as transboundary lake or river systems, or high seas areas, for example. Nor would the conceptual extension of such a rule *per se* cover situations of regional or global environmental degradation composed of dispersed indications of environmental damage such as that encountered when considering the causes and effects of global climate change, for example, where a handful of mainly Western, industrialised States historically and contemporaneously contribute to a disproportionately significant increase in greenhouse gases in the earth's atmosphere, while the negative effects of this greenhouse gases build-up in the atmosphere in respect of global mean temperature rises, sea-level rise, and extreme weather conditions are disproportionately felt by other, small island States. Shaw neatly encapsulates this last difficulty in respect of the application of the classical State responsibility approach when he notes that:

> The need to demonstrate that particular damage has been caused to one state by the actions of another state means that this model can only with difficulty be applied to more than a small proportion of environmental problems. In many cases it is simply impossible to prove that particular damage has been caused by one particular source, while the bilateral focus cannot really come to terms with the fact that the protection of the environment of the earth is truly a global problem requiring a global or pan-state response and one that cannot be successfully tackled in such an arbitrary and piecemeal fashion. Accordingly, the approach to dealing with environmental matters has shifted from the bilateral state responsibility paradigm to establishment and strengthening of international co-operation.[68]

A further indication of the uncertainty surrounding the imputation of State responsibility and consequent liability for transboundary environmental damage, as opposed to the normally accepted liability for pollution damage to persons and property can be discerned from Principle 13 of the Rio Declaration. This provides that:

> States shall develop national law regarding liability and compensation for victims of *pollution and other environmental damage.* States shall also co-operate in an expeditious and more determined manner to *develop further* international law regarding liability and compensation for adverse effects of *environmental damage* caused by activities within their jurisdiction or control to areas beyond their jurisdiction. (emphasis added)

This statement thus implies that, despite the wider conceptualisation of damage envisaged by this phrase (pollution and other environmental damage) within international environmental law, States themselves have arguably still not fully accepted the principle

[67] Principle 2(d) *ibid.*
[68] Shaw (2003) above, n 45, at 771.

of liability for environmental damage, both within their national laws applying within their domestic jurisdictions, as well as to areas beyond their national jurisdiction. More than fifteen years since the Rio 'Earth Summit', we are still awaiting a definitive international instrument on this issue. Moreover, it is also possible to argue that the reality of the situation on the ground as regards the application of this extended rule covering transboundary environmental damage is less certain when State practice in relation to major, environmentally damaging, incidents is taken into account. Boyle for example has noted 'the difficulty of reconciling doctrinal support for state responsibility for environmental damage with the realities of state practice'.[69]

Such cases of State practice are, for example, the Chernobyl nuclear reactor disaster in 1986, and the Southeast Asian 'haze' incidents arising from burning rainforest in land-clearing exercises during the late 1990s. In each of these cases, transboundary environmental harm undoubtedly occurred, alongside damage to human health and property damage, from a single country source. Yet no form of international liability, nor even responsibility under international law, has ever been accepted by the States concerned, namely the (then) Soviet Union in relation to the Chernobyl nuclear reactor explosion,[70] and Indonesia in respect of the Southeast Asian 'haze' incidents,[71] the latter of which continue to occur intermittently even to this day.

Finally, even where international liability for transboundary *environmental* damage (as opposed to 'mere' human health detriment and property damage) has been accepted in principle by the polluting States concerned, it is apparently confined to well-known and accepted ultra-hazardous activities, such as the nuclear energy and oil industries.[72] For example, in Canada's ultimately successful Statement of Claim against the (then) USSR for compensation for the expense incurred in locating, removing, recovering and testing radioactive debris and cleaning-up affected areas surrounding the Soviet Union's Cosmos 954 satellite crash landing site within its territory, the Canadian government relied on the argument that '. . . (international) liability applies to fields of activity having in common a high degree of risk . . . (and) had been accepted as a general principle of international law'.[73] The payment of compensation as a consequence of international liability for transboundary damage is also in any case symbolic of a reactive, compensatory type of approach to such damage,[74]

[69] AE Boyle, 'Remedying Harm to International Common Spaces and Resources: Compensation and Other Approaches', in Peter Wetterstein (ed) *Harm to the Environment: The Right to Compensation and the Assessment of Damages* (Oxford, Clarendon Press, 1997) at 89.

[70] Sands notes that several affected countries, including the Federal Republic of Germany, Sweden and the UK, expressly reserved their right to make formal inter-State liability claims against the (then) Soviet Union government for the various types of damage they suffered but no State ultimately did so. See Philippe Sands, *Chernobyl: Law and Communication* (Cambridge, Grotius, 1988) in 'Introduction', 1–49, at 27–28.

[71] For an appraisal of Indonesia's potential responsibility and hence liability to neighbouring Southeast Asian States such as Malaysia and Singapore for the transboundary damage caused by the 'haze' as a result of these deliberately-set, forest fires for cash crop plantation land-clearing, see Tan (1999) above, n 56.

[72] Brunnée, for example, notes that after 'decades of work on international environmental liability, the only liability regimes that are actually in force are those relating to nuclear and oil pollution liability'. See Jutta Brunnée, 'Of Sense and Sensibility: Reflections on International Liability Regimes as Tools for Environmental Protection', *International and Comparative Law Quarterly*, Vol 53, Part 2 (April 2004) 351–368, at 365.

[73] Canadian Statement of Claim, 18 *ILM* 902–30, at 907.

[74] On the compensatory rather than preventive approach favoured by international financial institutions, banks and corporations in their risk assessment strategies on a variety of issues including individual and community rights as well as environmental protection, see Sheldon Leader, 'Human Rights, Risks, and New Strategies for International Investment' *Journal of International Economic Law,* Vol 9 (2006) 657–705.

rather than the more pro-active type of approach favoured by international environmental lawyers, and encapsulated by the advent of the preventive principle in environmental law, both international and domestic. Moreover, questions continue to persist as to the accepted definition or meaning of 'pure' environmental or ecological damage.[75]

Perhaps most insidiously of all, where liability for transboundary environmental and other types of damage is shifted on to the relevant polluting industry through the use of international civil liability schemes, the prospects for the imputation of traditional State responsibility under international law for such transboundary damage are undoubtedly detracted from. While this well-charted trend in the provision of international civil liability for environmental damage can clearly be seen as a progressive development for international environmental law;[76] for example, by noting that it apparently applies yet another well-known general environmental principle, namely the polluter-pays principle;[77] it should nevertheless be explicitly recognised that this trend neatly substitutes industry-based civil liability for State responsibility and consequent international liability in fact, if not in law. It thereby impinges upon the possible evolution of the State responsibility doctrine to encompass such liability for environmental damage, most notably through the development of the 'due diligence' requirement for States to prevent such transboundary environmental harm. It should be noted that an emphasis on 'private', civil liability schemes for polluting industries or those undertaking ultra-hazardous activities may detract from, an ultimately undermine, efforts at establishing a rigorous due diligence requirement against the inaction or omission by States to act against polluting and/or ultra-hazardous industries. After all, why undertake the fraught conceptual enterprise of expanding the scope of State responsibility and liability for the transboundary environmental damage incurred when it is being compensated for, or otherwise re-dressed, by alternative means and arguably more appropriately, by the actual perpetrator of the damage concerned?

This is an especially pertinent question when we consider that most polluting activities, whether domestic or transboundary in nature are in fact likely to be committed by private persons, both natural and legal. Knox, for example, argues that the *Trail Smelter* remedial device, incorporating an international arbitration procedure, has not

[75] Observe, for example, the compensation practice of the 1996 Civil Liability for Oil Pollution Damage and Oil Pollution Compensation Fund Conventions, as amended, wherein the compensation for 'pollution damage' has been extended to include 'impairment of the environment . . . limited to costs of reasonable measures of reinstatement actually undertaken or to be undertaken'. As I have noted previously, this attempted limitation of the compensation headings available for 'impairment of the environment' neither fully covers the possible cost of the required measures as these will not necessarily be limited to reinstatement costs alone, nor has it gone unchallenged in domestic courts/ tribunals that have been charged with interpreting this phrase for the purposes of determining the levels of compensation required following oil spills within their territories. See Ong (2002) above, n 44, at 201–204.

[76] For the legal implications in respect of corporate governance of this and another related trend in the growth of corporate environmental management systems, see David M Ong, 'The Impact of Environmental Law on Corporate Governance: International and Comparative Perspectives', *European Journal of International Law*, Vol 12, Issue 4 (2001) 685–726.

[77] As noted above in the Introduction, there are different conceptions of this principle, ranging from a simple interpretation requiring the actual polluter to be liable for the environmental consequences of their activities, to the more sophisticated interpretation that envisages this principle as the application of a well-known concept within economics of requiring the internalisation of environmental costs incurred from polluting activities that are usually left to society as a whole to absorb. Principle 16 of the 1992 Rio Declaration favours the latter approach.

been followed since because it has proved to be an impractical mechanism for resolving what are essentially private environmental disputes. As Knox notes, 'although scholars differ on which method is best suited to limiting which types of private environmental harm, they generally agree that private rights have strengths that public limits do not. Relying on private rights to limit environmental harm may force private actors to compensate those injured by their actions and thereby *internalize* the actions' environmental costs'.[78] (emphasis added) Thus, it may ultimately be the case that the exhaustive efforts by the ILC and other bodies to provide for such public limits under international environmental law to private actions are destined to be superseded by the increasing provision of private or individual remedies for environmental harm, at both the international and domestic levels of jurisdiction. In Section/Part VI (below) we will consider a particular type of 'private' right in the form of a human right to a healthy environment as a possible means of seeking redress for environmental harms.

II. THE CONSEQUENTIAL DEVELOPMENT OF GENERALLY APPLICABLE (BUT NON-BINDING) ENVIRONMENTAL PRINCIPLES

Due to its essentially reactive nature, the inability of the traditional golden or primary rule of customary international environmental law to require States to actively protect even their domestic environments, let alone the environment they share with their neighbouring States and the environment beyond all national jurisdiction, has forced States to reconsider exactly how the global environment can be saved from the multitude of environmental threats facing it. The international community's response to this particular dilemma for the progressive development of international environmental law has been two-fold.

First, it has continued to develop other general environmental principles through various international legal and policy instruments, a striking example of the latter type of instrument being the documents adopted at the ten-year follow-up conference to the 1992 Rio de Janeiro UN Conference on Environment and Development (UNCED), namely, the 2002 Johannesburg Declaration on Sustainable Development,[79] and the Plan of Implementation of the World Summit on Sustainable Development,[80] both of these documents adopted by Resolutions at the World Summit on Sustainable Development (WSSD) held at the eponymous South African city. The latter, Plan of Implementation, document constitutes an admirable effort to identify the main challenges to 'sustainable development in a globalizing world' and on the 'means of implementation' for achieving sustainable development, through the current 'institutional framework for sustainable development'.[81] However, in keeping with the overall thrust of the 2002 WSSD, it is perhaps inevitably focused on increasing the participation and capacity of especially developing States to implement the sustainable development agenda. Within this context, the Commission on Sustainable Development is enjoined, *inter alia*, to take 'into account significant legal developments in the field of sustainable

[78] John H Knox, 'The Flawed *Trail Smelter* Procedure: The Wrong Tribunal, the Wrong Parties, and the Wrong Law', in Bratspies and Miller (2006) above, n 25, at 66–78, at 67.

[79] Adopted as an Annex to Resolution 1 (Political Declaration) at the 2002 WSSD, above, n 22.

[80] Adopted as Resolution 2 at the 2002 WSSD, above, n 22.

[81] In Chapters V, X and XI, of the WSSD's Plan of Implementation, respectively, above, n 22.

development, with due regard to the role of relevant intergovernmental bodies in promoting the implementation of Agenda 21 relating to international instruments and mechanisms'.[82]

Second, the international community has embarked on a veritable negotiating spree of multilateral environmental conventions, attempting to address separately almost every conceivable threat to the global environment. In nearly all such cases, the multilateral global or regional treaty concerned establishes a specific, often highly technical set of rules and obligations to constrain State behaviour in relation to the perceived environmental threat that the treaty is aimed at containing. These treaty regimes also seek to apply the appropriate environmental principles to their subject matter. Thus, aside from the golden rule apparently establishing inter-State responsibility and therefore liability for transboundary environmental damage, a number of other general environmental principles have now been accepted and applied by States in specific treaties. These include the integration principle, the preventive and precautionary principles, the polluter-pays principle, the principle of public participation in environmental decision-making processes, and—last but certainly not least—the principle of co-operation, which at least in part requires notification and consultation for environmentally hazardous activities.[83]

Of these well-accepted but not necessarily well-implemented environmental principles, the preventive principle occupies centre stage as the main underlying principle for many pollution control treaties in particular. Indeed, it can be argued to be at least implicitly part of the Principle 21/Principle 2 golden rule in that States are enjoined to prevent or otherwise ensure that transboundary harm does not occur. From a general, public international law perspective, however, these specific treaty regimes pose a *systemic* dilemma for the development of an over-arching set of generally applicable customary 'rules', as opposed to guiding 'principles', providing for the environmental protection of *all* States against *all* environmental threats. This is due to the fact that even a very well accepted, globally applicable, environmental treaty addressing a specific environmental threat will not necessarily be held to be applicable to any third party State that is not actually a contracting party to the treaty in question.[84] Thus, even when these well-known environmental principles are included within almost universally well-accepted environmental treaties, this does not mean that these principle have transcended these individual global environmental treaties to become rules of customary international environmental law applying to any environmental threat beyond the individual treaty concerned. Hence, the difficulties faced by the 1997 Kyoto Protocol to the 1992 Framework Convention on Climate Change, without the participation of the United States, even though the US is still a party to the 1992

[82] Para 148(e) of the Plan, above, n 22.

[83] Cassese for example, formulates this principle as 'requiring every State immediately to notify other States of the possible risk that their environment may be damaged or affected by an accident that has occurred on its territory or in an area under its jurisdiction'. See Antonio Cassese, *International Law*, 2nd edn (Oxford, Oxford University Press, 2005) at 489.

[84] The pacta tertis or third-party rule in international treaty law in respect of the possible application of treaty-based obligations upon non-parties to the treaty in question is relatively clear-cut, as enunciated by the Vienna Convention on the Law of Treaties, 1969. Art 35 provides as follows: 'An obligation arises for a third State from a provision of a treaty if the parties to the treaty intend the provision to be the means of establishing the obligation and the third State expressly accepts that obligation in writing' (emphasis added).

Framework Convention itself.[85] The fact that this Protocol establishes a specific greenhouse gases emissions reduction requirement that is in itself an application of the preventive and precautionary principle or approach embodied in the Convention does not mean that this specific emissions reduction limit is binding on the United States. This dilemma is a clear example of the kind of *systemic* problem that international environmental law, and especially environmental treaty law, poses for the development of comprehensive rules for environmental protection under public international law generally.

Moreover, the legal status of the preventive and other environmental principles is arguably far from being as certain under international law, as opposed to the original 'golden' rule providing for international liability for transboundary damage. As Sands notes in relation to these principles, 'The status and effect of the other principles is less clear, although they may bind as treaty obligations or, in particular contexts, as customary obligations. Whether they give rise to actionable obligations of a general nature is open to question'.[86] It is precisely this uncertainty surrounding the preventive and other environmental principles, when their possible invocation before a court of law is considered, which forms their collective Archilles' heel. Indeed, it is possible to suggest at this juncture that the well charted emphasis of international environmental law in the negotiation and adoption of not only more, but also more specific, international regulatory frameworks addressing specific pollution and other types of environmental threats, upon reflection serves only to highlight more clearly than ever the inability of even the most well-accepted principle of international environmental law, namely, the preventive principle, to transcend its legal sub-discipline and restrict States actions at the level of general or customary international law.

A good example of the hesitance displayed by international adjudicatory bodies when they seek to ascertain the precise limits of State action in the face of environmental concerns can be seen in the *Legality of Nuclear Weapons* case already discussed above. Here, despite acknowledging the fact that nuclear weapons 'have the potential to destroy all of civilization and *the entire ecosystem of the planet*' the Court could not bring itself to outlaw nuclear weapons, even on the basis of such global concerns, in every sense of the word. Instead, the Court merely held that 'States must take environmental considerations into account when assessing what is necessary and proportionate in the pursuit of legitimate military objectives'.[87] This statement prompts Nanda and Krieger to observe that while international environmental law does not prohibit the use of nuclear weapons, it does provide limiting environmental factors to their deployment under international law.[88] The fact remains however that none of these apparently limiting environmental factors are enumerated in any detail within the Advisory Opinion itself. Moreover, it is difficult, if not impossible, to see under what circumstances nuclear warfare could be pursued without breaching some if not all of these allegedly limiting environmental factors, apparently established by international environmental law, as the Dissenting Opinion by Judge Weeramantry highlights in relation to the rights of future generations.[89]

[85] Accessible at: http://www.unfccc.org/

[86] Sands (2003) above, n 20, at 232.

[87] *Legality of Nuclear Weapons case*, (1996) ICJ Rep, above, n 49, at para 30. Emphasis added.

[88] Ved P Nanda and David Krieger, *Nuclear Weapons and the World Court* (Ardsley, New York, Transnational Publishers, 1998) at 115–6.

[89] At pp 454–456 of the *Legality of Nuclear Weapons* case, ICJ Rep (1996) above, n 49.

Apart from the more conceptually controversial, and therefore normatively challenging, principles such as the precautionary and polluter-pays principles, international environmental law has also secured the wide acceptance of at least two relatively clear-cut procedurally-oriented principles, namely, the principle of public participation and Environmental Impact Assessment. These principles were enunciated at the global level in Principles 10,[90] and 17,[91] respectively, of the 1992 Rio Declaration and more recently, generally re-affirmed in the 2002 the World Summit's Plan of Implementation for Sustainable Development, with a particular emphasis on the participation of women.[92] They have also found their way in more specific fashion into a number of initially regionally-oriented Economic Commission for Europe (ECE) treaties such as the 1991 Espoo,[93] and 1998 Aarhus,[94] Conventions. A significant difference here lies in the potential for these initially regional-specific treaties, adopted under the auspices of the UN-ECE regional programme, to expand their application beyond the confines of the UN-ECE membership. Thus the stage is set for their eventual acceptance as applicable customary international rules between all States. However, again the required step from generally accepted principle, articulated as specific treaty rules and requirements in regional or subject specific treaties, to attainment of customary international law status, has arguably failed to materialise. This can be readily surmised, for example, from the reticence manifested by the International Tribunal for the Law of the Sea (ITLOS) when considering whether the reclamation works under taken by Singapore required a prior, transboundary environmental impact assessment exercise involving Malaysia, as argued by the latter State in the *Land Reclamation (Provisional Measures)* case (considered below in Section IV).

And what of the over-arching and ultimate goal or objective of 'sustainable development' itself? Lowe has highlighted several difficulties with this concept from a legal perspective,[95] but it is still very much the lynchpin of international environmental law. As the central tenet of international environmental law, however, 'sustainable

[90] As noted earlier, Principle 10 of the Rio Declaration on Environment and Development, 1992 (see www.unep.org) provides that '(E)nvironmental issues are best handled with the participation of all concerned citizens, at the relevant level'. It then goes on to highlight three aspects of such citizen participation, beginning with the need to have access to environmental information, especially in respect of hazardous activities; moving on to providing opportunities for public participation, and finally, allowing effective access to judicial proceedings to seek redress for any failings in respect of the first two aspects.

[91] As noted earlier, Principle 17 of the Rio Declaration *ibid.*, states that: 'Environmental impact assessment, as a national instrument, shall be undertaken for proposed activities that are likely to have a significant adverse impact on the environment and are subject to a decision of a competent national authority'.

[92] Para 164 of the 2002 WSSD's Plan of Implementation above, n 22, states that: 'All countries should also promote public participation, including through measures that provide access to information regarding legislation, regulations, activities, policies and programmes. They should also foster full participation in sustainable development policy formulation and implementation. Women should be able to participate fully and equally in policy formulation and decision-making'.

[93] Full title: Convention on Environmental Impact Assessment in a Transboundary Context (Espoo, 1991)—the 'Espoo (EIA) Convention'. Adopted 25 February, 1991; entered into force 10 September, 1997. Accessible at: http://www.unece.org/env/ This instrument heralds a significant conceptual development of the EIA principle to include projects that have potential transboundary impacts, an issue taken up in both the *MOX Plant* and *Land Reclamation* cases considered below in Section IV.

[94] Full title: Convention on Access to Information, Public Participation in Decision-making and Access to Justice in Environmental Matters. Adopted 25 June, 1998; entered into force 30 October, 2001. Accessible at: http://www.unece.org/env/.

[95] See Vaughan Lowe, 'Sustainable Development and Unsustainable Arguments', in Alan Boyle and David Freestone (eds) *Sustainable Development and International Law* (Oxford, Oxford University Press, 1999) 19–37, especially at 23–31.

development' can be likened to the 'King' piece on a chessboard—simultaneously the most important and yet also the most vulnerable piece in the game. If 'the name of the game' so to speak, is the achievement of 'sustainable development', then it must become the ultimate goal or objective of international environmental law as a whole, rather than as a separate and individual principle or rule in itself. Indeed, according to Victor, in order to be attained 'sustainable development' must arguably become '. . . a framework for every aspect of governance rather than as a special interest'.[96] Moreover, '(g)etting serious about sustainable development requires redrawing the lines of sovereignty; if sustainable development is a universal concept, then governments have a universal responsibility to promote it'.[97] Unfortunately, explicit manifestations of such responsibility are few and far between, whether in the international relations, or domestic policies, of States. As Lowe concludes in this context: 'The argument that sustainable development is a norm of customary international law, binding on and directing the conduct of states, and which can be applied by tribunals, is not sustainable'.[98]

Thus, in order to achieve the goal or objective of 'sustainable development', international environmental law has begotten other environmental principles. Chief among these is the principle of inter- and intra-generational equity,[99] as well as what is arguably the most important principle for our purposes here, namely, the principle of integration of environmental considerations within socio-economic development policies and plans.[100] This particular principle has been both upheld in terms of its legal status as an 'emerging' principle in itself, and perhaps more significantly, elaborated upon as to its implications for the application of the preventive principle, in a recent international arbitration case between Belgium and the Netherlands.[101] Here, the Tribunal stated that:

> Today, both international and EC law require the integration of appropriate environmental measures in the design and implementation of economic development activities. [. . .] Environmental law and the law on development stand not as alternatives but as mutually reinforcing, integral concepts, which require that where development may cause significant harm to the environment there is a duty to prevent, *or at least mitigate*, such harm. [. . .] This duty, in the opinion of the Tribunal, has now become *a principle of general international law*.[102]

Further on in the same decision, the Tribunal re-affirmed that '(t)oday, in international environmental law, a growing emphasis is being put on the duty of prevention. Much international environmental law has been formulated by reference to the

[96] Victor (2006) above, n 58, at 95.

[97] *Ibid*, at 96.

[98] Lowe (1999) above, n 95, at 30.

[99] This is provided in Principle 3 of the 1992 Rio Declaration on Environment and Development, as follows: 'The right to development must be fulfilled so as to equitably meet developmental and environmental needs of present and future generations'.

[100] This principle is described in Principle 4 of the 1992 Rio Declaration as follows: 'In order to achieve sustainable development, environmental protection shall constitute an integral part of the development process and cannot be considered in isolation from it'.

[101] *Arbitration Regarding The Iron Rhine ('Ijzeren Rijn') Railway between The Kingdom of Belgium and the Kingdom of The Netherlands*, Award of the Arbitral Tribunal, The Hague, 24 May 2005. Accessed at: http://www.pca-cpa.org/.

[102] *Ibid*, at para 59, at p 29 of the Arbitral Award. Emphasis added.

impact that activities in one territory may have on the territory of another'.[103] The Tribunal then referred in this context to the statement of ICJ's *Nuclear Weapons* Advisory Opinion quoted above.

Significant as these judicial statements are for confirmation of the legal status of the duty of transboundary harm prevention, it is submitted here that they do not necessarily advance the normative argument that much further. After all, few international lawyers would argue against the duty of prevention against transboundary harm being an accepted *principle* of general international law. What is needed here is a considered judicial reflection as to whether this preventive duty now extends to being a *rule* of customary international law. However, the Tribunal conspicuously circumnavigated this question in the *Iron Rhine* arbitration, merely noting that there 'is considerable debate as to what within the field of environmental law, constitutes "rules" or "principles"; what is "soft law"; and which environmental treaty law or principles have contributed to the development of customary international law. Without entering further into those controversies, the Tribunal notes that in all of these categories "environment" is broadly referred to as including air, water, land, flora and fauna, natural ecosystems and sites, human health and safety and climate. The emerging principles, whatever their current status, make reference to conservation, management, notions of prevention and of sustainable development, and protection for future generations'.[104] Moreover, the arguably qualified nature of the Tribunal's statement on the duty of harm prevention in that this duty can apparently be discharged merely by mitigating, rather than preventing, significant harm to the environment, suggests that it is less stringent than what most international environmental lawyers would prescribe. Here it should be emphasised that the primary rule stated in Principle 21/Principle 2 (as opposed to its enunciation in the *Trail Smelter* decision) appears to provide for a much lower threshold of environmental damage to occur for the rule to be breached.

Further evidence that even the duty to prevent significant environmental harm has been interpreted by States to allow for a certain amount of pollution to occur can be discerned from Uruguay's arguments against Argentina's provisional measures application in the ICJ *Pulp Mills* case (considered further below, in Section IV). Uruguay argued inter alia before the ICJ that 'even if it were to be considered that the operation of the mills might lead to "contamination of the river", the gravity of the "alleged peril to Argentina" was not "sufficiently certain or immediate as to satisfy the Court's requirement that it be "imminent or urgent"'.[105] The Court appears to have accepted Uruguay's argument as to the lack of imminent threat of irreparable prejudice to Argentina's rights in denying her provisional measures application, although it should be emphasised here that such applications inevitably carry a high standard or burden of proof which Argentina was adjudged not to have fulfilled in her application.[106]

Thus, while the application of these consequential environmental principles is vitally necessary for the achievement of 'sustainable development' and has clear normative implications for the behaviour of all States, and even international

[103] *Ibid*, at para 222, p 90 of the Arbitral Award.

[104] *Ibid*, at para 58, p 28 of the Award.

[105] Para 46, at p 12 of the ICJ Order in *Case Concerning Pulp Mills on the River Uruguay* (*Argentina v Uruguay*) Request for the Indication of Provisional Measures, 13 July 2006, at http://www.icj-cij.org/.

[106] *Ibid*, at para 62, p 16 and paras 73–76, pp 18–19.

institutions,[107] their continuing lack of clear judiciable content is still evident, despite their invocation within all manner of subsequent international environmental, and even other more general, albeit regionally applicable, treaty instruments, for example, within Article 3 (sustainable development) and Article 274 (preventive, precautionary and polluter-pays principles) of the much amended 1957 Treaty establishing the European Communities.[108]

In this context, and clearly alluding also to the *diffused* nature of international pollution sources and the *dispersed* nature of environmental damage caused by such pollution highlighted in Section I above, Brownlie notes that '(a) particular difficulty in the sphere of environmental hazards and damage is the selection and deployment of an appropriate cause of action or basis of claim. The process of contamination is often, in physical terms, incremental and may involve complex causal mechanisms. Apart from the finding of a cause of action, the requirement of damage as a necessary condition of claim bears an uneasy relation to the scientific proof of a certain threshold of damage caused by an overall rise in radiation or other forms of pollution and problems of multiple causation then arise'.[109]

A further problem, already alluded to earlier, that is associated with the possibility of invoking such environmental principles relates to the nature of any such international obligation arising from the acceptance by States of these principles. Are they only bilateral in their application and thus limited in terms of their possible invocation only by negatively affected States? Or do they provide for obligations *erga omnes*, with the further implication that they can be relied upon as the basis for an *actio popularis* action by interested, but not necessarily negatively affected States? As Okowa notes presciently, 'the multi-faceted nature of environmental disputes is bound to place considerable strain on an institution (the ICJ) largely structured to deal with bilateral issues on a private-rights basis'.[110]

The notion that these general environmental principles have an *erga omnes* character that may allow for *actio popularis* actions was relied upon by the New Zealand application in the 1995 *Nuclear Tests (New Zealand v France)* case.[111] In the event, the ICJ held that the basis of its 1974 decision had not been affected as required by paragraph 63 of that judgment and that it therefore lacked the competence to re-commence those proceedings. The Court also arrived at its decision by distinguishing between the facts of the initial 1974 claim brought by New Zealand and Australia regarding *atmospheric* French nuclear tests and the 1995 claim presented to it by New Zealand seeking to re-open the previous proceedings on the basis of *sea-bed* nuclear

[107] See, for example, Gunther Handl, 'The Legal Mandate of Multilateral Development Banks as Agents for Change Toward Sustainable Development', *American Journal of International Law,* Vol 92 (1998) 642. For a more recent account of the role played by the principle of sustainable development in the work of the United Nations Compensation Commission (UNCC), see Olufemi Elias, 'Sustainable Development, War Reparations and Environmental Damage', in Malgosia Fitzmaurice and Milena Szuniewicz (eds.) *Exploitation of Natural Resources in the 21st Century* (The Hague, Kluwer Law International, 2003) 67–90.

[108] Consolidated Version of the Treaty Establishing the European Community, as amended in accordance with the Treaty of Nice (OJ 2002 C325/1-184) and the 2003 Accession Treaty (OJ 2003 L237/17).

[109] Ian Brownlie, *Principles of Public International Law* 6th edn (Oxford: Oxford University Press, 2003) at 274.

[110] Phoebe N Okowa, Environmental Dispute Settlement: Some Reflections on Recent Developments, in Malcolm Evans (ed) *Remedies in International Law: The Institutional Dilemma* (Oxford, Hart Publishing, 1998) 157–172, at 164.

[111] Accessible at: http://www.icj-cij.org/.

testing. While undoubtedly correct within the narrow confines in which the Court construed its jurisdiction, the case nevertheless highlights the dilemma faced by the Court, and it is suggested here other international tribunals as well, when faced with claims from individual States that in fact relate to community, rather than self, interest.

III. THE CONTINUING GROWTH OF SPECIFIC ENVIRONMENTAL TREATY REGIMES

As has been noted, international environmental law has also developed through the adoption of a multitude of multilateral treaty regimes addressing specific environmental threats. In the main, these treaties can be categorised in the following manner: First, there are globally applicable but issue-specific treaties. Examples of such treaties include the 1987 Montreal Protocol to the 1985 Vienna Convention on Substances that deplete the Ozone Layer, and the 1973 Convention on International Trade in Endangered Species. Second, there are treaties that are expressly confined to a clearly defined regional space, most usually in the form of a semi-enclosed sea for example, but which encompass within their overall regulatory framework several pollution sources into that well-defined region. Examples of these types of treaties include a whole slew of regionally-focused marine environmental protection conventions. Several of these are managed by the United Nations Environment Programme (UNEP) Regional Seas Programme, such as the Barcelona Convention for the Mediterranean Sea (1976), the Cartagena Convention for the Wider Caribbean Region (1983),[112] and the Nairobi Convention for Eastern African Region (1985),[113] respectively, to name but a few of these regional seas conventions. Many others also form part of the global network of regional seas programmes even if they are not actually managed by the UNEP itself, such as the Bucharest Convention for the Black Sea (1992),[114] the Lima Convention for the Protection of the Marine Environment and Coastal Areas of the South-East Pacific (1981),[115] as well as the regionally-oriented (but not exclusively so) Economic Commission for Europe treaties such as the 1979 Geneva Convention on Long Range Transboundary Air Pollution,[116] and its eight related Protocols.

[112] Convention for the Protection and Development of the Marine Environment of the Wider Caribbean Region; Short title: Cartagena Convention; Adopted: Cartagena de Indias, Colombia on 24 March 1983. Entered into force: 11 October 1986. Text of the Convention accessible at: http://www.cep.unep.org/pubs/legislation/cartxt.html.

[113] Convention for the Protection, Management and Development of the Marine and Coastal Environment of the Eastern African Region; Short title: Nairobi Convention. Adopted: Nairobi, Kenya, on 21 June 1985, entered into force: 30 May 1996. Text of Convention accessible at: http://www.unep.org/regionalseas/Programmes/UNEP_Administered_Programmes/Eastern_African_Region/default2.asp.

[114] The Convention on the Protection of the Black Sea against Pollution; Short Title: Bucharest Convention. Year adopted: 21 April 1992 (UNEP 2001); Year entered into force: 15 January 1994 (with the ratifications of Bulgaria, Romania, Russian Federation and Georgia). Turkey ratified on 29 March 1994, Ukraine on 15 April 1994. Text of convention accessible at: http://www.blacksea-commission.org/main.htm.

[115] Adopted: 12 November 1981, entered into force: 1986. Full text of the Convention accessible at: http://sedac.ciesin.org/entri/texts/marine.environment.coastal.south.east.pacific.1981.html.

[116] Adopted in Geneva on 13 November, 1979, entered into force: 1983, accessible at: http://www.unece.org/env/lrtap/.

The combination of these globally applicable environmental treaties that cover certain specific environmental issues and regional treaties which in turn cover several different but related environmental threats gives much succour to international environmental lawyers. Indeed, it is possible to suggest that a gradual knitting process is underway here, with the global and regional regulatory threads becoming entwined over time to form a warming blanket of universal regulation (whether global and/or regional in form) covering all manner of general and specific environmental threats. Against this apparently serendipitous outcome, however, it is certainly possible to ask whether this veritable topsy of Multilateral Environmental Agreements (MEAs) is either necessary, or effective. Certainly von Moltke is not a lone voice when he suggests that '(t)he current number of international environmental regimes is clearly too large to be optimal'.[117]

Moreover, from the vantage point of general, public international law, certain *systemic* problems persist. These are at least two-fold in nature. First, gaps remain in both the coverage and participation of global and regional environmental treaties. As to the latter issue, it is noticeable that certain regions in the world are much better regulated than others. In particular, the western and northern European regions, incorporating Scandinavia and also including their marine regions, namely, the north eastern Atlantic ocean, inter alia, encompassing the Bering, North and Baltic Seas, as well as the Mediterranean Sea, are the subject of a range of regional environmental treaties.[118] Moreover, given the geo-political, economic and other circumstances of other, relatively under-developed regions, there is little prospect in the short- to medium-term time frame for this regulatory gap to be bridged, at least in terms of the range of environmental threats covered by individual regional instruments. In respect of the former issue, as noted above, the third-party (*pacta tertis*) rule of international treaty law prevents the imputation of arguably any treaty obligation on a non-party State, no matter how well-supported the treaty is, short of its universal acceptance by all States. Neither can this *systemic* difficulty be easily bridged by the reference to soft law instruments. Although as Shelton notes, 'such soft law instruments often serve as an authoritative way to allow treaty parties to resolve ambiguities in a binding text or fill in gaps',[119] this function of soft law as a supplement to hard law instruments is by definition limited in its application to the parties to the hard law, treaty instrument in the first place.

Second, even the present international regulatory framework of global and regional treaties covering a whole range of environmental threats—general and specific—cannot be easily expanded to cover newly perceived environmental threats. Indeed, the growth in environmental treaty specialisation sometimes occurs in the full knowledge of existing environmental treaty regimes related to, and even overlapping, the subject matter of the new instruments.[120] This legal reality serves yet again to highlight the disparity inherent in international environmental law between the multitude of global

[117] von Moltke, (2005) above, n 21, at 177.

[118] Examples are as follows in chronological order: the 1976 Barcelona Convention on Mediterranean Sea, 1979 Geneva Convention on Long Range Transboundary Air Pollution, the 1991 Espoo Convention, 1992 Paris Convention, the 1994 Baltic Convention, the 1998 Aarhus Convention. This is notwithstanding all of the environmental protection Regulations and Directives promulgated by the relevant European Union institutions, to be implemented and enforced within each of the (currently) 25 Member States of the EU.

[119] Shelton (2006) above, n 12, at 320.

[120] Von Moltke (2005) above, n 21, at 177.

and regional environmental treaties and the relative paucity in the development of accepted general customary rules, or even principles, to address new environmental threats.

Thus, the steady accretion of international environmental treaties that include provisions purporting to apply these environmental principles does not necessarily lead us to the assumption that these principles can or will be invoked, and perhaps more importantly, applied within international dispute settlement proceedings as rules of customary or general international law.[121] This much can be discerned from the jurisprudence of the International Tribunal for the Law of the Sea (ITLOS) and associated arbitral tribunals, as in the *MOX Plant* case (below) for example. As we shall see below, ITLOS refused to grant the provisional measures requested by Ireland in this case relying on the application of the precautionary principle, even though it was expressly provided for in at least one of the treaties invoked by Ireland, namely, the 1992 Paris Convention on the Protection of the Marine Environment of the North East Atlantic.[122] Notions of applying 'best treaty practice', in this context, where several different treaty instruments are arguably equally applicable to the matters at hand, appear to have fallen on stony ground, at least at the provisional measures stage of such proceedings. Neither have arguments based on Article 31.3(c) of the 1969 Vienna Convention on the Law of Treaties (hereinafter, VCLT) regarding the application of other 'relevant international rules' to the interpretation of a treaty,[123] proved successful at ensuring the cross-fertilisation and thus possible application of principles and rules from one treaty to another.[124] At least not within the World Trade Organization (WTO) context and not in respect of the precautionary principle. For example the WTO Panel in the recent *EC-Biotech Products* case held that this provision was limited in its application strictly to treaty instruments that *all* WTO Members to the dispute were party to.[125] This meant that neither the 1992 Biodiversity Convention, nor its 1999 Cartagena Protocol on Biosafety, could be regarded as falling within the scope of Article 31.3(c) and thus deemed to be applicable to the United States in this context. As Prévost notes, 'this finding would seem to practically exclude the possibility of a Panel being obliged to have regard to other treaties in the interpretation of WTO Agreements, since it is improbable that all 150 WTO Members would be parties to another treaty'.[126]

In the face of these difficulties, calls for a 'World Environment Organization' have arisen.[127] However, as von Moltke notes succinctly, attempts 'to create a single World

[121] See Robin Churchill 'Some Reflections on the Operation of the Dispute Settlement System of the UN Convention on the Law of the Sea During its First Decade', in David Freestone, Richard Barnes and David M Ong (eds), *The Law of the Sea: Progress and Prospects* (Oxford, Oxford University Press, 2006) 388–416, at 400–401.

[122] Adopted on 22 September 1992; entered into force on 25 March 1998. See www.ospar.org.

[123] Article 31.3(c) of the VCLT provides that: 'There shall be taken into account, together with the context: . . . (c) any relevant rules of international law applicable in the relations between the parties'.

[124] As mooted by Philippe Sands, 'Treaty, Custom and the Cross-fertilization of International Law', *Yale Human Rights and Development Law Journal,* Vol 1 (1998) 58–106.

[125] Full title: *EC-Biotech Products*, US, Canada, Argentina, v EC, WT/DS291R, WT/DS292R, WT/DS293R, 29 September, 2006.

[126] Denise Prévost, 'Opening Pandora's Box: The Panel's Findings in the EC-Biotech Products Dispute, *Legal Issues of Economic Integration*, Vol 31, No 1 (2007) 67–102, at 88.

[127] For a range of views on the viability of such a new international organisation, see the collection of essays in Frank Biermann and Steffen Bauer (eds), *A World Environment Organization: Solution or Threat for Effective International Environmental Governance?* (Aldershot: Ashgate, 2005).

Environmental Organization face extraordinary difficulties of both a theoretical and a practical nature'.[128] Neither is the alternative UNEP-sponsored efforts at the 'clustering' of Multilateral Environmental Agreements (MEAs) along the lines of their common characteristics likely to resolve either the *substantive* or *systemic* difficulties highlighted above.[129] MEA 'clustering' in this context is described by Moltke as the grouping of a number of international environmental regimes together through a variety of institutional and organisational arrangements so as to improve their efficiency and effectiveness, but crucially for our purposes here, 'without requiring elaborate changes in legal or administrative arrangements'.[130] Thus, currently envisaged modes of MEA 'clustering' can be seen as seeking to enhance only the *institutional* efficiency of their implementation by States Parties, rather than extending their *legal* application to non-Parties to one or other of the 'clustered' MEAs. Nor does there appear to be any formal legal mechanism by which to incorporate, or otherwise transfer, the environmental 'best practice' of individual MEAs within a particular 'cluster', apart from facilitating the dissemination of information on such 'best practice' among the clustered MEAs.

IV. THE RETICENCE OF INTERNATIONAL TRIBUNALS IN ENFORCING GENERAL ENVIRONMENTAL PRINCIPLES BETWEEN STATES

Nowhere is international environmental law's dilemma more pronounced than when the general environmental principles that have been articulated in various non-binding instruments, and applied in specific treaty rules within individual environmental treaty regimes, are then assessed in the context of international judicial settlement of disputes between States, where one party claims they should be applied to the dispute between them and the other attempts to deny the application of such environmental principles. Several cases have been brought before various international tribunals, where general environmental principles have been invoked. Thus, it is simply not possible to suggest anymore, as Bodansky did more than a decade ago, that international courts and tribunals play a relatively minor role in addressing international environmental issues,[131] although it remains true that '(t)hird-party dispute resolution has resolved few environmental problems'.[132]

On the other hand, this observation should not be taken to mean that the international adjudication of environmental disputes is either imperative, or even necessary to ensure their resolution. Paulus, for example, observes that judicial dispute settlement in the environmental field is the exception rather than the rule and tends to use general, rather than specific environmental treaty mechanisms, although he emphasises its 'non-negligible effect of clarifying the rules and developing the law'.[133]

[128] von Moltke (2005) above, n 21, at 176.

[129] For the latest information of UNEP efforts on the subject of International Environmental governance (IEG), see www.unep.org/IEG/background.asp.

[130] von Moltke (2005) above, n 21, at 178.

[131] Bodansky (1995) above, n 57 at 117 and 119.

[132] Bodansky (1995) above, n 57, at 117.

[133] Andreas L Paulus, 'Dispute Resolution', Chapter 14 in Geir Ulfstein (ed), in collaboration with Thilo Marauhn and Andreas Zimmermann, *Making Treaties Work: Human Rights, Environment and Arms Control* (Cambridge, CUP, 2007) at 362.

As von Moltke notes presciently, 'Environmental regimes pursue effectiveness and implementation through entirely different institutions (transparency and participation in particular) and there is no reason to assume that the availability of a reinforced dispute settlement mechanism will change that in any way. [. . . Moreover], the nature of legal obligations entailed in multilateral environmental agreements—and the structure of the ensuing regime—is such that environmental regimes rarely generate the kind of [legal] dispute that is characteristic of the WTO system'.[134] Indeed, the following section, Section V, focuses upon alternative non-compliance mechanisms developed by environmental treaty regimes that are at least in part aimed at stimulating greater adherence and implementation to the relevant international environmental treaty norms and standards by the States parties to these treaty regimes.

What will be highlighted in the rest of this Section is the apparent reluctance displayed by these tribunals when presented with opportunities to invoke and apply the relevant environmental principles to the international dispute at hand in such a way as to enhance overall environmental protection, which is presumably why these principles were developed in the first place. In subjecting this international case law to such scrutiny, the argument is not being made for a favourable outcome in respect of environmental protection in all circumstances. Rather, what will be shown is the lack of specific guidance offered by the relevant judgments as to the legal status and parameters of application of the environmental principles invoked before the international tribunals concerned. It is this significant judicial function that the international tribunals appear to have singularly failed to discharge in the following case law examples adduced here (and above in Section II).

These observations of course tap into a continuing general debate as to the nature of the international judicial function. In broad terms, this debate is divided between those who advocate only the resolution of the particular dispute at hand, through the application of the specific rules found to be applicable to the States concerned and, on the other hand, those that first require a more general rendition of the applicable principles for all States, from which specific rights and duties are then imputed upon the parties to the dispute.[135] In reality, the rendering of generally applicable rules to any particular situation usually requires the application of both these approaches and it very much depends on the individual circumstances of the dispute before the tribunal concerned as to how it will appropriately discharge its judicial function in this respect.

However, the shortcomings exhibited by the adjudicative decisions examined in this Section serve to highlight an important, arguably even imperative, aspect of the international judicial function when adjudicating between States in respect of well-accepted but, in legal status and definitional terms, relatively vague and recently established environmental principles. As Boyle and Chinkin pose the question: 'if an international court concludes that there is no applicable rule of customary international law what should be its response?'[136] In their view, reliance on 'general principles of law' in such cases is fraught with uncertainty as Article 38(1)(c) of the ICJ Statute does not provide specific guidance on how such general principles are to be

[134] von Moltke (2005) above, n 21, at 197.

[135] From a significant literature on this issue see, for example, Sir Gerald Fitzmaurice, *The Law and Procedure of the International Court of Justice*, Vol II, (Cambridge, Grotius Publications, 1986) at 647–648, where he elaborates on this apparent dichotomy.

[136] Alan Boyle and Christine Chinkin, *The Making of International Law* (Oxford: OUP, 2007) at 286.

ascertained, nor how they should be implemented by an international tribunal, with the attendant implication being that the exercise of judicial discretion in such cases would be of a subjective nature.[137]

There are at least two related arguments that can be made in favour of an enhanced judicial role in response to this concern. These arguments are relevant notwithstanding the fact that there is arguably a material difference here between the essentially *procedural* general principles alluded to in Article 38(1)(c), and the *substantive* environmental principles that are the subject of this essay. First, in a situation where the environmental principles concerned are still uncertain, both in terms of their legal status, definition, and scope of application, it is arguably incumbent that the relevant international tribunal's judicial function should extend beyond merely resolving the precise dispute before it. In other words, the discharge of the international judicial function in such cases should also include a clear, definitive statement of the rights and duties of *all* States finding themselves in similar situations, in light of the application of the relevant environmental principles.[138] Klein for example argues in the context of the compulsory and binding dispute settlement procedures laid down by the 1982 UN Convention on the Law of the Sea (UNCLOS) that 'many environmental obligations imposed on States are far from determinate and to this extent lack clarity of content. . . . Through the dispute settlement procedures, UNCLOS could also collaterally strengthen the obligations found in other international environmental treaties'.[139]

Second, this enhanced judicial role is especially significant when it is realised that in many cases the judicial pronouncements on the legal status and application of these principles are not only concerned with the simple adjudication of a State's bilateral responsibility for implementing these principles in the relation to a neighbouring State, but also its multilateral and indeed, global responsibility. This is because these principles are meant to govern a State's behaviour in respect of environmental protection not only *erga omnes*, against all other States, but also on behalf of the international community, in relation to international common spaces such as the high seas, the deep sea-bed and the global atmosphere. This is especially pertinent given the fact that no other entity can currently act for the international commons. Furthermore, *actio popularis*-type claims by States that are individually unaffected themselves have not to date received judicial succour,[140] despite being advocated by certain eminent commentators.[141]

[137] Boyle and Chinkin (2007) above, n 136, citing U Fastenrath, 'Relative Normativity in International Law', *European Journal of International Law*, Vol 4 (1993) 305, at 321.

[138] This view is clearly aligned to the Lauterpacht attitude towards the international judicial function, most famously rendered in the South-West Africa case, *ICJ Reports* (1955) 67, at 90. See also Fitzmaurice (1986) above, n 135, at 649.

[139] Natalie Klein, *Dispute Settlement and the Law of the Sea Convention* (Cambridge, Cambridge University Press, 2005) at 163.

[140] See for example the reluctance of the International Court of Justice to accept this notion in the South West Africa cases; South West Africa (Second Phase) (*Ethiopia v South Africa; Liberia v South Africa*) 1966 ICJ Rep. 6. Klein notes that '(I)t is not evident whether such a broad basis of standing would be acceptable before the courts and tribunals available under the (1982) Convention'. See Klein (2005) above, n 139, at 161–162.

[141] Charney for example has argued that '(b)ecause a violation by any state party is a legal injury to every other state party, any state party may bring an action in dispute settlement to enforce compliance'. See Jonathan I Charney, 'The Protection of the Marine Environment by the 1982 United Nations Convention on the Law of the Sea', *Georgia International Environmental Law Review*, Vol 7 (1995) 731, at 737.

Thus, in situations where the customary legal status of these environmental principles is still in question, the above arguments would strongly advocate in favour of a careful judicial consideration of both their legal status and perhaps more importantly, any limitations in their scope of application. As Lowe observes in this context, '(w)here disputes are submitted to such (judicial) tribunals by agreement between the parties to the dispute, as is always the case in international law, the submission entails an authorization to "reason judicially" even where that reasoning implicates *norms that may not have been established through the classic processes of international law formation*'.[142] The proactive judicial stance advocated here for a reasoned examination of the now well-known and well-accepted (by States) but still normatively uncertain environmental principles noted above is therefore vindicated by Lowe's view that it is precisely in this type of situation that the concept of sustainable development can play a legal role: 'Sustainable development can properly claim a normative status as an element of the process of judicial reasoning'.[143]

Such an exercise of the international judicial function would also be essential due to the 'regulating' effect and influence that judicial pronouncements have on future State behaviour in this field. Indeed, it is possible to argue that the uncertain legal nature and scope of application of general environmental principles necessitates more than ever the definitive exercise by international tribunals of their judicial function in this manner. This function is, as Rosenne puts it in relation to the International Court, first and foremost to 'declare the law, *jus dicere*', through 'pronouncements that are solely concerned with the law as it is'.[144] This function should therefore be fulfilled even if the resulting judicial application of the enunciated and invoked principles and rules does not favour a presumption for environmental protection, as against the discretionary exercise of State sovereignty in ways which may result in environmental damage. It should be noted however that the above statement by Rosenne can also be construed narrowly, as he notes further on in his discourse on the judicial role of the ICJ: 'Secondly, in principle it is the duty of the Court, in deciding on the basis of the international law the disputes that are submitted to it, to limit itself to the terms of its remit—the special agreement, the submissions, or the question put for an advisory opinion, as the case may be'.[145]

Another eminent commentator, Kwiatkowska has advocated this apparently long-standing narrow approach to the judicial function of the ICJ for application by the ITLOS as well,[146] noting that it was re-affirmed recently in the *Arrest Warrant* case between Congo and Belgium, where the Court recalled the well-established principle that 'it is the duty of the Court not only to reply to the questions as stated in the final submissions of the parties but also to abstain from deciding points not included in the submissions'.[147] On the other hand, Kwiatkowska also highlights the Court's view

[142] Lowe (1999) above, n 95, at 31. Emphasis added.

[143] *Ibid.*

[144] Shabtai Rosenne, *The Law and Practice of the International Court, 1920–2005, Vol I: The Court and the United Nations*, 4th edn (Leiden/Boston, Martinus Nijhoff, 2006) at 169.

[145] *Ibid.*, at 170, citing the *Asylum (Interpretation)* (*Colombia v Peru*) case, *ICJ Reports* (1950) 395, at 402.

[146] Barbara Kwiatkowska, 'The Ireland v United Kingdom (MOX Plant) Case: Applying the Doctrine of Treaty Parallelism', *International Journal of Marine and Coastal Law (IJMCL)* Vol 18, No 1 (2003) 1–49, at 45.

[147] *Arrest Warrant of 11 April 2000* (*Congo v Belgium*) Judgment (2002) *ICJ Rep.* at para.43, quoting from the Asylum case Judgment (1950) above, n 146, at 402.

that it was not precluded from dealing 'with certain aspects of the question at hand in the reasoning of its Judgment, should it deem this necessary or desirable'.[148] Indeed, she relies on this ICJ statement to argue that the ITLOS should have elaborated on the duty to co-operate under Part XII and general international law in the *MOX Plant* case, *inter alia*, to 're-affirm the critical importance of implementation of this basic duty by the procedural triad of principles of a prior EIA, information and consultation'.[149]

Returning to the main theme of this study, namely the attempt discern the precise legal status and application of well-known and accepted environmental principles, the above discussion highlights the paradox at the heart of the evolution of international environmental law. The paradox is as follows: Well-known and arguably well-accepted environmental principles by States enunciated in various international environmental instruments have nevertheless not been fully applied when invoked before the pre-eminent international judicial institutions such as the International Court of Justice, the World Trade Organization's dispute settlement mechanism consisting of the Panel and Appellate Body, and the International Tribunal on the Law of the Sea. The lack of full application of these principles has not been accompanied by sufficiently robust legal explanations as to their stilted application by the international tribunals concerned. Moreover, the relatively loose and compromised language used to articulate these environmental principles within formally non-binding, international 'soft' law instruments often exacerbates the uncertainty faced by States and hence also international adjudicatory bodies as to their precise nature and application. Thus, the apparent paradox at the heart of international environmental law between general environmental principles and specific environmental treaty rules only serves to throw the spotlight on the gulf between the apparent *acceptance* of these environmental principles at the international level and continuing difficulties with their *application*, especially in respect of their implementation by States and the enforcement of such implementation by international adjudicatory bodies. This in turn perpetuates uncertainties as to their international legal status and therefore their prospective enforcement by international tribunals tasked with the duty of applying them to any disputes between States in which they are invoked. This underlying and arguably inherent uncertainty as the legal status and enforcement of even well-known, much invoked, and apparently well-accepted international environmental principles serves as an appropriate backdrop for the subsequent examination of a number of cases adjudicated before various international tribunals, discussed below.

A further difficulty that must be borne in mind when examining such international case law is, to paraphrase Brownlie, the fact that many so-called 'environmental' disputes arise in the context of multilateral or bilateral treaties that are not explicitly environmental in their remit. Okowa too distinguishes between what she considers to be strictly 'environmental' disputes, presumably meaning disputes over the precise level of prescribed environmental protection standards; and other cases that do not in themselves raise questions of environmental protection, but where the legality or illegality of State action has to be determined by reference to applicable environmental standards.[150] It is precisely within this latter type of case, where applicable envir-

[148] Kwiatkowska (2003) above, n 146, at 45.
[149] *Ibid*, at 46.
[150] Okowa, (1998) above, n 110, at 160–1.

onmental principles, rules and/or standards are invoked by one State against another State that is at least ostensibly acting within the parameters of its sovereignty and sovereign rights under international law that international adjudication is needed but arguably has not been completely forthcoming until now. Case law examples from the jurisprudence of the ICJ, and the WTO Panel and Appellate Body decisions, as well as the ITLOS jurisprudence, serve to illustrate the nature of this problem.

For example, the *Gabcikovo-Nagymaros case* between Hungary and Slovakia before the ICJ,[151] was really concerned with whether Hungary could repudiate the terms of a bilateral 1977 treaty agreed between herself and the then Czechoslovakia purporting to put into place a plan to build a series of dams and other river diversions in the Danube River that passed through both countries. Hungary attempted to rely on environmental concerns to justify its unilateral refusal to fulfil the terms of the 1977 bilateral treaty,[152] and in this context was successful in getting the Court to acknowledge that later developments in environmental protection law should be allowed to colour the nature of the treaty obligations entered into: 'The Court wishes to point out that newly developed norms of environmental law are relevant for the implementation of the [bilateral] Treaty'.[153] However, the Court prefaced this statement with the observation that neither of the Parties had 'contended that new peremptory norms of international environmental law had emerged since the conclusion of the 1977 Treaty',[154] thus neatly side-stepping the need to assess the potentially very serious legal implications of these new environmental norms being ascribed such status.

Moreover, the Court neither articulates the precise terms of these new environmental norms, nor does it offer specific guidance to the disputing parties before it as to how these norms are to be implemented between them, merely stating in this respect that '(i)t is for the Parties themselves to find an agreed solution that takes account of the objectives of the [bilateral] Treaty, which must be pursued in a joint and integrated way, as well as the norms of international environmental law and the principles of the law of international watercourses'.[155] As we shall see below, this approach is replicated in the jurisprudence of the various law of the sea tribunals that have been seized of similar questions. Even when the Court in the present case alludes to the preventive principle, it does not explain the legal implications of the application of this principle: 'The Court is mindful that, in the field of environmental protection, vigilance and prevention are required on account of the often irreversible character damage to the environment and of the limitations inherent in the very mechanism of reparation of this type of damage'.[156] Thus, in the 'Danube Dams' case, as it is also known as; the Court appears to have accepted the legal concept of 'sustainable development' and the fact that the preventive and possibly even the precautionary principles are now part of international law.[157] But it failed to articulate exactly how these were to be applied by these States to the dam development project concerned.

On the other hand, the Court was at pains to confirm that 'neither of the two Parties contended that new peremptory norms of environmental law had emerged since the

[151] *Gabcikovo-Nagymaros Case* (Hungary/Slovakia) ICJ Rep (1997) above, n 52.
[152] *Ibid*, considered in the judgment from para 111 onwards.
[153] *Ibid*, at para 112.
[154] *Ibid*.
[155] *Ibid*, at para 141.
[156] *Ibid*, at para 140.
[157] *Ibid*, at para 140.

conclusion of the 1977 Treaty'.[158] Moreover, the Court pointed out that although these newly established environmental norms had to be taken into consideration by these two States when implementing their bilateral treaty, they did not provide the States concerned with specific obligations of performance.[159] Therefore, these States were jointly responsible for transforming these general environmental norms into specific obligations of performance through a process of consultation and negotiation in good faith.[160] As will be seen below, this reluctance on the part of the Court to elucidate the specific rights and duties of States incurred as a result of the application of apparently binding environmental norms of international law is a recurring theme of the various international tribunal judgments considered here. For Paulus, the *Gabcikovo* judgment, 'with its insistence on negotiation rather than a clear and unequivocal pronouncement', exemplifies the fact that 'litigation usually does not lead to definitive results'.[161] According to him, 'environmental situations are often too complex and technical to be adjudicated in a classical manner. Negotiation between the parties cannot be substituted by judicial *fiat*'.[162]

In the *Beef Hormones* case before the WTO dispute settlement system,[163] and involving the EU on the one hand, and the US and Canada on the other, the legal question posed was at least in part as to whether the EU was entitled to invoke the precautionary principle to justify its ban on the import of US beef derived from growth hormone-treated cattle. Both the WTO Panel and Appellate Body considered this issue and took a fairly narrow view of the legal status of the precautionary principle under international law. Significantly, these judicial bodies held that the mere invocation of the precautionary principle as a legal basis for justifying the ban, without further evidence derived from the required scientific risk assessment exercise under the terms of the Sanitary and Phytosanitary (SPS) Agreement would not be acceptable. This is notwithstanding the fact that as Van den Bossche notes, 'while the SPS Agreement uses science as a touchstone against which SPS measures are judged, it also recognises the fact that science does not always have clear answers to regulatory problems. Situations may arise where there is insufficient scientific evidence regarding the existence and extent of the relevant risk, but where governments nonetheless consider they need to act promptly and take measures to avoid possible harm. Thus, governments act with precaution without waiting for the collection of sufficient scientific information to conclusively assess the risks. This is commonly referred to as acting in accordance with the "precautionary principle". Under certain conditions, Article 5.7 of the SPS Agreement allows [WTO] Members to take provisional SPS measures where scientific evidence is insufficient'.[164]

The WTO Panel and Appellate Body *Beef Hormones* decisions on the uncertainty surrounding the legal status of the precautionary principle have been recently upheld

[158] *Ibid*, at para 112.

[159] *Ibid*.

[160] *Ibid*.

[161] Paulus (2007) above, n 133, at 362.

[162] *Ibid*.

[163] Re: *European Communities—Measures Concerning Meat and Meat Products (Hormones)* case, DS26. Accessible at: http://www.wto.org.

[164] Peter Van den Bossche, *The Law and Policy of the World Trade Organization: Text, Cases and Materials*, Cambridge: Cambridge University Press (2005) at 465–66, citing Article 5.7 of the SPS Agreement.

by the Panel decision in the *EC-Biotech Products* case.[165] Specifically, the Panel noted that: 'there has, to date, been no authoritative decision by an international court of tribunal which recognizes the precautionary principle as a principle of general or customary international law'.[166] Thus, the Panel concludes that 'the legal status of the precautionary principle remains unsettled, like the Appellate Body before us' in the *Beef Hormones* decision.[167] Moreover, the Panel in the EC-*Biotech Products* case declined to resolve this issue of the uncertain legal status of the precautionary principle and noted further that it was unnecessary to do so. Prévost however observes that it 'is difficult to see how it could be regarded as 'unnecessary' in this dispute. As pointed out by the Panel itself, 'if the precautionary principle has become a general principle of law or a rule of customary international law, it *must* be taken into account in the interpretation of the SPS Agreement under Article 31.3(c) of the VCLT. (emphasis in original) It therefore seems imperative for the Panel to decide whether the precautionary principle has achieved this status, in order for it to know whether it is obliged to have regard to this principle'.[168]

A further, cautionary, implication for the invocation and application of environmental principles by States that arises from the outcomes of both the WTO *Beef Hormones* and subsequent *EC-Biotech Products* cases relates to the fact that the reliance on the precautionary principle by the European Community in both these cases was ostensibly to protect human health, rather than guard against environmental threats, *per se*. Thus, it is pertinent to ask just how far the precautionary principle or approach could be invoked by a WTO Member against a product to ensure protection against 'pure' environmental or ecological damage to the natural environment, especially damage to wildlife, as opposed to its arguably more highly prioritised application to human health and food safety issues. In other words, as the invocation of the precautionary principle on the latter issue was unsuccessful, there is arguably little chance that it will be more successfully invoked and applied to the former issue, where the perceived threat is 'merely' to elements of the 'natural' rather than 'human' environment.

A completion of this admittedly impressionistic picture of the invocation of environmental principles before international tribunals by considering three cases decided by the ITLOS, namely, the *Southern Bluefin Tuna* (Australia and New Zealand v Japan), *MOX Plant* (Ireland v UK) and *Land Reclamation* (Malaysia v Singapore) Provisional Measures cases. Each of these ITLOS cases involved requests by applicant States for provisional measures against the allegedly environmentally damaging actions of the respondent State. It should first be noted in this respect that applications for provisional measures to the ITLOS under the 1982 Convention incorporates a significant legal innovation in favour of enhancing the opportunities for environmental protection in that such provisional measures can be requested not merely in respect of the traditional legal basis of potential damage to the interests of the State concerned, but also in respect of potential or actual damage or harm to the marine environment.[169] So far however there has been little judicial endorsement or application of this additional legal basis for the activation of provisional measures.

[165] *EC-Biotech Products*, WTO Panel decision, 29 September 2006, above, n 125.

[166] *Ibid*, at para 7.88, on p 339 of the Panel Report.

[167] *Ibid*, at para 7.89, on p 340–341.

[168] Prévost (2007) above, n 126, at 91.

[169] Article 290.1 of the 1982 UN Law of the Sea Convention provides that 'If a dispute has been duly submitted to a court or tribunal, which considers that prima facie it has jurisdiction under this Part or Part XI,

The first observation to make about this trio of cases is that none of them in fact proceeded to their *Merits* phase. This was particularly unfortunate in the *Southern Bluefin Tuna* case(s), which despite being the first of these cases from a chronological perspective, can now be seen in retrospect as perhaps the high point of the Tribunal's jurisprudence on the legal status and application of several environmental principles under general international law in the maritime context, notably that of the precautionary principle. The inchoate nature of these three ITLOS cases has also had a tantalising effect among legal commentators, leading to much speculation as to the possible outcomes of each of these cases. While not wishing to detract from these valiant efforts, it should be noted that definitive answers to the questions raised during the proceedings in each of these three cases are still elusive, with one being settled (*Land Reclamation*), another not proceeding to the merits phase (*Southern Bluefin Tuna*), and the last one currently (and possibly terminally) suspended in its proceedings (*MOX Plant*).

In the *Southern Bluefin Tuna* (Provisional Measures) case before the ITLOS on the other hand, the Tribunal stated in its Order granting the measures requested by the plaintiff States, Australia and New Zealand, that the parties should act 'with prudence and caution to ensure the effective conservation measures are taken to prevent serious harm to the stock of southern bluefin tuna'.[170] According to Rashbrooke, '(i)t is the reference to acting with "prudence and caution" in the face of scientific uncertainty which has led commentators to welcome the Tribunal's decision as showing it to be open to application of the precautionary principle'.[171] However, she concludes that 'the contribution of this case to the normative currency of the precautionary principle would have been much greater if ITLOS had made explicit reference to the precautionary principle in the Order itself . . .'.[172]

The *MOX Plant* litigation brought the invocation of the precautionary principle to the ITLOS once again. Indeed, it is possible to see that the abortive *MOX Plant* provisional measures cases before both the ITLOS and OSPAR tribunal as neatly encapsulating the dilemma that international environmental law currently finds itself, between generally applicable but non-binding principles and specific treaty rules that may not however be applicable to the dispute in the instant case between two (or more) States. In summary, Ireland's strategy in this case was to impute the inclusion of certain environmental principles within the generally-worded provisions of Part XII of the 1982 Convention seeking to protect and preserve the marine environment as a whole. The stumbling block here was the apparently restrictive nature of the provision for the applicable international law to resolve such disputes under Part XV of the 1982 UNCLOS. Article 293.1 states as follows: 'A court or tribunal having jurisdiction under this section shall apply this Convention and other rules of international law not incompatible with this Convention'.

section 5, the court or tribunal may prescribe any provisional measures which it considers appropriate under the circumstances to reserve the respective rights of the parties to the dispute or to prevent serious harm to the marine environment, pending the final decision'. (emphasis added)

170 *Southern Bluefin Tuna* cases Nos 3 and 4 (1999) At para 77 of the ITLOS Order of 27 August 1999.

171 Gwenaele Rashbrooke, 'The International Tribunal for the Law of the Sea: A Forum for the Development of Principles of International Environmental Law?', *International Journal of Marine and Coastal Law*, Vol 19, No 4 (December, 2004) 515–535 at 523, citing Philippe Sands (2003) above, n 20, at 275.

172 Rashbrooke, above, n 171, at 523.

Ireland pursued arguments on two main fronts in this respect. First, that the tribunal should have regard to the detailed regulation found in separate but not un-related marine pollution treaties covering the issue at hand, namely, discharges of low-level nuclear wastes into the Irish Sea lying between the British and Irish isles.[173] Ireland maintained that recourse to these related treaties would assist the tribunal in interpreting the generally worded provisions contained in Part XII of the 1982 UNCLOS. Second, Ireland argued that these related treaties were in any case implicitly brought within the scope of the applicable international law to the dispute at hand by virtue of the so-called *renvoi* clauses in several provisions within Part XII making explicit reference to 'applicable international rules and standards established through competent international organizations or diplomatic conferences'.

Klein submits that Ireland's approach to this case is entirely consistent with the substantive obligations of the 1982 Convention.[174] In so far as this is taken to mean that the applicable international law established sometime previous to the actual dispute at hand needs to be interpreted in the light of evolution in general international law, with particular reference in this instance to the subsequent development of general environmental principles, this argument replicates that which was made by the ICJ itself in the *Gabcikovo* case,[175] considered above. However, this progressive approach is somewhat undermined by the arbitral tribunal's finding on jurisdiction which clearly distinguishes the claims Ireland could make under the 1982 Convention, as opposed to those other related instruments. Although Klein rightly observes that this decision does not render inadmissible resort to other related international instruments to interpret and apply the provisions of Part XII,[176] she has to accept that the 'Convention does not create a complete system that automatically implements all necessary environmental rules and standards'.[177]

Boyle and Chinkin on the other hand are clear that the Irish arguments advocating the application of 'more detailed rules on environmental impact assessment and the precautionary principle found in European law and European regional treaties' to buttress similar, but admittedly more generally-worded, principles within the 1982 Convention would have had the effect of turning a specific, treaty-based dispute settlement system that confers only 'limited compulsory jurisdiction' into a 'general jurisdiction clause over non-UNCLOS aspects of the dispute'.[178] They conclude categorically that: '(u)sing an applicable law provision for this purpose is not an argument that any international tribunal has so far found persuasive'.[179] This view is arguably correct in relation to the Irish arguments in favour of the specific implementation of the precautionary principle, which is in any case not explicitly mentioned within the 1982 Convention itself. Thus, the difficulties posed by both the invocation and attempted application of the precautionary principle within this bilateral situation can

[173] The specific treaties whose provisions were relied upon by Ireland include the 1992 OSPAR and the 1998 Aarhus Conventions.

[174] Klein (2005) above, n 139, at 151.

[175] As Fitzmaurice notes, '(t)he Court has made a very forceful statement as to the importance of taking into consideration new environmental standards and norms', citing para 140 of the *Gabcikovo-Nagymaros* ICJ Judgment (1997) above, n 52. See: Fitzmaurice (2002) above, n 59, at 383.

[176] Klein,above, n 139, at 151, fn.106.

[177] Klein above, n 139, citing Jonathan I Charney, 'The Protection of the Marine Environment by the 1982 UNCLOS', *Georgia International Environmental Law Review*, Vol 7 (1995) 731, at 735.

[178] Boyle and Chinkin (2007) above, n 136, at 274.

[179] *Ibid.*

be equated with the WTO's *EC-Biotech* case whereby the Biosafety Protocol was invoked as an applicable legal authority, despite the fact that the several of the disputing WTO Members in that case were not parties to the Protocol. However, one might be less sanguine about the application of the Boyle and Chinkin view equally to the EIA principle, which is after all expressly incorporated within the 1982 Convention by Article 206,[180] and also forms the subject of more precisely-worded regional obligations that are directly applicable between the two States involved in the form of both the Espoo, and Aarhus Conventions, and relevant EC EIA and Strategic Environmental Assessment Directives. Moreover, the fact that these relevant UN-ECE treaties were initially exclusively regional in terms of their geographical scope is negated by the fact that they are now open to all States, therefore becoming potentially global treaties within their specific issue areas.

Notwithstanding the jurisdictional issues that later swallowed up this particular litigation, as to whether the correct tribunal to hear the merits of the case is an UNCLOS Annex VII arbitral tribunal, or an arbitral tribunal established under the 1992 Paris OSPAR Convention, or even, as appears now to be in fact the case—the European Court of Justice (ECJ), on the basis that it is a dispute between fellow European Union Member States over a matter that comes within the competence of the 1957 Rome Treaty establishing the European Communities (as amended),[181] Ireland's application for provisional measures before the ITLOS again afforded the Tribunal the opportunity to consider whether such measures could be applied at least in part on the basis of the prevention of serious harm to the marine environment, especially as a consequence of the application of the precautionary principle. As the Tribunal acknowledged in its Order in respect of Ireland's request, 'Ireland argues that the precautionary principle places a burden on the United Kingdom to demonstrate that no harm would arise from discharges and other consequences of the operation of the MOX plant, should it proceed, and that this principle might usefully inform the assessment by the Tribunal of the urgency of the measures it is required to take in respect of the operation of the MOX plant'.[182] In the event, the ITLOS declined to prescribe the provisional measures requested by Ireland, notably a moratorium on the authorisation and operation of the MOX plant and the discharge of any radioactive substances into the Irish Sea area.[183] Instead, the Tribunal noted the

[180] Article 206 (Assessment of potential effects of activities) of the 1982 UNCLOS provides that:

> Where States have reasonable grounds for believing that planned activities under their jurisdiction and control may cause substantial pollution of or significant and harmful changes to the marine environment, they shall, as far as practicable, assess the potential effects of such activities on the marine environment and shall communicate reports of such assessments in the manner provided in Article 205.

[181] The European Court of Justice ECJ has now delivered a judgment to this effect, ruling that the ECJ has exclusive jurisdiction to rule on disputes concerning the interpretation and application of the provisions of the Convention which form part of the Community legal order and therefore, by bringing proceedings against the United Kingdom within the framework of the Convention on the Law of the Sea, Ireland has breached Community law See: Commission of the European Communities v. Ireland, Judgment of the Court of Justice, Case C-459/03, 30 May, 2006. For an account of the MOX plant litigation culminating with the European Commission's action against Ireland before the ECJ, see: Robin Churchill and Joanne Scott 'The MOX Plant Litigation: The First Half-Life', *International and Comparative Law Quarterly*, Vol 53, Part 3 (July 2004) 643–676.

[182] MOX Plant Case, (*Ireland v UK*) ITLOS Order of 3 December 2001, at para 71.

[183] Para 29 of ITLOS Order of 3 December 2001.

fundamental nature of the duty of co-operation in the prevention of marine pollution under both Part XII of the Law of the Sea Convention and general international law, declaring that, 'prudence and caution require that Ireland and the United Kingdom co-operate in exchanging information concerning risks or effects of the operation of the MOX plant and in devising ways to deal with them, as appropriate'.[184] The significant disparity between the Irish and Tribunal articulations of both the invocation and application of the precautionary principle to this case is evident in the relative strengths of the wording employed. In particular, the Tribunal neither acknowledges the legal status of the precautionary approach as an accepted international legal principle, nor does it explicate in any detail on the legal implications of the application of 'prudence and caution', beyond relying on this term to enjoin the Parties to co-operate in the manner it prescribes. It then delivered an alternative declaration of provisional measures that specifically enjoined the Parties to co-operate towards the settlement of the dispute by entering into bilateral consultations to exchange information as to the possible consequences of the commissioning and operation of the MOX plant for the Irish Sea, and devising measures to prevent marine pollution which might result for the operation of the MOX plant.[185]

This aspect of the Order has been criticised by a number of distinguished commentators.[186] Kwiatkowska, for example, is critical of the apparent conjoining of what she regards as the separate requirements of 'urgency', under Article 290.5 of the 1982 UNCLOS, and the need to preserve the rights of the parties, or to prevent serious harm to the environment, under Article 290.1.[187] While accepting that the success or failure of such a provisional measures application 'depends on the quality of the evidence presented to the Tribunal [ITLOS] and [. . .] the urgency of the situation at hand',[188] Rothwell too, expresses disappointment at the outcome of the Irish provisional measures application before ITLOS. He notes that '. . . it was clear that there existed a potential environmental threat from the commencement of the operations of the Sellafield site and given the relatively short period of time until proceedings were to commence before the Annex VII Arbitral Tribunal, it would not have seemed inappropriate in this instance to issue the orders that were sought',[189] contrasting the ITLOS approach in this case with its approach in the *Southern Bluefin Tuna* case, where the requested provisional measures by Australia and New Zealand were granted. Kwiatkowska however explains this apparent discrepancy by observing that in this case both sides, namely, Australia and New Zealand on the one side and Japan on the other, accepted that the Bluefin Tuna stocks in question were depleted to the extent that this constituted 'serious harm to the environment', thus achieving the threshold for provisional measures to be prescribed; unlike in the *MOX Plant* case, where the triggering or activating

[184] Para 84 of ITLOS Order of 3 December 2001. Also cited in Churchill and Scott (2004) above, n 181, at 648.

[185] Para.1 (a)-(c) of the ITLOS Declaration in the Order of 3 December 2001.

[186] As cited in Churchill and Scott, see Chester Brown, Provisional Measures Before the International Tribunal for the Law of the Sea', *International Journal of Marine and Coastal Law,* Vol 17 (2002) 267; and Kwiatkowska (2003) above, n 146.

[187] Kwiatkowska (2003) above, n 146, 33–38.

[188] Donald R Rothwell, 'The International Tribunal for the Law of the Sea and Marine Environmental Protection: Expanding the Horizons of International Oceans Governance', in Elisabeth Mann Borghese, Aldo Chircop and Moira McConnell (eds) *Ocean Yearbook*, Vol 17 (2003) 26–55, at 47–48.

[189] Rothwell (2003) above, n 188, at 48.

threshold finding of a 'serious harm to the environment' was heavily contested between the two parties, namely, the UK and Ireland.[190]

Perhaps more contentiously, Kwiatkowska also objects to the distinction made by ITLOS between substantive environmental obligations, which include preventing the marine environment from harm; and procedural obligations, most notably comprising the requirements to conduct environmental impact assessment (EIA), provide access to environmental information, and engage in consultations with neighbouring States. In particular, she suggests that the ITLOS application of the precautionary approach and hence a lower threshold of proof for breach of the latter, procedural rights, followed by the reluctance by ITLOS to adopt a precautionary stance for the former substantive obligations, resulting in a higher threshold of proof for breach of these, 'is seriously flawed'.[191]

However, the apparent ITLOS distinction between the substantive and procedural rules for environmental protection is explicable on the basis that States can only be found responsible, and thus potentially liable, for causing 'serious harm to the marine environment' of other States, or beyond national jurisdiction. Therefore, the culpability of a State, in the absence of any outright and voluntary acceptance of its responsibility under international law, must be proven for such responsibility to hold. Within this context, the lack of due diligence on the part of the allegedly responsible State can infer such culpability. Such due diligence can in turn be surmised or implied on the part of the responsible State if it is able to show that it has been transparent in its dealings with its neighbouring States, for example, through including them in the EIA process, allowing them access to environmental information and consulting them in good faith on their major infrastructure plans, especially where these are to be located in frontier areas. Failure to evidence these efforts renders the State concerned vulnerable to the suggestion that it is not exercising due diligence and therefore susceptible to an application of provisional measures against it. However, in the absence of concrete evidence of both damage and the culpability of the State concerned in such damage, this would not be sufficient to render this State responsible under international law. This would explain the need to apply a lower threshold of proof for finding a breach of these procedural duties, hence implying the lack of due diligence on the part of the responsible State; and a higher threshold, or burden, of proof for the much more serious legal implications of State responsibility following a finding of a breach of a substantive obligation 'to prevent serious harm to the marine environment'.

Following the ITLOS Order on provisional measures in this case, the Annex VII arbitral Tribunal convened, and after first inviting and then considering a further provisional measures application from Ireland, ultimately decided it was not appropriate to issue such measures on the basis of the prevention of serious harm to the marine environment, as allowed under Article 290.1 of the Law of the Sea Convention. According to the Tribunal, Ireland had not established that any harm that might be caused to the marine environment would be 'serious'. Churchill and Scott note that like the OSPAR Convention Tribunal before it, the Annex VII Tribunal 'appears to regard the burden of proof as falling on Ireland to show significant damage'. However, they point out that if either of these Tribunals had applied the precaution-

[190] Kwiatkowska (2003) above, n 146, at 39

[191] Kwiatkowska (2003) above, n 146, at 41.

ary principle, which is explicitly incorporated in Article 2.2(a) of the OSPAR Convention, then they may have reached different views as to which of the two parties had the burden of proof in this provisional measures application.[192]

Finally, in the *Land Reclamation (Provisional Measures)* case between Malaysia and Singapore,[193] Malaysia requested inter alia that Singapore:

a) suspend land reclamation activities it was undertaking in the vicinity of the common maritime frontier between the two States parties to the 1982 UN Convention on the Law of the Sea (UNCLOS, 1982);
b) provide Malaysia with full information of the reclamation works; and
c) affording Malaysia a full opportunity to comment upon the reclamation works and their potential impacts.

However, the ITLOS declined to prescribe the provisional measures requested by Malaysia, preferring again to substitute the requested measures for its own provisional measures. The Tribunal arrived at this decision despite observing that 'an assessment concerning the land reclamation works on waters under the jurisdiction of Malaysia has not been undertaken by Singapore',[194] thus apparently acknowledging the need for an EIA procedure for such large infrastructure development projects, with transboundary implications as in the present case.[195] An EIA procedure incorporating a precautionary approach would arguably have had a wider, transboundary remit, encompassing the legitimate interests of such a close neighbouring State as Malaysia in this case,[196] but this view was not necessarily accepted by the Tribunal. Instead, in terms remarkably similar to its pronouncements in the *MOX Plant* case (discussed above), the Tribunal confined itself to holding that 'prudence and caution' required both Parties to establish mechanisms for exchanging information, assessing the risks of the reclamation projects and devising ways to deal with them.[197] By requiring the parties to this dispute to come to an agreement by themselves, the Tribunal certainly progressively developed the principle of co-operation as the preferred means to resolve such bilateral disputes.

On the other hand, it is possible to argue that this emphasis on achieving a suitable solution through the judicial imposition of bilateral negotiations between the Parties themselves merely serves to highlight the reluctance of the Tribunal to insist on the terms of the bilateral solution as a matter of the correct application of the international law to this dispute in the first place. Thus, the Tribunal alighted on the next best solution, namely, enjoining the Parties to co-operate in a suitably constrained way that rendered it difficult, if not impossible, to envisage them arriving at any other type solution

[192] Churchill and Scott (2004) above, n 181, at 651.

[193] *Case Concerning Land Reclamation by Singapore in and around the Straits of Johor (Malaysia v Singapore)*, Request for Provisional Measures, Order, ITLOS Case No 12, 8 October 2003. Accessible at: http://www.itlos.org.

[194] *Ibid*, at para 95 of the Order.

[195] As noted earlier in relation to the *MOX Plant* litigation, the obligation to conduct such an assessment and communicate the resulting report of this assessment, through the competent international organizations involved, to all States is arguably required by Arts 206 and 205, respectively, of the 1982 UN Law of the Sea Convention.

[196] In this respect, see the 1991 ECE Convention on Transboundary Environmental Impact Assessment, adopted in Espoo, Finland, which expressly requires that neighbouring States need to be consulted for significant infrastructure projects that would have transboundary effects.

[197] Para 99 of the ITLOS Land Reclamation Order, above, n 193, cited in Rashbrooke (2004), above, n 171, at 532.

to the dispute at hand than the one they did eventually reach.[198] The Tribunal specified the type of bilateral forum (in the form of a group of independent experts) that should be established to hear the scientific and other arguments put forward by both sides.[199] It also specified time limits for the bilaterally negotiated solutions to be arrived at and presented back to the Tribunal itself as the concrete results of this constrained bilateral negotiations procedure.[200] Lo and behold, this is exactly what in fact occurred, with the resulting Settlement Agreement now officially constituting the end of the dispute.[201]

The fact that the appropriate resolution to the dispute was eventually arrived at by the parties themselves, while wholly to be commended in itself, unfortunately leaves unanswered the all-important question as to whether this resolution is actually required by the applicable international law on the issues raised by the dispute. As Klein notes in this context, the 'Tribunal's desire to facilitate the parties' agreements reached during the course of proceedings obscured how, or if, the criteria of Article 290 (regarding Provisional Measures) were met'.[202] Thus, vital jurisprudence that could have been developed, and enunciated by the Tribunal in arriving at this solution as a binding judgment for the two States concerned has not taken place and therefore cannot be relied upon in future cases of this genre. While it is true that, in common with other international tribunals, ITLOS does not apply the *stare decisis* doctrine, whereby their decisions would form legal precedents for other States finding themselves in similar situations to the case at hand; nevertheless, it is submitted here that the resulting final Settlement Agreement of 2005 presents us with only the conclusions of what must have been a very interesting and informative debate between the two parties as to the true extent of their international legal obligations and rights inter alia towards each other, and the protection of their shared marine environment. This debate is in itself vitally important for the progressive development of applicable international environmental principles to future bilateral disputes involving similar circumstances. It is a debate that should have been addressed in a definitive judgment on the issues by ITLOS, rather than left to the parties to work out on their own.

In calling for such a definitive judgment, one should be conscious that this argument can be construed as requesting too much of the international judicial function. It is as well to recall Kwiatkowska's gentle rebuke of the Separate Opinions of both Judge *ad hoc* Szekely in the *MOX Plant* case,[203] and Judge *ad hoc* Shearer in the *Bluefin Tuna* case,[204] in which they criticised, inter alia, the excessively *diplomatic,* as opposed to

[198] Churchill notes how the Tribunal used the opportunity rendered to it by the provisional measures decision to enforce this extended principle of co-operation upon the two parties to the dispute in an arguably quite different manner to what had actually been initially requested by Malaysia in her original application. See Churchill (2006) above, n 121, at 412.

[199] By para 106(1)(a)(i) of the Order of the International Tribunal for the Law of the Sea in the Case Concerning Land Reclamation by Singapore In and Around the Straits of Johor (*Malaysia v Singapore*), Request for Provisional Measures, 8 October 2003.

[200] The Group of independent Experts (GOE) established pursuant to the above ITLOS Order submitted their report to the Parties on 5 November 2004.

[201] On the basis of the GOE report above, the Parties were able to conclude an agreement, signed on 26 April 2005 that constitutes a full and final settlement of the dispute. See *Case Concerning Land Reclamation by Singapore In and Around the Straits of Johor (Malaysia v Singapore) Settlement Agreement* (hereinafter, 2005 Settlement Agreement) the text of which is accessible at http://www.mfa.gov.sg/internet/press/land/Settlement_Agreement.pdf.

[202] Klein (2005) above, n 139, at 78.

[203] *MOX Plant* case (2001), Separate Opinion of Judge *ad hoc* Szekely, at para 21.

[204] *Southern Bluefin Tuna* case (1999) Separate Opinion of Judge *ad hoc* Shearer.

judicial, role the ITLOS fulfilled in both these cases. In this context, she responds with the rejoinder that multiple forms of 'preventive diplomacy' have always played an important role in ICJ and latterly, ITLOS judicial practice.[205] On the other hand, problems persist over the true nature of the role played by the Tribunal in these two cases. Apart from the lack of transparency as to how the conclusions presented in the 2005 Settlement Agreement were ultimately arrived at, it is also undoubtedly the case that the Agreement itself by definition has less international legal authority than a Judgment of the Tribunal would have. Indeed, this whole process could perhaps rather uncharitably be described as the application of an enforced negotiation procedure by recourse to international tribunal, which while yielding the desired result, contributes little by way of the elucidation and application of the relevant international environmental principles to the specific circumstances of the case at hand by a competent and authoritative international tribunal established to perform exactly this role.

Thus, whatever useful conclusions were achieved by the 2005 Settlement Agreement, notably, the acceptance and implementation by Singapore of arguably significant modifications to the land reclamation project to take into account Malaysia's interests in the area concerned,[206] and the payment of compensation by Singapore to Malaysia on behalf of losses suffered by Malaysian fishermen as a result of the reclamation works;[207] we are none the wiser as to the reasoning behind these conclusions in the 2005 Agreement. In particular, can it be assumed that Singapore's undertakings to modify the reclamation works concerned constitute an implicit acceptance that these changes should have been introduced at an earlier stage of the project as a result of the implementation of a more comprehensive and transboundary EIA? Does the acceptance of liability on the part of Singapore as implied by the compensation payment to the negatively affected livelihoods of Malaysian fishermen nevertheless also signal that Malaysia's concerns in respect of the alleged serious harm to the shared marine environment between the two neighbouring countries ultimately did not result in remedial action that required compensation? We are unable to do much more than speculate about the answers to these questions at the moment. Nor can we necessarily derive any legal implications from them for application to future situations of similar circumstances. Indeed, it may be noted that the title of Rashbrooke's article is both prescient and suitably apt: the ITLOS has only *developed,* rather than actually *applied,* the environmental principles that have been invoked in the cases held before it so far.[208] The collective effect of these ITLOS decisions is to undermine the initially optimistic outlook presented by Rothwell when he suggests that '(t)he lesson from these early ITLOS decisions is that coastal States seeking to rely upon existing and developing marine environmental (protection) principles do have open to them clear means by which they can seek some resolution from the new UNCLOS institutions'.[209] Indeed, given the uncertainty in the application of the relevant environmental principles between States themselves as evidenced by the above cases, it is surprising to note that they are nevertheless considered to be applicable to domestic activities within States. Perhaps the best

[205] Kwiatkowska, IJMCL (2003) above, n 146, at 43.
[206] Paras 1–5 of the 2005 Settlement Agreement, above, n 201.
[207] Para 7 of the 2005 Agreement, above, n 201.
[208] Rashbrooke, IJMCL (2004) above, n 171.
[209] Rothwell (2003) above, n 188, at 51.

thing that can be said about this assumption is that they are only applicable within States in accordance with the States' individual interpretations of the nature of their implementation.

A further opportunity for the International Court of Justice to clarify the uncertainties as to both the legal status and implications of the application of accepted environmental principles in the international relations between States presented itself with the application brought by Argentina against Uruguay before the Court in relation to a bilateral treaty between these two States called the Statute of the River Uruguay, adopted in 1975. In its application before the Court, Argentina alleged that Uruguay unilaterally authorised the construction of pulp mills and a port for servicing these mills, without complying with the prior notification and consultation procedure required by the 1975 Statute agreed between the two countries. Moreover, Argentina claims that if the pulp mills are allowed to be built, they will, inter alia, 'damage the environment of the River Uruguay'. A number of important legal questions will therefore hopefully be addressed by the ICJ's consideration of the present application in the *Merits* stage of this case.[210] These are as follows: 1) the legal status of the obligation to notify and consult with neighbouring States over environmentally hazardous activities; 2) whether the implementation of the preventive principle against potential environmental damage now also includes the obligation to prepare a full, objective study on the environmental impact of the proposed hazardous activity, and finally, 3) whether Uruguay has incurred international responsibility for its failure to undertake the above actions, assuming these were applicable to it as a matter of conventional and/or customary international law.[211]

The Court's consideration of these issues in the forthcoming judgment at the *Merits* stage of these proceedings is therefore eagerly anticipated. However interesting the content of this judgment is for the further development of international environmental law, it is as well to recall Paulus's neat summation of the essential nature of the implementation of environmental accords: 'it is informal rather than formal, dominated by negotiation rather than adjudication; often applies informal standards rather than precise rules, and is facilitative rather than confrontational'.[212] Hence, international environmental law has developed international institutional mechanisms to facilitate these very characteristics, in the form of treaty non-compliance mechanisms, as will be considered below, in the next Section of this essay.

V. THE DILEMMA OF INTERNATIONAL ENVIRONMENTAL LAW RESOLVED? ENVIRONMENTAL TREATY NON-COMPLIANCE MECHANISMS

Faced with the reality that few, if any, of the environmental principles invoked before various international tribunals in the still nascent case law jurisprudence on the application of international environmental law have in fact been applied in such a way as to directly constrain the environmentally degrading actions of a sovereign State, international environmental law has arguably pursued an alternative pathway towards

[210] The ICJ decision on Argentina's provisional measures application has already been discussed in Section II, n 105.

[211] *Pulp Mills case (Argentina v Uruguay)* ICJ (2006). See ICJ Press Release, 2006/17, 4 May 2006.

[212] Paulus (2007) above, n 133, at 362.

ensuring adherence to its obligations, namely, through the establishment of non-compliance mechanisms aimed at securing the co-operation of the errant States concerned to first accept and then act upon its non-compliant behaviour. The emergence of these mechanisms at least implicitly highlights the shortcomings of the dispute settlement systems established by the multilateral environmental agreements (MEAs). As Churchill and Ulfstein note in this context, allegations of non-compliance to environmental treaty obligations 'could in theory be resolved through traditional forms of dispute settlement. MEAs, however, offer fairly limited possibilities for binding dispute settlement'.[213] Fitzmaurice and Redgwell make the same point, noting that '(m)any recent environmental agreements also incorporate traditional dispute settlement mechanisms, though rarely with provision for compulsory third party dispute settlement'.[214] Thus, Churchill and Ulfstein observe that rather 'than place much emphasis on traditional dispute settlement procedures, some MEAs establish specific bodies to determine and deal with cases of non-compliance with substantive commitments'.[215] However, Fitzmaurice and Redgwell caution against the easily arrived at conclusion arising from these progressive developments in non-compliance procedures, to the effect that the availability of traditional dispute settlement mechanisms does not assist in the prevention of environmental harm, as these are usually only engaged in after the damage has occurred as a result of the alleged non-compliance, and hence, breach of environmental treaty obligation. While the preventive effect of traditional dispute settlement mechanisms should not be doubted, it is nevertheless the case that these mechanisms must be both compulsory in procedure and binding in result to be capable of exerting the maximum preventive effects on States parties contemplating the non-compliance of their environmental treaty obligations.

A further legal difficulty relates to the constraining effect on the capability of traditional international dispute settlement mechanisms, especially those of a judicial character, to resolve disputes arising over the alleged non-compliance or breaches, of environmental treaty obligations. This legal problem relates to the nature of environmental treaty obligations, specifically their non-reciprocal yet arguably *erga omnes partes* nature (denoting obligations owed to all parties to a particular regime). As Fitzmaurice and Redgwell note, 'Obligations *erga omnes partes* are of particular relevance in the environmental context',[216] where all States party to a particular environmental treaty regime have a common interest in its implementation but at the same time will not necessarily be able to make a claim against a non-compliant State party, as 'injured' States under international law, despite the recent broadening of this concept within Article 43 of the International Law Commission (ILC)'s Draft Articles on State Responsibility.[217]

[213] Robin R Churchill and Geir Ulfstein, 'Autonomous Institutional Arrangements in Multilateral Environmental Agreements: A Little-Noticed Phenomenon in International Law', *American Journal of International Law*, Vol 94, No 4 (2000) 623–659, at 644.

[214] MA Fitzmaurice and C Redgwell, 'Environmental Non-Compliance Procedures and International Law', *Netherlands Yearbook of International Law*, Vol 31 (2000) 35–65, at 43–44.

[215] Churchill and Ulfstein (2000) above, n 213.

[216] Fitzmaurice and Redgwell (2000) above, n 124, at 53.

[217] See references in Boyle (2005) above, n 34, and Fitzmaurice and Redgwell (2000)above, n 214, at p.41. For a comprehensive analysis of the ILC's Draft Articles on State Responsibility, see James Crawford, *The International Law Commission's Articles on State Responsibility: Introduction, Text and Commentaries* (Cambridge: Cambridge University Press, 2002).

The first of these treaty-based non-compliance procedures was introduced in the 1987 Montreal Protocol to the 1985 Vienna Convention on Substances that Deplete the Ozone Layer.[218] More recently, these non-compliance mechanisms have arisen in the context of, inter alia, the 1997 Kyoto Protocol to the 1992 Framework Convention on Climate Change,[219] and the 1989 Basel Convention on Transboundary Movement of Hazardous and Other Wastes.[220] By far the most interesting of these environmental treaty compliance mechanisms so far adopted must be the mechanism agreed by the State parties to the 1998 Aarhus Convention on Environmental Information, Participation in Environmental Decision-Making and Access to Justice,[221] which will be elaborated upon below. That these non-compliance mechanisms are clearly formulated as alternatives rather than replacements for the traditional means of international law enforcement by recourse to peaceful dispute settlement is a fact that can easily be discerned by the continuing presence of such dispute settlement provisions within these treaties.

It is possible therefore to envisage the various modes of peaceful international dispute settlement as different points along a single continuum or spectrum. This spectrum ranges from bilateral negotiations at one end of the scale, through to the introduction of various third-party roles within the dispute settlement process. At this intermediate stage of the international dispute settlement continuum or spectrum, the use of third parties ranges from use of the good offices of the UN Secretary-General, through other types of third-party mediation, and moving on towards more judicially-oriented, independent third-party dispute settlement procedures, using various types of international (judicial) arbitration, ultimately ending with recourse to the International Court. Treaty compliance regimes occupy a suitable point on this scale within the section of the continuum or spectrum devoted to the introduction of a third-party judicial-type role in dispute settlement. Within this section of the dispute settlement continuum or spectrum, treaty compliance regimes would be placed somewhere before, or prior to, the formal arbitration or judicial dispute settlement procedures. As Fitzmaurice notes presciently in this respect, the established environmental treaty compliance mechanisms 'allow for the resolution of these problems without recourse to international adjudication'.[222] Churchill and Ulfstein offer a couple more reasons for the utilisation of these non-compliance procedures: 'The advantages of using the non-compliance [sic] mechanisms rather than traditional dispute settlement procedures are twofold. First, because questions of compliance with MEA commitments are multilateral in character and usually affect all parties equally rather than any particular party or parties specifically, they should preferably be addressed in a multilateral context, rather than in a bilateral dispute settlement procedure. Second,

[218] Established pursuant to Article VIII of the Montreal Protocol. Accessible at: http://hq.unep.org.

[219] Established at the 7th Meeting of the Parties (COP7) by Decision 24/CP.7. Accessible at: http://www.unfccc.int/kyoto_mechanisms/compliance/items/2875.php

[220] Established at the 6th Meeting of the Parties (COP6) (VI/16). See Mechanism for Promoting Implementation and Compliance, Terms of Reference, accessible at: http://www.basel.int/legalmatters.

[221] For a recent and comprehensive discussion of the compliance mechanism established by 1998 Aarhus Convention treaty regime, see Veit Koester, 'The Convention on Access to Information, Public Participation in Environmental Decision-Making and Access to Justice in Environmental Matters (Aarhus Convention)', Chapter 8 in Ulfstein (ed) (2007) above, n 133, 179–217.

[222] See 'The Kyoto Protocol Compliance Regime and the Law of Treaties', Chapter 8 in Malgosia Fitzmaurice and Olufemi Elias, *Contemporary Issues in the Law of Treaties* (Utrecht, Eleven International Publishing, 2005) 289–313, at 292.

non-compliance procedures may promote the resolution of compliance problems in a co-operative, rather than adversarial, manner'.[223]

Indeed, with the exception of the Kyoto Protocol, which established enforcement as well as facilitative branches in the Compliance Committee,[224] these environmental treaty compliance mechanisms do not include provisions for exerting sanctions against the non-compliant States. In other words, they are designed to play mainly facilitative, rather than enforcement, roles in ensuring compliance with specific environmental treaty obligations. For example, all these compliance regimes adopt, as an alternative to the traditional confrontational-style of international judicial dispute settlement, the possibility for a 'confessional'-type procedure whereby a State party that is aware of the very real possibility that it will not be able to comply with its international obligations under the specific environmental treaty regime is able to present itself before the appropriately established compliance committee/commission in order for its case to be considered by the committee with a view to assisting the errant State party to achieve compliance using similarly appropriate co-operative methods, rather than relying upon possible economic or other types of international sanctions, as would usually be the case.

When set against the backdrop of internationally recognised and well-established dispute settlement procedures traditionally utilised by States, it is possible to suggest that these environmental treaty compliance mechanisms have endeavoured to 'cherry pick' only the non-confrontational aspects of such established international dispute settlement procedures or mechanisms. This perception is strengthened when it is coupled with the trend noted above in respect of the role played by ITLOS in the *MOX Plant* and *Land Reclamation* cases in facilitating the negotiated settlement of these disputes through the judicious use of its unchallenged legal authority to guide the disputing parties back to the negotiating table in a formalised, time-constrained and fully accountable manner.

Thus, it would appear at first glance that international environmental law has once again developed an innovative means to ensure compliance with substantive rules and standards provided within the individual environmental treaty regimes. So far, so good. However, taking a step back to view the broader picture and consider how far the resulting practice from these individual non-compliance mechanisms may be able to inform the general development of international environmental law in terms of arriving at an optimum standard for State compliance to adopted environmental rules and standards, we are again confronted by the fragmented nature of individual treaty regimes which does not bode well for the development of a general rule or standard on compliance that could be applied either to non-party States to a particular environmental treaty, or when addressing new (or remaining) areas of environmental threats that are yet to be subject to a separate treaty instrument dealing specifically with this new (or remaining) threat.

A comparison of the various environmental compliance mechanisms provides further evidence of the regime-specific nature of these compliance mechanisms in that there is no possibility of innovative best practice within one of these regimes being held to apply to any other treaty compliance regimes, let alone to non-party States as a

[223] Churchill and Ulfstein (2000) above, n 213, at 644–645.
[224] Accessible at: http://www.unfccc.org/.

matter of general or customary international law. A good example of this legal disability afflicting the potential application of international environmental law to all States, and not merely those States that are not parties to the individual environmental treaty regimes, is in respect of the innovative extension of the right to complain against a State party's alleged non-compliance under the Aarhus Convention to individual members of the public and even environmental and/or human rights Non-Governmental Organizations (NGOs) without them necessarily having to prove a direct interest in the environmental information requested.[225] Moreover, any person complaining need not be a citizen of the State party concerned, nor in the case of an NGO complaint, need it be based in the State party concerned. However, this clearly progressive right cannot be invoked outside the confines of the immediate (Aarhus) regime, nor can it be implied within any other environmental protection or human rights treaty regime.[226] Still less can it be said to be an enforceable right under general or customary international law. As von Moltke notes in relation to the 1998 Aarhus Convention, this agreement 'represents a first step towards developing universally applicable rules—although they do not apply to (other) international agreements but rather are binding countries that are party to the Convention only'.[227]

VI. FURTHER ALTERNATIVE REMEDY: AN INTERNATIONAL HUMAN RIGHT TO A HEALTHY ENVIRONMENT?

Leaving the traditional, bilaterally-based litigation responses and the more recent institutionally-focused solutions mooted for the resolution of global environmental disputes, we shall now examine a further, alternative remedy advocated by international environmental lawyers, namely, the invocation of human rights for environmental protection.[228] Given the evolving individual and community procedural rights to access to environmental information, participation in environmental decision-making procedures, and even access to environmental justice in the form of a right to challenge public authority decisions, the parallel development of an individual right to a healthy or clean environment has also been mooted.

Here too, the initial prognosis was positive but the previously encountered *substantive* and *systemic* problems raised by general public international law remain and indeed return to haunt the potential development of such an individual human right to a healthy or clean environment. Chief among these difficulties is of course the conceptual dilemma that the provision of 'environmental' rights, while ostensibly empowering human beings to be able to assert their interest in living and working within a healthy or clean environment in legal terms, nevertheless still leaves the 'natural' or wildlife elements of the environment without legally enforceable rights, except possibly by dint of a proxy voice in

225 Information about the Aarhus Compliance Committee, which was established under Article 15 of the Convention, is accessible at http://www.unece.org/env/pp/compliance.htm.

226 As the fact sheet on 'Communications from the public' notes, 'Only Parties to the Convention have legal obligations under it, and therefore issues of compliance arise only with respect to Parties.

227 von Moltke (2005) above, n 21, at 195–6.

228 The clearest indication of the international community's human rights response to international environmental protection issues can be seen in the appointment of Ms Ksentini as the Special Rapporteur on the 'Human Rights and the Environment' by the UN Economic and Social Council's Sub-Commission of the Human Rights Commission on the Prevention of Discrimination and Protection of Minorities, and her subsequent reports on this subject. See: http://www.unhchr.ch/.

the form of an interested NGO that is expressly granted legal standing to pursue such interests in wildlife or 'natural' environmental protection. This is despite the fact that a serious pollution incident is apt to pose a threat to both human health and the wider, natural environment. As Cook notes these twin threats are not always related or co-extensive with each other: 'There are many situations where demonstrable harm to the environment, the loss or species or habitat, or an incidence of pollution away from human settlement, does not have immediate consequences for human welfare'.[229] International human rights law has not evolved to recognise such natural environmental damage as a matter of violation of 'environmental' rights. Thus, there is still no actual human right to ensure the protection of the natural environment *per se*.

Moreover, although it has long been argued that there exists a human right to a healthy and decent environment under international law,[230] and this assertion is substantiated by the presence of a number of international instruments to this effect,[231] 'environmental' rights *per se* have not yet been expressly included in any binding global, as opposed to regional or bilateral, environmental or human rights treaty. While there is a growing body of cases involving the assertion of 'environmental' rights within various global and regional human rights treaty mechanisms, such as the Human Rights Committee under the 1966 International Covenant on Civil and Political Rights and the Inter-American human rights system,[232] these 'environmental' rights have arguably been claimed in the absence of, rather than due to, relevant treaty provisions for these rights. None of these 'environmental' rights have so far been specifically incorporated within the global treaty texts concerned. Moreover, even when such a right is expressly incorporated and implemented within regional human rights treaty frameworks such as the San Salvador Protocol to the Inter-American human rights system as noted above, and the African Charter alluded to below, litigation and enforcement issues remain.

This much can certainly be discerned from the evolving jurisprudence of the European Court of Human Rights in this context which, due to the space constraints of this article, will form the main focus of this section. As Cook notes in this respect, 'situations in which human welfare is not directly implicated are unlikely to give rise to a violation of rights' under the European Convention for Human Rights (ECHR).[233] For example, in the recent ECHR case of *Hatton* involving alleged noise pollution from night-time flights over Heathrow airport, the Court found that 'there is no explicit right in the Convention to a clean and quiet environment'.[234] As

229 Kate Cook, Environmental Rights as Human Rights', *European Human Rights Law Review (EHRLR)*, Issue 2 (2002) 196–215, at 197.

230 See, for example, WP Gormley, *Human Rights and the Environment: The Need for International Co-operation* (1976) More recent contributions to this literature include: Michael Anderson and Alan Boyle (eds) *Human Rights Approaches to the Environmental Protection* (Oxford, OUP, 1996).

231 For example, the 1989 Hague Declaration on the Environment, 11 March 1989, in 28 ILM (1989) at 1308. See also the 1981 African Charter on Human and Peoples' Rights (hereinafter, African Charter) discussed further below, which was adopted on 27 June 1981 and entered into force on 21 October 1986. See OAU Doc CAB/LEG/67/3 rev 5, reprinted in 21 ILM 58 (1982).

232 The Inter-American system for the protection and promotion of human rights is composed of two bodies, namely, the Inter-American Commission on Human Rights (IACHR) and the Inter-American Court of Human Rights, both of these established under the auspices of the regional Organization of American States (OAS) and accessible at: http://www.oas.org./OASPage/humanrights.htm.

233 Cook (2002) above, n 229, at 197.

234 *Hatton and others v United Kingdom*, European Court of Human Rights (2003) 37 *European Human Rights Reports (EHRR)* at para 96.

Loucaides asserts at the beginning of his survey of the Court's jurisprudence on this issue, 'The European Convention on Human Rights does not expressly protect the environment nor does it address environmental issues in any way—it does not provide for any relevant rights in respect of the environment as such'.[235] Thus, while environmental issues are growing in importance, the evolution of human rights in this field has focussed on the possible invocation of *procedural*, rather than *substantive*, rights. The relevant case law on environmental issues decided so far by the European Court of Human Rights is in the main devoted to the protection of the exercise of a relevant human right from environmental interference, or some other type of polluting activity, rather than the positive invocation of a substantive right to a clean or healthy environment *per se*. Unsurprisingly, the usual rights invoked in this context relate to Article 2—the right to life—and Article 8—the right to privacy and a family life.

Notable European Court of Human Rights case law in this respect includes the *Lopez Ostra* and *Guerra* decisions, to name but two. In *Lopez Ostra v Spain*,[236] the Court held that major environmental pollution can affect the well-being of individuals and thus impede the enjoyment of their home in such a manner as to constitute a breach of Article 8, without necessarily threatening human health seriously. Moreover, the Court balanced the competing interests of the individuals concerned with that of the community as a whole and found in favour of the individuals concerned. As Fitzmaurice notes the significance of this Judgement 'is the fact that the European Court discerned environmental issues within the human rights structure and that even without explicit environmental right in the [Convention], it found in Article 8 a proper and sufficient link between the two'.[237] In *Guerra v Italy*,[238] the Court appears to go even further in its recognition of the application of Article 8 of the Convention to situations of pollution interference with the individual's enjoyment of privacy and family life, holding that the rights under this Article extend to the right to receive essential information from public authorities about the environmental risks of hazardous activities conducted in close proximity to their place of residence. This in turn meant that there was a positive obligation on the part of the public authorities concerned to ensure respect for individual privacy and family life, which they had failed to fulfil by not informing the applicants in the instant case of the risks posed by these environmental interferences.[239] Such environmental interferences can also take the form of noise pollution, as was argued in both the *Powell and Rayner*,[240] and *Hatton*[241] cases.

The latest in this line of European Court of Human Rights cases involving alleged breaches of Article 8 rights is the *Fadeyeva v Russia* case,[242] where the Court accepted the applicant's claim that her prolonged exposure to excessive pollution levels from a

[235] Loukis Loucaides, 'Environmental Protection through the Jurisprudence of the European Convention on Human Rights', *British Year Book of International Law*, Vol.75, 2004 (Oxford, Oxford University Press, 2005) 249–267, at 249.

[236] *Lopez-Ostra v Spain*, European Court of Human Rights, Series A, No 303-C; 20 EHRR (1995) 277.

[237] Fitzmaurice (2002) above, n 59, at 320.

[238] *Guerra and Others v. Italy*, European Court of Human Rights, EHRR (1998) 357.

[239] *Ibid.*, at para 58. See also Fitzmaurice (2002) above, n 59, at 325.

[240] *Powell and Rayner v. the United Kingdom,* European Court of Human Rights, Vol 12 EHRR (1990) at 355.

[241] *Hatton and Others v. UK*, European Court of Human Rights, Application No 36022/97, Judgment of 2 October 2001. Later overturned by the Grand Chamber of the Court (see below).

[242] *Fadeyeva v Russia,* European Court of Human Rights, Application No 55723/00, Judgment of 9 June 2005, published on 30 November 2005.

nearby steel plant had 'adversely affected the quality of life at her home' and therefore, that 'the actual detriment to the applicant's health and well-being reached a level sufficient to bring it within the scope of Article 8 of the Convention'.[243] This initial conclusion as to the acceptability of the claim was reached by the Court despite its earlier finding in the same judgment that the only medical report produced by the applicant 'did not establish a causal link between environmental pollution and the applicant's diseases',[244] and moreover, no other medical evidence was presented which clearly connected her poor state of health to the high pollution levels at her place of residence.[245] The Court subsequently concluded that there was 'a sufficient nexus between the pollutant emissions and the State to raise an issue of the State's positive obligation under Article 8',[246] and moreover, that 'despite the wide margin of appreciation left to the respondent State, it has failed to strike a fair balance between the interests of the community and the applicant's effective enjoyment of her right to respect for her home and private life. There has accordingly been a violation of Article 8'.[247]

While the above European Court judgment is to be welcomed, attention should nevertheless be paid to the two-step jurisprudential process adopted by the Court in these cases. Although the Court has re-iterated in several cases now (including those cited above) that severe environmental pollution may be held to affect an individual's enjoyment of their home is such a way as to adversely affect their right to privacy and a family life under Article 8, it has also in each instance examined the balance between this adverse environmental effect upon the individual's rights and the wider, community interest in the benefits to be had from the environmentally hazardous activity in question. In doing so, the Court has usually allowed the respondent State concerned a wide margin of appreciation consistent with its general reluctance to substitute its own view for that of a democratically elected, or at least representative, government. This in turn makes for a high threshold of proof to be surmounted by the applicant when attempting to prove a breach of Article 8 of the Convention, a threshold that was ultimately not achieved by the applicants in the *Hatton* case, for example.[248] As Loucaides notes, the Grand Chamber decision in *Hatton* case, 'provides another example of the reluctance of the Court to find a breach of the Convention in respect of big projects for which "the economic well-being of the country" is invoked'.[249] Commenting on the outcome of the more recent *Fadeyeva* case, however, Leach suggests that governments must now be able to show that they have considered all the competing interests within a local community when regulating environmentally degrading socio-economic activities affecting such communities.[250] He argues that this 'due diligence'-type obligation 'appears to go further than the requirement laid down in the *Hatton* case'.[251]

243 *Fadeyeva v Russia*, ECHR (2005) *ibid*, at para 88.

244 *Ibid*, at para 80.

245 *Ibid*.

246 *Ibid*, at para 92.

247 *Ibid*, at para 134.

248 See the Judgment of the ECtHR's Grand Chamber of 8 July 2003, in *Hatton and Others v UK*, overturning the initial judgment of the Third Section of the Court, Application No 36022/97.

249 Loucaides (2005) above, n 235, at 264.

250 Philip Leach, 'Stay inside when the wind blows your way—engaging environmental rights with human rights, Fadeyeva v Russia, Judgment of the European Court of Human Rights, 9 June 2005', 4 Environmental Liability (2005) 91–97, at 96.

251 Leach (2005) *ibid*.

It is also significant to note that when considering the applicability of Article 8 generally to the *Fadeyeva* case, the Court had this to say under the sub-title *(a) General principles*: 'Article 8 has been invoked in various cases involving environmental concern, yet it is not violated every time that environmental deterioration occurs: *no right to nature preservation is as such included among the rights and freedoms guaranteed by the Convention* (emphasis added)'.[252] Cook summarises the limited possibilities of litigation in favour of nature conservation on the basis of Conventional provisions aptly as follows: 'There is widespread public interest in the conservation of natural habitats and species but in cases where a development project threatens a site containing even specially protected habitats and species, it is difficult to see what the Convention might add: if there is no proprietary interest at stake Article 1 of Protocol One (the protection of property) will not apply; if the threat to the environment does not impinge on the home or family life of any individual (as will often be the case in this type of situation) it is difficult to see how Article 8 (right to respect for private and family life) might be engaged'.[253]

Within this context, an arguably more progressive approach that may have implications for both wildlife protection and other 'natural' elements of the environment and the ability of NGOs to bring claims on their behalf before international human rights bodies can be seen in the so-called 'Ogoni' decision of the African Commission on Human and Peoples' Rights.[254] Here the Commission first held, inter alia, that such *actio popularis* actions were useful and as such 'wisely allowed under the African Charter',[255] before finding that the right to 'a general satisfactory environment', under Article 24 of the African Charter, 'imposes clear obligations upon a government', inter alia, to take reasonable and other measures to prevent pollution and ecological degradation, to promote conservation, and to secure an ecologically sustainable development and use of natural resources'.[256] The Commission clearly felt that States parties' obligations under the African Charter extended to the prevention of 'ecological degradation' and promotion of nature 'conservation' *per se*, even where these are unrelated to the exercise of human and peoples' rights, although this did not necessarily provide a right for NGOs to bring claims on behalf of these issues.

Finally, in this section, it is possible to suggest that the still fledgling *substantive* human right to a healthy or clean environment, and the more established *procedural* rights to participation in environmental decision-making processes,[257] are both in fact merely 'personalised' or 'individualised' extensions of the original inter-State duty to

[252] *Fadeyeva v Russia*, ECtHR (2005) above, n 243, at para 68, citing *Kyrtatos v Greece*, Application No 41666/98, ECHR 2003-VI, at para 52.

[253] Cook (2002) above, n 229, at 199.

[254] Decision Regarding Communication 155/96 (*Social and Economic Rights Action Center/ Center for Economic and Social Rights v Nigeria*) African Commission on Human and Peoples' Rights, 27 May 2002. Case No ACHPR/COMM/A044/1. Accessible at: http://www.umn.edu/humanrts/africa. For a comment on this decision by Dinah Shelton, see 'International Decisions' section, American Journal of International Law, Vol 96 (2002) at 937–942. See also, Fons Coomans, 'The Ogoni Case Before the African Commission on Human and Peoples' Rights', *International and Comparative Law Quarterly*, Vol 52 (July 2003) 749–760.

[255] *Ibid.*, at para 49 of the African Commission Decision. The 1981 African Charter on Human and Peoples' Rights (hereinafter, African Charter), was adopted on 27 June 1981 and entered into force on 21 October 1986. See OAU Doc CAB/LEG/67/3 rev 5, reprinted in 21 ILM 58 (1982)

[256] *Ibid*, at para 52 of the Decision.

[257] See in this regard, Malgosia Fitzmaurice, 'Some reflections on public participation in environmental matters as a human right in international law', *Non-State Actors and International Law*, Vol 2 No 1 (2002) 1–22.

notify and consult neighbouring States in the event of a transboundary environmental disaster, such as Chernobyl.[258] In other words, the international obligation to notify and consult owed by any State to other potentially affected States over significant environmental matters has now been given a personal or individual aspect in the form of procedural rights to be informed, consulted, and even in some cases challenge, environmental decision-making processes. In this respect, it is possible to trace a direct line from the inter-State obligation owed between States, to the domestic environmental duty owed by a State to an individual. Both these inter-State and domestic legal obligations owed by a State are, as far as the type of information, as well as notification and consultation procedures that should be applied in each instance, arguably much the same in their formal requirements.

This particular phenomena of the provision of personal or individual rights (which are also available to qualifying NGOs, where standing for their participation is provided for) can in turn be seen as an important aspect of an arguably wider trend that may be described as the 'privatisation' of international environmental law. Apart from the phenomena noted here in terms of the provision of individual procedural rights, further evidence of this wider trend is arguably shown by the provision of private, industry-based, civil liability for environmental damage as a viable alternative to the more difficult imputation of State responsibility under international law, as noted above, in Section I of this article.[259] Thus, 'privatisation' is taking place both in terms of the provision of individual rights of access to information, notification and consultation on environmental issues and in respect of the shifting of liability for transboundary or global commons damage from the State directly upon the individual polluter or, more usually, the hazardous industry concerned.

CONCLUSION

This study is uncompromising in its outlook on the current state of international environmental law. While not in any way seeking to deny the growing significance and influence of international environmental law in the overall development of public international law, it nevertheless argues that in the absence of a globally applicable environmental treaty, or sufficient confirming judgments of international tribunals, as to the customary legal status of the most important environmental principles; international environmental law will always be caught on the horns of a dilemma betwixt generally applicable principles contained in non-binding instruments and individual treaty rules thoroughly regulating specific environmental problems, but without the ability to transcend these individual treaty regimes to inform the *corpus* of universally applicable customary rules of international environmental law itself. International environmental law has thus fallen between the development of general environmental

[258] In respect of the nuclear energy-generating industry, these obligations to notify and consult neighbouring States in the event of a transboundary nuclear incident are now embodied with the 1986 Notification and Consultation Conventions, respectively. For an early assessment of the Notification Convention, see: Sharon McBrayer, 'Chernobyl's Legal Fallout—The Convention on Early Notification of a Nuclear Accident, 26 September 1986', *Georgia Journal of International and Comparative Law*, Vol 17 (Summer 1987) 303–319

[259] See also Ong, *EJIL* (2001) above, n 76, at 698–700, where this latter aspect of the phenomenon, namely the move from State to collective industrial liability for environmental damage is highlighted.

principles, mainly enunciated in non-binding international instruments (such as the 1992 Rio Declaration on Environmental and Development) and binding international environmental treaties which are nevertheless sector-specific in their orientation, or even when comprehensive in their approach to (several) environmental threats, are *regional* in their geographical scope of application. This developmental 'gap' between general environmental principles and specific treaty rules points towards a *substantive* failing within international environmental law as a viable sub-discipline of public international law generally. The lack of general application of even cornerstone principles of international environmental law can be seen by the examination (above, in Section I) of the evolution of the so-called 'golden' rule providing for State prevention and thus responsibility for transboundary environmental damage. Other well-known environmental principles are also conspicuous in their lack of full application by international tribunals even when circumstances apparently warrant their application (as noted in Sections II and IV). Instead, international environmental law has proceeded along at least *three* main pathways to secure better acceptance and especially implementation by States.

These three alternative but compatible modes are as follows: first, through the negotiation of a multitude of increasingly sophisticated treaties, in terms of their substantive rules and standards for addressing specific environmental threats, which are nonetheless dependent on States adopting and implementing them to have any impact. Second, by the development of treaty compliance mechanisms, the highlights of which are the enforcement branch of the 1997 Kyoto Protocol's compliance committee and the 1998 Aarhus Convention which allows individuals and even NGOs to make complaints against errant States parties. Third, through the progressive development of human rights protection to encompass environmental threats as potentially in breach of Articles 1 and 8 of the 1950 European Convention on Human Rights.

Useful though these developments are for the progress of international environmental law generally, they suffer from the following *systemic* difficulties inherent to public international law. First, it is difficult to impute generally applicable customary rules of international environmental law from globally applicable but sector-specific treaties, or even comprehensive regional treaty networks addressing several common environmental threats. This situation is both highlighted and exacerbated by the lack of an equally comprehensive, globally applicable treaty covering all major environmental threats. The *pacta tertis* rule regarding the applicability of treaties to non-parties is a further obstacle in this respect, as is the lack of authoritative jurisprudence in the decisions of international courts and tribunals seized of environmental issues to date. Second, environmental treaty compliance procedures, while performing a valuable role in ascertaining compliance to the specific treaty regime concerned, do not yield authoritative judgments contributing to an understanding of the application of the accepted environmental principles for the wider international community as decisions of international courts and tribunals would do. Finally, the progressive development of individual human rights protection from environmental interferences do not address the issue of 'pure' environmental or ecological threats to wildlife and their habitats, or natural ecosystems.

Thus, the sooner international environmental law, as a branch or sub-discipline of public international law generally, faces up to this reality of the intrinsic lack of an 'animating spirit of the law' at its heart that is focused upon ensuring environmental protection, the better it will be for all those who are genuinely concerned with the ability of international law as a whole to require States to provide for, and achieve, both global and domestic environmental protection. In this respect, well-known and arguably well-accepted concepts and principles of international environmental law such as sustainable development, the preventive and precautionary principles, the polluter-pays principle, the principle of co-operation, as well as the principle of notification, consultation and, consequently, citizen participation in environmental decision-making processes, must as far as possible be fleshed out into specific, and therefore enforceable, legal rules rather than remaining vague concepts or principles, relying on their claim of flexibility as a virtue, rather than a handicap, to the progressive development of international environmental law.

Finally, there should be a greater appreciation of the normative significance of the regulatory *process* of international environmental law-making,[260] encompassing its initial articulation of environmental principles to its acceptance by States as applicable rules and standards within individual treaties and the implementation of all these general principles, and specific rules and standards. This is notwithstanding both the *substantive* and *systemic* difficulties highlighted in this essay, or the relative paucity of definitive international tribunal decisions articulating the applicable rules to any given bilateral dispute. As Birnie and Boyle conclude in their major work on the subject of *International Law and the Environment*:

> Having started as a system of rules limited largely to liability for transboundary damage, resource allocation, and the resolution of conflicting uses of common spaces, international law now accommodates a preventive, and in this sense, precautionary, approach to the protection of the environment at the global level. This is a necessary and inevitable development if international environmental law is to address major global and regional environmental issues; it involves much greater emphasis on environmental regulation and gives less prominence to liability for damage as the law's main response to environmentally harmful activities.[261]

This view at least suggests that international environmental law is evolving along a slightly different trajectory than other, also comparatively recently established sub-disciplines of international law, such as international human rights and WTO law. Its effective implementation by States is often the outcome of a focused and detailed iterative multilateral regulatory *process*, rather than as a result of an established set of rules enunciated in a globally applicable treaty and confirmed in a series of definitive judgments by international tribunals resolving mainly bilateral dispute situations. Thus, it is the increasing numbers and strength of patterns and networks of international environmental *governance,*[262] rather than the development of coherent international

[260] In this sense, it may be observed that international environmental law arguably embodies the process-based explanation for the normative effects of international laws generally, as articulated by Rosalyn Higgins (presently, Her Excellency, Judge Higgins, President of the ICJ), in Higgins, *Problems and Process: International Law and How We Use It* (Oxford, Clarendon Press, 1994) where she argues that international law is an authoritative process of systematic decision-making directed towards the attainment of certain declared values, which within the present context would be towards environmental protection.

[261] Patricia Birnie and Alan Boyle, *International Law and the Environment*, 2nd. edn, (Oxford, Oxford University Press, 2002) at 753.

[262] As noted above, recognition of this growth in international environmental governance has stimulated calls and even efforts to establish a global organization aimed at consolidating the many disparate strands of such regimes. For a catalogue of such calls and efforts and an assessment of their viability, see: Steffen Bauer and Frank Biermann, 'The Debate on a World Environment Organization: An Introduction' and 'Conclusion', in Frank Biermann and Steffen Bauer (eds) (2005) above, n 127, at 1–23 and 257–269, respectively.

environmental law *jurisprudence,* arising from mounting instances of international environmental litigation, which defines the progress of international environmental law as a viable sub-discipline of public international law. In any case, the relative unsuitability of international litigation for ensuring global environmental protection is well-documented. Birnie and Boyle, for example, note that 'any examination of the functioning of the international legal system as regards protection of the environment must start with the realization that the role of the courts is inevitably secondary in this context, limited to the settling of bilateral problems'.[263] Given the reactive nature of such litigation, which generally arises only when a breach of an international obligation is deemed to have occurred, often already resulting in environmental damage; it may be seen that an institutionalising, process-based approach would better fulfil a preventive role than relying on litigation. Such an approach will arguably be more successful in attempting to *internalise* these well-known and well-accepted environmental principles, which have nevertheless until now still not been fully implemented within domestic legal regimes. This approach also accords with what is surely the ultimate priority of both international and domestic environmental law world-wide; namely, the prevention of environmental harm, rather than the allocation of fault, blame, and liability for its remediation. Indeed, the prevention of environmental damage can arguably only be fully achieved as a result of the *internalisation* of these environmental principles within both international and domestic societies. Should such an *internalisation* process be ultimately successful, then the need for traditional international legal remedies, which are still largely predicated upon the notion of bilateral (State v State) disputes, would arguably be obviated. In this context, an *internalising* approach can also be discerned within continuing efforts to strengthen the global governance of,[264] and remedies against, private non-State actors in respect of the environmental impact of their activities.[265]

[263] Birnie and Boyle (2002) above, n 261, at 753.

[264] Knox (2006) above, n 78, at 67, citing Daniel C Esty, 'Toward Optimal Environmental Governance', *New York University Law Review*, Vol 74 (1999) 1495, at 1508-1518.

[265] See, David M Ong, 'The Contribution of State-MNC Transnational Investment Agreements to International Environmental Law', *Yearbook of International Environmental Law*, 2006 Vol 17 (Oxford, OUP, 2008).

The Power of the UN Security Council to Determine the Existence of a 'Threat to the Peace'

Alexander Orakhelashvili*

INTRODUCTION

This article addresses one specific element of the United Nations system of collective security, the concept of a 'threat to the peace' under Article 39 of the Charter—which is the precondition for the application of Chapter VII enforcement measures[1]—and examines it in a systematic matter so as to clarify its content. According to the widespread doctrinal approach, the concept of a 'threat to the peace' is subjective and depends on discretionary determinations of the Security Council. This approach has not been questioned on many occasions and perhaps for this reason not many attempts have been made in recent years to (re)examine the concept or locate the criteria of its identification in specific cases. Given the abundance of writings on this issue in the earlier periods, it has become a conventional wisdom that this subject is well-researched and, consequently, very few contributions on this subject have appeared during the last decade.[2] Despite the end of the Cold War and the expansion of the Council's Chapter VII activities which have resulted in an unambiguous doctrinal recognition of the concept of 'threat to the peace', it is right to say that during the last five years, a further expansion of the use of the concept has taken place, which consists of the intensification of the exercise of Chapter VII activities as never before. Therefore, the Chapter VII material regarding determinations under Article 39 to be analysed is, in 2006, greater than at any point in the history of the United Nations, including early post-Cold War period in which the doctrinal debate were most intensive.

The abundance of recent practice on this subject makes it clear that the debate on the issue remains. In addition, the existing literature does not cover the practice of the Security Council involving determinations of a threat to the peace in situations in the Congo, Liberia, Sierra Leone, Cote d'Ivoire, Somalia, Angola, Ethiopia/Eritrea, the former Yugoslavia, Iran, Iraq, North Korea or Afghanistan, the Council's action with regard to international terrorism, prevention of proliferation of the weapons of mass destruction, and the exemption of certain categories of peacekeepers from the jurisdiction of the International Criminal Court (ICC). This Article responds to this doctrinal gap; it aims not to summarise the doctrinal treatment of the issue thus far, but focuses on its systemic treatment. This requires an examination of the practice and

* LLM *cum laude* (Leiden); PhD (Cantab.); Fellow, Jesus College, Oxford.

[1] Article 39 reads as follows: 'The Security Council shall determine the existence of any threat to the peace, breach of the peace, or act of aggression and shall make recommendations, or decide what measures shall be taken in accordance with Articles 41 and 42, to maintain or restore international peace and security'.

[2] But see K Wellens, 'The UN Security Council and New Threats to the Peace: Back to the Future', 8 *JCSL* (2003), 15–70.

evidence emanating from the UN Security Council in broad terms. The principal purpose of this contribution is to demonstrate, by reference to the recent practice, that the concept of a 'threat to the peace', although initially dependent on discretionary determinations of the Security Council, nevertheless is a concept whose content can be identified by reference to objective and observable criteria. Consequently, the principal issue addressed relates to the criteria according to which the field in which the discretionary political discrimination can be made can be delimited from the field in which the Council's activities are subjected to legal limitations.

THE CONCEPT OF A 'THREAT TO THE PEACE' IN THE GENERAL CONTEXT OF THE CHAPTER VII POWERS OF THE SECURITY COUNCIL

The contextual analysis of the Charter demonstrates that dangers and threats to international peace and security may vary in degree and kind, and consequently require different responses. The Charter provides for the distribution of powers and competences among the Organisation's principal organs. The Security Council is vested with primary responsibility for the maintenance of international peace and security 'to ensure prompt and effective action by the United Nations' (Article 24). Such competence of the Security Council has material and formal aspects. The material competence is functional. Under Chapter VI of the UN Charter, the Council may deal with disputes and situations; not with each and every one, but rather only with those likely to endanger international peace and security. Chapter VII empowers the Council to deal with actual threats to the peace, breaches of the peace and acts of aggression. The competences set out in both chapters make clear, on the whole, that the Council's role in the international legal system is strictly functional.

The formal competence of the Security Council relates to the nature of the acts it is empowered to adopt. The Council has recommendatory and enforcement powers. Recommendations may be adopted in the context of preventing a given situation from endangering international peace and security (Articles 36 to 38 of the Charter) or in the context of the restoration of international peace (Article 39). Under Chapter VII the Council may adopt military and non-military enforcement measures in accordance with Articles 41 and 42, to counter threats to the peace, breaches of the peace or acts of aggression.

While the concept of aggression is more or less clear,[3] the Charter does not define a threat to or breach of the peace. In its enforcement practice under Chapter VII, the Council has rarely used the concept of aggression[4] and has, on most occasions, characterised situations as threats to or breaches of the peace. This holds true even for those situations involving a clear example of an armed attack, such as the invasion of

[3] See Definition of Aggression, UNGA res 3314 (1974). The International Court of Justice confirmed in the *Nicaragua* case that UNGA res 3314 (1974) is part of customary international law, *ICJ Reports* 1986, 103. Furthermore, the definition of aggression is given in the regional instruments, such as the 1947 Inter-American Treaty of Reciprocal Assistance (Article 9), the 1975 Rio Protocol on Amendment of the Inter-American Treaty of Reciprocal Assistance (Article 9), and the African Union Common Defence and Security Pact, adopted in Abuja on 31 January 2005 (Article 1). These definitions overlap and consolidate the generally accepted standard of the definition of aggression in international law.

[4] The determination of aggression was made in Resolution 573 of 4 October 1985 on Israel and Resolution 577 of 6 December 1985 on South Africa.

Kuwait by Iraq or the invasion of the Falkland Islands by Argentina.[5] In most cases, the Council tends to characterise situations as 'threats to the peace'. Such a policy is without prejudice to the objective nature of the situation in question. For example, having determined an armed attack as a threat to the peace, the Council cannot be taken to hold that the same situation does not constitute aggression. The significance of labelling certain situations as threats to the peace is that the Council sees further action under Chapter VII justified and required. Therefore, the general concept of a threat to the peace does not objectively denote a specific factual or legal situation, nor does it have any inherent, or specific, substantive content and scope. The notion is merely the key necessary for unlocking measures under Chapter VII with regard to a specific situation. Only the Security Council can determine that the threat to the peace exists and the relevant situation, however grave, is not a threat to the peace unless and until the Security Council determines it to be so. This cannot be determined by other organs of the United Nations, regional organisations or individual States. The crucial question, however, is whether anything that the Security Council covers with its determinations is subsumable within this concept.

The need to maintain and restore international peace and security, for which the Security Council was established, derives not from an abstract concept nor has any inherent value—it is relevant only because and insofar as it is recognised in the Charter of the United Nations as a treaty. As is correctly emphasised, the powers of the Security Council are based on the constitution of delegated and limited powers.[6] It is evident that the lawfulness under the UN Charter of the use by the Council of its Chapter VII powers often depends on whether a threat to the peace is properly identified as such by the Council. This question is crucial for determining whether a specific Chapter VII action falls within the scope of the limited and delegated powers of the Council under the UN Charter. Once again, this issue becomes more acute in terms of the legal certainty of the exercise of delegated powers as the Council's activities comprise new fields hitherto untouched by the organ.

The treaty-based character of the Security Council's mandate prompts the crucial question of whether the Charter as a treaty manifests the consent of member States that the Council shall possess an unfettered discretion in identifying threats to peace; and that it is the only judge in determining whether there is such threat. There are not many instances, in practice, directly tackling the issue of the permissible content of Article 39 determinations. As the Appeals Chamber of the International Criminal Tribunal for the former Yugoslavia observed with regard to Article 39:

> It is clear from this text that the Security Council plays a pivotal role and exercises a very wide discretion under this Article. But this does not mean that its powers are unlimited. The Security Council is an organ of an international organization, established by a treaty which serves as a constitutional framework for that organization. The Security Council is thus subjected to certain constitutional limitations, however broad its powers under the constitution may be. Those powers cannot, in any case, go beyond the limits of the jurisdiction of the Organization at large, not to mention other specific limitations or those which may derive from the internal division of power within the Organization. In any case, neither the text nor the spirit of the Charter conceives of the Security Council as *legibus solutus* (unbound by law). . . . the "threat to the peace" is more of a political concept. But the determination that there

[5] UNSC Res 660 (1990), UNSC Res 502 (1982).

[6] T Franck, *Fairness in International Law and Institutions* (Oxford, OUP, 1995) 218–220.

exists such a threat is not a totally unfettered discretion, as it has to remain, at the very least, within the limits of the Purposes and Principles of the Charter.[7]

The standards of ascertainment of the compatibility of Article 39 determinations with the purposes and principles of the Charter are necessary above all for the considerations of legitimacy. In general, international law has the genuine degree of legitimacy, sometimes greater than national law, in that it is created by the express will of the legal person to which it applies. The accumulation of wide enforcement powers within the Council is based on the delegation by States, but this very delegation produces the result that is rather exceptional in terms of the basic nature and structure of international law. Even more so, as the indeterminate concept of the 'threat to the peace' can trigger the measures seriously affecting the rights of States.

The clause in Article 39 that the Council 'shall determine the existence of any threat to the peace' inherently requires the application of the pre-existing concept to facts, albeit with the use of discretion. It does not result in the authorisation to legislate; viewing it as doing so would contradict the basic nature of international law which knows of no legislative power over States. Under the Charter framework, the Council possesses political discretion as to the initial determination of the substance of threats to the peace, but the legal limitation on this discretion following from the text of Article 39 is that the such determination must relate to something that exists and threatens the peace. The discretion provided enables the Council to cover the range of situations not specified in the Charter; it does not empower the Council to extend its determination to anything it likes.

Therefore, the Council should abstain from intervention in situations, including determining threats to the peace, where such intervention is not required by the imperatives of its functional competence. The principle of subsidiarity, known in several systems of national law, can be applied to the United Nations system, requiring that the Council not intervene unless its intervention is necessary or indispensable for the settlement of the relevant problem. In the practice of regional peace-keeping, for instance, there is the established pattern that the Security Council intervenes, through establishing peace-keeping forces or perfecting their mandate, where the regional organisations do not have enough military power or funds to perform the task.[8]

The foregoing requires viewing the Council from the perspective of the conceptual and normative framework to which it belongs—the perspective cleansed of clichés. The expansion of the executive and enforcement activities of the Council to the variety of fields of international life is attendant not only with the prospects of success, but also with risks, because international law remains a decentralised legal system knowing of no sovereign power beyond States. To give these factors due consideration, the analytical and scientific, presumably to some extent contrarian, approach shall be adopted to consider the various implications that the Council's Article 39 power entail.

The Security Council being a political organ, its decision can be based on the outcome of political bargain and consensus, and thus can sometimes be at odds with the purposes and principles of the Charter in that it is motivated by considerations other

[7] *Tadic*, IT-94-1 (Appeal Chamber), 2 October 1995, paras 28–29.

[8] See A Orakhelashvili, The Legal Framework of Peace Operations by Regional Organisations, 11 *International Peacekeeping: Yearbook of International Peace Operations* (2006), 111–143.

than the desire to take measures genuinely addressing a verified threat to the peace. The adoption of any decision depends on securing the majority in the Council, including the votes of the five permanent members. The use of veto, or its likelihood, hampers the Council's speedy and efficient action in certain cases. But it can also prevent the adoption of ill-thought out and unreasonable decisions, especially those motivated by political whims and economic interests rather than genuine efforts to counter threats to international peace and security. Attempts to confer legality to such actions are based on the attempts to invoke Article 39 and thus justify coercive, including military, measures where those measures would not be objectively justified. In the case of war against Iraq in 2003, both the absence of a majority in the Council supporting the US/British proposal to authorise the use of force against Iraq, and the likelihood of vetoes of several permanent members prevented the Council from adopting a resolution approving the military action.[9] Despite a lack of Security Council mandate, the military action did take place and claimed many thousands of civilian lives in Iraq. It also perpetuated the deterioration of the economic and social situation of the country to such extent that it fails to approach the level of economic and social development manifest during the rule of the Hussein Administration.[10] The weapons of mass destruction—the stated cause of the war—have never been found, nor has any conclusive evidence been put forward that they had ever been there in the period of few years preceding the war. Whether the situation in Iraq as it stood in 2003 posed a genuine threat to the peace and security of the world, or the Middle East, this was never established as an objective justification for the Security Council to determine a threat to the peace which would allow for the sanctioning of the use of armed force. In situations like this, the veto of permanent members remains a useful tool to ensure that when the United Nations cannot prevent the illegal and unjustified use of force, it can at least refuse the stamp of legality from being placed upon it.

On the other hand, it is still possible that the procedural requirements of the Council's decision can be met, and the required majority is secured and the right to veto is not used. In such circumstances, the need to define the parameters of the Council's powers under Article 39, and the limits on these powers becomes even more pressing. The fact that the members of the Security Council achieve consensus on a certain issue may, under certain circumstances, be seen as a remarkable achievement, but the mere fact of reaching the consensus as to the existence of the 'threat to the peace' does not mean that those who reach this consensus are the ultimate and exclusive judges of the characterisation of the relevant situation and the selection of the means of address it. In other words with regard to the determining of *what* the threat is, *how* it is identified, *what* means are justified to be used in addressing it, and *how* the

[9] The stated justification for using force was the Iraqi programmes of weapons of mass destruction and, where the United Kingdom was concerned, especially the claim that Iraq possessed the capability to assemble and use nuclear weapons within 45 minutes. On the arguments invoked in support of the Coalition war against Iraq in 2003 see Y Dinstein, *War, Aggression and Self-Defence* (2005), 183ff, 297ff; C Gray, *International Law and the Use of Force* (2004), 179–184; see also the views of international lawyers published in *The Guardian*, 8 October 2002, and 7 March and 14 March 2003.

[10] This has been confirmed in the Report of the International Committee of the Red Cross, emphasising that for millions in Iraq the situation has worsen. See ICRC, *Civilians without Protection—the Ever-Worsening Situation in Iraq*, 11 April 2007. Similarly, the 2007 Easter *Urbi et Orbi* address of Pope Benedict XVI stresses that 'nothing positive comes from Iraq, torn apart by continual slaughter as the civil population flees'.

use of those means will contribute to the removal of the threat. The very fact that this process involves the application of the treaty framework requires that some degree of legal certainty be guaranteed. The exemplary way of achieving this level of transparency is demonstrated in the Council's Resolution 1676 (2006) on the situation in Somalia, addressing the aftermath of the imposition of arms embargo on this country. In this Resolution, the Council:

> *Condemning* the significant increase in the flow of weapons and ammunition supplies to and through Somalia, which constitutes a violation of the arms embargo and a serious threat to the Somali peace process,
>
> *Concerned about* the increasing incidents of piracy and armed robbery against ships in waters off the coast of Somalia, and its impact on security in Somalia,
>
> *Reiterating* its insistence that all Member States, in particular those in the region, should refrain from any action in contravention of the arms embargo and should take all necessary steps to hold violators accountable,
>
> *Reiterating* and *underscoring* the importance of enhancing the monitoring of the arms embargo in Somalia through persistent and vigilant investigation into the violations, bearing in mind that strict enforcement of the arms embargo will improve the overall security situation in Somalia,
>
> *Determin[ed]* that the situation in Somalia constitutes a threat to international peace and security in the region.

Another similar instance is provided by Resolution 1735 (2006), in which the Council ordered States to take the range of antiterrorist measures against Al-Qaeda. The Council:

> *Reaffirming* the need to combat by all means, in accordance with the Charter of the United Nations and international law, threats to international peace and security caused by terrorist acts, stressing in this regard the important role the United Nations plays in leading and coordinating this effort,
>
> *Stressing* that terrorism can only be defeated by a sustained and comprehensive approach involving the active participation and collaboration of all States, and international and regional organizations to impede, impair, isolate, and incapacitate the terrorist threat [. . .]
>
> *Noting* the need for robust implementation of the measures in paragraph 1 of this resolution as a significant tool in combating terrorist activity [. . .]
>
> *Expressing* its deep concern about criminal misuse of the internet by Al-Qaida, Usama bin Laden, and the Taliban, and other individuals, groups, undertakings, and entities associated with them, in furtherance of terrorist acts,
>
> *Noting with concern* the changing nature of the threat presented by Al-Qaida, Usama bin Laden and the Taliban, and other individuals, groups, undertakings and entities associated with them, in particular the ways in which terrorist ideologies are promoted,
>
> *Stress[ed]* the importance of meeting all aspects of the threat that Al-Qaida, Usama bin Laden and the Taliban, and other individuals, groups, undertakings and entities associated with them represent to international peace and security,

and went on to order a range of Chapter VII anti-terrorist measures, such as the freezing of assets and the reinforcement of arms embargo.

These two resolutions identify the specific and objectively observable situations as 'threats to the peace', explain how these phenomena can and should be combated or eliminated, and adopt the relevant Chapter VII measures in pursuance of these transparently stated goals. The link between the threats identified and measures adopted is transparently maintained. Under this approach, the international community can have a clear picture on how and for which purposes the mandate it entrusts to the 15-member Council is used and enforced.

CONSEQUENCES OF THE DETERMINATION UNDER ARTICLE 39

The Security Council does not always consider that the existence of the threat to peace necessarily requires taking any Chapter VII action. For instance, while identifying the threat to the peace in situations involving terrorist bombings in Bogota, Colombia, by Resolution 1465 (2003), and Istanbul, Turkey, by Resolution 1516 (2003), the Council merely condemned the attacks and urged States 'to work together' in providing to the respective Governments necessary support to find and bring to justice the perpetrators, organisers and sponsors. But under the legal framework, the finding by the Security Council that the threat to the peace exists entails certain legal consequences both within the realm of the Charter as well as of general international law, which include:

(a) Upon finding a 'threat to the peace', the Security Council is empowered, by virtue of Articles 41 and 42 of the Charter, to initiate coercive non-military or military measures against a State or non-State actor, such as the severance of communications, trade, economic and/or diplomatic relations. In the event that they are or would be ineffective, the Council may decide on the use of armed force.
(b) By virtue of the operation of Articles 2(5), 25, 48 and 103 of the Charter, all member States of the United Nations are obliged to support and implement coercive measures initiated by the Security Council.
(c) The Security Council, acting pursuant to its enforcement powers under Chapter VII, may disregard the domestic jurisdiction of States, which the United Nations is otherwise obliged to respect (Article 2(7) of the Charter).

It is thus clear that by determining a situation as a 'threat to the peace', the Council is empowered to bring about wide-reaching legal consequences with significant impact on sovereign rights, interests and obligations of the target State and third States, and drastic changes in existing legal relations. The enforcement function, as well as the discretion afforded to the Council, is very wide indeed. The outer limit of this enforcement function, especially under Article 39 that is initially based on political consensus, has to be seen in terms of the general framework which determines the relationship between the Security Council's powers and international law. Thus, the legal constraints on the political process under Article 39 follows both from the provisions of the Article which requires the factual existence of a threat to the peace, and from the relevant standards of the Charter.

The International Court of Justice clearly emphasised that the political character of organs of an international organisation does not release them from the observance of legal provisions which constitute limitations on their powers or criteria for their judgement.[11] As is suggested by Franck, 'it is apparent that the Council has broad discretion, but that is to be exercised bona fides and intra vires, in accordance with these specific procedural and substantive standards spelled out in the Charter'.[12] The compliance with the principles of the UN Charter is crucial. The issue of good faith is also acute and this principle clearly applies to the Council's determinations under Article 39, with the consequence that the threats to the peace identified by the Council shall be real threats and not just invented or imagined ones.[13] This once again confirms that a threat to the peace, in specific situations, must be clearly identified, ie explicitly determined. In addition, in order to ascertain whether the Council observes this principle while acting under Article 39, it is necessary to have a clear view of what types of situation could be encompassed by the concept of a 'threat to the peace', to ensure the minimum certainty and predictability of the legal position.

THE REQUIREMENT OF THE EXPLICIT, SPECIFIC, AND TRANSPARENT DETERMINATION

As the legal framework governing the Council's political decision-making requires the observance of minimum level of transparency and legal certainty, the Council must make it clear if it considers the relevant situation a threat to the peace. Some authors suggest that implied determination is possible under Article 39, without the explicit reference to the existence of a threat to the peace.[14] This argument fails the test of legal certainty. If the Council's Article 39 determination is about proving something,[15] then the relevance of implicit determinations is doubtful; the Council must demonstrate to the satisfaction of the international community that there is objectively the well-attested and verified situation that warrants the application of Chapter VII measures. Without an explicit determination of a threat to the peace, it would be unclear in each specific case which facts, events or circumstances warrant the application of such measures. Depending on specific circumstances, enforcement measures under Chapter VII may be targeted against either a State or non-State actor, or at some broader general situation. The Council shall make it clear what are the facts, situations or circumstances which warrant the application of enforcement measures. This required by the considerations of proportionality.

Even the reference to certain resolutions that have triggered Chapter VII action without explicit reference to that article is insufficient to prove that explicit reference is not necessary. Resolutions adopted under Chapter VII refer either to situations considered a threat to the peace under Article 39 or to a prior resolution of the Council that has already so characterised the relevant situation.[16] Implicit determination is

[11] *Admission of a State to the Membership of the United Nations* (Advisory Opinion), *ICJ Reports*, 1947–48, 64

[12] T Franck, *Fairness in International Law and Institutions* (Oxford, OUP, 1995) 220.

[13] F Kirgis, 'Security Council Governance of Postconflict Societies: A Plea for Good Faith and Informed Decision Making', 95 *AJIL* (2001), 581.

[14] H Freudenschuß, 'Article 39 of the UN Charter Revisited: Threat to Peace and the Recent Practice of the UN Security Council', 46 *Austrian Journal of Public and International Law* (1993) 31; R Lapidoth, 'Some Reflections on the Law and Practice Concerning the Imposition of Sanctions by the Security Council', 30 *Archiv des Völkerrechts* (1992) 115.

[15] Wellens, above, n 2, at 23.

[16] See, for instance, SC Res 819 (1993), 820 (1993), 824 (1993); and SC Res 1171 (1998), referring to SC Res 1132 (1997); SC Res 1448 (2003) on Angola, referring to several earlier resolutions; SC Res 1333 of 19 December 2000 referring to SC Res 1267 of 15 October 1999.

only theoretically conceivable where the Council explicitly mentions that it is acting under Chapter VII and does not specifically refer to the circumstances mentioned in Article 39. But requirement of legal certainty contradicts the viability of such option. When 'acting under Chapter VII', the Council engages in 'action with respect to threats to the peace'[17] and it is therefore bound to indicate what amounts to a threat to the peace in the specific situation, for the very reason that the power of the Council to apply enforcement measures is not absolute and unlimited but strictly functional and designed to be used only in circumstances where it is necessary and appropriate to respond to a threat to the peace.

That being said, it has happened that the Council neglects this requirement; for instance, the Council adopted the Resolution 1160 (1998) imposing an arms embargo on the Federal Republic of Yugoslavia, as that Resolution did not make a clear determination of a threat to the peace, nor referred to an earlier resolution including such finding. Such practice is dangerous as it reveals the trends of the abuse of power: the arms embargo, as a coercive measure under Article 41 of the Charter, can only be imposed in a situation satisfying the requirements of Article 39. Otherwise, it would exceed the Council's mandate under the Charter. The question is not whether the relevant situation addressed by the Council is grave; it relates rather to the Council's objective identification of the situation, as a threat to the peace, which warrants the application of measures specified under Chapter VII. This is even more so as the express labelling of the events referred to in Resolution 1160, namely 'the use of excessive force by Serbian police forces against civilians and peaceful demonstrators in Kosovo, as well as all acts of terrorism by the Kosovo Liberation Army or any other group or individual and all external support for terrorist activity in Kosovo, including finance, arms and training', could presumably qualify for the Article 39 determination.

This approach may be seen as formalistic. But the reality of this problem is illustrated by sharper examples, such as Resolution 1737 (2006), which imposed certain sanctions on Iran to address its non-compliance with the international demands to freeze its uranium enrichment programme. The Council refers, in the preamble to the Resolution, to the concerns expressed by the International Atomic Energy Agency regarding Iran's nuclear programmes. The Council's entire reasoning is based on the concern not that Iran has actually been doing something problematic, but that it failed to prove the opposite to the Council's satisfaction. The problems identified were that certain Iranian nuclear programmes '*could* have a military nuclear dimension' and that 'Iran has not established full and sustained suspension' of its presumed activities.

That said, Resolution 1737 does not specify the Iranian conduct that constitutes the threat to the peace. The imposition of sanctions for the presumed or expected conduct of the State cannot amount to the proper discharge of Chapter VII responsibilities either. One only needs to recall Resolution 1441 (2003), whereby the Council vigorously demanded the cooperation of Iraq in the matter of weapons of mass destruction which, as it transpired, Iraq no longer possessed. For its part, Resolution 1441 does not link the Article 39 determination to Iraq's actual conduct either, although it states in paragraph 1 that Iraq is in material breach of Resolution 687 (1991) requiring full disclosure of its programmes of weapons of mass destruction and ballistic missiles.

[17] The title of Chapter VII is 'Action with Respect to Threats to the Peace, Breaches of the Peace, and Acts of Aggression'.

The lack of monitoring of weapons programmes was, in effect, pronounced as the threat to the peace under Article 39. These cases thus illustrate the abovementioned phenomenon of achieving consensus among the Council Members on taking the Chapter VII action, without proper and transparent identification of the threat at hand.

When making use of its Chapter VII powers, the Security Council has therefore to ensure that the existence of a threat to the peace is duly determined. The practice of the Council encompasses findings of 'danger to peace and security', 'situations endangering peace', 'situations seriously disturbing international peace and security' and 'situations likely to threaten or endanger international peace and security'. A determination of this kind is not a suitable basis for action under Chapter VII. A determination must make it clear that the Council considers an actual 'threat to the peace' to exist, consisting of certain objective facts, events or circumstances which may, in the Council's view, warrant the application of Chapter VII enforcement measures. Some resolutions refer not to 'threats to the peace' as such but to threats to peace and security in the region, or emphasise that the consequences of the given situation as threating the peace. It seems that such determinations fall within the purview of Article 39. This Article requires simply a finding of a 'threat to the peace'. The determination of a threat to peace and security in the region is in fact a permissible determination under Article 39 because the peace in a given region is part of international peace, as it goes beyond the national boundaries of one single State. As regards the determination of the consequences of a given situation as a 'threat to the peace',[18] such determination would be permissible under Article 39 only if these consequences referred to in the Council's resolution actually exist and are not merely expected to occur.

THE EXPANDED NOTION OF A THREAT TO THE PEACE AND THE CRITERIA FOR ITS DETERMINATION

Even if there is no straightforward definition of threats to the peace, the factor of legitimate expectations requires that the Council's determination is genuine, that is relates to situations that warrant the application of coercive measures. Even if, allegedly, fifteen members of the Council believe in the ambiguity of this concept and the consequent open-endedness of the Council's competence on this issue, the rest of the international community is certainly entitled to ask where the limits lie and, in appropriate cases, to pass judgment on the Council's determination. The parties to the United Nations Charter should not be considered as having consented to the Council's power to make arbitrary or ambiguous determinations under Article 39; the considerations of good faith and legitimate expectations rather requires that United Nations Members be understood as having delegated to the Council the power to address the facts and situations genuinely justifying the invocation of Article 39 and make transparent determinations.

The concept of peace, a term of the foremost importance in Article 39, is not positively defined in the Charter. In its ordinary meaning, peace denotes the absence of war. But peace as understood by the Security Council has a much broader meaning:

[18] See, for instance, SC Res 688 (1991).

peace under the Charter includes not only the absence of inter-State wars but also other factors pertaining to the economic, ecological and humanitarian dimensions of international relations.[19] As suggested, 'the concept of the threat to the peace can be understood in an extraordinarily broad manner when there is unanimity within the Security Council'.[20] The Council has made its Article 39 determinations, and consequently applied its Chapter VII powers, in situations both involving and not involving inter-State armed conflict. In the case of Southern Rhodesia, the establishment of the minority rule and racist policies was characterised by the Council as a threat to the peace, and enforcement measures comprising the arms and oil embargo were applied. Resolution 688 (1991) declared the mass flow of refugees from Iraq as a threat to the peace. In Resolution 940 (1994), the removal of the legitimate government of Haiti was also considered a threat to the peace, notwithstanding the apparent domestic charcterisation of the situation. In Resolution 794 (1993), the Council addressed the failure of statehood and 'magnitude of human tragedy' in Somalia as a threat to the peace. The non-extradition by Libya of the two individuals suspected of having organised the explosion of Pan-Am 103 over UK territory was also deemed a threat to the peace under Resolutions 748 (1992) and 843 (1993). In each of these cases, the Council imposed extensive enforcement measures including, in some cases, the authorisation of member States to use armed force.

This practice shows that the Council considers it appropriate to make Article 39 determinations in a wide variety of situations. At the same time, the repertoire of such determinations does not help clarifying the content of a threat to the peace. The analysis based on past determinations under Article 39 would be simply retrospective and descriptive. The necessity to find some objective or objectivised criteria for defining the scope of peace, and threats to the peace, and thus clarifying the legal limits on the Council's political discretion, is obvious.

It is often suggested that determinations under Article 39 are conclusive and within the absolute discretion of the Security Council.[21] A formalistic definition of a threat to the peace is often used; and has been defined as 'a situation which the organ, competent to impose sanctions, declares to be an actual threat to the peace'.[22] This definition places the emphasis on the discretionary power of the Security Council and not upon the content of concept. From this perspective, the Council was designed to adopt purely political decisions, and the determination of a 'threat to the peace' is viewed from this angle.[23] This argument is widely shared in the scholarly doctrine. According to Reisman, the UN collective security mechanism was intended to operate according

[19] Statement of the Heads of States and Governments of Members of the Security Council, 31 January 1992: 'The absence of wars and military conflicts among States does not in itself ensure international peace and security. The non-military sources of instability in the economic, social, humanitarian and ecological fields have become threats to peace and security. The United Nations membership as a whole, working through the appropriate bodies, needs to give the highest priority to the solution of these matters' (UN doc S/PV.3046).

[20] J Frowein, 'On article 39', in Simma (ed), *The Charter of the United Nations. A Commentary* (1994) 612.

[21] R Lapidoth, 'Some Reflections on the Law and Practice Concerning the Imposition of Sanctions by the Security Council', 30 *Archiv des Völkerrechts* (1992) 115.

[22] Definition by J Combacau, quoted in P Kooijmans, 'The Enlargement of the Concept "Threat to the Peace', in Dupuy (ed), *The Development of the Role of the Security Council* (1993) 111.

[23] P Kooijmans, 'The ICJ: Where Does It Stand?' in S Muller, D Raic and H Thuranzsky (eds), *The International Court of Justice. Its Future Role after Fifty Years* (1997) 416.

to the will and discretion of the permanent members of the Security Council.[24] Kooijmans for his part refers to 'the complete discretion the Security Council has with regard to the interpretation of the three concepts "threat to the peace", "breach of the peace" and "act of aggression" '.[25] A 'threat to the peace' under the Charter is therefore supposed to be equivalent to what the Council determines it to be. Nevertheless, the relevant Charter provisions as well as the imperative of legal certainty require the rejection of the view that the power of the Council under Article 39 is based exclusively on political discretion, free of all visible limitation.

While the determination of the 'threat to the peace' involves political judgment of the Council members, Article 39 is a treaty provision subject to normal rules of treaty interpretation.[26] The practice of the Council is definitely helpful and important. But the primary importance in determining what may or may not be encompassed within that concept of a 'threat to the peace' depends on a textual, contextual and systematic interpretation of Article 39 as a treaty provision. The Council's practice, for its part, can be useful as subsequent practice in terms of treaty interpretation.[27]

The textual meaning of a 'threat to the peace' does not, by itself, divulge its potential legal and political connotations. Resorting to context, however, one can easily discover that no provision of the Charter envisage the role of the Council as entitled to adopt the decisions on the basis of its unfettered discretion. The general stipulation under Articles 24 and 25 of the UN Charter is that the Council shall act in accordance with the purposes and principles of the Charter and that its decisions must correspond to the Charter. Even as these provisions do not expressly mention the power under Article 39, they cannot be without relevance for it. The Yugoslav Tribunal also resorts to the subsequent practice argument in specifying that the conduct or situation can 'constitute a "threat to the peace" according to the settled practice of the Security Council and the common understanding of the United Nations membership in general'.[28] There is, however, very little common understanding amongst of the UN membership which can be inferred, apart from the silence of members which is in most cases inconclusive. Thus, the interpretative principles, falling short of providing affirmative guidance of understanding as to what facts and situations 'threats to the peace' covers can only provide the general criteria dictated by the factors of good faith and legal certainty, for ascertaining the area within which the Council can make its Article 39 determinations, and for judging the propriety and legality of these determinations in individual cases.

The general framework within which the Council operates suggests the relevance of such criteria. The criteria for the exercise of the Council's power under Article 39 are of both a factual and a legal nature. Factual limitations on the Council's discretion

[24] M Reisman, 'Peacemaking', 18 *Yale Journal of International Law* (1993) 418

[25] P Kooijmans, 'The Enlargement of the Concept "Threat to the Peace" ', in P-M Dupuy (ed), *The Development of the Role of the Security Council* (1993) 111. But Kooijmans adds: 'Although the Security Council is completely free to decide whether a situation constitutes a threat to the peace, one may ask whether it is fully in conformity with the spirit of the Charter to impose sanctions if the threat is not actual and efforts to resolve the dispute have not been completely exhausted', at 117.

[26] The UN Charter is subject to the normal rules of treaty interpretation as embodied in the 1969 Vienna Convention on the Law of Treaties, Article 5.

[27] According to Art 31 of the 1969 Vienna Convention, a treaty must be interpreted in accordance with the ordinary meaning of its terms and in the light of its object and purpose. Subsequent practice establishing an agreement as to the meaning of the treaty shall also be taken into account.

[28] *Tadic*, Appeal Chamber, para 30.

relate to its power to make a finding of a threat to the peace, that is, to identify certain facts, events or circumstances as amounting to such, because that is what Article 39 requires—to 'determine the existence' of a threat to the peace. It is correctly indicated that, although the notion of a threat to the peace is very open and flexible, it is nevertheless subject to interpretation.[29] In this regard, it must be asked whether the competence of the Security Council to identify threats to the peace has only a formal or also a material content, namely whether that competence relates to the genuine identification of facts and situations that give rise to the threat to the peace. According to Schilling:

> It is however disputed whether the determination of a threat to the peace shall relate to the defined subject-matter, whether it also is the legal consequence of the fact placed within the discretion of the Security Council, or the threat to the peace is always present where the Security Council so determines, whether in this case the so-called determination is constitutive. It is disputed whether the determination is legally bound to the fulfilment of a defined fact, or is a purely political decision.[30]

If the determination of threats to the peace is a purely political task:

> Thus at the top of the United Nations, by virtue of the international treaty, namely the UN Charter, the possibility would be present to adopt the decisions that are purely politically motivated, legally unbound, but binding for the members.[31]

And, as such:

> Breaking through the sovereignty of the members of the United Nations on the basis of the privilege of the Security Council is only permissible in so far as there is genuinely a threat to the peace in discussable sense. [. . .] A purely political determination of a threat to the peace, which would have its basis in the formal powers of the Security Council, without being based on the material threat to the peace, would be no sufficient justification for breaking through the State sovereignty; it would not be necessary for the maintenance of peace. Besides, it would not be compatible with the text of Article 39 of the UN Charter, under the factual composition of which subject-matters of life are subsumed.[32]
>
> The determination of a threat to the peace by the Security Council is permissible only where its factual composition is fulfilled.[33]

[29] T Schilling, 'Die "Neue Weltordnung" und die Souverenität der Mitglieder der Vereinten Nationen', 33 *Archiv des Völkerrechts* (1995) 78–79

[30] *Ibid*, 87; translated from the original: 'Umstritten ist hingegen, ob sich die Feststellung der Friedensbedrohung auf einen bestimmten Sachverhalt stützen muß, ob sie also die—in das Ermessen des Sicherheitsrates gestellten—Rechtsfolge eines Tatbestandes ist, oder ob eine Bedrohung des Friedens immer dann vorliegt, wenn der Sicherheitsrat dies feststellt, ob also die dann nur sogenannte—Feststellung konstitutiv ist. Umstritten ist damit, ob die Feststellung eine rechtlich an die Erfüllung eines bestimmten Tatbestands gebundene oder eine rein politische Entscheidung ist'.

[31] *Ibid.*, 79–80. "so bestünde an der Spitze der Vereinten Nationen kraft völkerrechtlichen Vertrags, nämlich der VN-Charta, die Möglichkeit zu rein politisch bestimmten, rechtlich ungebundenen, für die Mitglieder aber verbindlichen Entscheidungen".

[32] *Ibid*, 84–86. 'Eine Durchbrechung der Souverenität der Mitglieder der Vereinten Nationen aufgrund der Vorrechte des Sicherheitsrats ist nur zulässig, soweit tatsächlich eine Bedrohung des Friedens in einem noch zu erörtendem Sinne gegeben ist. . . . Eine rein politische Feststellung einer Bedrohung des Friedens, die ihre Grundlage nur in den formellen Befugnissen des Sicherheitsrates hätte, ohne daß ihr materiell eine Friedensbedrohung zugrunde läge, wäre keine ausreichende Rechtfertigung für eine Durchbrechung der staatlichen Souverenität; sie wäre zur Friedenswahrung nicht erforderlich. Sie wäre zudem mit dem Text des Art. 39 VNC, unter dessen Tatbestand sich Lebenssachverhalte subsumieren lassen, letzlich nicht vereinbar'.

[33] *Ibid*, 88. 'Die Feststellung einer Friedensbedrohung durch den Sicherheitsrat ist nur zulässig, wenn ihr Tatbestand erfüllt ist'.

Therefore, the use of the Council's power to determine the situation as the threat to the peace, the initially undefined notion, has to relate to a situation that can actually and transparently be seen as the threat to international peace and security.

This factual aspect of any limitation on the Council's powers is necessarily intertwined with its legal aspect. The discretion of the Council under Article 39 is not absolute and must be understood in the light of the purposes and principles of the United Nations. The text and context of Article 39 make it clear enough that the enforcement powers of the Security Council are functionally dependent on the UN's purposes and principles as enshrined in the Charter. Although the Council's discretion is wide and empowers it to adopt a wide range of coercive and non-coercive measures, the Charter makes it clear that the Security Council shall maintain a clear and inviolable link between its activities and the purposes and principles of the Organisation. The Council is bound by the purposes and principles of the Charter.[34] This limitation extends to all areas of the Council's activities. The text of the Charter does not provide that in making determinations under Article 39 the Council is free to disregard the Organisation's purposes and principles. Thus, in making a determination under Article 39, and in applying subsequent measures, the Council is bound to maintain the link between the steps it takes and the purposes and principles of the Organisation. It is presumably true that the discretion of the Council is based on the subjective judgement of its members, but the need to maintain a link to Organisation's purposes and principles means that this subjective discretion has observable and objective limitations.

It is admittedly impossible to enumerate fully what facts, events and circumstances fall within the notion of a 'threat to the peace' under Article 39. The practice of the Council offers a range of illustrations, but, on an empirical and illustrative basis, it is hardly feasible to identify the whole spectrum of situations which may threaten the peace. In exercising its mandate, the Council might perceive new imperatives for the maintenance of international peace and security, in line with the Organisation's purposes and principles, and identify new situations as threats to the peace, warranting enforcement measures. All interested parties can do is survey the Council's activities retrospectively, without prejudicing its subjective substantive discretion. However, it is in keeping with the methods and approaches of legal scholarship which allow for the identification of objective limitations of the Council's discretion, and thus allow for the judging of whether the link between its activities and the Organisation's purposes and principles are maintained in specific cases.

The purposes and principles of the UN must therefore be viewed not merely as abstract political or moral aspirations but as legally valid rules and principles capable, in themselves, of providing the legal basis for action by the Organisation and for the limitations to which such action must be subject. The subjective discretion of the Security Council is not a power of unlimited auto-interpretation but is connected with the appreciation of facts and circumstances in the light of the UN's purposes and principles, and with the clarification of the relationship between those facts and the operation of the UN Charter. Thus, the Council's discretionary power under Article 39 is not unlimited. Therefore, the Council must demonstrate in each concrete case which facts, events, situations or circumstances constitute a 'threat to the peace', warranting application of enforcement measures. In the event the Council decides to use

[34] UN Charter, Articles 24 and 25; *Namibia*, Advisory Opinion, *ICJ Reports*, 1971, 16ff.

enforcement powers, it must further demonstrate that the facts, events or circumstances involved are appropriate objects of enforcement powers which, in turn, are appropriate to the effective elimination or reduction of those facts, events or circumstances and their consequences.

As these general categories are clear, the specific criteria for clarifying the content of a threat to the peace must be identified and examined. The suggested criteria relate to the analysis of the concept of a threat to the peace *in kind* and *in degree*; these criteria are suggested as tools of checking the plausibility of the Council's determinations of a threat to the peace in specific cases. A type-oriented analysis of the notion of threat to the peace relates to the nature of facts, events or situations the Security Council labels as a 'threat to the peace'. The crux of such an analysis is the question of whether a given fact, event or circumstance is capable of constituting a threat to the peace by its nature or due to its context. A degree-oriented analysis of the notion of a threat to the peace centres on the development and evolution of specific situations, and the identification of their various stages. It might be suggested, for instance, that a determining factor in identifying a 'threat to the peace' is the spread of a given situation to or beyond national frontiers, or to or beyond a given region; or that the aggravation of a given situation constitutes a 'threat to the peace'.

The factual and legal criteria examined above, and the criteria of identification of threats to the peace in terms of the kind and degree of development of the relevant situation, especially the need of the compliance with purposes and principles of the United Nations Charter, can provide the more specific guidance in terms of the areas to which the Council shall properly direct its enforcement activities, including the Article 39 determination. The purposes and principles of the United Nations broadly reflect the basic principles of international law, such as the sovereign equality, non-intervention, non-use of force and respect for human rights,[35] and thus the structure of the international legal system within which the Council operates. As the international legal system is decentralised and based on the concept of State sovereignty, one focus of understanding the content of the determinations under Article 39 can be the interaction with the sovereign domain of States. Another, equally useful, focus is provided by the dichotomy between peace and war, and the evolution of the interaction between these concepts, on which international law has traditionally been based.

The following analysis will demonstrate that the Security Council is entitled to use its Article 39 determination power both in peacetime and wartime, and both with regard to international and internal situations. Article 39 determinations do not have to relate to the commission of an internationally wrongful act, even though this is the most regular practice. However, the Article 39 determinations cannot be legitimately made to justify the application of coercive measures against what does not constitute the breach of international law. Any opposite conclusion necessarily implies that the Council's power to make determinations under Article 39 with the adoption of consequent measures is not subject to limitation.

[35] On basic, or fundamental, principles of international law see A Cassese, *International Law* (2005), 46–68.

IDENTIFICATION OF THE POSSIBLE SOURCES OF A 'THREAT TO THE PEACE'

The source of a threat to peace has been identified in various ways in the practice of the Council. It has been interpreted as consisting of the conduct of a State or of a government or of a government or regime itself or in some process or situation (such as a humanitarian emergency or terrorism). The conduct of a State or government has been identified as a threat to peace on several occasions. Resolution 660 (1990), for example, states that the invasion of Kuwait by Iraq's armed forces—conduct by a State—constitutes a breach of the peace. Another noteworthy example of this approach is Resolution 1343 (2001), in the preamble of which the Council focused on the conduct of a State interfering in a civil war within another State by supporting one of the factions. The Council determined that 'the active support provided by the Government of Liberia for armed rebel groups in the neighbouring countries, and in particular its support for RUF in Sierra Leone, constitutes a threat to international peace and security in the region', and, acting under Chapter VII, demanded that Liberia stop such conduct. In paragraph 5 of the same Resolution, an arms embargo was imposed on Liberia. Resolution 864 of 15 September 1993 on Angola identified a non-State actor as the source of a 'threat to the peace', stressing that 'as a result of UNITA's military actions, the situation in Angola constitutes a threat to international peace and security'. In Resolution 941 (1994), the Council also addresses the conduct of non-State actors. The Resolution emphasises its concern with 'grave violations of international humanitarian law affecting the non-Serb population in those areas of the Republic of Bosnia and Herzegovina under the control of Bosnian Serb forces', and the consequent ethnic cleansing, and then determined this situation as threat to international peace and security. Likewise, in Resolution 1526 (2004), the Council was very specific in linking the existence of the threat to the peace to the conduct of the non-State actor—Al-Qaeda. Following the previous Resolutions, the Council reiterated 'its condemnation of the Al-Qaeda network and other associated terrorist groups for ongoing and multiple criminal terrorist acts, aimed at causing the deaths of innocent civilians, and other victims, and the destruction of property, and greatly undermining stability', stressed that States are committed to respond to threats caused by the attacks of Al-Qaeda to the international peace and security, and ordered States to strengthen sanctions against this organisation.

A process or situation was seen as a threat to peace and security in Resolution 794 (1993), in which the Council characterised the 'magnitude of human suffering'—not based on State conduct—as a threat to the peace. The expulsion of the Kurdish population from northern Iraq and the potential consequential destabilisation of the neighbouring countries was characterised as a threat to peace in Resolution 688 (1991). This resolution combines in a finding of a threat to the peace both a governmental conduct and a wider process or situation extending beyond the frontiers of a single country. These two facts are, however, linked, the conduct of the Government being the source of the consequent fleeing of the civilian population.

In the qualification adopted in Resolution 1306 (2000) on Sierra Leone the distinction between these two categories is blurred: the Council refers to the fact that the trade in illicit diamonds in Sierra Leone is a factor fuelling the conflict in that country and thus finds a 'threat to the peace' in the region. Furthermore, the Council demands in paragraph 1 under Chapter VII that 'all States shall take the necessary measures to prohibit the direct or indirect import of all rough diamonds from Sierra Leone to their territory'.[36] It can be argued that this Resolution is quite unique as an attempt by the Council to engage in resolving the structural causes of the conflict in Sierra Leone, and not just addressing the ensuing situation or conduct. Similarly, the two Resolutions addressing the situation in Cote d'Ivoire identify the 'threat to the peace' in the situation combining multiple events. Resolution 1572 (2005) refers to the repeated violations of the ceasefire agreement, the deterioration of the humanitarian situation, especially the use of radio to incite hatred, and determines that the situation in this country 'continues to pose a threat to international peace and security in the region'. Therefore, the Resolution imposes, in paragraph 7, an arms embargo on Cote d'Ivoire for thirteen months. Resolution 1643 (2005), similar to the above Resolution on Sierra Leone, identifies the threat to the peace in the illegal trade and exploitation of diamonds in and from Cote d'Ivoire and recognises 'the linkage between the illegal exploitation of natural resources such as diamonds, illicit trade in such resources, and the proliferation and trafficking of arms and the recruitment and use of mercenaries as one of the sources of fuelling and exacerbating conflicts in West Africa'. The Council identifies the existence of the threat to the peace and in paragraph 6 it decides 'that all States shall take the necessary measures to prevent the import of all rough diamonds from Côte d'Ivoire to their territory'. It seems that this Resolution, like Resolution 1306, addresses the roots of the conflict and thus contributes to the resolution of that conflict. Finally, the Resolution 1373 (2001), on anti-terrorist measures, confirms that the Council could refer to a general situation as a threat to the peace, without blaming a specific State in its determination under Article 39, and introduced the wide range of anti-terrorist enforcement measures.

'THREATS TO THE PEACE' AND THE LINK TO ARMED CONFLICTS

Although the Security Council explicitly rejected the idea that the concept of threats to the peace is limited to inter-State armed conflicts, this factor is a good starting point in examining the scope of the concept of the 'threat to the peace'. According to Arntz, a 'threat to the peace' may arise only in a case where the prohibition of the use of force in international relations is violated.[37] Schilling suggests that a threat to the peace can be found in situations where the possibility of occurrence of an international armed conflict increases and the Council is bound to find the existence of that circumstance when making a determination.[38] Instances where the Council has characterised as threats to the peace situations not involving the likelihood of occurrence of an international armed conflict, are held to constitute practice incompatible with the principle of sovereignty.[39] It is also stressed that a threat to the peace would be present if 'a danger of the use of force on a considerable scale arises', and the definition of a 'threat to the peace' would not encompass situations which 'do not involve the danger of forcible action'.[40] These

[36] This prohibition was imposed for the initial period of 18 months and further extended by Resolution 1446 (2002), para 2.

[37] J Arntz, *Der Begriff der Friedensbedrohung in Satzung und Praxis der Vereinten Nationen* (1975) 50.

[38] Schilling, above, n 29, at 90, 92.

[39] *Ibid*, at 91.

[40] Frowein and Krisch, 'On Article 39', in Simma (ed), *The Charter of the United Nations, A Commentary* (2002), 726.

opinions seem to reflect the approach expressed in the pronouncement of the Yugoslav Tribunal that the existence of an armed conflict will provide a *prima facie* and starting-point justification for the Council's determination that the relevant situation constitutes a threat to the peace.[41]

The suggestion that the finding of a 'threat to peace' shall be based on a situation involving transboundary armed conflict has an inherent value.[42] The fact that to address such armed conflicts is at the core of the Council's mandate is clear from Resolutions 1227 (1999), 1297 (2000) and 1298 (2000), in which the Council labelled as a threat to the peace the ongoing fighting between Eritrea and Ethiopia and ensuing humanitarian consequences. With Resolutions 1343 (2001) and 1497 (2003) on the situation in Liberia, the Council demanded 'that all States take action to prevent armed groups and individuals and groups from using their territory to prepare and commit attacks on neighbouring countries and refrain from any action that might contribute to further destabilization on the borders between Guinea, Liberia and Sierra Leone'. Consequently Resolution 1497 authorised the establishment of the Multinational Force to address this crisis.

At the same time, it must be admitted that the occurrence of an international armed conflict cannot be the sole situation governed by the Charter provisions on collective security. The Chapter VII enforcement powers of the Council can, by their very essence, be applied in situations not transcending national borders of one State or not involving the use of systematic and organised force. The Council possesses the power to make choice among various enforcement measures under Chapter VII. It is empowered to resort to non-forcible compulsory sanctions in a situation not amounting to an armed conflict. Therefore, the suggestion that the notion of a threat to the peace is inextricably linked with armed conflicts is unfounded.

'Threats to the Peace' and Internal Situations

The next issue to be examined is whether the notion of a threat to the peace is limited to inter-State conflicts or encompasses internal situations, such as civil war and insurgencies. The Council's practice may indicate the trend of the internationalisation of domestic conflicts.[43] In some cases, the Council addresses situations not extending beyond the borders of a State as threats to the peace. This approach is explicitly supported by Article 2(7) of the Charter which allows the Council to disregard the domestic jurisdiction of States if it applies the enforcement measures under Chapter VII. This is not really about the existence of some criteria as to the Council's action in relation to the fields that initially belong to domestic jurisdiction. Such criteria have indeed been suggested by reference to the necessity of the Council's response to systematic and massive human rights violations. The starting-point for those suggestions is the justifiability of unilateral action by States or groups of States in response to a humanitarian emergency, which are substantially based on the doubtful doctrine of

[41] As emphasised in *Tadic*, Appeal Chamber, para 30.

[42] Cf Frowein and Krisch, 'On Article 39', in Simma (ed), *The Charter of the United Nations, A Commentary* (2002), 722.

[43] Frowein and Krisch, 'On Article 39', in Simma (ed), *The Charter of the United Nations, A Commentary* (2002) 720–721.

humanitarian intervention.[44] But the question whether a unilateral action by States is justified in the relevant case does not prejudice the Council's power to pass its own judgment on the issue of measures under Chapter VII. It seems that the conceptual background of allowing 'Chapter VII exceptions' to domestic jurisdiction clause is the need to eliminate threats to the peace as such, regardless of whether their source lies in domestic or international sphere. The Council may, under certain circumstances, be entitled to intervene in domestic affairs of States even if the individual States would not be entitled to a similar intervention.

Nevertheless, the principle that domestic situations are generally not subject to international concern still stands. According to O'Connell, reference in the Charter to 'international peace' is intended to restrict the authority of the Security Council to intervene in domestic situations, such as a civil war, despite such wars being breaches of the peace. Article 39 refers to international peace. Internal wars and changes of governments are therefore situations the outcomes of which may not be dictated by the Security Council.[45] This position is no doubt correct. Certain domestic situations, however, may well have international implications. An obvious example of this may be a situation where domestic conflicts produce consequences transcending national frontiers, such as refugee flow, environmental pollution or terrorism. Does this mean that the Security Council is prevented from addressing under Chapter VII a situation which has no transboundary implications? Obviously this is not the case. The guidance for characterising internal situations as dangers or threats to international peace will therefore be the compatibility of a given internal situation with purposes and principles of the United Nations as enshrined in Articles 1 and 2 of the Charter, as well as with international obligations of the States concerned. As the Appeals Chamber observed in *Tadic*, internal situations may as such give rise to the Article 39 determination.[46] Nevertheless, it should be observed that even in such cases, the Council has sought to tie its response to circumstances which extends a given domestic situation or its consequences beyond the national frontiers, wherever such circumstances are present. Certain authors consider that the imposition by the Council of arms embargo on South Africa by Resolution 418 (1977) was an example of intervention by the Council into a purely domestic situation. As Franck has suggested, this resolution contributed 'to create a threshold of conduct by a government towards its own people which, when crossed, may be deemed a threat to the peace'.[47] However, if one tries to understand Resolution 418 as a unity, Franck's conclusions have to be considered as misinterpreting the reach and content of that resolution. In Resolution 418 (1977), the Council characterised the military build-up in South Africa and its persistent acts of aggression against neighbouring States as seriously disturbing the security of those States. The Council referred also to the fact that South Africa was 'at the threshold of producing nuclear weapons'. Pursuant to those assumptions,

[44] R Lillich, 'Humanitarian Intervention through the United Nations', 53 *Zeitschrift für ausländisches öffentliches Recht und Völkerrecht* (1993) 562–563; M McDougal and M Reisman, 'Rhodesia: The Lawfulness of International Concern', 62 *American Journal of International Law* (1968) 1ff.

[45] ME O'Connell, 'Regulating the Use of Force in the 21st Century: The Continuing Importance of State Autonomy', 36 *Columbia Journal of Transnational Law* (1997) 481.

[46] *Tadic*, Appeal Chamber, para 30.

[47] T Franck, *Fairness in International Law and Institutions* (1995) 230; See also N White, *Keeping the Peace* (1997) 35.

in operative paragraph 1, the Council determined 'that the acquisition by South Africa of arms and related *materiel* constitutes a threat to maintenance of international peace and security'. Acting under Chapter VII, the Council imposed an arms embargo on South Africa.

In the light of these considerations, the assumption that Resolution 418 (1977) was the case of application of Chapter VII enforcement measures to intra-State situations, seems not to be in accordance with the Council's intention as clarified in the text of the Resolution. The Council referred, of course, to the policy of apartheid in South Africa. However, the finding of a threat to the peace and response to it by Chapter VII enforcement measures can be understood as a coherent process, demonstrating that the *action* by the Council in case of Resolution 418 (1977), as distinguished from mere expression of concerns and condemnations, was directed against a situation having transboundary character and involving the use of force. The Council expressed concern with the military build-up, characterised the acquisition by South Africa of arms as a threat to the peace and then responded with concrete measures directed against that threat to the peace as identified in operative paragraph 1 of the resolution.

The final argument in this regard relates to the need to explain why exactly an arms embargo was imposed by Resolution 418 and not measures of economic character which are more suitable for addressing human rights situations. Arms embargos seem to be more suitable to threats to the peace of military character. Hardly could it be considered as an adequate response to human rights violations, due to its insufficiency to induce governments to change their domestic policies. One may argue, of course, that it was because of political considerations that the Council did not reach the consensus necessary for the adoption of more extensive enforcement measures. It must be borne in mind, however, that it is political considerations which lead the Council to adoption of almost each and every Chapter VII decision. And it was clearly the lack of political will which might have precluded the Council from addressing a purely domestic situation as a threat to the peace in that concrete case. Accordingly, Resolution 418 is limited to enforcement measures which are directed exclusively against the threats to the peace with transboundary implications.

For its part, Resolution 688 (1991) refers to the large-scale flow of Kurdish refugees as a threat to international peace and security. Although the Council condemned the large-scale repressions of the Kurdish population in Iraq, in operative paragraph 1 of the Resolution it declared that the consequences of those repressions (and not the repressions as such) were threatening international peace and security. In the preamble, the Council emphasised that repressions which led 'to a massive flow of refugees towards and across international frontiers' was threatening international peace. This case clearly illustrates that the Council found a threat to the peace not in repressions of Kurdish population as such, but in consequences thereof having transborder and international effects.

Despite this, the Council has not hesitated to qualify situations not crossing international borders as threats to the peace.[48] By Resolution 217 (1965), the Council imposed non-military sanctions on the racist regime of Southern Rhodesia demanding the end of the racist regime and its substitution by a government constituted on the

[48] One of the purposes of UN intervention in purely domestic conflicts may be, as White suggests, to prevent expansion of threats to the peace beyond the frontiers of a country which is the target of intervention. N White, *Keeping the Peace* (1997), 34.

basis of the right of peoples to self-determination in accordance with the UN General Assembly Declaration on Granting Independence to Colonial Peoples—Resolution 1514 (XV). In the case of Somalia, the Security Council in Resolution 794 (1993) has found a 'threat to the peace' in 'the magnitude of human tragedy, further exacerbated by the obstacles being created to the distribution of humanitarian assistance', which required 'an immediate and exceptional response' through the quick delivery of humanitarian assistance. The Resolution does not refer to any transboundary impact or consequence which would internationalise the situation in Somalia. Moreover, paragraphs 7 and 10 authorise the establishment of an operational force for establishing the secure environment for humanitarian relief operations. Therefore, Resolution 794 (1993) leaves no doubt that the Security Council addressed a purely internal situation as a threat to the peace. It has been correctly suggested, however, that in Somalia the action by the Council was caused by the absence of a government. It may therefore not be considered as an action against oppression by a government of its own population.[49]

The *coup d'etat* in Haiti was also a situation taking place within the frontiers of one State. By Resolution 940 (1994), the Council, having stated that 'the goal of the international community remains the restoration of democracy in Haiti and the prompt return of the legitimately elected President' to the country, determined the existence of a threat to international peace and security in the region. The Council was addressing in this case a purely domestic situation having no transboundary impact capable of constituting a threat to the peace in itself. In the preamble the Council referred to deterioration of humanitarian situation and systematic violations of civil liberties causing 'the desperate plight of Haitian refugees'. This circumstance does not permit, however, to conclude that this flow of refugees by sea towards the United States as such was the decisive factor having led the Council to make a determination under Article 39. First, Resolution 940 (1994) does not offer any evidence to consider the flow of refugees as a central issue addressed under that resolution. The Council directly refers to the goal of the international community to restore democracy in Haiti. Second, the final paragraph in the preamble to Resolution 940 (1994) refers to 'situation in Haiti' and not its consequences as a source of a threat to the peace. These criteria prompt the conclusion that in question of Haiti the Security Council has addressed the purely domestic situation as such under Chapter VII and applied enforcement measures to it.

The most recent practice of the Council focuses on several internal situations as threats to the peace, including Resolutions 864 (1993) and 1173 (1998) which state that the situation in Angola constitutes a threat to international peace and security. The fact that the operative provisions of these resolutions required taking certain measures only with regard to domestic actors, such as UNITA, is a further confirmation that the Council focuses on a purely internal situation as a threat to the peace. With regard to the Democratic Republic of the Congo, the Council *prima facie* has addressed an internal situation, but the latter has involved to take into effect, transboundary element. For instance, in the preamble of Resolution 1445 (2002), the Council considered that the situation in the DRC constituted a threat to the peace. On the other hand, that Resolution, as well as Resolutions 1457 (2003), 1468 (2003) and

[49] P Baehr, 'The Security Council and Human Rights', in Lawson and De Blois (eds), *The Dynamics of the Protection of Human Rights in Europe. Essays in Honour of Henry G Schermers* (1994) 25.

1493 (2003) demonstrate that the source of the threat to the peace is not merely domestic, but also international. This holds true in terms of the plunder of the DRC's natural resources, as well as large-scale human rights violations. However, by 2006, the Council addressed the purely internal situation, emphasising, in Resolution 1671 (2006), 'the importance of elections as the foundation for the longer term restoration of peace and stability, national reconciliation and establishment of the rule of law in the Democratic Republic of the Congo'. Having identified the threat to the peace in this situation, this Resolution, in the operative paragraphs 1 and 2, authorised the deployment of the European Union force in the period of presidential and parliamentary elections in the Congo, determining its tasks in terms of stabilising the internal situation.

This practice shows that the Security Council does not consider its mandate to be limited to inter-State conflicts. However, in order to ascertain whether or not in a given case the Council applies its Chapter VII powers to an internal situation as such, the decision of the Council must be examined in their context. The mere presence of a concern with or condemnation of certain internal situations by the Council does not justify assumption that Chapter VII powers are applied to an internal situation as such. The context of a decision of the Council consisting of motivation, of identification of a target and of the type of specific measures applied should be examined before one arrives at such a conclusion.

'THREATS TO THE PEACE' AND VIOLATIONS OF INTERNATIONAL LAW

There are different opinions as to whether a threat to the peace should necessarily involve a violation of international law by a State against which the measures under Chapter VII are applied. The Council was established arguably not to enforce the law but to maintain peace, these two tasks being distinct from each other.[50] It can thus be argued that a threat to the peace can exist even if no wrongful act is involved, as no link with a wrongful act is positively required under Article 39. Whether a threat to the peace should involve a breach of international law can be an open question, but the answer can be facilitated by a reverse question—can a situation, or the conduct of a State, which is in accordance with international law, be a threat to international peace and security? The fact that the Council's powers are limited by the principles and purposes of the Charter, whose basic principles are fundamental principles of international law which the Council is bound to safeguard not to undermine, which militates towards the attitude that the Council should not see too much of a threat to the peace in situations not involving breaches of international law, when a State follows its rights and entitlements under international treaties or general international law.

This may be exemplified by reference to the economic policies of States. Bowett, for instance, considers that a State's refusal to open up economically to other States can be a basis for the Council's determination of a threat to the peace, and refers to the fact that in the Second World War Japan launched its war in Asia-Pacific to secure its access to certain economic resources and markets.[51] Bowett's line of reasoning is

[50] H Kelsen, *The Law of the United Nations* (1951), 294; T Gill, 'Legal and Some Political Limitations on the Power of the UN Security Council to Exercise its Enforcement Powers under Chapter VII of the Charter', XXVI *Netherlands Yearbook of International Law* (1995) 46.

[51] D Bowett, *Self-Defence in International Law* (Manchester, 1958), 114.

defective as it ignores the aggressive character of Japan's war which was duly certified and prosecuted by the Tokyo War Crimes Tribunal. At the same time, every State has absolute entitlement under international law to conduct and control its economic policies. Already Vattel recognised that, for instance, 'every State has the right to forbid the importation of foreign goods; and the Nation which is thus prohibited has no right to complain, as if it had been refused an office of humanity. The complaint would be ridiculous'.[52] This is a clear evidence that the Council cannot see a threat to the peace in a State's behaviour that is fully in accordance with its rights under international law, especially the rights that are protected under the Charter which serves as a limitation on the Council's powers.

The approach that the determination of the threat to the peace does not have to involve the breach of international law is arguably supported by the Council's role in the context where the considerations of peace differ from those of justice. However, it is the practice of the United Nations organs to refute any inherent relevance of such dichotomy. In its Resolutions regarding the Middle East, the UN General Assembly clearly stated that the maintenance of international peace is integrally linked with the enforcement of legal norms violated in a given situation, such as the withdrawal from occupied territories and return of displaced persons.[53] Similarly, the Security Council itself has stated in several resolutions that for the restoration of international peace in former Yugoslavia the enforcement of certain legal norms, such as those imposing individual criminal responsibility on those perpetrating international crimes, was a necessary precondition.[54] In that case, the Council has in fact intertwined violations of international law and threats to the peace with each other. In Resolution 941 (1994), the threat to the peace has been determined on the basis of violations of international humanitarian law in Bosnia-Herzegovina. In Resolution 1638 (2005), the Council emphasised that the former President of Liberia, Charles Taylor, was indicted by the Special Court of Sierra Leone, and his return to Liberia, that is the avoidance of his trial, 'would constitute an impediment to stability and a threat to the peace of Liberia and to international peace and security in the region'. Therefore, the Council authorised the UN peace-keeping force to arrest Taylor if he returned to Liberia and transfer him to Sierra Leone so that he would be prosecuted before the Tribunal. In Resolution 1688 (2006) regarding the operation of the Special Court for Sierra Leone, the Council manifests its 'determination to end impunity, establish the rule of law and promote respect for human rights and to restore and maintain international peace and security, in accordance with international law and the purposes and principles of the Charter'. The Council further points out that 'the proceedings in the Special Court in the case against former President Taylor will contribute to achieving truth and reconciliation in Liberia and the wider sub-region'. Consequently, the Council praises the

[52] E Vattel, 'The Law of Nations or the Principles of Natural Law applied to the Conduct and to the Affairs of Nations and of Sovereigns' in Scott (ed), *Classics of International Law* (Washington, 1916), 40. Similarly, Hersch Lauterpacht observes that while the clash of economic interests, consisting of high tariffs, economic discrimination, restriction upon export and import, and other governmental interferences with the natural flow of commerce, may cause international friction, they 'should not be treated as constituting a direct menace to international peace'. This is so because 'in an international society living under the reign of law the clash of economic interests need not in itself constitute a danger to the cause of peace'. (H Lauterpacht, *The Function of Law in the International Community* (Oxford, 1933), 367).

[53] GA Res 41/162 (1986), paras 2–3; GA Res 39/146A (1984); GA Res 34/65 (1979) A, para 2.

[54] UNSC Res 771 (1993), 817 (1993), 827 (1993).

efforts to bring Taylor before the Court and decides in paragraph 7 of the Resolution that the Special Court would maintain its exclusive jurisdiction over him. A clearer evidence of the Council's perception of the interdependence between peace and justice would be hard to find.

Most significantly, Resolution 242 (1967) views the compliance with legal requirements as the essential element of international peace. According to the Resolution, 'the establishment of a just and lasting peace in the Middle East [. . .] should include the application of both the following principles: (i) Withdrawal of Israeli armed forces from territories occupied in the recent conflict; (ii) Termination of all claims or states of belligerency and respect for and acknowledgement of the sovereignty, territorial integrity and political independence of every State in the area and their right to live in peace within secure and recognized boundaries free from threats or acts of force'.

In the great majority of cases of the application of Chapter VII measures, the threats to the peace involved the breaches of international law by States or non-State actors. The Council has referred to the acts of aggression, to massive violations of human rights and humanitarian law as immediate threats to the peace. In the case of Rhodesia, the minority regime was systematically offending against internationally recognised human rights standards. In the case of Haiti, human rights violations have also been involved. In the case of Iraq, massive repressions of minorities took place in direct violation of Iraq's international obligations. In the case of Former Yugoslavia, the violations of international humanitarian law have reached such a large extent that the Council considered these violations to constitute in themselves a threat to international peace and security. The reference to terrorism, a notion not even defined in international law, as the threat to the peace in a number of resolutions may raise some thoughts in this regard, but most of these references relate to the conduct of non-State actors and acts that are outlawed under the number of anti-terrorist treaties. Even in cases where the Council fails to demonstrate in the conduct of a target State the degree of wrongfulness adequate for application of enforcement measures, it nevertheless appeals to certain rules of international law as justification for its action. For instance, in the case of the imposition of sanctions on Libya under Resolution 748 (1992), the Council extensively interpreted Article 2(4) of the UN Charter as imposing the prohibition on States 'to refrain from organising, instigating, assisting or participating in terrorist acts in another State or acquiescing in organised activities within its territory directed towards the commission of such acts, when such acts involve a threat or use of force'. These circumstances illustrate that where the Council decides to make a determination under Article 39 and to adopt enforcement measures, it prefers, if possible, to refer to a certain degree of wrongfulness, which it considers to be present in a given situation.

The fact that the Council's determinations under Article 39 are linked to a serious breach of international law cannot be without consequences in terms of the concept of a threat to the peace. Professor Graefrath considers that the determination under Article 39 is based not only on a political judgement, but also on the finding of a serious breach of international law. Such determinations are merely declaratory of the existence of a wrongful act and presuppose that a wrongful act has already occurred.[55]

[55] B Graefrath, 'International Crimes and Collective Security', Wellens (ed), *International Law: Theory and Practice. Essays in Honour of Eric Suy* (1998), 242–243.

Those unwilling to accept the presence of a legal element in the concept of a threat to the peace cannot contradict the reality that the determinations under Article 39 regularly involve serious breaches of international law.

The existence of the *acquis* linking the concept of a threat to the peace to internationally wrongful acts and the absence of a formal link between these two concepts under Article 39 need to be reconciled with each other. In this context, the practical question is whether the enforcement measures under Chapter VII may be taken against a State without prior commission of an internationally wrongful act by that State. According to the UN International Law Commission Articles on State Responsibility, the existence of a prior wrongful act is a precondition for applying countermeasures against a State.[56] The measures under Articles 41 and 42 of the Charter constitute only part of the Council's powers under Chapter VII (along with the powers to issue the recommendations under Article 39 and the provisional measures under Article 40). These measures are coercive measures, countermeasures, or sanctions[57] that necessarily presuppose the commission of an internationally wrongful act. Graefrath considers that countermeasures are not justified purely and simply by virtue of the Council's decisions; rather, they have to be justified in terms of the specific situation under general international law. Unless such measures are legitimate under the law of State Responsibility, they themselves are breaches of international law.[58] If so, and if the Council finds a threat to the peace in a situation not involving an international wrong, it is not empowered to impose sanctions on a State under Chapter VII. In such situations the Council is limited to making recommendations under Article 39 or ordering provisional measures under Article 40. For instance, the Council would, under certain circumstances, be justified to call upon the State to stop large-scale military exercises near the frontier of another State without duly notifying it; but it would hardly be justified to resort to enforcement measures in this case.

However, the fact that coercive measures under Articles 41 and 42 may only be applied against a State in response to its prior commission of an internationally wrongful act, does not render the enforcement powers of the Council inapplicable in cases where no wrongfulness in conduct of a State is involved. The facts, events or situations which the Council may address are not limited to situations where a State violates international law. The Council may determine, for instance, that certain environmental situations, or activities by non-State actors such as terrorists or rebels, are threats to international peace, for instance, because of their transnational effect. In such cases, the Council is empowered to use the powers under Articles 41 and 42 in order to coordinate activities by States in maintaining and restoring peace and security, provided that it does not target the State with sanctions. This was the case with Resolution 1526 (2004), paragraphs 1(a)–(c) which introduce a number of sanctions against Al-Qaeda to hamper its activities, without actually targeting any particular State with sanctions.

From the methodological point of view, it might be asked whether the involvement of wrongfulness shall be a cause for determination of the existence of a threat to the peace by the Council or just an accompanying determinative criteria in making

[56] Article 49(1), *ILC Report*, 2001, 56.

[57] V Gowlland-Debbas, 'Security Council Enforcement Action and the Issues of State Responsibility', 43 *ICLQ* (1994), 73.

[58] Graefrath, above, n 53, at 243.

findings under Article 39. Whatever interpretation shall be adopted, the Council, when it makes determinations under Article 39, should be considered to be bound by the duty of proportionality, which implies that the encroachment on the rights of a State must be commensurate with the degree of wrongfulness involved in the conduct of that State. It is, in this regard, undisputable that the Chapter VII powers of the Council are constrained by the principle of proportionality, and there seems to be no reason to assume that this principle could have in this context a meaning different from its meaning in the law of State Responsibility, particularly bearing in mind the generic similarity between State countermeasures and Chapter VII enforcement measures.

'THREATS TO THE PEACE'—A DEGREE-ORIENTED PERSPECTIVE

A degree-oriented analysis of the notion of a 'threat to the peace' deals with the development in time, space and extent of situations where the Council acts under Chapter VII. The primary question in this regard is the relationship between the notions of a threat to the peace and a situation the continuation of which may endanger international peace (Article 34 of the Charter). As suggested, hardly any firm and uniform distinction between these two notions is identifiable.[59] However, the Council's practice may indicate whether, and to what extent, a situation which was previously dealt by the Council under Chapter VI, can be eligible to be dealt with under Chapter VII.

The fact that the determinations under Article 39 relate to objectively observable and identifiable situations is confirmed in the Council's practice. In the Spanish case, the Council established the Sub-Committee charged with the task to determine whether the situation in Spain during Franco regime amounted to a threat to international peace and security.[60] According to the Sub-Committee, the situation in Spain had not yet resulted in a threat to the peace in terms of Article 39, but was a situation likely to endanger international peace and security in terms of Chapter VI. The Sub-Committee emphasised in particular that 'no threat of the peace has been established' and Chapter VII enforcement measures were not applicable.[61] The communication by Poland concerning the situation in Spain was concerned not merely with the fact of the existence of the Franco regime, but also with its connections with the former Nazi and fascist regimes in Germany and Italy. However, the communication of Poland did not refer to any transboundary implications of the situation in Spain. Moreover, no reference to the actual circumstances, based on actions by Franco regime, which might have constituted a threat to the peace, was made. And the Polish representative characterised the situation as falling not under Article 39 but under Article 34.

The Council's investigations with a view to ascertain the existence of threat to the peace in sense of Article 39 were performed also in other cases.[62] This practice indi-

[59] Frowein and Krisch, 'On Article 39', Simma (ed), *The Charter of the United Nations. A Commentary* (2002) 723; Goodrich, Hambro and Simmons, *Charter of the United Nations. Commentary and Documents* (1969) 295–296.

[60] 'The Security Council thereby resolves: to make studies in order to determine whether such a situation exists; to this end, the Security Council appoints a sub-committee of five its members . . .', *Yearbook of the United Nations* (1946–1947) 346.

[61] *Yearbook of the United Nations* (1946–1947) 347–348.

[62] For the overview of such cases see B Conforti, *The Law and Practice of the United Nations* (2005) 155–160.

cates that in case of doubt as to whether a threat to the peace is actual and not merely expected, the investigation of objective facts, events and circumstances surrounding the relevant case must be performed. Therefore, the presumption is that in cases where the Council does not initiate an investigation procedure, it holds for granted and undisputed that an actual threat to the peace exists and no additional inquiries are necessary to examine the obvious. But there is still a real possibility that the majority in the Council could agree to avoid objective scrutiny of a situation, which could result in the abuse of Chapter VII powers.

It can also happen that a threat to the peace matures after the Security Council has considered a given situation. This is illustrated in the Council's practice relating to Eritrea and Ethiopia, particularly Resolutions 1227 of 10 February 1999, 1297 of 12 May 2000 and 1298 of 17 May 2000. In these Resolutions, the Council refers to its earlier Resolutions on the same subject, the concern expressed therein with regard to the expected fighting between the two countries and the possible implications of the latter for international peace; having said this, the Council is 'deeply disturbed by the continuation of the fighting between Ethiopia and Eritrea', and ensuing humanitarian problems.[63] Due to this, the Council determines the situation in question as a threat to the peace and responds to it through the imposition of an arms embargo on both parties.

Similar trends are observable in the Council's practice in relation to Afghanistan. In Resolution 1214 (1998), which was not adopted under Chapter VII, the Council demanded from the Taliban to 'stop providing sanctuary and training for international terrorists and their organisations, and that all Afghan factions cooperate with efforts to bring indicted terrorists to justice'. After non-compliance, the Council determined, in the preamble to Resolution 1267 (1999) that the Taliban's non-compliance with paragraph 13 of Resolution 1214 constituted a threat to international peace and security. One could indeed wish to see more coherence in this approach, as it is more plausible to consider that a 'threat to the peace' is created by harbouring terrorist organisations rather than by a simple fact of non-compliance with the request to stop such activity. But this lack of coherence could perhaps be mitigated, though not necessarily justified, by the fact that the Council was dealing with a situation objectively involving a threat of international terrorism.

CASE STUDIES

The general framework examined above must be illustrated by reference to some specific situations from the Security Council's practice involving its exercise of the power to determine a threat to the peace. These case studies are aimed at testing in practical terms what has been examined more generally so far. It is worth examining certain resolutions which are thought to be adopted by the Council acting at the margins of its Charter mandate, and which combine in themselves the treatment of the range of issues examined above in the systematic perspective.

[63] This can be contrasted to earlier resolutions adopted on the same subject and referred to by the Council, in which the Council spoke in the language of the peaceful settlement of disputes (resolution 1177 of 26 June 1999) or expressed the concern about the implications 'over the risk of armed conflict between Ethiopia and Eritrea' (Resolution 1226 of 29 January 1999) and not an actual conflict.

a) Cases of Constructive Expansion of the Use of Article 39 Power

Some of the situations dealt with here involve transparent and consistent determinations under Article 39, and thereby demonstrate how the powers concentrated within the Chapter VII framework can be used in different contexts for combating threats of different natures.

Resolution 1373 (2001) on Anti-terrorist Measures

After the terrorist attacks on the World Trade Centre in New York on 11 September 2001, the Security Council has been dealing with the issue of international terrorism as a threat to international peace and security. At first, the Council adopted Resolution 1368 of 12 September 2001, in which it condemned the attacks and stressed the need to bring the perpetrators to justice. But the Council has also adopted a set of general anti-terrorist measures in its Resolution 1373 of 28 September 2001 adopted under Chapter VII. The Council made a general determination that the acts of international terrorism constitute threats to international peace and security. In this regard, the Council underlined the need of international co-operation to combat such acts, and imposed on States certain obligations to prevent terrorist acts, identify terrorist groups, cut their funding and bring perpetrators to justice.

This resolution is peculiar in that it identified a threat to the peace not in the action of a specific State or non-State actor, but in the general phenomenon of international terrorism. Consequently, it does not subject a specific State or non-State actor to coercive measures, but requires from all States to perform certain measures of cooperation aimed at destruction of terrorist networks and bringing perpetrators to justice. It must be emphasised that the determination by the Council of a 'threat to the peace' and the scope and nature of consequent measures under the resolution are logically consistent to each other; in other words, the measures ordered by the Council are proportional to the 'threat to the peace' identified by it and is clearly directed at its elimination. Therefore, it must be concluded that Resolution 1373 is a clear example of how the Council's discretionary power to determine the existence of a threat to peace should be properly exercised without involving any abuse or excess of powers of this organ.[64]

Resolution 1540 (2004) against the Proliferation of Weapons of Mass Destruction

This Resolution is another example of the Council's effort to use its Chapter VII powers to coordinate the activities of States to respond to the common threat, without addressing the conduct of the single State and targeting it with sanctions. The Council '*Affirm[s]* that proliferation of nuclear, chemical and biological weapons, as well as their means of delivery, constitutes a threat to international peace and security', and 'its resolve to take appropriate and effective actions against any threat to international peace and security caused by the proliferation of nuclear, chemical and biological weapons and their means of delivery, in conformity with its primary responsibilities, as provided for in the United Nations Charter'. The Council is '*Gravely concerned* by

[64] This is, of course, without prejudice to the legality, proportionality, and propriety of measures adopted consequent to such determination, which is the subject of a separate doctrinal debate.

the threat of terrorism and the risk that non-State actors [. . .] may acquire, develop, traffic in or use nuclear, chemical and biological weapons and their means of delivery', '*Recogniz[es] further* the urgent need for all States to take additional effective measures to prevent the proliferation of nuclear, chemical or biological weapons and their means of delivery', and '*Reaffirm[s]* the need to combat by all means, in accordance with the Charter of the United Nations, threats to international peace and security caused by terrorist acts'.

These passages show that the identification of the threat to the peace is transparent, and so is the reference to the source of it, namely the activities of non-State terrorist organisations. The Council does not address the conduct of any specific State nor apply the sanctions against the State. As a response, the Council decides that 'all States shall refrain from providing any form of support to non-State actors that attempt to develop, acquire, manufacture, possess, transport, transfer or use nuclear, chemical or biological weapons and their means of delivery', and introduce the measures of domestic control over such activities. Resolution 1540 also emphasises the legal element in the threat to the peace in this case. The Council emphasises 'the need for all Member States to fulfil their obligations in relation to arms control and disarmament and to prevent proliferation in all its aspects of all weapons of mass destruction', and 'its support for the multilateral treaties whose aim is to eliminate or prevent the proliferation of nuclear, chemical or biological weapons and the importance for all States parties to these treaties to implement them fully in order to promote international stability'. Thus, Resolution 1540 is of multiple importance for understanding how the concept of 'threat to the peace' is and ought to be treated. It offers transparent identification of the threat, explains why it should be combated and links it to the observance of the international obligations of States.

b) Cases of Inconsistent or Non-transparent use of Article 39 Determination Power

In contrast to the cases looked at above, the Council's use of the Article 39 power has given rise to determinations that do not really address the objectively existing situations that can be subsumable within the Chapter VII framework. This can be seen from the failure of the Council in these cases to demonstrate how the relevant situations threaten international peace and security and how the measures adopted are adequate in addressing the relevant situation.

Resolution 748 (1992) on Libya

The Lockerbie crisis has been analysed on multiple occasions,[65] and this analysis will only be concerned with the use of the Article 39 power by the Security Council. By adopting Resolution 748 (1992), the Security Council ordered States to introduce large-scale non-military coercive measures against the Libyan Arab Jamahiriya for the refusal of the latter to hand over to the United States or the United Kingdom two of its nationals accused of organising the explosion of Pan-Am Flight 103. Before seizing

[65] For the most recent analysis of this question see J Allain, ,The Legacy of Lockerbie: Judicial Review of Security Council Actions or the First Manifestation of "Terrorism" as a Threat to International Peace?' (2004) 44 *Indian Journal of International Law* 74.

the Council of the matter, the United States or the United Kingdom have demanded from Libya the extradition of the suspects. Libya refused by reference to the rule *aut dedere aut judicare* enshrined in Article 7 of the 1971 Montreal Convention on Suppression of Illegal Acts against Civil Aviation. Libya maintained that it had a freedom of choice between trying suspects in its own courts and extraditing them, and that it favoured the former option, thus acting fully in accordance with its international obligations. Despite those arguments, the United States and the United Kingdom managed to re-write their demands towards Libya into Resolution 731 (1992), adopted under Chapter VI. Libya thereafter instituted proceedings before the International Court of Justice by arguing that it was fully complying with its international obligations under international law. Libya also referred to threats of force against it by the United States and the United Kingdom and requested the Court to enjoin them from enforcing such threats. After the hearings before the Court were finished, but before the Court's Order was delivered, the Security Council adopted Resolution 748 (1992) under Chapter VII, which reiterated the demands of Resolution 731 (1992), supporting them by large-scale non-military sanctions.

The Council determined that State-sponsored terrorism constitutes a serious threat to international peace and security. The Council seems thus to be referring to a general phenomenon of terrorism. But along with that the Council determined that Libya's non-compliance with Resolution 731, that is the failure to extradite the suspects to the United States or the United Kingdom, constituted a threat to international peace and security and demanded compliance. As far as the Council determined that State-supported terrorism as such was as a threat to the peace, it was supposed to adopt measures for eliminating it or essentially reducing its impact in international relations. However, the Council simply linked its coercive measures to the demands for the extradition of the two suspects to the United States or the United Kingdom.

It is thus clear that while labelling a general phenomenon as a threat to the peace, the Council directed its enforcement measures not against that threat but a specific fact of non-extradition. It is obvious that the non-extradition of two suspects to a particular country cannot in itself be viewed as a threat to the peace, however wide the discretion of the Council in making determinations under Article 39 can be. Although the general phenomenon of international terrorism was also mentioned in the Resolution, it is clear from the operative paragraphs 1, 4, 5 and 13 of the Resolution that the Council's action was aimed specifically at obtaining the extradition of the suspects to the United States or the United Kingdom, and not the general elimination of international terrorism. The measures of the Council were thus not properly directed at the elimination of a threat to the peace as determined in the Resolution.

The extradition of two Libyan suspects could hardly ensure removal of a threat to the peace as identified by the Council. As is known, the Council made suspension of its sanctions conditional upon extradition of the two Libyan suspects. However, the extradition or punishment of two suspected terrorists is not equal to elimination of general threats to international peace, such as State-sponsored terrorism, nor can the mere fact of non-extradition of the two suspects amount to a threat to the peace in whichever way this notion is understood. Resolution 748 (1992) has therefore served purposes other than the maintenance and restoration of international peace and security in the sense of the Charter.

For the elimination of State-supported terrorism the enforcement of provisions of relevant multilateral conventions is the best option. Even in a wider conceptual sense, the goal to suppress and punish terrorism is to bring suspects before justice and not to try them in any particular country. Whether or not a terrorist will be tried in a country in which he/she committed a crime is not essential for elimination of terrorism. If the Security Council has considered that the punishment of suspects was necessary for the maintenance of peace, it did not provide adequate evidence why the trial in any particular country would be the best option. Instead of demanding extradition, the Council could have demanded from Libya to accept international observation and supervision in order to ensure that a trial in Libya was not used as a tool to shield suspects from true prosecution. Moreover, the Council, by adoption of Resolutions 731 (1992) and 748 (1992) has in fact supported the threats of the use of force against Libya which were unlawful under international law. This conduct of the Council is contrary to Article 2(4) of the UN Charter, and thus amounts to a violation of Article 24(1) of the Charter according to which the Council is bound to act. Therefore, the determination of a threat to the peace in Resolution 748 (1992) was inadequate and unjustified under Article 39 of the Charter from a kind-oriented perspective. But it was also defective under the degree-oriented perspective.

As shown above, a degree-oriented analysis of the notion of a threat to the peace involves the analysis of development and evolution of situations considered by the Council to be a 'threat to the peace' in specific cases. The factual circumstances leading to the adoption of Resolution 748 (1992), including the text of Resolution 731 (1992) which contains no reference to threats to the peace, demonstrate that the situation addressed by that Resolution had not developed to an extent warranting application of coercive measures. There was no peace-threatening development in Libya's conduct in the period between the adoption of Resolutions 731 (1992) and 748 (1992), but in the latter Resolution the Council determined the existence of a threat to the peace. Even if the Council referred to State-sponsored terrorism generally as a threat to the peace, it could not be believed seriously that it acquired such nature in the time between the adoption of those two Resolutions. Moreover, it is highly doubtful that State-supported terrorism may over time acquire a peace-threatening nature just because two suspects are not extradited to a particular country. Consequently, the Council has failed to demonstrate by virtue of which facts, events or circumstances has the conduct by Libya become a threat to the peace. Its judgment was therefore unjustified also under the degree-oriented perspective.

The Council and the sponsoring members were undoubtedly aware that Libya's refusal to extradite the suspects was fully in accordance with international law. Presumably, this is the reason that they tried to counterbalance this factor by referring, in Resolution 748 (1992), to Article 2(4) of the Charter and interpret it extensively as encompassing the prohibition of the State-supported terrorism and thus assume the role of law-enforcers. They failed, however, to demonstrate the coherent link between the general prohibition of State sponsored terrorism, the relevance of that prohibition in that particular case in the context of Libya's conduct and the measures adopted to enforce that prohibition.

In view of all the aforesaid, it has to be concluded that Resolution 748 (1992) cannot be considered as a step towards maintenance of international peace and security in terms of Article 39. As this resolution has been adopted in excess of powers of the

Council under Article 24 of the Charter, it must be considered *ultra vires*. The legal consequence thereof is the invalidity of Resolution 748 (1992) and it having no legal force from the moment of its adoption. In practice, this assumption is confirmed by the Organisation of African Unity, which decided in 1998 that it was not bound to observe the air embargo imposed on Libya by Resolution 748 (1992).[66] Further developments of this issue took place both before the Security Council and the International Court. Libya instituted proceedings before the Court, where it lost at the provisional measures stage in 1992,[67] but succeeded at the preliminary objections stage in 1998.[68] In the meantime, the problems arose with the observance of the sanctions imposed by Resolution 748 (1992).[69] Given this, there was no real prospect that Libya would comply with the demands of the United States or the United Kingdom embodied in Resolution 748 and other related Resolutions. The United States or the United Kingdom thus had to suggest a compromise solution—trial of the suspects by the Scottish court in the Netherlands—which they had consistently opposed during the preceding years.[70] The United Kingdom enacted the necessary statutory instruments and concluded the agreement with the Netherlands with a view to arranging the trial in that country.[71] On 27 August 1998, the Security Council adopted Resolution 1192. Paragraph 1 of this Resolution demanded 'once again' that Libya comply with Resolutions 731 (1992), 748 (1992) and 883 (1993). Paragraph 4, however, demanded Libya 'to ensure the appearance in the Netherlands of the two accused'. These two provisions of the resolution required Libya to do different things. It was clear, however, that extradition of the suspects to the United States or the United Kingdom was not really the goal which the Council or the sponsoring States were trying to achieve. That proved to be unrealistic. Therefore, upon arrival of the suspects in the Netherlands on 5 May 1999, the sanctions imposed on Libya by Resolutions 748 and 883 were suspended in accordance with paragraph 8 of Resolution 1192, which, in effect, meant that they were lifted because to re-impose them would have require a further decision of the Security Council.[72]

Resolution 1422 (2002) on the International Criminal Court

The establishment of the International Criminal Court (ICC) through adoption of its Statute at the 1998 Rome Conference was opposed by the United States as a threat to its military personnel stationed in different parts of the world. Despite this opposition, the Statute entered into force on 1 July 2002, and has been viewed by the United States as a factor obstructing its peace-keeping and peace-enforcement commitments. Ensuing efforts of the United States finally led the Security Council to adopt Resolution 1422 (2002),[73] whereby it exempted the personnel of UN-established or UN-authorised peace operations from jurisdiction of the ICC for the initial 12-month period.

[66] See pp 95–98 below.
[67] *ICJ Reports*, 1992, 3ff.
[68] *ICJ Reports*, 1998, 10ff.
[69] A Aust, 'Lockerbie: The Other Case', 49 *ICLQ* (2000), 283.
[70] *Ibid*. For the text of the UK/US Letter to the UN Secretary-General embodying these proposals, see 117 *ILR* 687–689.
[71] For the texts of these documents see 117 *ILR* 666ff.
[72] Aust, above, n 66, at 295–296.
[73] SC Res 1422 of 12 July 2002.

The Resolution was adopted under Chapter VII; it refers to 'the importance to international peace and security of United Nations operations' and considers it 'in the interests of international peace and security to facilitate to the Member States' ability to contribute to operations established or authorised by the United Nations Security Council'. But the Resolution does not determine a 'threat to the peace' under Article 39; nor does it suggest that preventing certain States from participating at UN operations would amount to a threat to the peace. The Resolution claims that it is in accordance with the ICC Statute, as it refers to its Article 16. This provision states that 'No investigation or prosecution may be commenced or proceeded with [. . .] for a period of 12 months after the Security Council, in a resolution adopted under Chapter VII of the Charter of the United Nations, has requested the Court to that effect; that request must be renewed by the Council under the same conditions'. But this provision, regardless of its general scope, cannot justify the action of the Council in the case of Resolution 1422. Article 16 requires that the Security Council act under Chapter VII if it is willing to exempt certain cases from the ICC jurisdiction. But this is where the reach of Article 16 ends; this provision refers to Chapter VII, but it is not meant to replace any provision of the UN Charter or modify the criteria applicable to the Council's decision-making under Chapter VII. That said, Article 16 would justify such action by the Council only where this organ would properly identify a specific situation as a threat to the peace under Article 39 and consider that the elimination of that threat requires certain exemptions from the ICC jurisdiction. This, however, is not what Resolution 1422 states, and this Resolution is therefore not justifiable either under Chapter VII of the Charter or Article 16 of the ICC Statute.

A logical conclusion is that Resolution 1422 (2002) is *ultra vires* for its inconsistency with the UN Charter standards on the Chapter VII decision-making, and for this reason it produces no legal effects. Consequently, it does not affect the scope of jurisdiction of the ICC as stipulated in its Statute. However, the Security Council has, in Resolution 1487 (2003),[74] prolonged the exemption from the ICC jurisdiction for a further 12-month period. This latter resolution is identical in terms with Resolution 1422, and the conclusions reached with regard to the latter should be deemed applicable to the former as well. This legal regime was not prolonged for a further year, which presumably reflects the incompatibility with the Charter and the impropriety of the use of Chapter VII in this case. The United States decided not to proceed with submitting a resolution prolonging the exemption from the ICC jurisdiction, because most members of the Council refused to vote for such.

Resolution 1718 (2006) on the Claimed Nuclear Test by the North Korea

Resolution 1718 has been adopted in the process of six-party talks regarding the policies and conduct of the Democratic Peoples' Republic of Korea in terms of the development of nuclear weapons. North Korea had earlier announced its withdrawal from the 1968 Non-Proliferation treaty, Article X of which gives States-parties such right. The Resolution proceeds with identifying the 'threat to the peace' in the combined circumstances of the North Korea's withdrawal from the Treaty and its claim of having performed the nuclear test. The Council is '*Expressing the gravest concern* at

[74] SC Res 1487 of 12 June 2003.

the claim by the Democratic People's Republic of Korea (DPRK) that it has conducted a test of a nuclear weapon on 9 October 2006, and at the challenge such a test constitutes to the Treaty on the Non-Proliferation of Nuclear Weapons and to international efforts aimed at strengthening the global regime of non-proliferation of nuclear weapons, and the danger it poses to peace and stability in the region and beyond'. The Council is further:

> *Expressing* its firm conviction that the international regime on the non-proliferation of nuclear weapons should be maintained and recalling that the DPRK cannot have the status of a nuclear-weapon state in accordance with the Treaty on the Non-Proliferation of Nuclear Weapons, *Deploring* the DPRK's announcement of withdrawal from the Treaty on the Non-Proliferation of Nuclear Weapons and its pursuit of nuclear weapons, *Deploring further* that the DPRK has refused to return to the Six-Party talks without precondition . . .
>
> *Expressing* profound concern that the test claimed by the DPRK has generated increased tension in the region and beyond, and *determining* therefore that there is a clear threat to international peace and security.

Therefore, in the relevant parts of operative paragraphs of the resolution, the Council:

1. *Condemns* the nuclear test proclaimed by the DPRK on 9 October 2006 in flagrant disregard of its relevant resolutions . . . including that such a test would bring universal condemnation of the international community and would represent a clear threat to international peace and security;
2. *Demands* that the DPRK not conduct any further nuclear test or launch of a ballistic missile;
3. *Demands* that the DPRK immediately retract its announcement of withdrawal from the Treaty on the Non-Proliferation of Nuclear Weapons;
4. *Demands* further that the DPRK return to the Treaty on the Non-Proliferation of Nuclear Weapons and International Atomic Energy Agency (IAEA) safeguards [. . .];
5. *Decides* that the DPRK shall suspend all activities related to its ballistic missile programme and in this context re-establish its pre-existing commitments to a moratorium on missile launching;
6. *Decides* that the DPRK shall abandon all nuclear weapons and existing nuclear programmes in a complete, verifiable and irreversible manner [. . .] and shall provide the IAEA transparency measures extending beyond these requirements, including such access to individuals, documentation, equipments and facilities as may be required and deemed necessary by the IAEA.

But most unusually, paragraph 8 imposes on the DPRK sanctions that do not really address the threat to the peace identified in the Resolution. Apart from the prohibition to supply items of nuclear technology to North Korea, the Resolution also bans supplying a number of items that have no relation whatsoever to its nuclear programmes, such as tanks, military aircraft, helicopters, artillery systems, warships and even luxury goods. The Council does not explain why the application of such measures is necessary for halting the North Korean nuclear programme and in which way will it contribute to this goal. Such a disproportionate response is even more unjustified as the two of the principal facts addressed by the Council were not the straightforward threats to the peace. One of them was the merely *claimed* nuclear test, and the second one related to the legal right of North Korea to leave the Nuclear Non-Proliferation Treaty.

THE REMEDIES AGAINST IMPROPER DETERMINATIONS UNDER ARTICLE 39

The United Nations Security Council's practice demonstrates that in certain cases the determinations under Article 39 are made beyond its competence. Assuming that an improper finding of a threat to the peace by the Council would offend against the letter and spirit of the UN Charter and would hence be *ultra vires* and void, the question of the possible reaction by individual States and their courts naturally arises. In practice, the challenge of Security Council resolutions does not happen very often, and when it does happen, it relates to the legality and propriety of coercive measures adopted in consequence of the Article 39 determination rather than the determination itself. For instance, in the above-examined case of sanctions against Libya, several regional organisations such as the League of Arab States, Organisation of the Islamic Conference and the Non-Aligned Movement deplored these sanctions.[75] The Organisation of African Unity declared that its membership, which includes more than fifty States, would no longer obey these sanctions, 'owing to the fact that the said resolutions violate Article 27 paragraph 3, Article 33 and Article 36 paragraph 3 of the United Nations Charter, and the considerable human and economic losses suffered by Libya and a number of other African peoples as a result of the sanctions'.[76]

Thus, the decision not to carry out the Council Resolution in this case related to the *ultra vires* character of the measures adopted and did not directly refer to the propriety of the Article 39 determination itself. However, if the challenge by States of *ultra vires* resolutions is generally possible, there is no reason to assume that the same does not extend to cases where the relevant resolution is *ultra vires* for its improper identification of the threat to the peace. While in legal terms the affected State can do this on its own, for the practical success of the challenge a group response, as was observable in the case of Libya, can be more efficient to induce the Security Council to reconsider.

In terms of the specific ways to challenge unlawful determinations made by the Security Council, this can in principle done by every branch of the government—legislative, executive or judicial. In terms of common sense, one would expect that executive organs would be more likely to challenge the resolutions that affect their State, while judicial organs may end up considering the legality of resolutions that affect either the forum State, or the third State. The outcome in national legal systems would depend on the status of the relevant sources of international law in the national legal system and the mandate of national courts.

In addition to the reaction by individual States and their groups, the question arises whether the correctness of the finding by the Security Council under Article 39 can be scrutinised judicially. The issue arose during the hearings of the *Lockerbie* case before the International Court of Justice where Judge Schwebel addressed the following

[75] Kalala, 'La décision de l'OUA de ne plus respecter les sanctions décrétées par l'ONU contre la Lybie: désobéissance civile des états Africains a l'égard de l'ONU', *Revue Belge de Droit International* (1999/2), 549–553.

[76] *The Crisis between the Great Socialist People's Libyan Arab Jamahiriya and the United States of America and the United Kingdom*, AHG/DEC 127 (XXXIV), 8–10 June 1998, 6 *African Yearbook of International Law* (1998), 390–391.

question to the applicant State after the latter had submitted to the Court that the Security Council had exceeded and abused its powers by holding in Resolution 748 (1992) that Libya's failure to respond to the Council's previous resolution constituted a threat to international peace and security:

> Does this mean that it is the position of Libya that the Court may substitute its judgment as to what constitutes a threat to the peace for the decision of the Security Council as to what constitutes a threat to the peace?[77]

The question was asked at the end of the oral proceedings, and the Judgement of the Court on Preliminary Objections does not focus on this issue. But despite the silence of the Court, the answer to Judge Schwebel's question may well be affirmative. The practice of the International Court of Justice suggests that this organ has never ruled out the possibility of judicial review of decisions of other principal organs of the United Nations. One is directed to the dictum of the Court in *Namibia*, according to which 'the Court does not possess powers of judicial review or appeal in respect of the decisions taken by the United Nations organs concerned'. But this passage does not rule out the power of judicial review by the Court for at least two reasons. First, the Court indicated that its attitude was based on the limited scope of the request for the advisory opinion by the General Assembly. Second, the Court has indeed undertaken to scrutinise certain resolutions in order to respond to the objections put before it.[78] In *Certain Expenses*,[79] as well as later in *Lockerbie*[80] the Court, while dealing with the effect of decisions of UN bodies, used the language of presumption of validity of those decisions and did not suggest that such decisions enjoy absolute validity and are immune from judicial review. Such an approach perhaps evidences the readiness of the Court to examine the findings of the Security Council in the appropriate cases where a party to those proceedings challenges their legitimacy.

The decision of the Appeals Chamber of the International Criminal Tribunal for the Former Yugoslavia in the *Tadic* case may provide useful guidance. Having concluded that 'neither the text nor the spirit of the Charter conceives of the Security Council as *legibus solutus* (unbound by law)', the Tribunal went on to examine the issue which falls directly within the ambit of the Council's powers under Article 39. The Tribunal examined the determination of a 'threat to the peace' by the Council, questioned whether the concrete situation dealt with by the Council indeed was a threat to the peace, and passed its own judgment on all of these issues.[81] The judgment of the

[77] CR 97/24

[78] It seems necessary to quote the relevant passage from the Opinion in full, in order to avoid misunderstandings. The Court said:

> It was argued that the Court should not assume the powers of judicial review of the action taken by the other principal organs of the United Nations without specific request to that effect, nor act as a court of appeal from their decisions. Undoubtedly, the Court does not possess powers of judicial review or appeal in respect of the decisions taken by the United Nations organs concerned. The question of the validity and conformity with the Charter of General Assembly Resolution 2145 (XXI) or of related Security Council resolutions does not form the subject of the request for advisory opinion. However, in the exercise of its judicial function and since objections have been advanced the Court, in the course of its reasoning, will consider these objections before determining any legal consequences arising from those resolutions.

ICJ Reports (1971) 45.

[79] *ICJ Reports* (1962) 167.

[80] *ICJ Reports* (1992) 15.

[81] *Tadic*, Decision by Appeals Chamber (1995) IT-94-1-AR72, paras 28–30.

tribunal is unambiguous on these issues and this makes it unclear how one could be serious in suggesting that the International Court of Justice which is the principal judicial organ of the United Nations, does not possess the powers which has been exercised by a tribunal established as a subsidiary organ of the Security Council.

The political element in the Council's power to make determinations under Article 39 and the issue of judicial review can be examined also from another perspective suggested by the practice of the European Court of Human Rights concerning the margin of appreciation of the States-parties to the European Convention on Human Rights. These two issues have hardly ever been compared to each other in doctrine. But they have certain common aspects relating to the judicial examination of decisions and determinations which are initially outside the judicial function.

As is known, the European Convention on Human Rights leaves the States-parties the freedom to impose restrictions on the exercise of certain rights on the basis of considerations of national security, public safety, protection of morals or other circumstances (Articles 8 to 11 of the Convention). The Convention also allows the States-parties to derogate from certain substantive rights in case of an 'emergency threatening the life of the nation' (Article 15 of the Convention). The Convention does not define any of these notions which may be invoked by States in order to justify the non-observance of rights and freedoms. Like a 'threat to the peace', each of these notions are applied on a case-by-case basis and in the context of political decisions. That means that it is the States-parties who, in the first place at least, determine in which cases and to what extent the limitations on and derogations from the rights enshrined in the Convention should take their effect. Such an approach from the European Court of Human Rights is illustrated in case of *Ireland v United Kingdom*, where the Court said:[82]

> The limits on the Court's powers of review are particularly apparent where Article 15 is concerned. It falls in the first place to each Contracting State, with its responsibility for 'the life of [its] nation', to determine whether that life is threatened by a 'public emergency' and, if so, how far it is necessary to go in attempting to overcome the emergency. By reason of their direct and continuous contact with the pressing needs of the moment, the national authorities are in principle in a better position than the international judge to decide both on the presence of such an emergency and on the nature and scope of derogations necessary to avert it. In this matter Article 15 para. 1 leaves those authorities a wide margin of appreciation.
>
> Nevertheless, the States do not enjoy an unlimited power in this respect. The Court, which, with the Commission, is responsible for ensuring the observance of the States' engagements (Article 19), is empowered to rule on whether the States have gone beyond the 'extent strictly required by the exigencies' of the crisis. The domestic margin of appreciation is thus accompanied by a European supervision.

The general feature of the European Court's practice in this field is the recognition of an initial freedom of States-parties to make determinations in the areas which normally belong to the ordinary fields of their responsibility. These are the maintenance of national security, public safety as well as situations of emergency threatening the life of the nation. States possess the initial freedom to determine what they understand under their national security and national interest and to decide on the measures to be taken in such cases, including the restrictions on and derogations from the rights

[82] *Ireland v United Kingdom* (1978), para 207 (references omitted).

recognised under the Convention. This freedom is, however, not unlimited but 'goes hand in hand with a European supervision'. The European Court is therefore empowered to pass its judgment on the political decisions adopted by States within the areas of their ordinary responsibilities and to decide whether these decisions are in accordance with the Convention. Most importantly, the European Court is entitled to verify the legitimacy of aim of the measures and steps taken by the States-parties to the European Convention. By the same token, there seems to be no visible limitations on the International Court's power to decide whether a determination of the Security Council under Article 39 of the Charter, made within the area of primary responsibility of this organ, is by its content or by its consequences compatible with the Charter of the United Nations. A further logical confirmation of this is the language used in *Ireland v UK*, where the Court described the primary responsibility of States-parties in a way perfectly suitable to describe the Security Council's responsibility with regard to the maintenance of international peace and security.

Generally, adjudicative organs may need to review discretionary institutional determinations to establish their own jurisdiction. In *Tadic*, the Yugoslav Tribunal referred to *competence de la competence* to support its power to review the decisions of the UN Security Council. Similarly, the Asian Development Bank Administrative Tribunal held, in *Lindsey*, that the determination of reviewability of discretionary powers of the Asian Development Bank falls within the powers of the Tribunal, as the latter has the power to determine its own competence.[83] Sometimes scholars and practitioners can be reluctant concerning the application at the United Nations' level of notions and concepts practised by other international tribunals. On the other hand, hardly any prevailing legal consideration prevents the judicial bodies from examining the lawfulness of the Council's determinations. Although the Security Council is in a better position than an international judge to determine the existence of a 'threat to the peace', judicial organs, above all the International Court of Justice, are entitled to review the Council's determinations in order to ensure their compatibility with the Charter.

CONCLUSION

At the current stage of development of international law, international tribunals increasingly assume the powers to review the decisions under Article 39 or other decisions in comparable situations, and the likelihood of the refusal of the target State or third States to comply with coercive measures following an improper determination under Article 39 cannot be excluded. All this requires from the United Nations Security Council is an increased degree of coherence in assessing the margins of its wide discretion.

The process of determining threats to the peace and ensuing measures of response includes some logically indispensable elements. Even if the Council possesses discretion in making determinations under Article 39, in using such discretion it must clearly identify a threat to the peace in its resolution as an objective fact. If that fact is targeted with enforcement measures, the Council has to demonstrate that it is of sufficient gravity and the use of enforcement powers to tackle it is both necessary and adequate. In deciding on the measures to be applied in response to the identified

[83] *Lindsey v Asian Development Bank*, 96 ILR 237–238.

threat, the Council should direct the measures to eliminate this threat in the objective sense. In other words, the measures applied by the Council should be directed to eliminate or reduce the identified threat, they should be logically required for countering the identified threat and be proportional. This is the purpose served by the discretionary powers under Article 39, which are delegated and limited powers; their exercise must be in accordance with the extent of delegation. The Council, in case it decides to act under Chapter VII, must ensure that its action is a coherent process of a genuine response to a threat to the peace. The direct link between an identified threat to the peace and the measures applied against it must maintain transparency at all stages of the Council's action. This entire process must, in its complexity, be consistent with the purposes and principles of the Organisation. This approach is dictated by the fact that the source of the Security Council's powers under Chapter VII is not the abstract need to maintain international peace and security or to enhance the implementation of certain common values, but the provisions of a treaty; the Charter which provides for the specific powers of the Council as well as limitations on those powers.

Life Sentences in Ireland and the European Convention on Human Rights

J Paul McCutcheon and Gerard Coffey*

The distinctive feature of the sentence of life imprisonment is that it is indeterminate. Unlike a prisoner serving a fixed term the life sentence prisoner does not know when, if ever, he or she will be released. Moreover, where the sanction is mandatory, life imprisonment is an inflexible instrument that does not take account of the culpability of the particular offender and such sentences are difficult to reconcile with the principle of proportionality.[1] It is not surprising that the compatibility of life sentences with human rights principles has become a matter of concern, as have the arrangements put in place to facilitate the release of life sentence prisoners.[2]

The European Court of Human Rights (ECtHR) has delivered a series of rulings in which life sentences have been evaluated in the light of the European Convention on Human Rights (ECHR). The Court has not declared that the life sentence *per se* involves a breach of the ECHR but it has pronounced on the review mechanisms and procedures that are required by the Convention. In short, once the punitive element of a life sentence has been served the prisoner is entitled to frequent and speedy review of the lawfulness of his or her imprisonment by an independent and impartial tribunal. The stated purpose underlying this regime is to protect the prisoner against the arbitrary prolonging of his or her incarceration.

The current Irish position is that the question of release is exclusively an executive matter and the courts have demonstrated a marked reluctance to interfere with the exercise of that power. The power of release has been assigned by statute to the Minister for Justice, Equality and Law Reform. The Parole Board, a non-statutory body, advises the Minister but crucially he or she is not bound by that advice. In a series of decisions the superior courts in Ireland have invoked separation of powers considerations to reinforce this stance and they have demonstrated a marked reluctance to interfere with the exercise of that executive power.

* Both authors are members of the School of Law, University of Limerick. Email: paul.mccutcheon@ul.ie and ger.coffey@ul.ie. This article is based on research conducted for the Irish Human Rights Commission. The authors gratefully acknowledge the support of the Commission.

[1] See T O'Malley, *Sentencing Law and Practice* 2nd edn (Dublin, Thomson Round Hall, 2006) p 536; also T O'Malley, 'Sentencing Murderers: the Case for Relocating Discretion' (1995) 5 *Irish Criminal Law Journal* 31. The Law Reform Commission, *Consultation Paper on Sentencing* (Dublin, 1993) p 311 queries whether the lack of judicial involvement that a mandatory sentence entails a breach of fair procedures in that it deprives the accused of a right to be heard in the matter of penalty.

[2] See N Padfield, *Beyond the Tariff: Human Rights and the Release of Life Sentence Prisoners* (Devon, Willan Publishing, 2002); G Richardson, 'Discretionary Life Sentences and the European Convention on Human Rights' [1991] *Public Law* 34; S Verelst, 'Life Imprisonment and Human Rights in Belgium' (2003) 3 *Human Rights Law Review* 279; D van Zyl Smit, 'Is Life Imprisonment Constitutional? The German Experience' [1992] *Public Law* 263; D van Zyl Smit, *Taking Life Imprisonment Seriously in National and International Law* (Kluwer Law International, 2002); D van Zyl Smit, 'Life Imprisonment: Recent Issues in National and International Law' (2006) 29 *International Journal of Law and Psychiatry* 405.

This article considers current Irish law on the review of life sentences, as opposed to fixed-term sentences, in the light of the ECtHR jurisprudence. The principal conclusion is that Irish law is incompatible with the ECHR. The question of how Irish law might be brought into compliance with the Convention is briefly considered.

ECHR AND LIFE SENTENCES

Since the enactment of the European Convention on Human Rights Act 2003, the Convention enjoys an enhanced profile in Irish domestic law.[3] The jurisprudence of the European Court of Human Rights has a greater purchase in domestic proceedings: Irish courts are now required to take judicial notice of declarations, decisions, advisory opinions and judgments of the European Court of Human Rights and to take 'due account' of the principles established by those instruments.[4] The courts are enjoined, where possible, to interpret national law in a manner that is compatible with the ECHR[5] and the superior courts are authorised to issue a declaration of incompatibility where a national law falls foul of the ECHR.[6]

A declaration of incompatibility does not invalidate a national legal measure, but of course it would place direct pressure on the *Oireachtas* (Parliament) to remedy the position in order to ensure alignment between Irish law and ECHR demands. This position may be contrasted with that which pertains under the Constitution where the superior courts may declare legislation to be invalid.[7] A measure that is so condemned by the superior courts is considered null and void. In the result, there are in effect two bodies of rights which operate in Irish law, namely national constitutional rights and the ECHR via the European Convention on Human Rights Act 2003. Although there might be significant overlaps between these two bodies the distinction between them must be borne in mind.[8]

The European Court has been presented with a growing number of cases concerning the determination of life sentences in recent years. This has provided the Court with the opportunity to spell out in some detail the requirements of the ECHR on the matter. Accordingly it is incumbent on signatory states to align their procedures governing the conditional release on licence of life sentence prisoners with rulings of the Strasbourg Court.

[3] See remarks of Kearns J in *Dublin City Council v Fennell* [2005] 1 IR 604 at 608: 'The 2003 Act . . . does not purport to incorporate the Convention directly into domestic law, but rather imposes an obligation that, when interpreting or applying any statutory provision or rule of law, a court shall, insofar as is possible, and subject to the rules of law relating to such interpretation and application, do so in a manner compatible with the State's obligations under the Convention provisions. The 2003 Act also provides that every organ of the State shall, subject to any statutory provision or rule of law, perform its functions in a manner compatible with the State's obligations under the Convention provisions. A party may also seek from the High or Supreme Court a declaration that a statutory provision or rule of law is incompatible with the State's obligations under the Convention provisions, and where such a declaration is made certain consequences as detailed in the Act then follow'.

[4] European Convention on Human Rights Act 2003, s 4.

[5] European Convention on Human Rights Act 2003, s 2.

[6] European Convention on Human Rights Act 2003, s 5.

[7] Constitution of Ireland, Art. 15.4.2.

[8] See further: G Hogan, 'The European Convention on Human Rights Act 2003' (2006) 12(3) *European Public Law* 331; G Anthony, 'Clustered Convergence? European Fundamental Rights Standards in Irish and UK Public Law' [2004] *Public Law* 283.

In general, European human rights law accepts that the detention of a prisoner following his or her being sentenced by a court of competent jurisdiction is lawful. However, the ECtHR has acknowledged that in some circumstances a prisoner may invoke the provisions of Article 5 to review his or her sentence.[9] In the context of the review of life sentences the Court has clearly established that the fact that a person has been convicted does not preclude future review of his or her continued incarceration: in this regard the prisoner may invoke the review provisions of Article 5(4).

Two key themes can be disinterred from the Court's jurisprudence. First, the underlying purpose of Article 5 is to protect individuals from being deprived of their liberty arbitrarily: in the context of life sentence prisoners a decision to continue their detention should not be taken arbitrarily. The required protection is achieved through the review mechanism prescribed by Article 5(4). Second, it may be inferred from the jurisprudence that prolonged detention can be justified on the limited grounds of risk and dangerousness. The second theme reflects the English tariff system under which a life sentence is in effect divided into punitive and preventive components. The thrust of the case law is to the effect that once the punitive element of the life sentence (as reflected in the tariff) has been served the continued detention of the prisoner can only be justified on the basis that he or she represents a continuing danger to the public, a matter that must be open to periodic review. Moreover, there must be a causal connection between the offence for which the prisoner has been convicted and the potential for re-offending.[10] Although it has not been required to rule on the matter directly, it is significant that the Court has indicated that public acceptability is not a relevant criterion on which to base a decision relating to a prisoner's release.[11]

The principle that the lawfulness of a life sentence prisoner's continued detention must be periodically reviewed once the punitive element of the sentence has been served, and the corresponding entitlement to challenge that detention in accordance with Article 5(4), was established in the late 1980s. In *Weeks v United Kingdom*,[12] the applicant, who had been convicted of robbery, received discretionary life imprisonment on the grounds that he was a dangerous offender. He was subsequently released on licence but the licence was revoked when he committed a further offence. The Court accepted that the freedom of a prisoner released on licence was 'more precarious' than that of a normal citizen. However, the restrictions on the applicant as an 'on licence' prisoner did not mean that he was not at liberty within the meaning of Article 5. Accordingly, he was entitled to invoke that provision. Nevertheless, the Court concluded that the decision to re-detain the applicant in this case was neither arbitrary nor unreasonable since it was based on his unstable and aggressive behaviour and it followed that there was no violation of Article 5(1). However, the Court went on to hold that once he was returned to custody the applicant was entitled to the review specified in Article 5(4) and in the circumstances it concluded that the procedures in the instant case were deficient.

European human rights law governing the determination of life sentences has evolved since the mid-1990s. At first the European Court drew a distinction between discretionary life sentences and mandatory life sentences, which coincided with the

[9] See eg *Iribarne Perez v France* (1996) 22 EHRR 153.

[10] *van Droogenbroeck v Belgium* (1982) 4 EHRR 443.

[11] *Stafford v United Kingdom* (2002) 35 EHRR 32, at para 80.

[12] (1988) 10 EHRR 293.

theory then underpinning English law that the latter were exclusively punitive whereas the former incorporated a preventative element. Hence in *Wynne v United Kingdom*,[13] the court held that a periodic review of a mandatory life sentence was not required: in these circumstances the review requirements of Article 5(4) were sufficiently complied with by both the trial court and appellate courts. The facts of this case merit consideration. The applicant, who had been convicted of murder and sentenced to a mandatory life sentence, was released on licence. Some time later he killed a woman. Ultimately, he pleaded guilty to manslaughter on the grounds of diminished responsibility and received a discretionary life sentence. His licence was also revoked so he continued to serve the life sentence for murder. Arguing that he was in reality serving the discretionary life sentence, the applicant contended that he was entitled to have that sentence reviewed. The court dismissed that claim concluding that his conviction for manslaughter did not alter the validity of either his original sentence for murder or the revocation of his licence. He continued to serve the mandatory life sentence and the discretionary life sentence for manslaughter merely added a supplemental basis for his detention. The Court reasoned that a review of the manslaughter sentence would be 'devoid of purpose'[14] since the applicant would continue to be held under the mandatory life sentence.

In *Thynne, Wilson and Gunnell v United Kingdom*,[15] the applicants, convicted sex offenders, were serving discretionary life sentences but their continued post-tariff detention had not been periodically reviewed. They claimed that this state of affairs violated Article 5(4) ECHR due to the absence of a review procedure to determine the lawfulness of the continued detention of the prisoners after the tariff period of the sentence had been served. This was not a challenge to the lawfulness of the imposition of the original sentence but rather against their continued indeterminate post-tariff detention. The ECtHR held that since the circumstances that gave rise to the applicants' initial detention may have changed in the intervening time they were entitled to periodic reviews of their continued indeterminate detention after the punitive element of their respective life sentences had been served. The ECtHR explained that:

> [. . .] the factors of mental instability and dangerousness are susceptible to change over the passage of time and new issues of lawfulness may thus arise in the course of detention. It follows that at that phase in the execution of their sentences, the applicants were entitled under Article 5(4) to take proceedings to have the lawfulness of their continued detention decided by a court at reasonable intervals and to have the lawfulness of any re-detention determined by a court.[16]

The Court eventually came to realise that the distinction between mandatory and discretionary life sentences lacked substance. The initial change in tack occurred in several cases dealing with juvenile offenders who had been convicted of murder. The mandatory sentence for such offenders was detention during Her Majesty's Pleasure—in effect, they were sentenced to indefinite detention with their release being determined by the Home Secretary. In *Hussain v United Kingdom*,[17] the applicant prisoner had been detained during Her Majesty's Pleasure for a murder he committed

[13] (1995) 19 EHRR 333.
[14] (1995) 19 EHRR 333, at paras 37–38.
[15] (1991) 13 EHRR 666.
[16] (1991) 13 EHRR 666, at para 76.
[17] (1996) 22 EHRR 1.

when he was a juvenile. The European Court held that under Article 5(4) ECHR such prisoners were entitled to have the lawfulness of their continued indeterminate detention considered by a court or quasi-judicial body. Subsequently, in *V and T v United Kingdom*,[18] the ECtHR in effect removed the Home Secretary's power to decide on the release date and, therefore, to set the tariff period of those detained at Her Majesty's pleasure. The ECtHR held that an 'independent and impartial tribunal', not the Home Secretary (an emanation of the executive), should set the tariff for juveniles convicted of murder. The setting of the tariff by the Home Secretary was held to be an infringement of the right to a fair trial under Article 6(1) ECHR.

Eventually, in *Stafford v United Kingdom*,[19] a uniform regime was adopted for mandatory and discretionary life sentences and for juvenile murderers. The applicant was a convicted murderer whose tariff period had been set by the Home Secretary in accordance with English domestic practice at the time. He had been released on licence but that was revoked on his later conviction for fraud. On completion of his fraud sentence the Parole Board recommended that the applicant be released but the Home Secretary rejected that advice on the grounds that there was a risk that the applicant would engage in further fraud offences. The ECtHR ruled that the applicant's rights under the provisions of Article 5(1) and 5(4) ECHR had been violated in that the setting of the tariff was a sentencing exercise for judges, not members of the executive. The ECtHR also held that the Home Secretary's power of veto over a recommendation by the Parole Board to release a post-tariff life prisoner contravened Articles 5(1) and 5(4) ECHR.

In *Stafford*, the ECtHR was particularly influenced by the fact that at this stage it had become widely accepted that the view that a mandatory life sentence amounts to punishment for life no longer corresponded with practical reality.[20] The UK government had sought to maintain the distinction between mandatory and discretionary life sentences by arguing that, unlike the latter, the former was not based on individual characteristics of dangerousness: accordingly, the argument ran, there was no issue of changing circumstances that might undermine the basis for continued detention. The Court rejected that argument, concluding that mandatory life sentences contain a punitive element that is reflected in the tariff. Once that period had been served, the Court reasoned, the grounds for continued incarceration, 'as in discretionary life and juvenile murder cases must be considerations of risk and dangerousness'.[21] Since those elements are liable to change over time, as in the case of other life sentence prisoners, the continued lawfulness of a prisoner's detention cannot be assumed. Departing from its judgment in *Wynne v United Kingdom* the ECtHR concluded that 'it can no longer be maintained that the original trial and appeal proceedings satisfied, once and for all, issues of compatibility of subsequent detention of mandatory life prisoners with the provisions of Article 5(1) of the Convention'.[22]

[18] (2000) 30 EHRR 121.

[19] (2002) 35 EHRR 32.

[20] In both Scotland and Northern Ireland the law had been altered to assign the function of setting the tariff to the trial judge: Convention Rights (Compliance) (Scotland) Act 2001; the Life Sentences (Northern Ireland) Order 2001, S.I. 2001/2564.

[21] (2002) 35 EHRR 32, at para 80.

[22] (2002) 35 EHRR 32, at para 87. The decision in *Stafford* had an impact on domestic law. In *R (Anderson) v Secretary of State for the Home Department* [2003] AC 1 the House of Lords bowed to the weight of ECtHR jurisprudence and concluded that the fixing of the tariff was legally indistinguishable from imposing a sentence. It followed that Article 6 ECHR applied and that the tariff should be set by a court ('an independent and impartial tribunal') rather than by the Home Secretary. Accordingly, the House

Following the decision in *Stafford* it is settled that, irrespective of the form the life sentence takes, once the punitive element of the sentence has expired a prisoner is entitled under Article 5(4) ECHR to have lawfulness of his continued indeterminate detention reviewed by a 'court'.[23] The concept of lawfulness embraces both domestic and Convention law: it requires the detention to conform with domestic substantive and procedural rules and to be 'in keeping with the purposes of Article 5, namely to protect the individual from arbitrariness'.[24] In the context of life sentences continued detention after the expiry of the punitive element has been served is justifiable only on grounds of risk and dangerousness. Factors that the Court has indicated that are relevant in assessing whether the continued detention is lawful include mental instability,[25] unstable, disturbed and aggressive behaviour,[26] youth and level of maturity[27] and personality factors such as anger, alcoholism and the ability to maintain relationships.[28] Given that these factors are liable to change over time a life sentence prisoner is entitled to frequent review of his or her sentence.[29]

It is also clear that the notion of lawful imprisonment insists that there is a sufficient connection between the prisoner's continued detention and the offence for which he or she was convicted. Thus, in *Stafford v United Kingdom*,[30] the Court condemned the imprisonment of a convicted murderer where his continued detention was based on a fear that he would commit fraud offences in the future. On the other hand, the circumstances of the original offence might be relevant to the issue of connection: in *Waite v United Kingdom*,[31] the Court held that there was a sufficient connection where the accused, who killed his grandmother while he was addicted to glue-sniffing, had his licence revoked following his arrest for possession of drugs.

Article 5(4) requires a speedy decision but it allows a measure of procedural flexibility. The ECtHR has acknowledged that the review period may vary according to the individual circumstances of the prisoner. In *Oldham v United Kingdom*,[32] the ECtHR held that an interval of two years between assessments did not fulfil the requirements of Article 5(4). The applicant attended a number of prescribed courses that were designed to deal with his anger and alcoholism problems and his difficulty in managing relationships. He completed these courses within eight months of his earlier review and a further 16 months passed before the next review. The UK government contended that the delay was necessary to monitor the applicant's progress but did not explain the nature or duration of that process. The Court concluded that:

of Lords declared s 29 of the Crimes (Sentences) Act 1997 [UK] to be incompatible with the ECHR. Following the decision in *Anderson*, the Criminal Justice Act 2003 [UK] transferred the function of setting the tariff, or 'minimum term' as it is now known, to sentencing judges, a development that has the advantages of being transparent and being undertaken by the official who is most familiar with the offender's circumstances. See D Thomas, 'The Criminal Justice Act 2003: Custodial Sentences' [2004] *Criminal Law Review*, 702.

23 What amounts to a 'court' is considered below in text accompanying fnn 38–42.

24 *Stafford v United Kingdom* (2002) 35 EHRR 32, at para 63.

25 *Thynne, Wilson and Gunnell v United Kingdom* (1991) 13 EHRR 666; *Stafford v United Kingdom* (2002) 35 EHRR 32.

26 *Weeks v United Kingdom* (1988) 10 EHRR 293.

27 *Waite v United Kingdom* [2002] ECHR 53236/99.

28 *Oldham v United Kingdom* [2000] ECHR 36273/97.

29 Discussed further in text accompanying fnn 32–37 below.

30 (2002) 35 EHRR 32.

31 [2002] ECHR 53236/99.

32 [2000] ECHR 36273/97.

> [. . .] in the circumstances of this case that the two year delay between reviews was not reasonable and that the question of whether his continued detention was lawful was not decided 'speedily' within the meaning of Article 5(4) of the Convention. There has, accordingly, been a violation of this provision.[33]

The ECtHR also considered the issue of frequency in *Blackstock v United Kingdom*,[34] which involved a gap of 22 months between reviews. The applicant received a discretionary life sentence for wounding a police officer. On the expiry of his minimum term (ie tariff) his detention was reviewed by the Parole Board who in June 1998 recommended that he be transferred to an open prison or, if that recommendation was not accepted by the Home Secretary, a further review in 12 months.[35] The Home Secretary rejected the recommendation and in September 1998 ruled that the applicant be transferred to a Category C prison. The appropriate transfer instructions were issued the following month but the applicant objected to the proposed prison to which he was to be sent, indicating his preference to be sent to one of several other named prisons. In December 1998 it was decided to transfer him to one of those prisons but that did not happen until April 1999 when a place became available. His next review took place in April 2000 with the Parole Board again recommending his transfer to open conditions. The Home Secretary accepted the latter recommendation.

In ruling in favour of the applicant, the Court's starting point was that the frequency of reviews required by Article 5(4) ECHR must be determined in the light of the circumstances of each case and it refused to lay down a firm rule stipulating a maximum period between reviews. Instead, the Court recognised that a flexible approach is to be preferred since the personal circumstances of prisoners will differ markedly. Thus the Court had ruled in some earlier cases that gaps of between 15 months and two years were unreasonable[36] while accepting a two-year lapse in another case.[37] In the instant case the UK government had sought to justify the delay on a combination of the delay (almost six months) in finding a place in the prison nominated by the applicant and a desire that he should spend 12 months in that facility before being considered for transfer to open conditions. The Court was not persuaded by that argument: no formal courses had been prescribed for the applicant when he was transferred and there was no evidence that, in the light of the administrative delays, consideration had been given to whether it was necessary to insist on the usual 12 months in Category C before reviewing his case.

The ECtHR has reflected on what constitutes a 'court' for the purposes of Article 5(4). In *Thynne, Wilson and Gunnell v United Kingdom*,[38] the ECtHR ruled that a 'court-like' body should determine the release date of life sentence prisoners. For these

[33] [2000] ECHR 36273/97, at para 37.

[34] [2005] ECHR 59512/00.

[35] At the time the Crimes (Sentences) Act 1997 [UK], s 28 invested the Parole Board with the power to order the release of discretionary life sentence prisoners once the tariff period had expired; where the Board chose not to order release it could make recommendations to the Home Secretary concerning the prisoner's future progress.

[36] Citing *Herczegfalvy v Austria* (1993) 15 EHRR 437; *Oldham v United Kingdom* [2000] ECHR 36273/97; *Hirst v United Kingdom* [2001] ECHR 40787/98.

[37] Citing *Dancy v United Kingdom* No 55768/00, 21 March 2002, where the applicant having benefited from previous 12-month reviews, failed to make progress and considerable offence-related work had been identified as being necessary.

[38] (1990) 13 EHRR 666.

purposes a 'court' does not have to be a permanent court in the legal system of a signatory state. In *Weeks v United Kingdom*,[39] the ECtHR explained that:

> The 'court' referred to in Article 5(4) does not necessarily have to be a court of law of the classic kind integrated within the standard judicial machinery of the country. . . . The term 'court' serves to denote 'bodies which exhibit not only common fundamental features, of which the most important is independence of the executive and of the parties to the case . . . but also the guarantees'—'appropriate to the kind of deprivation of liberty in question'—'of a judicial procedure', the forms of which may vary from one domain to another. . . . In addition, as the text of Article 5(4) makes clear, the body in question must not have merely advisory functions but must have the competence to 'decide' the 'lawfulness' of the detention and to order release if the detention is unlawful. There is thus nothing to preclude a specialised body such as the Parole Board being considered as a 'court' within the meaning of Article 5(4), provided it fulfils the foregoing conditions. . . .

Thus, a quasi-judicial body, such as a parole board, is a 'court' within the meaning of Article 5(4) ECHR provided that its deliberations are determinative rather than advisory. It is also clear that the body charged with deciding on whether the life prisoner should be released must be independent of the executive and of the parties involved.

In *Neumeister v Austria*,[40] the ECtHR addressed the issue of independence of the Court from the procedures adopted in the following terms:

> Nor is it possible to justify application of the principle of 'equality of arms' to proceedings against detention on remand by invoking Article 5(4) which, while requiring that such proceedings shall be allowed, stipulates that they should be taken before a 'court'. This term implies only that the authority called upon to decide thereon must possess a judicial character, that is to say, be independent both of the executive and of the parties to the case; it in no way relates to the procedure to be followed.

The central principle set out in *Neumeister* was amplified in *de Wilde and others v Belgium*,[41] where the ECtHR insisted that the procedures adopted must be judicial in nature and must provide 'the individual concerned [with] guarantees appropriate to the kind of deprivation of liberty in question'.[42]

It is essential that the body reviewing a prisoner's detention adopts procedures that are judicial in nature. In *E v Norway*,[43] the ECtHR outlined the general position under this provision in the following terms:

> Article 5(4) does not guarantee a right to judicial review of such a scope as to empower the court, on all aspects of the case including questions of pure expediency, to substitute its own discretion for that of the decision-making authority. The review should, however, be wide enough to bear on those conditions which are essential for the 'lawful' detention of a person according to Article 5(1).

Nevertheless, the ECtHR has held that domestic judicial review proceedings do not satisfy Article 5(4) ECHR on the ground that that procedure is not sufficiently wide to determine whether the prisoner's continued imprisonment was justified by the

[39] (1988) 10 EHRR 293, at para 61.
[40] (1979) 1 EHRR 91, at para 24.
[41] (1979) 1 EHRR 373.
[42] (1979) 1 EHRR 373, at para 76.
[43] (1994) 17 EHRR 30, at para 50.

objectives of the indeterminate sentence.[44] The Court has also taken the opportunity to provide some procedural detail. It has held that the review proceedings must be adversarial[45] with the prisoner being afforded an opportunity to attend an oral hearing that respects the rights to be legally represented and to call and question witnesses.[46] The Court has also ruled that a failure to disclose adverse material that the review body had in its possession did not satisfy the requirements of Article 5(4) ECHR.

The cardinal principles of ECHR law relating to the determination of life sentences can be summarised thus: (i) a life sentence is not *per se* a breach of Convention rights; (ii) once the punitive element of the sentence has been served a life sentence prisoner is entitled to a speedy and frequent review of the lawfulness of his continued detention by a court or quasi-judicial body; (iii) whether a review is sufficiently speedy or frequent is to be determined in the light of the circumstances of the particular case; (iv) the concept of 'lawfulness' embraces both domestic law and ECHR considerations and the permitted grounds for continued detention are risk and dangerousness; (v) the review must be sufficiently broad to allow a determination as to whether the grounds for continued detention still operate; and (vi) the body reviewing the detention must be invested with the power to determine the lawfulness of the prisoner's detention rather than acting in a merely advisory capacity and that body must be independent of the executive and of the parties and must adopt appropriate procedures in its hearings.

LIFE SENTENCES IN IRELAND

As is the case in many other jurisdictions, life sentences in Ireland fall into two categories. For some offences, most notably treason and murder, a mandatory life sentence is prescribed by law.[47] It was noted above that this form of sentence is a blunt instrument in that it cannot reflect the culpability of the particular offender. Thus, the mandatory life sentence is imposed for all murders ranging from the most heinous (eg serial killings) to those that some might feel merit less condemnation ('mercy' killing of a loved one is often cited in this regard). On the other hand, it may be contended that the mandatory life sentence amounts to a legislative assessment of the culpability associated with all murders and a corresponding judgement that it is not appropriate to draw a distinction between different types of murder. It might further be suggested that a mandatory life sentence is purely punitive (and perhaps deterrent) and eschews other sentencing goals such as rehabilitation and incapacitation. In a word, the mandatory life sentence may be taken to reflect the sentiment that 'murder is murder is murder' and deserves the severest punishment without mitigation. However these considerations are not borne out in practice. Most life sentence prisoners are

[44] *Weeks v United Kingdom* (1988) 10 EHRR 293; see also *Singh v United Kingdom* [1996] EHRC 23389/94.

[45] *Hussein v United Kingdom* (1996) 22 EHRR 1; *Singh v United Kingdom* [1996] ECHR 23389/94.

[46] *Hussein v United Kingdom* (1996) 22 EHRR 1; *Singh v United Kingdom* [1996] ECHR 23389/94; *Stafford v United Kingdom* [2002] ECHR 46295/99; *Waite v United Kingdom* [2002] ECHR 53236/99.

[47] Criminal Justice Act 1990, s 2. Juveniles (ie persons aged under 17 years) who are convicted of murder might be sentenced either to a determinate term or to indefinite detention: see T O'Malley, *Sentencing Law and Practice* 2nd edn (Dublin, Thomson Round Hall, 2006) pp 394–396; also D Walsh, *Juvenile Justice* (Dublin, Thomson Round Hall, 2005) pp 155–157; *The People (DPP) v DG*, Unreported, Court of Criminal Appeal, 27 May 2005.

eventually released and this, coupled with official or quasi-official pronouncements, creates an expectation that they will qualify for release.[48]

The second category consists of discretionary life sentences where a maximum sentence of life imprisonment is provided for by law. Discretionary life sentences are prescribed for a number of serious offences including manslaughter, rape, aggravated sexual assault, committing a sexual act on a child less than 15 years of age, causing serious harm, syringe attacks, false imprisonment, robbery, aggravated burglary and serious drugs offences. Discretionary life sentences are more easily reconciled with the principle of proportionality since the particular sentence imposed can be calibrated to match the culpability of the offender and the circumstances of the offence.[49] In such cases the sentencing judge enjoys the wide measure of discretion that is allowed in sentencing generally.

As far as discretionary life sentences are concerned, Irish courts have indicated that they are governed by the principle of proportionality and it has been ruled impermissible to include a preventive element in such a sentence. In theory, at least, a discretionary life sentence in Ireland is predominantly punitive in nature, designed exclusively to reflect the offender's culpability and the gravity of the offence. The dominance of the proportionality principle in the Irish sentencing process would appear to preclude the imposition of preventative sentences along the lines practised in the United Kingdom. Indeed, the Court of Criminal Appeal has handed down several decisions to the effect that a sentencing judge may not include an element of incapacitation, designed to protect the public from a potentially dangerous offender, in a sentence.[50] In *DPP v Jackson*,[51] the Central Criminal Court had imposed a discretionary life sentence on the defendant, a serious sex offender, but the Court of Criminal Appeal subsequently overturned that sentence on the basis that it constituted one of preventative detention. The Court clearly rejected the notion that preventative detention is a feature of Irish sentencing law, stating that: 'The Court is satisfied that preventative detention is not known to our judicial system and that there is no form of imprisonment for preventative detention'.[52] The decision in *Jackson* was applied in *The People (DPP) v Bambrick*,[53] where the Central Criminal Court refused to impose a sentence of preventative detention. The trial judge explained that he was:

[48] See the remarks of the Minister for Justice, Equality and Law Reform, 24 March 2006 (http://www.justice.ie/80256E01003A02CF/vWeb/pcJUSQ6N7FGB-en: accessed on 15 Feb 2007): '. . . nobody [convicted of murder] should expect even in the absence of aggravating factors and where guilt has been admitted, remorse shown, good behaviour demonstrated during imprisonment and a capacity for rehabilitation proven that there is a likelihood that he or she will be set at liberty on licence at least before the expiry of 12 to 14 years . . . I can tell you that, of those prisoners serving life sentences who have been released over the past ten years, the average sentence served in prison is approximately thirteen and a half years'. See also Chairman's Foreword, The Parole Board, *Annual Report 2005* (Dublin, 2006) p 3: 'The days of prisoners who have served 10 or 12 years expecting to be released from custody are now over. The sentence they must serve must be a long and salutary one. The Board must do everything it can to promote public confidence and to ensure that its attitude to the dreadful crime of murder will remain constant. The position of human life in society must be restored'.

[49] See further T O'Malley, *Sentencing Law and Practice* 2nd edn (Dublin, Thomson Round Hall, 2006) pp 114–115.

[50] See M Bolger, 'Judicial Discretion to Sentence Rapists to Life' (1997, April) *Bar Review* 249.

[51] Unreported, Court of Criminal Appeal, 26 April 1993.

[52] Unreported, Court of Criminal Appeal, 26 April 1993, *per* Hederman J.

[53] [1996] 1 IR 265.

> [. . .] precluded from approaching the case on the basis that over and above any considerations of punishment this dangerous accused should be preventively detained until in the opinion of the most qualified experts he is safe to be let back into the community.[54]

In view of this general policy, the sentencing process should not be concerned with the potential for future re-offending.[55] Probably as a result of this stance very few prisoners are sentenced to discretionary life sentences: the vast bulk of life sentence prisoners in the Irish prison system are serving mandatory sentences. Prisoners convicted of treason and certain forms of murder are required to serve a minimum of 40 years before becoming eligible for release.[56] In the case of other life sentence prisoners Ireland, unlike the United Kingdom, has not adopted a formal practice of setting tariffs or minimum terms to be served. Significantly, sentencing judges do not express an opinion on the length of time that should be served by life sentence prisoners although on occasion some judges have obliquely indicated their views on the matter without specifying a particular number of years. On the other hand, both the Minister for Justice, Equality and Law Reform and the Parole Board have proclaimed that a life sentence prisoner will not be considered for release until he or she has served at least 14 years.[57] By their very nature these pronouncements are political, stemming from a concern to be seen not to be overly lenient towards murderers, and do not bind the Minister. With the exceptions noted above, there is no legal impediment to releasing a life sentence prisoner early nor is there an entitlement to be considered for release after a certain period.

REVIEW OF SENTENCES IN IRISH LAW

A range of constitutional and statutory provisions governs the review of sentences in Ireland. In particular, the law accommodates the commutation and remission of punishment on the one hand, and the temporary release of prisoners on the other. Each is governed by separate legal provisions.[58] Article 13.6 of the Irish Constitution provides for the pardoning of offenders and the commutation and remission of punishment:

> The right of pardon and the power to commute or remit punishment imposed by any court exercising criminal jurisdiction are hereby vested in the President, but such power of commutation or remission may also be conferred by law on other authorities.

The Criminal Procedure Act 1993 prescribes the procedure to be followed by a person who seeks a presidential pardon. The power of pardon cannot be delegated but it is clear that the powers of commutation and remission are delegable. Section 23(1) of the Criminal Justice Act 1951 duly conferred the 'power to commute or remit punishment' on the executive.[59] Section 23A of the 1951 Act, inserted by section 17 of

[54] [1996] 1 IR 265 at 276–277.

[55] However, preventative considerations may feature in the decision to allow a prisoner temporary release; see further in text accompanying fn 71.

[56] Criminal Justice Act 1990, s 4.

[57] See remarks quoted in fn 48.

[58] See further on commutation and remission of sentences G Hogan and G Whyte (eds) *J.M. Kelly: The Irish Constitution* 4th edn (LexisNexis Butterworths, 2003) paras 4.1.38–4.1.50.

[59] Section 23(1) of the 1951 Act *inter alia* reads: '[t]he Government may commute or remit, in whole or in part, any punishment imposed by a court exercising criminal jurisdiction, subject to such conditions as they may think proper'.

the Criminal Justice (Miscellaneous Provisions) Act 1997, allows the government to delegate its powers of remission to the Minister for Justice, Equality and Law Reform.

The courts have considered the nature of the power of remission. In *The State (O) v O'Brien*,[60] Ó Dálaigh CJ drew a distinction between an act of sentencing and one that merely effects a remission.[61] Walsh J, drawing the same distinction, spoke of the judicial character of the power of remission:

> The power of commutation and remission . . . is a power which, although a power of a judicial character, is nonetheless expressly conferred by the provisions of the Constitution upon the President and, in certain instances, upon the Executive or members thereof. It was, of course, quite open to the People when enacting the Constitution to confer powers of a judicial character upon the Executive or to provide by the Constitution means whereby it could be done by Act of the Oireachtas; but that does not alter the nature of the power.[62]

In a dissenting judgment, McLoughlin J expressed a different view. He saw the power of commutation and remission as corresponding to the royal prerogative of mercy and, therefore, as being executive in nature. In *Brennan v Minister for Justice*,[63] Geoghegan J also preferred the view that the power of remission is executive in nature. However, he went on to state that that power should be exercised sparingly and, given the special nature of the power, the evidence supporting a decision to remit and the reasons for it should be recorded. Moreover, he ventured the opinion that the exercise of the power of remission is open to judicial review.

The constitutionally located powers of commutation and remission are complemented by the statutory power to order the temporary release of prisoners: in practice, it is the latter power that is employed to bring about the release of life sentence prisoners. A comprehensive statutory regime governing the temporary release was adopted in 2003 when section 2 of the Criminal Justice Act 1960 was amended by section 1 of the Criminal Justice (Temporary Release of Prisoners) Act 2003:

> The Minister may direct that such person as is specified in the direction (being a person who is serving a sentence of imprisonment) shall be released from prison for such temporary period, and subject to such conditions, as may be specified in the direction or rules under this section [. . .].

This provision establishes a clear legislative basis for the power of the Minister for Justice, Equality and Law Reform to grant temporary release of prisoners by setting down the principles that will apply to its exercise.[64] The Act stipulates the purposes for which temporary release may be ordered: to assess the prisoner's ability to be re-integrated into society, to prepare him or her for release on the expiry of his or her sentence or to assist the police in investigating crime;[65] where release is warranted on health or humanitarian grounds;[66] on the grounds of good prison management;[67] and where the Minister is of the opinion that the prisoner has been rehabilitated and is ready for re-integration into society.[68]

[60] [1973] IR 50.
[61] [1973] IR 50 at 60.
[62] [1973] IR 50 at 70.
[63] [1995] 1 IR 612.
[64] Criminal Justice (Temporary Release of Prisoners) Bill 2001, explanatory memorandum.
[65] Criminal Justice Act 1960, s 2(1)(a).
[66] Criminal Justice Act 1960, s 2(1)(b).
[67] Criminal Justice Act 1960, s 2(1)(c).
[68] Criminal Justice Act 1960, s 2(1)(d).

Section 2(2) of the Criminal Justice Act 1960 outlines the range of factors that the Minister is required to take into account in reaching a decision on temporary release:

(*a*) the nature and gravity of the offence to which the sentence of imprisonment being served by the person relates,
(*b*) the sentence of imprisonment concerned and any recommendations of the court that imposed that sentence in relation thereto,
(*c*) the period of the sentence of imprisonment served by the person,
(*d*) the potential threat to the safety and security of members of the public (including the victim of the offence to which the sentence of imprisonment being served by the person relates) should the person be released from prison,
(*e*) any offence of which the person was convicted before being convicted of the offence to which the sentence of imprisonment being served by him relates,
(*f*) the risk of the person failing to return to prison upon the expiration of any period of temporary release,
(*g*) the conduct of the person while in custody, while previously the subject of a direction under this section, or during a period of temporary release to which rules under this section, made before the coming into operation of the *Criminal Justice (Temporary Release of Prisoners) Act 2003*, applied,
(*h*) any report of, or recommendation made by—

(i) the governor of, or person for the time being performing the functions of governor in relation to, the prison concerned,
(ii) the Garda Síochána,
(iii) a probation and welfare officer, or
(iv) any other person whom the Minister considers would be of assistance in enabling him to make a decision as to whether to give a direction under subsection (1) that relates to the person concerned.

(*i*) the risk of the person committing an offence during any S.1 period of temporary release,
(*j*) the risk of the person failing to comply with any conditions attaching to his temporary release, and
(*k*) the likelihood that any period of temporary release might accelerate the person's reintegration into society or improve his prospects of obtaining employment.'

The Minister is prevented from ordering temporary release if he or she is of the opinion that it would not be appropriate to do so for reasons connected with any of the foregoing factors or if the prisoner has been remanded in custody by a court.[69] Moreover, section 2(3)(b) stipulates that a prisoner may not be released if another statute prohibits such release, a provision that is relevant in the case of those serving sentences for treason, certain forms of murder and some drug dealing offences.[70]

The power to order temporary release applies to life sentence prisoners and those serving a fixed term alike. It is noteworthy that both punitive and preventative considerations feature in the decision to allow temporary release. In particular, the factors listed in section 2(2)(a), (b) and (c) relate to the offender's culpability while the provision in paragraph (d) is clearly preventative in nature. Therefore, despite the courts' determination to avoid sentencing on a preventative basis[71] the Minister for

[69] Criminal Justice Act 1960, s 2(3)(a) and (c).
[70] Criminal Justice Act 1990, s 4 (prescribing a 40 year minimum term for treason and certain murders); Misuse of Drugs 1977, s 15A (specifying minimum terms for possession for supply of drugs worth more than €13,000).
[71] See text accompanying fnn 50–54.

Justice, Equality and Law Reform is statutorily obliged to take preventative considerations into account when deciding on the question of temporary release. As far as life sentence prisoners are concerned the net effect of this state of affairs is that the determination of their sentence is, in part, shaped by preventative concerns. To this extent, the fate of the life sentence prisoner in Ireland differs little from his or her English counterpart, despite the formal differences in sentence structure between the two jurisdictions.

The power to grant temporary release has been distinguished from the power to commute or remit punishment. In *Kinahan v The Minister for Justice, Equality and Law Reform*, the Supreme Court, *per* Hardiman J, stated:[72]

> It does not appear . . . that temporary release is a specific exercise of the general power of commutation or remission envisaged in the Constitution. Rather, it appears to be a statutory creation administered under the Prisoners (Temporary Release) Rules, 1960, which instrument was in turn made under the powers conferred by the Criminal Justice Act, 1960.

An administrative framework has been put in place to manage the temporary release of prisoners, including life sentences. The Parole Board, which was established in 2001 replacing the former Sentence Review Group, considers cases for release and advises the Minister for Justice, Equality and Law Reform. Significantly, the Parole Board was established on a temporary non-statutory basis and it lacks the power to determine cases: its role is merely advisory and the Minister is not obliged to act on their advice. Despite its non-statutory basis it is likely that the manner in which the Parole Board conducts hearings is open to judicial review: its predecessor, the Sentence Review Group has been successfully challenged in judicial review proceedings.[73] However, the susceptibility of the Parole Board to judicial review to ensure compliances with the principles of fair procedures is not matched by a similar judicial willingness to scrutinise the actual exercise of the power to allow temporary release.

The Irish courts have been consistent in their reluctance to engage in the review of sentences. Inspired by separation of powers considerations they have indicated that the question of early release is an executive matter and that the courts should exercise caution in encroaching on that territory. The executive enjoys a wide measure of discretion in the matter of release, which is seen as a privilege that is extended to prisoners rather than a right.[74] Judicial review of a refusal to order temporary release will be successful only on the limited grounds that the refusal was arbitrary, capricious or unjust.[75]

In *The People (DPP) v Tiernan*,[76] it was held that a court should not take account of the possible release of an offender when determining the appropriate sentence to impose. Finlay CJ emphasised the discretionary nature of temporary release:

[72] [2001] 4 IR 454 at 457.

[73] *Barry v Sentence Review Group* [2001] 4 IR 167.

[74] See *Ryan v Governor of Limerick Prison* [1988] IR 198 at 200, *per* Murphy J: '. . . temporary release is a privilege or concession to which the person in custody has no right . . .'; *Dowling v Minister for Justice, Equality and Law Reform* [2003] 2 IR 535 at 538, *per* Murray J: '. . . temporary release of a prisoner before the sentence imposed by the court has expired is a privilege accorded to him at the discretion of the executive'.

[75] This broadly corresponds with the grounds on which the courts will overturn an administrative decision: see *The State (Keegan) v Stardust Victims Compensation Tribunal* [1986] IR 642; *O'Keeffe v An Bord Pleanala* [1993] 1 IR 39; see further G Hogan and D G Morgan, *Administrative Law in Ireland* 3rd edn (Dublin, Round Hall Sweet & Maxwell, 1998) pp 641–649.

[76] [1988] IR 250 at 256.

> What is described in this ground as the conventional period a person who has been sentenced to life imprisonment might expect to serve is a matter of a policy pursued by the Executive at given times and subject to variation at the discretion of the Executive. It cannot, therefore, in my view, properly be taken into consideration by a court in imposing sentence.

In *Murray v Ireland*,[77] the Supreme Court refused to direct the executive to grant temporary release to the plaintiffs, a married couple serving life sentences for murder. Finlay CJ explicitly invoked separation of powers considerations:

> [. . .] it was said that a court should direct the executive to grant temporary release for this purpose. . . . The length of time which a person sentenced to imprisonment for life spends in custody and as a necessary consequence the extent to which, if any, prior to final discharge, such a person obtains temporary release is a matter which under the constitutional doctrine of the separation of powers rests entirely with the executive [. . .].[78]

However, the Court did concede that there is scope for a limited form of judicial scrutiny of the executive role. Finlay CJ explained:[79]

> The exercise of these powers of the executive is of course subject to supervision by the courts which will intervene only if it can be established that they are being exercised in a manner which is in breach of the constitutional obligation of the executive not to exercise them in a capricious, arbitrary or unjust way. It is not, however, in my view, permissible for the court to intervene merely on the grounds that it would [. . .] have reached a different conclusion on the appropriateness [. . .] of temporary release.

The Supreme Court has consistently reiterated these views. In *McHugh v Minister for Justice*,[80] the Court stressed that temporary release and any form of release under escort are exclusively matters within the Minister's discretion. In *Kinahan v Minister for Justice and Law Reform*,[81] the Court took the view that the same legal position governs the release of life sentence prisoners and those serving determinate sentences. Referring to the decision in *Murray*, Hardiman J stated:

> In my view, this decision properly emphasises the importance of the constitutional separation of powers in dealing with the implementation by the executive of a judicially imposed sentence of imprisonment. It also correctly identifies the sole circumstances in which the court would be justified in interfering with a decision in relation to temporary release.[82]

As to the exercise of the executive discretion in the matter, the Court rejected the notion that there is a presumption that a prisoner is entitled to temporary release.[83]

The Criminal Justice (Release of Prisoners) Act 1998 was enacted in the aftermath to the 'Good Friday Agreement' to provide a mechanism for the early release of prisoners. The Supreme Court, again emphasising the discretionary nature of the power to release, has held that the Act did not create a right to be released. In *O'Neill v Governor of Castlerea Prison*,[84] Keane CJ spoke for the Court:

[77] [1991] 2 ILRM 465.
[78] [1991] 2 ILRM 465 at 472.
[79] [1991] 2 ILRM 465 at 473.
[80] [1997] 1 IR 245.
[81] [2001] 4 IR 454.
[82] [2001] 4 IR 454 at 459.
[83] The Court also dismissed the argument that the recommendations of the Council of Europe of the Committee of Ministers to Member States on European Prison Rules were binding.
[84] [2004] 1 IR 298 at 314; see also *Doherty v Governor of Portlaoise Prison* [2002] 2 IR 252.

> The power to release itself, whether exercised on what might be called conventional grounds of a compassionate or humanitarian nature or for purely political considerations, as in the case of releases effected for the purpose of giving effect to the Belfast Agreement, is a quintessentially executive function.

The broad nature of the discretion to grant temporary release was central to the decision of the High Court in *Breathnach v Minister for Justice, Equality and Law Reform*,[85] where the applicant was granted temporary release on condition that he remained handcuffed during his release. He challenged that condition as being unreasonable and argued that since the respondent had not presented material to the court to show why handcuffing was necessary the court should conclude that there was no basis to support that condition. Rejecting the claim, Ó Caoimh J concluded that it was within the respondent's discretion 'to release the applicant subject to any conditions which he chose to impose'.[86] The Court also took the view that in the circumstances it was not necessary to give reasons for the imposition of the condition.

The revocation of temporary release where a prisoner had been charged with, but not convicted of, another offence was condemned by the Supreme Court in *The State (Murphy) v Kielt*.[87] While the Court acknowledged that the executive enjoyed a wide measure of discretion in the matter it ruled that in the circumstances the applicant should have been afforded the opportunity to refute the allegation. Griffin J explained:

> [. . .] the fact that the [applicant] had been charged with an offence is an insufficient reason for the revocation of his temporary release. Charges are frequently dropped or not proceeded with and, if temporary release can be revoked merely or solely because the person released has been charged with an offence, what of the apparent injustice done to such a person who, in the period intervening between the charge and the dropping of the charges, has lost the liberty to which he would otherwise have been entitled [. . .].[88]

It would appear that one response to the decision in *The State (Murphy) v Kielt* was to allow shorter periods of temporary release which could be renewed each time the previous period expired. The strategy was considered in *Dowling v Minister for Justice, Equality and Law Reform*.[89] The applicant in the latter case was a life sentence prisoner who had been granted temporary release on a monthly renewable basis: he was required to sign on at Mountjoy Prison on the 23rd day of each month. On 23 December 1999 the applicant was arrested and questioned in relation to a murder and, although he was released from police custody without charge, he was returned to prison the same day. The High Court refused to quash the revocation on the grounds that temporary release was a concession to which the prisoner had no right. The Supreme Court allowed the appeal and quashed the revocation. The Court again emphasised that temporary release is a privilege and that the executive enjoys a wide discretion in the matter. Moreover, Murray J, in language remarkably similar to that used by the ECtHR on the matter,[90] commented on the conditional nature of the

[85] [2004] 3 IR 336.
[86] [2004] 3 IR 336 at 343.
[87] [1984] IR 458.
[88] [1984] IR 458 at 473.
[89] [2003] 2 IR 535.
[90] *Weeks v United Kingdom* (1988) 10 EHRR 293.

liberty of a prisoner on temporary release: it is not 'on a par'[91] with that of the ordinary citizen.

The decision in *Dowling* turned on an interpretation of the nature of the release granted to the applicant. Was it, as the respondent contended, a series of separate one-month releases with a new one-month period of release being allowed each time? If that was the position it was clear that the executive could not be compelled to grant a fresh period of temporary release on the expiry of any particular period of release. However, the Court reached the different conclusion that in reality the applicant had been granted indefinite temporary release, not a series of separate monthly releases, which was revoked when he was returned to Mountjoy Prison: hence the relevance to this case of the decision in *The State (Murphy) v Kielt*.

Some judges adopted the practice of incorporating a review element into the sentence. Thus, an offender might have been sentenced to seven years' imprisonment, to be reviewed after 36 months with a view to determining whether the remainder of the sentence could be suspended. One purpose served by such a sentencing structure is that it allows the court to take account of the offender's progress in prison and if it is satisfactory to give him or her the benefit of that progress. However, there is also a suspicion that a sentence of this type has the darker attraction of preventing the executive from releasing the prisoner prior to the review date and that it was a judicial attempt to counteract the 'revolving door' phenomenon. The superior courts have condemned this sentencing practice on the grounds, inter alia, that such sentences seek to 'freeze' the exercise of executive discretion.[92]

The Supreme Court definitively resolved the matter in *The People (DPP) v Finn*,[93] where it rejected the idea that the sentencing judge could include a review date for possible release on licence. Keane CJ explained that:

> The making of such orders is not merely inconsistent with the provisions of s. 23 of the Act of 1951: it offends the separation of powers in this area mandated by Article 13.6 of the Constitution. That provision expressly vests the power of commutation or remission in the President but provides that the power may also be conferred by law on other authorities. Since under Article 15.2.1 of the Constitution the sole and exclusive power of making laws for the State is vested in the Oireachtas, it was for the legislative arm alone to determine which authorities other than the President should exercise that power. In enacting s. 23 of the Criminal Justice Act, 1951, the Oireachtas conferred the power of commutation or remission on the government or, where it delegated its power, the Minister for Justice. . . . It would seem to follow that the remission power, despite its essentially judicial character, once vested under the Constitution in an executive organ, cannot, without further legislative intervention, be exercised by the courts.[94]

Nevertheless, the Chief Justice offered the opinion that:

> It is also, of course, open to the Oireachtas to provide by legislation, as has been done in other countries, for the regular review of sentences by a parole board and such an approach might

[91] [2003] 2 IR 535 at 538.

[92] *The People v Cahill* [1980] IR 8; *O'Brien v Governor of Limerick Prison* [197] 2 ILRM 349. A different view was expressed by Walsh J in *The People (DPP) v Alymer* [1995] 2 ILRM 624. See T O'Malley, 'Principles of Sentencing: Some recent Developments' (2001) 1(1) *Judicial Studies Institute Journal* 50 at 56–63.

[93] [2001] 2 IR 25. See M O'Connell, 'The Supreme Court Decision in *DPP v Padraig Finn*' (2001, April) *Bar Review* 354.

[94] [2001] 2 IR 25 at 46.

> well be consistent with modern penological principles. These again, however, are entirely matters for the legislature and not within the competence of the courts, having regard to Article 13.6, to determine.[95]

This passage provides the Oireachtas with the reassurance that it is constitutionally permissible to enact legislation establishing a system of sentence review by an independent statutory body. It may be inferred that the Court was fully aware of the demands of sentence management and the desirability of providing a mechanism for the determination of life sentences: hence the reference to 'modern penological principles'.

CONCLUSION

The European Court of Human Rights' jurisprudence concerning the determination of life sentences is particularly relevant since the enactment in Ireland of the European Convention on Human Rights Act 2003. Rulings by the Court on the temporary release or release on licence of life sentence prisoners strongly indicate that current Irish law is not compatible with the ECHR.

The most significant deficiency in Irish law is that release is treated as an executive matter, a position that is in marked contrast to the position in European human rights law. Article 5(4) ECHR, as interpreted by the ECtHR, demands that a court or 'court-like' body should be entrusted with the release of life sentence prisoners. The key features of such a body is that it is independent of the executive and of the parties, that it has the power to determine cases, that it conducts adversarial hearings and accords to the prisoner the procedural rights that follow from such a hearing. The current Parole Board fails to satisfy ECHR requirements. The difficulty is that the Parole Board lacks the power to determine cases, its role being merely advisory. Moreover, the limited form of judicial scrutiny that Irish law allows does not meet the demands of the Convention. The ECtHR decisions have firmly indicated that judicial review proceedings do not provide the form of review required:[96] a mechanism that allows the review body to consider the factual basis for the continued detention of the life sentence prisoner is necessary.

The chasm between the Irish position and that required by the ECHR causes appreciable difficulties for Irish law given the Irish courts' reliance on the concept of separation of powers as underpinning their reluctance to engage in sentence review. There is a strange irony to the latter consideration given that the European Court and the House of Lords, in *Stafford*[97] and *Anderson*[98] respectively, have invoked the separation of powers in support of a very different conclusion: the view expressed in those cases is that the separation of powers demanded that sentencing and the setting of the tariff remain matters for the judiciary, not the executive. It is not beyond the bounds of possibility that the Irish courts will revise their position and bring Irish law into conformity with the ECHR. It is open to the courts to breathe life into the European Convention of Human Rights Act 2003 by interpreting it in a sufficiently expansive

[95] [2001] 2 IR 25 at 46.

[96] *Weeks v United Kingdom* (1988) 10 EHRR 293; see also *Singh v United Kingdom* [1996] ECHR 23389/94.

[97] (2002) 35 EHRR 32.

[98] [2003] AC 1. See M Amos, '*R v Secretary of State for the Home Department, ex p Anderson* Ending the Home Secretary's Sentencing Role' (2004) 67 *Modern Law Review* 108.

manner to ensure the reception of the relevant ECHR standards in domestic law: section 4 of the Act requires the courts to take 'due account' of the principles of European human rights law. To this end it is possible that the Irish courts, much like their English counterparts, will be driven to declaring the current legal position prescribed by section 2 of the Criminal Justice Act 1960[99] incompatible with the ECHR. This, of course, is a matter of speculation and it must be acknowledged that, to date, European human rights law has had a marginal impact on domestic Irish law and a decision along the lines of that in *Anderson* would represent a significant change in judicial attitude. However, it must also be observed that Irish case law on sentence review focused exclusively on questions of domestic law and that the ECHR issues were not raised in or considered by the courts. From a strictly doctrinal perspective the question whether Irish law can be interpreted in a manner that conforms to the ECHR, and the related question whether the courts would issue a declaration of incompatibility if the first question is answered in the negative, remain undecided.

It goes without saying that curing the defects in Irish law by judicial means requires an aggrieved litigant to initiate legal proceedings, an exhaustive process that leaves the law unchanged in the interim. Irish law might be aligned with the ECHR by a more direct legislative route. There is no constitutional impediment to transferring the power of release from the executive to a body that matches ECHR demands. As it happens the judgment in *The People (DPP) v Finn*,[100] quoted above, has opened the door to a development of the type required by ECtHR jurisprudence. The simple solution is to enact legislation that places the Parole Board on a statutory footing and assign to it the function of regularly reviewing sentences. In this way the Parole Board would acquire the vital qualities of a 'court like' body, namely that it is independent of the executive and acts impartially. It is clearly within the competence of the *Oireachtas* to enact such legislation. Whether it does so without prior judicial intervention remains to be seen.

[99] See text accompanying fnn 64-71.

[100] [2001] 2 IR 25.

Changing the Paradigm—the Potential Impact of the United Nations Convention on the Rights of Persons with Disabilities

Agustina Palacios* and Maria Walls**

After four years of intense negotiation, the much-awaited Draft United Nations Convention on the Rights of Persons with Disabilities was agreed on 25 August 2006 at the 8th Session of the Ad Hoc Committee. This was heralded as a great achievement, one of the fastest-negotiated treaties on record. The process continued when an open-ended drafting group, tasked to bring the text to uniformity, met on the 5 December to conclude the final text. At that final meeting of the Ad Hoc Committee, the United Nations High Commissioner for Human Rights, Louise Arbour warmly welcomed the Convention:

> In particular, I would like to highlight the importance of the Convention as a catalyst for change. We have often heard that the Convention enshrines a 'paradigm shift' in attitudes that moves from a view of persons with disabilities as objects of charity, medical treatment and social protection to subjects of rights, able to claim those rights as active members of society. Nowhere has this been so much in evidence as in this Ad Hoc Committee.[1]

The Convention on the Rights of Persons with Disabilities[2] went before the UN General Assembly on 13 December 2006 and was adopted by consensus. United Nations Secretary-General, Kofi Annan, for his part, noted:

> It is the first human rights treaty to be adopted in the twenty-first century; the most rapidly negotiated human rights treaty in the history of international law; and the first to emerge from lobbying conducted extensively through the Internet. On paper, [people with disabilities] have enjoyed the same rights as others; in real life, they have often been relegated to the margins and denied the opportunities that others take for granted.[3]

* Doctoral Fellow at the International, Ecclesiastic and Philosophy Law Department of the University Carlos III, Madrid, Spain; Lecturer in Philosophy of Law, University Carlos III of Madrid, Spain, since 2003. Member of the Experts Commission about the UN Convention on Disability created by the Royal 'Patronato' on Disability, Legislative Commission on Disability issues, Ministry of Social and Labor Affairs, Spain, since 2005.

** PhD Candidate, Faculty of Law, NUI Galway supported by a Government of Ireland IRCHSS Scholarship. Maria has worked for over twenty years in Disability Services, as Social Worker, Development Manager and most recently as Director of Research with the National Federation of Voluntary Bodies. She attended the August 2006 Ad Hoc Meeting in New York as a delegate with Rehabilitation International.

The authors wish to acknowledge the comments and support from Gerard Quinn, Professor at the National University of Ireland, Galway, and Rafael de Asís Roig, Professor at Carlos III University of Spain, in the elaboration of this article.

[1] Louise Arbour address to the 8th Session of the Ad Hoc Committee on 5 December 2006, New York, see: http://www.un.org/esa/socdev/enable/rights/ahc8.htm 14 December 2006.

[2] UN Convention on the Rights of Persons with Disabilities United Nations General Assembly Resolution, UN Doc A/61/611, 6 December 2006. Available at: http://www.un.org/esa/socdev/enable/rights/convtexte.htm.

[3] United Nations Secretary-General, 'Official Statement of the UN Secretary General', UN Doc SG/SM/10797, HR/4911, L/T/4400, 13 December 2006. Available at: http://www.un.org/News/Press/docs/2006/sgsm10797.doc.htm.

The Convention creates a paradigm shift in the recognition of, and respect for, the rights and dignity of people with disabilities throughout the world. Commentators have, in particular, praised the work of the International Disability Caucus (IDC) and other NGOs for their participation in the treaty-development process. This Article explores in detail this changing paradigm towards a human rights approach, including a discussion of the different models of disability; this is followed by an analysis of the definition of disabilities and of discrimination on the basis of disability, with an examination of the forces creating the impetus for the Convention. What then follows is an interpretation of the Convention through the lens of the key substantial rights of equality, protection, liberty, participation and basic social rights. Significant elements for the effective implementation of the Convention are explored, and a brief review is presented of the contribution of Ireland to the development of the Convention.

The main consequence of adopting the International Convention on the Rights of Persons with Disabilities ('the Convention') is an implied change of paradigm which, at an international level, has been steadily gaining momentum since the 1980s. This change of paradigm is summarised by considering disability as a matter of human rights. Ever since this approach was utilised, both the policies offered and the answers given to the problems faced by persons with disabilities has been thought of and elaborated upon, from beginning to end, by bearing in mind the respect for human rights of persons with disabilities.[4] To a great extent, this is a consequence of the fight that persons with disabilities have been carrying out since the 1970s. Persons with disabilities sought to be considered not as objects of assistance or paternalist policies, but to become subjects with full rights and with respect granted to their dignity and personhood. Fortunately, the Convention adopts such an approach, and binds States Parties to acknowledge this concept in the legislative policies to be adopted and implemented.

What then is required to assume a human rights-based approach to disability? To answer this question it is necessary to make a brief account of the treatment that persons with disabilities have been historically compelled to face, as well as how its implementation has been manifest in different models—one of which, the Social Model, sets the foundations for the new approach incorporated into the Convention on the Rights of Persons with Disablities.

THE DIFFERENT MODELS OF DISABILITY

Historically, very different approaches have been, it may be said, dispensed to persons with disabilities. These varied treatments have, consequently, been embodied in the various legal systems of States.[5] These approaches can basically be summarised from the perspective of two such models;[6] the rehabilitation model and the Social Model.

[4] See G Quinn and T Degener, *Human Rights and Disability. The current use and future potential of United Nations human rights instruments in the context of disability*, UN Doc HR/PUB/02/1, 2002. Available at: http://www.unhchr.ch/html/menu6/2/disability.doc

[5] See P Longmore and L Umansky (eds), *The New Disability History. American Perspectives* (New York University Press, New York, 2001); and HJ Stiker, *A History of Disability*, translated by William Sayers, (Ann Arbor, The University of Michigan Press, 1999).

[6] Note that a third model has been considered, that of the 'disregard model'; see A Palacios, *La discapacidad frente al poder de la normalidad. Una aproximación desde tres modelos teóricos* (Disability against the power of *normality*. An approach from three theoretical models'), Universidad Carlos III de Madrid, Instituto de Derechos Humanos 'Bartolomé de las Casas', Madrid, 2004.

Under international law, the treatment of disability has evolved from the former towards the latter.

The Rehabilitation Model

The first evidence of the rehabilitation or 'medical' model dates from the fifteenth century.[7] Nevertheless, the consolidation of the model itself, especially within the legislative field, can be traced to the beginning of the twentieth century and the end of the First World War. The causes which gave way to its foundation can briefly be summarised by two factors: war and work injuries. Jacques Stiker states that the first of these themes was manifest at the end of the First World War, as an alarming number of men had received life long injuries. These persons were called *the war crippled* in order to differentiate them from those who were disabled due to labour accidents. A *crippled* person was missing something, whether an organ, a sense, or a function. This way, the first image introduced with regard to disability was that of harm, of injury. The feeling was that the War had taken something which had to be replaced.[8] Thus, it happened that from that moment disability began to be related to those injured in war and it was seen as an insufficiency, a deficiency to be overcome. Also such injuries were acquired, not through an individual's own fault, but through the 'serving of their country'. Within the scope of law, this meant the implementation of legislative policies destined to guarantee social services for war veterans with disability, which somehow reflected the belief that there existed an obligation on behalf of States to compensate these persons through invalidity pensions, rehabilitation benefits and employment quotas.

Such measures were extended, by the 1960s, to all persons with disability, leaving aside the *cause* of deficiencies. Rehabilitation then became the objective, independent of the origin of the person's deficiencies. Within such recovery or 'normalisation' process the essential tools were special education, benefits of medical and vocational rehabilitation, employment quotas and institutionalised assistance services. In this way, persons with disabilities received benefits from social security because their disability was seen exclusively as a problem of an individual person who was not able to face society. Such persons with disabilities had the right to rehabilitation, but this included control, by *experts*, over many areas of their daily lives. These measures of positive action were introduced because, unlike other protected groups, it was not considered that persons with disabilities were capable of working on their own.[9]

Such measures can be easily put into a context and understood, as from the perspective of the rehabilitation model, disability is exclusively considered a person's problem directly caused by illness, accident, or a health condition and requires individual medical care to be rendered by professionals. Consequently, the treatment of disability is undetaken with the aim of obtaining a cure, a better adaptation of the person, or a change in his or her conduct. In this way, from the legal point of view, disability is primarily if not exclusively dealt with through assistance and social security laws, or

[7] Puig De La Bellacasa, *La Discapacidad y la Rehabilitación en Juan Luis Vives*. Homo homini par, Real Patronato de Prevención y de Atención a Personas con Minusvalía, Madrid, 1993.

[8] See HJ Stiker, *A History of Disability*, above, n 5, p 124.

[9] See T Degener and G Quinn, *A survey of international, comparative and regional Disability Law Reform*. Available at: http://www.dredf.org/international/degener_quinn.html.

as a part of certain issues of civil law related to the deprivation of legal capacity (legal incompetence) and guardianship.[10]

The rehabilitation model is criticised for several reasons.[11] Fundamentally as regards its theoretical justification, it requires the adoption of a variety of assimilation strategies. The rehabilitation model denotes the existence of a disturbing ideology, which Stiker calls *the social ideal of erasure.*[12] Thus, integration turns out to be the disappearance, or rather the concealment, of difference. This is because the disabled person is considered a deviation from a supposed standard of normality. Yet, it must not be forgotten, as Courtis points out, that the configuration of standards is not neutral, but implies an inclination in favour of the physical and psychic parameters of those who constitute the dominant stereotype.[13]

The Social Model

The Social Model essentially originated and was developed and articulated from a denial of the principles expressed in the rehabilitation model. One of the fundamental presumptions of the Social Model is that the causes of disability are not individual, but rather are primarily societal. According to this model, individual limitations are not the fundamental issue, but rather it is the limits of society in rendering appropriate services and adequately ensuring that the needs of the disabled are taken into consideration within social organisation.[14]

It is possible to situate the origins of the Social Model, or at least the time when the first thinking emerged, towards the end of the 1960s in the United States and in the United Kingdom. Previously, disability in Western societies had been considered as the sole result of an individual person's limitation, which implied a *personal tragedy* for the party affected, and a *problem* for the rest of society.[15] Nevertheless, towards the end of the 1960s such orthodoxy started to be the target of campaigns by persons with disabilities, particularly those who lived in residential institutions. Thus, activists with disabilities and organisations for disabled people took the political initiative and condemned their status as 'second class citizens'. They turned attention to the impact of social and environmental barriers, such as transportation and non-accessible buildings, discriminating attitudes and negative cultural stereotypes, which, they

[10] See World Health Organisation, the International Classification of Functioning, Disability and Health, 54th World Health Assembly A54/18 Provisional agenda item 13.9, 9 April 2001.

[11] The criticisms of the rehabilitation model touches on the underlying ideology and not to the so-called *rehabilitation process*, which is an element of considerable importance in the life of a disabled persons. See: C Barnes and G Mercer, *Disability*, (Cambridge, Polity Press, 2003); C Barnes, *Disabled People in Britain and Discrimination. A case for Anti-discrimination Legislation*, 3rd edn, (London, Hurst and Company, in association with the British Council of Organizations of Disabled People, 2000); A Silvers, D Wasserman and MB Mahowald, *Disability, Difference, Discrimination. Perspective on Justice in Bioethics and Public Policy*, (Rowman & Littlefield Publishers, Inc., United States of America, 1998).

[12] See HJ Stiker, *A History of Disability*, above, n 5, p 12.

[13] C Courtis, *Discapacidad e inclusión social: retos teóricos y desafíos prácticos. Algunos comentarios a partir de la Ley 51/2003*, 51 Jueces para la Democracia, 2004, p 7. With regard to 'the standard', see Marion Young's idea of impartiality; IM Young, *Justice and the politics of difference,* (Princeton University Press, 1990).

[14] See C Barnes, M Oliver and L Barton (eds), *Disability Studies Today*, (Oxford, Polity Press, 2002); M Oliver,*The Politics of Disablement*, (Hong Kong, Macmillan Press, 1990); M Oliver, *Understanding Disability. From theory to practice*, (Malaysia, Palgrave, 1996).

[15] See C Barnes and G Mercer, *Disability,* above, n 11, Chapter 1; P Abberley, 'The concept of oppression and the development of a social theory of disability', in *Disability, Handicap and Society*, vol 2, pp 5–19.

made plain, *disabled* persons with impairments.[16] In so doing, persons with disabilities and their organisations opened a new front of civil rights and helped create anti-discrimination legislation.

This process initially started in the United States, where a tradition of political campaigning based on civil rights had emerged. Thus, the struggle for the civil rights of Afro-Americans, combining conventional lobby tactics and mass political actions, greatly encouraged an emerging 'movement for the rights of people with disability' which focused on civil rights, mutual support, demedicalisation and deinstitutionalisation, among other issues.[17] From a rather different perspective, the disabled people's movement in the United Kingdom pursued changes either in social politics or human rights legislation. Their strategic priority was to emphasise the existence of the systems sponsored by the 'Welfare State'[18] to cover the needs of people with disabilities. In the United Kingdom, disabled people's organisations initially mobilised opinion against their traditional categorisation as a vulnerable group in need of protection. They defended the right to define their own needs and priority services, and declared themselves against the traditional domain by providers of services.[19]

Although it is possible to underline many similarities between the British and American models, there are some differences—especially those related to the origin and the rationale—which required separate approaches for their development. This however falls beyond the scope of this article; it remains to be said however, that both models had an important influence at international level. This influence was manifest by the consideration that disability has its origin in social causes, and the solutions, thus, should not be aimed at the individually-affected person, but rather should address society as a whole. Thus, whereas the previous model centred on rehabilitation or normalisation of persons with disabilities, the Social Model promotes the rehabilitation or normalisation of a society which should be conceived and designed to meet the needs of everyone.

In general terms, the social approach to which persons with disabilities would be subject to would be based on the search for inclusion through equality of opportunity. According to this perspective, for example, disabled children are to have the same development opportunities as children without disabilities; and education should tend to be inclusive, adapted to the needs of all, and as a rule ought to preserve special education as last resort. In relation to maintenance requirements, the Social Model advocates that social security and open employment are to be the appropriate means, and only exceptionally protected employment is to be accepted. It is worth remarking that the connotation of employment as an exclusive means of social integration, sustained

[16] During the same period and contrastingly, as Colin Barnes relates: academic literature continued accepting the orthodox point of view, which considered disability as a medical and individual matter. In spite of the fact that both gender and race were recognised as characteristic causes of social oppression. See C Barnes, M Oliver and L Barton (eds), *Disability Studies Today,* above, n 14, ch 1.

[17] C Barnes and G Mercer, *Disability,* above, n 11, p 33.

[18] According to the Cambridge Advanced Learner's Dictionary, welfare state is a system of taxation which allows the government of a country to provide social services such as health care, unemployment pay, etc. to people who need them. For further details see Pierre Pestieau, *The welfare state in the European Union: economic and social perspectives,* (Oxford, Oxford University Press, 2006); David A Gerber (ed), *Disabled Veterans in History*, Corporealities: Discourses of Disability, (Ann Arbor, University of Michigan Press, 2000).

[19] See C Barnes, M Oliver and L Barton (eds), *Disability Studies Today,* above, n 14, ch 1.

by the rehabilitation model, is questioned by the Social Model, which establishes that employment is not the only way of inclusion in society.[20]

The Social Model, it should be noted, is closely related with the assumption of certain intrinsic values of the human right discourse, and seeks to strengthen the respect of human dignity, personal equality and liberty, promoting social inclusion, relying on certain specific principles, such as, independent life, non-discrimination, universal accessibility, participation on decision making, among others. The Model departs from the premise that disability is a social construction and a way of social oppression, and the consequence of a society which does not consider nor bear in mind persons with disabilities. Instead, the Model aims to allow for the full autonomy of persons with disabilities to decide about their own lives and, in this way, focuses on the elimination of barriers in order to ensure an adequate equalisation of opportunities. At its most fundamental level, the Social Model considers disability as a complex phenomenon which does not simply restrict a person, but is the result of a combination of circumstances, for the most part created by a social context. This requires, therefore, the adoption of necessary modifications or adjustments in order to achieve the full participation of persons with disabilities in all areas of community life. The described situation—which is more an ideological than a biological matter—demands the implementation of social change which implies the adoption of a human rights perspective. The Social Model is thus intimately related with the assumption of disability as a human rights issue. It focuses on the intrinsic dignity of the human being and only when necessary, on the medical characteristic of the person. Consequently, the individual is placed at the centre of all self-concerning decisions and the core of the problem is outside the person, ie with society.

In this context, possible solutions towards unfavourable situations of persons with disabilities are addressed from the respect of certain essential values which are precisely the rationale of the human right discourse.[21] Accordingly, the development of a different answer for the needs of persons with disabilities has, in the recent decades, been based on the intrinsic values supporting human rights. This has triggered a shift in awareness towards the disabled person, focusing, first, on the person as a human being, in equality with others; and, second, on the person's attached condition (disability) which requires, in certain circumstances, special measures to ensure the full enjoyment and exercise of their rights in equality with others. For such purposes, law utilises a series of promotional techniques (such as affirmative action measures, or reasonable accommodations) and enshrines a series of principles which have an important impact on disability policies (non-discrimination, independent living, universal accessibility, design for all, mainstreaming, among others). These principles have, at

[20] In this model, the importance of approaching disability phenomena from a holistic point of view is remarked. Thus, leisure, culture, sports—among others—are activities that allow persons with disabilities to participate in social life, and at the same time develop their expectations. That is why, as it will be seen, so much importance is given to accessibility—as a previous requirement—for the enjoyment of such activities on an equal basis with others.

[21] As professor Rafael de Asís asserts: 'the inspiring principles of current legal norms (or public policies) in the field of disability are, in theory, totally compatible with the equality of rights discourse' in de Asís Roig, Rafael, 'La incursión de la discapacidad en la teoría de los derechos', en *Los derechos de las personas con discapacidad: perspectivas sociales, políticas, jurídicas y filosóficas,* I Campoy Cervera (coord), (Dykinson, Madrid, 2004), p 62.

their root, and pursue the same goal: that persons with disabilities have the same opportunities as everyone in the design and development of their own life.[22]

THE CONVENTION ON THE RIGHTS OF PERSONS WITH DISABILITIES

The shift towards a human rights-based perspective has engendered great support within the United Nations during the last three decades. In the first place, a series of tools exists within the universal system for the protection of human rights which, although they do not address disability expressly or exceptionally, they are applicable to persons with disability, and must be taken into account when it comes to ensuring the enjoyment and exercise of their rights. As Quinn and Degener state, the United Nations' treaties on human rights offer great possibilities for the legal protection of persons with disabilities, but surprisingly the experts on the topic note that to date no true advantage has been garnereed from them.[23] These human rights instruments include: the 1966 International Covenant on Economic, Social and Cultural Rights, the 1966 International Covenant on Civil and Political Rights, the 1984 Convention against Torture and Other Cruel, Inhuman or Degrading Treatments or Punishments, the 1989 International Convention on the Rights of the Child, the 1982 Convention on the Elimination of all forms of Discrimination against Women, and the 1963 Convention on the Elimination of all forms of Racial Discrimination.[24] The first general treaty that includes a specific provision with regard to people with disability is the 1989 Convention on the Rights of the Child, which refers specifically to children with disability in Article 23.[25]

For its part, the UN Human Rights Commission urged the treaty monitoring organs to bear in mind the rights of persons with disabilities when carrying out their activities; while Degener and Quinn have pointed out that this is of great importance as it acknowledges the need to channel the potential of the various international legal instruments for the benefit of persons with disabilities.[26]

Likewise, disability has been addressed within the United Nations system through rules of *soft law* within the following non-binding but significant instruments:[27] the Declaration on the Rights of Mentally Retarded Persons 1971,[28] which was followed by the Declaration on the Rights of Disabled Persons in 1975. In 1982 the World Programme of Action concerning Disabled Persons was launched,[29] which aimed to promote rehabilitation, effective measures for preventing disability, and the realisation

[22] For further details see R De Lorenzo García, *El futuro de las personas con discapacidad en el mundo. Desarrollo humano y Discapacidad,* (Fundación ONCE, Ediciones del Umbral, Madrid, 2003).

[23] United Nations General Assembly Resolution 34/180, 34 UN GAOR Supp (No 46) at 193, UN Doc A/34/46 (1979).

[24] See Office of the High Commissioner for Human Rights, 'A Compilation of International Instruments Volume 1, 2002, (First Part) Universal Instruments United Nations. GA Res 2106 (XX), Annex, 20 UN GAOR Supp (No 14) at 47, UN Doc A/6014 (1966).

[25] United Nations Convention on the Rights of the Child, 1989, Article 23 reads 'States Parties recognize that a mentally or physically disabled child should enjoy a full and decent life, in conditions which ensure dignity, promote self-reliance and facilitate the child's active participation in the community'.

[26] It is now acknowledged that there exists huge potential within these treaties, see G Quinn and T Degener, *Human Rights and Disability,* above, n 4, pp 41–164.

[27] *Ibid.*

[28] United Nations General Assembly Resolution 2856 (XXVI), 20 December 1971.

[29] United Nations General Assembly Resolution 37/52, 3December 1982.

of the goals of 'full participation' of disabled persons in social life and development, and of 'equality'. The emphasis was on equality of opportunities: this programme recognised that 'physical and social barriers in society' significantly limit the full participation of people with disability. This shift from impairment as the barrier, to society imposing the barriers, is important. Beyond the 1991 Principles for the Protection of Persons with Mental Illness and the Improvement of Mental Health Care[30], most significant and far-reaching effects resulted from the Standard Rules on the Equalization of Opportunities for Persons with Disabilities 1993[31], which was the key outcome of the Decade of Disabled Persons. Although not legally binding, the Standard Rules exerted strong moral and political pressure on States to take action to achieve the equalisation of opportunities for persons with disabilities.

Towards the Convention

If existing international binding human rights instruments are applicable to people with disabilities, why was a specific Convention on the Rights of the Persons with Disabilities necessary? In order to answer this question it is worth looking to two UN reports. The first was delivered by Leandro Despouy in 1991, and reported that among other issues, that persons with disabilities were legally disadvantaged when compared to other vulnerable groups such as women, refugees, and children, and pointed out that these other groups are protected by the specific Conventions whereas persons with disabilities are not[32]. While remarking on the United Nation's treaty-based system's shortcomings, the Report noted that persons with disabilities are as equally protected as all individuals by the general rules, international conventions, regional agreements, etc., but when compared to other vulnerable groups they did not benefit from international monitoring organs offering particular and specific protection.[33] The Report recommended, inter alia, that all treaty monitoring bodies ensure the application of their respective human rights treaties in relation to persons with disabilities.

The second report was prepared by Gerard Quinn and Theresia Degener, and is entitled 'Human Rights and Disability—The current use and future potential of United Nations human rights instruments in the context of disability' prepared in 2002.[34] The document analyses the applicability of human rights values and doctrine on disability and the perspective of evolution from a model that the authors call medical to one of human rights. They analyse binding human rights instruments and their potential application to the specific area of disability. The Report reached the conclusion that persons with disability were somehow 'invisible' within the human rights system of the United Nations. The difference between persons with disabilities and other groups, such as women and children is, according to the Report, that

[30] United Nations General Assembly Resolution 46/119, 17 December 1991.

[31] Resolution Approved by the General Assembly—48th period sessions, 20 December 1993. (A/RES/48/96 Standard Rules on the Equalization of Opportunities for Persons with Disabilities—85th Plenary Meeting 20 December 1993).

[32] See Sub-Commission on the Promotion and Protection of Human Rights, Mr Leandro Despouy, Special Rapporteur, Final Report, on Human Rights and Disability UN Doc E/CN.4/Sub.2/1991/31, 1991.

[33] Committee on Economic, Social and Cultural Rights, General Comment No 5, Persons with disabilities (Eleventh session, 1994), UN Doc E/1995/22 at 19 (1995), reprinted in Compilation of General Comments and General Recommendations Adopted by Human Rights Treaty Bodies, UN Doc HRI/GEN/1/Rev 6 at 24 (2003).

[34] See GQuinn and T Degener, *Human Rights and Disability,* above, n 4.

persons with disabilities do not rely on the legally binding instruments or the monitoring bodies for the protection of their rights in any explicit manner. This means that even when people with disabilities are covered—just like other individuals—by the protection established in the treaties, such rules in fact do not truly apply or are applied in a different manner which is disadvantageously towards the group. Having analysed the use and possibilities of the existing instruments on disability issues, the Report determined that the existing machinery does not work for disability concerns. Potential use of the treaties for disability issues were identified, and practical recommendations were made to improve the system, but the core of the Report contained a series of arguments referring to the need for a new specific treaty on disability: This new instrument would not replace, but broaden and reinforce the existing system.

The International Convention for the Rights of Persons with Disability was approved on 13 December 2006. Clearly, the Convention is the result of a long process in which several actors participated: UN Member States, UN Observers, important bodies and organisations of the United Nations, Special Rapporteurs on disability, national human rights institutions, and NGOs in which persons with disabilities' organisations had a key role.

As it has been remarked, this new instrument has important consequences for persons with disabilities, among the main ones the fact that the 'visibility' of people with disabilities in the UN human rights protection system can be highlighted, plus the undoubted assumption of the disability experience as a matter of human rights, and the fact of relying on a legal binding tool at the time of exercising these peoples' rights. At the same time, it is important to emphasise that, the Convention is not and should not be interpreted as an isolated instrument; on the contrary, it is the expression of a global trend in favour of restoring the visibility of persons with disabilities, in both social and legal spheres.

The first time the possibility of creating a convention for the rights of persons with disabilities was discussed was in 1987, at a meeting with experts in charge of examining the application of the 1982 UN World Action Program concerning Disabled Persons.[35] But more than thirteen years passed before a proposal by the President of Mexico to the General Assembly was approved, and an Ad Hoc Committee established with the object of analysing the possibility of creating a specific Convention on the rights of persons with disabilities.[36] The idea was backed by States and international NGOs dealing with the protection and promotion of the rights of people with disabilities. The Ad Hoc Committee was open to the participation of all States and UN Observers and worked from a holistic approach to the spheres of social development, human rights and non-discrimination.[37] The Ad Hoc Committee held eight meetings and the text of the Convention was adopted and promptly approved by the UN General Assembly on 13 December 2006.

[35] World Programme of Action concerning Disabled Persons. United Nations General Assembly Resolution, UN Doc A/RES/37/52, 3 December 1982.

[36] United Nations General Assembly Resolution 56/168, 19 December 2001.

[37] Note that after Resolution 56/168, the Social Development Commission adopted on 21 February 2002 and the Human Rights Commission on 26 April 2002 similar resolutions.

The Negotiation Process

The First Session of the Ad Hoc Committee, which lasted for two weeks, was held in August of 2002[38] and was chaired by Ambassador Luis Gallegos of Ecuador.[39] Previously, in June of the same year, the Mexican Government had organised a Seminar of Experts in Mexico City and had developed a draft text.[40] The document contained a series of indicators about the rights that the eventual treaty should include, as well as a series of principles that the treaty should address. This work had an important influence on this First Session of the Committee. As Professor Quinn asserts, this first session was difficult, while many delegations had no clear instructions from their respective governments, others had instructions to negotiate an international treaty. The Ad Hoc Committee ultimately decided that it would move to an elaboration of an international instrument. An important and innovative aspect of the negotiation process to emerge was that representatives of the civil society (read NGO) were invited to participate actively in the negotiations. Despite not necessarily having consultative status, groups of NGOs were able to be present in formal sessions and to speak to the plenary of State delegations.[41]

The Second Session of the Committee has held in June 2003,[42] and decided that the establishment of a Working Group with the mandate to elaborate a draft text would be necessary. The Working Group held its first session on January of 2004, which resulted in the elaboration a first draft text for future discussions.[43] The Third Session, held in May 2004, undertook the first reading of that text,[44] with members of the Ad Hoc Committee proposing modifications which resulted in a new document with a compilation of all the suggested modification being approved. As a result of differences and disagreements expressed in the working sessions, the Committee decided to delay until later in the process the addressing of certain issues, most notably the definitions and the possibility of a treaty monitoring mechanism. At the Fourth Session of August 2004, revisions of the suggested modifications during the first reading were considered. For its part, the Fifth Session on January 2005, led to a reduction in the ambit of the draft convention, while the Sixth Session of August 2005[45] saw the chairing of the Ad Hoc Committee taken over by Ambassador MacKay from New Zealand. Informal meetings were held during this Session, as they had been in the previous sessions, in order to consolidate a new, shorter working draft text. At the end of the meeting Ambassador MacKay announced that he would submit to the delegations

[38] First Session, 29 July to 9August 2002. For further details see Report of the first session UN Doc A/57/357.

[39] For further details about the development of the sessions see 'Ratification Toolkit', Disabled People International, 2006. Available at: http://www.icrpd.net/ratification/en/index.htm.

[40] Documents of the Seminar are available at: www.sre.gob.mx.discapacidad.

[41] See G Quinn, 'Next steps—Towards a United Nations Treaty on the Rights of Persons with Disabilities', in P Blanck (ed) *Disability Rights,* (Ashgate, England, 2005), pp 519–541.

[42] Second Session, 16 to 27 June 2003. For further details see Report of the second session, UN Doc A/58/118 & Corr 1, 3 July 2003.

[43] Working Group to the Ad Hoc Committee, 5 to 16 January 2004. For further details see Report of the Working Group to the Ad Hoc Committee, UN Doc A/AC.265/2004/WG/1.

[44] Third Session, 24 May to 4 June 2004. For further details see Report of the third session, UN Doc A/AC.265/2004/5, 9 June 2004.

[45] Sixth Session, 1 to 12 August 2005. For further details see Report of the sixth session, UN Doc A/60/266, 17 August 2005.

a new draft text containing the suggested modifications thus far. The document, called 'Chair's text', was provided to State delegations and NGOs in October 2005.[46]

As a result, a Seventh Session of the Ad Hoc Committee was held in January 2006[47] and a first reading of the Chair's text was completed. This resulted in a revised version of the Chair's text being adopted by the Committee as its 'Working Text'.[48] The last and final session (Eight Session) was held in August and December of 2006,[49] wherein participants conducted a final reading, analysed and discussed the text presented by the Chair and established, after tough and intense debate a general consensus on a definitive text. It was this text which the UN General Assembly adopted on 13 December 2006.

Even though a number of issues proved to be contentious during the negotiation process, it was clear from the beginning of the debates that the convention would assume the Social Model of disability as its philosophical foundation, as most delegations considered disability as a human rights issue.[50] This is made evident by the consensus towards the Convention's inspiring principles: equality of opportunity, non-discrimination, human dignity, accessibility, independent living, equality between men and women, respect for difference and acceptance of persons with disabilities as part of human diversity and humanity, and respect for the evolving capacities of children with disabilities, and respect for the right of children with disabilities to preserve their identities.[51]

The first relevant debate that quickly arose was with regard to the type of Convention that delegations where willing to adopt. Some delegations where supportive of a Convention including only substantive rights, while others where more inclined to adopt a Convention principally based on a non-discrimination approach, in order to ensure an equal treatment on the enjoyment and exercise of human rights without reference to any particular policy or subject-area. Finally, a third and more successful position, supported the adoption of a Convention including a mixed formula. As we will see, in the final text prevailed the idea that a rights approach would require the adjustment of existing relevant human rights treaty provisions to the specific context of disability. That is to say, that despite reaffirming the existing human rights already enshrined in treaty law, the new Convention would require the establishment of relevant mechanisms to ensure the full enjoyment of those rights to persons with disabilities on an equal basis with others.

[46] Letter dated 7 October 2005 from the Chairman to all members of the Committee, UN Doc. A/AC.265/2006/1, 14 October 2005.

[47] Seventh Session, 16 January to 3 February 2006. For further details see Report of seventh session UN Doc A/AC.265/2006/2, 13 February 2006.

[48] See Annex II of the Report of the Ad Hoc Committee on a Comprehensive and Integral International Convention on the Protection and Promotion of the Rights and Dignity of Persons with Disabilities on its seventh session, UN Doc. A/AC.265/2006/2, 13 February 2006.

[49] Eighth Session, 14– 25 August and 5 December 2006. For further details see Interim report of the eighth session, UN Doc A/AC.265/2006/4, 1 September 2006) and Final report of the Ad Hoc Committee UN Doc A/61/611, 6 December 2006.

[50] See A Palacios and F Bariffi, *La discapacidad como una cuestión de derechos humanos. Una aproximación a la Convención Internacional sobre los Derechos de las Personas con Discapacidad*, (Cinca, Madrid, 2007).

[51] See Article 3 of the Convention at: Final Report of the Ad Hoc Committee on a Comprehensive and Integral International Convention on the Protection and Promotion of the Rights and Dignity of Persons with Disabilities, UN Doc A/61/611, 6 December 2006.

In relation to the subjects of the Convention, (ie protected persons), from the beginning it was clear amongst delegations that the future instrument would include collectively persons with different kinds of disabilities. In other words, the outcome of the negotiations would result in an international legal body directed to the protection and promotion of the rights of persons with disabilities in general.[52] This did not avoid an intense debate with regard to the definitions of disability and of persons with disability, although it is important to underline that there was consensus that such definitions would have to enshrine the Social Model of disability as was noted in the footnote of the drafted article of definitions which stated that 'if a definition was included, it should be one that reflected the Social Model of disability, rather than the medical model [. . .]'.[53]

Another difficult issue, which was only settled in the final moments before the adoption of the final text was that related to legal capacity. The core of the discussion addressed the aspect of the legal capacity of persons with disabilities, especially in those situations when a person has a limitation or a restriction with regard to adopting a personal decision and therefore, some sort of third-party intervention becomes necessary. While the traditional system –influenced by the medical model—is clearly based on a 'substitution model' (ie the decision-taking of the person with disability is displaced and assumed by a third party), the new paradigm shift towards a human rights perspective based on the intrinsic dignity of all persons—influenced by the Social Model—advocating a 'support model' (ie the decision-taking ability of the persons with disability is not displaced but assisted or guided in a way compatible with the person's autonomy).[54] Although most delegations acknowledged and supported the trend towards this paradigm shift, there were many and deep discrepancies on how to deploy this new model within the emerging instrument.

Employment, for its part, was another issue in which, throughout the negotiation process, it is possible to discern a paradigm shift, and a move towards a Social Model perspective, as some delegations and, above all, NGOs repeatedly advocated the inclusion in a convention of a State obligation to ensure open, inclusive, accessible labour markets and work environments, to persons with disabilities, including the obligation to make reasonable accommodations. Social Model supporters also advocated for the inclusion in the final text, of a State commitment to promote the employment of persons with disabilities in the private sector through appropriate policies and measures, which might include affirmative action programmes, incentives, and other measures.[55]

[52] UN Doc A/AC.265/2004/WG.1, Annex I, p 10. See footnote 12 with regard to the concept of disability in the (first) draft comprehensive and integral international convention on the protection and promotion of the rights and dignity of persons with disabilities which reads:

> Many members of the Working Group emphasized that a convention should protect the rights of all persons with disabilities (i.e. all different types of disabilities) and suggested that the term 'disability' should be defined broadly. Some members were of the view that no definition of 'disability' should be included in the Convention, given the complexity of disability and the risk of limiting the ambit of the Convention. Other delegations pointed to existing definitions used in the international context, including the World Health Organization's International Classification of Functioning, Disability and Health (ICF) [. . .].

[53] *Ibid.*

[54] See Cabra De Luna, Bariffi and Palacios (coord), *Derechos Humanos de las Personas con Discapacidad: la convención Internacional de las Naciones Unidas*, (Editorial Centro de Estudios Ramón Areces, Madrid, 2007).

[55] *Ibid.*

Finally and despite all other contentious issues, it is important to underline the negotiation's debates on the matter of education. The debate focused on a dispute between inclusive or special education. While some delegations advocated the need to ensure an inclusive education system as a general rule, but leaving aside the special needs of persons with specific visual and hearing disabilities, which usually demands certain special educational environments; others defended the adoption of an inclusive educational system without any exception. As we will see, the final text sees advantage in inclusive educational systems, while keeping some special educational elements.[56]

Scope and Definitions

The scope or purpose of the Convention is:

> to promote, protect and ensure the full and equal enjoyment of all human rights and fundamental freedoms by all persons with disabilities, and to promote respect for their inherent dignity.[57]

In this manner, and applying the non-discrimination principle, one of the fundamental objectives of the Convention was to *adapt* the rules pertaining to the existing human rights treaties, to the specific context of disability. This required the establishment of mechanisms that guarantee the exercise of such rights on behalf of persons with disabilities, without discrimination and with equality of opportunities. The objectives of the instrument were the subject of debate during the process of creating the Convention, and as Gerard Quinn[58] notes, the object of the Treaty could have been different. A Convention containing only the development of substantive rights, such as the Convention on the Rights of the Child, could have been created, or simply a Convention containing a series of prescriptions against discrimination in order to ensure the equality of treatments in an abstract manner, without referring to any particular policy or area. The formula which was ultimately adopted within the Convention, however, was mixed, or integrated. The Treaty deals with protection against discrimination, and at the same time provides tools so that the enjoyment and exercise of the rights of persons with disabilities is not just a written statement, but its results can be applicable in each particular right or area. Therefore the objective was not to create new rights, but to ensure the usage of the non-discrimination principle with regard to each one of the rights in order that they might be equally be executed by persons with disabilities. Thus, at the time of regulating each right, it was necessary to identify the specific needs that had to be guaranteed so as to adapt such rights to the specific context of disability.

[56] See Article 27 of the Convention at Final report of the Ad Hoc Committee on a Comprehensive and Integral International Convention on the Protection and Promotion of the Rights and Dignity of Persons with Disabilities (A/61/611, 6 December 2006). There were strong disagreements even within the movement of persons with disability. The NGO dealing with disability from a general perspective was supportive of an inclusive system. The NGO representing the group of hearing disabled sign language users was supportive of special education. Lastly, the NGO representing the group of visual-hearing disabled was supportive of a formula that would allow the option to have special or inclusive education. For further details see: Cabra De Luna, Bariffi and Palacios, (coord), *Derechos Humanos de las Personas con Discapacidad*, above, n 54, at 17–56.

[57] UN Convention on the Rights of Persons with Disabilities, above, n 2, art 1.

[58] G Quinn, *The UN Human Rights of Persons with Disabilities Treaty. A Blueprint for Disability Law & Policy Research and Reform*, Conference given in Dublin, National Disability Authority, Annual Research Conference, on 16 November 2006.

With regard to definitions, Article 1 of the Convention defines disability. Nevertheless, for a proper interpretation of that provision, not only must Article 1 be read but also the Convention's Preamble so as to give context to the object and purpose of the treaty. The Convention acknowledges on the one hand, within its Preamble, that:

> disability is an evolving concept and that disability results from the interaction between persons with impairments and attitudinal and environmental barriers that hinders their full and effective participation in society on an equal basis with others'[59]

On the other hand, it also understands that, according to Article 1:

> Persons with disabilities include those who have long-term physical, mental, intellectual or sensory impairments which in interaction with various barriers may hinder their full and effective participation in society on an equal basis with others.[60]

From these provisions it can be understood that there is a social disability model implied when assuming that disability results from interaction with barriers due to attitude and environment. In addition, it can also be asserted that the definition remains open-ended, as it *includes* the mentioned persons, but does not exclude other situations or persons that might emerge or be protected by the domestic laws of the States. In light of the disability Social Model, the provision emphasises two essential issues. First, disability is an evolving concept. It could be added that it is also a cultural concept that varies amongst different cultures and societies.[61] Second, disability is a result of the interaction between the individual limits of the persons, impairments, and the existing barriers in attitudes and environments of society.

It must be said that the Convention establishes a minimum: in relation to the protection purpose of this instrument, the 'persons with disabilities' include those who have long-term physical, mental, intellectual or sensory impairments which, upon interacting with several barriers, may prevent their full and effective participation in society, under the same conditions as others. This does not mean that if a State in its domestic legislation, adopts a broader definition of disability, this would hamper the application of the Convention. On the contrary, it is understood that this Article must be interpreted as a minimum standard, from which can emerge other interpretation that benefits or broadens its field of protection.

With regard to discrimination, the Convention uses the term 'discrimination on the basis of disability' and defines it in Article 2 as such:

> any distinction, exclusion or restriction on the basis of disability which has the purpose or effect of impairing or nullifying the recognition, enjoyment or exercise, on an equal basis with others, of all human rights and fundamental freedoms in the political, economic, social, cultural, civil or any other field. It includes all forms of discrimination, including denial of reasonable accommodation.[62]

[59] UN Convention on the Rights of Persons with Disabilities, above, n 2, Preamble, Item e.

[60] *Ibid*, Art 1, para. 2.

[61] See B Ingstad and S Reynolds White (eds), *Disability and Culture,* (University of California Press, 1995).

[62] UN Convention on the Rights of Persons with Disabilities, above, n 2, Art 2.

According to the Convention, reasonable accommodation means:

> necessary and appropriate modification and adjustments not imposing a disproportionate or undue burden, where needed in a particular case, to ensure to persons with disabilities the enjoyment or exercise on an equal basis with others of all human rights and fundamental freedoms.[63]

This article was debated thoroughly by the Working Group. The majority of NGOs wanted to see reflected in the text a direct link between the failure to adopt reasonable accommodation and the non-discriminatory idea. This is why it was established that not adopting reasonable accommodation is discrimination in and of itself. NGOs sought to have the obligation linked to, but separated from, non-discrimination.[64] Finally, the adopted formula defines discrimination on the basis of disability, as covering all forms of discrimination, including that of denial of reasonable accommodations.

Article 2 should be considered along with Article 5 on Equality and Non-Discrimination, which establishes that:

1. States Parties recognize that all persons are equal before and under the law and are entitled without any discrimination to the equal protection and equal benefit of the law.
2. States Parties shall prohibit all discrimination on the basis of disability and guarantee to persons with disabilities equal and effective legal protection against discrimination on all grounds.
3. In order to promote equality and eliminate discrimination, States Parties shall take all appropriate steps to ensure that reasonable accommodation is provided.
4. Specific measures which are necessary to accelerate or achieve de facto equality of persons with disabilities shall not be considered discrimination under the terms of the present Convention.

Both Article 2, which defines discrimination on the basis of disability, and Article 5, which establishes measures against discrimination on the basis of disability coincide on an essential point. What is forbidden is discrimination 'on the basis of' disability. Therefore, as Gerard Quinn argues, it can be said that such a formulation focuses on the discrimination phenomena and not so much on the peculiarities of the person. This would avoid limiting, as for example Spanish Law does through Law 51/2003,[65] the benefits of anti-discriminatory regulations to certain types or degrees of disability.[66] Likewise, it would mean that persons can be discriminated 'due to' or 'on the basis of' disability, not having a disability themselves, but treated discriminatorily considering they have a disability. An example would be a facial disfigurement, which is not a disability in itself, but the person could be treated as if it were.[67]

Second, Quinn notes that those persons who are susceptible to having a disability are also susceptible to being treated in a discriminatory manner 'due to' or 'on the

[63] *Ibid.*

[64] Documents available at: http://www.un.org/esa/socdev/enable/rights/adhoccom.htm.

[65] Ley 51/2003, de 2 de diciembre, de Igualdad de Oportunidades, No Discriminación y Accesibilidad Universal de las Personas con Discapacidad, (BOE 3 de diciembre de 2003). Available at: http://www.mtas.es/sgas/Discapacidad/ConsejoDisca/Ley51-2003.pdf.

[66] See T Degener, *Definition of Disability*, EU Network of Legal Experts on Disability Discrimination Law, 2004. Available at: http://ec.europa.eu/employment_social/fundamental_rights/pdf/aneval/disabdef.pdf.http://www.europa.eu.int/comm/employment_social/fundamental_rights/pdf/aneval/disabdef.pdf.

[67] *Ibid*, para 77.

basis of' disability, although they do not have it at present. In this case, once again, if the focus is kept on the discrimination phenomena, it makes sense to assert that this category would also fit within the protective framework of anti-discriminatory rights outlined by the Convention. Third, there may be persons without a disability but who work with, or are associated with, persons with disability. This would include, for instance, a mother or father of a boy or girl with disability, who would be looking for a new position in the labour market, or a voluntary role within an institution working with people with HIV/AIDS. Such persons may well be treated in a discriminatory way 'on the basis of' or 'due to' disability, even though they have no disability. Considering the given arguments, it could be said that the Convention adopts a wide approach in relation to the framework protecting the rights to non-discrimination and equal opportunities.

Principles

The following section examines some of the principles enshrined in the Convention, which evidently will be of great importance at the time of either interpreting or applying the Convention provisions and when assessing the rights protected and the obligations established that will be assumed by State Parties at the moment of entry into force of the Convention.

The principles of the Convention are, as noted in Article 3:

(a) Respect for inherent dignity, individual autonomy including the freedom to make one's own choices, and independence of persons;
(b) Non-discrimination;
(c) Full and effective participation and inclusion in society;
(d) Respect for difference and acceptance of persons with disabilities as part of human diversity and humanity;
(e) Equality of opportunity;
(f) Accessibility;
(g) Equality between men and women;
(h) Respect for the evolving capacities of children with disabilities and respect for the right of children with disabilities to preserve their identities.

Item (a) refers to three principles or values that are closely linked—dignity, autonomy and independence—and that could be summarised in the first one (ie dignity). Gerard Quinn invites the consideration of the postulation of human dignity, which incorporates the simple idea that all persons are ends in themselves. In practice, however, Quinn says that most of our societies value human beings for their use value or utility. If this is perceived as diminished or limited, then the value as a human being also tends to decrease.[68] The notion of human dignity is the foundation stone upon which human rights are established. This idea of human dignity should thus reinforce the idea that persons with disability have a role in society, which must be considered absolutely independent from any consideration of social or economic utility. Nevertheless, to consider that persons have a social role independent of their utility might not be clearly justified, either from the modern conception of human dignity or from the claim of the Social Model. Therefore, this topic deserves to be considered in two respects.

[68] G Quinn, 'Next steps –Towards a United Nations Treaty on the Rights of Persons with Disabilities', above, n 41.

The first touches on the same idea of human dignity—typically characterised, since the Renaissance, by a series of features of mankind that would hardly apply to persons with certain types of disabilities.[69] Maybe because this idea of dignity was never characterised without making reference to certain contents, dignity is reduced to certain factors. Thus, it could be said that the justification of dignity was manifest in intelligence (Classic Age), God (Middle Age), nobility (Baroque Period), or finally to be subsumed by to reason and virtue (Modernity). This presents some philosophical problems concerning the way in which idea of dignity in a person whose capacity to reason is questioned is justified.

The second refers to one of the element introduced from the Social Model, which potentially could be contradictory. From the Social Model perspective, it is asserted that persons with disabilities have much to offer society. It would seem that the Social Model falls into the trap it is trying to avoid, when it gives value to persons in accordance with their conditional contribution to society. This does not imply the denial of such a statement, but it simply reinforces the misconception that the human value in itself is separated and independent from any social utility. In other words, persons with disabilities are not equal in dignity due to their capacity for contribution to society, but due to their essence—as being an end in themselves. If this was not so, the main content of the Kantian categorical imperative would be infringed, since if we value the person for his or her contribution to the community, we would be considering the human being as a means and not as an end in itself.[70]

A component of dignity that is intimately related to disability is autonomy, which can be understood as a reserved space without restrictions for the voluntary action of the person. The value of autonomy is based on the previous assumption of a capacity of action and of self-directed behaviour. Therefore it stands on the implicit image of a morally free person. As Rafael de Asis explains, moral freedom would be the referent of rights:

> We propose to define it as an individual utopian moment in which life plans, vital projects, needs satisfaction are performed, conditioned by the social dimension of human activity. Thus, the sense of this moral freedom should be subject to generalisation in a way that all persons should be able to attain it. Accordingly, the goal of social freedom and rights as instruments is to enable the moral subject to reach this moral freedom.[71]

It is evident that one of the key principles of the Social Model, which is clearly reflected in the philosophy related to independent life. In this sense, as Quinn and Degener state, in the context of disability the image of a moral subject sets up at least two important problems.[72]

[69] In this sense, upon performing interesting research on the idea of human dignity from the Philosophy of Law, Gregorio Peces-Barba understands that 'human dignity is formulated from two perspectives . . . a more formal one with a Kantian root, and another more related to contents, with a humanist and renaissance character. By the first one, dignity derives from our decision to show capacity for choosing, from our autonomy; by the second dignity consists in the study of the features that differentiate us from the rest of the animals. They are two complementary perspectives, we could almost say the form and the contents of our value as persons'. In G Peces-Barba, *La dignidad de la persona desde la Filosofía del Derecho*, col Cuadernos 'Bartolomé de las Casas', núm 26, (Dykinson, Madrid, 2003), p 65–66.

[70] I Kant, *The Metaphysics of Morals* (trans Mary J Gregor) (Cambridge, Cambridge Universtiy Press, 1996).

[71] R De Asis Roig, *Sobre el concepto y el fundamento de los derechos: una aproximación dualista*, col. Cuadernos 'Bartolomé de las Casas', núm 17, (Dykinson, Madrid, 2001), p 28.

[72] See G Quinn, G and T Degener, *Human Rights and Disability*, above, n 4.

One is that disability, especially intellectual disability, is generally associated with the lack of capacity to exercise moral freedom. This supposition, it must be said, is based on a pure prejudice or on a very restricted idea of autonomy. In this sense, from the Social Model a wider idea of autonomy is defended, one that does not incline itself to detecting incompetence[73] and thus grants the same importance to the need for an effective protection of the rights and interests of people with intellectual disabilities.[74] The fact that autonomy in certain cases is more restricted does not imply that it should be annulled or ignored. Autonomy is not so much a starting point as an end point; this acknowledges that an individual has limitations in theoretical and practical knowledge. In this sense, as regards persons with intellectual disabilities, it is evident that in many cases the autonomy can be limited, but it is precisely in those cases where the role of the law should be highlighted, guaranteeing the full development of the existing autonomy degree, whatever this may be.

A second difficulty this value faces in the context of disability is that many times society does not take seriously this autonomy of persons with disabilities that have such absolute 'capacity' for the exercise of the moral freedom mentioned. This is the typical case for persons with physical or sensory limitations. On many occasions, their life choices are not considered as deserving of the social support enjoyed by persons without disability. This situation, which seems to start from the consideration that these persons' lives do not deserve the same value, has led to the fact that the material conditions persons with disability need in order to have control over their lives has been ignored. In this sense, Quinn and Degener state that most societies have not carried out what was needed to enable people with disabilities to have the clear freedom to develop fully as moral subjects.[75]

The principle of freedom, which along with dignity, autonomy and independence constituted the principles enshrined in Article 3(a) of the Convention, should be understood as the basis upon which the instrument is interpreted and applied. This principle underlies every one of the rights that the Convention mentions, but it is specially reflected in Article 19, which regulates the right of persons with disabilities to live independently and to be included in community. The Article establishes that States parties:

> [. . .] recognize the equal right of all persons with disabilities to live in the community, with choices equal to others, and shall take effective and appropriate measures to facilitate full enjoyment by persons with disabilities of this right and their full inclusion and participation in the community, including by ensuring that:

[73] As Christian Courtis points out, defining a person only in relation to what he or she can not do, or in relation to his/her limitations, would suppose to label as 'useless or worthless' the entire body of humanity. Nearly every human being has a limitation to carry out some activities: sing, perform maths calculations, orient in an unknown place, run, practise sports, dance, remember data, recite poetry, cook, sew hand work, etc. For most people the actual information regarding their limitations to carry out certain activities is simply irrelevant. However, persons with disabilities have been historically characterized by the limitations they face in caring out certain activities, instead of putting the emphasis in the activities they can carry out without difficulties. See C Courtis, 'Discapacidad e inclusión social: retos teóricos y desafíos prácticos. Algunos comentarios a partir de la Ley 51/2003', above, n 13, at 8.

[74] See T Degener G Quinn, *A survey of international, comparative and regional Disability Law Reform*, above, n 9, at p 13.

[75] *Ibid*, at, p 13. The authors assert with irony that one issue is to have the possibility to study astrophysics regardless of the disability, and another issue is to be able to do it if that person does not have available accessible transport to use.

(a) Persons with disabilities have the opportunity to choose their place of residence and where and with whom they live on an equal basis with others and are not obliged to live in a particular living arrangement;
(b) Persons with disabilities have access to a range of in-home, residential and other community support services, including personal assistance necessary to support living and inclusion in the community, and to prevent isolation or segregation from the community;
(c) Community services and facilities for the general population are available on an equal basis to persons with disabilities and are responsive to their needs.

The Article foresees, among other issues, a principle which is closely related to the idea of human dignity and autonomy, and that is shaped into the right of persons with disabilities to choose their place of residence and where and with whom they live, with the appropriate community services and facilities.[76] This can be summed up by in the idea of independent life. Through the foundations of this principle, an answer has been given to one of the main claims of persons with disabilities—the opportunity to be part of decision-making related to their own lives. In this sense, persons with disabilities are no longer seen as passive subjects, or as subjects of paternalist policies that try to segregate them from decisions impacting their lives. The claim of persons with disabilities also originating in the Independent Life Movement, which seeks to have persons with disabilities be the author of their own decisions. The motto 'Nothing about us without us', which originated with this mode of independent life, sums up this position.[77]

The clauses (b), (c), (d), and (e) embrace four principles: Non-Discrimination, Full and effective participation and inclusion in society, Respect for difference and acceptance of persons with disabilities as part of human diversity and humanity, and Equality of opportunity. These four principles contain different aspects that can be reduced to one idea: that of equality. One of the fundamental premises of the Social Model of disability is the idea that everybody not only has intrinsic value, but also are intrinsically equal in value, beyond any physical, mental, intellectual, or sensorial difference. That does not mean that there are no differences between persons, rather that a society that truly respects the principle of equality is one that adopts an inclusive criterion regarding human differences, and takes it into consideration in a positive way.[78] In this regard, one of the essential arguments used by the defenders of the Social Model is based on the fact that persons with disability are socially oppressed. As we know, the term 'social oppression' is usually used in the analyses of groups that in a greater or lesser manner are systematically discriminated against.[79]

Here we have to consider several complex questions that could be summarised by asserting that persons with disabilities are socially excluded. It means, among other things, being unable to participate in a great number of activities that sustain social

[76] Some people require the assistance of another person in the day-to-day activities such as personal care, physiological needs, including sexual activities, and nursery care, dressing and undressing, shopping, home errands, etc. But the services of personal assistance support also activities outside home, such as studying, working, or leisure or sports.

[77] See JI Charlton, *Nothing About Us Without Us: Disability Oppression and Empowerment*, (Berkeley, University of California Press, 1998).

[78] See T Degener and G Quinn, *A survey of international, comparative and regional Disability Law Reform,* above, n 9.

[79] Ie, inter alia, women in relation to men, black people in relation to white people, homosexual people in relation to heterosexual people, older people in relation to young people, and people with disability in relation to people without disability.

life, and eliminates the normal flow of everyday life. And that is because all the means of access to the structures of daily life, education, work, family, social interaction, etc. are established mostly in relation to the prevailing standard—in this particular case, persons without disability. Thus, as adaptation is not usually anticipated to the 'deviations or differences' as regards the selected norm to follow, the difference helps to establish subtle—sometimes not so subtle—discrimination.[80] Lately, the immediate answer given by law to these questions has been addressed through anti-discriminatory legal formulae. While there exist different ways to consider the right to equality, within the context of the Convention agreement on this right was reached as meaning equality of opportunities.

The Convention assumes through its principles, and in the regulation of the right it enshrines, a broad conception of equality, that does not remain one of simple non-discriminating treatment (ie formal equality), but it assumes equality of opportunity, which in many cases requires active measures (ie material equality). The latter implies respect for differences and acceptance of persons with disabilities as part of the diversity of the human condition—which necessarily implies the adoption of politics of recognition,[81] approaching participation with a total and effective inclusion in the society. In this respect Mike Oliver does well to note that while the idea that the old vision of integration considers that those people who are different must be accepted and tolerated by the rest, the new vision of integration as inclusion is sustained by a completely different philosophy, which may be called one of personal identity. From this point of view, it is clear that difference should not only be tolerated and accepted, but it should be positively praised. To reach this goal, according to Oliver, not only is a legal framework necessary, but also the reinforcement of that framework with moral and political fervour to ensure its validity.[82] Thus, the previous approaches to disability were concerned with allowing excluded groups to integrate 'into the game', while a new vision conceives or creates a 'new game', in which nobody would be excluded beforehand.

The next principle, which is closely related to that of equality, is the universal accessibility principle. The Convention notes this in Article 3(f) and expands on it as a right in Article 9. We will come back to this point later, but, it is worth at this stage pointing out how important it is that universal accessibility is manifest, not only as a right but also as a principle of the Convention, since the principle becomes an unavoidable condition to exercise the rights, with equality of opportunities, by everybody, and finally to achieve human dignity and free development of the personality. That being said, the Convention assumes that disability is a complex phenomenon, and that integration is premised on social factors with its resulting barriers yet; arguably, universal accessibility becomes one of the most apt ways to prevent disablement. Thus, the prevention of disabilities should be understood as much as by what it prevents—traffic accidents, for instance—as for the avoidance of the construction of inaccessible buildings. Evidently, because of the subject the Convention regulates and protects, the prevention we are interested in as established at Article 9 corresponds to the second type of prevention, ie by means of accessibility. Nevertheless, it should be recalled that

[80] T Degener and G Quinn, *A survey of international, comparative and regional Disability Law Reform,* above, n 9, p 15.

[81] On the subject, see IM Young, *Justice and the politics of difference,* above, n 13.

[82] M Oliver, *Understanding Disability. From theory to practice,* above, n 14, p 89.

the construction of inaccessible buildings, following the previous discussion on the denial of reasonable accommodation, is a form of discrimination.

A further principle established by Article 3(g) is equality between men and women. For many years, women with disabilities have been invisible within the UN human rights system; as a result, there was no protection afforded to them in the Convention on the Elimination of All Forms of Discrimination against Women.[83] Thus the inclusion of women with disabilities in the International Convention on The Rights of Persons with Disabilities was an important step. Fortunately, the Convention adopted a double approach in relation to the situation of women with disabilities. On the one hand, a specific article on the subject is included and, on the other hand, a mainstreamed gender approach throughout the instrument was sought, though it can be said that this was not achieved in all the articles of the Convention.

The advantage to having a specific article included in the Convention was to ensure that the States remained attuned to the most important gender issues and the specific actions designed to achieve such a goal. The risk, as some delegations argued, was having the same results as with the Convention on the Rights of the Child where States interpreted the provisions of Article 23 as the sole provision addressing and protecting children with disabilities at the expense of the application of the rest of the instrument to such children. The specific provision in the Convention touching on women with disabilities is Article 6:

1. States Parties recognize that women and girls with disabilities are subject to multiple discrimination, and in this regard shall take measures to ensure the full and equal enjoyment by them of all human rights and fundamental freedoms.
2. States Parties shall take all appropriate measures to ensure the full development, advancement and empowerment of women, for the purpose of guaranteeing them the exercise and enjoyment of the human rights and fundamental freedoms set out in the present Convention.

In this Article it is recognised, among other issues, that multiple forms of discrimination are suffered by women with disabilities, and as a result of the adoption of the measures, States parties are required to guarantee the full enjoyment of equal conditions of human rights and fundamental freedoms.

Beyond the specific Article, as has been mentioned, the Convention adopts a mainstream gender approach when guaranteeing certain rights, as with regard to awareness-raising wherein Article 8 requires that 'States Parties undertake to adopt immediate, effective and appropriate measures' which include the combating of 'stereotypes, prejudices and harmful practices relating to persons with disabilities, including those based on sex and age, in all areas of life'. This article is important because of the prejudices that are often present regarding women with disabilities, their individual autonomy and their private life, such as those related to their sexuality, reproduction and the design of their professional lives. Likewise, Article 16 regarding freedom from exploitation, violence and abuse mandates that:

1. States Parties shall take all appropriate legislative, administrative, social, educational and other measures to protect persons with disabilities, both within and outside the home, from all forms of exploitation, violence and abuse, including their gender-based aspects.

[83] GA Res 34/180, 34 UN GAOR Supp (No 46) at 193, UN Doc A/34/46 (1979).

But further mandates that:

> 2. States Parties shall also take all appropriate measures to prevent all forms of exploitation, violence and abuse by ensuring, inter alia, appropriate forms of gender- and age-sensitive assistance and support for persons with disabilities and their families and caregivers, including through the provision of information and education on how to avoid, recognize and report instances of exploitation, violence and abuse. States Parties shall ensure that protection services are age-, gender- and disability-sensitive.
>
> [. . .]
>
> 4. States Parties shall take all appropriate measures to promote the physical, cognitive and psychological recovery, rehabilitation and social reintegration of persons with disabilities who become victims of any form of exploitation, violence or abuse, including through the provision of protection services. Such recovery and reintegration shall take place in an environment that fosters the health, welfare, self-respect, dignity and autonomy of the person and takes into account gender- and age-specific needs.
> 5. States Parties shall put in place effective legislation and policies, including women- and child-focused legislation and policies, to ensure that instances of exploitation, violence and abuse against persons with disabilities are identified, investigated and, where appropriate, prosecuted.

Further examples of mainstreaming gender issues are manifest in Article 25 dealing with health, which reads, inter alia:

> States Parties recognize that persons with disabilities have the right to the enjoyment of the highest attainable standard of health without discrimination on the basis of disability. States Parties shall take all appropriate measures to ensure access for persons with disabilities to health services that are gender-sensitive, including health-related rehabilitation. In particular, States Parties shall:
>
> a) Provide persons with disabilities with the same range, quality and standard of free or affordable health care and programmes as provided to other persons, including in the area of sexual and reproductive health and population-based public health programmes. [. . .]

This Article was controversial, mainly due to sexual and reproductive health, which proved to be a very sensitive subject for some delegations. The primary discussion was provoked by the sentence 'sexual and reproductive health services', which ultimately was removed from the text of the Convention.[84] Yet the Chair clarified that the objective of the Article was to eliminate discrimination, not to create or recognise a new right.[85] The goal was, therefore, the elimination of discrimination on grounds of disabilities, but there was no intention of creating a new right to that service; instead the provision is meant to ensure their availability and enjoyment for users of such a

[84] UN Convention on the Rights of Persons with Disabilities, above, n 2, art 25.

[85] See footnote 4 in the Report of the Ad Hoc Committee on a Comprehensive and Integral International Convention on the Protection and Promotion of the Rights and Dignity of Persons with Disabilities on its seventh session, (UN Doc A/AC.265/2006/2, 13 February 2006) which reads as follows: 'The Ad Hoc Committee notes that the use of the phrase 'sexual and reproductive health services' would not constitute recognition of any new international law obligations or human rights. The Ad Hoc Committee understands draft paragraph (a) to be a non-discrimination provision that does not add to, or alter, the right to health as contained in article 12 of the International Covenant on Economic, Social and Cultural Rights or article 24 of the Convention on the Rights of the Child. Rather, the effect of paragraph (a) would be to require States Parties to ensure that where health services are provided, they are provided without discrimination on the basis of disability'.

service who are persons with disabilities of such a service, whenever they exist and on an equal basis with others. The Ad Hoc Committee understood that this was a non-discriminatory provision that neither added to nor modified the right to health recognised in Article 24 of the International Covenant on Economic, Social and Cultural Rights, or Article 24 of the Convention on Rights of the Child. Its effect was rather that States would insure whenever a health service is given, that it be provided without discrimination on grounds of disabilities. These services, it should be noted, are generally denied to women with disabilities as such women are frequently considered asexual.

One further substantive right should be mentioned in the context of mainstreaming of gender equality and that is Article 28: Adequate standard of living and social protection, which reads in part:

> 2. States Parties recognize the right of persons with disabilities to social protection and to the enjoyment of that right without discrimination on the basis of disability, and shall take appropriate steps to safeguard and promote the realization of this right, including measures:
>
> [. . .]
>
> b) To ensure access by persons with disabilities, in particular women and girls with disabilities and older persons with disabilities, to social protection programmes and poverty reduction programmes.

Such lack of access to social protection or poverty reduction programmes creates multiple difficulties and barriers for women and girls with disabilities in different situations. One of those is related to literacy and education. Many parents, incapable of seeing a future for their daughters with disabilities as women, mothers and workers, do not see advantage in sending them to school. As a result, the number of illiterate women with disabilities is higher than that of men.[86] Also, in relation to professional training and employment, it is well known that 75 per cent of women with disabilities in the developed world and near 100 per cent in developing countries are excluded from the employment market. As a result, in fact, most women with disabilities live in poverty.[87]

Finally, one final provision regarding gender mainstreaming should be mentioned, which touches on the procedures regarding the implementation of the Convention, and that is with regard to Article 34 and the make up of the Committee on the Rights of Persons with Disabilities. Article 34 of the Convention requires, in part that:

> 4. The members of the Committee shall be elected by States Parties, consideration being given to equitable geographical distribution, representation of the different forms of civilization and of the principal legal systems, balanced gender representation and participation of experts with disabilities. (. . .).

The Substantial Rights

Turning now from the principles enshrined in the Convention to the substantive rights, the text enshrines a series of rights and principles that, irrespective of their

[86] See A Bruce, S Quinlivan and T Degener, 'Gender and disability: the Convention on the Elimination of all Forms of Discrimination against Women', in G Quinn and T Degener, *Human Rights and Disability,* above, n 4.

[87] *Ibid.* See also, ML Belaza, *Discrimination against women with disabilities*, (Council of Europe, 2003).

autonomy as individual articles, form an interrelated normative core requiring a systematic and mainstreamed approach for its proper comprehension, and above all for their effective enforcement. Thus, in the following section a description of the treaty provisions is put forward which groups together the rights enshrined in the Convention and divides them into five subject-areas, namely: equality rights, protective rights, liberty and personal autonomy rights, participation rights and basic social rights.

Equality Rights

The substantive equality rights found in the Convention include Article 5 (Equality and non-discrimination); Article 9 (Accessibility); Article 12 (Equal recognition before the law); and Article 13 (Equal access to justice). If we keep in mind that the main purpose of the Convention is to promote, protect and ensure the full and equal enjoyment of all human rights and fundamental freedoms by all persons with disabilities, and to promote respect for their inherent dignity, it is easy to see why the right to equality constitutes the core of the Convention. The main provision about equality and non-discrimination found in Article 5(1) recognises the so-called 'equality under the law' or 'formal equality':

> 1. States Parties recognize that all persons are equal before and under the law and are entitled without any discrimination to the equal protection and equal benefit of the law.

Immediately following this provision, the Convention goes beyond the acknowledgment of the formal equality by establishing a safeguard against real and substantial discrimination in a provision which should clearly inspires the rest of the legal text:

> 2. States Parties shall prohibit all discrimination on the basis of disability and guarantee to persons with disabilities equal and effective legal protection against discrimination on all grounds.

Evidence of the mainstreamed application of this provision is the fact that the Convention not only establishes a general prohibition of non-discrimination, but it establishes a specific non-discrimination clause on the basis of disability among a number of provisions of the Convention.[88] Likewise, the next paragraph recognises that, in certain circumstances, and in order to achieve real or substantial equality, States Parties must promote the adoption of reasonable accommodation:

> 3. In order to promote equality and eliminate discrimination, States Parties shall take all appropriate steps to ensure that reasonable accommodation is provided.

Including an express reference to 'reasonable accommodation'—a concept of paramount importance within the disability context—is critical. Unfortunately, however, the definition leaves out, or at least does not expressly mention, a similar reference in relation to accessibility. Last, paragraph 5 recognises the legality of what is called

[88] See Art 2 about definitions; Art 4 para 1(b) about general obligations; Art 23 para 1 about respect for home and the family; Art 24 paras 1 and 5 about education; Art 25(e) and (f) about health; Art 27 para 1(a) about work and employment; Art 28 paras 1 and 2 about adequate standard of living and social protection; and Article 29(b) about participation in political and public life (UN Convention on the Rights of Persons with Disabilities, above, n 2).

'affirmative action measures' or 'inverse discrimination', which allows the State to address long-term discrimination by special programmes targeted specifically to people with disability.

> 4. Specific measures which are necessary to accelerate or achieve de facto equality of persons with disabilities shall not be considered discrimination under the terms of the present Convention.

Article 9, Accessibility, refers to access in its broadest sense including the environment, communication and informed attitudes, as the essential basis from which to achieve real equality for persons with disabilities. By creating a universally accessible environment it creates the opportunity to live in an inclusive society, and removes discriminatory barriers as identified in the Social Model wherein *the environment disables the person*. Consequently, the Convention devotes an article to addressing accessibility, which is defined broadly as:

> 1. To enable persons with disabilities to live independently and participate fully in all aspects of life, States Parties shall take appropriate measures to ensure to persons with disabilities access, on an equal basis with others, to the physical environment, to transportation, to information and communications, including information and communications technologies and systems, and to other facilities and services open or provided to the public, both in urban and in rural areas. (. . .).

The provision goes on to comprehensively outline measures to adopt in order to achieve full accessibility, including the identification and elimination of obstacles and barriers in buildings, roads, transportation and other indoor and outdoor facilities; including schools, housing, medical facilities and workplaces; provision of information, communications and other services; including electronic services and emergency services; in both public and private environments. It also requires the adoption of communication measures, such as signage in Braille and easy-to-read and understandable formats; and measures such as the provision of live assistance and intermediaries, including guides, readers and professional sign language interpreters, to facilitate accessibility to buildings and other facilities open to the public. Finally, Article 9 acknowledges that this requires an active role by States in promoting, monitoring and implementing minimum standards and guidelines for the accessibility of facilities and services; the provision of training for stakeholders on accessibility; promotion of access for persons with disabilities to new information and the efficient availability of communication technologies, including the Internet; and to promote other appropriate forms of assistance and support to persons with disabilities to ensure their access to information.

A further provision under the rubrics of Equality Rights is Article 12—Equal recognition before the law. The legal capacity issue arose as one of the most controversial issues throughout the negotiations, even jeopardising the final adoption of the text.[89] The controversy involved on the one side those States supporting a full recognition of both acting and legal capacity, represented basically by the European Union, and on the other hand those States supporting the non-inclusion of an express reference to the capacity to act, represented by an important number of Islamic countries, China and

[89] For further details see A Palacios and F Bariffi, *La discapacidad como una cuestión de derechos humanos. Una aproximación a la Convención Internacional sobre los Derechos de las Personas con Discapacidad*, above, n 50, pp 104–106.

Russia. The dispute was settled at the time of the adoption of the text by the Ad Hoc Committee, by the insertion of a footnote in Article 12 which reads as follows: 'In Arabic, Chinese and Russian, the term "legal capacity" refers to "legal capacity for rights", rather than "legal capacity to act". Fortunately the final adoption of the text by the General Assembly omitted the footnote, giving rise to a pioneering and important universal provision for persons with disabilities. This provision imposes obligations on States with regard to the recognition of the legal capacity of persons with disability which, in many cases, will require domestic legislative review.

The rule established by Article 12 implies a paradigm shift in the embracing of a model regarding legal capacity of persons with disability, especially in situations where the person has a restriction or limitation of decision-taking and therefore some sort of third party intervention is required. While the traditional practice tends towards a 'substitution model', the human rights approach—based on the intrinsic dignity of persons with disability—demands a 'support model'. Thus the first part of Article 12 stands on the equal recognition of the legal capacity between persons with or without disabilities:

> 1. States Parties reaffirm that persons with disabilities have the right to recognition everywhere as persons before the law.
> 2. States Parties shall recognize that persons with disabilities enjoy legal capacity on an equal basis with others in all aspects of life.

Second, the provision establishes a support system for the decision-taking of persons with disability:

> 3. States Parties shall take appropriate measures to provide access by persons with disabilities to the support they may require in exercising their legal capacity.

At the same time it establishes a set of safeguards meant to prevent situations of abuse:

> 4. States Parties shall ensure that all measures that relate to the exercise of legal capacity provide for appropriate and effective safeguards to prevent abuse in accordance with international human rights law. Such safeguards shall ensure that measures relating to the exercise of legal capacity respect the rights, will and preferences of the person, are free of conflict of interest and undue influence, are proportional and tailored to the person's circumstances, apply for the shortest time possible and are subject to regular review by a competent, independent and impartial authority or judicial body. The safeguards shall be proportional to the degree to which such measures affect the person's rights and interests.

Finally the provision ensures, at least from a legal perspective, that all persons with disability have access to certain basic patrimonial rights essential to achieve equality of opportunities for persons with disabilities in society.

> 5. Subject to the provisions of this article, States Parties shall take all appropriate and effective measures to ensure the equal right of persons with disabilities to own or inherit property, to control their own financial affairs and to have equal access to bank loans, mortgages and other forms of financial credit, and shall ensure that persons with disabilities are not arbitrarily deprived of their property.

The final substantive provision touching on equality rights is Article 13, which speaks of equal access to justice. As regards the participation of persons with disability on an equal basis with others in the access to justice, the Convention offers a set of provisions designed to ensure the participation of persons with disabilities, in all instances, as both direct and indirect participants. Paragraph one seeks to support effective access to justice through provision of procedural and age-appropriate accommodations. Paragraph two for its part, establishes the important provision and adoption of measures for the training of persons and officials working in the administration of justice.

Protective Rights

The Convention contains a set of provisions with the main object of ensuring an adequate and specific level of protection of persons with disabilities. These provisions rely on the premise that in all the aspects regulated by the Convention dealing with protective rights, there is a situation of greater vulnerability or risk for persons with disability. These include Article 10 (Protection of life); Article 11 (Protection from situations of risk and humanitarian emergencies); Article 16 (Protection from exploitation, violence and abuse); Article 15 (Protection from torture or cruel, inhuman or degrading treatment or punishment); Article 17 (Protection of the integrity of the person); Article 22 (Protection of privacy); and Article 23 (Protection of home and the family).

With regard to Article 10, Protection of Life; while the right to life has a universal character, the Convention finds it necessary to insert an express reference in the text: 'States Parties reaffirm that every human being has the inherent right to life and shall take all necessary measures to ensure its effective enjoyment by persons with disabilities on an equal basis with others'. The main support towards this provision in the drafting process came from the organisations of civil society which alleged that the right to life, even though it has a universal recognition, is too often denied on the basis of the existence of a disability.[90] Therefore, this apparent duplicated reference in an international human rights instrument to the right to life acquires particular importance in the context of disability. If we take into account that there are still societies or cultures in which disability is considered a godly punishment, and therefore the elimination or denial of a quality of life of persons with disabilities is justifiable, or in those legislations where abortion is allowed when the foetus is known to have a disability, and is not allowed in other situations.

Article 11 speaks of protection from situations of risk and humanitarian emergencies. Statistically, it is clear that in extraordinary situations such as man-made or natural disasters, persons with disability are severely affected or placed in a higher level of vulnerability than others, and this demands the adoption of special measures in order to assure specific protection.[91] Article 17, for its part, seeks to protect the

[90] See for instance the EDF (European Disability Forum) Contribution to the Second Ad Hoc Committee in relation to the right to life: 'Current developments in population demography, ethics and medical technology present increasing challenges to the right to life for disabled people. Prenatal diagnosis aiming to prevent the birth of persons with disabilities and dangerous developments in the field of euthanasia, will require a special attention in the future UN Convention'. Available at: http://www.un.org/esa/socdev/enable/rights/contrib-edfvision.htm; also the Statement of the International Disability Alliance for 2nd Ad Hoc Committee Session asserting that: 'The lives of people with disabilities are threatened e.g. by denial of the necessities of life such as food and water, shelter, medical treatment (or conversely by the imposition of unwanted medical treatment) and eugenic threats'. Available at: http://www.un.org/esa/socdev/enable/rights/contrib-ida.htm.

[91] Article 11 reads: 'States Parties shall take, in accordance with their obligations under international law, including international humanitarian law and international human rights law, all necessary measures to ensure the protection and safety of persons with disabilities in situations of risk, including situations of armed conflict, humanitarian emergencies and the occurrence of natural disasters'.

integrity of the person of those with disabilities by the following provision: 'Every person with disabilities has a right to respect for his or her physical and mental integrity on an equal basis with others'. While having broad application, this article reinforces the idea that relying on others for personal care requires that it is provided in such a way as to protect the dignity of the person. Article 15 looks to provide individual protection from torture or cruel, inhuman or degrading treatment or punishment as like in the previous case, persons with disabilities require special protection from such physical abuse by the State. The importance of this right depends on the recognition of situations in which the lack of attention to the specific needs of persons with disability can be regarded as a degrading or inhuman treatment, eg detention of a person with disability where the person is not allowed to use a wheelchair, or an essential communicating device. Moreover, the provision acknowledges the possible tortuous or degrading situations in which persons with disability may be involved as a consequence of medical treatment or scientific experimentation.

Article 16 has been considered with regard to gender mainstreaming, but the provision is meant in essence to protect persons with disabilities from exploitation, violence and abuse. The circumstances of people with disability and in particular their reliance on their families, services or institutions, often places them at higher risk of exploitation, violence or abuse. Therefore, the Convention devotes special attention to the establishment of measures of prevention:

> 1. States Parties shall take all appropriate legislative, administrative, social, educational and other measures to protect persons with disabilities, both within and outside the home, from all forms of exploitation, violence and abuse, including their gender-based aspects.

The Article goes further by establishing a set of safeguards to avoid or prevent situations of abuse:

> 2. States Parties shall also take all appropriate measures to prevent all forms of exploitation, violence and abuse by ensuring, inter alia, appropriate forms of gender- and age-sensitive assistance and support for persons with disabilities and their families and caregivers, including through the provision of information and education on how to avoid, recognize and report instances of exploitation, violence and abuse. States Parties shall ensure that protection services are age-, gender- and disability-sensitive.

The need to effectively monitor facilities and programmes by independent authorities is recognised. Paragraph 4 requires the need to support the recovery, rehabilitation and social reintegration of persons with disabilities who become victims of any form of abuse. This area is often overlooked, and requires that counsellors among others develop specific skills in the areas of communication. Paragraph 5, for its part, speaks of effective measures in the identification, investigation and prosecution of instances of exploitation, violence or abuse.

Beyond protecting the physical person the Convention provides at Article 22 protection of privacy, and at Article 23 protection of home and the family. With regard to Article 22, no persons with disabilities, regardless of place of residence or living arrangements, shall be subjected to arbitrary or unlawful interference with his or her privacy, family, home or correspondence or other types of communication or to unlawful attacks on his or her honour and reputation. For such purposes, persons with disabilities shall have the right to be legally protected against such interference or attacks. Further on, the provision requires States parties to take specific measures to ensure the privacy of persons with disability: 'States Parties shall protect the privacy of personal, health and rehabilitation information of persons with disabilities on an equal basis with others'.

As for Article 23, it was especially controversial during the negotiation process on religious grounds.[92] The *chapeau* of Article 23 stresses that States parties shall take effective and appropriate measures to eliminate discrimination against persons with disabilities in all matters relating to marriage, family, parenthood and relationships, on an equal basis with others. Such measures shall ensure the rights of persons with disabilities:

(a) [. . .] who are of marriageable age to marry and to found a family on the basis of free and full consent of the intending spouses is recognized;
(b) [. . .] to decide freely and responsibly on the number and spacing of their children and to have access to age-appropriate information, reproductive and family planning education are recognized, and the means necessary to enable them to exercise these rights are provided;
(c) [. . .] including children, retain their fertility on an equal basis with others.

Additionally the text requires State parties to guarantee the right and responsibilities of persons with disabilities with regard to guardianship, wardship, trusteeship, adoption of children or similar institutions, ensuring in all these cases appropriate assistance to persons with disabilities in the performance of their child-rearing responsibilities. Such support has not always been available and led to the undermining of respect for the home and family of people with disabilities. Notably, this provision recognises an important set of rules regarding the protection of children with disability. State parties shall ensure:

3. [. . .] that children with disabilities have equal rights with respect to family life. With a view to realizing these rights, and to prevent concealment, abandonment, neglect and segregation of children with disabilities, State Parties shall undertake to provide early and comprehensive information, services and support to children with disabilities and their families.
4. ensure that a child shall not be separated from his or her parents against their will, except when competent authorities subject to judicial review determine, in accordance with applicable law and procedures, that such separation is necessary for the best interests of the child. In no case shall a child be separated from parents on the basis of a disability of either the child or one or both of the parents.
5. where the immediate family is unable to care for a child with disabilities, undertake every effort to provide alternative care within the wider family, and failing that, within the community in a family setting.

Liberty and Personal Autonomy Rights

Another cornerstone of the rights of persons with disability is formed by a framework of rights and measures directed to ensure the liberty and personal autonomy of

[92] This was mainly motivated by the inclusion in the Draft text of a reference to right of persons with disabilities to 'experience their sexuality'. See Compilation of proposals received from Government delegations electronically, during the Eight Session of the Ad-Hoc Committee (Revised as of 23 August 2006) in relation to article 23 'Respect for home and the family'. Available at: http://www.un.org/esa/socdev/enable/rights/ahc8docs/ahc8govcomp10.doc.

persons with disabilities, and this usually requires the adoption of positive measures by the State and society. That is to say that while traditionally the right to liberty has been regarded in terms of State or social passivity or abstention, through the perspective of the equality and non-discrimination principles this right rather requires an active role by the State that needs to adopt measures allowing for the exercise of this right to equality of conditions with others. These include Article 14 (Liberty and security of the person); Article 18 (Liberty of movement and nationality); Article 19 (Living independently and being included in the community); and Article 20 (Personal mobility).

Turning first to Article 14—Liberty and security of the person—as mentioned previously, if an accessible environment is not ensured, or if proper reasonable accommodations are not provided, the liberty and security of persons with disabilities will likely be jeopardised. Thus, persons with disability all too often find themselves constrained to live in government residences or institutions, without a real assessment of how this confinement affects the person's liberty, or if such confinement takes place in real conditions of liberty of choice. The provisions of Article 14 read:

> 1. States Parties shall ensure that persons with disabilities, on an equal basis with others:
>
>   (a) Enjoy the right to liberty and security of person;
>   (b) Are not deprived of their liberty unlawfully or arbitrarily, and that any deprivation of liberty is in conformity with the law, and that the existence of a disability shall in no case justify a deprivation of liberty.

Likewise this provision demands that, in situations of legitimate deprivation of liberty of a person with disability, his/her specific needs are taken into account and entitled to guarantees in accordance with the principles noted in the Convention, including that of reasonable accommodation.

Within the framework of provisions designed to ensure personal liberty, the Convention requires, under Article 18, that States parties recognise the right of persons with disability to liberty of movement, to freedom to choose their residence and to a nationality. For such purposes, the provision ensures that persons with disability have the right to acquire and change nationality and are not deprived of their nationality arbitrarily or on the basis of disability. It also insists that people with disability are not deprived of their ability to obtain, possess and utilise documentation of their nationality, or to utilise relevant processes such as immigration proceedings, that may be needed to facilitate exercise of the right to liberty of movement; that they are free to leave any country, and not deprived of the right to enter their own country.

The third liberty which can be grouped under the auspices of 'Liberty and Personal Autonomy Rights' is found at Article 19 which speaks of 'living independently and being included in the community'. An important step towards the fulfilment of the liberty and personal autonomy of persons with disability is the possibility of independent life. This obviously connects the right with the rest of the provisions of the Convention that together form a set of rules directed towards the full realisation of the right to liberty and personal autonomy. If we assume that the natural places for persons with disabilities are not governmental institutions or residences but their own homes, and if we connect this assumption with the rest of the rights enshrined in the Convention, improved autonomy and a proper social inclusion are achieved. Hence, the Convention recognises the right of persons with disability to live in the community, with equal options like everyone else, and for that reason requires that:

(a) Persons with disabilities have the opportunity to choose their place of residence and where and with whom they live on an equal basis with others and are not obliged to live in a particular living arrangement;
(b) Persons with disabilities have access to a range of in-home, residential and other community support services, including personal assistance necessary to support living and inclusion in the community, and to prevent isolation or segregation from the community;
(c) Community services and facilities for the general population are available on an equal basis to persons with disabilities and are responsive to their needs.

Following on this, Article 20 deals with personal mobility, which is another essential element which moves towards an adequate fulfilment of the right to liberty and personal autonomy of persons with disability. It is an acknowledgment of the need to ensure a level of personal mobility that would allow such persons to attain the maximum possible independence. For these purposes, the Convention imposes upon State Parties the obligation to take measures pointing at:

(a) Facilitating the personal mobility of persons with disabilities in the manner and at the time of their choice, and at affordable cost;
(b) Facilitating access by persons with disabilities to quality mobility aids, devices, assistive technologies and forms of live assistance and intermediaries, including by making them available at affordable cost;
(c) Providing training in mobility skills to persons with disabilities and to specialist staff working with persons with disabilities;
(d) Encouraging entities that produce mobility aids, devices and assistive technologies to take into account all aspects of mobility for persons with disabilities.

Participation Rights

Historically, persons with disabilities have been compelled to deal with marginalisation and social exclusion, generating the resultant phenomenon of invisibility. Such invisibility has prevented persons with disability from participating in society on an equal basis with others. The human rights perspective enshrined in the Convention promotes better visibility for persons with disability, requiring the adoption of measures to improve social awareness towards those persons, while demanding, at the same time, the adoption of measures to achieve social participation of persons with disability in diverse aspects of normal day-to-day activities. The provisions related to participation rights include Article 21 (Freedom of expression and opinion, and access to information); Article 29 (Participation in political and public life); and Article 30 (Participation in cultural life, recreation, leisure and sport).

The first so-called participation right, Article 21 relates to freedom of expression and opinion, and access to information. In the context of disability, access to information becomes an essential element to ensure that persons with disability are able to fully exercise their right to freedom of expression. This supposes inter alia the freedom to seek, receive, and impart information and ideas on an equal basis with others and through all forms of communication of their choice. For this reason, the Convention lists a series of measures for States Parties to provide, including: accessible formats and technologies appropriate to different kinds of disabilities in a timely manner and without additional cost; accepting, facilitating and promoting the use of sign languages, Braille, augmentative and alternative communication, and all other accessible means of communication of choice by persons with disabilities in official interactions;

and urging compliance by private entities; encouraging the mass media, including providers of information through the Internet, to make their services accessible to persons with disabilities.

The second participation right is found at Article 29 and deals with political and public life. Even though it is clear that political rights of persons with disabilities are essential for an adequate participation of citizenship, they are frequently ignored. Whether, as a result of the existence of barriers in the exercise of the right to vote, or of obstacles with regard to holding office, persons with disability usually face discrimination in the exercise of their political rights. The Convention requires States parties to ensure that persons with disabilities can effectively and fully participate in political and public life on an equal basis with others, directly or through freely chosen representatives, including the right and opportunity for persons with disabilities to vote and be elected. This provision requires States parties 'to actively promote an environment in which persons with disabilities can effectively and fully participate in the conduct of public affairs, without discrimination and on an equal basis with others, and encourage their participation in public affairs, including non-governmental organizations and associations concerned with the public and political life of the country, and in the activities and administration of political parties'; and importantly, 'organizations of persons with disabilities to represent persons with disabilities at international, national, regional and local levels'.

Article 30 turns to participation in cultural life, recreation, leisure and sport, as the Convention recognises the right of persons with disabilities to take part on an equal basis with others in cultural life, and requires States parties to ensure that persons with disabilities have the opportunity to develop and utilise their creative, artistic and intellectual potential, not only for their own benefit, but also for the enrichment of society. This includes the right of persons with disabilities to enjoy access through accessible formats to 'cultural materials'; 'to television programmes, films, theatre and other cultural activities; to places for cultural performances or services, including sites of national cultural importance'. This article includes recognition of persons with disabilities' creative, artistic and intellectual potential, assuring non-discriminatory practice with regard to intellectual property rights.

Paragraph 4 recognises that persons with disabilities are entitled to recognition and support of their specific cultural and linguistic identity, including sign languages and deaf culture. The final paragraph of Article 30 also recognises the right of persons with disabilities to participate on an equal basis with others in recreational, leisure and sporting activities, it includes the encouragement and promotion of people with disabilities in mainstream sporting activities at all levels and in disability-specific sporting and recreational activities, and to this end encourages the provision of appropriate instruction, training and resources; and access to sporting, recreational and tourism venues. Ensuring support for children with disabilities to participation in play, recreation and leisure and sporting activities, including those activities in the school system on an equal basis with others.

Basic Social Rights

The Convention recognises a set of basic social rights that together constitute a legal framework of norms and principles of evident social character, whose recognition and enforcement becomes essential in order to achieve real equality of persons with disabilities. These include Article 24 (Education); Article 25 (Health); Article 26 (Habilitation and rehabilitation); Article 27 (Work and Employment); and Article 28 (Adequate standard of living and social protection).

The first of these basic social rights is education found at Article 24. As regards the education of persons with disabilities, the key point of discussion lies in the apparent dilemma between special and inclusive education. Although the new trends in education of persons with disabilities clearly point towards the inclusion of those persons in the general educational system, there are some groups of persons with disabilities, or some specific situations, which require special education. Nevertheless, as the different groups among persons with disabilities are aware, access to education is the door towards the full realisation of the rights enshrined in the Convention.

The text recognises the rights of persons with disabilities to education without discrimination and on the basis of equal opportunity. For the realisation of this right the Convention requires States parties to ensure provision of an inclusive education system at all levels, with lifelong learning, directed to the full development of human potential, with a sense of dignity and self-worth, and the strengthening of respect for human rights, fundamental freedoms and human diversity; to the development by persons with disabilities of their personality, talents and creativity, as well as their mental and physical abilities, to their fullest potential; and enabling persons with disabilities to participate effectively in a free society. The safeguards attached to this are that:

(a) Persons with disabilities are not excluded from the general education system on the basis of disability, and that children with disabilities are not excluded from free and compulsory primary education, or from secondary education, on the basis of disability;
(b) Persons with disabilities can access an inclusive, quality and free primary education and secondary education on an equal basis with others in the communities in which they live;
(c) Reasonable accommodation of the individual's requirements is provided;
(d) Persons with disabilities receive the support required, within the general education system, to facilitate their effective education;
(e) Effective individualized support measures are provided in environments that maximize academic and social development, consistent with the goal of full inclusion.

Regardless of the inclusion of persons with disabilities in the general educational system, the Convention requires States parties to enable persons with disabilities to learn life and social development skills, and to facilitate their full and equal participation in education and as members of the community. To this end, States parties are to take appropriate measures, including:

(a) Facilitating the learning of Braille, alternative script, augmentative and alternative modes, means and formats of communication and orientation and mobility skills, and facilitating peer support and mentoring;
(b) Facilitating the learning of sign language and the promotion of the linguistic identity of the deaf community;
(c) Ensuring that the education of persons, and in particular children, who are blind, deaf or deafblind, is delivered in the most appropriate languages and modes and means of communication for the individual, and in environments which maximize academic and social development.

The provision emphasises the need for States parties to employ teachers, including teachers with disabilities, who are qualified in sign language and/or Braille, and to train professionals and staff who work at all levels of education. Such training shall incorporate disability awareness and the use of appropriate augmentative and alternative modes, means and formats of communication, educational techniques and materials to support persons with disabilities. The final provision of Article 24 guarantees the access of adult persons to the higher education:

> 5. States Parties shall ensure that persons with disabilities are able to access general tertiary education, vocational training, adult education and lifelong learning without discrimination and on an equal basis with others. To this end, States Parties shall ensure that reasonable accommodation is provided to persons with disabilities.

The second basic social right is health, which is found at Article 25 of the Convention. The health issue received special attention in the negotiations of the Convention.[93] This can be understood if we bear in mind that for many decades health has been used as the base to address disability. Therefore, and considering the need for this Convention to dissociate itself from the so-called 'medical' or 'rehabilitation' model of disability, health issues were addressed with special care. Consequently, and despite the fact that in its first reading health and rehabilitation were together in a single provision, soon the delegations decided to divide these two related though distinguishable issues into two different articles.[94] As a result, the Convention requires States Parties to recognise that persons with disabilities have the right to enjoy the highest attainable standard of health without discrimination on the basis of disability; undertaking, to this end, all appropriate measures to ensure access for persons with disabilities to health services that are gender-sensitive, including health-related rehabilitation. In particular, States parties shall:

> (a) Provide persons with disabilities with the same range, quality and standard of free or affordable health care and programmes as provided to other persons, including in the area of sexual and reproductive health and population-based public health programmes;
> (b) Provide those health services needed by persons with disabilities specifically because of their disabilities, including early identification and intervention as appropriate, and services designed to minimize and prevent further disabilities, including among children and older persons;
> (c) Provide these health services as close as possible to people's own communities, including in rural areas;
> (d) Require health professionals to provide care of the same quality to persons with disabilities as to others, including on the basis of free and informed consent by, inter alia, raising awareness of the human rights, dignity, autonomy and needs of persons with disabilities through training and the promulgation of ethical standards for public and private health care;

[93] See Report of the UN Secretary-General, Issues and Emerging Trends related to Advancement of Persons with Disabilities, UN Doc A/AC.265/2003/1. 'Traditionally disability advocates have sought to decouple disability and health issues, urging that society reject the notion of people with disabilities as 'sick'. There is a growing body of evidence that suggests that persons with disabilities are at greater risk of acquiring what have been termed secondary conditions. Formulation of options for prevention of secondary conditions for persons with disabilities is an important goal of public policy and introduces the urgent need to reconsider the conceptual bases and terminology on disability' (para 14).

[94] See The Sixth Ad Hoc Committee Daily Summaries prepared by Rehabilitation International, in particular Volume 7, #5, August 05, 2005 and Volume 7, #6 August 08, 2005. Available at: http://www.un.org/esa/socdev/enable/rights/ahc6summary.htm

(e) Prohibit discrimination against persons with disabilities in the provision of health insurance, and life insurance where such insurance is permitted by national law, which shall be provided in a fair and reasonable manner;
(f) Prevent discriminatory denial of health care or health services or food and fluids on the basis of disability.

Turing now to Article 26 which deals with habilitation and rehabilitation, it is necessary, as noted earlier, to distinguish between the aspects of rehabilitation on the one hand, and the access of persons with disabilities to health services on an equal basis with others, on the other hand. Hence, the Convention demands from States parties the adoption of effective and appropriate measures, including peer support, to enable persons with disabilities to attain and maintain maximum independence, full physical, mental, social and vocational ability, and full inclusion and participation in all aspects of life, as well as the organisation, strengthening and extended comprehensive habilitation and rehabilitation services and programmes, particularly in the areas of health, employment, education and social services. Such services and programmes shall be designed in a way that:

(a) Begin at the earliest possible stage, and are based on the multidisciplinary assessment of individual needs and strengths;
(b) Support participation and inclusion in the community and all aspects of society, are voluntary, and are available to persons with disabilities as close as possible to their own communities, including in rural areas.

Finally, the provision asserts that States parties' obligations about habilitation and rehabilitation shall also include the development of initial and continuing training for professionals and staff working in habilitation and rehabilitation services, as well as the availability, knowledge and use of assistive devices and technologies, designed for persons with disabilities, as they relate to habilitation and rehabilitation.

Following from Article 26, Article 27 deals with probably one of the most regulated fields of disability law—work and employment—yet it remains one of the major areas of discrimination of persons with disabilities. At an international level, the International Labour Organization, and at the regional level, the European Union, have enacted binding instruments to prevent and penalise discrimination on the basis of disability in employment, though discrimination rates do not seem to decrease. The formula adopted by the Convention begins with the recognition of the right of persons with disabilities to work on an equal basis with others; this includes the right to the opportunity to gain a living by work freely chosen or accepted in a labour market and work environment that is open, inclusive and accessible to persons with disabilities.

As a safeguard of the exercise of the right of persons with disabilities to work, including the right of those who acquire a disability during the course of employment, the Convention requires States Parties to take all appropriate measures including the enactment of legislation directed to:

(a) Prohibit discrimination on the basis of disability with regard to all matters concerning all forms of employment, including conditions of recruitment, hiring and employment, continuance of employment, career advancement and safe and healthy working conditions;
(b) Protect the rights of persons with disabilities, on an equal basis with others, to just and favourable conditions of work, including equal opportunities and equal remuneration for work of equal value, safe and healthy working conditions, including protection from harassment, and the redress of grievances.

This Article also requires that reasonable accommodation is provided to persons with disabilities in the workplace; and in the ability to exercise their labour and trade union rights on an equal basis with others; with effective access to general technical and vocational guidance programmes, placement services and vocational and continuing training; and employment in the public sector.

Article 27 establishes the responsibility to promote the employment of persons with disabilities: in the private sector through appropriate policies and measures, which may include affirmative action programmes, incentives and other measures; in the acquisition of work experience in the open labour market; in vocational and professional rehabilitation, job retention and return-to-work programmes; in employment opportunities and career advancement in the labour market, as well as assistance to finding, maintaining and employment; and in promoting opportunities for self-employment, entrepreneurship, the development of cooperatives and starting one's own business. Finally, the provisions of Article 27 require States parties to ensure that persons with disabilities are not held in slavery or in servitude, and are protected, on an equal basis with others, from forced or compulsory labour.

Moving on from employment, Article 28 speaks of an adequate standard of living and social protection. As manifestly shown in the latest reports and statistics, there is—at least in a large part of the world—a direct and close relation between disability and poverty.[95] Persons with disabilities are habitually compelled to live in conditions of extreme poverty. Therefore, and irrespective of its progressive character of economic and social rights as envisioned in the Covenant on Economic, Cultural and Social Rights, it is of vital importance that States Parties recognise that persons with disabilities have a right to an adequate standard of living for themselves and their families. According to Article 28, this includes the right to adequate food, clothing and housing, and to the continuous improvement of living conditions. Likewise, State parties are required to take appropriate steps to safeguard and promote the realisation of this right without discrimination on the basis of disability.

The Convention then recognises the right of persons with disabilities to social protection and to the enjoyment of that right without discrimination on the basis of disability, and also requires State parties to take appropriate steps to safeguard and promote the realisation of this right, including measures: in particular for women and girls with disabilities and older persons with disabilities, to social protection programmes and poverty reduction programmes; disability-related expenses, including adequate training, counselling, financial assistance and respite care; to public housing programmes; and to retirement benefits and programmes.

Implementation of the Convention

The Convention can clearly be viewed from the perspective of substantive rights touching on equality rights, protection rights, liberty and personal autonomy, participation rights and basic social rights. A key question remains as to how effective it

[95] See Disability, Poverty and Development, Department for International Development of the British Government, February 2002. Available at: http://www.dfid.gov.uk/pubs/files/disability.pdf; UNESCO, Overcoming Obstacles to the Integration of Disabled People, Report Contribution to The World Summit on Social Development Copenhagen, Denmark March 1995; International Labor Organization, Disability and Poverty Reduction Strategies, Discussion Paper, November 2002. Available at. http://www.ilo.org/public/english/employment/skills/disability/download/discpaper.pdf

can be in ensuring those rights. Despite the progress made to date through the 1993 UN Standard Rules on the Equalization of Opportunities for Persons with Disabilities, there remain real and difficult challenges ahead. The October 2006 Report of the Global Survey on Government Implementation of the UN Standard Rules on the Equalization of Opportunities for Persons with Disabilities,[96] reporting thirteen years after the introduction of the Standard Rules found that although some progress had been made, there was a serious lack of achievement of the rights of people with disabilities. Surveys were sent to the most relevant government departments and to two national NGOs in each participating State. However, given that only 114 of 191 UN Member States responded, there is concern that the worst case scenario has not yet emerged, with 77 states (of which half are developing countries) not reporting.[97] While it reports progress, the Global Survey also gives cause for concern on a wide range of issues, with nearly 30 States reporting no opportunity for integrated education. Accessibility, rehabilitation, awareness-raising and medical care continue to require a high level of attention while exclusion from medical care was further highlighted.

Regarding employment, the Report calls for a wide range of measures to shape a positive legal, cultural, attitudinal and physical environment, that would enable persons with disabilities to participate in the labour market as productive, contributing citizens. The Report identifies the need for gainful employment and a productive life as a source of dignified life as a prerequisite for psychological well-being and social adjustment. Persons with disabilities were found to be invisible in the labour market and remain, throughout the world, economically marginalised.[98] The Report questions whether governments view income maintenance as a priority for persons with disabilities on several counts: because of the lack of resources, because there is simply no recognition on their part that income and social security are necessary to maintain a certain standard of self-reliance and dignity, and because the financial support of persons with disabilities is considered the responsibility of their families rather than society at large or the government in particular.[99] With the Global Survey as a backdrop it is clear that the effective implementation of the Convention is crucial for significant progress to be made. The following sections thus consider those elements of the Convention that relate to mechanisms for its development, monitoring and enforcement, as well as the international implications and benefits of the Convention.

International Cooperation

It is estimated that of the 600 million people with disabilities worldwide, 70 per cent live in developing countries, and according to UN statistics 82 per cent live below the poverty line.[100] People with disabilities are among the most vulnerable and marginalised

[96] Global Survey on Government Action on the Implementation of the Standard Rules on the Equalization of Opportunities for Persons with Disabilities, administered November 2004 to June 2005 analysis October 2006.

[97] E/CN.5/2007/4 Commission for Social Development Forty–fifth session—Monitoring of the implementation of the Standard Rules on the Equalization of Opportunities for Persons with Disabilities.

[98] Global Survey on Government Action on the Implementation of the Standard Rules on the Equalization of Opportunities for Persons with Disabilities, administered November 2004 to June 2005 analysis October 2006. p 53.

[99] *Ibid*, p 57.

[100] White Paper on Irish Aid 2006, p 116.

in developing countries.[101] As a result of this reality, much debate took place during the treaty drafting process on the importance of international cooperation.[102] Some States attached such significance to international cooperation, that they wished to have it included in Article 1 of the Convention.[103] It then became a stand alone provision: Article 32. International cooperation thus is seen as an important element of the process towards achieving the aims and objectives to the Convention. Article 32 prescribes the following actions:

(a) Ensuring that international cooperation, including international development programmes, is inclusive of and accessible to persons with disabilities;
(b) Facilitating and supporting capacity-building, including through the exchange and sharing of information, experiences, training programmes and best practices;
(c) Facilitating cooperation in research and access to scientific and technical knowledge;
(d) Providing, as appropriate, technical and economic assistance, including by facilitating access to and sharing of accessible and assistive technologies, and through the transfer of technologies.

The discussion during the drafting of the Convention suggests reading Article 32 in conjunction with Article 4, para 2,[104] which states:

> With regard to economic, social and cultural rights, each State Party undertakes to take measures to the maximum of its available resources and, where needed, within the framework of international cooperation, with a view to achieving progressively the full realization of these rights, without prejudice to those obligations contained in the present Convention that are immediately applicable according to international law.

During the drafting to the Convention, the International Disability Development Consortium informed the Ad Hoc Committee that only 3 per cent to 4 per cent of people with disability were currently included in development programmes.[105] Similarly, it is estimated that only 1 per cent to 5 per cent of children with disability in developing counties attend school.[106] Ensuring international development programmes were inclusive of people with disabilities at all stages of the process became a key target of the Convention drafters.[107]

[101] The White Paper on Irish Aid 2006, notes at p 116, states that:

> Disabled children are the least likely to go to school and the mortality rate of children with disabilities in developing countries is comparatively much higher than that of non-disabled children. Much disability in developing countries is preventable and is closely related to malnutrition, poor sanitation, disease, poverty and conflict. Traditionally disability has received limited attention from aid agencies and donors. It is clear now that, if the Millennium Development Goals are to be achieved, the needs of disabled people must be considered alongside other development challenges by national governments, donors, international organisations and NGOS. Our existing work in this area includes programmes to remove landmines and ongoing water and sanitation programmes, which are central in of tackling trachoma, the leading cause of preventable blindness in the world.

[102] See discussion in all stages of drafting process on international cooperation beginning on www.un.org/esa/socdev/enable/rihgts/ahcstata32wgtext up to www.un.org/esa/socdev/enable/rihgts/ahcstata32sevscomments.htm.

[103] See Working Group proposal on Article 1 at www.un.org/esa/socdev/enable/rights/ahcstata1wgtext.htm.

[104] See www.un.org/esa/socdev/enable/rihgts/ahcstatasevscomments.htm. page 2–4.

[105] See Ad Hoc Committee, Background Documents, Article 32 at http://www.un.org/esa/socdev/enable/rights/ahcstatabkgrnddocs.htm page 6–7.

[106] SJ Peters, *Inclusive Education: An EFA Strategy for All Children* (World Bank, 2004).

[107] See Ad Hoc Committee, Background Documents, Article 32 athttp://www.un.org/esa/socdev/enable/rights/ahcstata32sevscomments.htm. Note also the UN Declaration on the Right to Development

Regional Integration Organisations

The Convention is unique in that, for the first time in an international instrument, in addition to being open to signature by States, it allows for 'regional integration organisations' to become signatories (Article 42). Throughout the negotiating process the State holding the Presidency of the European Union negotiated on behalf of all European Union States. Article 44 defines regional integration organisations as: 'an organization constituted by sovereign States of a given region, to which its member States have transferred competence in respect of matters governed by the present Convention'. On 30 March 2007 the then current EU presidency embraced this new opportunity and signed the Convention.

Reservations

A developing and sometimes controversial role for the Committee as a treaty monitoring body will be its consideration of reservations made to the treaty. as their remains a schism between general international law where invalidated reservations nullify the consent of the State to be bound to a treaty and international human rights law where an invalid reservation is decoupled from the treaty leaving the State bound to the treaty as a whole, without its reservations being considered in force. This example of fragmentation of international law has emerged as a result of the involvement of treaty monitoring bodies in determining the status of reservations. While it remains to be seen how the yet to be established Committee will deal with the issue, the Convention, for its part, at Article 46 allows States to make reservations while noting that 'reservation incompatible with the object and purpose of the present Convention shall not be permitted' and 'reservations may be withdrawn at any time'. There are a number of key areas where reservations are predicted, most notably in relation to Article 12 on Equal Recognition before the Law.[108]

Committee on the Rights of Persons with Disabilities

The Convention provides a road map with clear indicators of what is expected from a State to promote the rights of persons with disabilities. Enforcement of the Convention is essential. Accordingly, Article 34 establishes the treaty-monitoring body called the Committee on the Rights of Persons with Disabilities, which will consist of twelve international experts, will materialise within six months of the treaty coming into force and will be responsible for establishing its own rules of procedures. The functions of the Committee will include considering State reports (Article 35) on

adopted 4 December 1986 GA Res 41/128 UN GAOR, 41st Session, at 3, Annex, UN, Doc. A/Res/41/128 Annex (1987) Article 1 of the Declaration states:

1. The right to development is an inalienable human right by virtue of which every human person and all peoples are entitled to participate in, contribute to and enjoy economic, social, cultural and political development, in which all human rights and fundamental freedoms can be fully realized.
2. The human right to development also implies the full realization of the right of peoples to self determination, which includes, subject to the relevant provisions of both International Covenants on Human Rights, the exercise of their inalienable right to full sovereignty over all their natural wealth and resources.

[108] See as an introduction the letters from the Arab States and the EU at the final meeting on 5th December available on http://www.un.org/esa/socdev/enable/rights/ahc8documents.htm.

which it will make suggestions and recommendations (Article 36). Close cooperation between the States and the Committee is expected. In addition, the Committee is requested to explore avenues to enhance national capacities for the implementation of the Convention (Article 37).

States are required, inter alia, to collect appropriate data to identify and address the barriers experienced by people with disabilities (Article 31). In keeping with the operation of other treaty-monitoring bodies, the Committee is entitled to encourage NGOs and other competent parties to prepare reports and to comment on State reports (Article 38). The Committee will report on suggestions and recommendations to the UN General Assembly and to the Economic and Social Council every two years (Article 39). Article 40 provides for a 'Conference of State Parties'—an ongoing mechanism for consideration of any future matter concerning the implementation of the treaty including consideration of proposed amendments (Article 47).

The Committee will therefore be a key force in ensuring that the Convention is being implemented and that progress is being achieved through the avenue of State reports. It is disappointing that the avenue of communications from or on behalf of individuals became too controversial to be included within the main text of Convention.[109] A key feature of the general treaty monitoring body process is to encourage and accept reports, particularly from NGOs. This has proved invaluable in offering a more comprehensive picture of States' actual progress. Owing to the centrality and essential involvement of disabled and other NGO groups in the drafting process, it is hoped that this will continue in the ongoing monitoring process. The sense of working together towards a common objective has the potential to achieve positive results.

Optional Protocol

An important strand of enforcement lies in the Optional Protocol to the Convention. Following intense and protracted discussion, due in part to contemporary political tensions, it was not possible to agree on the inclusion of an individual complaints procedure within in the main body of the Convention. Consequently, the Optional Protocol was written and agreed to in great haste in the last week of negotiations in August 2006.[110] The Protocol was open for ratification with the Convention. The Optional Protocol to the Convention on the Rights of Persons with Disabilities begins with Article 1 which states:

> 1. A State Party to the present Protocol ('State Party') recognizes the competence of the Committee on the Rights of Persons with Disabilities ('the Committee') to receive and consider communications from or on behalf of individuals or groups of individuals subject to its jurisdiction who claim to be victims of a violation by that State Party of the provisions of the Convention.

[109] The issues of communications was dealt with in the discussions on Monitoring see Compilation of proposals on a monitoring mechanism for an International Convention on the Rights of Persons with Disabilities New York, New York, 12 May 2006 by Mexico at www.un.org/esa/socdev/enable/documents/mntrng_cmpltn.doc. At the meeting in August 2006 in informal meetings on Monitoring, in being unable to agree on a solution for inclusion of individual communications in the main draft it was agreed to prepare an optional protocol. See Ad Hoc Committee on a Comprehensive and Integral International Convention on the Protection and Promotion of the Rights and Dignity of persons with Disabilities Summary of the 8th Session on International Service for Human Rights www. www.ishr.ch p 16.

[110] See Ad Hoc Committee on a Comprehensive and Integral International Convention on the Protection and Promotion of the Rights and Dignity of persons with Disabilities Summary of the 8th Session on International Service for Human Rights www. www.ishr.ch, p 16.

2. No communication shall be received by the Committee if it concerns a State Party to the Convention that is not a party to the present Protocol.

Article 2 describes the circumstances when such communications are inadmissible. These include anonymity; if they are incompatible with the provisions of the Convention; if the matter has already been examined by the Committee or has been or is being examined under another procedure of international investigation or settlement; and similar to all procedures when all available domestic remedies have not been exhausted. While processing communications the Committee, if concerned, may request that the state party take protective measures to avoid possible 'irreparable damage to the victim or victims of the alleged violation'. When examining communications, the Committee will hold closed meetings and subsequently communicate its suggestions and recommendations to the relevant state party and petitioner. The heart of the work of the Committee is detailed in Article 6:

1. If the Committee receives reliable information indicating grave or systematic violations by a State Party of rights set forth in the Convention, the Committee shall invite that State Party to cooperate in the examination of the information and to this end submit observations with regard to the information concerned.
2. Taking into account any observations that may have been submitted by the State Party concerned as well as any other reliable information available to it, the Committee may designate one or more of its members to conduct an inquiry and to report urgently to the Committee. Where warranted and with the consent of the State Party, the inquiry may include a visit to its territory.
3. After examining the findings of such an inquiry, the Committee shall transmit these findings to the State Party concerned together with any comments and recommendations.
4. The State Party concerned shall, within six months of receiving the findings, comments and recommendations transmitted by the Committee, submit its observations to the Committee.
5. Such an inquiry shall be conducted confidentially and the cooperation of the State Party shall be sought at all stages of the proceedings.

The Committee may follow up with State parties on any measures taken in response to an inquiry. Gerard Quinn emphasises that just such a complaints procedure 'enables the raw edge of human experience to be expressed' and rather importantly, means that the Committee can develop case law in key areas and provide clarification on state obligations.[111]

IRELAND AND THE CONVENTION

Ireland has played an important role in various key stages of the treaty drafting process. A key international event took place in 2000, in which the disability organisations worked together to create the Beijing Declaration on the Rights of People with Disabilities in the New Century.[112] Led by the Chair of the Irish Rehabilitation

[111] G Quinn, *The UN Human Rights of Persons with Disabilities Treaty: A Blueprint for Disability Law & Policy Research and Reform*, (NDA Conference, Ireland, 2006).

[112] See Beijing Declaration on the Rights of People with Disabilities in the New Century Adopted on 12 March 2000 at the World NGO Summit on Disability Beijing, People's Republic Of China 'In 1999, on the basis of a unanimous call from its Governing Assembly, RI revived efforts to establish a UN Convention on the Rights of People with Disabilities. RI played a major role in the 2000 Disability Sector Summit in

International Network, Arthur O Reilly, it called for a Convention to be established. The final impetus towards a binding convention on the rights of persons with disabilities was achieved through the seminal study *Human Rights and Disability Report*.[113] This Report was commissioned by the then UN Human Rights Commissioner and former Irish President, Mary Robinson and authored principally by Professors Gerard Quinn and Theresia Degener, with the research undertaken by Irish lawyers. The Report argued for the need for a separate thematic Convention on the rights of people with disabilities because of the lack of an integrated human rights approach and the untapped potential of the existing treaties for the rights of people with disabilities. This central involvement in the treaty development process continued through Gerard Quinn being a significant member of the Working Group that developed the draft working text and participated in the Ad Hoc Committee.

The Department of Foreign Affairs of Ireland supported the move towards the Convention as, in 2002, it jointly hosted an important international conference[114] with strong international participation, which brought the possibility of a convention to the attention of the Irish NGO community. The then UN Special Rapporteur on Disability, Bengt Lindqvist, speaking at a critical juncture in the debate, endorsed the twin track approach of optimising the value of existing instruments while developing a new instrument.[115] This event came in quick succession, following the Mexican Government's successful initiative at the UN General Assembly of sponsoring an international instrument dedicated to people with disabilities.

Subsequently, representatives from Ireland participated in a wide range of groups involved at various levels of negotiation in the treaty drafting process over the four years of its gestation. The formal Irish delegation included the Department of Foreign Affairs, the Department of Justice, Equality and Law Reform, and members of People with Disability Ireland. The Disability Law and Policy Unity NUI, Galway, the Irish Law Reform Commission (LRC) and a number of Irish NGOs which were linked through various international representative bodies (including Rehabilitation International) and participated at both the formal and informal sessions.

With regard to the challenge of implementing the Convention within the domestic system, Article 33 is of particular relevance as it reads:

> 1. States Parties, in accordance with their system of organization, shall designate one or more focal points within government for matters relating to the implementation of the present Convention, and shall give due consideration to the establishment or designation of a coordination mechanism within government to facilitate related action in different sectors and at different levels.

China, which together with other international disability organizations issued the 'Beijing Declaration', calling for the development of such a UN Convention. In 2000 and 2001, RI representatives presented its Charter for the Third Millennium, calling for a UN Convention on the Rights of People with Disabilities, to nearly 100 national and international leaders'. http://www.rehab-international.org/advocacy/beijing_declaration.html DL February 2007.

[113] T Degener, G Quinn *et al*, *Human Rights and Disability—The Current Use and Future Potential of United Nations Human Rights Instruments in the Context of Disability*, (United Nations, New York and Geneva, 2002).

[114] Entitled 'Towards a United Nations Convention on the Human Rights of Persons with Disabilities' RHK, February 2002. Jointly hosted by Department of Foreign Affairs of Ireland, the National Disability Authority and the Irish Human Rights Commission.

[115] Bengt Lindqvist was appointed in 1994, and replaced Leandro Despouy, who had held the position since 1984.

2. States Parties shall, in accordance with their legal and administrative systems, maintain, strengthen, designate or establish within the State Party, a framework, including one or more independent mechanisms, as appropriate, to promote, protect and monitor implementation of the present Convention. When designating or establishing such a mechanism, States Parties shall take into account the principles relating to the status and functioning of national institutions for protection and promotion of human rights.
3. Civil society, in particular persons with disabilities and their representative organizations, shall be involved and participate fully in the monitoring process'.

The idea of one focal point noted in Article 33(1) had previously been proposed in the Irish Law Reform Commission Report 'Strategy for Equality',[116] and a Junior Ministry of the Irish Government was established under the rubric of 'Disability'. The National Disability Authority was established in June 2000, and it, along with the Equality Authority and the Central Statistics Office is working together on designing frameworks from which to gather information about the lives of people with disabilities, both separate and embedded in mainstream statistical data.[117] Many disability-specific functions have been mainstreamed. Despite such progress, NGOs report the need for significant improved coordination and cooperation.[118] The Convention can potentially add new energy to this challenge.

Capacity Legislation

One long standing area that requires significant legal reform in Ireland relates to capacity. Capacity is a key area to be addressed to enable Ireland to be in a position to ratify the Convention. Thankfully such legislative reform is currently being considered in Ireland.[119] The present lacunae in Irish law (including the archaic and in present standards insulting language currently on the statutes book—Lunacy Regulation (Ireland) Act 1871) in the area of capacity have long been recognised, and as such received particular attention from the Irish Law Reform Commission, which, in December 2006, released its third report on Vulnerable Adults and the Law.[120]

The first of the consultation documents produced by the Irish Law Reform Commission in 2003[121] began from the point of view of older people, where the focus is on diminishing capacity largely because of degenerative conditions. Irish intellectual disability[122] organisations, among other groups, sought to place the capacity debate in the wider discourse on promoting capacity in decision-making through person-centred

[116] *A Strategy for Equality* Report of the Commission on the Status of People with Disabilities Ireland, 2006.

[117] In the most recent Irish Census specific questions on disability were included, a post Censual Survey called National Disability Survey is currently underway to people with disabilities. See www.cso.ie/nds/default.htm

[118] Example report Ed M Walls *Making Appropriate Education a Reality for Pupils with Severe and Profound Intellectual Disability through Partnership*, (NFVB Ireland, 2002).

[119] PT Clarke, 'Capacity and Vulnerable Adults: A National Perspective'. (NDA Capacity Conference, Dublin, 2006).

[120] LRC 83 2006 Report: Vulnerable Adults and the Law is the third report in a series which began in 2003 entitled Law and the Elderly. The initial report focused more on older people; the spotlight of the debate widened to include all adults where questions of capacity arise, and consequently a second report was produced in 2005 which included a broader look at the circumstances of individuals. This final report includes a Draft Scheme of a Mental Capacity and Guardianship Bill.

[121] Law Reform Commission. (2003) *Consultation Paper—Law and the Elderly*. LRC CP 23-2003, Ireland

[122] National Federation of Voluntary Bodies 2004: RESPECT Symposium, Killarney www.fedvol.ie.

planning[123] and service delivery principles,[124] which places the person at the centre of key decisions in their life. In engaging with the Law Reform Commission, the focus was on promoting autonomy of persons with disability in decision-making. The second Commission report adopted a broader approach of including all vulnerable adults. The third Report adopts a similarly broad approach and includes a draft outline of proposed Guardianship Legislation. This highlights the Irish Law Reform Commission's commitment to the complex area of capacity to research and consult to achieve the right balance of protection and promotion of rights within the legislation. It is expected that a draft Mental and Guardianship Bill will be proposed in 2007 and need to be considered in light of the provisions of the Convention, specifically that of Article 12 which touches on equal recognition before the law.

CONCLUSION

By the end of 2006 an internationally binding Convention on the Rights of Persons with Disabilities had been drafted. Louise Arbour identifies the Convention 'as a catalyst for change' and as an important instrument in moving forward on a world agenda of the 'paradigm shift from viewing persons with disabilities as objects of charity, to individual subjects with rights'.[125] Yet, there are a number of challenges ahead; each State needs to start raising awareness about the Convention and building capacity and information, so that awareness turns to action. This needs to happen at the level of the civil society and at the State level to ensure that the message of the potential of the Convention is understood. This may also involve campaigning to ensure that States ratify both the Convention and the Optional Protocol. Many States will need to amend national legislation and address areas where State legislation and provisions do not meet the requirements of the Convention. Consultation with people with disability will be an essential requirement to determine priorities and the means of addressing such priorities.

The International Disability Caucus played a central role throughout all stages of the development of the Convention. Their role continues to be crucial in the implementation of the Convention, in encouraging State parties to sign and ratify it, and to support the work of the future Committee. They will also have a frontline role to play in ensuring that people on the ground are aware of the potential of a binding treaty in their day-to-day affairs. In all human rights debates, it can be difficult to make the link from everyday experiences and struggles to how these relate to international human rights treaties. With this Convention creating a paradigm shift in thinking and expectations there is also the need to ensure that this important message filters though to those who need it. But most important is the development of tools to maximise the potential of the Convention, to bring a human rights-based perspective to people with disability, to endorse their rights and to provide them with the tools to be use locally, nationally, regionally and internationally.

[123] Person Centred Planning for People in Ireland who have Disabilities, (NDA Dublin, 2005).

[124] National Federation of Voluntary Bodies 2004: Person Centred Services, National Federation of Voluntary Bodies, Galway www.fedvol.ie.

[125] Louise Arbour address to the 8th Session of the Ad Hoc Committee on 5 December 2006, New York, see: http://www.un.org/esa/socdev/enable/rights/ahc8.htm. 14 December 2006.

With regard to States, they play the crucial role in the implementation of the Convention; they need to review domestic legislation in order to adjust it to international requirements. There is a clear onus on States to develop and implement policy. States, in consenting to the Convention, will then be required to submit detailed reports to the Committee on the Rights of Persons with Disabilities as to how they are respecting the dignity and equality and ensuring non-discrimination of people with disabilities. NGOs and other bodies will be encouraged to submit and comment on reports, to ensure that there is a real and meaningful dialogue about the experience of individuals between States and the Committee. The Committee, based on the functioning of existing treaty monitoring bodies, will then issue its comments on progress and importantly set targets to be met by the time of the next report. In this way, an international spotlight will focus on a State's practice to illuminate to the world how that State is performing. It is hoped that the Convention will enlighten areas where rights are not respected and highlight progress towards equal citizenship for people with disabilities. The large number of States involved in the treaty drafting process reflects the full diversity of developing and developed countries. On the international agenda, people with disability have too often been invisible. The Millennium Development Goals[126] have set targets to be reached in the developing world across a baseline of human development indicators. It is vital that people with disability are identified in the targeting of the resources directed by the Goals, which could facilitate both mainstream inclusion and affirmative action programmes.

The Convention provides a new world vision of the rights of people with disabilities—the semblance of an international constitution of the rights for people with disabilities. The Convention shifts the paradigm and implies a strong moral and political commitment to take action to respect and promote the rights of persons with disabilities. By focusing on the right to be seen as a subject whose dignity is to be respected, it endorses the right for the individual experience and choices of people with disabilities to be heard. In legitimising the rights of people with disabilities, it empowers people to negotiate with all governments, with or without ratification. It offers the opportunity for the beginning of a new era in the rights of persons with disabilities.

[126] United Nations 2006: The Millennium Development Goals Report, available athttp://www.un.org/millenniumgoals/.

To The Rescue, All Hands!: The Good Neighbour Principle In International Law

Peter Hulsroj*

Sovereignty can be the best friend of humanitarian action—or its worst enemy.[1]

Recent history illustrates both extremes. The relief efforts of the 2005 tsunami provides impressive proof of how the State can be the key player in humanitarian support, both at the giving and the receiving end. The cases of Darfur, and before it Rwanda, demonstrate how sovereignty can stand in the way of humanitarian help, so obviously and demonstrably necessary. In Darfur and Rwanda sovereignty was an obstacle, because it, as so often, was misunderstood. Sovereignty is an emblematic expression of the right of a people, in the international system, to determine its own affairs. Sovereignty is, in other words, an expression of 'devolution'. Yet no sovereignty is absolute. Competition of sovereignties abound in an interdependent world, and the international legal system is precisely there to regulate the situations where sovereignties overlap.[2] But the international legal system is also there to regulate the obligations State *erga omnes*. Article 2(7) of the Charter of the United Nations does not enshrine a right for a State to disregard its obligations *erga omnes*,[3] by allowing for absolute exclusive State competence within its domestic jurisdiction, it only ensures that a people determines its own destiny within the bounds created by the regulation of competing sovereignties and by its *erga omnes* obligations.

The respect of human rights is one of these *erga omnes* obligations, and the human rights of millions of human beings were so egregiously violated in Rwanda and continue to be so in Darfur. Hesitancy does not become the Security Council, which had and has all legal tools necessary at its disposal for early intervention. This article however, does not seek to analyse when and how humanitarian intervention can take place, that is, when force can be used to remedy gross violations of human rights. Suffice it to say that the Security Council is the instrument for such intervention and its Chapter VII powers are almost unlimited in this respect[4]. The purpose here is,

* Legal Adviser, Preparatory Commission for the Comprehensive Nuclear-Test-Ban Treaty Organization. Email: peter.hulsroj@ctbto.org. The views expressed in this article are those of the author in his personal capacity. I am indebted to my colleagues, Mehrunnissa Mehdi and Lisa Tabassi, whose support has been instrumental in producing this article.

[1] See Report of the High-Level Panel on Threats, Challenges and Change, UN Doc/A/59/565 or under www.un.org/secureworld. On sovereignty and human rights in general see *Michael Reisman*, Sovereignty and Human Rights in Contemporary International Law, AJIL 84 (1990) 866–76.

[2] See *Peter Hulsroj*, Three Sources—No River, Zeitschrift für öffentliches Recht (ZÖR) 54 (1999) 219–259.

[3] Regarding a State's international obligations under Art 2(7) see Georg Nolte in Bruno Simma (ed) *The Charter of the United Nations, A Commentary*, Vol 1 (2002) 157, where he states, inter alia, 'in order to remove an area from the sphere of domestic jurisdiction, it is sufficient that this area be regulated by international law only in certain respects'.

[4] Ulrich Beyerlin, *Die humanitäre Aktion zur Gewährleistung des Mindeststandards in nicht-internationalen Konflikten*, (1975) 70–1; Yoram Dinstein, *War, Aggression and Self-Defence*, 2nd edn, (1994)

instead, to analyse whether a 'good neighbour' principle exists under international law, and what obligations such a 'good neighbour' principle might entail. For the 'good neighbour' the issue is not intervention or the use of force, but a readiness, or rather an obligation, to assist a neighbour in distress. Good neighbour obligations presuppose a need of help, a readiness to receive help and an ability of the good neighbour to provide help. The distress situations are typically natural disaster situations.

The issue at hand is, in a way, the flip side of the question of the legitimacy of humanitarian intervention. The question is not the right to intervene, but the obligation to help. Reisman and McDougal[5] suggested in the 1970s, though unsubstantiated, that States were under an international law obligation to intervene militarily when gross violations of human rights took place in another State. This is not assumed here, because it is so obviously contradicted by practice (or absence thereof) and is not even proposed as part of the 'duty to protect', now so hotly debated in the United Nations[6]. The more modest ambition here is to see whether States are under an international law obligation to assist States to avoid or mitigate natural disasters.

It may be argued that the present investigation is bound to arrive at a negative conclusion for the same reasons that the Reisman and McDougal thesis fails, namely that there is no State practice to support a supposition that 'good neighbour' obligations exist. This is too easy, however. Positive law develops not only through the passing of new laws, or, on the international plane, through new treaties, customary norms or general principles, but also through the application of existing norms to new situations. Hence Reisman and McDougal failed, not only because of the lack of practice, but also because they could not clothe the obligation they alleged in the robes of positivism. Reisman and McDougal did not point to any existing norm which, correctly applied, would lead to an obligation of forcible humanitarian intervention. It is the aspiration of this article to demonstrate that existing norms of international law lead to 'good neighbour' obligations.

The central argument is that disasters are characterised by an immediacy and immensity of adversity which render assistance obligations under existing human rights norms tangible and achievable. The right to life, shelter and health becomes a quest to overcome short term threats and the good neighbour only becomes obliged to shoulder a time-bound logistical and financial burden. The perennial objection of prosperous nations to a right to 'development' for poverty stricken nations, with a corresponding obligation on the prosperous to give effect to such a right, is that the prosperous cannot know what their obligation would mean in specific terms, since development is tied to domestic strategies and domestic implementation which other States cannot and should not interfere with. Such objection does not hold in the case of disasters, where admittedly the logistical challenges are often huge, but where the good neighbour's efforts to overcome them do not raise any macropolitical issue. The

294; Alexander Pauer, *Die humanitäre Intervention*, (1985) 86–90, 120; Peter Malanczuk, *Humanitarian Intervention and the Legitimacy of the Use of Force*, (1993) 16; Peter Hulsroj, *Unsanctioned Sanctions*, German Yearbook of International Law 43 (2000) 241, 245.

[5] See Michael Reisman and Myres S McDougal, 'Humanitarian Intervention to Protect the Ibos' in Richard B. Lillich (ed) *Humanitarian Intervention and the United Nations* (1973) 177–178.

[6] The Secretary General of the United Nations, In Larger Freedom, UN Doc/A/59/2005 or under www.un.org/largerfreedom, section III E, Report of the High-Level Panel on Threats, Challenges and Change, above, n 1, paras 53–7.

good neighbour may often fail, but it is clear that not trying is failure without fail! Furthermore, it is worth remembering that failure is not failure at the inter-State level, but failure vis-à-vis individuals who have received the covenant of the international community not to be left alone when they are left without shelter and are faced with immediate threats to life and limb. The letter and spirit of the key human rights instruments implore obligations towards individuals, and it is a perversion of legal interpretation if the international aspect of those obligations is not acknowledged, particularly when they are both tangible and achievable.

THE MEANING OF HUMAN RIGHTS

The human rights community has, understandably though regrettably, focused its attention on how to understand the defined rights from the perspective of their objects. By focusing on the object and not looking also inquisitively at the subject of the obligations some in-depth discussions of the proper meaning of human rights have been missed. Discussions such as whether all organs of States are direct subjects of human rights obligations individually or only as a conglomerate, and more esoteric discussions as to whether the individual is not only the object of human rights but also, in certain cases, the subject of the corresponding obligation, that is: must an individual respect the right to life even beyond the positive legislation of his or her country, beyond war crimes, beyond universal jurisdiction situations?[7] These issues are, however, far beyond the scope of this piece. The lament of this article is specifically that the human rights community has not tested the assumption that the subject of the human rights obligations is always the home or host State of individuals—and not third States via obligation *erga omnes*. The gut feeling, nurtured by sovereignty thinking, has been that it is always each State on its own when it comes to 'enforceable' rights. Yet, mirroring Article 55 of the Charter of the United Nations, Article 2 of the Universal Declaration of Human Rights proclaims that: Everyone is entitled to all the rights and freedoms set forth in this Declaration, without distinction of any kind, such as race, colour, sex, language, religion, political or other opinion, national or social origin, property, birth or other status.

This sweeping language gives cause for pause, particularly when discussing 'good neighbour' obligations. The literal meaning of Article 2 in this respect is that a human being cannot be discriminated against in the enjoyment of the listed rights because of his nationality.[8] But that does not answer the question: discriminated against by whom? In 1946, when the Universal Declaration was adopted, the addressee was clearly the home or host State. But is the answer the same now, and if we look beyond the confines of Article 2, does a State, even when it is not the host State, have obligations towards citizens of other States elsewhere? The language of the Declaration, in fact, supports an internationalist perspective on human rights entitlements very explicitly in Article 28, where it is said that: 'Everyone is entitled to a social and international order in which the rights and freedoms set forth in this Declaration can be

[7] Cf Peter Wismer, *Bring Down the Walls*, 2006 Chinese Journal of International Law, 511.

[8] See Sigrun Skogly in Asbjørn Eide (ed), *Economic, Social and Cultural Rights: a Textbook* (2001) 57–71.

fully realised'. It cannot be stated more strongly than this, and it is truly remarkable considering its 60 years provenance.[9]

The primacy of the home or host State for ensuring the enjoyment of human rights within its jurisdiction is not called into question.[10] The internationalist perspective on human rights only means that where the State cannot, or even will not,[11] ensure the enjoyment of human rights then there is an obligation for other States to become involved. 'Good neighbour obligations' mean the obligation to help a host or home State ensure human rights when that State cannot or will not do so effectively. The 'good neighbour' obligations arise when devolution no longer works.

The Universal Declaration is an authoritative expression of the minimum human rights ensured under public international law. The scene was set for the Universal Declaration by the Preamble and Articles 1, 55 and 56 of the Charter of the United Nations,[12] which proclaim a general obligation for the UN and its Member States to cooperate to find solutions to international economic, social, health and related problems. With the aid of the Charter, custom and 'general principles of law'[13] have enabled the Declaration to transcend its more humble origin as a non-binding declaration.[14] The Declaration invites the conclusion that a subsidiary obligation exists for States to help others which cannot ensure the enjoyment of human rights to all human beings within their jurisdiction.

The concepts enunciated in the Universal Declaration have been developed further in many treaties, prominently amongst these the International Covenant on Civil and Political Rights (ICCPR) and the International Covenant on Economic, social and Cultural Rights. The ICCPR states in Article 2(1):

[9] Asbjorn Eide (ed), *The Universal Declaration of Human Rights, A Commentary*, (1993) 433, states that: '[a]rticle 28 cannot, even by the most imaginative judge, be handled as a justiciable and enforceable subjective right for individuals . . .'. This, arguably, misses the point. The first question in interpreting a treaty is whether there are enforceable rights for the other State Parties, not whether there are subjective rights for individuals. As will be demonstrated below in relation to Article 2 of the Covenant on Economic and Social Rights, it is perfectly possible to derive rights for States to be helped when disaster strikes. In fact, Article 28 of the Universal Declaration provided the genesis for the rights of States to be helped to secure the rights of individuals.

[10] Cf General Assembly Resolution 46/182 on the Strengthening of the Coordination of Humanitarian Emergency Assistance of the United Nations, Annex, Para. 4.

[11] See for example Alston in Philip Alston and Katarina Tomasevski (eds), *International Law and the Human Right to Food* (1984) 42, who illustrates the duties contained in the Covenant by way of the tragedy that occurred in Ethiopia in 1973 (albeit before the coming into force of the Covenant), when the government of Emperor Haile Selassie refused to admit the existence of serious famine within the country: 'A duty of a different type which flows directly from the obligation of States Parties to co-operate internationally, is the duty of governments to seek international assistance in situations where widespread starvation would otherwise occur'. He concludes that (now that the Covenant has come into force) 'at least in theory, the Covenant does provide a mechanism by which attention could be called to such a serious violation of a State Party's duties under the Covenant'.

[12] See also General Assembly Resolution 2625: Declaration on Principles of International Law Concerning Friendly Relations and Co-operation Among States in Accordance with the Charter of the United Nations (1970) underlining the rights encapsulated by Articles 55 and 56.

[13] 'Custom' and 'general principles of law [as recognised by civilised nations]' are the second and third sources of international law defined by Article 38 of the Statute of the International Court of Justice.

[14] See John Peter Humphrey, 'The International Bill of Rights and Implementation', William and Mary Law Review 17 (1976) 259. See also Anthony D'Amato, *International Law: Process and Prospect* (1986) 123–147; Myres Smith McDougal, H Lasswell and L Chen, *Human Rights and World Public Order* (1980) 273–274, 325–327, who argue that the Universal Declaration should be regarded as customary law and is therefore binding on all States; cf Bruno Simma and Philip Alston, 'The Sources of Human Rights Law: Custom, Jus Cogens, and General Principles', Australian Yearbook of International Law 12 (1992) 82–108.

> Each State Party to the present Covenant undertakes to respect and to ensure to all individuals within its territory and subject to its jurisdiction the rights recognised in the present Covenant, without distinction of any kind, such as race, colour, sex, language, religion, political or other opinion, national or social origin, property, birth or other status.

Article 2 is a full-blooded expression of the reliance on the home or host State to ensure the enjoyment of human rights. It appears wedded to its times, and raises the issue of whether one must conclude *a contrario*, that no 'good neighbour' obligations exist, because the ball is put squarely in the court of the home or host State. An *a contrario* conclusion is not mandatory. It may instead be concluded that the Covenant neither supports the assumption of 'good neighbour' obligations, nor disproves them.[15] The aim of Article 2 is innocent, in the sense that it strives to exclude 'exceptionalism'. It was not its aim to settle an issue, which had not yet arisen, and indeed, Article 5(2) states explicitly that the Covenant does not restrict obligations which States may have by virtue of other instruments or norms. More importantly, the ICCPR has a natural emphasis on the State as enabler, because the State is the only entity which can grant rights such as voting rights, non-discrimination rights or can ensure protection to the family as a foundation of society. This also means, however, that the ICCPR is not highly relevant to good neighbour obligations simply because the good neighbour in reality has no possibility to help. Civil and political rights depend mainly on the will of the home or host State. One exception is the right to life under Article 6, but even there the ICCPR must be understood to mainly protect against arbitrary deprivation of life.[16] When it comes to ensuring the right to life from a material perspective, it is the International Covenant on Economic, Social and Cultural Rights that is really relevant with its provisions on the right to be free from hunger and preventable disease.

The International Covenant on Economic, Social and Cultural Rights (ICESCR) does not have an equivalent of Article 2 of the ICCPR. Quite to the contrary the ICESCR has emphatic internationalist language in its Article 2, where States agree to 'take steps, individually and through international assistance and co-operation, especially economic and technical, to the maximum of its available resources, with a view to achieving progressively the full realization of the rights recognised in the present Covenant by all appropriate means [. . .]'. This language, strong as it is, cannot, from a teleological perspective, be interpreted to abandon the primacy of the home or host

[15] Cf Manfred Nowak, *UN-Pakt über bürgerliche und politische Rechte und Fakultativprotokoll: CCPR-Kommentar* (1989) 29, who states that Art 2 of the ICCPR *primarily* refers to the domestic affairs of a State, however, not exclusively so: ‚Er bringt fuer den gesamten internationalen Menschenrechtsshutz geltenden Grundsatz zum Ausdruck, dass die konkrete Durchsetzung voelkerrechtliche normierter Menschenrechte *primaer* eine innerstaatliche Angelegenheit ist'.

In this regard see also Art 41(1)(c) of the Covenant which stipulates that the Committee shall deal with the failure of a State Party to give effect to the provisions of the Covenant after it has 'ascertained that all domestic remedies have been invoked and exhausted in the matter, in conformity with the generally recognized principles of international law'. Nowak further argues that a literal interpretation of the wording in Art 2(1) ('within its territory and subject to its jurisdiction') would lead to absurd results and defeat the purpose of the rest of the Covenant, as for instance Art 12(4), which states that 'no one shall be arbitrarily deprived of the right to enter his own State'. A literal interpretation would make this impossible to ensure as the individual seeking to enforce the right would not be on the territory of his own State in the first place. Nowak therefore argues in favour of a teleological interpretation of what he calls a clumsily formulated provision ('ungeschickt formulierten Bestimmung'), see pp 45–46.

[16] Nowak, *ibid.*, p 9.

State to ensure the relevant human rights, but is, in fact, superbly supportive of 'good neighbour' obligations, waffling in the *travaux préparatoires* notwithstanding.[17] Whatever the situation may have been when the Covenant was created, the general normative interdependency caused by globalisation means that provisions like Article 2 of the Covenant must be assumed to have also firmed up.[18] Still, the sweeping nature of the 'good neighbour' obligations outlined in the ICESCR results in the perception that the obligations are intangible, unenforceable.[19] This is hardly true, but this article will shy away from addressing the point in its generality, because its aim is only to address 'good neighbour' obligations in relation to emergency situations of an immediate nature, such as famine and natural disasters. In relation to such disasters, 'good neighbour' obligations are both tangible and as enforceable as any other obligation under public international law. As pointed out by Alston and Quinn, even if one may be reluctant about the overall binding effect of Article 2 in 'the context of a given right it may, according to circumstances, be possible to identify obligations to cooperate internationally that would appear to be mandatory on the basis of the undertaking contained in Article 2(1) of the Covenant'.[20]

It could be argued that the obligations in disaster situations are not tangible for individual States, because the obligations are on all States and therefore not attributable on an individual basis. Properly understood the obligations are 'jointly and severally' held, with the only restriction being 'within their means' in a both financial and practical sense. In the financial sense, 'within their means' could, again, be said to

[17] See Philip Alston and Gerard Quinn, 'The Nature and Scope of States Parties' Obligations under the International Covenant on Economic, Social and Cultural Rights', HRQ 9 (1987), 186–192, who state that 'the framers did not intend to let states arbitrarily and artificially determine for themselves the level of commitment required by the Covenant. Moreover, the reference to resources was deemed by many states to include whatever international as well as national resources were available'.

See also 'The Limburg Principles on the Implementation of the International Covenant on Economic, Social and Cultural Rights' HRQ 9 (1987) 126, underlining states' international obligations. For example, Principle 25 states: 'its available resources' refers to both the resources within a state and those available from the international community through international cooperation and assistance'. See further Evo Dankwa and Cees Flinterman, 'Commentary by the Rapporteurs on the Nature and Scope of States Parties' Obligations', HRQ 9 (1987) 140, in relation to Principle 25:

> whatever the resources and level of their economic development, States Parties should assure minimum subsidence rights for all. While a State Party should not make the fulfilment of its obligation dependent on the receipt of assistance from outside, it is envisaged that local resources may be augmented through international cooperation and assistance.

The language of Article 2.1 mirrors that used in other regional conventions such as Article 26 of the American Convention on Human Rights of 1969 and Article 1 of the Additional Protocol to the American Convention on Human Rights in the Area of Economic, Social and Cultural Rights 'Protocol Of San Salvador' 1988; see also Articles 22 and 24 of the Banjul (African) Charter of Human and Peoples' Rights.

[18] Note 14 of General Comment 3 of the Committee on Economic and Social Rights, emphasises the need for international cooperation in the realization of economic, social and cultural rights and that 'It is particularly incumbent upon those States which are in a position to assist others in this regard'.

http://www.unhchr.ch/tbs/doc.nsf/(symbol)/CESCR+General+comment+3.En?OpenDocument

[19] A good example of an unfounded defeatist perspective on economic, social and cultural rights, above, n 9, at 386–9, where unwittingly fuel is added to the intangibility fire by heavily conceptualising the issue, see also *ibid* 433 specifically on international obligations to help. Contrast this with the Declaration on the Right to Development, Article 3 'states have a duty to co-operate with each other in ensuring development and eliminating obstacles to development'.

Cf Louis Henkin (ed), *The International Bill of Rights: The Covenant on Civil and Political Rights* (1981) 10, who emphasises the binding nature of the rights contained in the ICESCR: 'the rights it recognizes are "human", universal and fundamental as are those of the Civil and Political Rights Covenant'.

[20] See Alston and Quinn, above, n 17, at 192.

introduce intangibility, as could the stated progressive implementation of rights. This is, however, only true from a very conceptual perspective. In practice, the goal of developed countries to provide 0.7 per cent of GDP as development aid,[21] leads naturally to the conclusion that as long as fulfilment of 'good neighbour' obligations would not bring expenditure of more than 0.7 per cent of GDP then, at least, there is no question of being beyond means and, therefore, no question of only progressive implementation. This is not a facile argument, but really only an illustration of how far the international community is from being a cohesive, caring community. Not long ago Christian religious thinking demanded tithe. Nowadays, our responsibility for our fellow human beings does not even bring us to a 'hundrethe'!

In any event it is wrong to focus on enforceability, because 'almost all nations observe almost all principles of international law and almost all of their obligations almost all of the time'.[22] What is required is that States understand what their obligations concretely are—because when they do, they are likely to comply. The issue is, hence, whether obligations are tangible, and this is where there may be a differences between the sweeping 'good neighbour obligations' generally and the 'good neighbour' obligations in disaster situations. If there is a famine, the obligation is to provide foodstuffs; if there is flooding, the obligation is to provide medical support, shelter, clean water and food. It is much easier to make concrete these obligations than, say, the long term obligation to assist in raising educational standards.

SPECIFIC HUMAN RIGHTS PROVISIONS

As mentioned in the introduction, this article seeks the normative effect of good neighbour obligations primarily in a correct and targeted interpretation of the existing human rights instruments. To a large extent this normative effect has lain dormant since the inception of the various instruments, because of the sovereignty considerations obscuring our view to this day. First principle analysis shows that on the conceptual level there are no bounds on the defined human rights justifying that the potentially good neighbour absolves itself from fulfilling perfectly achievable duties when disaster strikes. In a globalising world with ever freer trade, it becomes ever clearer that a neighbour cannot be seen only as a trade partner. Societies become interwoven and the obligation part of the equation must be reassessed whilst rights are invoked and opportunities continue to be chased.

A possible absence of supporting State practice does not bar a fresh look at the Universal Declaration and the two Covenants, the so-called 'International Bill of Rights', from the perspective of 'good neighbour' obligations. The International Bill of Rights is constitutional in character and shares an organic nature with domestic constitutions. The principles that are defined in the International Bill of Rights, and

[21] General Assembly Resolution 2626 of 1970 set the target for official development assistance (ODA) to developing countries by economically advanced countries at 0.7% of each country's gross national product (GNP) at market prices.

See further Mathew Craven, The International Covenant on Economic, Social and Cultural Rights, a Perspective on its Development (1995) 150, who states that few developed states have actually achieved the widely accepted ODA target of 0.7% of GNP. In fact in a number of developed countries official aid is less than half that figure. (To date only five countries have met or surpassed the 0.7% target: Denmark, Luxembourg, Netherlands, Norway and Sweden).

[22] See Louis Henkin, *How Nations Behave, Law and Foreign Policy*, 2nd edn (1979) 47.

in domestic constitutions, must be interpreted in light of the times and the involved rights are necessarily evolutionary. In fact, even constitutional scholars of the 'original intent' persuasion would agree that constitutional interpretation cannot be static, only they believe that the interpretation must be devolutionary rather than evolutionary. Hence, State practice should be understood as assisting in interpreting the International Bill of Rights in but a limited manner. Of far greater importance is the matching of the core of established norms with present-day societal exigencies in a holistic fashion.

The Universal Declaration, the ICCPR, ICESCR and other instruments weave a fabric of obligation with many potential overlaps—making a word-for-word interpretation of the various clauses unnecessary in order to conclude what the 'good neighbour' obligations are in disaster situations. In order to understand the fabric it is, however, necessary to understand its key constituents. The Universal Declaration is emphatic in stating in Article 3 that 'everyone has the right to life, liberty and security of person'. The statement is fundamental, absolute and unspecific. It only gains meaning when specific issues are tested against its protective aim. This notwithstanding, Article 3 has a strong, independent normative effect.[23] It is, however, supplemented by more specific provisions within the Universal Declaration, and, indeed, in separate instruments seeking to flesh out more concretely the protected domain; the ICESCR being the most prominent of these instruments.

On the more specific level, Article 25(1) of the Universal Declaration[24] provides that 'everyone has the right to a standard of living adequate for the health and well-being of himself and of his family, including food, clothing, housing and medical care and necessary social services, and the right to security in the event of unemployment, sickness, disability, widowhood, old age or other lack of livelihood in circumstances beyond his control'. Article 25(1) flags up an unambiguous obligation to provide care for the individual struck by disaster, even if the aim of Article 25(1) is much wider. The words 'beyond his control' are significant, because they underscore both an obligation of the individual to care for himself, and the obligation for others to help when an individual is rendered unable to do so. Disasters are archetypal for the latter case.

Article 22 of the Universal Declaration,[25] for its part, speaks of the right to social security and to the free development of personality. Article 22 was conceived as an umbrella provision, setting the scene for the subsequent substantive provisions (Articles 23 to 29). The idea is, inter alia, that the free development of personality presupposes a minimum of subsistence. In a very general, but inoperative sense, Article 22 can then be said to support the obligation to provide disaster assistance—by making clear that the obligations under the Declaration go far beyond securing mere survival.[26] Finally, Article 28 of the Universal Declaration[27] should be men-

[23] See inter alia the position of Chile in the negotiations leading to the Universal Declaration, where it is assumed that the right includes a right to subsistence for persons unable to support themselves, quoted above, n 8 (Lars Adam Rehof), at 75–6.

[24] On Art 25(1) in general, see Eide (ed), above, n 9, at 385–399.

[25] On Art 22 in general, see Baard Anders Andreassen in Eide (ed), above, n 9, at 319–353.

[26] The mention of social security in Art 22, and in Art 9 of the ICESCR has stirred much debate and confusion, see Baard Anders Andreassen, above, n 9, at 319–53. On the relationship between the right to develop one's personality and health, see summary reference above, n 8, at 74 (Lars Adam Rehof).

[27] On Art 28 in general, see Eide, above, n 9, at 433–447.

tioned again, because it not only bears on the question of who is obliged under the Universal Declaration, but sets out a wider obligation to create an international order which fosters the realisation of the enumerated rights. The creation of an international order which fosters human rights entails obligations not only to help in concrete situations, but also to establish effective institutions that can safeguard human rights and monitor compliance.

The International Covenant on Civil and Political Rights contains in Article 6 the provision regarding an individual's a right of life. It echoes Article 3 of the Universal Declaration,[28] yet is far more limited in scope, because of the distribution of tasks between the ICCPR and the International Covenant on Economic, Social and Cultural Rights. In the ICCPR, the right refers primarily to the right not to be arbitrarily deprived of life, as it is, indeed, made specific in the succeeding sentence of the clause. But also the further elements of the Article, on death penalty etc, make it clear that it is difficult to derive 'good neighbour' obligations from Article 6. The ICCPR can be said to address one dimension of the Universal Declaration, the one which is less applicable to disaster relief obligations. Yet, Philip Alston, quoting the Human Rights Committee, questions whether, indeed, there is such a clear distribution of tasks between the ICCPR and the ICESCR, when the right to life is concerned,[29] The right to life is said to conceptually embrace more than protection against arbitrary deprivation and should be understood to include protection against malnutrition and epidemics. The value of such an interpretation in relation to Article 3 of the Universal Declaration of Human Rights, as a monolithical legal structure, is clear but could be seen as introducing unwarranted fluidity when applied to Article 6 (right to life) of the ICCPR, because there is such strong coverage of hunger and illness issues in the ICESCR.

Hence the ICESCR is the most highly relevant treaty for the purposes of this investigation. Article 11 of the ICESCR, for instance, is a wonderful example of how the international community moves from 'good neighbour' intentions to 'good neighbour' obligations. Article 11(1) establishes the right to an adequate standard of living, but premises the foreseen international cooperation on the free consent of the parties. So a considerable softening up.[30] In contrast, Article 11(2) stipulates the right to be free from hunger, and puts international co-operation as an absolute, albeit taking 'into account the problems of both food-importing and food-exporting countries, to ensure an equitable distribution of world food supplies in relation to need'. Taking into account the problems of food-importing and food-exporting States does not detract from the nor-

[28] Alston, above, n 11, is, due to the *travaux préparatoires*, reluctant to acknowledge that Art 3 of the Universal Declaration embraces rights to be free from hunger and illness.

[29] Alston, above, n 11.

[30] The reference to 'based on free consent' was included during the drafting of the Article due to the fact that many states opposed the inclusion of a sentence referring to international cooperation as they felt that this would put too much emphasis on Article 11 and detract from the general obligation of states to cooperate internationally as provided for under Art 2 and Part IV of the Covenant. See Craven, above, n 21, at 296.

At the Commission on Human Right's seventh meeting, the concept of 'adequate standard of living' was interpreted by many states as applying to all of the economic, social and cultural rights under discussion, see Craven, above, n 21, at 290. See further at 291 where he states that Art 11 of the Covenant was drafted so as to strengthen the right encompassed by Art 25 of the Universal Declaration which guaranteed more than just an 'adequate' standard of living.

mative character of Article 11(2), it only introduces a further operative element into the normative equation. The fact remains, however, that Article 11(2) should be considered as one of the linchpins of 'good neighbour' obligations.[31]

The other significant provision of the ICESCR is Article 12(1) which recognises the right of everybody to enjoy the highest attainable standard of physical and mental health. The words 'highest attainable' might seem to relativise the right, and are followed up by paragraph 2 talking of 'steps to be taken [. . .] to achieve the full realisation of this right'. One of the steps is the prevention, treatment and control of epidemic, endemic, occupational and other diseases. It is perhaps tempting to conclude from this that neither host or home State nor the 'good neighbour' is the subject of any absolute obligation to provide for health, and that even achievable prevention of disease in disaster situations is 'best efforts' only. This is not correct, however. 'Attainable' is both moderating the obligation, and, by implication, describing what the minimum obligation is. Where resources allow prevention, clearly the obligation exists, and translated to the disaster situation, the 'good neighbour' obligation in this regard is to do what is practically possible to prevent disease and epidemics. As explained above, the resource element is normally not an issue for the 'good neighbour', since most developed countries lag far behind their means in terms of their humanitarian effort, and hence practicability is the only moderator.

Ironically, one must also conclude that Article 12 is the provision obliging the 'good neighbour' to provide for emergency shelter in disaster cases. Article 11(1) addresses housing as part of the right to an adequate standard of living. However, the right to an adequate standard of living shall, inter alia, be achieved by international cooperation 'based on free consent'. As mentioned above, the language of Article 11(1) implies that only best efforts are required from the international community when assisting in ensuring an adequate standard of living. However, when lack of adequate shelter becomes a threat to health, as in disaster situations, then the absolute 'good neighbour' obligation becomes incumbent under Article 12 .

[31] See Craven, above, n 21, at 297–301; Eide, above, n 8, at 90–105, United Nations Economic and Social Council, E/C.12/1995/5.

See further Alston, above, n 11, at 36, where he states in respect of Art 11:

> by imposing a duty on all states to act by international co-operation, the article implicitly vests rights in certain states as a corollary of the duty of all states to act. Moreover, in practical terms, the obligation of States Parties 'to ensure an equitable distribution of world food supplies in relation to need' can only be operationalized on an inter-state basis. The shield (or the sword) of state sovereignty severely restricts the possibility of implementing such an obligation at any other level.

Alston further states at 41 'it is submitted that in fact the Covenant does import a legally binding obligation to co-operate internationally (which may sometimes involve the provision of aid) with other states, in certain circumstances, to ensure the realization of inter alia the right to food'. He then goes even further: 'the duty to co-operate internationally to ensure the realization of the right to food is not limited to the need under appropriate circumstances to provide assistance. Indeed, given the extent to which food self-reliance is now recognized as a fundamental goal of most countries, the duties to avoid depriving and to protect from deprivation are almost certainly of greater importance'.

Cf Food Aid Convention 1999, aiming at contributing to world food security and improving the ability of the international community to respond to emergency food situations and other food needs of developing countries; and General Assembly Resolution 3180 of 1973: Universal Declaration on the Eradication of Hunger and Malnutrition; stressing the fact that eradication of hunger is a common objective of all countries of the international community, especially developed countries and others in a position to help, and that it is the fundamental responsibility of Governments to co-operate in order to achieve these ends.

NOT A SUBSPECIES OF THE RIGHT TO DEVELOPMENT

It may be tempting to assume that good neighbour obligations can exist only if international law in general confers a right to development on disadvantaged States.[32] This temptation may be particularly strong as many of the norms adduced as supportive of good neighbour obligations have been invoked also as a foundation for the right to development.[33] Going from the more general to the specific, one could argue that good neighbour obligations represent merely an application of the *a majore ad minus* principle vis-à-vis the general right to development. There could be reason to happily apply this logic, if the right to development was, indeed, generally assumed. Notwithstanding the Declaration on the Right to Development,[34] there is, however, great disagreement on whether a general right to development exists.[35] This does not mean that this disagreement as a matter of logic necessarily carries over to the issue of good neighbour obligations, because most of the legal reasoning utilised to question the general right to development does not apply to the assumption of good neighbour obligations. The perennial argument against hard obligations for developed countries to assist developing countries achieve development has been that no tangible obligation can be defined, and if an obligation is not tangible then it is, in fact, not an obligation.[36]

Take the two linchpins for good neighbour obligations, Articles 11(2) and 12(1) of the ICESCR. Article 11(2) establishes, as mentioned above, a right to be free from hunger. In relation to good neighbour obligations there is no lack of specificity in the obligation: if starvation occurs or is imminent, the obligation is to provide food. If, however, the argument is made that Article 11(2) means that there is an international obligation to create boundary conditions in developing countries which would mean that hunger disasters would become unlikely then, like most preventative measures, the obligation starts to become vague. How can it be assured that funds provided will be spent on schemes that are effective measures against future starvation, how can it be made sure that the preconditions for effective measures are in place, etc. Sadly, it is perhaps not surprising that developed countries will be reluctant to assume that a firm norm exists in the latter respect.[37] Article 12(1) provides for a right of everybody to

[32] On the right to development generally, see R Rich, *The Right to Development as a Human Right* E/CN.4/1334; Kéba Mbaye, *Le Droit du Developpement comme un Droit de L'Homme*, 5 Revue des Droits de L'Homme (1972); Oscar Schachter, 'The Emerging International Law of Development', 15 Columbia Journal of Transnational Law (1976); Subrata Chowdhury (ed), *The Right to Development in International Law* (1992); Gräfrath Bernhard, 'Gibt es ein Menschenrecht auf Entwicklung?' Humanitaeres Voelkerrecht Informationsschriften 1 (1994), 7 et seq.

[33] See Philip Alston and Gerard Quinn, above, n 17, at 186, on the right to development under the ICESCR.

[34] General Assembly Resolution 41/128

[35] See Jack Donnely, 'In Search of the Unicorn: The Jurisprudence and Politics of the Right to Development', 15 California Western International Law Journal 473 (1985), at 482, underlining the difficulty in establishing a right to development. Cf Mohammed Bedjaoui, 'The Right to Development', in Bedjaoui (ed), *International Law: Achievements and Prospects* (1991) at 1182 and Georges Abi-Saab, *The Legal Formulation of a Right to Development in Academy of International Law, The Right to Development at the International Level* (1980), at 163.

[36] See Donnely, above, n 35, at 482.

[37] See Philip Alston, 'Revitalising United Nations Work on Human Rights and Development', 18 Melbourne University Law Review 216 (1991) at 218, on the reluctance of Western states to accept a general right to development.

enjoy the highest attainable standard of physical and mental health. There is relativity built into the norm, and obviously there cannot be an obligation for developed nations to fund ever-increasing standards of health in other countries. Yet, the relativity does not mean that there is no minimum standard of health which must be ensured also by the good neighbour. The fact that the threshold of ultimate achievement is not described does not mean that there is no lower threshold to be achieved—by the host State, as well as by the good neighbour.[38]

The inherent two-pronged nature of Articles 11(2) and 12(1) in imposing both good neighbour obligations, as a minimum, and in parallel less tangible general development goals, set these human rights norms on a different footing than, for instance, the Declaration on the Right to Development, which addresses only assistance from developed to developing States. Good neighbour obligations apply to rich and to poor, meaning that in these disaster scenarios even a developing State is obliged to come to the aid of another State whether developed or developing, if it has a reasonable opportunity to do so. Good neighbour obligations are then, in the final analysis, not a subspecies of the right to development, even if partly they draw on the same human rights norms. They are separately identifiable obligations, because of their immediacy and tangibility, and the range of addressees is much wider.

TYPOLOGY OF STATE 'GOOD NEIGHBOUR' OBLIGATIONS

The above general review of the key components of the 'International Bill of Rights' shows that for disaster situations there is a general obligation to provide relief, be it in the form of food, shelter, clean water or medical care. These obligations are underwritten by norms that are both complementary and overlapping. By this an inclusive and strong fabric of obligation is created for emergency relief situations.[39] Yet, even when discussing disaster scenarios, different forms of assistance merit consideration. Some of these forms of assistance constitute instances of State practice underpinning, to some extent, the assertions of normativity of good neighbour activities.

Not surprisingly the practice of States has more readily embraced passive rather than active assistance. And, in fact, the most modest configuration of good neighbour obligations is the obligation of a State to allow help to be provided via its territory—an essentially passive duty even if waiving or simplifying visa and customs formalities may be involved.[40] Based on the reality of widespread State acceptance of allowing help to be provided via their territories, along with parallels from the Geneva Conventions on safe passage of relief consignments in war situations,[41] it might be

[38] Supra, n. 15, p 10.

[39] Contra, without reasoning. Eide, above, n 9, at 399.

[40] In order to be as affective as possible in this respect, states should, and often do, prepare general national legislation on these issues, so that an implementation system is in place when disaster strikes and assistance becomes necessary. The International Disaster Response Laws, Rules and Principles (IDRL) project initiated by the International Federation of Red Cross and Red Crescent Societies (IFRC) aims to raise awareness and promote the implementation and strengthening of the laws, rules and principles that ensure a timely, adequate and efficient international response to disasters. One aim is to assist States with identifying legal barriers that would impede the receipt of foreign disaster relief assistance and the IFRC maintains a database of case studies of legal issues that arose in disaster relief in various countries, http://www.ifrc.org/what/disasters/idrl/research/casestudies.asp .

[41] On this see Yoram Dinstein, *The Right to Humanitarian Assistance*, Naval War College Review, Autumn 2000, www.nwc.navy.mil/press/Review/2000/autumn/art5-a00.htm.

tempting to conclude that, at least, an international obligation exists for a State to allow relief operations to take place from or through its territory in favour of another State. In support of this view one may also adduce recent developments, such as the ASEAN Agreement on Disaster Management and Emergency Response of July 2005, Article 16 of which obliges States to seek to facilitate transit of persons and goods in disaster situations, and which obliges the transit State to exempt such transit goods from taxation and duties. With a correct interpretation of the human rights norms, however, obligations cannot stop there. States habitually come to the aid of others stricken by disaster proactively, and although the practice might not be sufficiently universal or uniform to be said to constitute custom, both the willingness of States, and, perhaps doctrinally more dubious, the willingness of populations to help through voluntary contributions to aid organisations, support the interpretation of the key human rights instruments leading to the assumption of active good neighbour obligations of States generally. A growing *opinio juris* in world society counteracts any suggestion of desuetude and helps allow a proper first principles interpretation of the International Bill of Rights.

In these circumstances it might be salutary to seek to match the above rather conceptual approach with concrete examples of how assistance has been effected in the past, and with concrete examples of the direction assistance would have to take in the future to achieve compliance with the general good neighbour norm. A starting point for such consideration can be constituted by the Cotonou Agreement 2000 (amended 2005) which is a remarkable document, not only in how it demonstrates the *opinio juris* of an important part of the international community, but also in providing evidence of how the 'good neighbour' obligations are implemented. In fact, the Cotonou Agreement defines in very practical terms the various elements that form part of effective disaster assistance. It mirrors in aim and methodology the Resolution of the United Nations General Assembly on the 'Strengthening of the coordination of humanitarian emergency assistance of the United Nations'.[42] Part 4, Chapter 6 of the Cotonou Agreement contains the provisions on humanitarian and emergency assistance. It establishes absolute obligations within an over-all financial ceiling. The obligations break down into essentially three categories, based on the time-line of disasters: (1) warning systems; (2) direct relief and (3) short-term rehabilitation and reconstruction.

Looking first at warning systems, it is interesting to note that the emphasis is on the 'setting up of disaster prevention and preparedness mechanisms'. This emphasis, of course, chimes with the general aspiration of self-sufficiency but ignores a potentially more difficult angle, namely, the provision of relevant disaster prevention data in the possession of the European Commission or its Member States. Both elements of this equation became highly topical as a result of the tsunami disaster, where questions abounded about whether warning could have been expressed earlier and about the reasons why no tsunami warning system existed in the Indian Ocean region. It is easy to conclude that assistance with the establishment of disaster prevention systems is sensible, and perhaps even part of complying with 'good neighbour' obligations, although the setting up of such systems typically involves a considerable lead-time and therefore is only emergency assistance in a very wide understanding of this concept. It is more the fishing rod than the fish.

[42] Above, n 10.

The provision of disaster prevention data already in the possession of a 'good neighbour' is more immediately associated with preventative disaster assistance. Should one conclude *a contrario* from the absence of such obligations in the Cotonou Agreement that the least costly, easiest, and potentially most effective assistance is not a 'good neighbour' obligation? Surely such a result is neither supported by the right to life provision in the Universal Declaration nor by the 'good neighbour' provision of the ICESCR.[43] In an age where pre-emption of aggression has become a dangerous fashion, prevention of disaster must be an obligation incumbent on the 'good neighbour', who in any event would have only disadvantage by waiting for the disaster to strike and then be called upon to alleviate the consequences as a 'good neighbour'.[44]

The reason that data provision was omitted from the Cotonou Agreement can presumably be found in jurisdictional reasons, namely that the European Commission itself would possess little relevant data. For the Commission to dispose of relevant data in the possession of the Member States was probably found to be too intrusive or even *ultra vires*. What is more, the relevance of this topic might also not have been fully realised in the negotiations leading to the Cotonou Agreement, considering that the focus was a completely different one. A 'good neighbour' obligation to provide available disaster prevention data seems a logical and uncontroversial conclusion, but a conclusion which invites a more problematic issue. The 'good neighbour' obligation would be to provide the data relevant for disaster prevention which would be in the possession of the neighbour. The issue is then whether the data covered by the obligation is only the data which is in the direct possession of the State, or also data which belongs to private entities within the State, for example, private weather companies. Arguing from a traditional public international law perspective one would be tempted to conclude that obligations of a State are obligations on all entities in a State whether private or not.[45] If a State is obliged to refrain from testing nuclear weapons then it is an obligation which the State must also enforce vis-à-vis private persons.[46] Yet, it is important both from a practical and conceptual perspective to distinguish between obligations incumbent on State organs themselves and obligations which State organs, in addition, are obliged to enforce domestically in respect of all its citizens, natural or other. The latter is a kind of second-level obligation, which it is prudent to consider separately in specific instances.

[43] The importance of early warning information is stressed in General Assembly Resolution 46/182, which, however, has as its focus the provision of such data through UN channels.

[44] An exception would be the situation where a custom-made disaster alert system is set up as a multilateral undertaking. If a disaster prone country deliberately refuses to participate in such an undertaking, and in the resultant cost, the other participants should not be obliged to cover for this country—although there may be a more general obligation for rich countries to fund the participation of the disaster prone country, if lack of participation is due only to a lack of funds. Yet, even in these situations the participants in the disaster alert system are obliged to alert the non-participating country if the disaster alert system in a concrete case identifies an avoidable danger. The participating countries are only free to withhold the continuous data-stream, which the disaster alert system may generate. In clear and present danger the non-participant must be alerted. Humanity beats principle!

[45] Part III, section 18 of the Maastricht Guidelines on Violations of Economic, Social and Cultural Rights, HRQ 20 (1998) 691–705, regarding 'acts by non-state entities', stipulates ie 'The obligation to protect includes the state's responsibility to ensure that private entities or individuals, including transnational corporations over which they exercise jurisdiction, do not deprive individuals of their economic, social and cultural rights'.

[46] See the Comprehensive Nuclear-Test-Ban Treaty (CTBT), especially Articles I and III regulating states' basic obligations and national implementation measures.

Considering the nascent stage of 'good neighbour' obligations, it is advisable to impose the second-level obligations only when such obligations have clear jurisprudential support. This is not the case for the provision of disaster prevention data, because such an obligation in respect of private entities would open a host of difficult practical and economic issues. Practically, the private entity would seek strong safeguards against misappropriation of the data, particularly if continuous data streams are involved. These safeguards could be difficult to implement and costly for the 'neighbour' if violations were to take place. And from a macroeconomic perspective the generation of data might be impeded if private entities would not be in sovereign charge of the data utilisation. The route to take, if such data would be important for disaster prevention, is probably the route ordinarily taken for domestic disaster prevention, namely, to enter into commercial agreements as required. But that goes beyond 'good neighbour' obligations, unless the 'neighbour' already has access to the data for use in its own, domestic disaster prevention systems.

Turning to direct relief and short term rehabilitation and reconstruction, the question of second-level obligations comes up in a somewhat different configuration. The 'good neighbour' obligation in relation to direct relief and short term rehabilitation and reconstruction is in the first instance an obligation to commit resources for these purposes. Yet, funds on their own do not suffice, so the issue becomes how the 'good neighbour' can make available relevant resources, food, medicine etc. If the neighbour already has the relevant resources within its ownership there is only a logistical problem to be overcome. But if part or all of the necessary resources are available only from private sources, the question on the second-level obligation becomes relevant again. For direct relief, and to a lesser extent for short term rehabilitation and reconstruction, there would not be the same reluctance to invoke a second-level obligation as in the case of disaster prevention data, the reason being that the immediate need to avoid mass death or misery would override all macro-economic concerns about sweeping aside the protective veil of private ownership. Expropriation would be a relevant tool to do so, and the loss of private ownership would be compensated through the expropriation mechanism, if the private entity was unwilling to assist in the disaster relief. The problem with using expropriation is a practical one, however. Expropriation takes time, and time is a scarce commodity when relief must be provided. The conclusion must be that in rare cases the 'good neighbour' might have to step to expropriation, when time allows and no other practical way of complying with the 'good neighbour' obligation exists. But normally the good neighbour is under no public international law obligation to utilise a specific method to comply with obligations, as long as obligations are, indeed, met.[47] The reality will then mostly be that resource

[47] Cf. Andreassen, above, n 9, at 351, citing the Limburg Principles (above, n 45): 'it must be born[e] in mind that the Covenant affords to a State Party a margin of discretion in selecting the means for carrying out its objectives . . .'.

See Antonio Cassese, International Law (2001) 167, who argues that although a duty for states exists to bring national law in conformity with obligations under international law, state practice has shown that states are only interested in the final result, namely whether there has been fulfilment or non-fulfilment of an obligation.

Cf the decision of the International Court of Justice in the *North Sea Continental Shelf Cases*, ICJ Reports 1969, paras 83–101, where it held in respect of the delimitation of the continental shelf between the Federal Republic of Germany and Denmark on the one hand, and between the Federal Republic of Germany and the Netherlands on the other, that the use of the equidistance method or any other method of delimitation was not obligatory between the Parties and that delimitation was to be effected by agreement in accordance

needs will be met by the good neighbour using commercial channels to obtain required relief supplies.

Finally, one intriguing question with regard to providing assistance in times of natural disaster is whether a 'good neighbour' is obliged to utilise all types of resources within its control, as long as they can be spared. Or, more explicitly, whether a neighbour is obliged to utilise its military resources for relief, if otherwise adequate relief could not be provided. The tsunami relief effort showed how instrumental foreign military forces and equipment can be for providing effective relief. Utilising military forces for relief touches, however, a core sovereignty nerve. In this respect it is important to note that the point here is whether military resources might have to be utilised when they can be spared; there is no suggestion that the 'good neighbour's' own security should be compromised by relief deployment.

It is a natural corollary to the general principle of the 'good neighbour' being responsible for its own implementation measures, that the 'good neighbour' must also deploy its military resources, if this is necessary to fulfil obligations. Whether the stricken State will allow foreign troops as part of the relief effort is another question, however, since here we are speaking of a sovereign preserve and the possible sentiment of vulnerability of the receiving State. The question then turns out to be the inverse: is a stricken State obliged to receive foreign troops, as part of a relief effort—or even more fundamentally: is a stricken State obliged to allow foreign relief? It is conceptually easy to dismiss the notion that a stricken State should be obliged to receive foreign troops as part of a relief effort—for the simple reason that such an obligation would open avenues for abuse by the 'good neighbour' and, as a matter of principle, would be such an imposition on sovereignty that an obligation would become unpalatable, particularly in the current unintegrated state of the international community.

On the more general question of whether there is an obligation to accept relief by the stricken State, it might appear radical to suggest that such an obligation is a direct result of the obligation to ensure the right to life, freedom from hunger etc, with the consequence that when the State cannot do so itself then it must allow the 'good neighbour' to help. What triggered the 'good neighbour' obligation must, in this logic, be understood to have triggered also the lesser obligation to receive the assistance,[48] at least from States with which diplomatic relations are maintained. The radical appearance of this argument stems from our metaphysical perception of sovereignty. In the bright light of analysis, an obligation to accept assistance in disaster situations does not trample on any protectable element of sovereignty, given the supremacy of the right to life, to freedom from hunger. A stricken State might be reluctant to receive assistance because of mistaken sovereign pride, yet true pride must be founded first and foremost in the care a State shows for its own population. This is what States have recognised through the Universal Declaration and by ratifying the human rights covenants.

with equitable principles, taking account of all relevant circumstances. This principle was confirmed by the Court in the subsequent case of *Tunisia/Libya*, ICJ Reports 1982, para 70: 'It is however the result which is predominant; the principles are subordinate to the goal . . .'.

[48] See Alston, above, n 11, using the example of Ethiopia as a country, subject to the ICESCR, under an obligation to receive assistance. The drift of General Assembly Resolution 46/182, para 3, might appear to contradict this assumption. Resolution 46/182 is, however, not couched in mandatory terms, and could, in any event, not be taken to be dispositive of the issue. The same is true for the statement in the 2006 Report of the International Law Commission that disaster assistance requires a request from the stricken state, http://untreaty.un.org/ilc/reports/2006/2006report.htm, 479

A further issue with regard to the stricken State exists with regard to compensation. The Cotonou Agreement can, in many respects, be considered as a paradigm for disaster assistance from developed countries to less developed countries. The Cotonou Agreement assumes that there is no obligation for the recipient of disaster assistance to ultimately compensate the 'good neighbour' for the assistance provided. This is natural in the context, but does not resolve the issue of whether a recipient of disaster assistance must compensate the provider of the assistance, in the absence of specific agreement. In support of an obligation to eventually compensate it could be said that the domestic parallel of emergency assistance normally entails an obligation for the recipient of help to compensate third parties, if the goods of third parties have been sacrificed in order to save goods of higher value belonging to the recipient of the assistance.[49]

This parallel, and overall macroeconomic consideration, would normally lead to the conclusion that an obligation to compensate exists also on the international plane. However, the Universal Declaration, together with the ICESCR, leads to the opposite result, if the provider of the assistance is a developed country and the recipient a developing country. Article 28 of the Universal Declaration sets out a right for everyone to enjoy an international order in which the rights and freedoms of the Declaration can be fully realised. This, in conjunction with Article 2(1) of the ICESCR, which mirrors this right, and adds the inter-State obligation to assist 'to the maximum of its available resources', means that the assisting developed State is not entitled to compensation from a developing country recipient. The situation is different where there is an equality of prosperity: rich to rich, or poor to poor. In these situations the normal principles, aiming to avoid unjust enrichment, kick in. This is particularly noteworthy in the poor-to-poor relationship, because the distress of a country cannot be allowed to add to the distress of a 'good neighbour'. Would it be otherwise, it would ensure that the neighbour would never be good, to the obvious detriment of international cohesion and human rights.

In this context, it is remarkable that the world is rich on multilateral and bilateral defence pacts, but almost devoid of dedicated multilateral or bilateral disaster assistance pacts.[50] Disaster-prone regions, subjected to hurricanes, droughts, flooding,

[49] Cf § 904 of the Buergerliches Gesetzbuch (BGB) on 'Notstand' which stipulates that the owner of property is not entitled to deny someone the use of his property if such use is in order to avert an imminent danger and the damage that would be averted by use of the property is much higher than that which would occur to the property in order to avert such danger. In such an event, the property owner has the right to compensation from the user of the property, and the user has a right to compensation from the person/owner of the property he was trying to rescue. See also §§ 683, 670 of the BGB.

See also the principle of *negotiorum gestio* in Roman and civil law which governs the conduct of business without mandate. In such a situation a quasi-contract arises in which the actor, who has undertaken of his own accord to manage the affairs of another (to the benefit of the absentee) and who thus has the 'tacit responsibility to continue such affairs up until completion and to deliver the proceeds to the owner, who likewise is bound to reimburse the actor for any expenses incurred'. See *Black's, Law Dictionary* 7th edn (1999) 1060. See the decision of the Bundesgerichtshof in *Funkenflug*, BGHZ 40, 28 VII. Civil Senate (VII ZR 263/61). The concept of 'constructive trust' under the doctrine of equity is used in common law.

[50] Of note, however, is the exhortation in General Assembly Resolution 46/182 for the UN 'to make appropriate arrangements with interested Governments and intergovernmental and non-governmental organizations to enable it to have more expeditious access, when necessary, to their emergency relief capacities, including food reserves, emergency stockpiles and personnel, as well as logistic support'.

Fact Sheet 6 of the International Disaster Response Laws, Rules and Principles (IDRL) of the International Federation of Red Cross and Red Crescent Societies, contains a preliminary overview of treaties addressing disaster response. In Europe quite a number of treaties exist, whereas in other regions treaties appear to be missing. Special studies of Southern Africa showed that disaster assistance was mainly addressed in passing in treaties of a broader scope, or the subject of dedicated treaties on specific disasters.

would appear to have a strong interest to create effective formal frameworks for disaster assistance, so that the role of each State would be defined before disaster actually strikes. By this, reluctance might be overcome, for instance, due to uncertainty on the obligation for the recipient to ultimately compensate, and speed would obviously be greatly served. It is sad that the world is so much more preoccupied with war than with disaster avoidance!

OBLIGATIONS OF INTERGOVERNMENTAL ORGANISATIONS

Given the large number of States Parties to the ICESCR, it might be less necessary to discuss whether States that are not party to the Covenant are, nevertheless, bound by its provisions. Suffice it to say that the provenance of the Covenant in the Charter of the UN and in the Universal Declaration, together with its large number of ratifications, would lend credence to an assumption that a general *opinio juris* about its normative effect have made its scope universal through the vehicle of 'general principles of law'.[51]

However, separate consideration must be given to the normative effect vis-à-vis intergovernmental organisations, if it would be assumed that the ICESCR has not achieved universal validity. It goes with the territory of the United Nations and its specialised agencies that they are subject to the norms which are derived from their constitutive documents. It is more problematic whether other intergovernmental organisations, as independent subjects of international law, are bound by norms derived from the ICESCR, to which they neither are, nor can become, parties.[52] For almost universal treaties of fundamental importance normative effect vis-à-vis an intergovernmental organisation might be found in the *opinio juris* of its constituency, its Member States. If the Member States have committed themselves to such a treaty it is an expression of an intention to be bound which can be considered transposed to the intergovernmental organisation by way of a kind of 'local general principle of law'.[53] Consider the

Hence, one must conclude that there is a lack of coverage of effective treaties on general disaster relief. One exception is in the highly relevant field of telecommunications, where The Tampere Convention on the Provision of Telecommunications Resources for Disaster Mitigation and Relief Operations seeks to ensure effective access in disaster cases. The ASEAN Agreement on Disaster Management and Emergency Response of 2005 is a welcome development. Also noteworthy is that Switzerland has concluded Memoranda of Understanding on disaster assistance with all of its neighbours; all four can be found at: www.admin.ch.

[51] See Hulsroj, above, n 2, at 244–254;. See also below, n 53.

[52] See Art 26 of the Covenant on conditions of accession, which stipulates that the Convention is only open for signature by State Parties to the Statute of the International Court of Justice, or any state which has been invited by the General Assembly to sign, and State Members of the United Nations or any of its specialised agencies.

[53] On general principles of law as a source of substantive legal norms see Hulsroj, above, n 2, at 244–254; and Theodor Meron, *Human Rights and Humanitarian Norms as Customary Law* (1989) 79–106.

See further Henry G Schermers and Niels M Blokker, *International Institutional Law* (1995), 984–988, who state that: 'states who have founded an international organization are bound by general principles of law. . . . It may be difficult to find principles of law applicable in specific cases. They will have to be derived from the national legal orders of the member states and from treaties into which the majority of member states have entered'; and further in respect of situations where treaties exclude international organisations, 'they will have to apply the main substantive provisions of general law-making treaties such as Red Cross Conventions. Regional organizations will also be required to apply the main substantive provisions of regional law-making treaties such as the European Convention on Human Rights. The legal foundation of this obligation lies not in its character as an international treaty but rather in its character as a general principle of law codified by treaty'.

example of the European Union. All Member States of the EU are parties to the European Human Rights Convention, but the EU itself is not and cannot be. Does this mean that the EU is not bound by the substantive provisions of the Convention, which is an instrument under the aegis of the Council of Europe? That cannot and should not be assumed. The procedural and recourse provisions clearly require party status, which the European Union cannot achieve. Yet, the defined substantive rights of the Convention must also apply mutatis mutandis to the EU. So, for instance, the European Union must ensure its staff the right to liberty and security of person[54] while on European Union extraterritorial terrain.

The binding effect on intergovernmental organisations of fundamental treaties which have been ratified by a majority of its Member States could also be sought in State succession theory. In fact, there are parallels to the issues facing the International Law Commission in drafting the Convention on Responsibility of Intergovernmental Organisations and their Member States. The State succession argument would run that the intergovernmental organisation derives its functional powers from the Member States by their transfer of part of their sovereign powers to the organisation. A transfer of sovereign powers comes with the liens already attached to the sovereign power transferred.[55] Thus it becomes an obligation on the transferring State to seek to ensure that the intergovernmental organisation does not act contrary to the liens on the received power.[56] At least if a majority of Member States had the same liens attached to the transferred power, they must be obliged to exercise their majority rights in the organisation to ensure respect of the liens. It should, however, be remembered that these theoretically complex issues only become relevant if it is assumed that that the ICESCR has not become part of general international law.

The Advisory Opinion of the ICJ on *Certain Expenses of the United Nations*[57] made it clear that intergovernmental organisations have international personality commensurate with their functional scope. With this starting point and with the caveats discussed above, it can probably be said that 'good neighbour' obligations apply to intergovernmental organisations to the extent that fulfilment would fall within the scope of their functional role, but that intergovernmental organisations cannot be obliged to move *ultra vires* in order to be 'good neighbours'. Hence the World Bank might have 'good neighbour' obligations of a financial nature, and the European Organisation for the Exploitation of Meteorological Satellites might have 'good neighbour' obligations of a data provision nature, but the European Organisation

[54] See Art 5 of the European Convention on Human Rights 1950. see also Schermers and Blokker, above, n 53, at 985, noting that although the EU is not a party to the European Convention and the EU Court has held that it is not bound thereby, the Court has nonetheless declared that it will ensure respect for the general principles of Community law and has translated some of the provisions of the Convention into Community law, in line with basic principles of human rights and general principles of law. Thus, the Court has adopted an 'interpretative' approach, whereby it will give effect to the principles guaranteed by the Convention by making sure that relevant norms, to the extent possible, are construed so as to be in line with the Convention.

[55] Cf Art 12 of the Charter of Economic Rights and Duties for an example of this line of thought.

[56] See the Maastricht Guidelines on Violations of Economic, Social and Cultural Rights, above, n 45, Part II, s 19: 'Acts by international organizations', states, ie, 'The obligations of states to protect economic, social and cultural rights extend also to their participation in international organizations, where they act collectively. It is particularly important for states to use their influence to ensure that violations do not result from the programmes and policies of the organizations of which they are members . . .'.

[57] ICJ Reports, 1962, 151.

for the Exploitation of Meteorological Satellites would not have a 'good neighbour obligation' to provide financial funds for disaster relief purposes.

THE DOMESTIC PARALLELS?

In *foro domestico* it is remarkable to note how reluctant the legal systems are to establish duties to assist. In some jurisdictions there are criminally sanctioned obligations to assist if somebody's life is acutely endangered.[58] Obligations to assisting in fighting fires and other specified hazards also sometimes exist.[59] But generally domestic legal systems do not impose a duty to assist, and even tort law is very restrained in allowing compensation if a bystander does not act to avert impending damage.[60] Looking at the rationale for this approach, there are probably three driving forces: first, not to oblige citizens to performance of actions which might not be clear; second, to avoid that a duty to assist turns out to be an obligation to meddle; and third, more fundamentally, it might be assumed that the duty to assist is a duty on society, not on the individual. It can be concluded from the lack of domestic duties to assist, that no norm to that effect has been established on the international scene by virtue of 'general principles of law'. Still, it may be relevant to investigate whether the reasons that led domestic legal systems to abstain from duties to assist would lead to the conclusion that also no 'good neighbour' obligations exist in public international law, notwithstanding the mentioned human rights norms.

Not to commit someone to obligations of unclear scope and the desire to avoid meddling are concerns that could be said to be equally valid in international relations. Nevertheless, international diplomacy and State systems are, of course, far more able to interpret the scope of obligations and far more able to counteract meddling. In fact, such issues are the reality of daily life in the international arena, and they cannot be considered a deterrent for seeking to avoid disasters. It is obviously not an argument against 'good neighbour' obligations that society should take care of disaster assistance instead of the individual State. Because such an argument presupposes that there is a society that could take on this task. Despite the good work of UN organisations, for example, and the coordination done by the UN,[61] it is woefully clear that in the international arena there is no 'society' which can provide consistent, effective disaster relief. The involvement of 'neighbours' is indispensable.

The only international institution which has a command authority similar to that of domestic governments is the Security Council in cases where threats to the peace,

[58] Danish Criminal Code, Art 253.

[59] Danish Criminal Code, Art 185.

[60] In the United Kingdom, there is generally no legal liability for a mere omission to assist. For example, there is no legal obligation on an individual to assist a person in need of resuscitation provided he was not the cause of the casualty requiring treatment.

[61] The United Nations Office for the Coordination of Humanitarian Affairs (OCHA) was established by General Assembly Resolution 46/182 in 1991 in order to strengthen the United Nation's response to both emergency situations and natural disasters.

For early efforts on disaster relief see the Convention Establishing an International Relief Union, 1927, 135 LNTS 247; General Assembly Resolution 281G of 1971 on 'Assistance in Case of Natural Disaster and Other Disaster Situations' and General Assembly Resolution 39/207 of 1984 on 'Special Economic and Disaster Relief Assistance: Office of the United Nations Disaster Relief Assistance'. Most recently, the General Assembly adopted Resolution 59/279 of 2005 on Strengthening Emergency Relief, Rehabilitation, Reconstruction and Prevention in the Aftermath of the Indian Ocean Tsunami Disaster.

breaches of the peace or acts of aggression exist.[62] Under this heading the Security Council has made a few forays into humanitarian action and disaster relief. Albania,[63] Somalia,[64] and Bosnia[65] spring to mind. Common to these cases was the fact that the Security Council action involved a military element, which might have made the Security Council comfortable with the link to 'threats to the peace'. The military element was directed at the State with the humanitarian crisis on its hands. So relief operations could be defended by foreign military means. In other words the 'good neighbour' could be militarily sheltered.

It is not advocated here that the Security Council should be expected to be an ingredient in all humanitarian efforts, or that the Security Council can or should replace the 'good neighbour'. It is, however, suggested that the possibilities of the Security Council to enable disaster relief and to reinforce the 'good neighbour' obligations is an important, and largely overlooked, part of the disaster relief tool-box; overlooked, in fact, even by the UN itself, despite its recent laudable effort to promote the concept of 'the duty to protect'. 'The duty to protect' embraces the much discussed concept of humanitarian intervention, and repackages it in Security Council terms. However, 'the duty to protect' involves, again, the use of force to protect the persecuted, but ignores inexplicably a much less politically sensitive duty for the Security Council to enforce good neighbour obligations.[66]

With the expansive interpretation of 'threat to the peace, breach of the peace and acts of aggression' which the Security Council has adopted,[67] it is clear that the Security Council cannot only allow that military force be used against a regime that will not allow that its citizens be helped in a humanitarian crisis, but it can positively demand that the 'good neighbour' rushes to the rescue, much as when the President of

[62] By virtue of Art 24 of the Charter of the United Nations, the Security Council has been vested with the sole power under Chapter VII of the Charter to determine when a threat to, breach of the peace or act of aggression has occurred and to order the necessary provisional or enforcement measures against a state. On the Chapter VII powers of the Security Council in general see Simma (ed), above, n 3, at 701–807; Danesh Sarooshi, *The United Nations and the Development of Collective Security* (1999).

[63] In March 1997 the Security Council passed Resolution 1101, authorising humanitarian action as a reaction to the crisis situation in Albania. The resolution enabled the Security Council to make full use of its Chapter VII powers by determining (in accordance with Art 39 of the Charter): 'that the present situation of crisis in Albania constitutes a threat to peace and security in the region'.

[64] In the case of Somalia, the Security Council made an Art 39 determination, enabling it to use its Chapter VII powers, through Resolution 794 in December 1992 where it stated that 'the magnitude of the human tragedy caused by the conflict in Somalia, further exacerbated by the obstacles being created to the distribution of humanitarian assistance, constitutes a threat to international peace and security'.

[65] In Bosnia, the Security Council passed Resolution 770 in August 1992 stating: 'the provision of humanitarian assistance in Bosnia and Herzegovina is an important element in the Council's effort to restore international peace and security in the region', thus enabling it to make use of its Chapter VII powers.

[66] See above, n 1; Report, 26–31, 56–58, where, very laudably, it is recommended that the Security Council develops a set of criteria for when to exercise its responsibility to protect. Unfortunately, neither the unwillingness of a state stricken by a natural disaster to receive help nor the unwillingness of not-so-good neighbours to provide help are included as criteria. The Secretary General of the United Nations' Report 'In Larger Freedom', UN Doc/A/59/2005 or under www.un.org/larger freedom, 65–6,177, 202–11, deals in some detail with the need for reform to be able to better handle disasters. However, there is no mention of the duties of the good neighbour and no effort to sensitivise the Security Council to the need to potentially exercise Chapter VII powers vis-à-vis recalcitrant receivers or givers of assistance.

[67] The term 'threat to the peace' might be understood to imply some actual or potential military manifestation; however, the Security Council has not always made use of its Chapter VII powers according to such criteria. See Alexander Orakhelashvili 'The Power of the UN Security Council to Determine the Existence of a "Threat to the Peace" *Irish Yearbook of International Law, 2006*, Volume 1, pp 61–99.

the United States commands the National Guard to assist when disaster strikes domestically. In jurisprudential analysis it is often overlooked that when the Security Council takes action to quell threats to the peace or breaches thereof, the action often has profound effects on third party States. When sanctions are applied they are normally directed at the peace violator, but must be executed by third party States. Embargoes hurt not only the violator but also the enforcing States. In this sense, sanctions are almost *Kelsenesque*[68] in their emphasis on compliance by the law-enforcing entities. This being so, the Security Council could, without swallowing conceptual camels, use its Chapter VII powers to call up 'good neighbour' obligations, even when the State experiencing a disaster is entirely receptive to getting assistance, and only the 'good neighbour' shows reluctance. Using the Chapter VII powers in this fashion is only a variation on the theme struck, for instance, in Somalia. There the providers were ready, but the receiver hostile. When the provider is hostile and the receiver ready, the threat to the peace is no less. In both cases, Chapter VII can be applied.

The concretisation of 'good neighbour' obligations through Chapter VII action can be said to not add to the commitment of the neighbour, because it was, in any event, committed to help. However, just like a judgment makes an obligation unambiguous, the exercise of Chapter VII powers vis-à-vis an unwilling neighbour can be highly motivating and make the obligation unambiguous. Nevertheless, the Chapter VII powers of the Security Council is not a panacea. Chapter VII powers must be used judiciously, and the Security Council may not be able to directly commandeer troops or military equipment, because of the absence of Article 43 agreements.[69] Nevertheless, the Security Council can in disaster cases be an important tool for progress, both by exercising Chapter VII powers in rare cases and by unlocking the benevolence of the willing, because they know that if they are not willing then they may be forced.

CONCLUSION

The human being is the object of all law.[70] Hence the measure and interpretation of all law must be the interest of the human being. Admittedly, the interest of the human being is a measure open to interpretation in much the same way as natural law. Positivism is the moderator of this subjectivity, yet even under positivism a realisation of the foundation of law is necessary for holistic or teleological interpretation. The interest of the human being is in this respect far easier to handle than subjective moral

[68] Kelsen distinguishes between primary and secondary legal norms: Primary legal norms addressed to officials are only valid if they have been enacted in accordance with higher-order procedural and substantive norms that govern the creation of secondary norms addressed to citizens. See Hans Kelsen, *The Pure Theory of Law* (1934, revised ed 1960), cf HLA Hart, *The Concept of Law* (1967). Kelsen's theory has been heavily criticised for his overemphasis on sanctions. See Stanley L Paulson (ed), *Normativity and Norms: Critical Perspectives on Kelsenian Themes* (1999). And, indeed, the focus on the law-enforcer is counter-intuitive. For a summary of Kelsen's pure theory of law and comparison with other philosophers see J.W. Harris, Legal Philosophies 2nd edn (1997), 64–82.

[69] See Hans Kelsen, *The Law of the United Nations*, who argues that the text of Chapter VII itself does not rule out direct commandeering, yet Art 106 seems premised on the assumption that military resources would only be made available to the Security Council for Chapter VII purposes in accordance with Article 43 agreements; see also Hulsroj, above, n 4, at 240–244.

[70] Cf. Alf Ross, *Laerebog i Folkeret*, 4 edn (1972) 35, 41, 124–5, on the various constituent elements of international 'personality'.

judgements wrapped in the guise of natural law. Concept inflation tends to give institutions and legal precepts a life of their own that obscure the understanding of the interest of the human being, and, indeed, obscure the fact that the human being, in the final analysis, is also the only subject of law. Hence the intimacy of human's concern for human has to some extent been lost in an institutionalised and depersonalised world, rendering it all too easy to stay ignorant of the immense and avoidable suffering of a large part of humankind.

The obligation to assist when disaster strikes is a most tangible duty and should be obvious to all when the blinding effect of sovereignty hypostasis is removed.[71] Positivistically, the obligation to assist is underwritten by the Universal Declaration and the ICESCR. In the same fashion, the International Bill of Rights mandates that the stricken State must allow for such assistance—only bizarre systemic distortion could lead to a different result. In a sense, all other issues are secondary. The obligation to compensate the underprivileged assisting State or the possibility for the Security Council to enforce 'good neighbour' obligations are implementation issues that should not be allowed to distract from the basic concept: that a viable and healthy globalised society requires unstinting humanitarian commitment by all the institutions that that are ultimately created by human beings to serve the interest of the human being. The 'good neighbour' obligation to provide relief in times of natural disaster is one such humanitarian commitment, which, as demonstrated in this article, finds voice in international law.

[71] It is an illustration of how blinded we have become by sovereignty, that we find wonderfully clear statements on international good neighbour obligations in the writings of E de Vattel in the 18th century. Leap-frogging 250 years of sovereignty embellishment allows us to see afresh what our moral and legal obligation is, Emer de Vattel, *The Law of Nations or the Principles of Natural Law Applied to the Conduct and to the Affairs of Nations and of Sovereigns*, (Carnegie Institution of Washington, 1916), vol III, 114.

The Interplay of the ACP-EU Economic Partnership Agreements and the Rules of the World Trade Organization: Double Jeopardy for Africa

Getahun G Seifu*

The Cotonou Agreement of 2000 re-defines the longstanding bi-regional relationship between the African, Caribbean and Pacific Group of States (ACP) and the European Union.[1] The colonial and exploitative relationship between European countries during colonial times has given way to a different arrangement with the apparent intention of continuing some old practices. Accordingly, the birth of the European Economic Community and particularly the adoption of the Treaty of Rome in 1957 created avenues for cooperation with European States' overseas countries and territories. Such possible economic relations, at least for European States, were established on the basis of a binding legal instrument.[2] Flowing from this was the establishment of essentially reciprocal trade agreement, which is the first and second Yaoundé conventions (1963 and 1969 respectively), between 18 francophone African countries and the European Economic Community. These conventions established the legal framework and guaranteed sustainable access to former colonies of the European Communities' States.[3]

In 1975, 46 ACP States and nine European Economic Community Member States signed the First Lomé Convention in Togo. Among the very important innovations of this Convention was the introduction of 'non-reciprocal trade concessions'[4] which guaranteed preferential market access for ACP products in the Community's market. The Lomé conventions signed since also introduced new issues partly as a tribute to the logic of gradualism and increamentalism that are at the root of ACP-European Union relations.[5] Poignantly, the logic of gradualism and increamentalism that

* The author wishes to thank Professor James H Mathis, from Amsterdam Law School, for his useful comments during his supervision as this Article was originally researched in preparation for an LLM dissertation. The author would also like to thank the Department of Trade and Industry of the African Union and the Foreign Trade Relations Department of the Ministry of Trade and Industry of Ethiopia for their kind assistance during the research. The author is a legal advisor at the Ministry of Foreign Affairs of Ethiopia and part-time lecturer of laws. The Article reflects the personal opinion of the author, he can be reached via e-mail at: getahunseifu@yahoo.com.

[1] The Cotonou Agreement stands for the 'Partnership Agreement between the Members of the African, Caribbean, and Pacific Group of States, of the One Part, and European Community and its Member States, of the Other Part signed in Cotonou (Benin) on 23 June 2000'; For the purpose of this research, the terms European Community and European Union will be used in terms of their chronological order regardless of issues of their respective areas of competence.

[2] See eg Olufemi Babarinde and Garrit Faber, 'From Lomé to Cotounou: ACP-European Union Relationship in Transition', in Olufemi Babarinde and Garrit Faber (eds), *The European Union and Developing Countries: The Cotonou Agreement*, (Kininklijke Brill NV, Leiden, 2005), 1–3.

[3] See Stephen Huger *Developing Nations and the Politics of Global Integration*, (The Brookings Institution, Washington, DC, 1995), 101 who comments that this partnership initially included strong principles of non-discrimination and reciprocity.

[4] O Babarinde and G Faber, above, n 2, at 4.

[5] *Ibid*, 3.

underpins ACP-European Union relations manifest in the signing of further Lomé conventions, has had limited effect. The preferential treatment which has been in place for more than a quarter of a century has provided little tangible gain for the ACP Group of States, as 40 out of the 77 of the Group are still categorised as low income, least-developed, States; of which 34 are African States.[6]

The Cotonou Agreement, for its part, significantly modifies this relationship, as it will introduce a special trade regime known as Economic Partnership Agreements (EPAs) as of 1 January 2008.[7] Economic Partnership Agreements are required to be compatible with the regime of the World Trade Organization (WTO).[8] This requirement ushers in the concept of regional trade agreements under Article XXIV of the GATT and allows, by way of Economic Partnership Agreements, for the establishment of free-trade areas. Such a free-trade area imposes trade liberalisation requirements[9] on States, and creates formidable challenge to the economies of the various ACP States. Such Economic Partnership Agreements constitute the essence of the Cotonou Agreement and are a significant point of departure from its predecessors.

Taking into account, inter alia, the imbalance created by regional trade arrangements between developed and developing countries along with the fact that they have become a central part of the 'development strategy' of developing countries, the Doha Declaration recognises the need for strengthening their developmental aspects.[10] Yet, ACP States are divided, for the purpose of Economic Partnership Agreements, into six regional blocs, four of which are in Africa.[11] This highly criticised configuration has posed myriad problems. Notwithstanding these problems, the Cotonou Agreement requires Economic Partnership Agreements to be concluded on the basis of reciprocity and to be WTO-compatible. If Economic Partnership Agreements are to be concluded under the existing WTO rules of Article XXIV, there lacks sufficient room for special and differential treatments. In this regard, it is worth noting that the regional trade arrangement exception of General Agreement on Trade in Services provides for flexible treatment in favour of developing countries.[12] The question is: why not with regard to the General Agreement on Tariffs and Trade (GATT)?

Thus, the major challenges involved in Economic Partnership Agreements comprise: (i) the issue of geographical configuration; (ii) the issue of whether Economic Partnership Agreements should be GATT-compatible or whether GATT should be flexible in accommodating development needs; (iii) the issue of reciprocal market access between the European Union and the African ACP States given the existing gap in their levels of development; and (iv) what Africa should do to overcome these challenges. This article aims to explain chiefly the liberalisation agenda of free-trade areas in the WTO legal system; what Economic Partnership Agreements mean to African

[6] Compare Annex VI to the Cotonou Agreement and United Nations Conference on Trade and Development (UNCTD), *Statistical Profile of the Least Developed Countries*, UNCTD, Geneva (2005), for the list of the countries. It can be observed that two more Least-developed countries have joined the list since the conclusion of the Cotonou Agreement.

[7] See eg Cotonou Agreement, Art 36(1) and Art 37(7).

[8] *Ibid.* Art 38(7) and (8) and Art 39(3).

[9] See below for analysis of the requirements of Art XXIV.

[10] WTO, *Doha Declarations*, Ministerial Declaration (adopted 14 November 2001), WTO, Geneva (2005), para 29.

[11] The six regional divisions are West Africa region; Central Africa region; East and Southern Africa region; Southern African Development Community region; the Caribbean region; and the Pacific region.

[12] The General Agreement on Trade in Services (GATS) (1994), Article V (3).

States and how such free-trade areas come into existence as well as the main flaws that emerge in seeking to establish such Economic Partnership Agreements. Accordingly, the first section of this article provides a general background as to the relationship of African States to the European Union and to the World Trade Organization. The second section gives a conceptual overview of regional trade arrangements under the GATT/WTO system and considers the ambiguous issues of Article XXIV of the GATT which appear to be systemic in light of Economic Partnership Agreements. The third section focuses on the major defects of Economic Partnership Agreements as they manifest themselves in Africa. The final substantive section sets forth the dual challenges to Africa, posed by Economic Partnership Agreements with the added perplexity caused by the Doha Development Agenda under the WTO.

FREE-TRADE AREAS AND THE EMERGENCE OF NEW REGIONAL TRADE ARRANGEMENTS UNDER THE COTONOU AGREEMENT

Regional Trade Arrangements under the GATT

Article XXIV of the GATT, together with the Understanding on Interpretation of Article XXIV of GATT 1994 (Understanding on Regional Trade Arrangements), sets forth the cornerstone principles for regional trade arrangements as part of the architecture of the GATT/WTO regime. The provisions of the GATT apply to customs territories, which is any territory with respect to which separate tariffs or other regulations of commerce are maintained for a substantial part of the trade of such territory with other territories.[13] It needs to be noted that for the purpose of the WTO, as well as regional trade arrangements, customs territories could be sovereign States or non-sovereign entities such as the European Union, which maintain separate tariff or other regulations of commerce for the substantial part of their trade with other territories.

The provisions under Article XXIV concerning regional trade arrangements can generally be classified as those dealing with substantive issues and those dealing with procedural or transparency issues.[14] Generally speaking, most of the provisions of Article XXIV dealing with regional trade arrangements define customs unions and free-trade areas and lay down their substantive requirements.[15] Paragraphs 6 to 7 of Article XXIV and paragraphs 4 to 12 of the Understanding on Regional Trade Arrangements largely deal with procedural issues such as notification and review and compensatory adjustment of tariffs, if any, as well as dispute settlement procedures relating to regional trade arrangements. GATT allows, under Article XXIV, sections (5) and (8), exceptions to the most-favoured nation principle[16] with regard to such

[13] GATT, Art XXIV(1) and (2).

[14] Article XXIV is a broad provision covering rules on the territorial application of the entire GATT (paras 1 and 2); facilitation of the so-called frontier traffic for adjacent countries (para 3); and specific rules on regional trade arrangements (paras 4 to 12). As the first two aspects of Article XXIV are beyond the scope of this paper, only the third aspect will be dealt with.

[15] GATT, Art XXIV, paras 4–5, 8–9 and 11–12; and Understanding on Regional Trade Arrangements, paras 1–3.

[16] Article I:1 of GATT enshrines immediate and unconditional extension of any most-favoured nation treatment for like products to all members of the WTO. However, Art XXIV makes an exception for parties to regional trade arrangements, exempting them from extending, on most-favoured nation basis, the treatment under the regional trade arrangement to non-parties to the regional trade arrangement. In this

regional trade arrangements where they are designated as so-called customs unions or free-trade areas.

Meaning of Customs Unions and Free-Trade Areas

The definitional provisions of Article XXIV on customs unions and free-trade areas are paragraphs 8 (a) (i) and (b). Article XXIV: 8(a) (i) defines customs union as:

> the substitution of a single customs territory for two or more customs territories, so that duties and other restrictive regulations of commerce (except, where necessary, those permitted under Articles XI, XII, XIII, XIV, XV and XX) are eliminated with respect to substantially all the trade between the constituent territories of the union or at least with respect to substantially all the trade in products originating in such territories.

Accordingly, a customs union substitutes two or more customs territories with one customs territory and eliminates duties and 'other restrictive regulations of commerce' on substantially all the trade between the constituent territories either (i) irrespective of origin of products, ie whether products originate from the member territories or not, or (ii) only for products originating from such territories. In addition, paragraph 8 (a) (ii) requires each member of a customs union to apply substantially the same duties and other regulations of commerce to the trade of third parties to the customs union. Building on this, sub-paragraph (b) of section 8 of Article XXIV defines free-trade areas as:

> a group of two or more customs territories in which the duties and other restrictive regulations of commerce (except, where necessary, those permitted under Articles XI, XII, XIII, XIV, XV and XX) are eliminated on substantially all the trade between the constituent territories in products originating in such territories.

Thus, a free-trade area brings together two or more customs territories to form a group that eliminates duties and other restrictive regulations of commerce on substantially all the trade among the constituent territories. To this extent, free-trade areas are similar to customs unions. However, they do not require liberalisation for products that do not originate from the constituent territories like customs unions. Hence, they impose lesser obligation than customs unions on their members particularly where rules of origin requirements are at issue. In addition, free-trade areas do not impose common external tariff requirements. Furthermore, from a legal point of view, they do not entail the substitution of a single customs territory for two or more customs territories in the sense of customs unions.

Finally, Article XXIV of the GATT does not expressly define an interim agreement for the formation of free-trade areas and customs unions. However, sub-paragraphs 5(a) and (b) allow for a transitional agreement 'leading to' the formation of a free-trade area or a customs union. Paragraph (c) requires interim agreements to include a plan and schedule for the formation of a customs union or free-trade area within a reasonable length of time. Evidently, the formation of such regional trade arrangements entails significant trade policy coordination among the parties, as well as extensive

regard, Art XXIV: 5 provides in particular: '. . . *the provisions of this Agreement shall not prevent*, as between the territories of contracting parties, the formation of a customs union or of a free-trade area or the adoption of an interim agreement necessary for the formation of a customs union or of a free-trade area . . .' (Emphasis added).

changes to the domestic regulations affecting trade.[17] As such, interim agreements provide members of regional trade arrangement with breathing space to prepare such blocks, as it is impossible to form regional trade arrangement overnight.

The definitions cited above also highlight some of the requirements of regional trade arrangements. These requirements could be classified as internal and external trade requirements.[18] While internal trade requirements generally refer, in the case of customs unions, to those laid down in Article XXIV(8)(a)(i) and, in the case of free-trade areas, to the criteria under Article XXIV(8)(b), the external trade requirements refer to the obligation of members of a regional trade arrangement not to raise barriers to the trade of other members of the WTO which are not members of the regional trade arrangement (Article XXIV(4) and (5)). For customs unions, the requirement of 'substantially the same duties and other regulations of commerce' in respect of third parties as well is regarded as an external trade requirement. As this Article focuses on free-trade areas, the following section will examine the systemic issues in free-trade areas, expressed in terms of internal and external trade requirements, as stipulated in the relevant provisions of Article XXIV of the GATT.[19]

The Internal Trade Requirements of Article XXIV on Free-Trade Areas

As mentioned, one of the conditions of Article XXIV is that within Member States of free-trade areas, 'duties and other restrictive regulations of commerce' shall be eliminated on substantially all of the trade conducted between the areas and for products originating in their territories. But to date, there is no clear definition of what is meant by 'duties and other restrictive regulations of commerce'. No panel or Appellate Body report of the WTO has expressly clarified these terms. It is evident, however, that the 'requirement of elimination applies only to regulations that have "restrictive" effect on commerce irrespective of whether the regulations impose duties or take some other form'.[20] It does not expressly state whether the restrictive regulation applies only to border measures between the parties to the free-trade area or to restrictions after goods have crossed the border such as requirements affecting internal sale, offering for sale, purchase, transportation, distribution or use. It appears from the phraseology of the preamble of the Understanding on Regional Trade Arrangements (ie 'if elimination between the constituent territories of duties and other restrictive regulations of commerce extends') that the 'restrictive regulation' in paragraph 8(b) applies to border measures for transactions between the parties to a free-trade area. To be specific, such restrictive border measures that affect imports include 'import bans, quantitative restrictions and the many administrative rules regulating importation'.[21]

Parties to a free-trade area are required to eliminate such duties and other restrictive regulations of commerce among themselves for products originating in their territories except as provided for under the bracketed exceptions (except, where necessary, those

[17] Nicholas Lockhart and Andrew Mitchell, 'Regional Trade Agreements under GATT 1994: An Exception and its Limits', in Andrew D Mitchell (ed), *Challenges and Prospects for the WTO*, (London, Cameron May Publishers, 2005), 225.

[18] See generally James H Mathis, *Regional Trade Agreements Under the GATT/WTO: The Internal Trade Requirements*, (TMC Asser Press, The Hague, 2002); and Joel Trachtman, 'Towards Open Recognition?—Standardization and Regional Integration under Article XXIV of GATT', *Journal of International Economic Law*, (Oxford, Oxford University Press, March 2003), Vol 6, No 1, 481 et seq.

[19] See discussion on Economic Partnership Agreements as free-trade areas below.

[20] Lockhart and Mitchell, above, n 17, at 236.

[21] *Ibid*, at 237.

permitted under Articles XI, XII, XIII, XIV, XV and XX) of Article XXIV (8)(b) itself. These bracketed exceptions apply only 'where necessary' for those duties and other restrictive regulations of commerce permitted under the GATT dealing with general elimination of quantitative restriction, restrictions to safeguard balance of payments, non-discriminatory administration of quantitative restrictions, exceptions to the rule of non-discrimination, exchange arrangements, and general exceptions. It should be noted that there is a debate as to whether this bracket includes other possible exceptions (such as safeguards, antidumping duties and security exceptions).[22] The Appellate Body of the WTO has faced, on various occasions, the issue of safeguards cases but thus far has avoided ruling on it, noting that either the issue was not raised in the particular case,[23] it makes no findings[24] or has found that it 'need not rule'[25] on the issue. Despite this, paragraph 8(b) sets a benchmark that, under normal circumstances, all free-trade areas need to eliminate duties and other restrictive regulations of commerce on substantially all the trade between their members. They could deviate from this rule, to impose the bracketed restrictions, only under 'exceptional' circumstances. Consequently, members to a free-trade area have two means to use should they prefer to act in a protectionist manner: (i) duties and other restrictive regulations of commerce mentioned under the bracketed exceptions and (ii) the vagueness of the substantially all the trade requirement, which will be discussed hereunder.

Another internal trade requirement that free-trade areas need to observe is the liberalisation of barriers to trade on substantially all the trade as between each of the parties. The elimination of the duties and other restrictive regulations of commerce explained above applies to substantially all the trade between the parties to the free-trade areas for products originating in their territories. This begs the question: what is meant by the term 'substantially all the trade'? Here again, there is no agreement among WTO members, and neither had the Panel nor the Appellate Body ruled on what this actually means. However, there is a common understanding that it has a 'qualitative as well as a quantitative aspect and that it should not be taken as allowing the exclusion of a major sector of economic activity'.[26] In this regard, the Appellate Body, in agreeing with the Panel, in *Turkey-Textiles* stated that, it is clear that:

[22] See JH Mathis, above, n 18, at 60–63; and Bonapas Onguglo and Taisuke Ito, *How to Make EPAs WTO Compatible? Reforming the Rules on Regional Trade Agreements*, European Centre for Development Policy Management (ECDPM) Discussion Paper No. 40 (July 2003), 52–53, available at www.acpsec.org.

[23] WTO, *Argentina- Safeguard Measures on Imports of Footwear*, WT/DS121/AB/R, adopted on 12 January 2000, para. 114. The ruling of the Appellate Body is as follows: 'We make no ruling on whether, as a general principle, a member of a customs union can exclude other members of that customs union from the application of a safeguard measure'.

[24] WTO, *US-Wheat Glutten*, WT/DS166/AB/R, adopted on 19 January 2001, para 99. The Appellate Body stated: 'In this case, the Panel determined that this dispute does not raise the issue of whether, as a general principle, a member of a free-trade area can exclude imports from other members of that free-trade area from the application of a safeguard measure. We see no error in this approach, and make no findings on these arguments'.

[25] WTO, *US-Definitive Safeguard Measures on Imports of Circular Welded Carbon Quality Line Pipe from Korea,* WT/DS202/AB/R, adopted on 8 March 2003, para 198. The Appellate Body stated: 'We need not, and so do not, rule on the question whether Article XXIV of the GATT 1994 permits exempting imports originating in a partner of a free-trade area from a measure in departure from Art 2.2 of the *Agreement on Safeguards*'.

[26] See eg Jean-Pierre DL Fletcher, *The Multilateral Rules on Free Trade Agreements and Customs Unions: Some Implications for the Accession of the Commonwealth Independent States (CIS) to the World Trade Organization (WTO)*, in Madeline Hoslid and Arild Saether (eds), *Free Trade Agreements and Customs Unions: Experiences, Challenges and Constraints*, (Tacis Services DG IA and the European Commission, Maastricht, 1997), 254.

> 'substantially all the trade' is not the same as all the trade, and also that 'substantially all the trade' is something considerably more than merely some of the trade. [. . . T]he ordinary meaning of the term 'substantially' in the context of sub-paragraph 8(a) appears to provide for both qualitative and quantitative components.[27]

Thus little guidance is provided as the Appellate Body only speaks of some figure in the continuum between all of the trade and some of the trade and does not demonstrate what it means by substantially all the trade. Be that as it may, from the way paragraph (b) of Article XXIV (8) is formulated, one thing is clear: that the level of dismantlement of the barriers to trade is not meant to apply to all the trade between the territories of parties to the regional trade arrangement. The third preambular recital of the Understanding on Regional Trade Arrangements notes that the contribution of regional trade arrangements to the expansion of world trade would increase 'if the elimination between the constituent territories of duties and other restrictive regulations of commerce extends to all trade' and becomes 'diminished if any major sector of trade is excluded'. This recital accentuates the notion that if barriers are dismantled in all trade, and not substantially all the trade as in GATT 1994, world trade would expand much further. On the other hand, its conditionality implies that it is simply aspirational. Nonetheless, although it does not provide a clear-cut elucidation, the Appellate Body's pronouncement demonstrates that the term 'substantially all the trade' does not mean all the trade but something less than that.

In the same vein, the omission of a major sector of trade from the requirement of substantially all the trade would in all likelihood jeopardise the realisation of the purpose of free-trade areas. Such a conclusion is informed by the preambular recital mentioned above. The crux of the problem then is where the benchmark should be as between 'all the trade' and the 'substantially all the trade' criteria. This is the bone of contention especially between developed countries that want to interpret it to mean close to all the trade (ie European Communities' 90 per cent standard) and developing and least-developed countries that want it to be interpreted to hold at lower standard.

The other issue that needs to be considered, of course, is what constitutes 'major sector of trade'? Is it possible to say that a free-trade area that excludes the entire agricultural sector violates Article XXIV(8)(b)? What if the exclusion applies only to a sub-sector of agriculture such as trade in fishery, cereals etc? The case of total exclusion of agriculture is very difficult, as it normally constitutes the major sector of most economies, substantially overshadowing all other trade requirements. As regards sub-sectors, one can only say that the answer depends on the kind and size or volume of trade the sub-sector contributes to the overall trade of a particular free-trade area.

A final internal trade requirement is the principle of reciprocity, which demonstrates the existence of mutuality of interests and operates on the basis of *quid pro quo*. It assumes that the parties have to be seen on equal footing and that no preferential treatment by one party towards the other can be claimed as of right.[28] Although it is not expressly stated in paragraph (b) of Article XXIV (8), a closer reading of the paragraph (ie 'eliminated [. . .] between the constituent territories') confirms the

[27] WTO, *Turkey- Restriction on Imports of Textile and Clothing Products*, WT/DS34/R (31 May 1999) adopted as amended by the Appellate Body Report, 19 November 1999, WT/DS34/AB/R, AB-1999-5, paras 48–49. Although this ruling was rendered in the context of customs unions, the interpretation presumably applies to free-trade areas as well.

[28] Compare addendum to para 8 of GATT Art XXXVI.

elimination of duties and other restrictive regulations of commerce under free-trade areas has to transpire on a reciprocal basis.

The addendum to paragraph 8 of Article XXXVI of GATT, though not expressly related to Article XXIV, defines non-reciprocal treatment in the context of trade and development. It is worth reciting the (negative) definition of non-reciprocity in the addendum simply for the sake of clarifying what is meant by the principle of reciprocity in the WTO legal system. According to the addendum, non-reciprocity is defined to mean that developing countries should not be expected, in the course of trade negotiations, to make contributions which are inconsistent with their individual development, financial and trade needs, taking into consideration past trade developments.[29] As Article XXIV: 8 does not make any distinction between developed and developing countries and as the addendum does not cover Article XXIV for its exception (Article XXIV could not be taken as a procedural provision according to the last bit of the addendum), it is impossible to link the non-reciprocity principle to Article XXIV.

External Trade Requirements of Article XXIV on Free-Trade Areas

A very unique aspect of Article XXIV is that it gives protection not only to WTO members or members of a regional trade arrangement but also to third parties to the WTO and regional trade arrangements. In general, Article XXIV prohibits members of a regional trade arrangement from raising barriers to trade to third parties as compared to the trade barriers they had before the formation of the regional trade arrangement but rather requires them to further liberalise international trade.

As explained above, parties to a free-trade area are not required to apply substantially the same duties and other regulations of commerce to third parties to the free-trade area. They are allowed to maintain their individual tariffs and apply their individual multilateral most-favoured nation concessions to WTO Members and continue with their existing tariffs towards third countries. Put differently, they are prohibited from raising barriers to the trade of third parties to the free-trade area. They are, instead, required to facilitate trade.[30] In respect of external trade requirements, paragraph 5(b) of Article XXIV provides:

> with respect to a free-trade area, or an interim agreement leading to the formation of a free-trade area, the duties and other regulations of commerce maintained in each of the constituent territories and applicable at the formation of such free-trade area or the adoption of such interim agreement to the trade of contracting parties not included in such area or not parties to such agreement shall not be higher or more restrictive than the corresponding duties and other regulations of commerce existing in the same constituent territories prior to the formation of the free-trade area, or interim agreement as the case may be.

[29] The addendum continues: '. . . This paragraph would apply in the event of action under Section A of Article XVIII, Article XXVIII, Article XXVIII *bis* (Article XXIX after the amendment set forth in Section A of paragraph 1 of the Protocol Amending Part I and Articles XXIX and XXX shall have become effective), Article XXXIII, or *any other procedure under this Agreement*'. (Emphasis added)

[30] GATT, Art XXIV (4): 'They [Contracting Parties] . . . recognize that the purpose of a customs union or of a free-trade area should be to facilitate trade between the constituent territories and not to raise barriers to the trade of other contracting parties with such territories'. Note that while interpreting para 5 of Art XXIV, the Appellate Body in *Turkey-Textiles,* expressed this as a 'purposive' provision than operative and concluded that it 'informs' the other relevant paragraphs of Art XXIV. See para 54.

Thus the measures covered are duties and other regulations of commerce. These requirements appear to be different from those discussed with regard to Article XXIV (8)(b) above. As such, they seem to include any measure that regulates commerce, be it restrictive or not.[31] However, a closer reading seems to suggest that paragraph 5(b) deals with the 'restrictiveness' of duties and other regulations of commerce as it prohibits them from being 'higher or more restrictive' than duties and other regulations of commerce that existed prior to the formation of the free-trade area.

An issue that remains is the criteria for determination of 'higher or more restrictive' measures. Paragraph 5(b) calls for a comparison of duties and other regulations of commerce applied or maintained before the formation of a free-trade area and those applied or maintained at the time of formation of the free-trade area. Therefore, what need to be compared are the specific duties and other regulations of commerce applied at the time of formation of a free-trade area or adoption of an interim agreement and the corresponding duties and other regulations of commerce in each of the constituent territories prior to the formation.

General Trade Requirements of Article XXIV on Free-Trade Areas

Additional requirements to the internal and external trade requirements of Article XXIV on free-trade areas, which could be referred to as general trade requirements, include rules of origin, the time requirement and the issue of review.

In general terms, rules of origin are defined as those laws, regulations and administrative determinations of general application applied by any member of the WTO to determine the country of origin of goods; or to determine whether goods qualify for preferential treatment under contractual or autonomous trade regimes.[32] They are the criteria used to determine the national source of a product.[33] They enable the parties to verify the formalities and procedures needed as to in which country goods are produced and whether they qualify for most-favoured nation treatment or preference under regional trade arrangement. Relating to regional trade arrangements, determination of rules of origin is an indispensable requirement of free-trade areas.[34] It should be noted that in as much as they could be used to give preference to members of a regional trade arrangement, they could also be used as barriers to the trade between the members as well as to the trade of third parties. That is why clear and predictable origin rules are of paramount importance for the facilitation of the flow of international trade.

[31] See the Panel Report in *Turkey-Textiles,* para 9.120, for instance, where the Panel, as adopted by the Appellate Body, concluded that other regulations of commerce, as 'evolving concept', include quantitative restrictions and could also be interpreted to include any regulation having impact on international trade, be it under WTO rules or outside the ambit of WTO rules.

[32] See Agreement on Rules of Origin, Art 1(1) cum para 1 of Annex II. This Agreement normally applies to non-preferential rules of origin and its Art 1(2) demonstrates that areas such as most-favoured nation, anti-dumping and countervailing duties, origin marking requirements, any discriminatory quantitative restrictions or tariff quotas, government procurement and trade statistics are covered for its non-preferential treatment. However, the annexed Common Declaration on Preferential Rules of Origin applies to preferential treatments under contractual or autonomous trade regimes.

[33] *Technical Information on Rules of Origin (Technical Information)*, available at:http://www.wto.org/english/tratop_e/roi_e/roi_info_e.htm. See also Antoni Estervaldeordal and Kati Suominen, *Rules of Origin: The Emerging Gatekeeper of Global Commerce*, in Mina Mashyekhi and Taisuke Ito (eds), *Multilateralism and Regionalism: The New Interface*, (United Nations Conference on Trade and Development, Geneva, 2005), 52.

[34] See Raj Bhala, *International Trade Law: Theory and Practice*, 2nd edn (Lexis Publishing, 2001), 660.

If products originating from members to a free-trade area could not be identified properly and accorded the preferential treatment (in this case the elimination of duties and other restrictive regulations of commerce), products coming from other WTO Members on most-favoured nation basis could compete equally with those originating from parties of the free-trade area and could thus render of no use such free-trade area arrangements. Therefore, the discrimination based on rules of origin between products originating from parties to the free-trade areas and the rest of WTO membership is crucial.

Although Article I(1) of GATT's most-favoured nation provision underscores the beneficiary 'like product' to originate in a Member State and the Agreement on Rules of Origin defines rules of origin as set out above, GATT/WTO does not provide detailed rules, despite laying down the general framework, governing the determination of the country of origin of goods, be it for preferential or non-preferential treatment.[35] Articles I(1) and XXIV of GATT simply require rules of origin, and leave the Member States to determine their content. Attempts at harmonisation under the Agreement on Rules of Origin have yet, it should be said, to materialise. As regards preferential rules of origin, the common declaration simply lays down the basic principles concerning transparency, with few substantive requirements and leaves the determination of the actual requirements of rules of origin to the Member States. This means that members to regional trade arrangements are free to adopt any type of origin rule that meets their purpose. The main problem, which thus emerges, is the method to be used in determining the origin of a product. Generally speaking, there are four different methods used by regional trade arrangements to determine the origin of a product. These are: 1) change in tariff classification; 2) value added; 3) specified process; and 4) substantial transformation.[36] Due to the overlap, complexity and shortcomings of these methods, States that have limited resourses are left at a disadvantage.[37] As a result, this lack of binding nature of what constitutes the origin of a product has led to a proliferation of protectionist and discriminatory origin rules that some refer to as 'gatekeepers' of international trade.[38] Therefore, though origin rules were meant to promote and liberalise international trade, they are in fact serving as hindrances to it being used excessively discriminatorily at borders.

Beyond the issue of the origin of a product, it should be recognised that interim agreements leading to the formation of a customs union or a free-trade area are transitional in nature. They are used for a preparatory time on the road to the formation of a regional trade arrangement and allow time for adjustment. Thus, Article XXIV(5)(c) requires interim agreements to transform into full-fledged free-trade areas or customs unions 'within a reasonable length of time'. The Understanding on

[35] See also Aly K Abu-Akeel, *Definition of Trade in Services under the GATS: Legal Implications*, (George Washington Journal of International Law and Economics, George Washington University, Washington, 1999), Vol 32, 201. However, the Uruguay Round resulted in certain principles for the harmonisation of non-preferential rules of origin (Agreement on Rules of Origin, Art 9) and the adoption of a common declaration on preferential rules of origin as mentioned above.

[36] See eg Donald Mackay, *The North American Free Trade Area Agreement: Its Possible Extension to South American Countries*, in Paul Demaret, Jean-Francois Bells and Gonzalo Garcia (eds), *Regionalism and Multilateralism after the Uruguay Round: Convergence, Divergence and Interaction*, (European Interuniversity Press, Brussels, 1997), Series European Policy No 12, 343–351.

[37] This is clearly the case in Generalised Systems of Preference and bi-regional economic relations such as between the ACP and the European Union that provide preferential treatment to the one side only.

[38] A Estervaldeordal and K Suominen, above, n 33, at 63.

Regional Trade Arrangements provides under paragraph 3 that the 'reasonable length of time' should exceed ten years only under exceptional cases upon full explanation of the need for a longer period. The Understanding on Regional Trade Arrangements was supposed to clarify the vagueness but it did not add much precision to solve all the problems associated with the provision. It shows that the time could be extended beyond ten years but only in exceptional cases and upon 'full explanation'. Due to this, Members' views still diverge on the issue of extension of the time beyond the maximum limit.[39] Paragraph 1 of the Understanding on Regional Trade Arrangements stipulates that for free-trade areas or interim agreements leading to their formation to be consistent with Article XXIV, they must satisfy the requirement, inter alia, of the provisions of paragraphs 5–8 of that Article. Paragraph 7(a) of Article XXIV in particular requires prompt notification to WTO Members to enable them to review the new interim agreement leading to the free-trade areas. The review is done by a Working Party that submits a report to the Council for Trade in Goods on its findings. The Council may present its recommendations to the WTO Members for consideration.

Strictly speaking, Article XXIV does not require approval of such regional trade arrangements. But paragraph 1 of the Understanding on Regional Trade Arrangements requires such arrangements to be consistent with Article XXIV. It is not clear whether consistency with Article XXIV should entail approval or rejection of a regional trade arrangement under review, particularly if viewed from the perspective of the permissive nature of paragraph 7 of the Understanding on Regional Trade Arrangements. This has left what appears to be a large gap in determining the status of regional trade arrangements within the WTO. This lack of precision, it can be said, has affected the entire review process. William Davy of the Legal Affairs Division of WTO has noted that this can be 'demonstrated most clearly by the fact that many free-trade areas [. . .] have been examined by GATT Working Parties for consistency with Article XXIV over the years but such Working Parties have seldom reached any concrete conclusion on the question of consistency'.[40] This obviously leaves regional trade arrangements to maintain discriminatory treatments until such time that they are challenged before the dispute settlement mechanism as has happened, for instance, in the *Turkey-Textiles* case.

In stark contrast, as regards interim agreements, the Understanding on Regional Trade Arrangements mandates the Working Party make in its reports appropriate recommendations on the proposed time-frame; on measures required to complete the formation of the free-trade area; and for the inclusion of a plan and schedule, if none exists. If the parties to the interim agreement are not prepared to modify their plans or schedule as recommended, they will not be able to maintain it or be allowed to bring it into force.[41] Nonetheless, under Article XXIV (10), WTO Members may, by two-thirds majority, approve interim agreements, which do not fully comply with the requirements of paragraphs 5 to 9; provided that the proposal leads to the formation of a free-trade area 'in the sense of Article XXIV'.

[39] Report by the Chairman of the Trade Negotiations Committee (Chairman's Report), TN/RL/15, 30 November 2005, para A.7.

[40] Serge Davos, *The Multilateral Rules and the New Dimension of Regional Integration: Weaknesses, Need and Scope for More Discipline*, in P Demaret, J Bells, and G Garcia, above, n 36, at 751.

[41] It worth noting that in practice, interim agreements are notified to the WTO only after they are signed and ratified by the parties, ie after they have entered into force. That undermines the rights of WTO Members to make recommendations for modification.

On the other hand, the waiver provision under Article XXV(5) of GATT is a mechanism widely used in relation to obligations under regional trade arrangements. It is used partly to curb challenges that resulted from the inconclusiveness of Working Parties. The waiver has 'been used to authorize regional agreements'[42] albeit these radically deviate from the most-favoured nation obligation, such as the Enabling Clause,[43] and do not fully satisfy the requirements of Article XXIV. For its part, the Understanding in Respect of Waivers of Obligations under GATT 1994 and Article IX(3) and (4) of the Marrakesh Agreement The Establishment the World Trade Organization tighten the rules for waiver[44] and make it nearly impossible to institute such a waiver. Onguglo and Ito summarise well the problems with waivers as follows:

> Members requesting a waiver [for regional trade arrangement inconsistency] must justify it with sound economic analysis and arguments, undergo a complex process of requesting WTO authorization and abide by stringent conditions for maintaining the waiver if it stretches over several years. . . . Thus in general, WTO members will not be able to easily obtain waivers.[45]

Finally, It should be noted that efforts to clarify the ambiguous rules under Article XXIV of the GATT have been manifest in the establishment of the Committee on Regional Trade Agreements, the attempt by the Dispute Settlement Body to clarify some of the thorny issues in regional trade arrangements,[46] the drawing up of the Doha Development Agenda and launching of negotiation through the Negotiating Group on Rules under the Trade Negotiations Committee.

The central functions of the Committee on Regional Trade Agreements, established in 1996, include examining individual regional agreements and considering the systemic implications of regional trade arrangements for the multilateral trading system. In so doing, it is expected to examine the ambiguous wordings in Article XXIV and provide clarifications. However, it could not finalise any report since its establishment 'because of lack of consensus'.[47] Due to this, WTO Members, meeting at the Fourth Ministerial Conference in Doha, while recognising that regional trade arrangements can play an important role in promoting trade liberalisation and in fostering economic development, stressed the need for a harmonious relationship between the multilateral and regional processes[48] and adopted the Doha Declaration (otherwise known as Doha Development Agenda). The Declaration envisages negotiation in all sectors of trade including regional trade arrangements. In an attempt to solve the problems faced by the Committee on Regional Trade Agreements, the Conference established another mechanism of negotiation under the scheme of the Doha Development Agenda. Paragraph 29 of the Declaration, in particular, states: 'We [the ministers]

[42] R Bhala, above, n 34, at 628.

[43] Formally referred to as *'Decision on Differential and More Favourable Treatment, Reciprocity and Fuller Participation of Developing Countries'*, Decision of 28 November 1979 (L/4903).

[44] Despite the long procedure, a decision by the Ministerial Conference by three-fourths majority to grant a waiver shall state the exceptional circumstances justifying the decision, the terms and conditions governing the application of the waiver, and the date on which the waiver shall terminate.

[45] B Onguglo and T Ito, above, n 23, at 17.

[46] The *Turkey-Textiles Case* is a good example where the Dispute Settlement Body went extra miles in attempting to clarify some of the ambiguities under Article XXIV that are being misused.

[47] See Work of the Committee on Regional Trade Agreements, available at http://www.wto.org/english/tratop_e/region_e/regcom_e.htm.

[48] *Ibid.*

agree to negotiations aimed at clarifying and improving disciplines and procedures under the existing WTO provisions applying to regional trade arrangements. The negotiations shall take into account the developmental aspects of regional trade arrangements'.

With the view to implementing this commitment, negotiations aimed at clarifying and improving the disciplines and procedures of Article XXIV commenced immediately although little progress has been registered after five years of negotiation.[49] During these negotiations, the ACP Group of States made the following major proposals to inject developmental dimension in Article XXIV of the GATT:

> With regard to duties, appropriate flexibility shall be provided for developing countries in meeting the 'substantially all the trade' requirement in respect of trade and product coverage, including in terms of the application of favourable methodology and/or lower threshold levels, if to be applied, in the measurement of trade and product coverage of developing country parties to a regional trade arrangement;
>
> With regard to 'other restrictive regulations of commerce', the term shall be interpreted in a flexible manner, so that the right of developing countries to apply contingency protection measures including safeguards and other non-tariff measures (e.g. rules of origin) on intra-regional trade is not unduly impeded, and that legal security and predictability is guaranteed for special and differential treatment measures in terms of asymmetry in rights and obligations of developed and developing country members under a regional trade arrangement in respect of such non-tariff measures;
>
> For the maximum length of the transition period permissible . . . to be established, the period should be determined in such a manner that is consistent with the trade, development and financial situation of developing countries, but in any case not less than 18 years; and
>
> Members agree that special and differential treatment for developing countries be formally and explicitly made available to developing countries in meeting criteria set out in paragraphs 5 to 8 of GATT Article XXIV in the context of regional agreements entered into between developing and developed countries.[50]

All these proposals—and principally the last proposal on special and differential treatment—have proved to be controversial. They are proposed on the basis of specific terminology ('take into account the developmental aspects of regional trade

[49] Paragraph 46 of the Doha Declaration sets the deadline for the conclusion of the Doha Round negotiations to be 1 January 2005. This timeline is already missed and the Hong Kong Ministerial Declaration, while lamenting that, instructs the negotiations to be concluded by the end of 2006. See Annex D, Regional Trade Agreements, para. 3, available at http://www.wto.org/english/thewto_e/minist_e/min05_e/final_annex_e.htm. See also WTO Secretariat, Trade Negotiations Committee, available at http://www.wto.org/english/news_e/news06_e/tnc_dg_stat_1may06_e.htm. However, the whole Doha Round of negotiations were suspended in June 2006 due to divergent interests of Member States. Though the negotiation could restart, the suspension is not a good sign for developing as well as least-developed countries.

[50] Submission on Regional Trade Agreements, Paper by the ACP Group of States, TN/RL/W/155, 28 April 2004 (ACP Submission hereafter). It has to be noted that the ACP Submission requests the preservation of the Enabling Clause as an *acquis* in the legal architecture of the WTO and accentuates that the negotiation on rules should not prejudice it: 'With regard to the Enabling Clause, the ACP Group of States proposes that Members reaffirm the legal validity of the Enabling Clause to cover regional trade arrangements entered into among developing countries (ie South-South agreements) to the effect that developing countries' right to form such arrangements under the Enabling Clause are not undermined by paragraphs 5 to 9 of GATT Article XXIV. . . . The Clause is an "acquis" in the legal architecture of WTO. The negotiations on Regional Trade Arrangement rules should not prejudice the coverage of South-South agreement under the Enabling Clause', paras 12 and 13.

arrangements'). The European Union agrees in principle with the ACP proposals as regards the appropriateness of flexibilities to include the length of the transitional period, the level of final trade coverage and the degree of asymmetry in terms of timetables for tariff reduction and elimination.[51] However, other developed countries such as Japan object to the inclusion of special and differential treatments in regional trade arrangements and insist that the mandate for negotiations is to improve and clarify the rules and procedures under the existing WTO provisions applying to regional trade arrangements.[52] In adition, Australia's proposal includes setting the substantially-all-the-trade requirement as a benchmark eliminating all duties on a minimum of at least 95 per cent of tariff-lines at the six digit level in the harmonised system of tariff classification with a short transition period and that such obligation should apply to all regional trade agreements currently in force to which WTO Members are a party.[53] This includes regional trade arrangements between developing countries as per the Enabling Clause, but later Australia reaffirmed its willingness to consider negotiating special and differential treatment-specific provisions that apply to all developing countries whose regional trade arrangements are notified.[54]

Due to the differences in perspectives on the developmental aspect, the Negotiating Group on Rules has yet to reach agreement on what is meant by the ambiguous clauses of Article XXIV, including 'substantially all the trade requirement', 'duties and other restrictive regulations of commerce', 'reasonable length of time', as well as special and differential treatment and issue of transparency.[55] As could be extrapolated from the foregoing, the viewpoint of the negotiation on Article XXIV has changed; since GATT 1947 the focus has been on interpretation and clarification of the ambiguous terms; however, of late the negotiations have been bogged with a consideration as to whether developmental aspects (especially special and differential treatments) in favour of developing countries should be considered.

What would be the implications of these imprecise and apparently far reaching liberalisation requirements of Article XXIV on Economic Partnership Agreements? The following section turns to consider the issue.

ECONOMIC PARTNERSHIP AGREEMENTS: THE NEW REGIONAL TRADE ARRANGEMENTS UNDER THE COTONOU AGREEMENT

As discussed at the outset, the evolution of the ACP-European Union bi-regional economic cooperation dates back to the 1960s when the First Yaoundé Convention was signed. It extends to the present Cotonou Agreement signed in Benin in 2000.[56] The number of countries taking part in the co-operation grew over the years from 18 to 77

[51] Submission on Regional Trade Agreements by the European Communities and their Member States, TN/RL/W/14 of 9 July 2002 and Second Submission on Regional Trade Agreements by the European Communities and their Member States, TN/RL/W/179 of 12 May 2005 (European Union Submissions hereafter).

[52] Japan's Comments on the ACP Paper TN/RL/W/155, TN/RL/W/165, 8 October 2004.

[53] Submissions on Regional trade arrangements by Australia, TN/RL/W/173, 1 March 2005, para 14.

[54] Submissions on Regional Trade Arrangements by Australia, TN/RL/W/180, 13 May 2005, para 22.

[55] Chairman's Report, above, n 39, para A.8. See also the Hong Kong Ministerial Declaration and the report of the Trade Negotiations Committee, above, n 49.

[56] See Dominique David, *40 years of European Union-ACP relationship*, (ACP-European Union Courier, Special Issue on the Cotonou Agreement), September 2000, 12.

on the ACP side and from 6 to 15 for European Union States by the time the Cotonou Agreement was signed.[57]

The Cotonou Agreement is a comprehensive agreement covering wide range of fields such as promotion and protection of human rights, democratisation, good governance, eradication of poverty, conflict prevention, management and resolution, and international trade. As such, it has a strong political dimension behind its objectives of liberalising international trade.[58] As noted by the European Centre for Development Policy Management, it is 'a comprehensive aid and trade agreement'[59] that stays in force for 25 years with a review at 5-year intervals.[60] One of its fundamental principles, according to Article 2, is that the parties are equal partners and they own and determine their development strategies for their economies and societies on the basis of total independence. The objectives of the Cotonou Agreement, as stated in Article 1, include promoting and expediting the economic, cultural and social development of the ACP States, reducing and eventually eradicating poverty and integrating these States into the world economy by sustaining economic growth, developing the private sector, increasing employment and improving access to productive resources. It is clear that the Agrement accentuates issues of economic development and poverty reduction that are pivotal to ACP economies.

Among the co-operation strategies of the Cotonou Agreement, economic and trade cooperation is but one. It embraces a broad range of framework agreements on international trade, which are to be WTO-compatible. In particular, it covers trade in goods (Articles 36(1) and 37(7)); trade in services including maritime services and information and communication technology (Articles 41–43); and trade-related areas such as competition policy (Article 45), intellectual property rights (Article 46), standardisation and certification or technical barriers to trade (Article 47), sanitary and phyto-sanitary measures (Article 48), trade and environment (Article 49); and trade and labour standards (Article 50). It also covers the promotion and protection of investment activities (Article 74) within Economic Partnership Agreements.[61] The Cotonou Agreement deals with these issues because its negotiation transpired in late 1990s, when most of these WTO-plus issues were under parallel deliberation commencing with the Singapore Ministerial Conference in 1996. This led to the commitments in the Cotonou Agreement and is manifest in Article 78 on investment, which aspires to endorse the best results agreed in the competent international fora; which despite their best endeavours were dropped from the WTO negotiations.

In spite of the comprehensiveness of the Cotonou Agreement and the vast agenda of trade liberalisation embedded in it, the Agreement enunciates, among other things, that the central aim of these economic and trade co-operations is to enhance the

[57] *Ibid.* See also B Onguglo and T Ito, above, n 23, at 9.

[58] See generally Cotonou Agreement, Arts 8–11 and 34–51.

[59] European Centre for Development Policy Management, *Cotonou Infokit, The Cotonou Agreement at a Glance (2),* European Centre for Development Policy Management, Maastricht (2001), available at http://www.ecdpm.org/Web_ECDPM/Web/Content/Navigation.nsf/index2?ReadForm.

[60] Cotonou Agreement, Art 95(1) and (2).

[61] Article 78(3) states: 'The Parties also agree to introduce, *within the Economic Partnership Agreements*, and while respecting the respective competencies of the Community and its Member States, general principles on protection and promotion of investments, *which will endorse the best results agreed in the competent international fora or bilaterally*' (emphasis added).

capacity of the ACP countries[62] in the production, supply and trading as well as attracting investment opportunities. Such so-called special and differential treatment provisions are included in the Agreement apparently to mask the challenges and to appear to be development-friendly. We now turn our attention to how Economic Partnership Agreements liberalise trade and problems associated with it.

Economic Partnership Agreements and Free-Trade Areas

It is difficult to discern from a reading of the Cotonou Agreement why the parties preferred to use the term 'economic partnership agreement' rather than the usual international trade term: free-trade area. At first glance, it seems to refer to a rather generous partnership/co-operation, but a cumulative reading of Articles 34(4), 36(1) and 37(7), which require the establishment of new, WTO-compatible trading arrangements, removing progressively barriers to trade with a fixed timetable, and introduce implicitly the requirement of reciprocal treatment is in stark contrast with the Lomé conventions. These would bolster the misnomer of a free-trade area. Instead, Economic Partnership Agreements bring an end to the existing preferential market access treatment to the ACP side and introduce equal treatment between the ACP Group of States and the European Union.

In plain language, the Cotonou Agreement has re-defined the entire relationship between the ACP countries and the European Union, marking a U-turn from the preferential treatments under the previous Lomé conventions. The Economic Partnership Agreements arrangement, which must be compatible with WTO rules in general—in particular Article XXIV of the GATT—be reciprocal in nature, require no common external tariff for third countries, and refer to full-fledged free-trade areas under the WTO architecture. Accordingly, all the internal and external trade liberalisation requirements discussed in relation to the elements of Article XXIV seem to be applicable to Economic Partnership Agreements.

The issue of making the trade regime between the European Communities and the ACP countries WTO-compatible started with the series of conflicts that arose over the preferential treatments to the ACP bananas (the so-called European Communities-Bananas disputes). Before the bananas cases were taken to the dispute settlement mechanism, GATT members, on the one hand, and European Communities and the ACP, on the other, held extensive deliberations since the review of the First Lomé Convention in Working Parties.[63] The European Communities attempted to justify the preferential market access to the ACP through, among others, Article XXXVI (8) (non-reciprocal treatment in favour of developing countries) in Part VI of GATT 1947 (Trade and Development), the Enabling Clause, and the need for extension of special and differential treatment to developing countries in the context of regional trade arrangements.[64]

[62] Article 35(3) shows that such efforts would take in to account the different needs and levels of development of the ACP countries and regions and maintains special treatment for ACP least-developed countries. See below for an in-depth discussion on this issue in relation to the issue of special and differential treatment.

[63] See JH. Mathis, above, n 18, at 92; Peter Hilpold, *Regional Integration According to Article XXIV GATT- Between the Law and Politics*, (Max Planck Yearbook of United Nations Law, Martinus Nijhoff Publishers, Leiden/Boston, 2003), Vol 7, n 88.

[64] See JH Mathis, above, n 18, at 89–92; and P Hilpold, above, n 63, at 255–256.

These justifications were not acceptable to some members; subsequently, Colombia, Costa Rica, Guatemala, Nicaragua, and Venezuela took the first and second bananas cases (European Economic Community—Member States' Import Regime for Bananas I and II) to the GATT dispute settlement mechanism. The first panel report was published in 1993 and the second report in 1994. The reports found, inter alia, that the preferential treatment to the ACP Group of States was inconsistent with some GATT obligations as the preference being given discriminated against other developing countries. As such, the preference was found to be in contravention of the Enabling Clause that applies to all developing countries across the board.[65] After finding inconsistency with GATT obligations in the second bananas case, in particular, the panel recommended that the parties to the Lomé Convention seek the achievement of their treaty objectives through 'other procedures'[66] available under the GATT. The parties heeded this advice and applied for waiver for the Fourth Lomé Convention with the aim of 'improv[ing] the legal certainty for the trade of ACP countries'[67] and secured a waiver from 9 December 1994 to 29 February 2000,[68] when the Convention expired. This waiver ensured that the otherwise WTO incompatible ACP-European Communities trade arrangement would, in fact, be compatible.

The other cause of WTO-compatibility of ACP preferential treatment is the failure of ACP States to take advantage of market access and show meaningful economic progress. It has been reported that ACP States could not achieve 'substantial market penetration in the European Union' and 'make substantial transformation [in] their economies' despite the duty-free access of 'about 92% of products originating from ACP states' for more than a quarter of a century.[69] This waiver procedure allows the current WTO-compatible Cotonou Agreement to remain in force until 30 December 2007, when the preparatory period provided under Article 36(3) expires[70] and it is replaced by Economic Partnership Agreements. The negotiation of Economic Partnership Agreements was launched as scheduled and the following Section examines in greater detail the predicaments Economic Partnership Agreements would cause to African countries.

[65] See eg Panel Report, *European Economic Community-Import Regime for Bananas*, DS38/R, 11 February 1994, para 167, available at http://www.worldtradelaw.net/reports/gattpanels/. It is worth noting, however, that both reports were not adopted due to European Union's persistent blocking under the consensus decision-making procedure of the GATT. This triggered the *Bananas III Case* (EC-*Regime for Importation, Sale and Distribution of Bananas*) in 1996 where, again, the panel, as adopted by the Appellate Body and the Dispute Settlement Body, found the bananas preference inconsistent with WTO obligations.

[66] *Ibid*, para 168.

[67] Friedl Weiss, *Manifestly Illegal Import Restrictions and Non-compliance with WTO Dispute Settlement Rulings: Lessons from the Banana Dispute*, in Ernst-Urlich Petersmann and Mark Pollack, *Transatlantic Economic Disputes: The European Union, the United States, and the WTO*, (Oxford, Oxford University Press, 2001), 129.

[68] The Fourth ACP-European Economic Communities Convention of Lomé, Decision of 9 December 1994 (L/7604).

[69] B Onguglo and T Ito, above, n 23, at 15–16. According to the European Center for Development Policy Management, currently 96.5% of all imports from the ACP already enter the European Union duty and quota free: Billal, Sanoussi and Rampa, Francesco, *Alternative (to) EPAs: Possible Scenarios for the Future ACP trade Relations with the European Union* (2006), Policy Management Report 11, Maastricht, European Center for Development Policy Management, available at http://www.ecdpm.org, footnote 1.

[70] Decision on Waiver for European Communities- the ACP- European Communities Partnership Agreement, WT/MIN (01)/15, 14 November 2001, para 1.

WEAKNESSES OF ECONOMIC PARTNERSHIP AGREEMENTS

Neglecting the Rules Under the Cotonou Agreement

As discussed already, Economic Partnership Agreements are being negotiated during a preparatory period of September 2002 to 30 December 2007.[71] The question that immediately comes to ones mind is which entities are qualified to negotiate such Economic Partnership Agreements—the ACP as a group, individual States, Regional Economic Communities in Africa, or some other body such as the African Union?—and whether all ACP States would agree to conclude Economic Partnership Agreements. Concerning the first question, Article 37(5) stipulates that the negotiations will be undertaken with the ACP countries which consider themselves in a position to do so, at the level they consider appropriate and in accordance with the procedures agreed by the ACP Group of States, taking into account regional integration processes within the ACP. Tellingly, this provision enunciates an element of freedom of choice by the individual States, which will be complemented by a procedure to be agreed upon by the ACP as a group, focusing on the promotion of the existing regional integration in the ACP countries. As regards the latter question, the European Union had agreed to assess the situation of non-least-developed ACP States that did not want to conclude Economic Partnership Agreements by 2004, and examine all possible alternatives in order to provide the ACP States with a new framework for trade, equivalent to their existing situation and in conformity with WTO rules.[72]

Nonetheless, as of mid-2007, all ACP countries (developing as well as least-developed) were negotiating Economic Partnership Agreements as groups, ignoring these provisions presumably for the following reasons. If countries were to opt-out of Economic Partnership Agreements and wait for a possible 'new framework', they would be uncertain of the type of relationship which would replace the transitional Cotonou preference. The legally dubious notion of equivalence of the existing situation and the future framework's WTO compatibility would leave them in no better a position than the European Union's unilateral Generalised System of Preferences schemes or the 'Everything But Arms' initiative (if this was to be retained). It is also believed that there could be potential advantages that the European Union would confer to Economic Partnership Agreement members such as increased assistance, aid and capacity building support,[73] which are not available in the 'Everything But Arms' initiative. More importantly, Economic Partnership Agreements are not only about tariffs and quotas or market access, which are the centrepiece of the Generalised System of Preferences and 'Everything But Arms' initiative. Economic Partnership Agreements cover several further areas of trade. As a result, these factors compelled

[71] Cotonou Agreement, Art 37(1).

[72] Cotonou Agreement, Art 37(6) (Emphasis added). It is noticeable that this provision exempts least-developed countries from obligation to conclude EPAs.

Later, the implementation of this review and assessment is delayed until some other future date. See San Bilal and Francesco Rampa, 'Reviewing Economic Partnership Agreements Negotiations and Alternative Scenarios', in *Trade Negotiations Insights: From Cotonou to Doha*, Vol 5 n 1, January-February 2006, 1, available at http://www.acp-European Union-trade.org/tni.html.

[73] Stephen Karingi *et al*, *Economic and Welfare Impacts of European Union-Africa Economic Partnership Agreements*, adopted as African Union document, AU/TI/TMIN/EXP/10(III), June 2005, 3.

ACP States to join Economic Partnership Agreements, at the expense of the flexibility of the rules found within the Cotonou Agreement.

Economic Partnership Agreements' Configuration Weakens Regional Integration

For the purpose of Economic Partnership Agreements, ACP States are divided into six regional groupings: 1) West Africa group;[74] 2) Central Africa group[75]; 3) Eastern and Southern Africa group;[76] 4) Southern African Development Community group;[77] 5) the Caribbean comprising 15 ACP members of the Caribbean Community (CARICOM) and the Dominican Republic; and 6) the Pacific, comprising 14 ACP members.[78] The divisions within Africa fall largely along the lines of the major Regional Economic Communities with some modifications, such as in the Eastern and Southern Africa, and the Southern African Development Community. It is well known that there is an intricate overlap of membership in different Regional and Sub-regional Economic Communities in Africa. For instance, in the Eastern and Southern Africa, and Southern African Development Community regions, there are a number of regional integration efforts through the Intergovernmental Authority on Development, the East African Community, the Common Market for Eastern and Southern Africa, the Southern African Development Community, Southern African Customs Union and Indian Ocean Commission.[79] The overlap of membership in these organisations and the ensuing Economic Partnership Agreement grouping has created, at least, three major problems resulting from the lack of harmonised policies in Africa.

First, the configuration disregards the principles under Article 35(2) and 37(5) that require Economic Partnership Agreements to build upon regional integration efforts of the ACP States. The Cotonou Agreement emphasises the importance of regional

[74] Comprising the 15 member stated-Economic Community of Western African States (ECOWAS) with eight of them members of the West African Economic and Monetary Union (Benin, Burkina Faso, Ivory Coast, Guinea-Bissau, Mali, Niger, Senegal and Togo) and Cape Verde, Gambia, Ghana, Guinea, Liberia, Nigeria, and Sierra Leon. Mauritania, which is a member of the Arab Maghreb Union (AMU), is also a member of this group for Economic Partnership Agreement negotiation.

[75] Comprising of Communauté Economique et Monétaire de l'Afrique Centrale (CEMAC), which is a customs and monetary union of Cameroon, Central African Republic, Chad, Republic of Congo, Gabon and Equatorial Guinea and São Tomé and Príncipe, which is related to the group through free-trade area arrangement.

[76] Comprising of eligible members of the Common Market for Eastern and Southern Africa (COMESA), which has 20 members (Angola, Burundi, Comoros, DR Congo, Djibouti, Egypt, Eritrea, Ethiopia, Kenya, Libya, Madagascar, Malawi, Mauritius, Rwanda, Seychelles, Sudan, Swaziland, Uganda, Zambia and Zimbabwe), and members of three other sub-regional organisations: Intergovernmental Authority on Development (IGAD) consisting of Djibouti, Eritrea, Ethiopia, Kenya, Somalia, Sudan and Uganda; the Indian Ocean Commission (IOC), which consists of 135 members from different continents; and the East African Community (EAC) consisting of Kenya, Uganda and Tanzania. Libya and Egypt are not members of the ACP. Angola, Tanzania, and Swaziland preferred to negotiate Economic Partnership Agreements together with the Southern African Development Community group.

[77] Comprising Angola, Mozambique, and Tanzania (an EAC member), as well as Botswana, Lesotho, Namibia and Swaziland that together with South Africa (observer to the Southern African Development Community negotiating group) belong to the Southern African Customs Union (SACU).

[78] See generally Common Market for Eastern and Southern Africa Secretariat, Geographical Configurations in the Eastern and Southern Africa Regions, May 2003, 1, available at http://www.comesa.int/trade/multilateral/epa/GEOGRAPHICAL%20CONFIGURATION%20IN%20THE/en.

[79] S Karingi et al, above, n 73, at 4 demonstrate that out of the 53 African negotiating countries, only 6 belong to just one Regional Economic Community; 26 are members of two groupings, 20 are members of three groupings and 1 belongs to four groupings. For the diagrammatic representation of the intertwinement of the membership, see Commission for Africa, *Our Common Interest: Report of the Commission for Africa* (March 2005), 264 available at http://www.number10.gov.uk/files/pdf/Chapter%208-final.pdf.

integration in Africa, which already has a very fragile foundation. This implies that integration should be sequenced in such a way that Economic Partnership Agreements would come after the regional integration efforts already underway are strengthened and streamlined. By dividing the negotiations to follow the major Regional Economic Communities rather than build on these small ones and strengthen their integration, Economic Partnership Agreements are creating a sense of rivalry amongst the old Regional Economic Communities. This has lead the Advisory Panel of Experts commissioned by the African Union to conclude that it 'will serve neither the interests of African countries nor that of the future Africa-European Union relationship for individual African Regional Economic Communities to be induced or coerced into Economic Partnership Agreements with the European Union'.[80]

Second, the States in the groups are not at the same level of economic development. Some are developing while most (about thirty-four States in Africa) are identifiable as least-developed countries,[81] which shows that States within a group require different special and differential treatment by the European Union and have presumably different interests and goals to achieve in Economic Partnership Agreements. This has meant that an antagonistic rather than co-operative spirit has developed between the member States especially for least-developed countries, as their 'Everything But Arms' preference would be eroded.

Finally, States are compelled to be party to two or more free-trade areas: one or more already among themselves and another with the European Union. If, for example, they have to eliminate duties and other restrictive regulations of commerce on substantially all the trade in Economic Partnership Agreements, then what would be the fate of the existing Regional Economic Communities established under the Enabling Clause with less stringent conditions than elimination of duties and other restrictive regulations of commerce? It is obvious that when ACP States join Economic Partnership Agreements with the European Union, they will need to eliminate duties and other restrictive regulations of commerce on substantially all the trade among themselves. That is an inherent nature of free-trade areas.[82] So, would the Regional Economic Communities under the Enabling Clause be subsumed by Economic Partnership Agreements? This will be very difficult, considering the overlap and the cross-Economic Partnership Agreement nature of the existing Regional Economic Communities. It may be said that these problems will have patent negative impact on efforts to strengthening regional integration in Africa, which has become one of the development strategies, which through Economic Partnership Agreements was meant to provide for the maximisation of the possible gains.

Two-phased Negotiation: Evidence of Disagreements

The negotiation of Economic Partnership Agreements started with a two-tier arrangement wherein it was intended that principal negotiations would be conducted at the level of all-ACP States with the European Union and another subsidiary negotiation

[80] The African Union Advisory Panel of Experts on International Negotiations, *EPA Negotiations between African Countries and the European Union: A Technical Note*, in Trade Policy Brief, Dossier for EPA Negotiations, Issue 2, Sept- Dec 2003, 6.

[81] See above, n 6.

[82] This issue becomes more complicated when viewed from the point of view of duty-and-quota free market access granted to least-developed countries under the Hong Kong Ministerial Declaration of December 2005.

would be conducted at the level of African Regional Economic Communities/regions with the European Union as a counterpart, to cover specific commitments. The first phase of the negotiation started on 27 September 2002 at the 'all-ACP level with the European Union with a view to concluding an all-ACP-European Union Agreement, focusing on objectives and principles of Economic Partnership Agreements and issues of common interest to all ACP states'.[83] The concern of the ACP States in this phase was discussing horizontal issues of interest to all ACP States and understanding the position of the European Union on how the negotiations should transpire. To that end, the ACP side raised horizontal issues such as the principles and objectives of Economic Partnership Agreements, WTO-compatibility, rules of origin, market access, agriculture and fisheries agreements, services, trade-related areas such technical barriers to trade and the development dimension of Economic Partnership Agreements. On the other hand, the European Union also raised some Cotonou-plus issues such as public procurement, personal data protection and non-execution clause (where economic sanctions could be imposed if a member fails to implement Economic Partnership Agreements).[84]

Due to these ambitious proposals by both sides and the insistence of the European Union not to conclude binding agreement in the first phase, this phase ended with more divergence than convergence. In the end, the parties were unable to conclude a formal all-ACP-European Union general agreement. Instead, a joint declaration and report on the progress of the first phase negotiation at all-ACP-European Union level was adopted. Reflecting the overwhelming divergence, the agreements in the report merely reiterate the agreements and principles already contained in the Cotonou Agreement.[85] Subsequently, an agreement was reached to continue the first tier negotiations through a Joint Technical Monitoring Committee, the remaining negotiations running parallel with the second tier negotiations.[86] Though the timing was slightly different for the various groups, the second tier negotiations started in 2003 and 2004.[87]

Though numerous divergences are seen at the Regional Economic Communities-level deliberations, the major point of divergence for all the groups, beyond that manifest in second tier negotiations is the development dimension of Economic Partnership Agreements. Getting additional resources through the European Union's Development

[83] Declaration on Economic Partnership Agreements (EPAs) Negotiation (Maputo Declaration), Assembly-AU/Decl.5 (II), adopted at Maputo, Mozambique, 12 July 2003, para 4; see also Developments and Issues in the Negotiations of EPAs between African ACP States and European Union, TI/TMIN/EXP/8-a (III), June 2005, 3; and Common Market for Eastern and Southern Africa Secretariat, above, n 78, at 4.

[84] See ACP-European Communities EPA Negotiations, Joint Report on the all-ACP-European Communities Phase of the Negotiations, 2 October 2003, available at http://trade-info.cec.European Union.int/doclib/docs/2003/november/tradoc_114136.pdf for a comprehensive discussion of the points raised by both sides and the results of the negotiation.

[85] *Ibid.* For example, see paras 4 to 6 of the Joint Report about the basic principles and objectives of Economic Partnership Agreements and market access which merely reiterate such provisions as Articles 1, 19(2), 28, 30, 34, 35 and 37(7) of the Cotonou Agreement.

[86] *Ibid*, paras 33–34. It needs to be underlined, however, that even if a Joint Technical Monitoring Committee was established to pursue the remaining first phase all-ACP-European Union negotiation, all the issues supposed to be handled by it are evidently passed down to the second tier and the negotiation is being conducted primarily at the level of Regional Economic Communities in Africa.

[87] For instance, the Central African Economic and Monetary Union and Economic Community of West African States groups launched the second tier in October 2003; the ESA group in February 2004; and the Southern African Development Community group in July 2004.

Fund, which they are already receiving through the Cotonou Agreement, has become the priority issue in Economic Partnership Agreements.[88] The stance of the African Union in this regard could be summarised as follows:

> The development dimensions, with emphasis on the provision of additional resources for the removal of production, supply and trade constraints, must be adequately addressed in the negotiations to make EPAs truly development-oriented.[89]

While the European Union argues that the ACP States are not fully absorbing the existing European Development Fund and they should rather improve their absorption capacity and utilise what is available to them than ask for more fund; the ACP-side says that European Development Fund has became inefficient not because they are unable to absorb it, but due to the rigorous procedures for accessing it and the stringent conditions attached to its implementation. The ACP States' argument is that access to European Development Fund should be improved as well as making additional funding available. The European Development Fund is available for implementing the entire Cotonou Agreement while the additional funds would be used for the reforms related only to Economic Partnership Agreements and improving competitiveness, which is a central objective of the Cotonou Agreement. In this connection, trade experts of the African countries, meeting in June 2005, emphasised 'the need for urgent and easily accessible substantial additional resources for building capacity, infrastructure development, diversification, competitiveness of African economies and to deal with anticipated adjustment costs'.[90] This would address the supply-side constraint and strengthen regional integration as well as regional markets of the ACP States. The point is that market access for ACP States, without being able to produce and supply, is meaningless and Economic Partnership Agreements should be used more as development tools than merely creating market access.

Despite the fact that the entire negotiation process is facing difficulties at various corners, the groups are discussing issues that are of common interest to all. Such issues of common interest include rules of origin, technical barriers to trade, and sanitary and phyto-sanitary measures and the groups are at different stages regarding such issues. The need to reach agreement on these common interests is vital. Consider for instance, if the groups establish a common position on rules of origin, this might lead to Economic Partnership Agreements having cumulated rules of origin, which would have a shattering effect on the continent.[91] If the Eastern and Southern Africa group agrees to rules of origin that excludes inputs originating from the Southern African Development Community, then it would be quite impossible to implement the agreement due to the overlap of membership at the sub-regional level and the inevitable mix-up.

As a result, one has to wonder why the various groups are moving at different speeds. The answer is simple: the difference emanates from the difference in the level of development of their membership. Some of the group members had already reached

[88] This debate started during the first phase all-ACP-European Communities negotiation. See Joint Report on the all-ACP- European Communities Phase of the Negotiations, above, n 84, at paras 28–30.

[89] Maputo Declaration, above, n 83, at para 6.

[90] Summary of Recommendations of the Meeting of Experts, AU/TI/Recom. I, Cairo (Egypt), 5–7 June 2005.

[91] Note that the Cotonou Agreement considers all the ACP states as one customs territory and allows cumulating rules of origin. If EPAs disregard this, that would mean lesser treatment for the ACP states.

the point of customs union among themselves; for instance, the Central Africa group is already a customs and monetary union; the West Africa group is largely an economic and monetary union; and the Southern African Development Community is contemplating a customs union by 2010.[92] In Eastern and Southern Africa group, there is a move to form a customs union among the East African Community members (Kenya, Uganda and Tanzania), and some of the countries are part of the Common Market for Eastern and Southern Africa free-trade area while others are not.[93] Consequently, Economic Partnership Agreement negotiations within a group as well as inter-group appear to be doomed to reflect these realities. This would certainly have an impact on the speed at which a group would agree on issues; thus this is the main reason why the groups are already moving with veritable speeds on the various issues even when they understand that the issues are of common interest. Considering the potential problems associated with this, the African trade ministers expressed concern that the various groups need to be properly coordinated.[94] No doubt, the process requires judicious monitoring and coordination. A question that should follow from these problems is what is being done with regard to harmonising Economic Partnership Agreements?

Generally speaking, there are two mechanisms established to supervise and coordinate activities related to Economic Partnership Agreements. These are mechanisms in the Cotonou Agreement itself and those that are established by the African Union. The African Union coordinates Regional Economic Communities participating in Economic Partnership Agreements through its Department of Trade and Industry. It can be said that there is an external and internal monitoring mechanism within the African Union. The joint African Union-European Union monitoring mechanism, which could be referred to as the external monitoring mechanism, is established with the view to considering the entire process of Economic Partnership Agreements and facilitating the regional integration programmes as envisaged in the Cotonou Agreement.[95] In this connection, the Africa-European Union Summit, which transpired in April 2000 in Cairo, Egypt, is worth mentioning. The Summit deliberated on various issues including trade, investment and regional integration, and established its own follow-up mechanisms. Since then, several high level and expert meetings, deliberating on, inter alia, Economic Partnership Agreements have taken place.[96]

While the external mechanism focuses on how the two sides—the African Union and the European Union—could effectively co-operate to live up to their commitments

[92] Southern African Development Community, *Updates on SADC-EC Economic Partnership Agreement Negotiations* (on file with author), 2; see also Regional Indicative Strategic Development Plan, available at http://www.sadc.int/key_documents/risdp/index.php.

[93] For instance, Angola, Eritrea, Ethiopia, DR Congo and Uganda have not yet joined the free-trade area. See http://www.comesa.int/trade/Folder.2005-09-06.3314/part%20III%20The%20FTA/view. It is also worth noting that COMESA Member States decided, on 23 May 2007, to become a customs union as of the end of 2008.

[94] *African Union's Declaration on EPA Negotiation*, AU/TI/MIN/DECL.(III), 5–9 June 2005, Cairo (Egypt), para 3.

[95] Maputo Declaration, above, n 83, para 10.

[96] It was agreed to hold the second Summit in European Union in 2003. See Cairo Declaration and Plan of Action, Africa-European Union Summit under the Aegis of the OAU and the European Union, Cairo (Egypt), 3–4 April 2000, paras 126–127 and 130; and European Union-Africa Ministerial Meeting, *Communiqué*, Luxembourg (11 April 2005), in *Follow-up of the Africa-European Union Summit: Catalogue of Commitments from Cairo (2000) to Bamako (2005)*.

under the Cotonou Agreement, the internal monitoring and coordination mechanism centres on how the various negotiating teams from the African side should be organised. As such, the internal mechanism coordinates the Permanent Representatives Committee of the African Union in Addis Ababa (Ethiopia), the African Group of Ambassadors and Negotiators in Brussels (Belgium) and Geneva (Switzerland) and member States negotiating Economic Partnership Agreements.[97] In this regard, the African Union is negotiating a separate protocol on its relations with the Regional Economic Communities. The draft is submitted to the policy organs of the Union for consideration and approval.[98] As a result, the African Union does not have a clear mechanism governing the activities of internal monitoring, coordination and harmonisation of Regional Economic Communities specifically in relation to Economic Partnership Agreements. This has inhibited the African Union from effectively dispensing its duties. A simple example of lack of proper coordination and monitoring is the fact that the various Regional Economic Communities are at startlingly different levels on cross-cutting issues, which incite undue competition and rivalry among the Regional Economic Communities, thus complicating the entire process.[99]

THE CONUNDRUM: GATT-COMPATIBLE ECONOMIC PARTNERSHIP AGREEMENTS OR DEVELOPMENT-COMPATIBLE GATT?

The previous section concludes that the imprecision in the systemic issues of Article XXIV of GATT are still unresolved and Economic Partnership Agreement free-trade areas are being negotiated to be, among other things, GATT-compatible. In addition, it has been demonstrated that the entire process of negotiating Economic Partnership Agreements appears to be defective, if not flawed. This following section examines the specific challenges emanating from the manifestly huge liberalisation obligations of the GATT/WTO and the additional pressures, which are created by Economic Partnership Agreements. In particular, the problem of the parallel negotiation of GATT Article XXIV and Economic Partnership Agreements; the unjustifiable dissimilar treatment of goods and services in the WTO; the problem of preference erosion against least-developed countries; the issue of forum-shifting in Economic Partnership Agreements; and the lack of due attention to Economic Partnership Agreements will be considered in turn.

The requirement of conformity with WTO-rules in accordance with Articles 34, 36 and 37 of the Cotonou Agreement primarily brings the issue of meeting the requirements of GATT Article XXIV on free-trade areas to the fore. To recapitulate, the major requirements of Article XXIV on free-trade areas relate to other restrictive regulations on commerce, other regulations of commerce, the rules of origin, the length of the transitional period, transparency and the reciprocity requirements. There is no

[97] Maputo Declaration, above, n 83, para 8, second limb. These teams are envisaged in the Cotonou Agreement as well.

[98] Final Report, African Union-Regional Economic Communities Relations, Committee of Secretariat Officials Fourth Meeting, 24–25 January 2005, Abuja (Nigeria), African Union-Regional Economic Communities/OFF/RPT (IV).

[99] See African Trade Policy Centre (UNECA), the African Union Commission and the ACP Secretariat, *Continental Review of EPA Negotiations: a Survey of African Countries' Perspectives*, in Trade Negotiations Insights: from Doha to Cotonou, Vol 6, n 2, March-April 2007, above, n 72, at 5–7.

common understanding or agreement among the WTO members as to what these terms exactly mean. The language of Article XXIV, as it stands, suggests that Economic Partnership Agreements must fulfil these requirements despite the difference in the level of development of the parties negotiating them. In other words, ACP States have to observe the trade liberalisation requirements of Article XXIV in their bilateral trade with the European countries. Certainly, it may be said, Article XXIV of the GATT does not have built into its provisions criteria for flexibility.

The only flexibilities available in derogation of the requirements of Article XXIV are: (i) the so-called de facto flexibilities[100] under Article XXIV, which exist due to their ambiguity and (ii) those provisions under the Enabling Clause where differential and more favourable treatment could be accorded to regional trade arrangements whose parties are only developing States. It should be remarked that de facto flexibilities apply to all parties of the WTO and do not favour specific developing States such as the ACP States. So ACP States cannot take special advantage of them. Besides, such flexibility is susceptible to dispute settlement proceedings as has already happened in the *Turkey-Textiles* case where Turkey's quantitative restrictions defence under Article XXIV(5) was challenged and found inconsistent with its obligations. Apart from the de facto flexibilities, the flexibility under the Enabling Clause covers only South-South regional trade arrangements, which does not include Economic Partnership Agreements.

As discussed earlier, the Negotiating Group on Rules still entertains sharp differences. There exist acute differences on the scope and substance of the negotiations on systemic issues.[101] This means that the Doha Development Agenda is a moving target for the foreseeable future. Regarding special and differential treatment, Article 34(4) of the Cotonou Agreement provides that the economic and trade cooperation, which is essentially Economic Partnership Agreements, shall be implemented in full conformity with the provisions of the WTO, including special and differential treatment, taking into account the parties' mutual interests and their respective levels of development. Article 35(3) reaffirms special and differential treatment for all ACP States and maintains special treatment for the ACP least-developed States and agrees to take due account of the vulnerability of small, landlocked and island States. Finally, Article 37(7) commits that negotiations will be as flexible as possible in establishing the duration of a sufficient transitional period, the final product coverage, taking into account sensitive sectors, and the degree of asymmetry in terms of timetable for tariff dismantlement, while remaining in conformity with WTO rules then prevailing.[102] As regards the level of differentiation, the catchwords are 'flexible' and 'asymmetry'. The Cotonou Agreement does not define these words. Neither does the WTO.[103]

According to Article 37(7), flexibility is used to include asymmetry such that flexibility will be used to establish the duration of a sufficient transitional period, the final product coverage (taking into account sensitive sectors) and the degree of asymmetry in terms of timetable for tariff dismantlement. Therefore, asymmetry is just a subset

[100] See *Turkey-Textiles*, above, n 27, paras 45–47; and ACP Submission, above, n 50, para 8.

[101] Chairman's Report, above, n 39, para A.1.

[102] Note the similarity of this provision with European Union's Submission for the negotiation under Article XXIV, above, n 51 (emphasis added).

[103] Even the General Agreement on Trade in Services, Article V, which provides for 'flexibility' for regional trade arrangements with developing countries, does not provide interpretation for the term 'flexibility'.

of flexibility and asymmetry will be used only in the determination of the timetable for tariff dismantlement, which could overlap with the requirement of transitional period. The question then is how 'flexibility' could be construed and whether it refers to special and differential treatment. Flexibility is a generic term that does not imply non-reciprocity or any departure from reciprocal treatment but implies some degree of differentiated treatment in favour of the ACP States.[104] Hence, it refers to special and differential treatment relating to transitional period, final product coverage and timetable for tariff dismantlement (with asymmetry) in favour of the ACP States provided the flexibility remains 'in conformity with WTO rules then prevailing'.[105]

Nonetheless, in so far as the Doha Development Agenda has yet to be finalised, the 'flexibility' envisaged under Article 37(7) would not assist in making a good case. Viewed from the angle of Economic Partnership Agreements, the request of the ACP countries to include special and differential treatment under Article XXIV faces a two-fold problem. First, agreement might not be reached in the WTO forum.[106] This is because the WTO adopts decisions by consensus and, as some states such as Japan, with significant share in world trade, are expressing serious concern about the issue, it appears very difficult, if not impossible, to forge consensus. Second, even if one is optimistic that WTO members would agree, there is a possibility that Economic Partnership Agreements could be concluded well before WTO's negotiations take place as the European Union is pushing to meet the deadline of December 2007. Thus Article XXIV and the Cotonou Agreement could leave ACP States out in the cold without any protection.

The natural implication of the GATT-compatibility requirement would be that Economic Partnership Agreements have to offer reciprocal treatment between the ACP and the European States. According to the Cotonou Agreement, ACP States have to progressively remove various barriers to trade to be compatible with the GATT rules under Article XXIV (Article 36(1) and 37(7) first sentence). Although criticised for not being comprehensive and being inconclusive, empirical data studies have showed that such a reciprocal arrangement would harm in the extreme the fledgling economies of the ACP countries.[107] A study conducted by the United Nations Economic Commission for Africa concludes particularly that its 'key finding [. . .] is that full reciprocity will be very costly for Africa in terms of revenue losses, adjustment costs associated with de-industrialization and its undermining effect of regional integration. Of major concern was this finding that even though the full reciprocity principle appears to be trade expanding globally (singularly in favor of European

[104] The third sentence of Art 37(7) states that negotiations shall take account of the level of development and the socio-economic impact of trade measures on ACP countries, and their capacity to adapt and adjust their economies to the liberalisation process.

[105] Cotonou Agreement, Art 37(7), fourth sentence.

[106] S Billal and F Rampa, above, n 69, 10 where they observe, 'under the current political climate, it appears unlikely that fundamentally new rules will be introduced at the WTO'.

[107] See generally S Karingi *et al*, above, n 73; See also Chris Milner, Oliver Morrissey and Andrew McCay, *Some Simple Analytics of the Trade and Welfare Effects of Economic Partnership Agreements*, (Journal of African Economies, Oxford University Press, Oxford, 2005), Vol 14, n 3, 346–348; Chris Milner, *An Assessment of the Overall Implication and Adjustment Costs for the ACP Countries of Economic Partnership Agreements with the European Union*: Report to the Commonwealth Secretariat (2005) (on file with the author); and United Nations Conference on Trade and Development, *Developments and Issues in the Negotiation of Economic Partnership Agreements between African ACP States and the EC*, adopted as African Union document, AU/TI/TMIN/EXP/8- a(III), June 2005.

Union), it will pose serious implications for deepening of regional integration in Africa'.[108]

No doubt, the infant industries of the ACP countries would not be in a good position to compete on equal footing with their technologically advanced and heavily subsidised counterparts in European Union. This is evident from the historical preferential trade relationship itself. As discussed in the introductory section above, ACP industries and economies have not shown any meaningful progress despite over a quarter of a century of preferential market access and, in fact, the vast majority of the countries are still low-income least-developed countries. Therefore, expecting them to open up and compete equally on a reciprocal basis with European industries armoured with Europe's Common Agricultural Policy would put them under even more complicated situation.

In reaction to these glaring facts, ACP countries repeatedly declared their position that the negotiation on systemic issues has to address the principle of less-than-full reciprocity, asymmetry in market access and their development concerns while entering into a regional trade arrangement with developed countries.[109] The African Union ministers of trade, while accentuating that Economic Partnership Agreements should serve as development tools and strengthen regional integration in Africa and expressing concern over the parallel negotiations under WTO and Economic Partnership Agreements (eg market access), reiterated that:

> Article XXIV of GATT needs to be appropriately amended to allow for necessary special and differential treatment, less than full reciprocity principle and explicit flexibilities that are consistent with the asymmetry required to make EPAs pro-development. Conclusions of the market access aspects of the EPAs should take place upon completion of the amendment.[110]

It is clear from this that African governments would perfer to deal with Economic Partnership Agreements only after the negotiation in WTO regarding regional trade arrangements is completed but for some reason Economic Partnership Agreements are about to be concluded with all their defects and challenges.

As a counterpart to the GATT Article XXIV, the General Agreement on Trade in Services provides for economic integration agreements under Article V. The criteria for economic integration agreements are similar or parallel to those in Article XXIV but adjusted in the context of trade in services. Accordingly, an economic integration agreement shall normally provide for (i) substantial sectoral coverage in terms of number of sectors, volume of trade affected, and all modes of supply; and (ii) absence or elimination of substantially all discrimination (elimination of existing discriminatory measures and/or prohibition of new or more discriminatory measures) in national treatment in the sectors covered.[111]

Article V (3) recognises economic integration agreements based on the level of economic development of the members. According to paragraph 3(a), if developing States are party to such an economic integration agreement (North-South regional trade

[108] S Karingi *et al*, above, n 73, 1.

[109] *Cairo Declaration and Road Map on the Doha Work Programme*, TI/TMIN/6-b(III)Rev.4, African Union Conference of Ministers of Trade Third Ordinary Session, Cairo(Egypt), 5–9 June 2005, para 16(f); *Livingston Declaration*, LDC/IV/2005/4, Fourth Least-Developed Country Trade Ministers Meeting, Livingston (Zambia), 26 June 2005, para 35.

[110] African Union's Ministerial Declaration on EPA Negotiations, above, n 94, para 6.

[111] General Agreement on Trade in Services, Art V(1).

arrangement), then flexibility will be provided in accordance with their level of development, both overall and in individual sectors and sub-sectors. In the same fashion, paragraph 3(b) articulates that when members of the economic integration agreement are only developing countries (South-South regional trade arrangements) they may grant more favourable treatments to each other. Put differently, the parties in the latter instance may make more discriminatory treatment derogating from the most-favoured nation obligation under Article II of the General Agreement on Trade in Services.

It is apparent that the General Agreement on Trade in Services differentiates between three categories of regional trade arrangements: North-North regional trade arrangements, North-South regional trade arrangements and South-South regional trade arrangements. In summary, North-North regional trade arrangements are required to meet the substantial sectoral coverage and elimination of substantially all discrimination requirements while North-South regional trade arrangements take into account the level of development of the parties and proffer flexibility in favour of developing countries. The South-South regional trade arrangements are even more favourable to the juridical persons operating within the particular arrangement. GATT Article XXIV does not, however, set such a differentiation on the basis of the levels of development of the parties to a regional trade arrangement. The only available differentiation for regional trade arrangements dealing with trade in goods (in the GATT legal system) is according to paragraph 2(c) of the Enabling Clause, wherein South-South regional trade arrangements could be accorded differential and more favourable treatment derogating from the most-favoured nation treatment.

Thus, in stark contrast with the General Agreement on Trade in Services, Article XXIV of the GATT treats North-South regional trade arrangements equally with North-North regional trade arrangements. This disharmony is bolstered by the fact that out of all exports of African countries to the world, agricultural exports alone constitute 20.1 per cent[112]. Evidently, for developing States producing primary (agricultural) products, trade in services, which is principally in the domain of developed States, is not of much help. Developing States have little to provide in the services sector. The irony is that developing States that are dependent on goods are given better treatment for services in the form of North-South and South-South regional trade arrangements and not for goods. In the case of goods, North-North and North-South regional trade arrangements are treated equally.

Although Economic Partnership Agreements cover several trade and trade-related areas in addition to goods, there is no doubt that trade in goods would constitute the heart of Economic Partnership Agreements. To ones surprise, a single Economic Partnership Agreement, say between the Eastern and Southern Africa group and the European Union, would treat goods and services differently in the same regional trade arrangement. That puts developing States in a vividly disadvantageous position, as it ignores the sector that boosts their development and requires them to compete equally with partners that are not equal in economic development.

As stipulated in several provisions of the Cotonou Agreement (generally Articles 84 to 90 and especially Article 35(3)), least-developed countries are entitled to special and

[112] United Nations Conference on Trade and Development, *Trade Negotiation Issues in the Cotonou Agreement: Agriculture and EPAs*, United Nations Conference on Trade and Development, Geneva (2003), 48.

differential treatment. In particular, Article 84(1) stipulates, in part: 'To enable least-developed, land-locked and island ACP states to take full advantage of the opportunities offered by the [Cotonou Agreement . . .], cooperation shall ensure special treatment for the least developed ACP countries and take due account of the vulnerability of landlocked and island ACP countries'. Article 85, dealing with least-developed countries reiterates that they shall be accorded a special treatment in order to enable them to overcome the serious economic and social difficulties hindering their development so as to step up their respective rates of development. When read in light of Article 86, that cross-references the underpinning principle of trade and economic cooperation and ensures special and differential treatment for ACP least-developed countries along with all other ACP States,[113] Articles 84 and 85 entitle the ACP least-developed States to special form of special and differential treatment.[114] This special and differential treatment is special because it grants the least-developed States a treatment that is separate from the general special and differential treatment to which they are entitled together with other ACP States. It is to be recalled that the European Union introduced the 'Everything But Arms' initiative allegedly to meet this commitment.[115] However, it is global in scope and, strictly speaking, is not special for ACP least-developed States alone. If this interpretation is correct, Economic Partnership Agreements present two problems. First, the special treatment for least-developed States would be severely undercut by Economic Partnership Agreements. That is so because, among other things, Economic Partnership Agreements are required to be 'implemented in full conformity with the provisions of the WTO, including special and differential treatment'.[116] In other words, as long as Article XXIV does not allow special and differential treatment for North-South regional trade arrangements, these provisions will become inconsistent with it and rendered inapplicable to Economic Partnership Agreements. Second, this creates a similar treatment of least-developed States with the ACP developing countries in their respective regional trade arrangements entailing enormous erosion of preference against the least-developed countries.

As already noted, the Cotonou Agreement was negotiated between the Singapore Ministerial Conference of the WTO in 1996 and the Doha Ministerial Conference in 2001. During this time, what became to be known as the 'Singapore issues': the relationship between trade and investment, trade and competition policy, trade facilitation and transparency in government procurement were being negotiated under the auspices of the WTO. The relationship between trade and labour standards was also under discussion in WTO at the time.

With the view to improving the legal regimes of ACP States in these fields and accommodating such developments (eg in the case of investment), the Cotonou Agreement covers competition policy, trade and labour standards and investment protection under Articles 45, 50 and 78 respectively without explicitly mentioning transparency in government procurement. It is clear that all of these issues, with the exception of trade facilitation, have already been dropped from the WTO forum.

[113] Cotonou Agreement, Art 35(3).

[114] For landlocked and island ACP states, most of which are also least-developed countries, the provisions guarantee only taking due account of their vulnerability, which could be in any other form.

[115] Compare the Cotonou Agreement, Art 37(9).

[116] *Ibid*, Art 34(4).

However, they may come back in Economic Partnership Agreements as 'WTO-plus' issues after failure in the multilateral forum. Vehemently objecting to this, the African Union ministers of trade reaffirmed 'the position of African countries that, except for trade facilitation, the other three Singapore issues of investment, competition policy and transparency in government procurement should remain outside the ambit of the WTO Doha Work Programme/EPA negotiations'.[117] Hence, Economic Partnership Agreements are not only intended to be WTO-compatible but also extend beyond WTO commitments. This would entail further liberalisation in addition to that sought in the WTO and has to be addressed by the ACP States very prudently.

As pointed out elsewhere, Economic Partnership Agreements are not well coordinated and the negotiations are at different levels, leaving the various States and groupings in rivalry rather than co-operating. On the other hand, the African Union, which is the only continental organisation with the mandate to oversee trade negotiations,[118] does not even have observer status in the WTO. This shows that the African Union does not have a direct supervisory or intervention mechanism with regard to trade within the WTO. In Economic Partnership Agreements, most of the issues supposed to be negotiated at the all-ACP level are transferred to group/ Regional Economic Communities levels and issues of continental interest (eg the developmental aspect of Economic Partnership Agreements and rules of origin) are being negotiated at the level of Regional Economic Communities. The Regional Economic Communities in Africa, the Caribbean region as well as the Pacific region, which need firm coordination, are moving at different speeds. Let alone coordinating the groups outside of Africa, even those in Africa are moving at markedly different speeds on critically cross-cutting issues. Evidently, this will have negative impact on the overall outcome of Economic Partnership Agreements. Thus, unless the Cotonou Agreement and Article XXIV of the GATT are judiciously managed and the processes in the two forums well harmonised, Economic Partnership Agreements will lose their essence and become development unfriendly. Needless to say, both the WTO and Economic Partnership Agreements attempt to liberalise international trade. What is actually happening is that the European Union is trying to secure through Economic Partnership Agreements what it has failed to get through the WTO. As discussed elsewhere, the WTO's requirements of disproportional liberalisation such as the substantially-all-the-trade requirement have proved to be very difficult to meet. Using these obligations as a justification, the European Union is pushing Africa to liberalise its market through Economic Partnership Agreements as well. This patently leaves African States in a precarious situation of 'double jeopardy'. The European Union appears to be reclaiming what it has lost, at least with respect to Africa, in WTO negotiations, through Economic Partnership Agreements, which would mean that African States are losing in both the WTO and Economic Partnership Agreement fronts.

[117] African Union's Ministerial Declaration on EPA Negotiations, above, n 94, para 8.

[118] See Art 13(1)(a) of the Constitutive Act of the African Union, adopted at Lomé (Togo), 11 July 2000, which confers the Union with the competence to coordinate and take decisions on policies in areas of common interest to member states, one of which is international trade.

CONCLUSION

The Cotonou Agreement is important and has tremendous implication on development endeavors of the African, Caribbean and Pacific Group of States. With this in mind, Article 34(1) and (2) shows that the Cotonou Agreement, and in particular Economic Partnership Agreements, have two underpinning rationales. First, they aim at the promotion of trade: intra-ACP trade and trade between the ACP countries and the European Union. Second, they target the reduction (and eradication) of the abject poverty in the ACP countries.

Though it is decorated with these lofty objectives, the reality is that there are two fundamental reasons behind Economic Partnership Agreements' quest for reciprocal market access. The first is the failure of the ACP countries to show any meaningful development through the preferential market access treatments to the European Union via the 25-years old Lomé agreements. The argument in this respect seems to be along this line: 'if preferential market access can not help, then let's try it the other way around'. Studies have shown that subjecting poor ACP States to opening their markets to European competitors (highly subsidised by Europe's Common Agricultural Policy) on a reciprocal basis would not solve the prevailing problem in ACP States.[119] The prevailing problem is lack of ability to structurally transform and build capacity to solve supply-side constraints (ie if the ACP States do not have the ability to produce, then it does not make sense to expect them to supply and compete). Even if ACP States produce something, there has to be the infrastructure to make it available to the market. If they cannot effectively compete, then they cannot be expected to show meaningful change. The other reason is the issue of WTO-compatibility. As is well known, the previous Lomé conventions, for instance, ended up generating a series of controversies with the banana disputes ruled by the dispute settlement mechanism of the WTO to be inconsistent with WTO laws. Economic Partnership Agreements with WTO-compatible and reciprocal market access obligations are allegedly introduced in reaction to this legal problem in the WTO.

As a result of this demonstrably unsound background, the framework provisions of Economic Partnership Agreements have proved to be extremely controversial. Despite this, however, Economic Partnership Agreements are to be concluded between six ACP groups, four of which are African, and the European Union. This is transpiring at a time when the WTO is also conducting negotiations under the umbrella of the Doha Development Agenda. One of the negotiations deals with the clarification and improvement of the WTO provisions on regional trade arrangements and consideration of their developmental aspect in accordance with paragraph 29 of the Doha Declaration. Accordingly, the systemic issues of free-trade areas are being negotiated among the WTO members. Reports about the negotiation show that there are sharp divergences on interpreting the provisions of Article XXIV and the issue of including special and differential treatment into Article XXIV has especially proved to be the most contentious.[120] Considering the tedious consensus decision-making procedure of the WTO (especially when developed countries are to be convinced), it appears that the negotiations would drag for a long time.

[119] See generally, above, n 107.

[120] Chairman's Report, above, n 39, paras A.1 and A.8.

In contrast, Economic Partnership Agreements will be signed at the latest by 30 December 2007. It is only logical to conclude that the European Union can push stronger for observance of its timeline than the WTO. This would mean that Economic Partnership Agreements would have a better chance of being concluded ahead of the Doha Development Agenda. The conclusion of Economic Partnership Agreements entails some form of agreement regarding the systemic issues under Article XXIV. To say the least, this puts ACP States that are WTO members in an adverse position to argue for a better regime in the WTO. In addition, the possible weighing of Economic Partnership Agreements in favour of the European Union could cause problems. Especially for the ACP States that hope to benefit from regional trade arrangements, where the outcome may well be the reverse, that is debilitating. This appears to ensure that African States will be 21st century losers in both *fora*.

Therefore, the following are recommended:

i) Search for Other Alternatives

First and foremost, taking into account the negative implications they could entail, Economic Partnership Agreements should be stopped or suspended until the Doha Development Agenda is finalised. One may ask, if Economic Partnership Agreements are stopped, then what? For this, Article 36(3) of the Cotonou Agreement lays down the possibility of examining possible alternatives to Economic Partnership Agreements in the form of 'new framework for trade'. What these 'alternatives' could be is not indicated in the Agreement but they could imply a form of improved and expanded (in terms of scope) Generalised System of Preferences equivalent to the present Cotonou preference, with predictable criteria and legal certainty; or substantial financial support that brings about speedy structural transformation on the economies of the ACP States; or even requesting waiver for further period showing the severe handicap posed by Economic Partnership Agreements, or a combination of these and continue looking for other options. It should be underscored that the WTO has adopted the aid-for-trade approach in the Doha Round of negotiations and hence liberalisation of trade must not be attached to aid. The WTO and European Union should support Africa to improve its economy and infrastructure in the short term after which the Economic Partnership Agreements project could be introduced.

ii) Amendment of the Enabling Clause

As regards the ACP Group of States' proposals for the amendment of Article XXIV of the GATT, which essentially requests less-than-full reciprocity, what constitutes a particular challenge to the ACP States is securing special and differential treatments in concrete, operational and mandatory terms while remaining WTO-compatible.[121] Surprisingly enough, instead of asking for amendment of the Enabling Clause in the proposals, the ACP States asked for reaffirmation of its legal validity.[122] This seems to be influenced by the proposals of other WTO Members. For example, Australia's proposal covers all regional trade arrangements in force and it is reported that 'some WTO members'[123] contested the status of the Clause earlier on. The ACP proposal

[121] For detailed discussion regarding the content of the proposals, see B Onguglo and T Ito, above, n 23, at 49–63.

[122] ACP Submission, above, n 50, paras 12 and 13.

[123] B Onguglo and T Ito, above, n 23, at 48.

appears to be strategic but it is not convincing at all. In as much as the Enabling Clause (for South-South regional trade arrangements) is already being contested and the ACP group is requesting legal validity for the same, there is no reason that its amendment should not be requested so that it includes North-South regional trade arrangements as well. That will have a two-fold advantage: 1) it ends up in asserting the validity of South-South regional trade arrangements under the Enabling Clause; and 2) it could be a logical alternative to amending Article XXIV per se, which touches on the core of WTO architecture (ie non-discrimination under the most-favoured nation treatment). Therefore, the ACP group must make another proposal for the amendment of the Enabling Clause, while asserting its legal validity, so that it also includes North-South regional trade arrangements with sufficient flexibility in favour of developing countries.

iii) Seeking Strong Asymmetry

Economic Partnership Agreements should draw experience from existing regional trade arrangements between developed countries and developing countries. The European Union's criterion of liberalisation of regional trade arrangements for WTO compatibility is an average of 90 per cent of the total value of trade.[124] The Trade and Development Cooperation Agreement between the European Union and South Africa signed in 1999, which the European Union attempts to use as a prototype for Economic Partnership Agreements, is a case in point. The coverage of this Agreement is asymmetric: the European Union, the richest region, committed to liberalising 95 per cent of its imports from South Africa, while the latter agreed to import only 86 per cent of the European Union products without customs restrictions.[125] But the problem is that even if the European Union liberalises 100 per cent, then ACP countries are to be compelled to liberalise at least 80 per cent to meet the 90 per cent threshold. Then the question is whether the criterion applies to an average liberalisation of members of a group or whether it applies on an individual country basis and if so, whether all ACP countries can meet this limit. Hence, individual Economic Partnership Agreement negotiating groups have to assess their economic structure and development needs. Regarding transitional periods for the interim agreements to form Economic Partnership Agreements/free-trade areas, there are instances where longer periods, up to 20 years, are applied in asymmetrical manner for regional trade arrangements between developed and developing countries (eg 20 years for the Australia-Thailand free-trade area and 17 years for the Canada-Chile free-trade area).[126] So Economic Partnership Agreement groups should secure longer asymmetrical transition periods that give sufficient space for deeper regional integration and dealing with the supply-side constraints before full formation of Economic Partnership Agreements.

iv) Closer Coordination

There is an urgent need for strengthened coordination and supervision of Economic Partnership Agreements. To play its proper role in the diplomacy of international trade and ameliorate the problems in Economic Partnership Agreements, the African Union has to secure observer status in the WTO. Various intergovernmental organisations

[124] S Billal and F Rampa, above, n 69, at 8.

[125] *Ibid*. However, it should be noted that there are instances where developing countries such as Tunisia liberalized trade more than the European Union in a bilateral free-trade area arrangement.

[126] *Ibid*, at 9; see also B Onguglo and T Ito, above, n 23, at 39 and 59.

including the ACP States have observer status in the WTO.[127] It is only then that it could play its rightful role in the system. The African Union cannot rely indefinitely on reports to oversee and harmonise the massive and multi-faceted activities under the WTO.

v) Political intervention

Political intervention could be taken as an option to use pressure in the WTO as well as for rectifying the flaws in the Cotonou Agreement. In other words, discussions at the highest political level could bring about some breakthroughs. In this regard, African States, along with the African Union, should conduct focused lobbying at various *fora*, including the targeting of influential actors within the WTO. In addition, the Africa-Europe Summit could be a good opportunity and thus Africa should push for an immediate reconvening of the proposed second Summit, in accordance with the agreement reached in Cairo,[128] and seek to have it focus on trade and development for Africa.[129]

[127] International Intergovernmental Organizations Granted Observer Status to WTO Bodies, http://www.wto.org/english/thewto_e/igo_obs_e.htm (accessed on 26 March 2006).

[128] See Cairo Declaration and Plan of Action, above, n 96.

[129] Perhaps this could also be viewed in light of the agreement for regular review of Economic Partnership Agreements as envisaged under Art 37(4) of the Cotonou Agreement.

The Right of Property for Refugees and Displaced Persons?: On the Progressive Development of Customary Law by the International Administrations in the Balkans

Leopold Von Carlowitz*

The last century has been termed the century of ethnic cleansing.[1] There are, however, no indications that the 21st century will see fewer massive refugee flows and mass expulsions in the course or aftermath of ethnic or national conflicts. Property issues often play an important role in the development of these conflicts, as property regimes are designed to control land and resources and can be subject to political agitation by one group against another.[2] In a post-conflict situation, the resolution of property issues is crucial to successful reconstruction and for the reconciliation of the conflicting parties. In many cases, the property rights of refugees and internally displaced persons (IDPs) have to be weighed against the needs of the post-conflict society, often characterised by a massive housing crisis and homelessness. In the context of post-conflict peace-building, property issues are extremely sensitive and complex matters whose settlement is replete with legal difficulty and questions of legislative legitimacy.[3]

After violent ethno-political conflicts, it is generally impossible to return to the *status quo ante* by means of property restitution. Moreover, the payment of full compensation would in most cases exceed the resources of a post-conflict society and might significantly hamper a peace process by putting an excessive economic burden on the perpetrators' side. For the sake of reconciliation, consideration should be given to more moderate compensation payments or to making use of alternative forms of reparations such as public apologies, memorials or 'future-funds' for the victims' descendents, in particular where the violation of property rights is undocumented or dates back a long time.[4]

Resolving property issues in post-conflict societies requires, in general, many painful compromises on behalf of the quarrelling parties. As the plan for a United Nations Comprehensive Settlement Plan for Cyprus ('Annan-Plan')[5] or the Model

* The author is Research Fellow with the German Center for International Peace Operations and Programme Officer with the Irmgard Coninx Foundation based at the Social Science Research Center Berlin.

[1] For example M Brumlik, *Wer Sturm sät. Die Vertreibung der Deutschen* (Berlin, Aufbau Verlag, 2005) 167.

[2] TW Waters, 'The Naked Land: The Dayton Accords, Property Disputes, and Bosnia's Real Constitution' (1999) 40 *Harvard International Law Journal* 517 at 520.

[3] For an overview of the different issues involved, see L Von Carlowitz, 'Crossing the Boundary from the International to the Domestic Legal Realm. UNMIK Lawmaking and Property Rights in Kosovo' (2004) 10 *Global Governance* 307–331.

[4] For an overview of different forms of reparations, see: D Bloomfield, T Barnes and L Huyse (eds), *Reconciliation After Violent Conflict. A Handbook* (Stockholm, IDEA, 200) 145–147.

[5] United Nations Comprehensive Settlement Plan for Cyprus, see at: www.un.org/Depts/dpa/annanplan/annanplan.pdf

Israeli-Palestinian Peace Agreement ('Geneva Accord')[6] demonstrate, such property-related compromise may also consist of a complex mix of individual property restitution and compensation and elements of voluntary population exchange. In these instances, it is necessary to distribute needed sacrifices on both sides in a fair and well-proportioned manner. Finding the appropriate solution involves a process of negotiation and balancing of interests in the grey zone between law and politics in which property claims of refugees and IDPs are only one of several factors.

In his theory of redress, Brooks found that the existence of a valid legal position is only one of four elements required for a successful reparations campaign. Besides a legal claim, he maintains that legislative (in contrast to judicial) action, a high degree of political pressure and strong support for the campaign within the victim group is required for realising redress.[7] In the context of international human rights law, Shelton emphasises the relevance of whether an historical injustice is based on legal or illegal conduct at the time of its commitment.[8] Claims that relate to actions that were originally not seen as illegal face the problem of retroactive application of (later) law. Contrary to this, reparation claims founded on clearly illegal action involve less difficulty in their implementation. In the first situation, Shelton argues, cases would have to be judged taking into account various factors including the (moral) persuasiveness of the claim, the need for reconciliation between the conflicting parties and practical issues relating to the implementation of remedies. According to her, claims not based on clear legal grounds can nevertheless successfully be advanced in a political process if certain conditions, including most notably much political pressure, are met.[9]

In this article the question will be explored whether refugees and IDPs possess a legal claim for the protection of their property. In principle, the study will be limited to universal human rights law. Regional human rights conventions and in particular the extensive property-related jurisprudence of the European Court of Human Rights concerning the communist expropriations in Central and Eastern Europe after the Second World War are only addressed in passing. The issue of a universal human right to property remains relevant for such post-conflict situations like Palestine, Northern Iraq or Afghanistan where claimants cannot make use of a regional human rights regime, or like with regard to many African States, where the regional system is not effectively implemented.

That refugees and IDPs possess a right to housing and property restitution has recently been stipulated by the UN Sub-Commission for Promotion and Protection of Human Rights in a Declaration of Principles in 2005.[10] The Sub-Commission calls

[6] Model Israeli-Palestinian Peace Agreement, available at: www.geneva-accord.org/Accord.aspx?FolderID=33&lang=en

[7] RL Brooks, 'The Age of Apology', in RL Brooks (ed), *When Sorry Isn't Enough. The Controversy over Apologies and Reparations for Human Injustices* (New York, New York University Press, 1999) 1 at 6–7.

[8] D Shelton, *Remedies in International Human Rights Law*, 2nd edn (Oxford, Oxford University Press, 2005) 459–463.

[9] As conditions to be met, Shelton lists that both perpetrators and victims (or their direct descendents) are identifiable and still alive; that the victim group is not too large; that political pressure is also mobilised through decisive and cohesive support within the victims group; that the human rights violations are properly documented; and that the injustices are ongoing. Shelton at 464.

[10] The Sub-Commission includes in its terminology a reference to the right of housing to remind that any restitution scheme needs to take into account the housing rights of present occupants. The term 'housing and property restitution' is also used to indicate the special urgency that restitution rights of refugees and IDPs possess in comparison to other restitution cases. Compare: UN Doc. E/CN.4/Sub.2/2002/17, Working Paper submitted by Mr Paulo Sérgio Pinheiro pursuant to Sub-Commission decision 2001/122, 12 June

upon States to establish and support the required institutions, procedures and mechanisms to assess and enforce restitution claims and notes that 'the international community [also] has a responsibility to act in ways which promote and protect the right to housing and property restitution[. . .]'.[11] Although this declaration is not binding, it is nevertheless a significant step in the history of the protection of property rights.

The cases of the Palestinian refugees and of the German expellees from Central and Eastern Europe demonstrate that this was not the international position after the Second World War. At this time, refugees and IDPs could neither effectively reclaim their properties left behind or taken away, nor demand individual compensation for it. While their fate might have been deplored internationally, the international community de facto followed a stability-oriented approach focused on a negative peace aiming at the absence of war between the States involved and not at pursuing individual rights. The creation of ethnically homogenous territories was seen as a suitable means to reach that goal.[12] In only a few cases, for example with respect to Poland's territorial shift to the West initiated by the Soviet Union, property issues were considered collectively in the course of exchanges of territories—a policy influenced by the 1923 Treaty of Lausanne which legitimised the involuntary population transfer between Greeks and Turks. On the international level, there was, however, no room for individual property claims—a situation that is not surprising in the light of a human rights system that was only just emerging.

In this article, I will first give a brief overview of the international efforts to codify a human right of property. In this context, I will also mention significant developments at the regional and national level. I will then shortly review the mandate and performance of the two international (quasi-) judicial bodies meant to settle property claims in Bosnia and Herzegovina (BiH) and in Kosovo, (ie the Commission for Real Property Claims of Refugees and Displaced Persons and the Housing and Property Directorate and Claims Commission). Finally, I will argue that the High Representative of the Dayton Peace Agreement, Paddy Ashdown, was right when claiming that the international community created, with its engagement, a human right to return for individuals to their former homes after a war.[13] It can thus be argued that the practice of the international administration in BiH (and in Kosovo) crystallised an international consensus recognising an emerging universal human right of property for refugees and IDPs. In this context, property is understood as the private property of individuals, their homes and land lost or taken in the course of a war and/or ethnic cleansing.

2002, para 9. See also S Leckie, 'New Directions in Housing and Property Restitution', in S Leckie (ed), *Returning Home: Housing and Property Restitution Rights of Refugees and Displaced Persons* (Arsdley Park, Transnational Publishers, 2003), at 3 FN 1.2002, para 9. See also S Leckie, 'New Directions in Housing and Property Restitution', in S Leckie (ed), *Returning Home: Housing and Property Restitution Rights of Refugees and Displaced Persons* (Arsdley Park, Transnational Publishers, 2003), at 3 FN 1.

[11] UN Doc E/CN.4/Sub.2/2005/17, *Final report of the Special Rapporteur, Paulo Sérgio Pinheiro. Principles on housing and property restitution for refugees and displaced persons*, 28 Juni 2005.

[12] For the international stance towards the Palestinians and the German expellees, see J Allain, *International Law in the Middle East. Closer to Power than Justice* (Aldershot, Ashgate, 2004) at 101; and AM de Zayas, *Nemensis at Potsdam. The Anglo-Americans and the Expulsion of the Germans* (London, Routledge/Kegan Paul, 1977) at 6–9.

[13] International Crisis Group, 'The Continuing Challenge of Refugee Return in Bosnia and Herzegovina', *ICG Balkans Report* 137, 13 November 2002, at 39.

PROPERTY-RELATED INTERNATIONAL CODIFICATION AND REGIONAL DEVELOPMENTS

Traditionally, only foreign property was protected by the law of diplomatic protection which is not of much use for refugees and IDPs. A human right of property applying to nationals and non-nationals alike did not exist. It is true that Article 17 of the Universal Declaration of Human Rights includes the right of property.[14] However, this right was not included in either of the international Covenants that codify the non-binding principles contained in that Declaration. The UN General Assembly and the Commission on Human Rights disagreed on the status of private property: the Western States regarded property as the foundation of the modern State, the Socialist States rejected private property in principle except in the very limited form of personal property which covered things for personal usage only. Moreover, consensus could not be reached on whether the right of property was a negative right of the 'haves' being part of the first generation of human rights, or a positive right of the 'have nots' entitling everyone to (a minimum amount of) property in the sense of the second or third generation.[15] The International Covenant on Civil and Political Rights merely included a general right to choose one's residence which was interpreted to comprise the right of refugees to return to their country of origin (but not to the individual home).[16]

Despite its non-codification in the international Covenants, the right of property and its protection against unlawful expropriation was, however, subsequently included in various regional human rights systems, (ie the American Convention on Human Rights,[17] the First Protocol to the European Convention on Human Rights and Fundamental Freedoms (ECHR),[18] and the African Charter on Human Rights and Peoples' Rights)[19]. The protection of property rights has been a central issue in many cases before the European Court of Human Rights.[20] In addition, property rights are mentioned in the International Convention on the Elimination of All Forms of Racial Discrimination,[21] the Convention on the Elimination of All Forms of Discrimination against Women,[22] and the International Labour Organization

[14] Article 17 of the UDHR reads: 'Everyone has the right to own property alone as well as in association with others. No one shall be arbitrarily deprived of his property'.

[15] K Malfliet, 'Property Rights as Human Rights: A Post-Communist Paradigm?', in F Feldbrugge and WB Simons (eds), *Human Rights in Russia and Eastern Europe. Essays in Honor of Ger P. van den Berg* (The Hague, Nijhoff, 2002) 163 at 185; A Rosas, 'Property Rights', in A Rosas and J Helgesen (eds), *The Strength of Diversity. Human Rights and Pluralist Democracy* (Dordrecht, Nijhoff, 1992) 133; For an overview of the drafting history, see WA Schabas, 'The Omission of the Right to Property in the International Covenants' (1991) 4 *Hague Yearbook of International Law* 135–170.

[16] See Art 12.

[17] See Art 23.

[18] See Art 1.

[19] See Art 14.

[20] For an analysis of the ECHR jurisprudence TRG Van Banning, *The Human Right to Property* (Antwerpen, Intersentia, 2002) at 80–125; AR Çoban, *Protection of Property Rights within the European Convention on Human Rights* (Burlington, Ashgate, 2004) at 143–216. To a lesser extent and mainly concerning collective property rights of indigenous people, property rights have also been subject before the Inter-American Court of Human Rights.

[21] See Art 5(d), (v) and (vi).

[22] See Art 16(1)(h).

Convention (No 169) Concerning Indigenous and Tribal Peoples in Independent Countries.[23]

With the fall of the Berlin Wall in 1989, the right of property received a further boost when most of the formerly Soviet States, which had worked against the codification of a liberal right of property in the Commission on Human Rights four decades earlier, adopted new constitutions that included the protection of private property against arbitrary interference by the State or third parties.[24] Many of these States also engaged in restitution and privatisation processes concerning property expropriated during previous Socialist land reforms.[25] In parallel to this, the UN General Assembly had resumed its considerations of the right to property in the late 1980s, which led to the issuance of an independent expert report in 1994 that analysed, in detail, the existing property-related State practice with a view to its contribution to economic and social development. Given the variety of forms of property and their social importance, the independent expert, Mr Luis Valencia Rodríguez, found that 'it is extremely difficult to establish a universal human right to individual private property in terms that one can substantiate as requiring incorporation in the national law of all States and capable of being given the same weight to in domestic courts'.[26]

Irrespective of this inconclusive finding, the South African post-apartheid Government decided in the same year to restore property rights or to provide equitable redress to those persons and communities that had been dispossessed after 1913 on the basis of racially discriminatory laws or practices. It thereby set an important precedent for the international response to the refugee crisis that was to follow in BiH in 1995.

INTERNATIONAL PROPERTY RESTITUTION IN POST-CONFLICT BIH AND KOSOVO

With more than half of the Bosnian population fled or displaced after the war,[27] the crisis was so serious that the international community decided to improve significantly the legal position of refugees and IDPs that had been international standard so far. Influenced also by the penalisation of mass expulsions and ethnic cleansing by the two ad hoc criminal tribunals for the former Yugoslavia and Rwanda, Annex 7 of the Dayton Peace Agreement granted refugees and IDPs an individual right to freely return to their homes of origin.[28] The Commission for Real Property Claims of

[23] See Art 14. The predecessor ILO Convention No 107 also contained a provision to recognise collective and individual property rights of indigenous people but did not include a positive obligation to protect these rights (Art 11).

[24] Malfliet, above, n 15, at 171; HI Sagel-Grande, 'Property Rights and Ownership in Eastern and Western Europe and Article 1 Protocol No. 1', in JP Loof, H Ploeger and A Van der Steur (eds), *The Right to Property. The Influence of Article 1 Protocol No. 1 ECHR on Several Fields of Domestic Law* (Maastricht, Shaker, 2000), 49 at 59–60.

[25] For an overview, see M Karadjova, 'Property Restitution in Eastern Europe: Domestic and International Human Rights Law Responses' (2004) 29 *Review of Central and East European Law* 325–363.

[26] UN Doc. E/CN.4/1994/19/Add.1, 'The Right of Everyone to Own Property Alone as well as in Association with Others', *Completed final report submitted by Mr Luis Valencia Rodríguez, independent expert*, 1 February 1994, para 475.

[27] At the end of the war, there were approximately 1.3 million refugees and nearly 1.3 million IDPs out of a total pre-war population of over 4.3 million.

[28] See Art 1(1).

Refugees and Displaced Persons (CRPC) was established to safeguard these rights internationally in a post-conflict situation characterised by a serious housing shortage, ethnic hatred, and the lack of an impartial judiciary and law enforcement agencies.

The CRPC operated as an internationally supervised institution mandated to receive and decide any claims for restitution or compensation of lost real property that was not voluntarily sold or otherwise transferred since the outbreak of the war in 1992. The CRPC consisted of six local members and three international members including the Chairman. The CRPC was a hybrid institution with mixed local and international staff that applied in its mass claims procedure both national property legislation and international human rights law.[29]

At the end of its mandate on 31 December 2003, the CRPC had issued nearly 312,000 decisions with 99 per cent of all cases closed. In line with the general distribution of international and local responsibilities prescribed by the DPA, enforcement responsibility for CRPC decisions fell on the Bosnian entities, the Federation of BiH and the Republika Srpska. The reliance on local implementation became, however, the major challenge and pitfall of the CRPC's work, as the entities and their nationalistic administrations refused to implement the decisions for several years.[30] Only new legislation adopted under pressure from the High Representative, as well as a concerted monitoring and coordination effort by all relevant international organisations operating in BiH, brought about an enforcement policy in late 1999.[31] To effect this change in local attitude and policy, it was important for the entities to adopt their own 'parallel' procedures for the confirmation of property rights that did not involve any CRPC decision-making. On the one hand, this led to considerable duplication of work, but on the other hand it allowed the enforcement of CRPC decisions (as well as local decisions) in the restitution process.[32]

At the end of the armed conflict in Kosovo in 1999, with more than half of Kosovo's population fled or displaced,[33] the international community protected property claims of refugees and IDPs in a similar way as in BiH. Invoking Chapter VII of the UN Charter, the Security Council mandated the UN Interim Administration in Kosovo (UNMIK), inter alia, to protect and promote human rights and to ensure the safe and unimpeded return of all refugees and IDPs to their homes in Kosovo.[34] For this purpose, UNMIK established the Housing and Property Directorate and Claims

[29] For an overview of the CRPC mandate and procedures, see L Von Carlowitz, 'Settling Property Issues in Complex Peace Operations: The CRPC in Bosnia and Herzegovina and the HPD/CC in Kosovo' (2004) 17 *Leiden Journal of International Law* 599 at 601–603.

[30] *Ibid*, at 603–605. See also M Garlick, 'Protection for Property Rights: A Partial Solution? The Commission for Real Property Claims of Displaced Persons and Refugees (CRPC) in Bosnia and Herzegovina' (2000) 19 *Refugee Survey Quarterly* 64 at 76–80.

[31] L Hastings, 'Implementation of Property Legislation in Bosnia Herzegovina' (2001) 37 *Stanford Journal of International Law* 221 at 226–249.

[32] Philpott argues the CRPC should have used a niche as a second instance for difficult cases, once domestic restitution procedures had been established. By continuing with its mass claims process, the CRPC wasted international resources by duplicating restitution work: C Philpott, 'Though the Dog is Dead, the Pig must be Killed: Finishing with Property Restitution to Bosnia-Herzegovina's IDPs and Refugees (2005) 18 *Journal of Refugee Studies*, 1 at 16–17. See also RC Williams, 'Post-Conflict Property Restitution and Refugee Return in Bosnia and Herzegovina: Implications for International Standard-Setting and Practice' (2005) 37 *New York University Journal of International Law and Politics* 441 at 507–508.

[33] An estimated 860,000 Kosovo Albanians of a total population of approximately 2 million Kosovars had fled or were deported during the armed conflict. Shortly thereafter, about 230,000 Kosovo Serbs and other non-Albanian Kosovars fled the province as a result of reprisals.

[34] Security Council Resolution No 1244, 10 June 1999, para 11 (j) and (k).

Commission (HPD/CC) to resolve property claims resulting from ethnic discrimination in Kosovo's post-autonomy period after 1989 and from the mass flight after NATO bombardment. Institutionally modelled after the CRPC, the HPD/CC also operated as a mixed local and international mass claims adjudication body with two international and one local Commission members. However, in contrast to BiH, the HPD/CC was also responsible for the execution of its decisions—through eviction of illegal occupants with the support of the law enforcement authorities.

Initially, the HPD/CC's work was delayed significantly by considerable funding shortages and administrative problems.[35] Only when it was made an independent legal entity with its own legal, administrative and financial capacity late in 2002, did its efficiency increase in claims processing and resolution. As of the deadline for filing claims on 1 July 2003, nearly 29,000 claims had been filed. When the HPD/CC terminated its activities, all but a few complex cases had been decided. The newly established Kosovar-run Kosovo Property Agency is to settle those cases.

In 2003, the HPD/CC had evicted over 900 occupants. This number was lower than expected due to many voluntary evacuations of property. Also, evictions were delayed where the owner was not ready to reoccupy immediately—in order to avoid destruction or reoccupation of properties following an eviction. Moreover, many successful claimants asked the HPD/CC to place their properties under administration to use as humanitarian housing, for example for evicted occupants in need of accommodation, until they had gained greater clarity about their return.[36] As procedures improved and more staff were employed, the implementation rate increased continuingly. Whereas, in April 2004 only 1,600 cases had been settled, over 25,000 cases (87 per cent of the decided claims) had been regularised and implemented by February 2006 when the HPD/CC was dissolved and partly transformed into the Kosovo Property Agency.[37]

Taking into account the lack of precedents for international legal intervention and the serious operational obstacles involved with international administration, overall, the CRPC, together with the domestic repossession procedures, and the HPD/CC can be marked as an international success, in as far as they safeguarded the property rights of refugees and IDPs in a post-conflict environment with continuing ethnic tensions. In this context, it should be noted, however, that the alternative to property restitution in BiH—compensation—remained unfulfilled due to a lack of funds and that, particularly in Kosovo, minority returns remain the exception. Instead of returning to their homes of origin once they could reclaim their properties, many refugees and IDPs decide to sell their property and to continue with their new life elsewhere. Although not intended, the restitution programmes created a viable property market that seems to set free the means for compensation payments that could not be raised otherwise.[38] International property rights protection in BiH and Kosovo has since served as a model worthy of emulating with regard to refugee and displacement issues in other conflict scenarios, most notably with regard to the 'Annan Plan' for Cyprus

[35] Von Carlowitz, 'Settling Property Issues', above, n 29, at 609–612.

[36] *Ibid*, at 612.

[37] Interview with HPD staff, 20 April 2004; HPD Statistics February 2006, available at: http //www.hpd-kosovo.org/newimplemented.asp

[38] Compare Philpott, above n 32, at 21; Williams, above n 32, at 553.

and in the context of redressing property-related wrongs emerging from Saddam Hussein's 'Arabisation' programme in Northern Iraq.[39]

PROGRESSIVE DEVELOPMENT OF PROPERTY-RELATED CUSTOMARY INTERNATIONAL LAW

Have these developments transformed customary international law in such way that there nowadays exists a universal human right of property for refugees and IDPs, as Ashdown's above-cited remark suggests? New norms of international custom emerge with a sufficient amount of consistent State practice confirmed by corresponding *opinio juris*.[40] A sound determination of sufficient practice and *opinio juris* is, however, very difficult to make. Due to a lack of capacity and resources, international courts and legal writing mostly avoid broad comparative studies on particular legal principles that would normally be required to prove the existence of practice and *opinio iuris*.[41] Exacerbated by the growing number of relevant State and non-State actors in a globalising world, there is also a large array of dogmatic ambiguities with respect to the elements and the development of international custom. For example, it is unclear how much State practice and for how long it needs to exist to qualify as sufficient. If the existence of a customary norm cannot be examined in the practice of all States, a selective approach focussing on particular precedents seems to be unavoidable. Consequently, the determination of customary norms does not only involve objective and empirical aspects but also subjective elements.[42]

Further, uncertainty exists as to whether and how the increasing relevance of international organisations, transnational companies and non-governmental organisations in the process of creating international norms should be taken into account when assessing customary international law.[43] With respect to the development of universal custom, the role of the UN as the only universal (or universally legitimised) organisation is particularly important.[44] As an inter-State forum, the UN does not only codify entire legal areas (such as the law of the sea), some of its organs such as the International Court of Justice and the Security Council may set law that is binding on States and serves as important precedents for international custom. Moreover, non-binding resolutions of the General Assembly and specialised agencies may contribute over time to the formation of customary international law.[45]

[39] See eg H Das, 'Restoring Property Rights in the Aftermath of War' (2004) 53 *International and Comparative Law Quarterly*, 429–444.

[40] Compare Art 38 I (b) of the ICJ Statute.

[41] DP Fidler, 'Challenging the Classical Concept of Custom: Perspectives on the Future of Customary International Law' (1996) 39 *Jahrbuch für Internationales Recht*, 198 at 216–217.

[42] J Kammerhofer, 'Uncertainty in the Formal Sources of International Law: Customary International Law and Some of Its Problems' (2004) 55 *European Journal of International Law* 523 at 524; R Kolb, 'Selected Problems in the Theory of Customary International Law' (2003) *Netherlands International Law Review* 119 at 133.

[43] S Hobe, 'Die Zukunft des Völkerrechts im Zeitalter der Globalisierung. Perspektiven der Völkerrechtsentwicklung im 21. Jahrhundert' (1999) 37 *Archiv des Völkerrechts* 253 at 261–264.

[44] R Higgins, *The Development of International Law through the Political Organs of the United Nations* (London, Oxford University Press, 1963) 2. See also JE Alvarez, *International Organizations as Law-makers* (Oxford, Oxford University Press, 2005) 1–3.

[45] See below, n 51.

A rigid focus on (predominantly) State practice is particularly problematic in the area of human rights. Whereas traditional international legal relations between States could potentially be examined empirically, this is impossible in the area of human rights given the abundance of State actions towards its citizens.[46] According to classical international law, the implementation of human rights belongs to the *domaine réservé* of States to which international access is especially limited. To determine State practice and *opinio juris* in this context, greater focus needs to be put on the ratification of relevant human rights treaties and to official statements rather than on States' observance of human rights norms in concrete inner-State relations. Furthermore, given the fact that human rights violations frequently occur without their status as customary law being questioned, one should concentrate more on the normative content of particular human rights norms and the corresponding international *opinio iuris* than on the 'hard' practice of particular State organs.[47]

This consideration lies at the heart of the so called 'words versus action' debate.[48] Asserting that talk is cheap, traditionalists argue that the relevant gauge for determining customary law remains 'hard' State practice despite the mentioned difficulties in measuring national implementation of international human rights standards.[49] In contrast to this inductive approach, modernists allow that State practice and *opinio juris* may be deduced from ratified international human rights treaties and national constitutions and laws that are human rights-friendly.[50] They argue that *opinio juris* (and not 'hard' practice) forms the real basis of international customary law. They also claim that, despite of its formal insistence on both the subjective and the objective element of custom, the International Court confirmed in the *Nicaragua* case the modernist stance by applying a deductive approach and abstaining from a proof of existing state practice in the light of a definite international *opinio iuris*.[51] In this context, resolutions of international organisations and conferences play an important role, as they can set international soft law which crystallises under certain circumstances the *opinio iuris* of States.[52] Traditionalists counter that the modernist approach not only

[46] C Tomuschat, *Human Rights. Between Idealism and Realism* (Oxford, Oxford University Press, 2003) 34.

[47] I Österdahl, 'The Exeption as the Rule: Lawmaking on Force and Human Rights by the UN Security Council' (2005) 10 *Journal of Conflict and Security Law* 1 at 14; C Tomuschat, 'Obligations Arising for States Without or Against Their Will' (1993) 241 *Receuil des Cours. Collected Courses of the Hague Academy of International Law*, 199 at 353–360.

[48] A good summary of the debate is provided by AE Roberts, 'Traditional and Modern Approaches to Customary International Law: A Reconciliation' (2001) 95 *American Journal of International Law* 757–760.

[49] B Simma and P Alston, 'The Sources of Human Rights Law: Custom, Jus Cogens, and General Principles' (1992) 12 *Australian Yearbook of International Law*, 82 at 83; AM Weisburd, 'The Effect of Treaties and Other Formal International Acts on the Customary Law of Human Rights', (1995–96) 25 *Georgia Journal of International and Comparative Law* 99 at 106, 140.

[50] See for example RB Lillich, 'The Growing Importance of Customary International Law', (1995–96) 25 *Georgia Journal of International and Comparative Law* 1 at 12–14; T Meron, *Human Rights and Humanitarian Norms as Customary Law* (Oxford, Clarendon Press, 1992), 99; O Schachter, *International Law and Practice* (Dordrecht/Boston/London, Nijhoff, 1991) 336.

[51] *Military and Paramilitary Activities in and against Nicaragua (Nicaragua v United States of America), Merits* (1986) ICJ-Reports, at 87–104, paras. 183–193.

[52] See for example R Lee, 'Rule-Making in the United Nations: Opinio Communitatis', (1995) 27 *New York University Journal of International Law and Politics* 571 at 574–575; M Bothe, 'Legal and Non-Legal Norms—A Meaningful Distinction in International Relations?' (1980) XI *Netherlands Yearbook of International Law* 65 at 75–79. See also International Law Association, 'Statement of Principles Applicable to the Formation of General Customary International Law', *Report of the Sixty-Ninth Conference* (London, 2000), principles 28–33, 55–66.

violates basic principles of international law but also runs the danger of separating itself from the actual realities on the ground. Such approach should be avoided because ' "pseudo-law" can be the worst enemy for the Rule of Law'.[53]

DEVELOPMENT OF PROPERTY-RELATED CUSTOM

That the right of property is meanwhile codified in all existing regional human rights conventions may be counted as growing State practice and *opinio juris* in support of the right. It is also relevant for the right's universal recognition that the formerly Socialist States of Central and Eastern Europe changed their position on property rights entirely and adopted market-friendly property legislation and often introduced restitution and/or compensation programmes after 1989. That precisely these States which had been critical in the Commission on Human Rights with respect to the codification of a human right of property, and whose systems had been built on large-scale expropriations of the property-classes without compensation, shifted to a liberal approach must be seen as an important turning point at the universal level. This tendency towards increasing property-friendly State practice and an emerging *opinio juris* of the international community supporting a human right of property was strengthened by other developments, such as the restitution programme instituted in post-apartheid South Africa and elsewhere.

There is also significant practice of the UN and other international organisations in support of a right of property for refugees and IDPs. Numerous resolutions by the General Assembly, the Commission on Human Rights and its Sub-Commission have called for the protection of property rights in concrete cases and in general terms, and thereby shape a corresponding international *opinio iuris*.[54] However, these resolutions only serve as non-binding recommendations for further state action. Despite their contribution as soft law to the crystallisation of international custom, it is undisputed that non-binding resolutions of international organisations cannot outweigh a lack of state practice.

In contrast to potential criticism of the General Assembly and many other UN organs and agencies, the UN Security Council can hardly be reproached for being a 'paper tiger'. Its resolutions are binding and can order compulsory measures in accordance with Chapter VII. It therefore possesses regulatory powers that can penetrate deeply into a State's *domaine réservé*. It is true that the Security Council was not intended to have 'quasi-legislative' powers like the General Assembly.[55] In principle, its resolutions address particular cases and do not possess general and abstract normative effect.[56] Moreover, its exclusive membership and the veto power of the five permanent members make it doubtful whether Security Council action can represent general international

[53] I MacGibbon, 'Means for the Identification of International Law. General Assembly Resolutions: Custom Practice and Mistaken Identity', in B Cheng (ed), *International Law: Teaching and Practice* (London, Stevens, 1982) 10 at 26.

[54] Leckie, above, n 10, at 9–12.

[55] K Harper, 'Does the United Nations Security Council Have the Competence to Act as Court and Legislature?' (1994) 27 *New York University Journal of International Law and Politics* 103 at 150–154.

[56] G Nolte, 'The Limits of the Security Council's Powers and its Function in the International Legal System: Some Reflection', in M Byers (ed), *The Role of Law in International Politics: Essays in International Relations and International Law* (Oxford, Oxford University Press, 2000), 315 at 321.

opinio juris.[57] Notwithstanding these considerations, it is recognised that Security Council resolutions do form, in practice, important precedents whose effects can exceed far beyond the particular case and which thereby contribute significantly to the development of customary law. In particular Alvarez pointed out that, though States are not obliged legally, they often do revert to the practice of the Security Council in their search for the actually applicable (customary) law. In the absence of a compulsory international judiciary, the Council is the only international organ on the universal level that is both legitimised collectively and able to adopt binding decisions of its own initiative.[58] Even if the Council is not always acting in a consistent manner as regards serious human rights violations because of a lack of resources and capacity, it is nevertheless presumed that it is acting in accordance with the applicable law and will treat similar cases similarly.[59] Therefore, it is appropriate to use Security Council resolutions as an indication of the current state of international custom.[60] In principle, this effect should also be assumed when subsidiary organs of the Council such as international tribunals and administrations engage in regulatory activity.

Since the end of the Cold War, international administrations have been established in different forms. Whereas the UN peace operations in Cambodia and Somalia were still only authorised to use limited executive and legislative powers, the administrations in East Timor East Slavonia, and Kosovo possessed a full executive and legislative mandate.[61] The international engagement in BiH holds a special position as the central administrative role is not performed by the United Nations but by a broad coalition of States. Within a Peace Implementation Council, this coalition oversees the activities of the High Representative of the Dayton Peace Accords who is endowed with far-reaching executive and legislative competences.[62] However, the Security Council has expressly endorsed the intervention in form and substance expressly and requires that the High Representative submits monthly reports on his work.[63]

International administrations with governance functions are characterised by a functional duality in the sense that they serve an international mandate to maintain peace and security, and a local mandate to govern a particular territory.[64] Their operations are particularly relevant for the determination of human rights-related

[57] V Gowlland-Debbas, 'The Functions of the United Nations Security Council in the International Legal System', in Byers, above, n 56, 277 at 300.

[58] Alvarez, above, n 44, at 188–189.

[59] This applies at least until the Council's legitimacy is not challenged in the face of continuous selectivity of norms application, one-sided power politics and/or inefficiency. Compare Alvarez, above, n 44, at 195.

[60] I Österdahl, 'The Exception as the Rule: Lawmaking on Force and Human Rights by the UN Security Council' (2005) 10 *Journal of Conflict and Security Law* 1 at 16.

[61] E de Wet, 'The Direct Administration of Territories by the United Nations and Its Member States in the Post Cold War Era: Legal Bases and Implications for National Law' (2004) 8 *Max Planck Yearbook of United Nations Law* 291 at 296–306. For a general overview of international administrations, see R Wilde, 'From Danzig to East Timor and Beyond: The Role of International Territorial Administration' (2001) 95 *American Journal of International Law* 583–603.

[62] On the composition and powers of the Peace Implementation Council, see K Oellers-Frahm, 'Reconstructing Bosnia-Herzegovina: A Model with Pit-Falls' (2005) 9 *Max Planck Yearbook of United Nations Law*, 179 at 192–193. On the 'Bonn Powers', see M Cox, 'The Right to Return Home: International Intervention and Ethnic Cleansing in Bosnia and Herzegovina' (1998) 47 *International and Comparative Law Quarterly* 599 at 607.

[63] UN Doc. S/Res/1031, 15 December 1995, paras 25–28.

[64] R Wilde, 'The Complex Role of the Legal Adviser When International Organizations Administer Territory' (2001) 95 *American Society of International Law Proceedings* 251 at 255–256.

customary international law, as they actively protect and promote human rights and engage in the building of democratic institutions and the rule of law in the territories concerned.[65] Authorised by Chapter VII of the UN Charter, the international administrators perform governance functions that have a direct impact on the local population and normally fall within the *domaine réservé* of a sovereign State.[66] Therefore, their legislative and executive activities may be regarded as 'quasi-State practice'.

The practice of international administrations in the area of human rights may be interpreted as reflecting the human rights standards that are underpinned by international consensus. If a peace operation is run by the UN, its activities to protect human rights and foster the rule of law primarily follow universal human rights standards that, at least in theory, are shared by the whole international community.[67] The same applies for the international engagement in BiH carried out by a multi-regional coalition of States with the support of the UN. In principle, international law only legitimises interventions in national sovereignty for the purpose of maintaining peace and security by international peace operations under UN auspices in which the various contributing states follow uniform, (ie universal) standards and practices. In a similar vein, Paris argued that international administrations engage in state and institution building as 'mission civilisatrice' following less particular but global values and norms characterised by an expanding Western liberalism.[68]

Promoting or protecting the right to return (including property rights protection) of refugees and IDPs was part of the mandate of all mentioned peace operations.[69] To count as 'hard' practice it is necessary that the international administrations also actively engaged in protecting and implementing these rights. Of the four missions with full governance powers only the administrations in BiH and in Kosovo actually established institutions and undertook programmes for the enforcement of property rights. This fact could lead to the conclusion that consistent practice in support of

[65] R Wolfrum, 'International Administration in Post-Conflict Situations by the United Nations and Other International Actors' (2005) 9 *Max Planck Yearbook of United Nations Law* 649 at 680–693; R Caplan, 'A New Trusteeship? The International Administration of War-Torn Territories' (2002) *Adelphi Paper* No 314, International Institute for Strategic Studies 30–46.

[66] L Von Carlowitz, 'UNMIK Lawmaking between Effective Peace Support and Internal Self-Determination' (2003) 41 *Archiv des Völkerrechts* 336–345.

[67] Compare UN Doc S/2004/616, 'The rule of law and transitional justice in conflict and post-conflict societies', *Report of the Secretary-General*, 23 August 2004, para 9. For an outline of the relevant human rights treaties, see ND White and D Klaasen, 'An Emerging Legal Regime?', in ND White and D Klaasen (eds), *The UN, Human Rights and Post-conflict Situations* (Manchester, Manchester University Press, 2005) 1 at 6–7.

[68] R Paris, 'Peacekeeping and the Contraints of Global Culture', (2003) 9 *European Journal of International Relations* 441 at 442; R Paris, 'International Peacebuilding and the "Mission Civilisatrice"', (2002) 28 *Review of International Studies* 637–656. See also E Barkan, *The Guilt of Nations. Restitution and Negotiating Historical Injustices* (New York, WW Norton, 2000) 309–311.

[69] The international presences in Cambodia, Somalia, BiH, East Slavonia and Kosovo all had a clear mandate to promote and protect return rights of refugees and IDPs. See Agreement on a Comprehensive Political Settlement of the Cambodia Conflict, 23 October 1991, art 20 (I) and Annex 4 in connection with UN Doc. S/Res/745, 28 February 1992, paras 2 and 9; UN Doc S/Res/814, 26 March 1993, paras 4 (b) and 12; Dayton Peace Agreement, 14 December 1995, art 1 and Annex 7 in connection with UN Doc S/Res/1031, 15 December 1995, para 8; UN Doc. S/Res/1037, 15 January 1996, para11(d); UN Doc S/Res/1244, 10 June 1999, para 11(k). Slightly different thereto, the resolution that established the international administration in East Timor reaffirmed the return rights of refugees and IDPs in its preamble, but contains the corresponding obligation to protect only indirectly in the context of maintaining public law and order and providing humanitarian and rehabilitation assistance. UN Doc S/Res/1272, 25 October 1999, preamble, para 2(a) and (d).

property rights of refugees and IDPs does not even exist within the relevant peace operations with legislative and executive powers. However, this argument can be countered with the finding that it has only been the administrations in BiH and in Kosovo that possessed a sufficiently wide mandate to carry out serious and effective measures to protect property rights.[70] Whereas their mandate is long-lasting and somewhat open-ended, the administrations in East Slavonia and in East Timor were only set up for an interim period of one and two years respectively until the Croatian and Timorese governments took over full governance functions.

Among the many forms of international conduct, it is maintained that the quasi-State practice of international administrations is in the rare position to combine 'hard' action with the crystallisation of international *opinio juris* typically attributed to international organisations. The approach is able to reconcile traditionalist and modernist positions contended in the 'words versus action' debate concerning the role international organisations play in the determination of customary international law. A further argument for a crystallising effect of the legislative and executive activities by international administrations can be drawn from an analogy with the jurisprudence of the Yugoslav and Rwanda tribunals that were also set up as subsidiary organs of the Security Council. These tribunals based their jurisdiction, it has been argued, in part on criminal norms for which no consistent State practice existed previously.[71] To avoid a violation of the principle *nullum crimen, nulla poena sine lege*, it is generally argued that the tribunals materialised an existing international *opinio iuris* concerning certain criminal norms to customary law.[72] The International Criminal Tribunal for the former Yugoslavia confirmed this view in the *Celebici* case and the International Court of Justice used the statutes of the criminal tribunals for the determination of customary international law in the *Arrest Warrant* case.[73] A similar argument may be applied for the regulatory activities of international administration, in particular if quasi-judicial mass claims proceedings are involved. Therefore, it is put forward that the efforts to protect property rights by the international administrations in BiH and in Kosovo hold a primary role as indicators of the present state of property-related international custom.

CONCLUSION

Of course, these ideas on a human right of property as well as on new ways of establishing international custom through international governance require much more reflection and theoretical development which exceeds the scope of this essay. The purpose of this essay has been to portray, in broad terms, that and how the international protection of property rights of refugees and IDPs has increased over the years, in particular in contrast to the situation shortly after the Second World War. In

[70] Von Carlowitz, 'Crossing the Boundary', above, n 3, at 207.

[71] C Greenwood, 'The Development of International Humanitarian Law by the International Criminal Tribunal for the Former Yugoslavia', (1998) 2 *Max Planck Yearbook of United Nations Law* 97 at 132.

[72] R Cryer, *Prosecuting International Crimes. Selectivity and the International Criminal Law Regime* (Cambridge, Cambridge University Press, 2005) 169 and 240; Tomuschat, above, n 46, 287.

[73] *Prosecutor vs. Delalic, Mucic, Delic and Landzo*, ICTY, IT-96-21-A, Appeals Chamber, paras 107–181; *Arrest Warrant of 11 April 2000 (Democratic Republic of the Congo vs. Belgium), Merits*, (2002) ICJ Reports, para 58, p 21.

the latter context, it should be emphasised that the essay does not intend to take sides or render support to certain property-related positions taken in ongoing controversies on past expulsions or expropriations. Reference should be made, though, to the jurisprudence of the European Court of Human Rights concerning the Socialist expropriations in Central and Eastern Europe. In several cases the Court ruled out *ratione temporis* any claims based on facts which occurred prior to the entry into force of the European Convention on Human Rights with respect to the State concerned. The deprivation of property is seen in principle as an instantaneous act that does not produce a continuing situation of deprivation of rights.[74]

While the outlined developments assume the existence of a human right of property for refugees and IDPs on a universal level, there is less clarity with respect to the legal consequences of conflict-related expropriations and other violations of property rights. The relevant cases in the context of racial discrimination, ethnic cleansing and expulsion demonstrate that dealing with past (property-related) injustices is subject to serious political negotiations especially with respect to the modalities of any restitution and/or compensation regime. It nevertheless does not seem to be mistaken to ascertain a right to a remedy as a minimum legal position for refugees and IDPs whose property was taken or lost in the course of ethnic cleansing or war. Time will demonstrate how far specific standards such as those contained in the Principles on housing and property restitution by the Sub-Commission on Human Rights will be implemented in future peacebuilding efforts following violent ethno-political conflicts.

By arguing that (future) refugees and IDPs can base their claims on an emerging universal human right of property, this article only addresses the negative aspect of the right that protects existing property against unlawful interference by the State or third parties. In this discussion, no statement has been made with respect to any potential positive obligation of a State to guarantee a minimum amount of property nor with respect to the social aspects of existing property. It is maintained, however, that at the beginning of the 21st century any disagreements the international community might have as to the appropriate ways of reconciling property rights protection with considerations of social justice no longer prevent the universal recognition of a human right of property for refugees and IDPs.

For considerations of justice it might be regrettable to limit this consideration to property-related custom to the 'haves'. On the other hand, the acknowledgement of the customary legal existence of the negative aspects of property might also be interpreted as a first step towards a more comprehensive crystallisation of property-related custom including the right's positive and social aspects. It is certainly not unlikely in a globalising world that concerns relating to a fair distribution of resources and in relation to social aspects of property rights remain an issue and will be contested more fiercely.[75] Ultimately, even if the right of property remains highly political, it has become more difficult and less acceptable for States to appropriate the property of particular groups by means of expulsion and expropriation, to declare such policy as serving the interests of peace, and to sit out potential property claims of the affected populations.

[74] See also Van Banning, above, n 20, at 123–125.

[75] For an interesting discussion on the implications of recent American (Western) legal policies, see A Carty, 'Marxism and International Law: Perspectives for the American Twenty-First Century?' (2004) 17 *Leiden Journal of International Law* 247–270.

CORRESPONDENT REPORTS

International Law in Ireland—2006

Fiona de Londras

UNIVERSITY COLLEGE CORK

In 2006 there were a number of areas of the domestic agenda in which international law featured prominently, most notably in relation to Irish neutrality and the 'Global War on Terror'.

In addition, the Irish Government outlined its executive policy in relation to certain types of munitions that have the potential to cause damage after war and attempted to steer the international community towards drafting an instrument related to such munitions. On the legislative front, a number of international instruments were incorporated into domestic law and executive policy in relation to the potential incorporation of others was put forward. The government and legislature also outlined their views on the international legal standards applicable to the situations in Israel, Palestine, and Sudan in particular.

In general terms the Irish approach to international law in 2006 did not indicate any shift in diplomatic policy or in the Irish approach to the role and substance of international legal provisions.

INTERNATIONAL TERRORISM

Ireland's role with regard to the 'Global War on Terror' loomed large on the domestic and international agenda in 2006. In general terms, the debate on this matter centred on two issues—(i) Ireland's view of the international law governing the United States' conduct of the 'Global War on Terror', and (ii) Ireland's potential liability should it be found that the United States used Shannon Airport for unacknowledged detentions and/or extraordinary detention; ie ' extraordinary rendition'.

The Irish Government repeatedly asserted that the US was bound by international human rights law and, where applicable, international humanitarian law with regard to the 'War on Terror'. In particular, the Irish Government made repeated domestic and diplomatic statements that those detained in Guantánamo Bay, Cuba, are entitled to the full protections of international human rights and, where appropriate, international humanitarian law.[1] The Government stressed that this viewpoint was regularly communicated to the United States Government. This position was consistent with the views of inter alia the Inter-American Commission of Human Rights[2], the

[1] See for instance, Minister for Foreign Affairs, *Dáil Debates*, col 545, 22 February 2006; Minister for Foreign Affairs, *Dáil Debates* col 1809, 1 March 2006; an Taoiseach, *Dáil Debates*, col 439, 29 March 2006; Minister for Foreign Affairs, *Dáil Debates* col 1199 and cols 1238–1239, 4 April 2006; Minister for Foreign Affairs, *Dáil Debates*, col 1942, 1 June 2006; Minister for Foreign Affairs, *Dáil Debates*, cols 1690–1691, 29 June 2006; 3 Minister for Foreign Affairs, *Dáil Debates* cols 1770–1771, October 2006.

[2] *Precautionary Measures in Guantanamo Bay, Cuba*, Inter-American Commission on Human Rights, 13 March 2002.

United Nations Working Group on Arbitrary Detention,[3] and the former United Nations Human Rights Commission.[4] It was also consistent with the views of the International Court of Justice that human rights law and international humanitarian law both apply during times of conflict; they are not mutually exclusive.[5] The Irish Government further made repeated statements that extraordinary rendition is contrary to international law and that torture is not acceptable in any circumstances.[6] In addition, the Irish Government clearly stated that the operation of alleged secret prisons would be a violation of international law and unequivocally stated that no such facilities operated on Irish territory.[7]

The debate relating to the unacknowledged deprivation of liberty, otherwise known as extraordinary rendition, was particularly prominent in Ireland this year and was framed to a great extent by European developments in this area. In late 2005 and early 2006 the Secretary General of the Council of Europe circulated a questionnaire to all Member States relating to their potential involvement in any such activities.[8] The Irish Government considered Ireland's potential involvement—active or passive—in any such scheme in the context of answering this questionnaire.[9]

The Government was of the opinion that extraordinary rendition would never be legal under Irish law as there are only two circumstances in which foreign governments are entitled to transfer prisoners through Ireland—extradition and transfer of sentences.[10] Extraditions may only take place pursuant to the Extradition Act 1965, which requires that there would be an extradition agreement with the recipient state and that the Minister for Justice, Equality and Law Reform would have consented to the extradition. The Minister for Justice, Equality and Law Reform may consent to the transfer of a prisoner under the European Convention on the Transfer of Sentenced Persons 1983[11] provided he is satisfied that Article 16 applies. Any other instances of deprivation of liberty by a foreign government constitute false imprisonment; a criminal offence under section 15 of the Non-Fatal Offences against the Person Act 1997.[12] As noted, the Government was of the view that the practice of extraordinary rendition was contrary to international law and communicated this view to the United States Government.

Although fully satisfied that there were no instances of unacknowledged deprivation of liberty within Irish facilities, the Irish Government was 'fully aware of their

[3] See, UN Working Group on Arbitrary Detention, 'Legal Opinion Regarding the Deprivation of Liberty of Persons Detained in Guantanamo Bay', in *Report of Working Group on Arbitrary Detention*, 16 December 2002, UN Doc E/CN.4/2003/8; *Report of the Working Group on Arbitrary Detention*, 12 December 2005, UN Doc E/CN.4/2006/7.

[4] See, eg, Commission on Human Rights, 'Situation of Detainees at Guantanamo Bay', 15 February 2006, UN Doc E/CN.4/2006/120.

[5] International Court of Justice, *Advisory Opinion on the Legality of the Threat or Use of Nuclear Weapons* [1996] 1 ICJ Rep. 226.

[6] See, for instance, Minister for Foreign Affairs, *Dáil Debates* col 545, 22 February 2006; Minister for Foreign Affairs, *Dáil Debates*, col 1809, 1 March 2006; Minister for Foreign Affairs, *Dáil Debates*, cols 1690–1691, 29 June 2006; Minister for Foreign Affairs, *Dáil Debates*, cols 1770–1771, 20 June 2006.

[7] Minister for Foreign Affairs, *Dáil Debates*, col 287–288, 7 March 2006.

[8] See, for instance, COE Press Release 703 (2005)—'Secretary general sets the parameters of the Council of European inquiry into alleged CIA activities in Europe', 16 December 2005.

[9] 'Article 52 Request in Respect of Unacknowledged Deprivation of Liberty: Reply of the Government of Ireland', 21 February 2006, available at www.foreignaffairs.irlgov.ie.

[10] *Ibid*, pp 10–11; Minister for Foreign Affairs, *Dáil Debates*, cols 523–524, 22 June 2006.

[11] ETS No 112.

[12] Above, n 9, p 11.

obligation to prevent involvement by omission in the unacknowledged deprivation of liberty and to fulfil all of their positive obligations in respect of this matter'.[13] Such a positive obligation arises in particular from the *jus cogens* nature of the prohibition on torture[14] and the well-established principle of *non-refoulement*.[15]

The Irish Government noted that assurances had been received from the United States Government to the effect that Shannon Airport was not being used to facilitate the transfer of individuals within its extraordinary rendition programme, and claimed that these were sufficient to fulfil Ireland's positive international obligations in this matter.[16] It appears that the assurances received by the Irish government comprise statements that people are not being rendered through Shannon Airport and, as a result, consist of promises both that there is no unacknowledged deprivation of liberty through Ireland and that people are not being transported to a place where they are at risk of torture, inhuman or degrading treatment or punishment through Irish territory. The Irish Government has consistently expressed its complete abhorrence for torture and has stated that the practice is 'unacceptable and unjustifiable in any circumstances'.[17]

In addition, Ireland is bound by an absolute obligation of *non-refoulement* in international law. According to the Irish Government, the assurances received are sufficient to fulfil Ireland's positive obligations because they relate to facts that are wholly in the control of the assuring nation (ie the United States). The assurances could, the Government noted, be distinguished from diplomatic assurances that the European Court of Human Rights had held to be inadequate to satisfy the *non-refoulement* obligation under Article 3 of the Convention, and such assurances had been reiterated over a long period of bilateral talks and cooperation between two States with especially friendly and long-standing diplomatic relationships.[18]

In *Chahal v United Kingdom*[19] the Strasbourg Court found that deporting the applicant to India on the basis of a diplomatic assurance that 'he would enjoy the same legal protection as any other Indian citizen, and that he would have no reason to expect to suffer mistreatment of any kind at the hands of the Indian authorities'[20] constituted a breach of the defendant government's positive obligation to protect against *refoulement*. The European Court of Human Rights felt that, notwithstanding the *bona fides* of the Indian government in making these assurances, the violation of human rights by some members of the Indian security forces was 'a recalcitrant and recurring problem'[21] and, as a result, that the Government was not in a position to make assurances of this kind. The Irish Minister for Foreign Affairs, Dermot Ahern

[13] *Ibid*, p 17.

[14] See, for instance, International Criminal Tribunal for the former Yugoslavia, *Prosecutor v Furundzija* Case No. IT-95-17/1-T, Trial Chamber Judgment, 10 December 1998.

[15] See Art 33, Convention relating to the Status of Refugees, 189 UNTS 150, entered into force 22 April 1954; Note also: *Soering v United Kingdom* [1989] ECHR 14 (7 July 1989).

[16] See Minister for Foreign Affairs, *Dáil Debates*, col 685, 22 February 2006; Minister for Foreign Affairs, *Dáil Debates*, col 1810, 1 March 2006; Minister for Foreign Affairs, *Dáil Debates*, col 290, 7 March 2006; Minister of State at the Department of Foreign Affairs, Noel Treacy TD, *Dáil Debates*, cols 1578–1579, 29 June 2006.

[17] 22 February 2006, Minister for Foreign Affairs, *Dáil Debates*, col 545.

[18] Statement by Mr Dermot Ahern TD, Minister for Foreign Affairs of Ireland to European Parliament—TDIP Committee, 30 November 2006, available at www.foreignaffairs.irlgov.ie.

[19] ECHR 15 November 1996, 1996-V No.22 (1996).

[20] Assurance as quoted in the judgment, para 37.

[21] *Chahal v UK*, para 105.

TD [*Teachta Dála*: Member of the legislative House of Representatives], expressly distinguished the assurances received from the United States government from assurances of this nature and was of the view that claiming such diplomatic assurances do not fulfil Ireland's international obligations is a misunderstanding and misapplication of the law.[22] While accepting, therefore, that Articles 2 and 3 of the European Convention on Human Rights create a positive obligation on the part of Ireland to ensure that the State does not facilitate human rights abuses, the Minister for Foreign Affairs noted that this positive obligation could not be imposed in such a manner as to create an impossible or disproportionate burden on the part of the relevant State.[23] According to the Minister, Ireland had not wilfully ignored potential illegality on its territory, rather it was the first country to raise concerns regarding extraordinary renditions with the US Government and had received full factual assurances in relation thereto thus fulfilling its international legal obligations.[24]

The Government did not assert that diplomatic assurances were the only manner in which these international obligations could be fulfilled, but rather that this was the most appropriate mechanism for compliance with international law in the circumstances. The Minister of State at the Department of Health and Children, Tim O'Malley TD, speaking for the Government, noted that the best way to fulfil Ireland's international obligations was through assurances and a policy of engagement, which creates a channel through which concerns can be expressed in an open manner and in which any questionable incidents can be discussed frankly. The Minister of State made these remarks in response to a Dáil [re *Dáil Éireann*: the lower house of parliament] motion proposed by Michael D Higgins TD, which called on the government to, inter alia, establish a credible independent investigation into the existence of secret and extralegal arrangements between Ireland and any other state regarding the use of Irish territory, and to use the full powers available under domestic law to investigate and inspect planes.[25]

The Government did not claim that the police—the *Gardaí*—had no authority to board and inspect planes. On the contrary, it acknowledged that inspection powers in relation to civilian aircraft are governed by the Tokyo Convention 1964,[26] which provides for criminal jurisdiction where offences have been committed on Irish territory and for the investigation of criminal offences alleged to have been committed on board an aircraft registered to another state where that aircraft is not in flight.[27] In addition, the Irish Air Navigation and Transport Acts 1988 and 1998 empower an authorised person (including a *Garda*) to board a civilian aircraft where it is suspected that, inter alia, a crime is being committed.[28] The Government also pointed to the Criminal Justice (UN Convention against Torture) Act 2000, giving the *Gardaí* search powers under warrant. The fact that such an action had never been taken was noted by the Government to be a result of the *Gardaí* not seeking such warrants, as opposed to the inadequacy of domestic law. Where military aircraft were concerned, the situation was different. In its

[22] Minister for Foreign Affairs, *Dáil Debates*, col 788, 13 June 2006.

[23] *Ibid.*

[24] *Ibid.*

[25] Michael D Higgins TD, *Dáil Debates*, cols 768–775, 13 June 2006.

[26] The Convention on Offences and Certain other Acts committed on board Aircraft, Tokyo 14 September 1963, as incorporated into Irish law by the Air Navigation and Transport Act 1973.

[27] Above, n 9, pp 7–8.

[28] Air Navigation and Transport Act 1988, s 33.

response to the Secretary General of the Council of Europe's questionnaire, the Government stated 'foreign military aircraft enjoy immunity from search by Irish officials unless permission [to land] is conditional upon the waiver of this immunity'.[29]

The Irish Government strongly opposed the finding of the Marty Report,[30] which resulted in part from States' responses to the Council of Europe Secretary General's questionnaire. In his Report, Senator Marty identified a number of countries—including Ireland—that could be held to be responsible for either active or passive collusion involving secret detention and extraordinary rendition.[31] As already outlined, the Government concluded that no such liability would arise because of the nature of the assurances received from the United States; Ireland's repeated representations to the US Government of its abhorrence for the illegal practices of extraordinary rendition and torture; and the fact that domestic law fully allows for steps to be taken to address any suspected violations occurring in Irish territory or within the control of the Irish Government.

The Government also co-operated with the Temporary Committee on the alleged use of European countries by the CIA for the Transportation and Illegal Detention of Prisoners, established by the European Parliament.[32] The Draft Report of the Temporary Committee (now the Final Report)[33] expressed 'serious concern about the 147 stopovers made by CIA-operated aircraft at Irish airports that on many occasions came from or were bound for countries linked with extraordinary rendition circuits and the transfer of detainees; deplores the stopovers in Ireland of aircraft which have been shown to have been used by the CIA, on other occasions, for [. . .] extraordinary rendition',[34] criticised the lack of parliamentary scrutiny of intelligence sources in Ireland that could result in abuse,[35] recommended that an investigation be launched into the CIA's use of Irish airports,[36] and recommended 'that, in the absence of a system of random searches, a ban should be imposed on all CIA-operated aircraft landing in Ireland'.[37] Commenting to the Temporary Committee on the Draft Report, the Minister for Foreign Affairs rigorously questioned the methodology applied to reach the conclusion that 147 flights used for suspicious and/or illegal activity stopped-over in Irish airports. The Minister also noted that the *Gardaí* have powers available to them under the criminal law that can be exercised if evidence of illegal activity arises in Ireland and that the *Gardaí* and the Director of Public Prosecutions are independent in their functions in this and every other regard.[38]

The concentration on the use of Shannon Airport for extraordinary rendition in 2006 followed a High Court decision in 2005 that confirmed the court's reluctance to

[29] Above, n 9, p 8.

[30] Committee on Legal Affairs and Human Rights (Rapporteur: Dick Marty), *Alleged Secret Detentions and Unlawful Inter-state Transfers Involving Council of Europe Member States*, Draft Report—Part II, 7 June 2006, AS/JUR (2006) 16 Part II, available at http://assembly.coe.int.

[31] *Ibid*, p 66.

[32] Decision setting up a temporary committee on the alleged use of European countries by the CIA for the transportation and illegal detention of prisoners B60051/2006 (12 January 2006).

[33] TCIP (Rapporteur: Giovanni Claudio Flava), *Report on the alleged use of European countries by the CIA for the transportation and illegal detention of prisoners*, 30 January 2007, A6-0020/2007.

[34] *Ibid*, para 123.

[35] *Ibid*, para 124.

[36] *Ibid*, para 126.

[37] *Ibid*, para 125.

[38] Statement by Mr Dermot Ahern TD, Minister for Foreign Affairs of Ireland to European Parliament—TDIP Committee, 30 November 2006, available at foreignaffairs.gov.ie.

involve itself in matters relating to the lawfulness of Ireland's 'involvement' in military operations in Afghanistan. In *Dubsky v Government of Ireland*[39] the High Court considered a number of international law questions, namely whether, by allowing overflight and refuelling rights for US military aircraft in Shannon Airport, the Irish government was participating in a war without the consent of the Dáil as required by Article 28.3.1 of the Constitution; whether the military action in Afghanistan is unconstitutional under Article 29.1, 29.2, 29.3 and 29.4 of the Constitution in particular by reference to the 1907 Hague Convention V respecting the Rights and Duties of Neutral Powers which Dubsky claimed represented customary international law; whether this military action is mandated by Security Council Resolution 1368 and, if so, whether that redeems an unconstitutional act.[40] The Government argued that the arrangement with the United States did not constitute participation in a war and that, in any case, the conflict in Afghanistan did not constitute a war in the sense of the term as employed in Article 28 of the Constitution; the decision to enter into such an agreement is in essence an executive one dealing as it does with the external relations of the state and matters relating to Articles 29.1–29.4 concerning, as they do, the external relations of the state, can not be employed by an individual litigant in the Irish Courts.[41]

Macken J held that Article 28.3 of the Constitution was not engaged as Dubsky had failed to satisfy the burden of proving that the military operation in Afghanistan could be considered a 'war', therefore the question of whether Ireland was participating in a war without the consent of the Dáil did not need to be considered. In addition, the High Court held that Articles 29.1–29.4 were long-established as binding on the state in its external relations only, therefore even if the 1907 Hague Convention V Respecting the Rights and Duties of Neutral Powers and Persons in Case of War on Land could be established as customary international law (which the applicant had failed to do) and therefore incorporated into Irish law under Article 29.3 these legal principles would apply to the State solely 'in its relations with other States' as expressly outlined in Article 29.3 itself. The Irish principle of military neutrality therefore retained its status as a matter of governmental policy and did not fall to be considered by the Court. Finally Macken J held that an Irish Court could not consider the meaning of a UN Security Council Resolution but that unconstitutional action by the state could not be saved by its being authorised by a Security Council Resolution.

Although *Dubsky* was a High Court decision, when taken in conjunction with *Horgan v An Taoiseach, Minister for Foreign Affairs*[42] it clearly signifies the Irish courts' unwillingness to involve themselves in determinations of the international lawfulness of current military campaigns in Afghanistan and Iraq and of Ireland's 'participation' therein.

[39] [2005] IEHC 442.

[40] Dubsky also argued (unsuccessfully) that domestic law (in the form of the Air Navigation (Foreign Military Aircraft) Order 1952, Air Navigation (Carriage of Munitions of War, Weapons, and Dangerous Goods) Order 1973, and Air Navigation (Carriage of Munitions of War, Weapons, and Dangerous Goods) Order, 1989) did not allow for the Minister for Justice, Equality and Law Reform to enter into agreements allowing over-flight and refuelling of US military aircraft or, if it did, then s 5 of the Air Navigation Act 1946 was an unconstitutional usurpation of legislative functions conferred solely on the Oireachtas by Art 15 of the Constitution.

[41] For a fuller consideration of the arguments raised in this case see Thornton, *Dubsky v Government of Ireland*, ILDC 486 (IE 2003) (OUP).

[42] [2003] 2 IR 468.

Also related to Shannon Airport was the July 2006 case of *DPP v Clancy et al*[43] wherein a jury in the Dublin Circuit Criminal Court acquitted Deirdre Clancy, Nuin Dunlop, Karen Fallon, Damien Moran and Ciaron O'Reilly of criminal damage to a military plane. The five, all of whom were members of the direct action Pitstop Ploughshares group, had caused some $2.5 million of damage to a US Navy cargo 737 plane that was parked in Shannon Airport on 3 February 2003. The defendants did not dispute that they had caused criminal damage, but claimed that they had 'lawful excuse' for their actions. The lawful excuse defence as pleaded is contained in section 6(2) of the Criminal Damage Act 1991, which provides in relevant part:

> (2) A person charged with an offence to which this section applies shall, whether or not he would be treated for the purposes of this Act as having a lawful excuse apart from this subsection, be treated for those purposes as having a lawful excuse
>
> [. . .]
>
> (c) if he damaged or threatened to damage the property in question or, in the case of an offence under *section 4*, intended to use or cause or permit the use of something to damage it, in order to protect himself or another or property belonging to himself or another or a right or interest in property which was or which he believed to be vested in himself or another and, at the time of the act or acts alleged to constitute the offence, he believed
>
> (i) that he or that other or the property, right or interest was in immediate need of protection, and
> (ii) that the means of protection adopted or proposed to be adopted were or would be reasonable having regard to all the circumstances.

In order to successfully make out the defence of 'lawful excuse' the defendants would have to show that, in the circumstances and with the knowledge they possessed, they carried out their actions in order to save lives in Iraq and their actions were reasonable in pursuit of that goal. This requires that a defendant would honestly believe that they were protecting property or life, and that their action would be reasonable taking into account all of the circumstances.[44]

Directing the jury, Judge Miriam Reynolds stressed the importance of the jury's analysis of the reasonableness of their actions. In his closing speech for the prosecution, Conor Devally SC claimed that the defendants' actions did not meet the 'reasonableness' requirement because they were directed towards aims additional to saving lives in Iraq—such as raising consciousness—that could have been achieved through lawful means such as government lobbying, working with NGOs etc. The defendants furthermore knew that these aims could be achieved by lawful means, and their actions were therefore unreasonable within the meaning of the Act. According to Mr Devally the expert testimony that the War in Iraq is contrary to international law ought not to be taken into account by the jury in assessing reasonableness.

The defence counsel argued that although the defendants may have had a number of objectives, their broader intention (of raising consciousness about the War in Iraq) does not take away from their main motivation (namely, saving lives in Iraq). What the jury ought to consider was (i) what the defendants honestly believed to be the case,

[43] Dublin Circuit Criminal Court, 25 July 2006, Reynolds J.

[44] See *Lloyds v DPP* [1992] 1 All ER 982; *Johnson v DPP* [1994] Crim LR 673; Cf Charleton, McDermott and Bolger, *Criminal Law*, (Dublin; Butterworths Lexis Nexis, 1999), pp 753–755.

(ii) what their objective was, and (iii) whether their actions were reasonable in light of these considerations. According to the defence the defendants believed that the war in Iraq was illegal and that their action in Shannon could help to save lives in Iraq; their objective was primarily to save lives, although there may have been a secondary 'consciousness raising' objective; and causing damage to the airplane was a reasonable way of achieving this objective in the circumstances as they knew them to be.

Following three and a half hours of deliberation, the jury accepted that the defendants had lawful excuse for carrying out the criminal damage and accordingly acquitted them. The trial lasted two weeks, during which the defence adduced evidence of the illegality of the war in Iraq in order to substantiate the defendants' claim that their actions were lawful as they were preventing the commission of war crimes by the United States in Iraq. This was the third trial of this action; two previous trials had been declared mistrials after the presiding judges accepted arguments that they might be said to be biased against the defendants.

Finally, in line with the Government's view that international law must be respected in the 'Global War on Terror', Ireland endorsed the creation of international counter-terrorism strategies that are consistent with international law and the rule of law, and outlined the Government's position that all counter-terrorism policies ought to be designed on the basis of the following principles: (i) engagement in terrorist activities ought to be dissuaded, (ii) terrorist organisations ought to be denied access to funds and materials, (iii) states ought to be deterred from supporting or sponsoring terrorism, (iv) states' capacities to defend against terrorism ought to be developed, and (v) human rights and the rule of law must be defended at all times.[45]

INTERNATIONAL PEACE AND SECURITY

International peace and security was a prominent theme in Ireland's dealings with international law in 2006. Within this area three issues arose as being of particular significance—the Middle East Peace Process, the situation in Darfur, and arms control. In addition, Ireland continued to support international peace and security through the provision of humanitarian aid and involvement in international peacekeeping missions.

The Middle East peace process has long been a high priority on Ireland's foreign affairs agenda and the events of 2006, including in particular the election of Hamas in Palestine and the armed conflict between Israel and Lebanon, attracted concerted governmental attention. In the main, Ireland approached these events from its position as a member of the European Union, therefore unilateral dealings with the Israeli, Palestinian and Lebanese governments were limited.

The Government showed particular concern for the human rights situation of those living in the Palestinian Occupied Territories and, in line with the Advisory Opinion of the International Court of Justice, expressed the view that Israel ought to comply with international human rights law and, where appropriate, international humanitarian law in its actions in the Occupied Territories.[46] Instead of raising human rights

[45] Minister for Foreign Affairs, *Dáil Debates*, col 799, 22 February 2006.

[46] See Minister for Foreign Affairs, *Dáil Debates*, cols 1520–1522, 17 May 2006; Minister of State at the Department of Foreign Affairs, Noel Treacy TD, *Dáil Debates*,, cols 417–418, 24 May 2006; Minister for Foreign Affairs, *Dáil Debates*, cols 1431–1432, 15 June 2006; Minister for Foreign Affairs, *Dáil Debates*, col 1639, 29 June 2006.

issues directly with the Israeli government, Ireland indicated that its approach to compliance with these standards was largely multilateral and assessed by reference to the human rights conditions contained in the EU-Israeli Association Agreement of 20 November 1995, which is monitored by the EU on a continuous basis.[47] In domestic commentary, the Minister for Foreign Affairs, Dermot Ahern TD, repeatedly expressed the view that many Israel's actions within the Occupied Territories were in violation of international law and, in particular, of the Fourth Geneva Convention.[48] The government expressed special concern in relation to the creation and expansion of Israeli settlements in the Occupied Territories,[49] the construction of 'the Wall',[50] the killings of civilians in Gaza,[51] and the practice of administrative detention within the Occupied Territories.[52] All of these practices were identified by Ireland as violations of international standards and of the Roadmap agreement. To this end, Ireland unequivocally stated that there is no potential for a military resolution to the situation in Israel and the Occupied Territories and expressed its support for the EU position, ie that a viable and lasting peace can only be achieved by means of a two-State solution, negotiated between the parties, and resulting in 'the coexistence of two viable, sovereign and independent states with agreed international borders'.[53]

Ireland also stressed the need for the Palestinian Authority to act in compliance with its international obligations.[54] Following the election of the Hamas Government in January 2006, Ireland participated in a review of the provision of humanitarian assistance and aid to Palestine in order to ensure that any monies and materials provided would be for the assistance of the people of Palestine and would not be directed towards illegal ends.[55] Despite the Irish Government's concern as to the potential ramifications of the election of the Hamas Government, Ireland did not revoke or freeze its aid to Palestine, feeling that the Palestinian people ought not to suffer for the actions of their Government. In the alternative to freezing the provision of aid, Ireland worked within the EU to devise a system of direct provision of 'necessary assistance' to the people of the Occupied Territories, operating on the basis of a flexible and expansive definition of 'necessary provision' to ensure that health and education were provided for as adequately as possible.[56]

It was the view of the Irish Government that the military conflict between Israel and Lebanon (July-August 2006) was inextricably linked with the Israeli-Palestinian conflict, and that this served to underline the view that there is no possible military or unilateral solution to the difficulties in the Middle East. Following the kidnap of Corporal Gilad Shalit the Irish government appealed directly to the Israeli Government to exercise

[47] Minister for Foreign Affairs, *Dáil Debates*, col 674, 22 February 2006.

[48] Minister for Foreign Affairs, *Dáil Debates*, col 1096, 4 April 2006.

[49] Minister for Foreign Affairs, *Dáil Debates*, col 273, 25 April 2006; Minister for Foreign Affairs, *Dáil Debates*, col 1042, 16 May 2006; Minister for Foreign Affairs, *Dáil Debates*, col 1297–1298, 30 May 2006; Minister for Foreign Affairs, *Dáil Debates*, col 1560, 29 June 2006.

[50] Minister for Foreign Affairs, *Seanad Debates*, col 697, 26 April 2006.

[51] Minister for Foreign Affairs, *Dáil Debates*, col 538, 23 November 2006.

[52] Minister for Foreign Affairs, *Dáil Debates*, col 1400, 3 May 2006.

[53] Minister for Foreign Affairs, *Seanad Debates*, col 693, 26 April 2006.

[54] *Ibid.*

[55] Minister of State at the Department of Foreign Affairs, Conor Lenihan TD, *Dáil Debates*, col 446, 10 May 2006.

[56] See, Minister for Foreign Affairs, *Dáil Debates*, cols 896–897, 26 April 2006; Minister for Foreign Affairs, *Dáil Debates*, cols 1405–1406, 3 May 2006; Minister for Foreign Affairs, *Dáil Debates*, cols 228–229, 23 May 2006; Minister for Foreign Affairs, *Dáil Debates*, col 1400, 29 June 2006.

restraint and the Minister of State at the Department of Foreign Affairs, Noel Treacy TD, stressed the Government's concern at the humanitarian ramifications of Israeli military actions in Gaza.[57] The Government also joined in the EU's call on Israel to act only in accordance with international humanitarian law and, in particular, to distinguish appropriately between civilians and combatants in its actions.[58] The Irish Government concluded that the cause of the tensions with Lebanon lay in the lack of a credible process for the settlement of issues related to the occupation of Palestine. The difficulties and frustrations association with this were then exacerbated by the actions of Hezbollah, which were met with a 'harsh and disproportionate' Israeli response.

In keeping with Ireland's commitment to the resolution of the situation in the Middle East, the Government continued to work for diplomatic solutions based on the Roadmap and welcomed UN Security Council Resolution 1701 calling for an immediate end to hostilities.[59] The Government further committed one hundred and fifty members of the armed services to the UN mission in Lebanon, identifying a number of roles for the forces in the reconstruction of the country including, in particular, the decommissioning of unexploded cluster munitions that pose a serious humanitarian risk to the civilian population of the Lebanon.[60] This was in furtherance of Ireland's stated policy that diplomacy is the only viable solution to international conflict. Ireland favours multilateral peace-making with the concerns of key players in the region, including in particular Syria and Iran, being taken into account in order to remove this major obstacle to peace and security in the Middle East and, as a result, in the world.[61]

Ireland expressed concern as to extensive use of cluster munitions by Israel in the conflict against Lebanon. The use of such weapons poses extensive risks to civilians, and the Irish Government repeatedly stressed the importance of retaining the distinction between civilian and combatant in relation to a number of international situations in 2006. As considered fully below, the Irish Government played a prominent role at the Review Conference of the Convention on Certain Conventional Weapons at which it strongly condemned the use of cluster bombs and called for the negotiation of an international legal instrument on the use of such weaponry.

The humanitarian situation in Darfur received significant Executive and Legislative attention in 2006, with the Government's statements becoming more critical of the parties involved as the year progressed. This culminated in an all-party Parliament—*Dáil*—motion requesting urgent international action in November 2006.[62] Early in the year, the Government identified the redevelopment of the infrastructure in Southern Sudan as a major priority. As this redevelopment would take an appreciable amount of time, the Government identified the provision of humanitarian aid as an important priority both for the people of the Southern Sudan and for the entire country whose stability is threatened by the unrest in the south. The Government expressed early

[57] Minister of State at the Department of Foreign Affairs, Noel Treacy TD, *Seanad Debates,* col 1037, 5 July 2006.

[58] *Ibid.*

[59] Department of Foreign Affairs Press Release, 'Statement by the Minister for Foreign Affairs, Dermot Ahern TD, on the adoption of UN Resolution 1701', 12 August 2006.

[60] Minister of State at the Department of Foreign Affairs, Noel Treacy TD, *Seanad Debates,* col 1733, 18 October 2006.

[61] Minister for Foreign Affairs, *Dáil Debates*, col 581, 23 November 2006.

[62] 28 November 2006

support for the completion of peace talks in Abuja and for the African Union's role in attempting to bring about this peace agreement, including a humanitarian ceasefire and a roadmap for implementation. When it became clear that the agreement was not being honoured, the Irish Government condemned the Sudanese Government's 'utter disregard' for it.[63] Ireland further condemned the Sudanese Government's failure to distinguish between combatants and civilians and identified this approach as inconsistent with the requirements of international humanitarian law.[64] Later in the year Ireland expressed, in principle, its support for the agreement reached by the five permanent Members of the UN Security Council and the Sudan in November 2006, for a joint African Union-United Nations force to be deployed in Darfur.[65]

The Minister for Foreign Affairs, Dermot Ahern TD, clearly acknowledged the situation in Darfur as a challenge for the United Nations and identified it as 'the first opportunity we have to put into practice the principle of responsibility to protect'[66] as contained in the UN Reform Agenda. As a result, Ireland expressed full support for the imposition of sanctions against those who failed to advance the peace process and engaged in attacks on humanitarian convoys, which the Irish Government characterised as being 'in direct contravention of international law'.[67] Furthermore, the Minister stated that the Sudanese government was in breach of Security Council Resolution 1591 (2005), expanding the scope of the pre-existing sanctions regime and imposing additional travel bans and assets freezing on particular individuals. As a result, the Minister for Foreign Affairs, speaking in October, stated that the 'Sudanese government has a clear responsibility to protect its citizens and if it fails to act the international community will have to consider possible further measures'.[68] As the year progressed and the situation in Darfur became more grave, the Irish Government began to advocate a more directly interventionist approach by the international community. The Minister for Foreign Affairs indicated[69] his full agreement with the statement of Michael D Higgins TD, to the effect that 'using sovereignty as a shield while massive loss of life and dislocation is taking place is an abuse of the concept of sovereignty [. . .]. The international community must have the right to intervene where a state is not protecting a significant part of its population'.[70]

Throughout the year, Ireland expressed unreserved support for a peaceful and diplomatic settlement to the situation in Darfur. This policy manifested itself in a number of ways. As already mentioned, the Government expressed enthusiasm for the negotiation of a peace settlement that included details of a humanitarian ceasefire. When this settlement appeared to be ineffective, the Government went on to express its support for the use of an international peace keeping force as mandated by the United Nations (Security Council Resolution 1706) and condemned the Sudanese government for its failure to accede to this proposal.[71] The Irish Government took a

[63] Minister for Foreign Affairs, *Dáil Debates*, cols 1502–1504, 3 October 2006.

[64] *Ibid.*

[65] Department of Foreign Affairs Press Release, 'Minister for Foreign Affairs Welcomes Progress on Darfur', 17 November 2006.

[66] Minister for Foreign Affairs, *Dáil Debates,* col 533, 23 November 2006.

[67] Minister for Foreign Affairs, *Dáil Debates*, col 886, 28 November 2006.

[68] Minister for Foreign Affairs, *Dáil Debates*, cols 1502–1504, 3 October 2006.

[69] Minister for Foreign Affairs, *Dáil Debates*, col 555, 25 October 2006.

[70] Michael D. Higgins TD, *Dáil Debates*, col 555, 25 October 2006.

[71] Department of Foreign Affairs Press Release, 'Minister for Foreign Affairs Welcomes Authorisation by UN Security Council of a United Nations Peacekeeping Force for Darfur, Sudan', 1 September 2006.

prominent role in attempting to persuade the Sudanese government that a United Nations humanitarian force would be appropriate. The Government welcomed a British proposal to hold a conference to negotiate such a move and stated that it would be willing to host such a conference. The Minister for Foreign Affairs considered that an action of this nature would be important in order to negotiate and try to predict what the potential impact of such a force would be; he was particularly conscious of the potential for the placement of a UN force to further aggravate matters if not handled appropriately. The Minister expressed doubt, however, as to the potential for such a conference to have any significant impact given the political situation in Sudan.[72]

The Government supported the International Criminal Court's investigation of alleged human rights and humanitarian abuses in Darfur,[73] but did not reach a conclusion as to whether the situation in Darfur was genocide. In the view of the Minister for Foreign Affairs, Dermot Ahern TD, such a question was 'academic' as the situation in the Darfur was dire and the international community ought to concentrate on the delivery what the Government felt were the three immediate needs of the people of the Sudan: (1) humanitarian assistance; (2) an international peacekeeping force with a strong mandate whose deployment the Sudanese Government should no longer oppose; and (3) full implementation of the Darfur peace agreement. The Irish Government advocated for a Special Session of the UN Human Rights Council to consider the situation in Darfur, which was convened on 12–13 December 2006, and urged full implementation of the Darfur Peace Agreement, calling for increased co-operation between the Sudanese government and the United Nations organisation, and the dispatching of a High-Level Mission to assess the human rights situation in Darfur and the needs of the Sudan in that regard.[74]

Throughout 2006, Ireland expressed strong statements of support for arms control both internationally and domestically. In the international sphere Ireland took a prominent role at the Review Convention of the Convention on Certain Conventional Weapons.[75] Ireland joined with some twenty-four other nations in declaring cluster munitions to be a grave humanitarian concern during and after armed conflict and, together with Australia, the Holy See, Mexico, New Zealand and Sweden, proposed that the Conventional Weapons Review Committee would draft a mandate for the preparation of a convention on cluster munitions. The proposed convention would prohibit the use of cluster munitions within areas of civilian concentration; and prohibit the development, production, stockpiling, transfer and use of cluster munitions that pose serious humanitarian hazards because they are either unreliable or inaccurate (or both). Despite gathering the support of a further nineteen states, the proposal could not acquire the required consensus. Consensus was reached, however, on the calling of a meeting at which the status of cluster munitions within international law

[72] Department of Foreign Affairs Press Release, 'Minister for Foreign Affairs Welcomes Authorisation by UN Security Council of a United Nations Peacekeeping Force for Darfur, Sudan', 1 September 2006.

[73] Minister for Foreign Affairs, *Dáil Debates*, cols 1253–1254; 25 October 2006, Minister for Foreign Affairs, *Dáil Debates*, cols 553–554, 4 April 2006.

[74] Decision Adopted by the Council at its Fourth Special Session as reported in *Report of the Fourth Special Session of the Human Rights Council*, UN Doc A/HRC/S-4/5 (22 January 2007).

[75] Convention on Prohibitions or Restrictions on the Use of Certain Conventional Weapons which may be Deemed to be Excessively Injurious or to have Indiscriminate Effects 1981 (as amended on 21 December 2001).

might be considered. In addition, Ireland successfully introduced wording into the Conference Final Declaration that will increase the onus on military commanders to give due regard to the foreseeable repercussions for civilians (including post-hostilities repercussions) of the weaponry deployed. Despite being disappointed that the Conference could not agree a more comprehensive mandate in relation to such weaponry, the Irish Government restated its commitment to working to seek agreement on an international instrument on such munitions.[76] Ireland's commitment to reducing the use of cluster munitions was echoed by the Joint Committee on Foreign Affairs which heard testimony on the matter in December 2006.[77]

In 2006, Ireland also expressed repeated support for the Nuclear Non-Proliferation Treaty, which the Minister for Foreign Affairs described as 'the Government's highest priority in the field of disarmament and non-proliferation'.[78] To that end, Ireland continued its work within the New Agenda Coalition (NAC)[79] to achieve the universalism of the treaty. Ireland also acted unilaterally and within the NAC to encourage commitment to the international dual approach to nuclear arms, ie non-proliferation and disarmament as outlined in Article VI of the Treaty.[80] In keeping with Ireland's long-standing practice, the Irish delegation introduced a General Assembly Resolution entitled 'Towards a nuclear-weapon-free world: accelerating the implementation of nuclear disarmament commitments' in October 2006, which was adopted by an overwhelming majority of States. Ireland also received special commendation for its efforts to strengthen and improve implementation of the Non-Proliferation Treaty in the Weapons of Mass Destruction Commission's 2006 report entitled *Weapons of Terror: Freeing the World of Nuclear, Biological and Chemical Arms*.[81]

While acknowledging that the international approach to nuclear weaponry had suffered a number of setbacks in 2006, the Government did not accept that the international approach was completely undermined or incapable of effective implementation. Rather, Ireland took the approach that breaches of the international system ought to be viewed with seriousness by the international community and that Ireland should continue to raise the questions of non-proliferation, disarmament and ratification of the Non-Proliferation Treaty in its bilateral and other dealings with relevant States. In this relation there were three particular issues that caused concern for the Irish government in 2006.

In March 2006, the United States and India concluded an agreement on civil nuclear co-operation that caused some concern for the Government as it had repeatedly called for India to accede to the Non-Proliferation Treaty and to terminate its

[76] Ambassador Kavanagh, Delegation of Ireland Statement at the Final Plenary Meeting of the Third Review Convention on the Convention on Certain Conventional Weapons, Geneva, 17 November 2006.

[77] Presentation of Tony D'Costa (Pax Christi Ireland) before the Joint Committee, 5 December 2006.

[78] Statement of Minister for Foreign Affairs to the Joint Committee on Foreign Affairs, 7 November 2006.

[79] The New Agenda Coalition was launched in Dublin on 27 June 1998 by the Ministers for Foreign Affairs of Brazil, Ireland, Egypt, Mexico, New Zealand, Slovenia, South Africa and Sweden. The NAC aims to persuade nuclear states to take decisive steps towards disarmament. See Joint Declaration: 'A Nuclear-Weapons-Free-World: The Need for a New Agenda', 27 June 1998.

[80] Article VI provides 'Each of the Parties to the Treaty undertakes to pursue negotiations in good faith on effective measures relating to cessation of the nuclear arms race at an early date and to nuclear disarmament, and on a Treaty on general and complete disarmament under strict and effective international control'.

[81] WMB Commission, 2006, p 64. Report available at: www.wmdcommission.org/files.

development programme.[82] In the view of the Government this agreement had the potential to undermine the Treaty, which is Ireland's preferred framework for international law and negotiations related to nuclear arms. The Government, however, committed to take into account the views of other members of the Nuclear Suppliers Group (NSG)[83] in reaching its conclusions on the agreement and continued to consider it throughout the remainder of 2006 and, particularly, in three later meetings of the NSG. As the United States is a member of the NSG the US-India Agreement can not be implemented until US domestic law has been changed[84] *and* a consensus has been reached within the NSG. The Minister for Foreign Affairs stressed that Ireland would take into account the broader political and economic context of the agreement in reaching its decision and confirmed that he had held direct talks with a member of the Indian Government in which India's lack of commitment to the NPT was discussed in full.[85]

Ireland unreservedly condemned North Korea's nuclear testing, which it characterised as a threat to the security and stability of the region and a direct contravention of the international objectives of nuclear disarmament and non-proliferation.[86] In the view of the Government, concrete action against North Korea was called for and, to this end, Ireland committed to taking all necessary steps to be in full compliance with Security Council Resolutions 1718 (2006) (condemning North Korea's nuclear tests and demanding, inter alia, that North Korea retracts its announcement of withdrawal from the NPT)[87] and 1695 (2006) (condemning North Korea's nuclear testing and demanding inter alia a re-enactment of the moratorium on missile launching).[88] Although Ireland considered Security Council Resolution 1718 to be a 'necessary measure'[89] in the case of North Korea, the Minister for Foreign Affairs remained committed to resolving the issue by means of diplomacy and multiparty talks.[90]

Despite expressing concern about Iran's nuclear programme, Ireland was of the view that the nuclear issues with Iran ought to be resolved by means of dialogue and negotiation, which in turn would open the way to developing further relations with Iran in which, inter alia, human rights concerns could be effectively addressed. In order to facilitate this approach, Ireland urged the immediate suspension of all enrichment activities, co-operation with the IAEA and the provision of the transparency required to resolve any remaining issues.[91] This view was fully in line with the EU's commitment to a diplomatic solution to the question.[92]

[82] Minister for Foreign Affair, *Dáil Debates*, col 1249, 4 April 2006; Minister of State at the Department of Foreign Affairs, Noel Treacy TD, *Dáil Debates,* col 421–422, 24 May 2006.

[83] The NSG is a group of supplier-nations that aims to ensure non-proliferation by the development and implementation on guidelines relating, mostly, to export policy and licensing.

[84] The Agreement requires amendment of the Atomic Energy Act of 1954 which was not secured during 2006.

[85] Statement of Minister for Foreign Affairs to the Joint Committee on Foreign Affairs, 7 November 2006.

[86] Department of Foreign Affairs Press Release, 'Minister for Foreign Affairs condemns underground nuclear test by DPRK', 9 October 2006.

[87] See further Paulus and Muller, 'Security Council Resolution 1718 on North Korea's Nuclear Test', (2006) 10(29) ASIL Insight.

[88] Minister for Foreign Affairs, *Dáil Debates*, col 558–559, 25 October 2006.

[89] Statement of Minister for Foreign Affairs to the Joint Committee on Foreign Affairs, 7 November 2006.

[90] *Ibid.*

[91] See Department of Foreign Affairs Press Release, 'Iran's decision to resume suspended nuclear research and development', 10 January 2006.

[92] Minister for Foreign Affairs, *Dáil Debates*, col 1249–1250, 4 April 2006.

On the domestic landscape, the Irish government began the drafting process on a Control of Exports Bill which would, *inter alia*, codify the principles upon which dual-use goods are exported from Ireland.[93] As it stands, the Department of Trade, Enterprise and Employment is the licensing body for exports and consults with the Department of Foreign Affairs on the export of any controlled dual-use goods. Licences for export are only granted following a case-by-case assessment of the destination country under a number of different criteria—human rights; the internal situation in the final destination country; the behaviour of the buyer country in the international sphere (especially in relation to terrorism, alliances, and respect for international law); regional peace and security; and the risk of diversion of materials under undesirable conditions.[94] This process is designed to meet Ireland's international obligations in this area.

The regulations concerning flights carrying munitions that wish to travel through Irish airspace were placed under review in 2006. As it stands all such flights must give notification to, and receive permission to land from, the Minister for Transport who makes the decision based on consultation with the Ministers for Foreign Affairs, Defence, Justice Equality and Law Reform, and the Irish Aviation Authority.[95]

On 27 June 2006 the Government moved a motion before the Dáil, which was referred for approval to the Committee on Justice, Equality, Defence and Women's Rights, to approve the terms of Protocol V on the Convention on Prohibitions or Restrictions on the Use of Certain Conventional Weapons which may be deemed to be Excessively Injurious or to have Indiscriminate Effects, 1980. Protocol V deals with Explosive Remnants of War and requires parties to take all feasible steps to protect civilians from the effects of explosive remnants of war, including marking, removing and destroying such remnants. Ireland expressed strong support for Protocol V with the Minister for Defence, Willie O'Dea TD stating that 'if widely adhered to and fully implemented [Protocol V] has the potential to significantly reduce the civilian casualties that regularly occur after the end of hostilities and to minimize the long-term socio-economic consequences that explosive remnants of war inflict on war-affected countries'.[96] The committee approved the motion on Protocol V. Throughout the year, Ireland continued to contribute forces and other resources to efforts to ensure international peace and security through humanitarian aid and peacekeeping missions. Ireland contributed aid unilaterally and by means of multilateral operations (mostly within the EU and UN).

In 2006, the Government produced a White Paper on Irish Aid[97] which outlined the 2015 goals of Irish Aid and the guiding principles for the programme, namely partnership, public ownership and transparency, effectiveness and quality assurance, coherence, and long-term sustainability. The White Paper signalled no change to Ireland's policy of attaching human rights and democratisation conditions to development aid, but rather was substantially concerned with codifying best practice and ensuring that

93 Minister for Defence, *Dáil Debates*, col 561, 11 October 2006.

94 Minister of State at the Department of Foreign Affairs, Noel Treacy TD, *Dáil Debates*, col 1572–1573, 28 June 2006.

95 Minister for Transport, *Dáil Debates*, col 1787, 4 May 2006.

96 Statement of Minister for Defence to the Select Committee on Justice, Equality, Defence & Women's Rights on the Motion on the Protocol on Explosive Remnants of War (Protocol V), 10 October 2006.

97 *White Paper on Irish Aid*, 18 September 2006, available at: www.irishaid.gov.ie/whitepaper. The White Paper is reproduced in the Document section of this *Yearbook*.

future policy was neither developed nor deployed in an *ad hoc* manner.[98] The attachment of human rights and democratisation conditions to aid is motivated by Ireland's belief that good government and democratisation is critical for eradicating poverty and increasing development.[99] The White Paper announced the introduction of a rapid response capability for Irish Aid, which comprises the pre-positioning of resources and compilation of information on skilled individuals who can be deployed speedily should the need arise.[100] The implementation of this programme involves logistical agreements with the World Food Programme. The first such agreement was completed by the Minister of State at the Department of Foreign Affairs, Conor Lenihan TD, in October 2006.[101] This agreement provides for the funding by Irish Aid of the pre-positioning of humanitarian supplies comprising shelter and housing equipment sufficient for 20,000 people in both locations in both Brindski (Italy) and the Curragh. The agreement also provides for additional financial provision by Ireland to the United Nations Humanitarian Response Depot.[102] The White Paper also announced the establishment of a dedicated unit for conflict analysis and resolution within the Department of Foreign Affairs in order to enable Ireland to 'forge a distinctive role in conflict prevention and resolution and peace building'.[103] Ireland will also create a dedicated 'hunger task force' comprising a number of Irish and international experts which will have the role of developing strategies for the effective tackling of root causes for food insecurity in Africa.[104]

The Government repeatedly affirmed its commitment to reducing corruption in recipient countries so that development aid can be used effectively for the benefit of those countries. To this end, Government departments were assessing the legal changes required by accession to the UN Convention on Corruption[105] and the Minister for Justice, Equality and Law Reform confirmed that he would be bringing proposals to Government to give effect to the Convention in due course.[106] The Convention aims to create shared responsibility among signatory states for the tracking of stolen money, the sharing of intelligence, the repatriation of assets etc. In addition, the Government committed to the development of increased parliamentary, audit and evaluation, and advisory board oversight mechanisms for Irish Aid within the domestic system and asked the Joint Committee on Foreign Affairs to consider

[98] Presentation of Minister of State at the Department of Foreign Affairs, Conor Lenihan TD, to the Joint Committee on Foreign Affairs, 10 October 2006.

[99] Minister of State for Development Co-Operation and Human Rights at the Department of Foreign Affairs, Conor Lenihan TD, *Dáil Debates*, col 705, 22 February 2006; Minister of State at the Department of Foreign Affairs, Conor Lenihan TD, *Dáil Debates*, col 1665, 29 June 2006.

[100] Above, n 97, p 35.

[101] Department of Foreign Affairs Press Release, 'Minister of State Conor Lenihan TD signs agreement on pre-positioning of humanitarian supplies with UN World Food Programme', 13 October 2006.

[102] *Ibid.*

[103] Presentation of Minister of State at the Department of Foreign Affairs, Conor Lenihan TD, to the Joint Committee on Foreign Affairs, 10 October 2006; above, n 86, p 58.

[104] Above, n 97, p 52.

[105] United Nations Convention against Corruption, adopted by the United Nations General Assembly by Resolution 58/4 of 31 October 2003.

[106] See Minister for Justice, *Dáil Debates*, col 1834, 1 March 2006; Minister for Foreign Affairs, *Dáil Debates*, cols 1212–1213, 4 April 2006; Minister for Foreign Affairs, *Dáil Debates*, col 1714, 29 June 2006. This commitment followed a motion from the Joint Committee on Foreign Affairs calling for the government to ratify the Convention at the earliest possible opportunity—Motion proposed by Michael D Higgins TD, Joint Committee on Foreign Affairs, 18 October 2005.

models by which effective oversight could be increased.[107] The December 2006 budget included an increase of 21 per cent in overseas aid for 2007.

The Minister for Defence made clear in 2006 that Ireland will continue to contribute to international peace and stability by supporting peace missions (indeed, the Minister for Defence repeatedly identified Irish participation in such missions as one of Ireland's obligations as a member of the United Nations, the European Union and the international community generally[108]), and that such involvement would not in any way threaten Ireland's military neutrality. As a matter of government policy[109] neutrality was secured through the so-called 'triple-lock' facility, which requires the approval of the United Nations, the Cabinet and the Dáil before Irish troops are committed to an operation. The integrity of Irish military neutrality was brought into focus throughout 2006 in relation to the debate on the EU 'Battlegroup' concept introduced by the Treaties of Amsterdam and Nice. The EU Battlegroup concept forms part of the European Security and Defence Policy. The objective is the creation of combat-ready units that would be readily deployable and could endure missions of a loner duration than the European Rapid Reaction Force. Each group will comprise 1500 combat soldiers and support and the Union aims to have approximately seven such groups ready for deployment by 2010.[110] The Minister for Defence identified the Battlegroup concept as a means of fulfilling a long-recognised need for a rapid response capability that could prevent situations of unrest from deteriorating into a major crisis and could deliver interim operations pending the deployment of United Nations forces. To this end, Ireland conceives of the substantive role of the EU Battlegroups as one of support for the United Nations, recognising the role of the United Nations and the primacy of the Security Council.[111] Because of the triple-lock procedure the decision to participate in missions would continue to be made on a case-by-case basis,[112] therefore it was noted that Ireland's participation in a Battlegroup 'in no way weakens or undermines Ireland's traditional policy of military neutrality . . . [or gives] rise to any constitutional issues'.[113] The Minister for Defence acquired Cabinet approval for participation in the Nordic Battlegroup on 14 November 2006.[114]

The Minister for Defence indicated his intention to introduce legislation that would ensure that the Defence Forces receive all necessary training, including international legal training, to enable their participation in overseas UN peace support operations and that would allow for the participation of the Defence Forces in humanitarian operations necessitated by natural disasters (for which personnel must currently

[107] Presentation of Minister of State at the Department of Foreign Affairs, Conor Lenihan TD, to the Joint Committee on Foreign Affairs, 10 October 2006.

[108] See Speech on Ireland's Future Participation in UN Peace Support Missions, McKee Barracks, 9 February 2006, available at www.defence.ie. Presentation by the Minister for Defence to the Joint Committee on European Affairs, 'Ireland's Participation in EU Battlegroups', 22 March 2006.

[109] *Horgan v An Taoiseach, the Minister for Foreign Affairs, the Minister for Transport, the Government of Ireland, Ireland and the Attorney General* [2003] 2 IR 468.

[110] See Headline Goal 2010 (6309/6/04)

[111] See Presentation by the Minister of Defence to the Forum on Europe, 'Ireland and the EU Battlegroups', 11 May 2006, available at: www.defence.ie.

[112] See *Ireland and the European Union: Identifying Priorities and Pursuing Goals*, 4th edn, (Dublin; Department of an Taoiseach, 2006), pp 12 and 67.

[113] Above, n 108.

[114] Department of Defence Press Release, 'O'Dea secures Cabinet approval for Ireland's participation in Battlegroups and rejects Joe Costello's false claims', 14 November 2006.

volunteer).[115] These proposals were brought before the Oireachtas in the Defence (Amendment) Bill 2006, which provides for deployment of defence forces to, inter alia, undertake military exercises and training for international forces.[116] The Bill was not promulgated in 2006.

In 2006 Ireland committed one hundred and fifty troops to the UN peace missions in Lebanon for an initial twelve-month period pursuant to Security Council Resolution 1701, Cabinet,[117] and Dáil approval.[118] Ireland also committed up to ten members of the Defence Forces for service with the EU military operation to support the UN Mission in the Democratic Republic of Congo during the Congolese elections.[119] Ireland renewed its commitment of Defence Forces to Liberia for a further six-month period,[120] to Bosnia and Herzegovina for a further twelve-month period,[121] and to Afghanistan and Kosovo for a further twelve-month period.[122]

LEGISLATION CONCERNING INTERNATIONAL LAW

2006 saw the introduction of a number of pieces of legislation that sought to give effect to Ireland's international obligations. In addition, a number of Bills were introduced for debate on international legal matters without being promulgated.

The International Criminal Court Act 2006 was signed into law on 31 October 2006 in order to incorporate the Rome Statute on the International Criminal Court[123] into Irish law. The Act lays out the interpretative and procedural rules relating to enforcement of the Statute[124] in Irish courts, co-operation with requests and orders from the International Criminal Court,[125] and the government's co-operation with the Court.[126] In addition, it provides for universal jurisdiction[127] for domestic prosecutions of 'ICC offences', meaning 'genocide, a crime against humanity, a war crime or an ancillary offence'.[128] The Act allows for the surrender of suspects to the International Criminal Court pursuant to a surrender order made by the High Court,[129] which has the further option of remanding the individual for trial in the Central Criminal Court.[130] Persons subject to such an Order will be entitled to apply for bail.[131] Furthermore, if the individual has not been surrendered within one month of the grant of the Order either the

[115] Department of Defence Press Release, 'O'Dea secures Cabinet approval for Ireland's participation in Battlegroups and rejects Joe Costello's false claims', 14 November 2006.

[116] See especially ss 1 and 3 of the Defence (Amendment) Bill 2006.

[117] Cabinet approval acquired 3 October 2006.

[118] Dáil approval acquired 11 October 2006.

[119] Department of Defence Press Release, 'Defence Minister O'Dea secures Cabinet approval to send troops to Congo', 9 May 2006.

[120] Department of Defence, Press Statement 'O'Dea Obtains Cabinet Approval for Continued Deployment of Irish Troops in Liberia and Bosnia', 29 November 2006.

[121] *Ibid.*

[122] Department of Defence Press Release, 'Irish troops to remain in Kosovo and Afghanistan following Cabinet approval—Minister for Defence Willie O'Dea TD', 27 June 2006.

[123] UN Doc 2187 U.N.T.S. 90, *entered into force* 1 July 2002.

[124] ICC Act 2006, Part 1.

[125] ICC Act 2006, Part 5.

[126] ICC Act 2006, Part 3.

[127] ICC Act 2006, s 12.

[128] ICC Act 2006, s 9(1).

[129] ICC Act 2006, s 25.

[130] ICC Act 2006, s 26(1).

[131] ICC Act 2006, s 26(2).

Minister for Justice (in consultation with the International Criminal Court[132]) or the High Court can order their release.[133] Release does not, however, bar a subsequent surrender order.[134] The Act further provides for assets to be frozen by a freezing order issued by the Minister for Justice pursuant to a request from the International Criminal Court,[135] and for the enforcement of orders issued by the International Criminal Court.[136]

Section 186 of the Criminal Justice Act 2006 amends the definition of torture contained in the Criminal Justice (United Nations Convention against Torture) Act 2000. The amended definition, with the amendment emphasised by the author, provides:

> 'torture' means an act or omission *done or made, or at the instigation of, or with the consent or acquiescence of a public official* by which severe pain or suffering, whether physical or mental, is intentionally inflicted on a person—
>
> (*a*) for such purposes as—
>
> (i) obtaining from that person, or from another person, information or a confession,
> (ii) punishing that person for an act which the person concerned or a third person has committed or is suspected of having committed, or
> (iii) intimidating or coercing that person or a third person,
>
> or
>
> (*b*) for any reason that is based on any form of discrimination,
>
> but does not include any such act that arises solely from, or is inherent in or incidental to, lawful sanctions.

This amendment was introduced in order to ensure that acts by private individuals would not be contained within the scheme of the 2000 Act. The Minister for Justice, Equality and Law Reform, Michael McDowell TD, invited this change at committee stage in order to synchronise the definitions of torture within Irish law and within Article 1 of the United Nations Convention against Torture,[137] which clearly restricts torture to acts 'inflicted by or at the instigation of or with the consent or acquiescence of a public official or other person acting in an official capacity'.

Part 7 of the Criminal Justice Act 2006 is intended to fulfil some of Ireland's obligations under the United Nations Convention against Transnational Organised Crime.[138] This Part only concerns activities that occur within the context of criminal organisations, defined as groups of three or more people, in existence over a certain period of time, and created with the objective of carrying out serious offence(s) for material gain.[139] In relevant part, the Act provides that it is an offence to conspire inside the State to commit a serious offence within or outside the State.[140] Furthermore, it is an offence to conspire

[132] ICC Act 2006, s 32.
[133] ICC Act 2006, s 33.
[134] ICC Act 2006, s 34.
[135] ICC Act 2006, s 38.
[136] ICC Act 2006, s 40.
[137] Minister for Justice, Equality and Law Reform, *Dáil Debates*, col 64, 28 March 2006; Minister for Justice, Equality and Law Reform, *Dáil Debates*, col 1143, 16 May 2006.
[138] GA Res 5, annex I, UN GAOR, 55th Sess, Supp No 49, at 44, UN Doc A/45/49 (Vol I) (2001), *entered into force* 25 December 2003; Minister for Justice, Equality and Law Reform, *Dáil Debates*, col 1321, 28 June 2006.
[139] Criminal Justice Act 2006, s 79(1).
[140] Criminal Justice Act 2006, s 71(1).

outside the State to carry out a serious offence within the State.[141] Where the conspiracy has occurred outside the state the DPP may only proceed with a prosecution if extradition or surrender has not been achieved, except where the offence was committed in Ireland or on board an Irish airplane or ship, intended to be perpetrated against an Irish citizen or to be committed by an Irish citizen or stateless person perpetually resident within the State.[142] Analogous provisions are introduced in relation to participation in organised crime or facilitation of organised crime to be committed inside or outside the state;[143] and the commission by someone who is not a member of a criminal organisation of a criminal offence for a criminal organisation.[144] Non-members of criminal organisations are liable to conviction under the Act regardless of whether they knew that the persons concerned were members of a criminal organisation.[145]

The Patents (Amendment) Act 2006 was signed into law on 11 December 2006. This is a largely technical piece of legislation that deals with four main areas—incorporation of the Agreement on Trade Related Aspects of Intellectual Property Rights (TRIPs Agreement) annexed to the Agreement establishing the World Trade Organisation; incorporation of the Patent Law Treaty 2000; giving effect to revisions and amendments to the European Patent Convention 2000; and corrections and clarification to pre-existing legislation.[146] Provisions relating to the revisions of the European Patent Convention and to the Patent Law Treaty were not commenced in December 2006.[147]

The Europol (Amendment) Act 2006 was signed into law on 23 December 2006. The Act incorporates the three protocols to the Europol Convention and, by so doing, extends Europol's competence to all cases of money laundering; clarifies the powers, privileges and immunities relating to Europol participation in Joint Investigation Teams; and reforms and streamlines the internal workings of Europol.

Significant Bills debated but not promulgated in 2006 include the Criminal Justice (Mutual Assistance) Bill 2005[148] and the Nuclear Test Ban Bill 2006.[149]

The Criminal Justice (Mutual Assistance) Bill 2005 is intended to give effect to a number of international agreements, including the Convention on Mutual Assistance in Criminal Matters between the Member States of the European Union and the Protocol thereto, by which Ireland pledges and receives mutual assistance in criminal matters. The Bill was met with heated debate at its second reading with a number of Deputies expressing concern about mutual assistance pacts with the United States in the current climate where the United States compliance with international legal standards is in question and when the United States has not ratified the Rome Statute of

[141] Criminal Justice Act 2006, s 71(2).

[142] Criminal Justice Act 2006, s 71(3). Stateless persons habitually resident within the state are defined as stateless persons who have had their principle residence in Ireland for twelve months or more (Criminal Justice Act 2006, s 71(4)).

[143] Criminal Justice Act 2006, s 72.

[144] Criminal Justice Act 2006, s 73(1).

[145] Criminal Justice Act 2006, s 73(2).

[146] Patents Act 1992 as amended by s 75 of theTrade Marks Act 1996; Intellectual Property (Miscellaneous Provisions) Act 1998.

[147] The immediately effective provisions were ss 1, 2, 7, 10, 12, 15, 16, 1–25, 29(c)(ii), 31(c), 32, 34–40, 42–51.

[148] Bill presented to the Dáil 2 March 2006 and available for consultation at www.oireachtas.ie.

[149] Bill presented to the Dáil 13 September 2006 and available for consultation at www.oireachtas.ie.

the International Criminal Court.[150] This concern emanated mostly from section 4 of the Bill which allows for information sharing with another state but does not appear to lay down guidelines as to how a decision to share information would be made, including whether human rights and other international legal considerations would be taken into account. The Irish Human Rights Commission also expressed concerns about the lack of human rights protections in the Bill.[151]

The Nuclear Test Ban Bill 2006 is intended to give domestic effect to the Nuclear Test Ban Treaty which, as considered above, is the lynchpin of Ireland's dual approach to nuclear weaponry, ie non-proliferation and disarmament.

UNITED NATIONS REFORM

The Minister for Foreign Affairs, Dermot Ahern TD, made clear Ireland's intention to remain involved in and at the forefront of United Nations reform early in 2006.[152] This position was reiterated by the Taoiseach, who identified United Nations reform as a necessary condition 'for the UN to remain an efficient and effective instrument of the international community in the twenty-first century'.[153] While welcoming the reform agenda agreed at the UN World Summit in 2005, the Taoiseach expressed particular concern that the matter of Security Council reform had not been fully considered and agreed upon at that time, and called for a 'more balanced and representative [Security Council] . . . which would properly reflect the contributions made by States to peace and security in their regions and the world'.[154] The Taoiseach later elaborated on this view in an interview with *The Irish Times* when he called for the number of permanent members of the Security Council to be expanded in order to more properly reflect economic, political and regional realities.[155]

Ireland welcomed the establishment of the new United Nations Human Rights Council which, although not displaying all of the characteristics that Ireland desired, was identified by the Minister for Foreign Affairs as a significant improvement on the former Human Rights Commission.[156] Ireland did not stand for election to the Council in 2006, but pledged to show support in the election for countries that have shown themselves to be fully committed to the promotion and protection of human rights; Ireland committed to not vote for any State that is subject to Security Council sanctions for human rights related reasons.[157] At the Inaugural Session of the Human Rights Council the Minister of State at the Department of Foreign Affairs, Noel Treacy TD, called on the Council to preserve the best aspects of the Commission

[150] See Catherine Murphy TD, *Dáil Debates*, cols 470–473, 8 June 2006; Michael D Higgins TD, *Dáil Debates*, cols 996–1001, 28 September 2006.

[151] IHRC, 'Observations on the Scheme of the Criminal Justice (International Co-Operation) Bill 2005', 10 May 2005, available at www.ihrc.ie.

[152] Department of Foreign Affairs Press Release, 'Ireland Will Remain at the Forefront of UN Reform Drive', 4 January 2006.

[153] Speech of an Taoiseach at the Nehru Memorial Museum and Library, New Delhi, 18 January 2006, available at www.taoiseach.gov.ie.

[154] *Ibid.*

[155] Hennessy, 'Reform of UN Security Council Overdue—Ahern', *The Irish Times*, 19 January 2006, p 9.

[156] Minister for Foreign Affairs, *Dáil Debates*, col 1015–1016, 9 March 2006; Department of Foreign Affairs Press Release, 'Minister for Foreign Affairs, Mr Dermot Ahern TD, welcomes agreement on establishment of United Nations Human Rights Council', 15 March 2006.

[157] Minister for Foreign Affairs, *Dáil Debates*, col 1221, 4 April 2006.

(especially civil engagement), nurture a constructive environment in which grave human rights breaches can be addressed in a frank manner, and to ensure its relevance by confronting 'the human rights challenges the world faces today'.[158]

Ireland continued to play a prominent role in the internal reform of the United Nations during 2006, with the Irish Permanent Representative to the United Nations, HE David Cooney, acting as Co-Chair of the Informal Working Group on UN Mandate Reform.[159] The task of the Co-Chairs was to achieve the broadest consensus possible on issues of oversight, accountability, management, governance and prioritisation of the work of the United Nations. This group began its work in June 2006 and was seized with the responsibility of reviewing all United Nations mandates that are over five years old; a task that the then Secretary General Kofi Annan described as 'a unique opportunity to strengthen and adapt our Organisation to the priorities of today'.[160] Although United Nations mandates have no definitive legal definition, the working definition for the purposes of the mandate review is 'a request or a direction for action by the UN Secretariat or other implementing entity, that derives from a resolution of the General Assembly or one of the other relevant organs'.[161] The process of mandate review was not completed in 2006, however the Working Group designated 74 mandates as 'completed' in November 2006.[162] Phase II of the review with a thematic cluster on drug control, crime prevention and international terrorism began in December 2006. This Phase will comprise an evaluation of all mandates over five years old that have been renewed.

INTERNATIONAL AGREEMENTS

During 2006 the Irish Government outlined its intentions in relation to a number of international agreements. The government indicated its plan to incorporate into Irish law the Vienna Convention on the Law of Treaties,[163] the United Nations Convention on Corruption,[164] the International Labour Organisation Maritime Labour Convention,[165] and the Aarhus Convention (Access to Information and Public Participation in Environmental Decision Making).[166] The Minister for Justice, Equality and Law Reform also confirmed that the drafting process for a statute (Criminal Law (Trafficking in Persons and Sex Offences) Bill 2006)[167] incorporating the Convention on

[158] Department of Foreign Affairs Press Release, 'Minister of State Treacy addresses inaugural session of UN Human Rights Council in Geneva', 20 June 2006.

[159] Department of Foreign Affairs Press Release, 'Irish Diplomat to Head Key UN Task Force', 7 March 2006.

[160] General Assembly Press Release, 30 March 2006—'Review of Mandates is "Unique Opportunity" to Strengthen United Nations, Secretary-General Says, Presenting Report to General Assembly'.

[161] As found at: webapps01.un.org/mandatereview/

[162] *Status Report on the Informal Working Group*, 27 November 2006.

[163] Minister of State at the Department of Foreign Affairs, Conor Lenihan TD, *Dáil Debates*, col 1552, 15 February 2006.

[164] Minister for Justice, *Dáil Debates*, col 1834, 1 March 2006; Minister for Foreign Affairs, *Dáil Debates*, cols 1212–1213, 4 April 2006; Minister for Foreign Affairs, *Dáil Debates*, col 1714, 29 June 2006.

[165] Minister for Transport, *Dáil Debates*, col 184, 7 March 2006.

[166] Minister for the Environment and Local Government, *Dáil Debates*, col 685, 8 March 2006; Minister for the Environment and Local Government, *Dáil Debates*, col 1906, 5 April 2006; Minister for the Environment and Local Government, *Dáil Debates*, col 1538, 3 May 2006.

[167] Bill announced by the Minister for Justice, Equality and Law Reform, *Dáil Debates*, col 1369, 3 October 2006.

Action against Trafficking in Human Beings had begun in 2006 and that the proposed legislation would also take into account the EU Council Framework Decision on combating trafficking in persons, and the Protocol to Prevent, Suppress and Punish Trafficking in Persons of the UN Convention against Transnational Organised Crime and the Optional Protocol to the UN Convention on the Rights of the Child and the Sale of Children, Child Prostitution and Child Pornography.[168]

The Government indicated that decisions as to the incorporation of the following international agreements would be taken on the basis of reviews underway in government departments: Optional Protocol to the United Nations Convention against Torture,[169] Protocol 12 of the European Convention on Human Rights,[170] the European Convention on Contact Concerning Children,[171] the European Convention on Human Rights and Biomedicine.[172]

The Government confirmed that it had no plans to ratify the United Nations Convention on the Protection of the Rights of All Migrant Workers as the rights of migrant workers are already protected under national legislation, the Constitution, and within already-ratified human rights instruments such as the International Covenant on Civil and Political Rights. It was noted that ratification of this Convention would require significant changes to Irish law and might affect the common travel area between the UK and Ireland.[173] Furthermore, the Government contended that the Employment Permits Act 2006 fulfils many of the aims of the Convention.[174]

The Government further confirmed that it has no intention to ratify the Antarctic Treaty of 1959 or the Madrid Protocol on Environmental Protection to the Antarctic Treaty (1991). Ireland is of the view that the Antarctic ought to be seen as part of the 'common heritage of mankind' and believes that a United Nations agreement in which all States had an input into its terms would be the best means of ensuring full accountability for actions taken in and in relation to Antarctica.[175] To this end, Ireland confirmed that it supports United Nations General Assembly Resolutions 57/51 and 60/47 affirming that the use of Antarctica ought to be in accordance with the purposes and principles of the Charter of the United Nations.[176]

The Government confirmed that it did not intend to ratify the European Convention for the Protection of Vertebrate Animals used for Experimental and other Scientific Purposes as it considered that many of the aims had already been met in Irish law.[177] The Convention treats of the care, accommodation, conduct of

[168] Minister for Justice, Equality and Law Reform, *Dáil Debates*, col 95, 9 March 2006; Minister for Justice, Equality and Law Reform, *Dáil Debates*, col 314, 28 March 2006; Minister for Justice, Equality and Law Reform, *Dáil Debates*, col 508, 10 May 2006; Minister for Justice, Equality and Law Reform, *Dáil Debates*, cols 570–574, 8 June 2006.

[169] Minister for Foreign Affairs, *Dáil Debates*, cols 1659–60, 29 June 2006.

[170] Minister for Justice, Equality and Law Reform, *Dáil Debates*, col 271, 9 May 2006.

[171] Minister for Justice, Equality and Law Reform, *Dáil Debates*, col 314, 28 March 2006.

[172] Minister for Health and Children, *Dáil Debates*, col 211, 28 March 2006.

[173] Minister for Foreign Affairs, *Dáil Debates* 272, 25 April 2006; Minister for Enterprise, Trade and Employment, *Dáil Debates*, col 386, 10 May 2006.

[174] Minister for Enterprise, Trade and Employment, *Dáil Debates*, cols 562–563, 11 October 2006; and Minister for Enterprise, Trade and Employment, *Dáil Debates*, cols 190–191, 21 June 2006.

[175] Minister for Foreign Affairs, *Dáil Debates*, cols 1396–1397, 3 May 2006.

[176] *Ibid.*

[177] Minister for Health and Children, *Dáil Debates*, cols 210–211, 28 March 2006 (referring to the EC (Amendment to the Cruelty to Animals Act 1876) Regulations 2002 giving effect to Council Directive 86/609/EEC).

experiments, humane killing, breeding and supplying of animals used in experimentation as well as the education and training of those conducting such procedures. Because of the pace with which scientific experimentation advances the Convention is subject to a Protocol of Amendment (ETS 170) which allows for the swift amendment of technical aspects of the Convention.

DIPLOMATIC RELATIONS

The Diplomatic Relations and Immunities (Amendment) Act 2006 was signed into law on 12 April. The act amends previous legislation[178] in order to ensure that the Government is limited by the Vienna Convention on Diplomatic Relations 1961 in the immunities and privileges that it confers on international organisations and bodies. The Diplomatic Relations and Immunities Act 1967, as amended by the Diplomatic Relations and Immunities (Amendment) Act 1976, allows the Government to confer diplomatic privileges and immunities on certain non-State entities, but prior to 2006 decisions on these matters were not subject to any definitive statement of principle. The 2006 Act introduces a principled statement of the guidelines for such government orders in the shape of the Vienna Convention on Diplomatic Relations 1961.[179] The Vienna Convention provides for the absolute inviolability of the person,[180] residence,[181] papers and correspondence[182] of a diplomatic agent; the immunity from suit of a diplomatic agent[183] except in stated limited circumstances;[184] non-compellability of diplomatic agents as witnesses;[185] immunity from social security provisions in the receiving state;[186] immunity from taxation;[187] Furthermore, the Act provides that any privileges or immunities conferred by government order prior to enactment will take effect as if they were an Act of the Oireachtas [*Tithe an Oireachtas*: the Houses of Parliament].[188]

In 2006 Ireland accepted credentials from Ambassadors representing Uruguay, Indonesia, Saudi Arabia, Australia, Moldova, Iraq, Estonia, Syria, Bangladesh, Ethiopia, Algeria, Rwanda, the United Kingdom of Great Britain and Northern Ireland, Greece, Israel, Poland, the United States of America, Canada, Zimbabwe and

[178] Diplomatic Relations and Immunities Act 1967, as amended by the Diplomatic Relations and Immunities (Amendment) Act 1976.

[179] Diplomatic Relations and Immunities Act 2006, ss 3–5.

[180] Vienna Convention on Diplomatic Relations, Art 29.

[181] Vienna Convention on Diplomatic Relations, Art 30(1).

[182] Vienna Convention on Diplomatic Relations, Art 30(2).

[183] Vienna Convention on Diplomatic Relations, Art 31(1).

[184] Vienna Convention on Diplomatic Relations, Art 31(1)(a), (b), (c)—property actions relating to private real property, actions in succession, and actions relating to commercial or professional activity outside of the agent's official obligations. In addition, in Ireland, there is no diplomatic or state immunity relating to domestic proceedings under the International Criminal Court Act 2006 or to co-operation with international proceedings by the International Criminal Court itself (International Criminal Court Act 2006, s 61).

[185] Vienna Convention on Diplomatic Relations, Art 31(2).

[186] Vienna Convention on Diplomatic Relations, Art 33(1).

[187] Vienna Convention on Diplomatic Relations, Art 34; there is no immunity from indirect taxes such as VAT (Art 34(a)), estate or other inheritance taxes (Art 34(c)), taxes on private income outside of official duties (Art 34(d)), charges related to specific services (Art 34(e)), and duties relating to private real property (Art 34(b) and (f)).

[188] Diplomatic Relations and Immunities Act 2006, s 6.

Uganda.[189] The Minister for Foreign Affairs confirmed that, in line with recent practice, Ireland would not be accepting the diplomatic credentials of a Burmese ambassador and would not deploy an Irish ambassador to Burma.[190]

Although Ireland has consistently supported the claim for self-determination of the Saharan people, the government confirmed in 2006 that Ireland does not recognise a Sahara Arab Democratic Republic as no such state has emerged that meets the internationally recognised criteria.[191] The Irish government denied that its policy on the Saharan people's claim of self-determination was in any way undermined by the EU's fisheries agreement with the Kingdom of Morocco, which allows for fishing in the seas claimed by the Saharans.[192] The Irish Government confirmed that Ireland's support for the Fisheries Partnership Agreement between the EU and Morocco does not entail a de jure recognition of Morocco's rights in respect of the area alleged to be the Saharan Arab Democratic Republic.[193]

CONCLUSION

2006 could not be said to signal any changes in Ireland's approach to international law at either the Executive, Legislative or Judicial level. The Government continued to pursue its policy of co-operation and open engagement with the United States in relation to the 'War on Terrorism' and took the view that, while the United States may not comply fully with its international legal obligations in its current military operations, Ireland is fulfilling its positive obligations under Articles 2 and 3 of the ECHR in relation to the alleged use of Shannon Airport in the extraordinary renditions programme.

The Irish Government's commitment to international peace and security through primarily diplomatic means was evident in its treatment of the conflicts in Israel, Palestine, Lebanon and the Sudan and in its approach to events that threatened the integrity and effectiveness of the international nuclear arms framework. This approach was accordingly reflected in the work of the Joint Committee on Foreign Affairs. In addition, Ireland's commitment to international peacekeeping and its conception of peace-keeping as an international obligation was evident in its continued provision of military service personnel to UN peace-keeping missions and its decision to join the Nordic Battlegroup. In keeping with Ireland's long-standing concerns in relation to particular types of munitions, the Government spearheaded an international campaign to limit cluster munitions and, while not achieving all of its objectives,

[189] See Department of Foreign Affairs Press Releases 'New Ambassadors present Credentials—Thursday, 2nd February 2006' (2 February 2006); 'New Ambassadors present Credentials' (21 March 2006); 'New Ambassadors present Credentials, Thursday, 11th May 2006' (11 May 2006); 'New Ambassadors Present Credentials' (28 June 2006); 'New British Ambassador presents Credentials' (12 September 2006); 'New Ambassadors present Credentials' (12 September 2006); 'New U.S. Ambassador presents Credentials' (18 October 2006); ' (24 October 2006).

[190] Minister for Foreign Affairs, *Dáil* Debates, col 721, 22 February 2006; Minister for Foreign Affairs, *Dáil* Debates, col 1208-1209, 4 April 2006; Minister for Foreign Affairs, *Dáil* Debates, cols 1300–1301, 30 May 2006.

[191] Minister of State at the Department of Communications, Marine and Natural Resources, John Browne TD, *Dáil* Debates, col 1259, 30 May 2006.

[192] *Ibid.*

[193] Minister of State at the Department of Communications, Marine and Natural Resources, John Browne TD, *Dáil Debates* col 1259, 30 May 2006.

succeeded in gaining consensus on wording that places an additional onus on military forces to give due regard to the implications of cluster munitions for the civilian population both during and after the completion of hostilities.

The Irish Government's commitment to playing a full role in the achievement of basic human security throughout the world was reflected in the publication of the first While Paper on Irish Aid and the decision to establish particular task forces to contend with the deprivation of food and safe water, particularly throughout Africa. Reflecting Ireland's commitment to the effective provision of aid, the Government also expressed strong support for the UN Convention on Corruption and helped to devise innovate methods of providing direct assistance to persons resident in the Palestinian Occupied Territories. Ireland also showed its commitment to a number of international agreements through incorporation and through the drafting of legislation to be debated and/or promulgated in the future.

Irish Practice Abroad—2006

Joshua Castellino

NATIONAL UNIVERSITY OF IRELAND, GALWAY

The goals of Irish foreign policy are summed up in the Mission Statement of the Department of Foreign Affairs *Strategic Statement 2005–2007*:

> . . . to advance Ireland's political and economic interests in the European Union and in the wider world, to promote Ireland's contribution to international peace, security and development both through the European Union and through active participation in international organizations, in particular the United Nations, to protect our citizens abroad, and to pursue reconciliation and partnership on the island of Ireland.[1]

In reporting on and assessing Irish foreign policy, the following structure will be adopted to enable a wide recitation of the various components that are included within activities undertaken during 2006:

(a) efforts at achieving reconciliation in Northern Ireland;
(b) Ireland's contribution within the United Nations;
(c) development cooperation and aid;
(d) Ireland's role in the World; and
(e) provision of Consular and Diplomatic Services.

This Correspondent's Report draws on the *Strategy Statement 2005–2007* published by the Department of Foreign Affairs in accordance with its obligation under the provisions of the *Public Service Management Act 1997*. The Statement is designed to reflect the framework under which the Department will operate until the end of 2007. Towards this end, the Statement provides an overview of the Department itself and seeks to identify and define its goals, objectives and strategies over the designated period. Most importantly, the Statement sets out the indicators which it suggests are the basis for measuring the effectiveness of the Department's performance.

The *Strategic Statement* identifies the following six 'high level goals':

1. Work to achieve the full implementation of the Good Friday Agreement and the sustained operation of all its institutions, promoting co-operation, mutual understanding and respect between both traditions on the island, between North and South in Ireland and between these islands.
2. Pursue Ireland's foreign policy in accordance with the ideals enshrined in the Constitution and in conformity with the principles of the United Nations Charter, through the development of our bilateral relations with other States, our participation in the European Union's Common Foreign and Security Policy, and our active and principled participation in international organizations.

[1] 'Mission Statement' Department of Foreign Affairs *Strategic Statement 2005–2007* p 3.

3. Promote and protect Ireland's interests at the heart of the European Union as it continues to evolve and enlarge, including through the further development of our relations with our current and future EU partners.
4. Promote Ireland's trade, investment and other interests, including its culture, in close co-operation with other Departments, State Agencies and the private sector, ensuring that the State's network of diplomatic and consular missions add real value to this task.
5. Make a substantive and effective contribution to the Millennium Development Goals, and to poverty reduction and sustainable growth in developing countries, through the policy and programmes of the Development Corporation Ireland, and by working for a just and stable international economic system.
6. Protect and support the interests of Irish citizens abroad, maintain and strengthen links with people of Irish ancestry, and to provide a modern and efficient passport and consular service.[2]

The Minister for Foreign Affairs, Mr Dermot Ahern TD stresses the importance of maintaining a clear focus on Ireland's fundamental interests, in light of the 'complex and volatile' global political situation. In his foreword to the Report, Minister Ahern stresses the importance of the first of the six high level goals: the implementation of the various aspects of the Good Friday Agreement as being at the core of Governmental priority. Towards this end, the Irish Government outlined its commitment to restoring the process of devolution at the earliest possible date, and on a basis that will be both inclusive and sustainable. Linked to this was the promise to work at relations between the North and South in a spirit of co-operation, reconciliation and understanding. The following section will seek to summarise departmental activities with regards to this issue.

EFFORTS AT ACHIEVING RECONCILIATION IN NORTHERN IRELAND

The primary responsibility for managing the process of reconciliation from the Dublin perspective is the Anglo-Irish Division within the Department of Foreign Affairs, though with the priority accorded to Northern Ireland issues, it has merited attention at the highest level with the *Taoiseach* devoting considerable amount of time to the issue. Among the core tasks identified for 2006 was working towards the restoration of institutions such as the Assembly and Executive for Northern Ireland as envisaged under the Good Friday Agreement. This was viewed within the Department as the best possible route towards ensuring power sharing while garnering support for policies concerning policing and the restoration and maintenance of rule of law in Northern Ireland. The Government's vision was published in a joint proposal with its United Kingdom counterpart, unveiled at St Andrews in Scotland on 13 of October 2006.

The St Andrews Agreement sought to give substance and determine a 'road-map' towards achieving the goal set in Armagh in April 2006: namely the restoration of political institutions in Northern Ireland. The agreement states the Irish Government's belief that 'the transformation brought about by the ending of the IRA's campaign provides the basis for a political settlement'.[3] Among the issues that have merited special attention in making the goals of the Agreement reality were:

[2] 'High Level Goals' as contained in *Strategic Statement 2005–2007* p 9.
[3] St Andrews Agreement 2006 para 1.

—support for devolution of policing and the criminal justice system;
—changes to the operation of the Agreement institutions;
—matters raised by the parties or flowing from the Preparation for Government Committee.

The Agreement discusses several issues, among them:

a. Power Sharing and Political Institutions
b. Policing and the Rule of Law
c. Human Rights, Equality, Victims, and other issues
d. Financial Package for the Newly Restored Executive.

In common with the Government of the United Kingdom, the Irish Government stressed its commitment to fundamental principles such as:

i) the requirement of consent for any constitutional change;
ii) the further commitment to use means that are exclusively peaceful and democratic in resolving the issues;
iii) to work towards a stable and inclusive government based on partnership;
iv) to seek a balanced institutional accommodation of the key relationships within Northern Ireland, cross border and between the two islands; and
v) for equality and human rights to be at the heart of the new dispensation in Northern Ireland.[4]

The Agreement also stressed the need for all parties to commit 'in good faith and in a spirit of genuine partnership, to the full operation of a stable power-sharing Government and the North-South and East-West arrangement'. The practical changes necessary for the operation of the institutions are published separately as Annex A appended to the Agreement.

The provisions on policing and the rule of law are contained under a specific heading which commences with the statement that 'support for policing and the rule of law should be extended to every part of the community'.[5] The Agreement states the importance of this:

> We believe that the essential elements of support for law and order include endorsing fully the Police Service of Northern Ireland and the criminal justice system, actively encouraging everyone in the community to co-operate fully with the PSNI in tackling crime in all areas and actively supporting all the policing and criminal justice institutions, including the Policing Board.[6]

The Agreement also endorses the progress made before the Preparation for Government Committee and requests that these discussions continue with a view to agreeing the necessary administrative agreements towards the creation of a new policing and justice department. Hope was further expressed by the two Governments that, by virtue of the St. Andrews Agreement, there would be sufficient momentum towards the building of community confidence necessary for the Northern Ireland Assembly to be able to request the devolution of criminal justice and policing from the British Government by May 2008.

Issues concerning the need for confidence-building measures among the communities, the need to pursue a shared vision in Northern Ireland's future and specifically,

[4] St Andrews Agreement 2006, para 3.
[5] St Andrews Agreement 2006, para 5.
[6] St Andrews Agreement 2006, para 6.

cultural rights were discussed under the heading 'Human Rights, Equality, Victims and Other Issues'. Importance is placed on creating a society where 'rights and aspirations of all are respected and valued, free from sectarianism, racism, and intolerance'[7] with further details appended to the Agreement as Annex B.

The provision of a financial package for the newly restored Executive are contained in Annex C to the Agreement. It requires the package to be negotiated in meetings between the British Chancellor of the Exchequer and Minister of Finance, with delegations from the First and Deputy First Minister.

In keeping with achievement of concrete results Annex D to the Agreement sets out a time-table for the implementation of the Agreement, with parties having been required to confirm their acceptance by the 10 November 2006, with the final restoration date identified as the 26 March 2007. One of the safeguards for the Agreement coming into effect was included in the joint statement made by the Governments at St. Andrews:

> The Prime Minister and the Taoiseach are determined that default by any one of the parties following restoration of the Executive should not be allowed to delay or hinder political progress in Northern Ireland.
>
> The Governments have made clear that in the event of failure to reach agreement by the 24 November we will proceed on the basis of the new British Irish partnership arrangements to implement the Belfast Agreement.
>
> It is clear to us that all the parties wish to see devolution restored. It is also clear to us that all parties wish to support policing and the rule of law. We hope they will seize this opportunity for bringing the political process in Northern Ireland to completion and establishing power-sharing government for the benefit of the whole community.[8]

The political parties in Northern Ireland confirmed their acceptance of the implementation time-table of the St. Andrews Agreement by the 10 November 2006 deadline.

In setting out its strategy for the period the Department identified the following key performance indicators of its work in Northern Ireland:

1. Extent of implementation of all aspects of the Good Friday Agreement.
2. Effectiveness of arrangements to support the operation of the institutions established under the Good Friday Agreement.
3. Effectiveness of co-ordination arrangements with other Departments with regard to policy development and strategies on Anglo-Irish and Northern Ireland issues.
4. Enhanced relationships with a wide range of representatives from all traditions in Northern Ireland, with a view to broadening and deepening support for the Good Friday Agreement.
5. Ongoing support from the United States, the EU and others for the implementation of the Good Friday Agreement and the peace process.

With a look to 2007 and the possible restoration of devolution to Northern Ireland, the issues that still remain would suggest that the Northern Ireland question will need to remain high on the agenda of Irish foreign policy for the foreseeable future.

[7] St Andrews Agreement 2006, para 8.
[8] St Andrews Agreement 2006, para 13.

IRELAND S CONTRIBUTION WITHIN THE UNITED NATIONS

In terms of Ireland's participation in international organisations outside the European Union, the United Nations remains the highest priority. In the *Strategic Statement 2005–2007*, Ireland reveals its strategy vis-à-vis the United Nations as consisting of the following:

1. Uphold the United Nations Security Council's primary responsibility for maintenance of international peace and security.
2. Support reform of the UN system, including reform of the Security Council and the revitalization of the UN General Assembly.
3. Contribute to the implementation of the United Nations Millennium Declaration and the achievement of the Millennium Development Goals.
4. Ensure implementation of the UN Security Council and EU sanctions, in conjunction with other Government Departments, the Central Bank and the Financial Services Authority of Ireland.
5. Coordinate with Department of Defence and Department of Justice, Equality and Law Reform to facilitate Ireland's participation, where appropriate and on a case-by-case basis, in humanitarian and crisis management operations in military and civilian areas, including ESDP operations, subject to the requirements of UN authorization and Government and Dáil approval.
6. Consider and develop, through the Standing Interdepartmental Committee on peacekeeping, Ireland's policy on peacekeeping.

Against these outlined 'strategies', Ireland played an active role in some areas of UN operations during 2005–2006. This Report will focus on peace-keeping, membership of organs, contribution to UN reform, and discussion regarding the ILC's Draft Articles on Responsibility of International Organisations.

Peace-keeping

Ireland's proud record of involvement in the United Nations is most visible in the number of peacekeeping missions undertaken by the Irish Defence Forces under UN auspices. Since Ireland's entry into the United Nations in 1955 and its first overseas mission in Lebanon (UNOGIL) in 1958, it has become a regular contributor to UN peacekeeping missions. Among the theatres where Irish soldiers have served are: Lebanon, Syria, Zaire, Eritrea, Liberia, Sierra Leone, Cyprus and the Balkans.[9] In more recent years, Ireland has also played a significant role in EU- and OSCE-led missions and joined the Partnership for Peace Programme in 2003.[10] According to Minister Ahern, Ireland will continue this rich tradition by working with the UN and European Union partners 'in the building of stability and justice in Iraq, the Middle East, the Balkans, Afghanistan and other areas of tension and conflict, and to address the longer-term issues which fuel such difficulties'.[11]

In 2006, Ireland had soldiers abroad in the following locations:[12]

[9] The full list of missions where Irish troops have served is accessible at http://www.military.ie/overseas/missions_list.htm (last accessed 31 March 2007).

[10] For a history of Irish Peacekeeping Operations see http://www.military.ie/overseas/missions.htm (last accessed 31 March 2007).

[11] *Strategic Statement 2005–2007* p 4.

[12] See www.military.ie/overseas/missions_list.htm.

Mission	Start Date	Strength[13]
UN Truce Supervision Organisation (UNTSO) Middle East.	18 Dec 58	427
UN Peacekeeping Force in Cyprus (UNFICYP).	27 Mar 64	9647
UN Interim Force in Lebanon (UNIFIL).	13 May 78	31,413
UN Headquarters New York (UNNY).	27 Nov 78	17
UN Mission for the Referendum in Western Sahara (MINURSO).	20 Sep 91	120
UN Observer Mission in Congo (MONUC).	27 Jun 01	12
UN Mission in Liberia (UNMIL).	Nov 03	971
Organisation on Security and Co-Operation in Europe (OSCE). Location: Vienna.	16 Jan 84	21
Organisation on Security and Co-Operation in Europe (OSCE) Location: Bosnia Herzegovina.	Jan 96	39
Organisation on Security and Co-Operation in Europe (OSCE). Location: Croatia.	Jan 98	21
Organisation on Security and Co-Operation in Europe (OSCE). Location: Albania.	Jan 97	11
Organisation on Security and Co-Operation in Europe (OSCE—Kosovo).	01 Jul 99	8
EC Monitor Mission (ECMM). Location: former Yugoslavia.	16 Jul 91	203
International Conference on the Former Yugoslavia (ICFY).	Sep 94	5
WEU Brussels.	09 July 96	11
ICC Mons.	12 June 97	3
Kosovo Force (KFOR).	29 August 99	1068
International Security Assistance Force (ISAF).	Jan 02	21
European Union Force (EUFOR).	Dec 05	53
Goal, Concern, Red Cross & Trócaire (Somalia, Angola, Rwanda, Russia, Albania & Macedonia)	14 Apr 93	44

As highlighted by the Defence forces, the task of peace-keeping missions in the modern context involves a range of different activities. Thus the missions abroad have been trained to address and perform a range of different tasks, including:

Investigation of Human Rights Abuses;
Disarming/Demobilising Forces;
Monitoring Withdrawal of Forces;
Monitoring Elections;
Mine-Clearance;
Preventive Deployment;
Protection of Humanitarian Aid;
Establishment and Protection of Safe Areas;
Assisting the Civil Administration;
Guarantee/Denial of Movement by Air, Land or Sea;
Dealing with other UN agencies and Non Government Organisations on an increasing basis.[14]

[13] This reflects cumulative tours of duty since the beginning of the respective mandate.
[14] For more details see www.military.ie/overseas/irl_un.htm.

The growing range of challenges faced by Missions abroad as well as the regular phenomenon of 'Mission-Creep'—whereby a mission established for one purpose is called on to deal with other challenges that arise on the ground—has made the task of preparing soldiers for such Missions challenging. The *United Nations Training School Ireland* (UNTSI), established at Camp Curragh, County Kildare in 1993 as a school of the Military College has been seeking to provide the necessary training, drawing on expertise from within and outside the Defence forces. As a result soldiers about to be deployed receive instruction in the development of peacekeeping in its different forms globally, and other instruction designed to ensure consistency and awareness of policies and issues. In addition to this UNTSI carries out other courses on a more regular basis such as:

—Mission specific training of Military Observers for all Irish supported peacekeeping missions world-wide;
—An International Course for Military Observers and Staff Officers (UNMOSOC) of Captain or Major rank. To date 198 Officers from 46 countries have been trained on this course;
—International Military Police Course;
—Debriefing—Personnel from all Irish peacekeeping missions worldwide.

The reputation of Irish soldiers abroad has been greatly assisted by the attitude of these personnel and their willingness to engage in providing humanitarian assistance to the target population. In the last few years troops posted to various missions have organized at their own initiative activities such as the provision of medical and dental care to the population, the restoration and repair of essential services and the rebuilding of local institutions (churches, mosques, schools etc) that have been damaged by conflict. Among missions taking place in 2006, are soldiers on secondment to the UN Relief and Works Agency in the Middle East and to Irish NGOs Goal and Concern and the Irish Committee of the Red Cross in Somalia, Sudan and Angola.

In May 2006 the 95th Infantry Battalion was deployed to Liberia (group strength of 420) as part of United Nations Mission in Liberia. They were tasked with the mandate to conduct long-range patrols throughout the State, particularly difficult in light of poor transport and communication facilities and the ambience of conflict. Among the more specific tasks mandated for the contingent were:

—Be prepared to act as the Force Commanders (FC) 'Quick Reaction Force' (QRF) in the Monrovia area;
—Act as the Force Advance Guard for the securing of key locations. Conduct 'Cordon and Search' operations for weapons held in areas that are declared 'weapons free zones';
—Assist in preparations for cantonment and DDRR;
—Ensure security and freedom of movement along the main lines of communication;
—Within capabilities provide security to civilians under threat of violence.[15]

The UNIFIL Mission in Lebanon is one of the longest missions served on by the Defence Forces. This mission received a renewed mandate in 2006 following the outbreak of conflict between Hezbollah and Israel, and in concordance with UN Security Council Resolution 1701 of August 2006. Following the end of hostilities and in response to a request from the UN Security Council, the Defence Forces returned in

[15] www.military.ie/overseas/africa.htm.

greater numbers to Lebanon on 31 October 2006. The mandate for operations included reconnaissance, patrolling and various other security roles alongside a Finnish military engineering unit as part of joint Irish-Finnish Battalion.

In a more humanitarian role, four officers of the Irish Defence Forces were deployed to Sri Lanka in January 2005 and remained through 2006 to assist the United Nations Joint Logistics Co-ordination Centre in its efforts to conduct a relief operation in the aftermath of the Asian Tsunami crisis. The main role of the team was detailing transport and logistics to enable coordination and distribution of aid and equipment to the worst affected regions of the country.

Membership of Principal Organs and Committees

Since the expiry of Ireland's term on the Security Council (2001–2002) its representation on the various other United Nations Charter-based bodies has ebbed. Besides the General Assembly there is no representation of the Irish government on any of the other Charter-based bodies. Ireland's membership of the Economic and Social Council terminated on the 31 December 2005.

Among the subsidiary organs to the General Assembly, Ireland will be a member of the Executive Board of UNICEF for 2007 but is not represented on any of the Commissions (Disarmament Commission, International Civil Service Commission, International Law Commission, the UN Commission on International Trade Law, or the UN Peacebuilding Commission). Neither was Ireland represented on any of the subsidiary bodies to the Security Council (Peacebuilding Commission, Counter-Terrorism Committee, Al-Qaida and Taliban Sanctions Committee, 1540 Committee, Sanctions Committee).

In terms of United Nations committees, Ireland has a representative on the Human Rights Committee (who sits in his independent capacity), but no such membership on the UN Population Award, Committee on Contributions, Committee Against Torture, Committee for the Elimination of Discrimination Against Women, Committee on the Elimination of Racial Discrimination, Committee on the Exercise of the Inalienable Rights of the Palestinian People, Committee on the Peaceful Uses of Outer Space, Committee on the Rights of the Child or the UN Scientific Committee on the Effects of Atomic Radiation.

United Nations Reform

As part of its active involvement in the United Nations, Ireland played an important role in the discussions pursuant to the United Nations reform proposed by UN Secretary-General Kofi Annan in his report entitled *In Larger Freedom: Towards Development, Security and Human Rights for All.*[16] Minister Ahern was appointed Special Envoy for UN Reform in April 2005 placing Ireland in a central role in what was ultimately a controversial reform process that was instigated by the need to garner greater accountability and clearer co-operation between the Member States, but instead yielded the dissolution of the United Nations Commission on Human Rights and the creation of its replacement, the Human Rights Council. The Irish position was

[16] Report of the UN Secretary-General, UN Doc A/59/2005 21 March 2005.

contained within the discussions of the European Union states, though Ireland appears to have played a significant role in framing the group arguments.

A more radical idea that Ireland become party to in 2006 vis-à-vis UN Reform was articulated in the position of what is referred to as the G13 (ie a group of 13 donor countries).[17] This Group proposes wide-scale reform of the United Nations, advocating major structural and operational change, including the closure or merger of several United Nations organisations. The dominant view within the G13 envisaged the reform resulting in three large UN agencies of 'pillars' dealing with development, humanitarian and environmental affairs, with some specialised agencies continuing though functioning under the rubric of 'centres of excellence' or 'think tanks'. The proposal was presented to the Prime Minister of Norway in his capacity as Co-chair of the *Panel on UN System-wide Coherence*.[18]

Ireland, along with its 12 partners raised the following principal issues vis-à-vis the functioning of the United Nations:

—Determining the core normative and operational roles in which the United Nations has a comparative advantage to other actors
—Understanding the optimal structure for the United Nations
—Determining optimal governance structure for United Nations operational systems
—Country level reform (including international developmental goals such as the MDGs)
—Determining optimal funding of UN operational activities
—Mainstreaming cross-cutting issues
—Managing change in human resources (with a large share of UN staff due to retire in the next five to ten years)
—Determining UN contribution to improving the effectiveness of aid.[19]

Ireland and the International Law Commission's Draft Articles on the Responsibility of International Organisations

The Department of Foreign Affairs submitted a Statement to the Sixth Committee of the General Assembly at its 61st Session vis-à-vis Agenda Item 78: Report of the International Law Commission on the work of its 58th session, dealing with Chapter VII, entitled 'Responsibility of International Organisations'.[20] The statement draws attention to two of the draft provisions, namely Article 22 on State Necessity and Article 28 on International Responsibility in the case of provision of competence to an international organisation.

While generally satisfied with the provisions of draft Articles 17–24 on circumstance precluding wrongfulness was expressed, concern was raised about the need to limit the scope of the exception within defined boundaries. The Statement expressed the view that Article 22 in its proposed formulation failed to adequately protect Member States' essential interests. The statement reads:

[17] The G13 consists of Canada, Belgium, Denmark, Finland, France, Germany, Ireland, Luxembourg, Netherlands, Norway, Sweden, Switzerland and the United Kingdom.

[18] This panel was created by Secretary-General Kofi Annan on 16 February as follow-up to para 160 in the Outcome of the 2005 World Summit, which calls for the Secretary General to launch work to strengthen the management and coordination of UN operational activities.

[19] More details on the proposal are available on http://www.reformtheun.org.

[20] See Statement by Ms Patricia O'Brien, Legal Adviser, Department of Foreign Affairs, UNGA 61st session (Sixth Committee), New York, 27 October 2006.

> A state may choose to entrust functions to an international organization. However, simply because a state has transferred functions does not mean that it no longer retains essential interests in relation to those functions. These essential interests of the state may be imperilled by an act or omission of the organization, even if the organization's conduct is consistent with, and indeed required by, its own legal obligations.
>
> However, according to the wording of the most recent draft article 22 adopted by the Commission, unless a member state's essential interest coincides with an essential interest of the international community as a whole, the international organization is unable to invoke necessity.
>
> Obviously, states may be reluctant to transfer powers to an international organization if their essential interests are not afforded sufficient protection. We therefore support the view held by some members of the Commission that an international organization should be entitled to invoke an essential interest of its member state when claiming necessity.[21]

In addition, concern was expressed as to whether Article 22, in its current formulation, reflected the 'present reality of movement towards international integration'. The Statement suggested that in its current formulation draft Article 22 makes the organisation's ability to invoke necessity dependent on its functions. It reasons further:

> While, in the modern era, international integration has led to states granting international organizations more and more functions, most of these organizations deal individually with discrete issues and are entrusted with a narrow range of functions, Draft article 22, in its present form, may fail to adequately accommodate this state of affairs. After all, it is quite plausible that the actions of an international organization might imperil an essential interest of a member state, or indeed of the international community as a whole, without that organization having as one of its functions the protection of that interest. In such circumstances, the current working of draft article 22 would leave the organization without recourse to the claim of necessity in order to safeguard the imperilled essential interest.[22]

The Statement endorsed the view of the International Law Commission's Special Rapporteur who highlighted that reference only to the constituent instrument of an international organisation in determining its functions, and as a consequence, the concept of necessity may be too restrictive.

The other draft provision which merited comment was draft Article 28 concerning international responsibility in case of provision of competence to an international organization. Once again support was expressed for the views of the Special Rapporteur, that place should be made within the article 'for member states to incur responsibility for acts of international organizations in certain circumstances'. However reservations were expressed as to the formulation of the article.

Draft Article 28, as proposed reads as follows:

> 1. A State member of an international organization incurs international responsibility if it circumvents one of its international obligations by providing the organization with competence in relation to that obligation, and the organization commits an act that, if committed by that State, would have constituted a breach of that obligation.
> 2. Paragraph 1 applies whether or not the act in question is internationally wrongful for the international organization.

[21] See Statement by Ms Patricia O'Brien, Legal Adviser, Department of Foreign Affairs, UNGA 61st session (Sixth Committee), New York, 27 October 2006, at p 3.

[22] *Ibid*, pp 3–4.

The Statement considers that the scope of the Article is inadequately defined with the insistence on the provision of competence in relation to the circumvented obligation, narrowing the scope of the Article, especially where a restrictive understanding of the requirement is employed. Thus:

> In such circumstances, the member state may not have provided the organization with competence in relation to the specific obligation being circumvented but may nevertheless, in the knowledge that the organization had a general competence that could impinge upon the obligation, have intended that it be breached by the organization.
>
> Conversely, a broad understanding of the provision of the competence requirement could result in a state responsibility where an international organization acts upon a general competence which may affect the obligation in question but without any intent on the part of the member state that the obligation be breached. In this regard, we welcome the Commission's commentary on draft article 28, which provides that the use of the term 'circumvention' is intended to exclude that international responsibility arises when an act of the organization, which would constitute a breach of an international obligation if taken by the state, has to be regarded as an unwitting result of providing the international organization with competence.[23]

The Statement closes by highlighting the practical difficulties of whether or not State has provided an organisation with competence in relation to an obligation. Additionally concern was expressed as to the absence of any requirement of intent in draft Article 28, which is deemed as limiting the potential scope of the provision.

DEVELOPMENT COOPERATION AND AID

One of the most dramatic manifestations of Ireland's changed international status is its move from a recipient country in terms of foreign aid, to one of the world's leading donor States per capita. As a result of this changed status, development co-operation was been placed high on the agenda of Irish foreign policy, under the supervision of a separate Minister of State who reports directly to the Minister of Foreign Affairs. This section narrates the main issues regarding aid that arose in 2006:

> Development cooperation policy has its absolute priority the reduction of poverty, inequality and exclusion in developing countries. It embraces the broad range of trade, investment and other issues which affect developing countries. Development assistance refers to support provided by developed to developing countries. Ireland is committed to achieving the UN target for official development assistance (ODA) of 0.7% of GNP. The budget for 2005 is €545m and €1.8 billion will be spent on ODA in the three years 2005–2007. This will ensure that further progress is made towards reaching the UN target.[24]

The stated objective of Irish Foreign Policy is 'to achieve the goal of making a lasting contribution to poverty reduction and sustainable growth in the world's poorest countries'.[25] Towards this end, the Department has engaged in a broad consultation with numerous groups throughout Ireland in a bid to understand the best possible route towards meeting the above stated objectives. The results of this consultation emerged

[23] *Ibid.* p5
[24] *Strategic Statement 2005–2007*, p 40.
[25] Dermot Ahearn 'Foreword' in *Strategic Statement 2005–2007* p 4.

as the *White Paper on Development Cooperation Policy* which is reproduced in the Documents Section of this volume of the *Irish Yearbook of International Law*.[26]

This White Paper begins by asserting the importance of development assistance to Irish Foreign policy, suggesting that this reflects the State's 'longstanding commitment to human rights, international cooperation and the peaceful resolution of conflicts'.

The distribution of the Official Development Assistance for 2006 was €734 million, with the budget managed by Irish Aid within the Department of Foreign Affairs. The structure of the Department itself is aligned to reflect the emphasis placed on development aid with Minister Conor Lenihan TD, responsible for the distribution of this aid under the aegis of his mandate as Minister of State for Development Cooperation and Human Rights. With the emphasis of the Department on poverty reduction programmes, Ireland has supported over sixty such programmes in the world's poorest countries, with a particular emphasis on sub-Saharan Africa.

With the Government committed to reaching the UN target of development assistance of 0.7 per cent of GNP by 2012, there is likely to be a significant increase each year in the budget for assistance. According to the Development White Paper the projection is to reach 0.5 per cent of GNP in 2007 and 0.6 per cent in 2010. Based on currently available levels of GNP growth this suggests that by 2010 Ireland's commitment to development aid will likely to be close to €1.5 billion in 2010, making its contribution significant in global terms.

According to Minister Lenihan, the fact that Ireland is identified in the *United Nations Human Development Report* as the tenth most developed State in the world, with the third highest per capita income, brings the responsibility to commit itself to addressing global issues:

> For Ireland, our new found prosperity brings both a responsibility and an opportunity; a responsibility to help reduce vulnerability and foster opportunity not just at home, but also abroad, and an opportunity to develop a set of foreign policy values that reflect out belief in the role of democracy.[27]

Minister Lenihan also sets out the manner in which development aid is likely to be distributed:

> Development assistance does not operate in a vacuum but rather within a broad political and economic environment. The reduction of poverty in developing countries depends not only on aid but also on the trade, investment, environment and other policies pursued by developed countries. Every country is responsible for its own development and the welfare and the well-being of its own citizens. Progress can only be made if primary responsibility is assumed by developing countries themselves. Outside assistance can greatly help but only if development is owned, driven and managed by developing country governments and their citizens.[28]

The objectives identified for Ireland's development co-operation policy have included ensuring that this policy is framed in line with international best practice, ensuring that the contribution increases the coherence and impact of international development co-operation, while working closely with Irish NGOs and missionary organisations on the ground in determining the role for development assistance. In seeking to achieve

[26] The full-text of this paper is available at www.irishaid.gov.ie/whitepaper/assets/Whitepaper.pdf.
[27] Conor Lenihan TD *Strategic Statement 2005–2007* p 6.
[28] Conor Lenihan TD *Strategic Statement 2005–2007* p 6.

these objectives, several key performance indicators are identified, among them: ensuring the quality and effectiveness of monitoring and evaluation processes, the use of international fora to advance Ireland's development cooperation policy and the inclusion of additional countries in Ireland's Bilateral programme on Development Cooperation.

The Government made several funding pledges during 2006, in response to various crises. Among these were €1 million to assist countries facing avian flu threats; €5 million for the reconstruction of Afghanistan; €5 million to ease the drought crisis in the Horn of Africa (subsequently raised to €7 million); €100,000 in humanitarian assistance to landslide victims in Philippines; €26 million in emergency humanitarian and recovery aid for Africa; €500,000 to support Fair Trade initiatives in Nicaragua; €300,000 for Global Alliance for Tuberculosis Drug Development; €20 million for Liberia and Sierra Leone; €500,000 for victims of the earthquake in Indonesia; €2 million New Public Private Partnership with Africa; €43.5 million for UN Funds and Programmes; €500,000 for humanitarian relief in Timor-Leste (subsequently raised by €1.14 million); €1.5 million for African Union Mission in Sudan; €1 million to meet crisis needs in Lebanon and Palestine (subsequently doubled); €250,000 for International Criminal Tribunal for Rwanda; €70 million agreement signed with the Clinton Foundation to fight HIV/AIDS in Africa; €9 million to victims of 2005 earthquake in Pakistan; €3 million Irish Aid Pledge for Crop Diversity; €40,000 to Irish community organizations in South Africa and Zimbabwe; €6 million for 'ongoing humanitarian emergencies'; €500,000 for Moldova; and €300,000 for victims of typhoon in Philippines.[29]

IRELAND'S ROLE IN THE WORLD

Closely linked to the distribution of development co-operation, Ireland has made a concerted effort in the last decade, to carve a niche for itself in terms of global affairs. These efforts continued in 2006 and this section will seek to reflect on some of the policies under the heading 'Ireland's role in the World'. The *Strategic Statement* lists the issue of 'Ireland's role in the world' as part of its strategic vision. Towards this end it identifies a list of institutions, issues, followed by regions in which it has strategic interests. These include:

a The United Nations (discussed above)
b. Security Policy
c. Human Rights (out of the scope of this report)
d. Disarmament
e. Terrorism
f. Africa
g. Asia/Oceania
h. Eastern Europe, Southern Caucasus and Central Asia
i. Western Balkans
j. Middle East Peace Process
k. Gulf Stability
l. North America, and
m. Latin America and the Caribbean

[29] Details compiled through an examination of Government of Ireland Press releases throughout the year.

The overall goal of the foreign policy is stated as follows:

> Ireland has an abiding interest in a stable, secure, inclusive and cooperative international environment. Through our bilateral relations and through our membership of international organizations and fora, we will continue to pursue Irish interests in this regard in a manner which is fully consistent with Ireland's foreign policy, including our policy of military neutrality.[30]

In terms of the issues highlighted, policy around security issues, disarmament and terrorism are particularly worthy of brief focus. Under the rubric of security issues the objective identified in foreign policy terms is the development of Ireland's role in the context of the European Union's Common Foreign and Security Policy (CFSP). This is seen as a vehicle for carrying Ireland's voice more forcefully in terms of global politics. With this in mind, a number of goals have been identified which emphasise Ireland's desire to participate within the CFSP and to contribute towards the development of the EU's capabilities for conflict prevention, humanitarian and crisis management, in accordance with UN and OSCE principles.

On the issue of disarmament, the objective outlined is the pursuit of 'the total elimination of nuclear weapons and the prevention of further proliferation of nuclear weapons capability'.[31] Other issues listed are the strengthening of regimes against the use of chemical and biological weapons, anti-personnel landmines and inhumane weapons. The strategy outlines is contained in eight points including promotion of the *New Agenda for the Achievement of a Nuclear-free World* as adopted during the Non-Proliferation Treaty Review Conference in 2000. Other specific strategies indicated include support for a number of regimes: the *EU Strategy on Non-Proliferation of Weapons of Mass Destruction*, the International Atomic Energy Agency, the Organisation for Prohibition of Chemical Weapons, the *Biological and Toxin Weapon Convention*, the *Mine Ban Convention* and the United Nations *Programme of Action to Prevent, Combat and Eradicate the Illicit Trade in Small Arms and Light Weapons*.

In keeping with the emphasis placed globally on countering terrorism, Ireland articulates its objective as:

> Promotion of increased international cooperation in the fight against terrorism, both bilaterally and through relevant multilateral organizations, including the UN, EU, OSCE and Council of Europe, emphasizing the need to respect human rights at all times in the fight against terrorism and to seek political solutions to international and regional problems which contribute to support for, and recruitment into, terrorism.[32]

The strategy drawn up to meet this objective consists of measures that Ireland has adopted in conjunction with EU and other partner-States. In addition, emphasis was placed on the particular experience of terrorism on the island:

> Drawing on the special understanding and insights derived from our own national experience, participate fully in the activities of international bodies addressing the problems presented by international terrorism.[33]

[30] *Strategic Statement 2005–2007*, p 32.
[31] *Strategic Statement 2005–2007*, p 34.
[32] *Strategic Statement 2005–2007*, p 34.
[33] *Strategic Statement 2005–2007*, p 34.

Among the regional objectives identified to raise Ireland's profile internationally, are greater ties with different parts of the world and increased political relations. In addition, with regard to Africa, Irish foreign policy seeks to contribute to peace and stability on that Continent. Similar aspirations were expressed in the context of relations between Ireland and States in Eastern Europe, the Southern Caucasus, Central Asia and the Western Balkans. In Asia/Oceania, the need to manage bilateral relations better was emphasised as was the need to work closely with regional and inter-regional organizations such as ASEM, ASEAN and SAARC.

In terms of the delicate issue of peace in the Middle East, Ireland's objective appeared to focus on facilitation and implementation of the Quartet's (the UN, EU, United States and Russia) 'Roadmap' approach to the peace process between Israel and Palestine. In addition the need to contribute to the wider issue of the restoration of peace and security to the Gulf region, and encouragement of the growth of democratic institutions were highlighted as being crucial to raising Ireland's role in the world.

Overall the following were identified as key performance indicators in assessing the extent to which Irish foreign policy was effective in raising its profile internationally:

1. Extent to which Ireland's foreign policy is reflected in the outcomes of our participation in international fora.
2. Implementation of improved liaison and coordination arrangements with our Missions abroad, other Departments, States Agencies and other relevant bodies, to ensure Ireland's interests are well represented in international bodies and to facilitate implementation of decisions, resolutions and agreements made by these bodies.
3. Quality, timeliness and accuracy of reports and briefing material.[34]

An important aspect that is linked to raising Ireland's international profile was the extent to which it garnered opportunities for advancing Ireland's external economic interests. In this context the objective of Irish foreign policy is to:

> Pursue Ireland's economic and commercial interests abroad by leveraging the resources of our diplomatic network in close cooperation with other Departments, State Agencies and the private sector.[35]

Of equal importance is the objective to provide 'a particular focus on the emerging markets in Asia, Latin America, Eastern Europe and the Middle East for Irish goods and services'.[36]

The *Strategic Statement* suggests that the success of the advancement of Irish economic interests can be measured by six key performance indicators:

1. Effectiveness of the contribution of the [Bilateral Economic Relations] Division to maintaining and extending access for Irish exports, particularly in emerging markets;
2. Successful implementation and effectiveness of coordination structures and processes with other Departments and agencies in further strengthening the business support role of the Department;
3. Number of new economic/trade agreements signed with Ireland's key partners and number of visits abroad with an economic component;
4. Quality and frequency of reports and briefing material prepared;

[34] *Strategic Statement 2005–2007*, p 37.
[35] *Strategic Statement 2005–2007*, p 38.
[36] *Strategic Statement 2005–2007*, p 39.

5. Creation of new organizational arrangements to improve the effectiveness of the operation of the Division;
6. Contribution to the opening of additional markets for Irish beef.[37]

PROVISION OF CONSULAR AND DIPLOMATIC SERVICES

In addition to securing a place for Ireland in the world, the Department of Foreign Affairs remains mindful of providing services of a diplomatic and consular nature to its own citizens, as reflected in this final section of the Report. Ireland maintains diplomatic relations with 158 States. While the size and scale of operations vary from State to State, they have common objectives to:

—deepen Ireland's relations with host governments and advance international priorities and objectives;
—report on political, economic, legal, commercial and, as appropriate, EU developments;
—advance Ireland's economic interests through working with others in the public and private sectors to expand trade and tourism, and to highlight the benefits of inward investment into Ireland;
—oversee the implementation of programmes in developing countries funded by the Government's overseas development programme, Development Cooperation Ireland;
—provide assistance to Irish citizens abroad and maintain contact with local Irish communities;
—promote Irish culture and disseminate information on Ireland.[38]

Ireland maintains six Missions accredited to multilateral organisations including the United Nations in New York and Geneva, to the European Union in Brussels, to the Organisation for Security and Cooperation in Europe, to the Organisation for Economic Cooperation and Development and UNESCO, and to the Council of Europe. In addition, it maintains 49 embassies and 12 Consulates-General offices. Besides these, the Government also draws on 24 Honorary Consuls-Generals and 62 Honorary Consuls, whose role is to provide assistance to Irish citizens in 50 countries.

Among the biggest issues that Ireland has been involved with under this heading has been in direct lobbying to the Government of the United States of America over the plight of illegal and undocumented migrants from Ireland. This has been motivated by the strong lobby of Irish-Americans and has resulted in various Ministers making strong statements in favour of the regularisation of the status of undocumented Irish migrants in the United States of America[39]

As part of the recent lobbying efforts, Minister Dermot Ahern met with US Senator Edward Kennedy, the Massachusetts Democrat, in December 2005. As a result, the Irish Government actively backed Mr Kennedy's Bill to grant illegal aliens resident in the United States a 'multi-step path to citizenship'. The Irish Government has distributed grants that were available to organisations in the United States that sought to provide advice and assistance to Irish immigrants as part of this multi-step path. The continued commitment to this issue was reflected in statements made by Taoiseach Bertie Ahern in the Dáil during 2006. The Taoiseach stressed that the Government

[37] *Strategic Statement 2005–2007*, p 39.

[38] *Strategic Statement 2005–2007*, p 12.

[39] See Stephen Dinan and Jerry Seper 'Ireland backs US legalizing illegal aliens' The Washington Times, 2 December 2005.

attached the highest priority to the issue of undocumented Irish workers in the United States, suggesting that the issue was regularly discussed with the United States administration and representatives both in Washington and with the United States of America's Ambassador to Ireland, in Dublin. The issue was also kept alive by the Irish Ambassador in Washington, through support for the Irish Lobby for Immigration Reform.

North-South Developments—2006

Ursula Kilkelly

UNIVERSITY COLLEGE CORK

This contribution to the *Irish Yearbook of International Law* aims to report on developments from a North-South perspective, that is from the perspective of the relations between Northern Ireland, a constituent part of the United Kingdom, and Northern Ireland and the Republic of Ireland. As this is the first such report, it will identify the beginnings of the north-south bodies as from their establishment under the 1998 Good Friday/Belfast Agreement, bringing the reader up to date on developments up to December 2006.

The Good Friday Agreement consists of two agreements both of which date from Good Friday 1998. The first Agreement was that reached at the Multi-Party Talks between the major political parties and the British and Irish Governments (Multi-Party Agreement) with the second agreement concluded between the British and Irish governments (referred to as the British-Irish Agreement) Each agreement is annexed to the other. The Multi-Party Agreement is a political agreement rather than a legally binding one. The British-Irish Agreement, however, is an international instrument, which on its entry into force, created obligations which are legally binding in international law on both States. Those elements of the Agreements which deal with constitutional arrangements and which required United Kingdom legislation are embodied principally in the Northern Ireland Act 1998.

The Agreements' principal elements clarify the status of Northern Ireland involving inter alia, the amendment of the Irish Constitution, the creation of a democratically-elected Assembly for Northern Ireland with executive and legislative authority and the formation of an Executive Committee of Ministers with executive functions drawn from the principal political parties to discharge executive authority on behalf of the Assembly. The Agreement also made provision for North-South and East-West bodies. The former comprises the North/South Ministerial Council consisting of ministers from Northern Ireland and from the Irish Government to develop consultation, co-operation and action, including through all-island and cross-border implementation bodies. The East-West dimension comprises the British-Irish Council comprising representatives of the British and Irish governments and of the devolved institutions in Northern Ireland, Scotland and Wales. The Agreements also created a British-Irish Intergovernmental Conference to bring together the British and Irish governments to promote bilateral co-operation on all matters of mutual interest including in relation to Northern Ireland.

The Multi-Party Agreement follows three strands:

Strand One concerned relationships within Northern Ireland, including devolved government;

Strand Two concerned relationships among the people of the island of Ireland, ie North-South relations;

Strand Three concerned the relationship between the British and Irish governments.

Given the purpose of this report, its focus will be Strand Two issues concerning the island of Ireland, principally the activities of the North/South Ministerial Council.

NORTH/SOUTH MINISTERIAL COUNCIL

The Multi-Party Agreement and British-Irish Agreement provide for a North/South Ministerial Council (NSMC) to be established. The role of the Council is to bring together ministers (those with executive responsibilities) from Northern Ireland and from the Irish Government to develop consultation, co-operation and action within the island of Ireland—including through implementation on an all-island and cross-border basis—on matters of mutual interest within the competence of the administrations, North and South.[1] On 8 March 1999 the British and Irish Governments entered into a further agreement which established on its entry into force the North/South Ministerial Council in furtherance of Article 2 of the British-Irish Agreement.[2] This set out the functions and structure of the North/South Bodies and the common arrangements applying to them and was given domestic effect North and South via the North/South Co-operation (Implementation Bodies) (Northern Ireland) Order 1999 and the British-Irish Agreement Act 1999 respectively.

The NSMC was established on 2 December 1999 and its inaugural plenary meeting took place in Armagh on 13 December 1999. Its first meeting in sectoral format took place on 24 January 2000 dealing primarily with issues relating to the Trade and Business Development Body.[3]

The work of the Council is supported by a Joint Secretariat located in Armagh which is staffed by personnel from the Northern Ireland Civil Service (under the aegis of the Office of the First Minister and Deputy First Minister (OFMDFM)) and the Irish Civil Service (under the aegis of the Department of Foreign Affairs). Amongst other duties, the Joint Secretariat is responsible for arranging NSMC meetings in both sectoral and plenary formats, co-ordinating the papers for the meetings and monitoring the work of the six implementing bodies and areas for co-operation.

The North/South Ministerial Council has four functions:[4]

> to exchange information, discuss and consult with a view to co-operating on matters of mutual interest within the competence of both Administrations, North and South;

[1] Article 1, Strand Two.

[2] Agreement between the Government of the UK of Great Britain and Northern Ireland and the Government of Ireland establishing a North/South Ministerial Council, 8 March 1999 (The Implementation Bodies Agreement).

[3] Achievements in Implementation of the Good Friday Agreement—16 July 2001: A Paper by the British and Irish Governments.

[4] Article 5, Strand Two of the Multi-Party Agreement.

to use best endeavours to reach agreement on the adoption of common policies, in areas where there is a mutual cross-border and all-island benefit, and which are within the competence of both Administrations, North and South, making determined efforts to overcome any disagreements;

to take decisions by agreement on policies for implementation separately in each jurisdiction, in relevant meaningful areas within the competence of both Administrations, North and South,

to take decisions by agreement on policies and action at an all-island and cross-border level to be implemented by the implementation bodies.

The implication here is that this is indeed an executive body or at least a body with executive functions. Moreover, although harmonisation does not appear in the description of the functions of the North/South Council, its duty to endeavour to reach agreement on the adoption of 'common policies' would appear to involve some harmonisation.

According to the Agreement, the Council is to meet in three different formats:

in plenary format twice a year with NI representation led by the First Minister and Deputy First Minister and the Irish Government led by the Taoiseach (Prime Minister);

in specific sectoral formats on a regular and frequent basis with each side represented by the appropriate Minister, and

in an appropriate format to consider institutional or cross-sectoral matters (including in relation to the EU) and to resolve disagreement.[5]

Agendas for all meetings are settled by prior agreement between the two sides, but it is open to either to propose any matter for consideration or action. The Assembly's approval is not required for every agreement entered into by Ministers in the Council but it is required where any agreement reached in the Council requires additional finance or fresh legislative provision.

According to the Multi-Party Agreement, all Council decisions are to be made by agreement between the two sides. Northern Ireland is to be represented by the First Minister, Deputy First Minister and any relevant Ministers, and the Irish Government is to be represented by the Taoiseach and relevant Ministers. All must operate in accordance with the rules for democratic authority and accountability in force in the NI Assembly and the Oireachtas (Parliament of the Republic of Ireland) respectively. Thus, Ministers on each side remain accountable to the Assembly and Oireachtas respectively, whose approval is required for decisions which go beyond the defined authority of the Ministers.[6]

The Multi-Party Agreement provides that there should be a work programme for the Council including at least six subject areas where existing bodies will be appropriate mechanisms for co-operation in each separate jurisdiction and at least six areas where co-operation will take place through 'agreed implementation bodies on a cross-border or all-island level'.[7] As to the latter, the Agreement clarifies that:

[5] Article 3, Strand Two.

[6] Section 52 Northern Ireland Act 1998 makes provision for the Council to be accountable to the Assembly in a number of ways.

[7] Strand 2, para 9.

The implementation bodies will have a clear operational remit. They will implement on an all-island and cross-border basis policies agreed in the Council.[8]

NSMC IMPLEMENTATION BODIES

In the Agreement of the British and Irish Governments to establish the implementation bodies[9] Six North-South implementation bodies were agreed, dealing with inland waterways, food safety, trade and business development, special EU programmes, language and marine sectors. These are outlined in turn in the sections that follow:

Inland Waters (Waterways Ireland)

Waterways Ireland's primary function is the management, maintenance, development and restoration of specified inland navigable waterway systems throughout the island, principally for recreational purposes. Waterways Ireland is responsible for navigation systems including the Erne Waterway and the Grand Canal, which were previously under the respective control of the Department of Community, Rural, and Gaeltacht Affairs in the South and the Department of Agriculture and Rural Development in Northern Ireland. It launched its Marketing and Promotion Strategy in 2004 representing the culmination of a two year formulation, research and consultative process. It recommends a pro-active role for Waterways Ireland with the objectives of creating awareness, developing a Waterways Ireland brand, promoting greater use of the waterways, building partnerships with other bodies and building a platform of sustained market development.[10] Major works have been completed by Waterways Ireland on the Erne and Bann waterways.

Food Safety (The Food Safety Promotion Board)

The Food Safety Promotion Board is charged with food safety promotion through public campaigns, conferences, training and advising professionals and the general public. It is involved in supporting North/South scientific co-operation and links between institutions working in the field of food safety operating under the brand identifier *safefood*.[11] It operates under three directorates—Scientific and Technical, Marketing and Communications and Planning and Resources—which ensures that the body is adequately resourced and fully supported to fulfil its mandate.[12]

Trade and Business Development (The Trade and Business Development Body)

The Trade and Business Development Body exercises a range of functions in the trade and business sector. Under the overall policy direction of the NSMC, Inter*Trade*Ireland works in close collaboration with the Department of Enterprise, Trade and Investment (in Belfast) and the Department of Enterprise, Trade and

[8] Para 11.

[9] Agreement between the Government of the UK of Great Britain and Northern Ireland and the Government of Ireland Establishing Implementation Bodies. The Agreement came into force on 2 December 1999.

[10] North South Ministerial Council, *Annual Report 2004* (Armagh: NSMC, 2005) p 25.

[11] See some of its activities in North South Ministerial Council, *Annual Report 2004* (Armagh: NSMC, 2005) pp 12–13.

[12] North South Ministerial Council, *Annual Report 2005* (London: The Stationery Office, 2006), p 14.

Employment (in Dublin). It has a focus on promoting North/South trade and business co-operation by building enterprise capability and competitiveness and its current mission for the 2005–2007 period is to enhance the global competitiveness of the all-island economy to the mutual benefit of Ireland and Northern Ireland.[13] Its overall objective is to promote North/South trade and business development and to achieve this Inter*Trade*Ireland works to develop the capability of businesses to trade on an all-island basis by increasing the knowledge and information required by business and policy-makers, and by improving the flow of such knowledge to those who can use it to create value.

In 2003, Inter*Trade*Ireland's achievements included the creation of all-island Research and Development portal (expertiseireland.com) achieved through collaboration with the nine universities on the island and the all-island Public Procurement Portal (go-source.com) which is a collaboration between Inter*Trade*Ireland, Enterprise Ireland and Invest Northern Ireland.[14] In 2004, it aided co-operation between the two communications regulators (OFCOM and COMREG) by producing research on all-island tariffs,[15] and in 2005, it continued this work by developing sector-specific networks in areas such as biotechnology, computer science and crafts.[16]

Special EU Programmes (The Special EU Programmes Body) (SEUPB)

The objective of SEUPB is to develop co-operation, understanding and action between people and organisations in Ireland and Northern Ireland through consultation and the implementation of EU social, economic, reconciliation and cultural programmes.[17] This body has significant managerial, including grant-making, and oversight functions in relation to the Community Initiatives under the 2005–2006 European Structural Funds, the EU Programme for Peace and Reconciliation (Peace II) and the INTERREG IIIA programme. The Body is also responsible for monitoring and promoting the implementation of the Common Chapter in the National Development Plan for Ireland and the Northern Ireland Structural Funds Plan.

Language (Irish and Ulster Scots) (The North/South Language Body)

The North/South Language Body is a single body reporting to the NSMC but composed of two separate and largely autonomous agencies—the Irish Language Agency (*Foras na Gaeilge*) and the Ulster-Scots Agency (*Tha Boord o Ulster-Scotch*). *Foras na Gaeilge* has a wide range of functions including the promotion of the Irish language on an all-island basis in the area of education, dictionaries and terminology. *Tha Boord o Ulster-Scotch* is responsible for promoting a greater awareness and use of

[13] See North South Ministerial Council, *Annual Report 2005* (London: The Stationery Office, 2006), p 12. Its previous mission was 'to lead the development of the island economy through distinctive knowledge-based interventions, which will produce significant returns in the areas of cross-border trade and business development. See the InterTradeIreland *Corporate Plan 2002–2004* in North South Ministerial Council, *Annual Report 2003* (Armagh: NSMC, 2004) p 10.

[14] North South Ministerial Council, *Annual Report 2003* (Armagh: NSMC, 2004) pp 10–11.

[15] North South Ministerial Council, *Annual Report 2004* (Armagh: NSMC, 2005) pp 10–11.

[16] North South Ministerial Council, *Annual Report 2005* (London: The Stationery Office, 2006) p 13.

[17] See the mission statement of the sector in North South Ministerial Council, *Annual Report 2005* (London: The Stationery Office, 2006), p 20.

Ullans and of Ulster-Scots cultural issues, both within Northern Ireland and throughout the island. Together this sector provides significant core funding to language and educational organisations and provides sponsorship to a wide range of small events and publications.[18]

Aquaculture and Marine Sector

Decisions and actions are implemented in this area by the Foyle, Carlingford and Irish Lights Commission (FCILC).[19]

AREAS OF CO-OPERATION

Six areas for co-operation were agreed at the inaugural meeting of the North/South Ministerial Council.[20] These are transportation, agriculture, education, health, environment and tourism. A summary of these follows:

Transport—strategic planning and development of cross-border co-operation (with respect to rail, road, port and airport sectors) and road and rail safety. Activity has been slow to take place in this sector with an apparent focus on discussion[21] although 2005 reported developments in the area of north-south rail links, road safety and co-operation between the respective roads authorities with respect to the development of strategic road networks.[22]

Agriculture—discussion of Common Agricultural Policy (CAP) issues, animal and plant health policy and research and rural development. Developments here have included the development of an all-island Animal Health Strategy for control of animal movements and the prevention, containment and eradication of epizootic diseases in Ireland. The ultimate objectives are to establish a common import regime and equivalent internal arrangements with a view to achieving free movement of animals and animal products within the island. To this end, no less than nine policy working groups have been established[23].

Education—work in this area focuses currently on the following issues:[24]

Education for children with special needs—the initial focus here was on autism and dyslexia and a number of actions were agreed including a special education exchange programme for teachers. In 2002, the decision was taken to establish a centre for excellence at Middletown near Armagh on best practice in diagnosis and

[18] See for example, North South Ministerial Council, *Annual Report 2004* (Armagh, NSMC, 2005) pp 19–21, and North South Ministerial Council, *Annual Report 2005* (London, The Stationery Office, 2006), pp 23–27.

[19] For difficulties that have arisen in the exercise of the mandate of the council in this area see North South Ministerial Council, *Annual Report 2003* (Armagh, NSMC, 2004), pp 14–16 and North South Ministerial Council, *Annual Report 2005* (London, The Stationery Office, 2006), pp 18–19.

[20] These six Areas were approved by the NSMC at its Inaugural Plenary Meeting in Armagh on 13 December 1999. See further North/South Ministerial Council, *Annual Report 2001* (Armagh, NSMC, 2002).

[21] See, for example, the report of 2004 activities in North South Ministerial Council, *Annual Report 2004* (Armagh, NSMC, 2005) p 36.

[22] See North South Ministerial Council, *Annual Report 2005* (London, The Stationery Office, 2006), p 39.

[23] North South Ministerial Council, *Annual Report 2003* (Armagh, NSMC, 2004), p 31.

[24] See North South Ministerial Council, Education Sector, Joint Communique, Dublin, 28 November 2001, para 6.

assessment of children with Autistic Spectrum Disorders, the training of professionals, support for parents, and the development of individual education plans. As an all-island facility, the Centre is the first of its kind and is funded jointly by both Departments and managed on a joint North/South basis.[25]

Educational underachievement—a number of proposed actions including the establishment of arrangements for the exchange of teaching materials on literacy and numeracy have been approved and the Council has considered the Joint Working Group's proposals for the dissemination of good practice in the area of promoting attendance and retention rates. The Council has also agreed to undertake a targeted Home/School/Community pilot project aimed at improving parental involvement in the North.

Child Protection—in November 2001, the Council agreed that there was a need to develop a confidential mechanism for the registration of teachers and other works in the education field who are deemed unsafe to work with children and young people. In 2002, the Council welcomed that the Department of Education and Science was preparing a discussion paper on proposals for a register of persons unsuitable to work with children and young people, and that these proposals would seek to provide a system compatible with that in Northern Ireland[26] although little further progress has been reached in this area due to the limits of Ireland's vetting procedures.

School, youth and teacher exchanges on a cross-border basis—in November 2001, the Council agreed in principle to establish an advisory Standing Committee on School, Youth and Teacher Exchanges with representation from across the various stakeholder groups;

Co-operation on EU Programmes—in November 2001, the Council noted the availability of over 5 million euro under Measure 5.5 of the EU Peace 2 Programme to promote school and youth co-operation. The Council noted that officials in both departments have been working closely together to set up administrative procedures so that bids could be invited shortly by the two Education Departments acting jointly for funding for cross-border projects under that Measure.

Health—priorities identified for co-operation are accident and emergency planning, emergency services, co-operation on high technology equipment, cancer research and health promotion.[27] A number of working groups have been set up and co-ordination has been developed in areas such as rapid response to road traffic accidents in border areas. Joint seminars, workshops and conferences have been held on a wide range of health related topics to explore the potential for co-operation in this sector.[28]

[25] *Ibid.*, para 10. The 2005 Report of NSMC noted that this facility was still at the design stage. See North South Ministerial Council, *Annual Report 2005* (London, The Stationery Office, 2006) p 34.

[26] North/South Ministerial Council, Education Sector, Joint Communique, Armagh, Thursday 11 April 2002.

[27] See North South Ministerial Council, Food Safety Promotion and Health Sectors, Joint Communique, London, 16 November 2001.

[28] North South Ministerial Council, *Annual Report 2003* (Armagh, NSMC, 2004), pp 32–33. See also North South Ministerial Council, *Annual Report 2005* (London, The Stationery Office, 2006), pp 37–38.

Environment—research into environmental protection, water quality management and waste management in a cross-border context. Developments here include work on developing an all-island strategic approach to market development for recyclable material, and agreement on an all-island contract for the management and disposal of waste fridges/freezers.[29] Cooperation in this sector includes the relevant government departments as well as the Environmental Protection Agency in Ireland and the Environment and Heritage Service in the North. It has been particularly effective in relation to implementation of the EU Water Framework Directive.[30]

Tourism—marketing of the island of Ireland overseas as a tourist destination.[31] In this sector, the NSMC oversees the work of Tourism Ireland, the publicly-owned limited company which is responsible for marketing the island of Ireland overseas as a tourist destination. There has been significant practical co-operation in this area including the launch in 2005 of an all-island, industry-wide, e-marketing partnership group.[32]

In addition to the areas detailed above, the Annex to Strand Two of the Multi-Party Agreement also envisaged social security and social welfare as an area for North-South co-operation and implementation.

A further area identified for co-operation is the proposal that the Offices of Ombudsman, North and South, would have jurisdiction in relation to complaints of maladministration against the Implementation Bodies. The Offices also intend to submit joint annual reports to their respective legislatures on the performance of their functions in relation to the Implementation Bodies.[33]

THE ST ANDREWS AGREEMENT

Following political difficulties, the Northern Ireland Assembly was suspended on 14 October 2002 and eventually reinstated following elections in 2007. Provision for this reinstatement was made in the Agreement between the British and Irish governments and Northern Ireland's political parties concluded at St Andrew's, Scotland in October 2006. Apart from setting out the timetable towards the restoration of devolution in Northern Ireland, the St Andrew's Agreement also made provision for transitional arrangements inter alia with respect to the North South Ministerial Council.[34] These arrangements were given royal assent in the Northern Ireland (St Andrews Agreement) Act 2006 which amended the Northern Ireland Act 1998 accordingly.

In line with the objective of requiring all members of the Northern Ireland Assembly to work towards devolution and to manage the affairs of the Assembly during the period of suspension, the 2006 Act made provision for a statutory Ministerial Code. This places a duty on all Ministers to act in accordance with the provisions on

[29] North South Ministerial Council, *Annual Report 2003* (Armagh, NSMC, 2004), p 32. This was completed in 2005 –when the WEEE directive entered into force—and deemed a success of north-south partnership. See North South Ministerial Council, *Annual Report 2005* (London, The Stationery Office, 2006), p 36.

[30] The 2005 Report noted that this facility was still at the design stage. See North South Ministerial Council, *Annual Report 2005* (London, The Stationery Office, 2006) p 36.

[31] Joint Communique issued after the inaugural meeting of the North-South Ministerial Council on 13 December 1999.

[32] North South Ministerial Council, *Annual Report 2005* (London, The Stationery Office, 2006), p 31.

[33] Office of the Ombudsman Report, 1998.

[34] Joint Statement of the Irish and British Governments, 13 October 2006, St Andrew's, Fife, Scotland.

ministerial accountability introducing a new section 28A into the 1998 Act. The Ministers' Pledge of Office was also amended to require them to attend the North South Ministerial Council (section 7 of the 2006 Act). It was further provided in section 6 of the 2006 Act that draft NSMC decision papers would be circulated to all Executive members in advance of a scheduled NSMC meeting and that any member of the Executive would have the right to seek an Executive discussion on such a paper. Notwithstanding the lead Minister's executive authority in his/her area of responsibility as defined in the Agreement, where the Ministerial Code provided that certain matters should be considered/agreed in the Executive Committee this would also apply to any draft NSMC decision papers falling within those agreed provisions. The same requirements were applied to the British Irish Council under section 6 of the 2006 Act.

Amendments to the 1998 Act by section 12 of the 2006 Act also provided for a Minister with lead departmental interest in an issue under consideration at an NSMC meeting to be entitled to attend and a power for the First Minister/Deputy First Minister to adjudicate where a Minister's lead departmental interest was disputed. In the circumstances where a lead Minister was not proposing to attend the meeting in question, and had not arranged for a replacement Minister to discharge his/her responsibilities, OFM/DFM was given a statutory obligation to nominate such a replacement. OFM/DFM was also given a statutory power to require such relevant information from the lead department as would be necessary for the meeting in question. Finally, reflecting the existing requirement for representation of the Executive on a cross-community basis at meetings of the NSMC/BIC, a statutory obligation was imposed on OFM/DFM to nominate the other Minister whose presence might be necessary to fulfil that requirement.[35]

However, the most significant measure affecting the Ministerial Council is the decision in Appendix A to the St Andrew's Agreement to undertake a review of the implementation bodies under Strand Two of the Belfast Agreement.[36] This will be undertaken by the Northern Ireland Executive and the Irish Government under the auspices of the North South Ministerial Council. In particular, a review group is to examine the efficiency and value for money of existing implementation bodies and the case for additional bodies and areas of co-operation within the NSMC where mutual benefit would be derived. The Group is to report with recommendations to the NSMC with any changes to the existing arrangements requiring the specific endorsement of the Assembly and the Oireachtas. In the meantime, the NSMC is to continue to oversee the ongoing work of the Implementation Bodies and work in the areas of co-operation.

A JOINT HUMAN RIGHTS COMMITTEE

According to the British-Irish Agreement, a joint committee of representatives of the two Human Rights Commissions—North and South—was to be established to act as a 'forum for the consideration of human rights issues in the island of Ireland'. It was envisaged that the joint committee would consider, among other matters, the possibility of establishing a charter, open to signature of all democratic political parties,

[35] See further Annex A to the St Andrew's Agreement.

[36] *Ibid*, para 19.

reflecting and endorsing agreed measures for the protection of the fundamental rights of everyone living in the island of Ireland.[37]

The Joint Committee was established in November 2001 and immediately identified its first two tasks as the drafting of a charter of rights for the whole island pursuant to the Belfast Agreement and the setting up of a sub committee on racism, a growing problem on both sides of the border.[38] The Committee subsequently met at various intervals between 2004 and 2006.[39] In relation to racism, the issues to come to the committee's attention were the need for judicial training on avoiding racist comments from the bench, the need for both governments to ratify the Convention on Migrant Workers and the need for research to identify the north/south movement of asylum seekers and refugees. Initial work took place on the Charter and a pre-consultation document was published in 2003 to which feedback and responses were invited. However, the project has not progressed significantly since that time due inter alia to the change of membership of the Northern Ireland Commission. It is expected to be revived in 2007.

The Joint Committee decided in December 2004 in the light of the change in membership in the Northern Ireland Human Rights Commission that it was an opportune time to review the operation of the Committee. The outcome of this review is not yet known. Apart from the work on racism and the Charter of Rights for the Island of Ireland, the Joint Committee appears to have spent most of its time sharing experiences and developing common approaches towards human rights issues of mutual concern. Joint submissions were discussed, for example, on the issue of reform of the European Court of Human Rights, on national human rights institutions and on issues of disability and migration and asylum. There is clearly much potential for collaboration and co-operation here.

POLICING

The Multi-Party Agreement focused predominantly on the need for policing reform in Northern Ireland and in particular mandated the Patten review which led to the overhaul of the former Royal Ulster Constabulary. In April 2002, An Garda Síochána (police force of the Republic of Ireland) and the newly established Police Service of Northern Ireland held their first joint annual conference in part fulfilment of the Independent Commission on Policing in Northern Ireland (the so-called Patten Commission) recommendation for greater co-operation between the two forces. The focus of the conference was on issues of community safety, disaster planning, road traffic issues and security and crime matters.

On 29 April 2002, the Irish Government signed an inter-governmental agreement on the implementation of Patten recommendations on co-operation between the Garda Siochana and the Police Service of Northern Ireland (PSNI). The Agreement provides a bilateral legal framework for enhanced co-operation between An Garda Síochána and the PSNI and in particular it allows for closer liaison, joint investiga-

[37] Strand Three, para 10.

[38] Monika Unsworth, 'Joint Study of Human Rights Issues' *The Irish Times,* 9 November 2001.

[39] Only the minutes from the meetings in April and September 2002, April 2003 and December 2004 are available on the website of the Irish Human Rights Commission at www.ihrc.ie.

tions, an annual conference and joint emergency planning. It also provides for extensive arrangements for exchange of personnel and experience as well as for co-operation in the area of training. Finally, the Agreement covers the implementation of reciprocal provisions for lateral mobility and secondment with policing powers between the two police services.

There is much potential for collaboration between the Police Service of Northern Ireland and An Garda Síochána and child protection is one area where there is clear imperative. In this regard, it is notable that a joint protocol was signed in 2006 between PSNI and An Garda Síochána to co-share information regarding the movement of sex offenders across the jurisdictions. The inadequacy of personnel vetting procedures in Ireland (no information short of a conviction for a sexual offence is recorded in the system) are still a hindrance to the effective operation of this protocol however.

CONCLUSION

It is clear from the North-South Ministerial Council's annual reports of its activities that they represent the quiet success story of the Belfast Agreement. Areas in which co-operation and coordination is of clear mutual benefit to both parts of the island have been identified and acted upon in a relatively short space of time and with positive and practical results. While in many areas the need for this co-operation is painfully obvious—such as in relation to roads, waterways, tourism and business—the Belfast Agreement provided a much needed impetus to develop it in other areas as well. In education and healthcare, for example, there are real economies of scale to be maximised and its full potential is yet to be realised. This potential is to be the focus of the review mandated by the St Andrew's Agreement.

At the same time, developments in other areas have been modest and hindered by slow political progress and other problems mainly in Northern Ireland. In particular, the work of the joint committee of the Human Rights Commissions might have been more dynamic but for the difficulties experienced by the Bill of Rights process in Northern Ireland. More generally, although the suspension of the Northern Ireland Assembly does not appear to have had a significant practical effect on the operation of the North South Ministerial Council,[40] it must mean that the work of the implementation bodies has not benefited from the full political weight which the Agreement intended to support them. This will hopefully now change.

[40] On the dissolution of the Assembly in 1999, an agreement was reached in 2002 between the British and Irish governments for the operation of the Council during suspension. It puts in place interim procedures for the processing of ministerial decisions by th (Armagh, NSMC, 2004), p 7.

Law of the Sea Developments in Ireland—2006

Clive Symmons

MARINE LAW AND OCEAN POLICY CENTRE, NUI, GALWAY AND TRINITY COLLEGE, DUBLIN

This Report deals primarily with various items which transpired in 2006 and touch on the Law of the Sea in Ireland. Both the partial and joint submissions involving Ireland to the Commission on the Limits of the Continental Shelf established under the Law of the Sea Convention are considered, while their Executive Summaries are reproduced in the Documents Section of this volume of the *Irish Yearbook*. The bulk of this Report focuses on the Sea-Fisheries and Maritime Jurisdiction Act, 2006, which incorporates various elements of the Law of the Sea regarding jurisdiction in maritime zones, considers cross-border issues, salmon fishing, maritime safety and registration of ships. Beyond this, issues of maritime pollution and the case of the United Kingdom's Sellafield nuclear plant are discussed briefly. Overall, 2006 was a year in which Ireland was active both at home and in international fora with regard to the law of the sea.

CONTINENTAL SHELF LIMITS: SUBMISSIONS TO THE CLCS

On 25 May 2005, Ireland lodged its partial submission to the 1982 United Nations Convention on the Law of the Sea (UNCLOS) Commission on the Limits of the Continental Shelf (CLCS).[1] The Minister of Communications, Marine and Natural Resources, Noel Dempsey, noted in the *Dail* that this had been done as part of the 'registration of exploration interests' and 'potential entitlement' outside the 200nm limit, with particular reference to the Porcupine Abyssal Plain. Both the Porcupine Basin and the Goban Spur seabed areas, it was noted, 'lie entirely within Ireland's exclusive economic zone (EEZ)'.

This submission was followed nearly a year later, on 19 May 2006, by a joint submission, the first of its kind, by Ireland, together with France, Spain and the United Kingdom, in respect of the outer limits in parts of the Celtic Sea and Bay of Biscay beyond two hundred nautical miles. The Note accompanying the Irish Executive Summary and the submission indicated that this area was 'not the subject of any dispute [between the four submitting States] nor any other State(s)'. It thus appears that Ireland and its neighbours utilised both paragraphs 3, on partial submissions, and 4, on joint submissions, of Annex 1 to the CLCS Rules because of this perceived 'non-dispute' situation; this having been exemplified by a pre-agreed stance based on shared research and data and a 'single document prepared collectively and collaboratively by the four coastal States concerned'.

[1] See Clive Symmons, (2006) 37 *Ocean Development and International Law* at 299–317.

In consequence, the four States viewed the joint submission of the portion of the seabed area in question as not prejudicing 'matters relating to the delimitation of boundaries between the four coastal States and any other States'. The Irish Note accompanying the Submission went on to refer to 'unresolved questions' with other 'neighbours', presumably Denmark/Faeroes and Iceland in respect of the Hatton-Rockall Plateau dispute further north, in which case Irish submissions could be made 'at a later date'. Ireland envisages that once the outer limits of the mutually-agreed submission area are determined by the CLCS, a lateral 'carve up' of the area can take place between the four States on an agreed basis in accordance with 'applicable principles of international law'.

In the *Dáil*, it was stated that Ireland expected a recommendation from the CLCS on this Biscay Abyssal Plain submission in 2007, following which it could proceed to 'establish its outer limits' and license exploration in such an area 'in the normal way'.

THE SEA-FISHERIES AND MARITIME JURISDICTION ACT 2006

The Sea-Fisheries and Maritime Jurisdiction Act 2006, which entered into force on 4 April was the most important piece of general law of the sea legislation to emerge in 2006 and was meant to modernise the legislative framework for sea fisheries found in the principal Act, the Fisheries (Consolidation) Act 1959, so as to clarify and strengthen the law against illegal fishing in line with European Union (EU) policy. A further aim of the 2006 Act was to update and replace the Maritime Jurisdiction Act 1959, and, in particular, to give effect to the concept of the EEZ in the UNCLOS.

In the context of Irish fisheries legislation, the Sea-Fisheries and Maritime Jurisdiction Act was designed to 'fill a major gap' in the legislation by implementing EU policy following an adverse Supreme Court judgment that led to pressure to enact new legislation by 31 December 2005 to avoid EU penalties. These gaps arose in part from the *Kennedy* and *Vincent Browne* cases, in which the Supreme Court had taken issue with a Ministerial Order, under Section 223A of the Fisheries (Consolidation) Act, 1959, that penalised any breach of an EU prohibition on drift netting within the Common Fisheries Policy (CFP) area, including and extending beyond the two hundred nautical mile limit. As a consequence, Section 224B was amended to extend the geographical scope of such regulations beyond two hundred nautical miles and to apply it to all activities in breach of the CFP.

It was aptly stated in the *Seanad* [the Senate of Ireland] that the Act had not only provoked widespread debate in the fishing industry but had attracted unusual publicity elsewhere with an alleged 'concerted and organised campaign against [the] legislation'.[2] Undoubtedly the most controversial part of the Bill concerned sea fisheries regulation, upsetting not only fishery organisations, whose boats made a day-long protest on 3 February 2006, but leading to protest by the ruling *Fianna Fáil* party's backbenchers.[3] Concern was voiced specifically with regard to section 28 of the Act, which updated and consolidated penalties dating from 1978 and gave effect to a deterrent system of penalties required under EU law. This was seen by some opposition members and several Irish Members of the European Parliament as not only disproportionate but also

[2] *Seanad Debates*, 2006, 183, col 234 (Mr Dempsey).
[3] See *Irish Times*, 3 and 23 February 2006.

discriminatory against 'Irish fishermen'.[4] In fact, the *Oireachtas* [National Parliament] Joint Committee on Communications, Marine and Natural Resources took the unusual step of engaging the services of senior counsel to advise them on the legislation in connection with proportionality and administrative sanctions. Counsel reportedly advised the Committee that administrative sanctions for fishery offences were constitutional.[5]

Another controversial issue which arose during the debates leading to the Sea-Fisheries and Maritime Jurisdiction Act was with regard to the use of force at sea, empowering fishery protection officers to use gunfire in fisheries enforcement. This particularly outraged the fishing lobby and several Members of the *Daíl*, despite the fact that this power was already contained in the 1959 Act. It was officially claimed in the Select Committee that 'removing the gun' would not amount to a major shift of policy as 'it had never been used'.[6] The latter assertion was, in fact, incorrect, as in the past the Naval Service has used its weapons in fisheries enforcement.[7] Even at the second stage of the reading of the proposed Act, there was unease about this 'use of gun' aspect, leading to an early pledge by Pat Gallagher, Minister of State for Communications, Marine, and Natural Resources, to make an amendment at Committee stage. This was duly undertaken early in 2006, though it was later enigmatically announced in the *Seanad*, that this matter was not finalised, as it was 'being addressed in other legislation'.[8]

Part 3 of the Sea-Fisheries and Maritime Jurisdiction Act contains the central law of the sea provisions which are dealt with in more detail below. The definitions in section 81 of the Act are essentially those of the various maritime zones as established by UNCLOS and are in large part reproduced verbatim from the Maritime Jurisdiction Act, 1959, except for the concepts of 'contiguous zone' and the exclusive economic zone, the 'EEZ', which are both new to Irish legislation.

Fisheries Jurisdiction and International/EU Law

Under section 3 of the Sea-Fisheries and Maritime Jurisdiction Act, Ministerial Regulations may be made, inter alia, for the conservation and management of straddling fish stocks. Sections 8 and 9 deal with sea fishery boats passing through Irish waters, rather than fishing therein as in Section 10. This provision updates and replaces old section 221 of the 1959 Act restricting the entry of foreign sea fishing boats into the exclusive fishery limits of the State, now defined by section 88 as being within 'the outer limit of the exclusive economic zone'. The reference to 'international law' in this Section includes, in particular, multilateral treaties, such as UNCLOS, the so-called 'Straddling Fish Stocks Agreement' of 1995, which was previously implemented in the Fisheries (Amendment) Act 2003, and customary international law. Section 9 of the Sea-Fisheries and Maritime Jurisdiction Act updates and replaces section 222 of the 1959 Act, which provision provided for control of foreign sea fishing boats when lawfully within exclusive Irish fishery limits, namely two hundred nautical

[4] See *Dail Debates*, 2006, 610, col 887 (Mr Perry); *Ibid*, cols 895/899 (Mr Broughan).

[5] *Dail Debates*, 2006, 615, col 572 (Mr O'Keefe); *Irish Times*, 7 February 2006.

[6] Select Committee on Communications, Marine and Natural Resources, Vol 29(16), 527 (Mr Gallagher).

[7] See Clive Symmons, *Ireland and the Law of the Sea,* 2nd edn (Dublin, Thomson Round Hall, 2000) 254–59.

[8] *Seanad Debates*, 2006, 183, col 101.

miles extending from the baselines, including the enforced exit of such boats from this zone.

The reference in sub-section 3(2) to the Minister being empowered to make regulations relating to 'good order' among fishing boats and persons on board while in the Irish territorial sea can be contrasted with the rest of the section inasmuch as the regulatory powers do not apply exclusively within the twelve nautical mile territorial sea and inasmuch as it does not relate to fishery offences *per se*. For example, the phrase 'good order' could take in offences relating to harassment and intimidation of Irish fishing vessels by foreign fishermen, as has happened in the past,[9] which the ill-fated Law of the Sea (Suppression of Piracy) Bill 2001, had aimed at dealing with in respect of such offences occurring outside the twelve nautical mile limit. Such public order offences committed by foreign fishermen outside the twelve nautical mile limit remain outside Irish control. Indeed, it was officially confirmed in the *Daíl* that such regulations have ever been made under the 1959 Act from which the wording was adopted.[10]

An attempt was made at the Report and Final/Select Committee stages of the consideration of the Act as a Bill to add a reporting requirement for foreign fishing vessels when entering the Irish territorial sea. Mr Dempsey stated that such a specific requirement could not be undertaken 'unilaterally'[11] but that section 9 dealt with situations where a foreign vessel enters Irish waters with a lawful excuse but fails to leave when the lawful purpose no longer exists. He confirmed that a 'sign-in' and 'check-out' notification system to the Irish authorities was already in place for Irish waters and mentioned the right of freedom of navigation in the Irish two hundred nautical mile zone for foreign vessels. It was further noted that Irish enforcement agencies already could, for example, direct such a vessel into a designated port if an incident were to transpire.

Section 11 of the Act makes it an offence (subject to penalties in section 28) to contravene certain directly-applicable EU Regulations relating to the Common Fisheries Policy. It was confirmed in Select Committee that although EU regulations directly apply throughout the EU, national legislation is required to penalise any contravention. Section 12 deals with the State's fishing quota and simplified, expedited and streamlined notices that allocate and manage Ireland's annual sea fishing quotas as decided by the EU Council. The Minister of State confirmed that a specific period of days' requirement in relation to notices coming into force was unnecessary and could infringe EU law; and that each vessel notified of a relevant prohibition or restriction had one day's grace between any notice being served on it and it taking effect. This was meant to ensure that fishing disruption would be kept to a minimum.[12]

Section 14 updates and replaces section 224B of the 1959 Act for the purposes of applying, by Ministerial Regulations, detailed requirements of the CFP in relation to matters for which the State has no discretion as regards both principle or policy, both beyond and within its exclusive two hundred nautical mile fishery limits; that is throughout the whole area to which the CFP applies. Previously, the 1959 Act had only applied within the exclusive fishery limits of Ireland and to illegal fishing *per se*.

[9] Above n 7, at 178–83.

[10] *Dail Debates*, 2006, 615, col 610.

[11] *Dail Debates*, 615, col 610.

[12] See the words 'not being a day earlier than the day after its first publication' in *Seanad Debates*, 183, col 93; 29 SCMNR no 18, cols 589, 594.

In effect, this section and the next were a direct response to the *Browne* and *Kennedy* cases. Section 15 updates the 1959 Act by empowering the relevant Minister by regulations to supplement the EU Common Fisheries Policy by prescribing national measures. A comparison with the former section shows the present Section to be broader in scope but with some regulatory matters changed from the Act as initiated, including, for example, requiring the master of an Irish sea fishing boat to inform a protection officer of the expected port of landing for catches. As was officially explained, this Section filled the gaps identified in the *Kennedy* case by specifically enabling Ministerial regulations to be made to supplement the CFP where Ireland has discretion to do so, such as in the case of lobster, mussel and oyster fisheries in Irish coastal waters. To some extent, it mirrors section 14, but it allows Ireland to regulate the 'local element' under its national fishery policy where EU law does not cover the issue, compatible with the CFP as reviewed in 2002.

Section 18 updates and replaces section 233 of the 1959 Act and sets out the powers of sea fisheries protection officers relating to sea fishing boats. This section, as initiated, had controversial sub-sections 5 and 6 which stated that if an order was given by a sea fisheries protection officer of the Defence Forces or Gardaí to a fishing boat to stop, etc, and that order was 'disobeyed or disregarded', the appropriate officers could, 'after causing a gun to be fired as a signal', 'fire at or into the boat'. These provisions were deleted, and thus, enforcement officers no longer have the statutory right to fire at recalcitrant fishing vessels for law enforcement purposes. This may cause practical problems in future for the Naval Service where, for example, the pursued fishing vessel persistently refuses to stop.

Section 28, which was designed to update and comprehensively restate penalty provisions for indictable sea fisheries offences which were originally enacted in the Fisheries (Amendment) Act 1978, as subsequently amended, and which had since that time been updated 'on an *ad hoc* basis, for a variety of sea fisheries offences',[13] proved to be controversial. The increased penalties proposed were claimed by the Minister of State to be sufficient to provide an effective range of fines for the courts to deal with both large and small-scale economic infractions by both 'large and small boats', as well as bringing in a system of fines and forfeitures which was as 'generally dissuasive' as EU law required. The initially-proposed increases in maximum penalties were officially viewed as 'reasonable' but were seen by most Opposition spokesmen as disproportionate or criticised as being the highest in Europe.[14]

In light of this early criticism, Mr. Gallagher announced in Select Committee that graduated fines based on vessel size were to be introduced, ranging from €20,000 for smaller vessels to €100,000 for larger ones, but without moving to a system of 'administrative penalties'. Thus, the levels of more serious fines set out in Table 1 of the proposed Bill were to be fine-tuned, according to three categories of sea fishing vessels, with a reduction of the original amounts, but with account still being taken of EU requirements on dissuasive fines and sanctions. It was officially acknowledged from the start that the fishing industry wanted administrative penalties and sanctions on a graduated basis. Such sanctions were claimed to be actively encouraged by the EU

[13] Gallagher, 610 Dail Debates, col 874.

[14] For example, see Mr Perry, 610 *Dail Debates*, cols. 885/889; Mr Broughan, *Ibid* at col 900; Mr O'Flynn, *Ibid* at col 914.

Commission.[15] The concept of administrative sanctions was, however, initially claimed to give rise to constitutional difficulties. As the *Taoiseach* [the Prime Minister] stated at one stage of the debate, administrative sanctions had been 'repeatedly considered by the Attorney General', who had advised that such penalties were permissible under Irish constitutional law only in the case of technical breaches of the law.[16]

This latter system was considered to have certain advantages, such as the potential to deal 'speedily' with fishery offences. However, it was constantly stressed that the CFP required 'deterrent' penalties and mandatory forfeitures at a substantial level. Thus, this required sanctions of a criminal nature that would be administered 'by the Courts', by virtue of Article 34 of the Irish Constitution. This official interpretation was challenged by several TDs and was not accepted by the legal adviser hired by the *Oireachtas* Committee on the issue, who reportedly stated that Articles 15 and 37 of the Constitution allowed for such a system.[17] The system was also officially criticised for allegedly causing impracticalities as to enforcement when fishery offences were committed by foreign-registered vessels, and it was officially stated that there might not be protection under the Constitution for this.[18] In the end, such concerted attempts to introduce 'fixed charge' offences into the Act were unsuccessful; and a late attempt during the Select Committee stage to introduce a new 'Chapter 6' into the Bill to allow for 'administrative penalties' failed.

Cross-Border Fisheries

Section 7 of the Sea-Fisheries and Maritime Jurisdiction Act ensures that sea fisheries law applies to those areas between North Ireland and the Republic of Ireland where jurisdictional issues are in doubt. This section relates to the Moville area on the northwest coast of the Island of Ireland and the 'Louth area', namely that part of Carlingford Lough located in the border region on the east coast but within the Irish Republic as defined by section 31 of the British–Irish Agreement Act 1999. For historical reasons, the Moville area was excluded from the old Foyle Commission joint jurisdiction under the 1952 Act. The recent Foyle and Carlingford Fisheries Bill, however, modifies the Fisheries (Amendment) Act 1997 to provide that in addition to the Moville area that Act also does not apply to the 'Louth area' as defined in the British-Irish Agreement Act, 1999.

During 2006, it was confirmed in the *Daíl* that the curious 'voisinage agreement' which applies to reciprocal fishing rights in seas both sides of the border and dates back to 1959 applies to the mussel seed fishery which is managed on an all-Ireland basis and that the Minister could authorise fishing by Irish-registered vessels not only in Irish waters but also in the waters around Northern Ireland for certain purposes. Furthermore, it was announced that a comprehensive set of guidelines had been drawn up by the Irish authorities, the Department of Agriculture and Rural Development in Northern Ireland, and the 'Loughs Agency' in respect of shellfish operations in Lough Foyle.

[15] Mr O'Keefe, 615 *Dail Debates*, col 572.
[16] 615 *Dail Debates*, col 524.
[17] See *Irish Times*, 7 February 2006.
[18] Mr N Dempsey, 615 *Dail Debates*, col.589); 610 *Dail Debates*, col 879.

It should be noted that there still do not exist agreed to maritime boundaries between the United Kingdom and the Republic of Ireland in the border loughs of Carlingford and Foyle. However, since the advent of the Belfast (or Good Friday) Agreement of 1998 and changes to Article 2 of the Irish Constitution (which had made territorial claims to the entire island), there must exist a notional boundary in both loughs which divides the respective jurisdictional areas, whether as territorial seas or internal waters, arguably along a median, or *thalweg* line (in the navigable channel, which follows the sinuosities on both sides of the shoreline). For practical reasons of fishery regulation and enforcement in the past, some purely administrative lines had to be drawn unilaterally on the Irish side in Carlingford Lough. Thus, a vague line was defined in the First Schedule to the 1980 Regional Fisheries Order. Since 1999, however, this boundary was overtaken by a new Order to take account of the new cross-border Loughs Agency's joint fishery jurisdiction in this Lough, and Lough Foyle, brought about by the Belfast Agreement.[19]

Despite amending the 1952 Act, the abovementioned Irish Order for the border loughs, which was published on 5 December 2006, makes no changes in such cross-border jurisdictional limits. However, the Order does extend the functions of the 'Loughs Agency' (the Foyle, Carlingford and Irish Lights Commission) in relation to the development of inland fisheries in the Foyle and Carlingford areas, in particular for regulation and licensing of aquaculture by the Agency in these border areas. It also establishes a new appellate body, the Foyle and Carlingford Aquaculture Licensing Appeals Board. Reciprocating legislation should be enacted in the United Kingdom along the same lines for Northern Ireland in the near future.

Salmon Drift–Netting

In April 2006, the National Salmon Commission (NSC) recommended a ban on drift-net fishing of salmon in Irish waters as of 2007 on conservation grounds,[20] and in October 2006, a three-man independent advisory salmon group recommended a similar ban. Outside pressure to stop commercial salmon-netting included statements from the North Atlantic Salmon Fund, which accused Ireland of evading constructive dialogue under Article 66 of the UNCLOS relating to anadromous stocks between concerned States and Ireland (dealing with a shared management plan concerning salmon whilst in Irish waters).[21]

At the end of 2006, the Irish Government decided to join other western European States in banning open-seas drift netting of salmon for 2007, stating that it was committed to accepting the scientific advice given by the expert bodies. As Mr Browne, Minister of State at the Department of Agriculture and Food, was to state in the *Daíl*, international best practice for management of North Atlantic salmon required 'adoption of the precautionary approach', as this was the recommendation under the North Atlantic Salmon Convention; and EU obligations required Ireland to comply with the Habitats Directive and put an end to 'mixed stock' fishing.[22]

[19] Note that the Eastern Fisheries Region (Alteration of Boundaries) Order, 1999, depicts an updated provisional territorial sea limit line projecting seawards, from a straight closing line between Ballagan and Cranfield Points.

[20] See *Irish Times*, 1 March 2006.

[21] See *Irish Times*, 4 January 2006.

[22] See 626 *Dail Debates*, cols 182/6; 627 *Dail Debates*, col 1670.

Maritime Jurisdictional Zones

Part 3 of the Sea-Fisheries and Maritime Jurisdiction Act largely restates the past maritime zones claimed by Ireland. Thus, section 82 of the Act of 2006 on the territorial sea essentially replicates the wording contained formerly in section 2 of the Maritime Jurisdiction Act 1959 (MJA 1959). Curiously, the phrase 'territorial seas' in the plural is still used here whereas international practice and treaty law put the phrase in the singular. It should be noted that the vague phrase 'territorial waters' is also still used in Irish legal parlance and legislation, and although it is not a legal term, it is often used to describe the totality of internal waters and the territorial sea as such.[23] Prior to the Belfast Agreement and changes to Articles in the Irish Constitution, Ireland's claim to the territorial sea of the northern six counties was catered to by vagueness of wording, as 'the baseline' did not specifically relate the baselines from which this maritime zone is drawn to the shores of the twenty six counties of the Republic as such. This wording, however, remains.

Section 83, dealing with the outer limits of the Irish territorial sea, essentially restates Section 3 of the MJA 1959, and incorporates the amended extension from three to twelve nautical miles in the Maritime Jurisdiction (Amendment) Act 1988. The technical method of calculating a point twelve nautical miles from the 'nearest point of the baseline' would be to use the so-called 'arcs of circles' method, which is based on a set distance from the baseline, whether normal, that is following the sinuosities of the low-water mark, or straight, rather than the 'traces parallel' system. The lateral limits at both extremities, in or from the border bays, of Northern Ireland relative to the Irish territorial sea remain vague in the absence of any delimitation agreement on this between the United Kingdom and Ireland.

Section 84 of the Sea-Fisheries and Maritime Jurisdiction Act deals with a contiguous zone and was a late addition to the Act. It implements for the first time such a zone around the State. Although the actual distance of this zone in Irish law is not spelled out as such, it amounts to a twelve nautical mile belt contiguous to the Irish territorial sea, a zone extending to twenty-four nautical miles in total from the baseline. Curiously, sub-section 3 does not explicitly spell out the jurisdictional rights which apply to this zone. The rights, and, indeed, duties, are simply defined as those 'provided for in international law'. This reference to 'international law' means that Article 33(1)(a) and (b) of UNCLOS notionally apply and implies an ability for the State to exercise the control necessary to prevent infringement of customs, fiscal, immigration or sanitary laws/regulations 'within its territory and its territorial sea', or punish (in the outer twelve nautical mile zone) infringement of any of the abovementioned types as may be intraterritorially committed. The lack of specificity in the Act as to the types of jurisdictional controls to be imposed may only be temporary, as it was confirmed in debate on the Bill that implementation of this particular regime in Irish waters would require further legislation to give effect to Article 33 of the UNCLOS.[24] This newly-proclaimed zone also gives Ireland potential control, under Article 302(2) of the UNCLOS, over the removal of archaeological objects from such zones. It was confirmed by Mr. Dempsey in the *Seanad* that provision was being made in 2006 for

[23] See Symmons, above, n 7, p 69.

[24] See 182 *Seanad Reports*, col 1729.

'further legislation' by the relevant Ministers for 'enhancing the power of the State to protect archaeological objects in the contiguous zone'.

The provisions in section 85 on Irish baselines essentially restate section 4 of the MJA 1959. It should be noted, however, that change of wording in sub-section 2 has meant that straight baseline provisions can now only lie within 'the State' as a consequence of the Belfast Agreement and the consequent constitutional amendment.

By the phrase '[s]ave as otherwise provided', subsection 1 indicates that the normal Irish baseline is the 'low-water mark', designated as the 'low water line' and 'normal baseline' in Article 5 of the UNCLOS, from the mainland or any island, or from a 'low tide elevation' within twelve nautical miles of either. The latter formation is defined in section 81 in essentially the same terms as in Article 13 of the UNCLOS.

Unfortunately, the *tidal datums* to be used in this section are not specified, particularly the meaning of 'low-water mark'. Exceptions to the abovementioned normal, 'low-tide' Irish baseline are contained in sub-section 2, whereby the Government may prescribe 'straight baselines'. Essentially (though this is not fully spelled out), this type of baseline may be used by a State where its coast is 'deeply indented' or where there is a 'fringe of islands along the coast in its immediate vicinity'. This was effected by Ireland in its Maritime Jurisdiction Act 1959 (Straight Baselines) Order 1959, as indicated in sub-section 3.

It is unfortunate that this Order has been expressly retained in sub-section 3 (subsection 3 of section 85 confirms the continuing relevance of the 1959 statutory instrument laying down straight baselines, preserving it without amendment) because the extensive baseline system decreed by it has many legal flaws. For example, it is based on unspecified chart data, so that its fixing points often are inland or, worse, out to sea when plotted on conventional United Kingdom Admiralty Charts (which, as will be seen in section 92(2), are the prescribed Irish charts for baseline purposes). Some of the lines also infringe the controlling provisions of Article 7 of the UNCLOS, such as the geographical and other requirements in paragraph 1 thereof and elsewhere. Furthermore, they tend to have no 'closing-off' lines to shore at their lateral limits, and in the sections elsewhere the baseline reverts to and from the low-water line. The new legislation offered an excellent opportunity for Ireland to rectify the abovementioned deficiencies of the law, not only to bring the situation in line with the requirements of the law of the sea but also to avoid possible domestic legal challenges to Ireland's exercise of its criminal jurisdiction in its territorial sea.

Another deficiency in respect of secondary legislation is that there has never been a prescribed 'closing line' for juridical bays, and, indeed, for ports and river mouths, which Ireland might claim on the *east* coast (most, though not all, of the southern, western and northern coastal bays already being enclosed by lines specified in the 1959 statutory instrument). These east coast bays would most obviously include Dundalk, Dublin and Wexford bays where, at the present time, no specified closing lines exist. As the appropriate points to be joined in these instances are unspecified in Irish law, the consequence is that the extent of claimed internal waters therein remains unclear.

It seems that an official view has been taken in the past that such bays are already notionally enclosed at *common law* under the general 'saving clause', which is now contained in section 91. The vague and opaque wording in section 86 ('in all respects as its ports, harbours, bays, lakes and rivers') might also imply an already-existing claim to internal waters in bays. However, this is obviously unsatisfactory: subsection

1 requires, in the words 'prescribe' and 'prescribed', that actual closing lines be sufficiently clear as to the internal waters to be claimed under section 86. This is compounded by the fact that Article 16(2) of the UNCLOS requires that coastal States give due publicity to their charts of straight baselines/closing lines and deposit copies of these with the United Nations Secretary-General. Ireland has not fully complied with these obligations with regard to relevant baselines.

With regard to the definition of 'internal waters', section 86 of the Act restates section 5 of the MJA 1959. As noted above, there is no definition of bays in the legislation, nor of ports or harbours. The lack of prescribed closing lines on the east coast, as seen, is unsatisfactory because there are presently no clear (that is 'prescribed'), enclosing lines, and therefore, there are no properly constituted 'internal waters' in these locations. Theoretically, the normal baseline rule could apply, meaning that the low water mark would follow the sinuosities of the *internal* coast of the indentation, thus making the waters seaward of this line territorial sea rather than internal waters.[25]

Another strange result of the restated wording of this section is in respect of the reference to 'innocent passage'. This phrase has still not been defined in Irish legislation, and indeed, there was justified criticism in the *Daíl* that the present Act only incorporated a very small number of UNCLOS provisions into Irish law. There is no express definitional 'saving clause' in this Part that would indicate that in default of inclusion of a technical definition, interpretative reference should be made to a background treaty such as the UNCLOS. Nonetheless, the definition of 'innocent passage' must comply with Articles 18 and 19 of the UNCLOS, which define 'passage' and 'innocent' in the law of the sea.

Additionally, as this writer has commented elsewhere,[26] the breadth of the latter wording, which indicates that the right of innocent passage shall extend to '*all sea areas*' which are *landward of the baselines* where the enclosed sea areas had been 'previously considered *as part of the territorial seas or the high seas*' is an unfortunate misapplication of the stricter rule of Article 8(2) of the UNCLOS, which only preserves such a right for foreign ships in the case of internal waters formally enclosed by the *more extensive* system of 'straight baselines' *under Article 7* (to which regime that Article *solely refers*), and not to those enclosed by the more restrictive rules which apply to *bays* per se under Article 10. The effect of this is that Ireland presently allows the right of innocent passage to foreign ships in the waters of its *notional* 'bays', *stricto sensu,* presupposing that the internal waters of formally unenclosed Irish bays have prospectively prescribe closing lines. However, it is possible to interpret the separate reference here to the legal regime of 'its' 'bays', 'ports', and similar terms as implying that the State already has (apart from any 'bays' incidentally enclosed under the 1959 Order), internal waters in such indentations *at common law* where rights of innocent passage do not apply.

Section 87, an entirely new provision, legislatively caters for the new concept of a two hundred nautical mile EEZ being established off Ireland in accordance with Articles 55 and 56 of the UNCLOS. Thus, Ireland's off-shore waters include, beyond the territorial sea, 'two distinct legal zones, known as the "contiguous zone" and the "exclusive economic zone"' which 'partially overlap with each other physically'.[27]

[25] See generally Clive Symmons, 'The Background to the Imposition of the Straight Baseline System Around the Irish Coast' (1998) 13 IJMCL 47, 50, 56–58.

[26] See *ibid*, at 65–66.

[27] Minister for Foreign Affairs, 621 *Dail Debates,* col 1430.

Article 55's 'specific legal regime' is expressly contained in Part V of the UNCLOS, the text of which is annexed to the Act as Schedule 2, so that the relevant treaty law on this zone is effectively incorporated into Irish law by reference. However, if only *ex abundanti cautela*, the essence of the specific regime for the EEZ is also laid out almost verbatim in sub-section 4, thus indicating that the sovereign rights that Ireland now claims in this zone includes rights to explore, exploit, conserve and manage not just natural resources in the water column of the zone (essentially free-swimming fish) but also mineral resources in its seabed and subsoil, including in the latter regard 'living organisms' of the 'sedentary species' as defined in Article 77(4) of the UNCLOS. Additionally, as allowed by Article 56(1)(b) of the UNCLOS, Ireland specifically claims the lesser three-fold 'jurisdictional rights' that are essentially dealt with in Articles 246–55 of UNCLOS.

In effect, therefore, the EEZ-based 'sovereign' rights now being claimed in this zone include those classically associated with an exclusive fishery zone, namely exploitation and other uses of fish, including sedentary species, within a two hundred nautical mile wide water column, and seabed mineral rights which have traditionally been associated with the continental shelf regime. The latter were, and still are, exercisable in Irish practice under section 2(1) of the Continental Shelf Act 1968. This particular regime, then, is still catered for in Ireland as a zone and legal regime in legislation that is separate from the more general maritime jurisdictional regime in the 2006 Act. Thus, it is to the 1968 legislation that reference must still be made in respect of licensing for exploration/exploitation, etc, for minerals and non-living resources. Mr Broughan criticised this disjunctive maritime law treatment in Select Committee and also attempted to include in the present Act a new provision on the continental shelf as such. He alleged that the 1968 Continental Shelf Act did not properly clarify the rights that were exercisable in this zone, particularly beyond the two hundred nautical mile limits which thus, was 'deficient'. The Minister of State, Mr Dempsey, was somewhat sympathetic to this claim and stated in response that the proposal was 'worthy of a separate Bill'.

Unfortunately, there is now a messy compromise in respect of water column and fishing rights within the new EEZ. It would have been preferable to have legislatively combined the fisheries aspect in the water column with the continental shelf aspect in the broader concept of the EEZ regime: yet, as a result,there is no cross-reference to seabed rights continuing to be governed under the continental shelf legislation referred to above. These anomalies suggest the potential merits of the amendment that Mr Broughan had argued for in Select Committee to more clearly define in Irish law the term 'continental shelf'.

Another problem which potentially arises is in connection with the outer limits of the new regime. Sub-section 2 states that these limits are normally two hundred nautical miles from the 'baseline' as defined in section 85. The uncertainties regarding existing Irish straight baselines from which the baseline, territorial sea and contiguous zones must be drawn has 'rebound' effects on the outer limits of Irish off-shore zones, even in cases of more extensive maritime zones. This is another reason why the Act should have legislated on amending the existing straight baseline system.

Equally problematic is the wording in sub-section 3 in respect of the rule which governs delimitations of potentially overlapping EEZs in sea areas less than four hundred nautical miles wide (because of 'proximity of a similar zone of another State'). This is an indirect allusion to the existing two hundred nautical mile overlap of zones between the United Kingdom and Ireland. In respect of past British and Irish two hundred nautical mile fishery zone claims, there has never been an agreed boundary delimitation for fishery purposes between the two States. In fact, since 1977, there has existed in the so-called 'grey zones' a de facto regime relating to the respective areas of overlap of fishery zones pending agreement.[28]

Consequently, the problem arising from the wording of sub-section 3 is that it unilaterally readopts for overlapping EEZ purposes the same self-styled Irish formula of so-called 'equitable equidistance'. This formula has been borrowed verbatim from a 1976 Order (the Maritime Jurisdiction Act (Exclusive Fishery Limits) Order 1976) and has been transposed to refer now to the EEZ. Prior to the advent of an Irish EEZ claim, this matter was not critical because *seabed* jurisdictional matters were, in effect, dealt with separately from water column matters. Now, however, these two jurisdictional rights have been purportedly rolled into a single notional unitary concept in the zone.

The practical effect of this ostensible amalgamation is that Ireland now seems to have 'paper' claims for both seabed and water column purposes within the same maritime boundary in sea areas less than four hundred nautical miles apart with, presumably, the same overlaps in the two hundred nautical mile zones in the North Atlantic and Irish Sea (in narrower sea areas) as previously existed for its two hundred nautical mile exclusive fishery zone (as such) based on the list of published coordinates. This is unfortunate from a continental shelf perspective, because the seabed boundary in such areas was already agreed with the United Kingdom (by treaty in 1988) along a quite different trajectory, and this has been subsequently amended by a protocol and Memorandum of Understanding. Despite the use of the categorical word 'is' in Subsection 3, treaty law does not permit new Irish-decreed delimitation lines to override an internationally agreed maritime boundary *ex-post facto*.[29] A 'hiatus' situation may thus now exist over the outer limits of the two hundred nautical mile water column in such overlapping areas. The 'parent Act', the MJA 1959, is expressly stated to be wholly repealed in Schedule 1 of the current Act, and this includes the revocation of most statutory orders emerging from it, such as those effecting Section 88. This seems to indicate in cases of Irish 'exclusive fishery limits' that the outer EEZ boundary per se is all-dominant in fixing the outer limits of Ireland's two hundred nautical mile fishery zone. However, no new 'outer limits *co-ordinates*' have been 'prescribed' under sub-section 3 as they were for fishery purposes previously. Even if the United Kingdom has not yet claimed a full EEZ, the reference to a 'similar zone' caters for potential overlaps and re-enforces the boundary enigma.

The agreed 'zig-zagged' continental shelf boundary is ill-suited for practical reasons within a conversion, even on an agreed basis, to a combined water column/seabed EEZ boundary.[30] Thus, for EEZ purposes, a new agreed boundary must be mutually agreed upon, as only for de facto fishery purposes, and non-economic seabed and water column-based jurisdictions, can any 'equitable equidistant' line meaningfully operate. In fact, the express retention of a vestigial Irish 'exclusive fishery zone' in

[28] See Symmons, above, n 7, pp 337–339.

[29] The Act's s 4(2) implicitly indicates, however, that the existing Maritime Jurisdiction Act (Fishery Limits) Order of 1976 has been revoked, as have statutory instruments based on a repealed statutory provision listed in the Schedule under s 4(2).

[30] See Symmons, above, n 7, p 339.

section 88 indicates that Irish seabed jurisdiction and water column claims are still separable issues in sea areas of less than four hundred nautical miles. To this extent, then, the newly-claimed zone is *pro tempore,* merely a grandiose fishery zone with other 'non-economic' EEZ elements, such as pollution control included, to an extending indeterminate limit in narrower areas of seas.

Section 88 follows on from section 87 by providing that the exclusive fishery limits of the State are coterminous with its EEZ. The Maritime Jurisdiction (Exclusive Fishery Limits) Order 1976 formerly specified the exclusive fishery zone limits in narrower areas *with co-ordinates*; but this has now been revoked by implication. As noted above, it is unfortunate that the old terminology of 'exclusive fishery zone' has been retained alongside the two hundred nautical mile EEZ regime which now expressly incorporates in the coastal State's jurisdiction 'natural resources, whether living or non-living, of the waters superjacent to the seabed'. This compromise may have been influenced by, among others, the legislative pattern in Ireland of treating sea fisheries as a self-contained area of statutory control.

Section 89 essentially restates section 10 of the 1959 Act in defining the prescriptive jurisdiction of Irish courts for offences committed within the territorial seas or internal waters of the State and treating them as if they were committed in areas completely intra-territorial. While section 90 provides for actual enforcement measures against 'non-nationals', the Minister for Foreign Affairs must confirm by certificate the expediency of such measures for offences committed on non-Irish ships in the Irish territorial sea. For this to apply, a non-national must have been connected with a non-Irish ship. Past problems have arisen in interpreting this provision in a drug interdiction case, *People (DPP) v Van Onzen* (1996), which concerned the certification process. A similar provision in section 36 of the Criminal Justice Act (1994) in relation to drug trafficking in the territorial sea has also caused problems.[31]

Another change in wording is that sub-section 2 now goes beyond exempting sea fisheries prosecutions, formerly the sole exception, from the 'advance consent' requirement. Thus such bureaucratic intervention is now also dispensed with in instances of pollution and dumping at sea, as well as in cases of maritime terrorism under the Maritime Security Act, 2004.[32]

Section 92 restates, in updated fashion, section 13 of the 1959 Act. This has the effect of allowing prescribed copies of charts (in fact Admiralty charts) to be conclusive proof in legal proceedings) of location of relevant baselines or features related such as a low-tide elevation or as to the outer limits of key maritime zones. A MJA 1959 (Charts) Order remains in force and establishes that charts published by the Admiralty, London, shall be the charts prescribed.[33]

Maritime Safety

Section 104 of the Sea-Fisheries and Maritime Jurisdiction Act amends the Maritime Safety Act 2005 in various ways. Most relevant to public international law are

[31] Symmons, above, n 7, at pp 115, 116.

[32] See the annotation in ICLSA R 99, October 2005, 29-01 at 29-12, noting, strangely, that drug trafficking legislation of 2004 did not itself dispense with this formality.

[33] There was an unsuccessful challenge to the Order in *People (DPP) v Van Onzen*. See Symmons, above, n 7, p 44.

paragraphs (d) and (e). Paragraph (d), which was a very late amendment to the draft of the Act, expressly provides, by way of clarification, for Ministerial direction concerning search and rescue and recovery operations to be conducted safely, including establishing temporary exclusion zones around the area of maritime casualties. In this, it supplements the Merchant Shipping (Investigation of Casualties) Act 2000, which makes similar provision in cases of marine casualties. It seems to have been prompted by representations made over the exclusion zone declaration in the '*Rising Sun*' fishing boat tragedy of November 2005.[34]

Paragraph (e) clarifies the prohibition on unlawfully interfering with access to or from ports and harbours in the State and the power to direct vessels to move in the interests of safety at sea. It also applies to foreign vessels transiting Irish waters, despite the fact that such vessels would have the right of innocent passage in the law of the sea.

Registration of Irish Ships/Fishing Boats

Section 97 of the Sea-Fisheries and Maritime Jurisdiction Act is a full, up-to-date provision on sea fishing boat registration. The three provisions in section 100 each amend the Mercantile Marine Act 1955, which provides for registration of Irish shipping. This was designed to reduce unnecessary bureaucracy by exempting from compulsory registration as a ship under the 1955 Act smaller sea fishing boats. These matters have been the responsibility of the Minister for Transport since January 2006.

Although attempts were made to incorporate the provisions of the UNCLOS regarding restrictions on re-flagging to situations where there is no genuine connection between the ship and the State into Irish law, this was unsuccessful. It may be noted more generally on the matter of 're-flagging' that in 2005 Irish Ferries reportedly tried initially to re-register their passenger ferry, the *MV Normandy*, under the flag of the Bahamas. This was in an apparent bid to remove the employment obligations of Irish and EU law. When the company then opted for registration in Cyprus, an EU Member, the Irish Government conceded that it could not stop the company from removing its vessels from the Irish registry under EU law. However, an official Irish spokesman added that the company had been asked to prove that it 'actually intended to operate from Cyprus' and that this was not just a 'paper registration'. [35]

MARINE POLLUTION

A major piece of legislation on marine pollution emerged as the Sea Pollution (Miscellaneous Provisions) Act (No 29 of 2006), which was signed into force on 31 October 2006. The purpose of this legislation was essentially to give effect in Ireland to a number of treaties which had been agreed to under the auspices of the International Maritime Organization relating to the protection of the marine environment,[36] namely:

[34] 29 SCMNR No 19, col 786.
[35] See *Irish Times*, 29 November 2006.
[36] See 587 *Dail Debates,* col 32; 174 *Seanad Debates,* col 546.

(i) The Protocol to the International Convention on Oil Pollution, Preparedness, Response and Co-Operation (OPRC) 2000 (see Part 3, sections 19–35). The Sea Pollution (Amendment) Act, 1999, implementing OPRC.
(ii) The International Convention on the Control of Harmful Anti-Fouling Systems 2001 (see Part 3, sections 34 and 37).
(iii) Annex VI (Regulations for Prevention of Air Pollution by Ships) as added to the International Convention on the Prevention of Pollution from Ships (1973/1978) in 1997 (see also Part 3, sections 34 and 37).
(iv) The International Convention on Civil Liability for Bunker Oil Pollution Damage 2001 (see Part 2, section 7). This complements past Irish legislation on civil liability and compensation for pollution damage by oil (in general) and noxious as well as hazardous substances at sea under the Sea Pollution (Hazardous Substances) (Compensation) Act 2005. It does this by including 'bunker oil', defined as 'any hydrocarbon mineral oil, including lubricating oil, used or intended to be used for the operation or propulsion of the ship, and any residues of such oil', in the compensable category.
(v) The International Convention for the Control and Management of Ship's Ballast Water and Sediments 2004 (see Part 3, section 34).

In a more limited manner, section 103 of the Sea-Fisheries and Maritime Jurisdiction Act amends the Dumping at Sea Act 1996. In effect, the addition of the EEZ reference in paragraph (a)(2)(III) of the 1996 Act is cosmetic, as that Act already applies in the two hundred nautical mile zone, as it did also to inland waters and the territorial sea. In the latter instances, this section tidies up loose drafting in the 1996 Act. In essence, this section adds improved definitions of these zonal areas; they had formerly been lumped together under the inapt generic title of 'territorial seas of the State' in section 1 of the 1996 Act.[37]

Apart from enacted legislation, there were other developments and incidents in the sphere of marine pollution in 2006 in Ireland. In February 2006, for example, a Dutch ship was impounded in Estonian waters on suspicion of being destined to dump European toxic waste in the Ivory Coast. The European Environment Commissioner reportedly wrote in this context to the Irish Government to seek immediate Irish ratification of the amendment to the Basel Agreement on dumping toxic wastes in developing countries. An Irish spokesman from the Department of the Environment was quoted as saying that Ireland did not have a date for ratification but that EU regulations on the issue were in force domestically.

BEYOND LEGISLATION

The passage of ships carrying nuclear materials off the Irish coast and marine pollution from Sellafield in Great Britain continued to cause problems for Ireland. In mid-November 2006, the Minister for the Environment, Mr Roche, announced that the Irish Coast Guard would be monitoring a shipment of mixed oxide nuclear fuel passing through the Irish Sea from Sellafield and that the Irish Government had conveyed its concerns relating to safety, security and environmental risk to the United Kingdom over such shipments. He confirmed that the Irish Government had been assured through its voluntary advance notification arrangements with the United

[37] For a critical comment on the old terminology, see Symmons, above, n 7, pp 69–70.

Kingdom that the fuel shipment would not enter 'Irish territorial waters' and that the shipment was 'governed by a stringent system of regulation established in line with internationally-agreed standards and recommendations'.[38]

Last, but most importantly, the end of 2005 saw the EU Commission challenge Ireland over its decision to bypass the European Court of Justice (ECJ) in its campaign to close the Sellafield nuclear plant, in the so-called 'MOX' case, by alleging various breaches by the United Kingdom of the UNCLOS relating to marine pollution. The International Tribunal for the Law of the Sea (ITLOS) applying the provisions of the UNCLOS had ordered several interim measures of protection in Ireland's favour. The EU Commission's subsequent intervention, arguing that environmental protection is a shared competence in EU law and, thus, that EU fora should take precedence in resolving such disputes, put other treaty-based proceedings before the ITLOS on hold. In May 2006, the Commission duly ruled that Ireland should have taken its case in a European forum rather than before an international one. As an Irish official commentator said at the time, the ECJ has, in consequence, enforcement powers over a wide range of international agreements on environmental law issues which Ireland cannot enforce before the ITLOS. This may mean that Ireland's past primary reliance on the marine pollution provisions of the UNCLOS, which are more marine-specific than those in EU law, may be forfeited in further litigation because of the precedence of EU law on environmental matters.[39]

[38] See *Irish Times,* 15 *Irish Times*, 15 November 2006.

[39] See G Biehler in *Irish Times*, 31 May 2006.

Human Rights—2006

Siobhán Mullally, Fiona De Londras, Darren O'Donovan, and Liam Thornton

CENTRE FOR CRIMINAL JUSTICE AND HUMAN RIGHTS, FACULTY OF LAW, UNIVERSITY COLLEGE CORK

2006 saw a significant number of changes to the criminal law in Ireland with human rights law and a changing system of criminal justice increasingly coming into conflict. These changes culminated with the appointment, during 2006, of a Criminal Law Review Group, mandated to assess whether a 'rebalancing' of rights was needed as between victim and accused in the Irish legal system. Much of the 'rebalancing' agenda had already borne fruit in legislative changes introduced throughout the year.

The Criminal Law (Insanity) Act 2006 reforms the law on criminal insanity, fitness to be tried and related issues, with the aim of bringing Irish law and practice into line with the jurisprudence of the European Court of Human Rights. The Criminal Law (Sexual Offences) Act 2006 provides a replacement provision for section 1(1) of the Criminal Law (Amendment) Act 1935 (Defilement of girl under 15 years of age), which was struck down by the Supreme Court in the *CC* case. In that case, the Supreme Court had concluded that the legislation did not provide a person charged with an offence under that provision with a defence of honest belief as to the age of the girl. The Criminal Law (Sexual Offences) Act 2006 enacts, in gender neutral terms, a replacement provision for the subsection struck down by the Supreme Court, and allows for a defence of *honest belief* that the child against whom the offence was alleged to have been committed had attained 15 years of age. The Criminal Justice Act 2006 contains a comprehensive package of measures designed primarily to strengthen the powers of law enforcement bodies. The main purpose of the Act was to improve the efficiency with which criminal offences are investigated and prosecuted. This legislation also introduced a new system of anti-social behaviour orders, leading to objections, particularly in light of the experience of the operation of anti-social behaviour orders in the United Kingdom under its Crime and Disorder Act 1998. The Irish Human Rights Commission, expressing apprehension at the introduction of such orders in Ireland, noted that the Council of Europe Commissioner for Human Rights had expressed concern at the high level of use of these orders in the United Kingdom.[1]

The enactment of the International Criminal Court Act 2006 gives effect to the Rome Statute of the International Criminal Court (ICC), signed by Ireland in July 1998. Because submission to the jurisdiction of the International Criminal Court entailed a partial transfer to the Court of the sovereign power of the State to administer criminal justice, it was necessary to amend the Irish Constitution prior to

[1] See report of the Commissioner for Human Rights on his visit to the United Kingdom 4 to 12 November 2004, Council of Europe document CommDH(2005) 6 of 8 June 2005 at p 36. For the *CC* Case see [2006] IESC 33 (23 May 2006).

ratification of the Rome Statute. The twenty-third amendment of the Constitution inserted Article 29.9, providing that the State may ratify the Rome Statute. The ICC Act 2006 creates domestic offences and associated penalties for ICC crimes of genocide, crimes against humanity and war crimes, repealing the Genocide Convention Act 1973. It enables assistance to be given to the ICC by permitting the arrest and surrender of persons requested. It also provides for freezing of assets and enforcement of orders for fines and other forms of assistance in the investigation of ICC offences.

The International Criminal Court Act was the subject of much lobbying by Amnesty International Ireland, in particular, concerning the non-retroactivity of the legislation and the implications for domestic prosecutions. The Act provides that proceedings cannot be taken in relation to conduct constituting an 'ICC offence' which occurred before the passing of this Act,[2] with the exception of offences occurring under the Genocide Act 1973.[3] This position raises broader questions as to the role of customary international law in domestic law and the difficulties that have arisen in attempting to invoke custom or general principles in domestic proceedings in the past.[4] The strict dualist position that has been adopted by the Irish courts[5] and the 'externalising' of custom and general principles is unlikely to provide good ground for the exercise of universal jurisdiction.

In July 2006 the Government published a Scheme for the Criminal Justice (Trafficking in Persons and Sexual Offences) Bill. The Bill was intended to provide a legislative framework to facilitate ratification of the UN Protocol to Prevent Suppress and Punish Trafficking (the Palermo Protocol), implementation of the EU Framework Decision on Combating Trafficking in Human Beings (overdue for implementation since 31 December 2004), and ratification of the 2005 Council of Europe Convention Against Trafficking. Ireland has been identified in the recent US State Department Report on *Trafficking in Persons* as a country both of transit and destination for traffickers. The Scheme of the Bill provides for criminalisation of the offence of trafficking. Its focus, however, is on law enforcement rather than on the protection of victims of trafficking. As such, measures such as the provision of residence permits, rights of access to legal aid, voluntary repatriation, are not provided for. The publication of the Scheme follows on from the Report of the Department of Justice, Equality and Law Reform and *An Garda Siochana* (national police force) in April 2006, which recommended that protections for victims of trafficking be provided for in the proposed Immigration and Residence Bill. The Scheme for the Immigration, Residence and Protection Bill, published in October 2006, however, does not include any provisions on trafficking.

[2] Section 9(4)

[3] Section 7(4)

[4] See Joe Noonan 'Case Report—*DPP v Clancy et al*' this volume of the *Irish Yearbook of International Law*, p 337; See also L Thornton *Horgan v An Taoiseach Case Report*, OUP International Law in Domestic Courts.

[5] *In Re O'Láighleis* [1960] IR 93; *Government of Canada v Employment Appeals Tribunal* [1992] IR 484; *The MV 'Toledo' ACT Shipping (PTE) Ltd v Minister for the Marine, Ireland and the Attorney General* [1995] 2 ILRM 30; *Kavanagh v Governor of Mountjoy Prison, the Special Criminal Court, the DPP the Minister for Justice, Equality and Law Reform and the Att Gen.* 29th, [2001] IESC 11 (1st March, 2001); *Horgan v An Taoiseach & Ors* [2003] IEHC 64 (28 April 2003); *Eoin Dubsky v Govt of Ireland, The Minister for Foreign Affairs et al* [2005] IEHC 442

MIGRATION LAW

Legislation

Within the legislative field, Ireland transposed two significant E.U. directives. The transposition of the Qualification Directive[6] by means of the Eligibility for Protection Regulations[7] made provision for the granting of subsidiary status to third country nationals who, although failing to qualify as refugees as per section 2 of the Refugee Act 1996 (as amended), could request the Minister for Justice, Equality and Law Reform to make a finding of entitlement to subsidiary protection. An individual is entitled to subsidiary protection where there is a risk of 'serious harm' which can consist of the death penalty or execution; torture or inhuman or degrading treatment or punishment, or a serious and individual threat to an individual's life or person by reason of indiscriminate violence in situations of international or internal conflict.[8] The Eligibility for Protection Regulations introduced a number of factors that those examining claims for refugee (or subsequently subsidiary) status must take account of, including, facts and circumstances in the country of origin, as well as providing definitions of actors of persecution and serious harm, actors of protection, acts of persecution and outlining in detail the precise reasons for persecution,[9] so as to be eligible for protection as either a refugee or subsidiary status. Those entitled to subsidiary status were granted the same social rights as refugees, although residence permits to those with subsidiary status were to be initially granted for a three year period.[10] The Irish Government did not transpose Qualification Directive measures[11] which could have differentiated certain social rights entitlements between those with refugee status and those with subsidiary status.[12] Family reunification of those eligible for subsidiary status[13] is on par with those entitled to refugee status.[14] The Regulations also outline the reasons for failing to grant, renew, revoke or exclude those from refugee and subsidiary status incorporating some of the provisions on these issues found within the Qualification Directive.[15]

[6] Council Directive 2004/83/EC of 29 April 2004 on the minimum standards for the qualification and status of third country nationals or stateless persons as regards refugees or persons who otherwise need international protection and the content of the protection granted.

[7] SI 2006/518 European Communities (Eligibility for Protection) Regulations 2006.

[8] Article 15 of the Qualification Directive as transposed by reg 2 of the Eligibility for Protection Regulations.

[9] See Articles 4(3), 6, 7, 9 and 10 of the Qualification Directive as transposed by reg 10 of the Eligibility for Protection Regulations.

[10] Regulation 17(1) of the Eligibility for Protection Regulations.

[11] Article 24(2) wherein an individual with subsidiary status would have been entitled to a one-year and renewable residence permit; Art 25(2) which would have restricted the right of an individual with subsidiary status from being granted a travel document but for 'serious humanitarian reasons'; Art 28(3) which allows a Member State to limit the social assistance to 'core benefits' provided under the same eligibility conditions as nationals; Art 29(2) wherein health care can be limited to 'core benefits' provided under the same eligibility conditions as nationals and Art 33(2) where Member State's have an option to extend access to integration facilities to those with subsidiary protection.

[12] Regulation 18(1) and reg 19 of the Eligibility for Protection Regulations.

[13] Regulation 16 of the Eligibility for Protection Regulations.

[14] Section 18 of the Refugee Act 1996 (as amended).

[15] Articles 11, 12, 14, 16, 17 and 19 of the Qualification Directive as transposed by regs 11, 12, 13 and 14 of the Eligibility for Protection Regulations.

The second important statutory transposition of EU law was in the immigration field in relation to the rights of EU citizens and their families to reside and move freely throughout the Union.[16] The transposition of this Directive by the Free Movement of Persons Regulations[17] made significant improvements in guaranteeing the rights of spouses and family members of Union citizens, as well as setting out clearly the right of Union citizens to move freely and reside within the Irish State. This Directive sets out inter alia the right of entry,[18] the right of both Union citizens and non-Union family member(s) to reside for varying periods and the conditions attached there to, including provisions on entitlement to remain in the State, registration of non-Union citizen family members, retention of right to residence by a non-Union citizen or due to death or departure or divorce or annulment[19] grounds for removal from the State, including restrictions that can be applied on the grounds of public policy, public security or public health.[20]

Scheme for the Immigration Residence and Protection Bill

This Bill, published in October 2006, proposes a 'radical' overhaul, consolidating, but also significantly adding to existing legislation in this field. Notable omissions from the Scheme include human trafficking and family reunification for migrant workers on short-term residence permits. The Scheme proposes stringent restrictions on the right to marry for foreign nationals, raising questions as to compliance, not only with the constitutional provisions on the family, but also with the European Convention on Human Rights (ECHR) and other human rights treaties. As the Irish Human Rights Commission has noted, a 'pressing social need' is not detailed to support the imposition of such restrictions, as required by article 12 ECHR. Safe country practices, following on from developments at EU level, are greatly expanded and include provision for the so-called 'super-safe' countries. Combined with stringent time limits and shifts in the burden of proof, such practices will pose significant obstacles to accessing the asylum process and, as commentators have noted, may increase the risk of *refoulement*. The Scheme includes a number of welcome proposals, such as the introduction of long-term residence permits and a legislative framework for subsidiary protection. The protections provided for separated children remain weak, however, and, in particular, do not provide for the appointment of a *guardian ad litem.* The Irish Refugee Council published a research report on Separated Children/Unaccompanied minors, seeking asylum in Ireland. Drawing on the General Comment No 6 (2005) on the Treatment of Unaccompanied and Separated Children, the Report highlights the failings of the current asylum process in Ireland, and the risks posed by such failings to separated children. Those failings are not addressed in the Scheme.

[16] Directive 2004/38/EC of the European Parliament and of the Council of 29 April 2004 on the rights of citizens to move and reside freely within the territory of the Member States amending Regulation (EEC) No 1612/68 and repealing Directives 64/221/EEC, 68/360/EEC, 73/148/EEC, 75/35/EEC, 90/360/EEC, 90/365/EEC and 93/96/EEC.

[17] SI 2006/226 European Communities (Free Movement of Persons) Regulations 2006.

[18] Article 5(1) and Art 5(2) of the Directive; reg 4(1) and reg 4(2) of the Free Movement of Persons Regulations.

[19] See Arts 6 and 7, 9, 12 and 13 of the Directive; reg 10 of the Free Movement of Persons Regulations.

[20] Article 27 to Art 33 of the Directive; regs 20 to 23 of the Free Movement of Persons Regulations.

Jurisprudence

Irish Courts' jurisprudence on the issues surrounding asylum has markedly grown, as has reference to international legal norms which effect the interaction of asylum law and human rights law. The interaction between Irish constitutional provisions and the ECHR has somewhat added to protection of the rights of asylum seekers within the Irish Republic. The case of *Bode and Others*[21] revolved around the right of the non-national applicants to remain in Ireland to ensure their citizen children had a right to their care, company and support. An administrative scheme had been established by the Department of Justice, Equality and Law Reform. The IBC/05 Scheme laid out the possibility for non-national parents, who did not have a right to reside within the State, to apply to the Department of Justice, to have their case for residency with their citizen child within the Republic of Ireland considered.[22] All the applicants within the eight cases had had their IBC/05 applications refused. The applicants argued that since this scheme gave no consideration to the rights of the Irish citizen child it was contrary to the rights of the citizen child under Article 40.3[23] and 41[24] of the Irish Constitution, *Bunreacht na hEireann* and, under Article 8, the right to family life, and Article 14 (in conjunction with Article 8), enjoyment of Convention rights without discrimination under the *European Convention on Human Rights and Fundamental Freedoms* (ECHR).[25]

Ms Justice Finlay Geoghegan accepted the constitutional argument that the IBC/05 Scheme failed 'in so far as is practicable' to defend and vindicate the personal rights of the citizen child to live in the State, be reared and educated with due regard for his/her welfare. In relation to the ECHR grounds, without needing to examine the Article 14 argument, the Court found, in relation to Article 8 and the protection of the family, that while there was no interference with the ability of the family to form relationships, each citizen child who lived in the State since his/her birth had a right to a private life, including the right to form and develop relationships as found by the European court in *Sisojiva and Others v Latvia.*[26] The child's exercise of rights is dependent on the presence of parents in the State, and on the parents' ability to provide for their children by inter alia working and providing a stable environment wherein to live so that the citizen child may develop. Ms Justice Finlay Geoghegan found a positive obligation under Article 8 in light of *Knutzer v Germany*[27] meaning that the parent of the citizen

[21] *Bode v Minister for Justice, Equality and Law Reform* [2006] IEHC 341 (14 November 2006) is the principle judgment in this series of seven other co-joined proceedings on the same substantive issues.

[22] This scheme arose as a result of the judgement in *Lobe and Osayende v Minister for Justice, Equality and Law Reform* [2003] 1 IR 1 which held that non-national parents do not have an automatic entitlement to remain in the Republic of Ireland with their Irish citizen child and non-national parents could be subject to deportations. As a result of this the Department of Justice set up the IBC/05 Scheme to deal with persons who had given birth to Irish citizen children. A general policy was adopted of granting those persons permission to remain in the State provided that they fulfilled certain criteria. All the applicants in these proceedings were deemed not to have fulfilled some of the criteria. In all there were 17,917 applications under the IBC/05 Scheme with 16,693 requests for residence granted and 1,119 refusals.

[23] This article outlines the duty of the State to respect, and as far as practicable, defend and vindicate, the personal rights of its citizens.

[24] This article sets out the 'inalienable and imprescriptable' rights accorded to the marital family.

[25] Ireland incorporated the ECHR by virtue of the European Convention on Human Rights Act 2003. Of particular significance to this case was s 3 of the 2003 Act which obliges all organs of State to perform its functions in a manner compatible with the ECHR.

[26] Application No 60654/00 *Sisojiva and Others v Latvia* (European Court of Human Rights, 16 June 2005), para 102.

[27] *Knutzer v Germany* (2002) 35 EHRR 653 at para 62.

child has a right to remain in the State and that a fair balance must be struck between the needs of the individual child and the community. Any decision to refuse a parent(s) residency without considering the right to the private life of a child violated Article 8(1). The State did argue that this was within its margin of appreciation under Article 8(2). The Court found that the Minister for Justice, Equality and Law Reform had acted contrary to the State's obligations under the ECHR by not examining the right to private life of the child citizen.

The deportation of individuals continued to raise questions of compatibility with European human rights law. In the case of *Cosma*,[28] the applicant claimed to be suicidal, and counsel argued that were a deportation order to be enforced and proceeded with, this would result in a violation of Article 3 and Article 8 of the Convention. The Court found that since the deportation order was made prior to the commencement of the ECHR Act 2003, the Article 3 and Article 8 jurisprudence could only be of a persuasive authority.[29] In relation to Article 3, Mr Justice Hanna examined both the *D*[30] case and the *Soering*[31] case, and found that the principles in these cases greatly contrasted with the situation of the applicant. The Court was referred to a British House of Lords case of *Razgar*[32] where the applicant was to be returned to Germany, which was the first safe country he reached. The House of Lords, in examining Article 8, noted that the ability to function socially and to preserve mental stability was a precondition to the effective enjoyment of ones human rights. In this case, Hanna J noted the circumstances of that particular case wherein the Secretary of State had not considered Mr Ragzar's asylum claim as he deemed it to be manifestly unfounded, and compared it to the situation of Ms Cosma, who had her full procedural rights respected with a process for determining both her asylum and leave to remain claims. Mr. Justice Hanna was not satisfied that the applicant established a 'real and substantial risk' of self-harm and found the medical reports to be far short of 'objective' diagnosis of her condition. None of the relevant ECHR related cases, Hanna J noted, deal with a bare threat of suicide in response to deportation; in any case, the applicant had not established that the deportation alone would avert threatened suicide.

The Irish courts have once again reasserted the principle that there is an obligation to consider refugee claims from asylum seeking children, where their parent/guardian 'as primary protector of the best interests of the child' requests such separate determination of claims.[33] The legal basis for such a decision is based on the Refugee Act 1996 in light of Article 12 (on measures to combat the illicit transfer and non-return of children abroad) and Article 22 (on the rights of asylum seeking children) of the United Nations Convention on the Rights of the Child (CRC).[34] With regard to procedures within the refugee determination process, the Irish High Court has found

[28] *Cosma v The Minister for Justice, Equality and Law Reform* [2006] IEHC 36 (15 February 2006).

[29] The issue of retrospective application was decided in *Dublin City Council v Fennell* [2005] 2 ILRM 288, where the Supreme Court found that the ECHR Act 2003, which incorporated the ECHR into Irish law, could not have a retrospective effect on actions taken or decisions made by organs of the State.

[30] *D v The United Kingdom* (1997) 24 EHRR 423.

[31] *Soering v. The United Kingdom* [1989] ECHR 14.

[32] *R(Ragzar) v Secretary of State for the Home Department* [2003] EWCA Civ 840.

[33] *Dada & Ors v Minister for Justice, Equality and Law Reform and Ors* [2006] IEHC 166 (31 January 2006).

[34] [2006] IEHC 166, (31 January 2006), per MacMenamin J.

that there is no right, either under the Constitution, or the ECHR Act 2003 for an applicant to demand that his/her interview with the status determination bodies be audio or visually recorded.[35]

FAMILY LAW

While asylum and migration cases had seen some developments from a human rights law perspective in 2006, international human rights treaties played a relatively minor role in other areas of Irish jurisprudence in 2006. In the light of cases such as *In re O'Laighléis*[36] and *Kavanagh v Governor of Mountjoy Prison*[37] in which the Irish Supreme Court clearly held that unincorporated international treaties were of merely persuasive authority, this position is perhaps unsurprising.[38] For example, the UN Convention on the Rights of the Child was certainly ripe for consideration in two adoption-related decisions that arose in 2006,[39] but was practically ignored in both. In the most prominent of these cases—*N & Another v Health Services Executive & Another*[40] (also known as 'the Baby Ann Case')—only McGuinness J mentioned the UN Convention on the Rights of the Child in her judgment and criticised the lack of individual legal representation for the child on its basis. In the case of *CC v Ireland & Others*,[41] the Supreme Court utilised the Canadian Charter of Fundamental Rights and resulting case law[42] in finding that the strict liability offence of statutory rape was contrary to personal rights provisions and the presumption of innocence under the Irish Constitution,[43] but did not make use of the provisions of international human rights treaties to which Ireland is a party.

MILITARY LAW

Addressing the often thorny question of human rights in the context of military justice, the Defence (Amendment) (No 2) Bill 2006 focuses in particular on the disciplinary provisions of Part V of the Defence Acts and seeks to amend and update its Code of Discipline having regard to prevailing human rights norms. The Bill makes significant structural and procedural changes to military justice, providing for the summary disposal of disciplinary charges; the establishment and jurisdiction of the summary court-martial; the appointment of the Court-Martial Administrator, the

[35] *Hakizmana v Minister for Justice, Equality and Law Reform & Ors* [2006] IEHC 355 (14 November 2006), per Feeney J.

[36] [1960] IR 93.

[37] [2002] 3 IR 97.

[38] See Art 29.6, *Bunreacht na hÉireann* ('Constitution of Ireland') requiring treaties to be incorporated in order for them to domestic effect in Ireland.

[39] *Attorney General v Dowse and another; Dowse and another v Adoption Board and another* [2006] I.E.H.C. 65—applicants seeking *in camera* hearing for the removal of an adoption from the foreign adoptions register following their highly-publicised decision to no longer parent the child; *N & Another v Health Services Executive & Another*[2006] IESC 60—concerning the decision of biological parents to revoke consent to adoption when the child was settled with the prospective adopters and had been resident with them for approximately two years.

[40] *Ibid.*

[41] [2006] IESC 33.

[42] *Hess and Nguyen v The Queen* [1990] 2 SCR 906.

[43] Arts 38.1, 40.3.1, 40.3.2 and 40.4 of the Irish Constitution.

Director of Military Prosecutions and a military judge. The Bill establishes the membership of a court-martial board and provides for the award and execution of punishments by courts-martial.

GENDER AND LAW

The Consortium on Gender Based Violence, a consortium of Irish human rights, humanitarian and development agencies, Irish Aid and Government agencies, published a *Guidance Note on Institutionalising Gender Based Violence Prevention and Response within Organisations.* This follows on from the recommendations published in a 2005 Report on *Gender Based Violence: A Failure to Protect, a Challenge to Action.* The Consortium is aimed at developing capacity on GBV prevention and response within Irish development agencies, both internally and within field work, and reflects a priority commitment in the *White Paper on Irish Aid* to address GBV as a human rights concern.

AMICI CURIAE

Amici Curiae and third party intervenors have played important roles in bringing international human rights law arguments into domestic legal proceedings. In Ireland, jurisprudence on the role of such intervenors and on *amici curiae* is relatively underdeveloped. In the *Doherty v South Dublin County Council* case, the Supreme Court considered the scope of the statutory power of the Equality Authority[44] to act as amicus curiae.[45] The Equality Authority sought to provide assistance to the court regarding the proper interpretation of the EU Race Directive[46] arguing that the issues raised had broad implications for the Travelling Community in Ireland. At first instance Quirke J found that the Equality Authority would be able to furnish assistance to the court at the direction of the Trial Judge.[47]

On appeal to the Supreme Court, the State reiterated its opposition to the granting of such a role, noting that the Equality Authority was expressly entitled to intervene in proceedings in a number of specified cases which, the State submitted, implied that the *Oireachtas* (the national parliament) had not intended to grant a broad power. This position was supported by the contrasting manner in which the Human Rights Commission Act 2000 conferred express power on the Commission to act as amicus curiae. The Supreme Court examined the more general provisions concerning the role of the Authority in the Equal Status Acts and the Equality Act 2004. Fennelly J delivering the majority verdict for the Court,[48] found that the power to act as an amicus curiae was included under the general powers of the Equality Authority, which tasked

[44] The Equality Authority is a statutory body.

[45] *Doherty v South Dublin County Council and Others (Equality Authority, Notice Party)*, Supreme Court [2006] IESC 57 (Hearing Date 31 October 2006).

[46] Council Directive 2000/43/EC of 29 June 2000 implementing the principle of equal treatment between persons irrespective of racial or ethnic origin.

[47] Ex tempore judgment of 22 May 2006.

[48] Macken J dissented, expressing concern that the role which the Equality Authority would play in the proceedings would an oppositional one, unsuited to a first instance consideration of the issues. He found that a role as amicus curiae was not reasonably incidental to any of the powers granted by the legislation.

it to 'work towards the elimination of prohibited conduct'.[49] However, he did describe it as a power of relatively modest proportions, likely to be exercised 'sparingly'[50] and contingent on the determination by the trial judge that the Equality Authority could provide assistance to the Court.

THE EUROPEAN CONVENTION ON HUMAN RIGHTS

In the main, the European Convention on Human Rights was the predominant international human rights treaty in operation in the Irish courts and, even then, its impact was relatively muted given its sub-constitutional incorporation by the European Convention on Human Rights Act 2003.[51] The case law relating to the Convention and, indeed, the ECHR Act 2003 tended to focus on two matters—(a) retroactive application of the ECHR Act 2003, and (b) the relationship between the Convention and the Constitution. In addition, the High Court did decide one significant case on the role of Convention considerations in extradition proceedings[52] and considered the Convention's role in determining the requirements of due process.[53]

Retroactive Application

Since its incorporation in 2003, the scope of the European Convention on Human Rights has been controversial. In *Dublin County Council v Fennell*[54] the Supreme Court had already held that the interpretive obligations contained in the ECHR Act 2003 did not apply to cases concerning matters that arose prior to 31 December 2003 (ie prior to incorporation), however the matter of the weight to be given to decisions of the Strasbourg Court relating to matters arising prior to that date had long been contentious.

Earlier cases relying on Convention arguments had resulted in the Irish courts rejecting the significance of those decisions to their deliberations. In *Norris v Attorney General*,[55] for example, the Supreme Court refused to follow *Dudgeon v United Kingdom*[56] notwithstanding its clear appositeness as both cases comprised challenges to the same piece of legislation (ie sections 61 and 62 of the Offences against the Person Act 1861). This can be contrasted with the later decision of the Supreme Court in *Society for the Protection of Unborn Children v Grogan (No 5)*[57] in which Keane J (as he then was) relied to a considerable degree on the Strasbourg court's decision in *Open Door Counselling v Ireland*[58] in his dissent. This situation of uncertainty as to the weighting to be given to Convention jurisprudence relative to matters arising prior to incorporation was not, as already mentioned, resolved by the *Fennell* decision.

49 Equal Status Act, 2004, s 39(a).
50 *Ibid.*
51 For more on the incorporation of the European Convention on Human Rights see generally Kilkelly (ed), *The ECHR and Irish Law*, (Bristol, Jordan, 2004).
52 *Attorney General v Russell* [2006] IEHC 164.
53 *Crowley v Roche Products Ltd & Others* [2006] IEHC 6.
54 [2005] 1 IR 604.
55 [1984] IR 36.
56 [1981] 4 EHRR 149.
57 [1998] 4 IR 343.
58 [1993] 15 EHRR 244

While the Court of Criminal Appeal did not completely resolve this matter in *People (DPP) v Matthews*,[59] it did shed some light on the current judicial approach to the question. The case concerned a challenge by Matthews to the use of anonymous statements by the Prosecution in the course of a trial by the Special Criminal Court. According to Matthews this practice undermined his right to a fair trial under Article 6, ECHR as the witnesses could not be cross-examined. The events that formed the basis of the prosecution in this case had taken place in June 2003—some six months before the introduction of the ECHR Act—and the Court therefore found that Convention case law was not binding in its considerations. Importantly, however, the Court went on to hold that even where the matters at issue had arisen prior to incorporation, the Convention case law ought to be given substantial weight in recognition of its importance.

Relationship between the ECHR and the Constitution

Section 2 of the European Convention on Human Rights Act 2003 imposes an interpretive obligation on the Irish courts *viz*:

> (1) In interpreting and applying any statutory provision or rule of law, a court shall, in so far as is possible, subject to the rules of law relating to such interpretation and application, do so in a manner compatible with the State's obligations under the Convention provisions.
>
> (2) This section applies to any statutory provision or rule of law in force immediately before the passing of this Act or any such provision coming into force thereafter.

Since its promulgation in 2003, however, section 2(1) has given rise to some difficulties, particularly in terms of the order of arguments before domestic courts. Because the Convention operates on a sub-constitutional level there are some uncertainties as to whether Convention arguments should be made before constitutional arguments, or whether they are to be set to one side and made only when constitutional arguments have been dispensed with and have not, of themselves, resolved the issues before the Court.

The case law from the High Court shows two distinctive approaches to this question. In *Carmody v Minister for Justice, Equality and Law Reform*[60] Laffoy J held that arguments based on the Convention ought to be heard before arguments based on the Constitution as a result of the doctrine of constitutional avoidance.[61] In contrast, O'Neill J in *Law Society of Ireland v Competition Authority*[62] held that constitutional matters ought to be considered before Convention arguments, which would then only be reached if constitutional argument did not settle the matter.

2006 saw the Supreme Court reject an opportunity to indicate a preference for either approach to this issue. In *Ward v Governor of Portlaoise Prison*[63] the applicant argued

[59] [2006] IE CCA 103.

[60] [2005] 2 ILRM 1.

[61] This doctrine requires judicial restraint in considering constitutional matters only where the issue at hand could not be resolved by reference to other sources of law. The doctrine was espoused by Finlay CJ in *Murphy v Roche* [1987] IR 106. For a critical discussion of Laffoy J's approach in this case see Hogan, 'The Value of Declarations of Incompatibility and the Rule of Avoidance' (2006) *Dublin University Law Journal* 408.

[62] [2005] IEHC 455.

[63] [2006] IESC 39.

that the High Court's refusal to hear arguments on the basis of the Convention deprived him of his right to a fair hearing. While this case did not deal directly with the *Carmody/Law Society* controversy, a decision that one had a right to make Convention arguments might well have indicated an unwillingness to relegate Convention-based argumentation to the extent suggested by *Law Society*. The Supreme Court, however, did not rule on this question and instead sent the case back to the High Court for reconsideration.[64]

There is also some question as to the relationship between the Convention and Constitution in terms of defining the scope of Constitutional rights. The incorporation of the Convention certainly created an opportunity for the substance of constitutional rights in Ireland to be expanded in certain cases in order to take into account relevant ECHR jurisprudence. However, as O'Connell et. al. noted in their 2006 study *ECHR Act 2003: A Preliminary Assessment of Impact* the Convention has not, thus far, played such a role.[65] This is reflected by the 2006 High Court decision in *Irish Municipal Public and Civil Trade Union v Ryanair Ltd.*[66]

This case concerned a claim by the applicant trade union that its members' right to association was violated by Ryanair's policy of not engaging in collective bargaining. Ryanair, on the other hand, claimed that the right to association was not infringed as it was prepared to listen to, although not negotiate with, the trade union and that this did not in any way violate its employees' right to association. The competing claims essentially focused on whether the right to association as contained in Article 40.6, *Bunreacht na hÉireann* could be interpreted as including a 'protection against an employer offering financial inducements to its employees and threatening to impose penalties upon such employees, or both, with the object or effect of inducing the employees to refrain from carrying on collective bargaining through a trade union' on the basis of the European Court of Human Right's decision on the scope of Article 11, ECHR in *Wilson v United Kingdom.*[67] This claim formed part of a wide matrix of litigation between these two parties based substantively in the Labour Court,[68] and as a result the High Court declined to decide the matter of the appropriate relationship between the Convention and Constitution:

> The instant case certainly involves the investigation of questions of general importance in the context of recent changes in domestic law, which raise issues as to the impact of the State's international obligations on its domestic law. Given that context it is impossible to conclude that the plaintiffs' claim must fail. Apart from that, and notwithstanding the comprehensiveness and thoroughness of the submissions made on behalf of the parties, It is

[64] The case was decided in January 2007 and, having considered constitutional arguments relating to the right to a fair trial and concluded that the applicant's constitutional rights had not been infringed, the Court found that there had been no violation of his Convention rights without consideration of any ECHR case law or other reference to the Convention—*Ward v Minister for Justice, Equality and Law Reform* [2007] IEHC 39.

[65] O'Connell, Cummiskey, Meneghan and O'Connell, *ECHR Act 2003: A Preliminary Assessment of Impact*, (Dublin, Dublin Solicitor's Bar Association & Law Society of Ireland, 2006), p 119.

[66] [2007] ILRM 45, [2006] IEHC 118.

[67] [2002] 35 EHRR 523, [2002] ECHR 30668/96.

[68] For more on the other litigation between these parties see, eg O'Sullivan, 'Employment Update' 2005 1(1) *Irish Business Law* 21, 22; 'Cases and Comment: Ryanair v Irish Municipal, Public and Civil Trade Union/Irish Airlines Pilots Association (Labour Court)' (2005) 2(1) *Irish Employment Law Journal* 31; 'Cases and Comment: Ryanair v The Labour Court and Irish Municipal Public and Civil Trade Union (Supreme Court)' (2007) 4(1) *Irish Employment Law Journal* 24.

rather unsatisfactory that the novel and difficult questions of law raised should be determined on an application of this nature.[69]

The High Court's eschewal of this issue is both understandable in the circumstances and disappointing; however it is unlikely that there will be too significant a delay before this matter arises before the Courts again, particularly since it is widely thought that the Convention offers 'value added' to the Constitution in relation to certain rights, particularly family-related rights.

The ECHR and 'Legal Process'

In *Attorney General v Russell*[70] the High Court was asked to prevent the extradition of Russell to the United States on the basis of Article 3 (prevention of torture, inhuman and degrading treatment or punishment) of the Convention. The extradition charges against Russell related to vehicular manslaughter, vehicular assault, forgery and theft, but Russell claimed that his extradition would violate Article 3 as he had been subjected to death threats prior to his flight from the United States which the police had not actively pursued. In addition, he claimed that he would be held in solitary confinement pending trial and if convicted and that such conditions would violate his Article 3 rights. Russell also claimed that the conditions in American prisons, including the alleged high incidence of 'male-rape' constituted inhuman and degrading treatment contrary to Article 3. Russell's claim was, therefore, that Ireland's positive obligations under Article 3 to not engage in *refoulement* extended to an obligation not to extradite him to the United States.

The High Court held that any death threats outside of the prison environs could not be acted upon as Russell would be in detention and that the solitary confinement to which he may be subjected would be for his own safety and not violatory of Article 3. Referring to Bingham LJ's interpretation of the European Court of Human Rights decisions on *non-refoulement*,[71] as cited with approval by Laws LJ in *R (Bermingham and others) v Director of the Serious Fraud Office*,[72] Peart J held that an applicant was required to show strong grounds for believing that the extradition would result in a violation of Article 3 rights. Russell had not succeeded in doing that in this case. It is worthy of note that Peart J based the majority of his reasoning on domestic legal considerations and comparative law, and referred to the Convention only in terms of its interpretation in *Bermingham* rather than engaging in any sustained consideration thereof himself.

Although the Convention has been utilised to a particularly significant degree in the consideration of due process requirements, last year the High Court in *Crowley v Roche Products (Ireland) Ltd & Others*[73] confirmed that the European Convention on Human Rights was not in itself a due process factor *per se*; rather it is one of a number of factors to be weighed in the traditional test for due process in civil litigation. This case related to delay. Crowley claimed that the delay in litigation was inordinate

[69] See above above n 66 *per* Laffoy J.

[70] Above n 62.

[71] *R (on the application of Ullah) v Special Adjudicator, Do v Secretary of State for the Home Dept* [2004] 3 All ER 785, [2004] 2 AC 323, *per* Binham LJ at para 24.

[72] [2006] All ER 268, para 111.

[73] [2006] IEHC 6.

and that any resulting trial would violate his Article 6 entitlements (fair trial). The pre-2003 Irish law on this matter is the so-called *Primor* test.[74] This provides that even where Rules of Court have been violated by inordinate and inexcusable delay, litigation may still proceed where the 'balance of justice' requires it.

Crowley's argument was that the incorporation of the European Convention on Human Rights essentially displaced the *Primor* test. The Court, however, held that the practical approach taken to Article 6(1) by the European Court of Human Rights (ie. to ask whether the litigation has proceeded within a reasonable time of the statements of claim etc having been served and concentrating in particular on delays caused by the State[75]) is analogous to the Irish 'balance of justice approach' (particularly in the assessment of 'reasonableness'). As a result, the court held, the appropriate role for the Convention in such circumstances is to be taken into consideration in the weighing operation, together with the other important considerations (ie nature of the litigation (with more weight given to civil rights litigation)[76], prejudice to the defendant arising from his status as defendant,[77] any loss of opportunity to seek an indemnity or contribution arising from the delay,[78] and whether the delay was caused by the client or by his legal representation).[79]

UN HUMAN RIGHTS TREATY BODIES

The Committee on the Rights of the Child issued its Concluding Observations on Ireland's Second Periodic Report under the Convention on the Rights of the Child on 29 September 2006.[80] The Concluding Observations include proposals for constitutional and statutory reform as well as more specific policy initiatives. The Committee noted legislation adopted since consideration of the First Report, and the ratification of international treaties relevant to the protection of the rights of the child, including: The Optional Protocol to the Convention on the Rights of the Child on the involvement of children in armed conflicts in November 2002; The International Convention on the Elimination of All Forms of Racial Discrimination in December 2000; and The Convention against Torture and Other Cruel, Inhuman or Degrading Treatment or Punishment in April 2002.

While welcoming the adoption of the National Children's Strategy 2001, the Committee expressed regret that some of its previous recommendations had not been fully addressed, in particular, those related to the status of the child as a rights holder and the need for a child rights-based approach in policies and practices. Noting the State's obligations under Article 12, it recommended that the State '. . . strengthen its efforts to ensure, including through Constitutional provisions, that children have the right to express their views in all matters affecting them and to have those views given due weight'.[81] The Committee also criticised the failure to provide for a comprehensive

[74] The test was espoused in *Primor Plc v Stokes Kennedy Crowley & Ors* [1996] 2 IR 459.

[75] See *Bucholz v Federal Republic of Germany* [1981] 3 EHRR 597; *Zimmerman and Steiner v Switzerland* [1983] 6 EHRR 17; *Guincho v Portugal* [1984] 7 EHRR 223; *Scopelliti v Italy* [1993] 17 EHRR 493.

[76] See, eg, *Manning v Benson & Hedges* [2004] IEHC 316.

[77] See, eg, *Southern Mineral Oil Ltd (in Liquidation) v Cooney*, [1997] 3 IR 549.

[78] See, eg, *Silverdale v Italiatour Ltd.*, [2001] 1 ILRM 464.

[79] See, eg, *Rogers v Michelin* [2005] IEHC 294.

[80] CRC/C/IRL/CO/2.

[81] Above n 1 at para 25.

national strategy or measures for the prevention of child abuse. Concerning the office of the Ombudsman for Children, the Committee welcomed the specific inclusion of powers to investigate complaints by children or on their behalf, but expressed concern that limitations related to children in prisons and *Garda* (police) stations could undermine the mandate of the Ombudsman.

Noting the failure to enact a number of outstanding provisions in the relevant Children Acts, the Committee called for further measures to incorporate the Convention into domestic law and to secure full implementation of existing legislation. Specific measures to secure compliance with the State's obligations under the *CRC* were highlighted by the Committee. These included the provision of comprehensive 24-hour services for vulnerable children and young people; the introduction of a statutory requirement for the vetting of all persons seeking to work with children and; the provision of mental health services appropriate to minors. In the context of child poverty, the Committee recommended the introduction of targeted supplements to existing universal child benefit payments and the greater subsidisation of services for vulnerable families.

Regarding the age of criminal responsibility, the Committee was 'very disappointed'[82] that the Criminal Justice Act 2006 lowered the age of criminal responsibility for serious crimes to ten years. On the introduction of anti-social behaviour orders, they recommended that all alternatives be explored prior to the imposition of such orders. The Committee reiterated its previous recommendation that all forms of corporal punishment in the family be prohibited,[83] taking into account the Committee's general comment No 8 (2006) on the right of the child to protection from corporal punishment and other cruel or degrading forms of punishment.

The Committee made a number of observations on the position of children within minority communities, including children belonging to the Traveller community, and refugee and asylum seeking children. The Committee reiterated the concern raised by the Committee on the Elimination of Racial Discrimination[84] that non-denominational or multi-denominational schools represent less than 1 per cent of the total number of primary education facilities. The Committee expressed concerned that unaccompanied children or children separated from their parents might still not receive adequate guidance, support and protection during the asylum process, in particular with respect to access to services and an independent representation. On family reunification, the Committee called for an expanded definition of the family reflecting changing social patterns.

In line with Articles 34 and 35 of the Convention, the Committee reiterated the recommendation by the Committee on the Elimination of Discrimination against Women[85] on the adoption and implementation of a comprehensive strategy to combat trafficking and to support victims of trafficking, including the provision of shelter, counselling and medial care. Finally, again referring to the recommendations of CERD, they called on the Government to work more concretely towards the recognition of the Traveller community as an ethnic group.[86]

[82] Above n 1, at para 66.
[83] CRC/C/15/Add.85 para 39.
[84] Concluding observations on the Initial and Second periodic reports of Ireland (CERD/C/IRL/CO/2).
[85] CEDAW/C/IRL/CO/4-5
[86] CERC/C/IRL/CO/2 para 20.

Mr Morten Kjærum, Co-ordinator on Follow-up of the Committee on the Elimination of Racial Discrimination (CERD), undertook a country visit to Ireland from 21 to 23 June 2006, [87] following an invitation from the Irish Government. Ireland was the first State Party to undergo this follow-up process, which seeks to strengthen the effectiveness of the treaty reporting process. As an additional focal point in the treaty reporting process, the follow up visit highlighted the importance of ongoing monitoring and evaluation, beyond the crisis points of treaty reporting. As part of his visit, Mr Kjærum met with Government officials, NGOs and the Irish Human Rights Commission. An on-site visit to an asylum accommodation centre was also made. In preparation for this visit, a follow-up report was submitted by the Government and by the NGO Alliance Against Racism.

In his report to the CERD Committee,[88] he noted the importance of the visit in the evolution of human rights monitoring, commenting that 'Ireland was viewed as a pioneer in the follow up processes and an example of good practice'.[89] Specific steps taken were welcomed, including the move towards establishing a Press Council and the commissioning of research on 'race hate crimes' and 'racially aggravated assaults', with a view to possible adoption of legislation in this field. Noting the adoption of the National Women's Strategy, he expressed regret that multiple discrimination was not acknowledged in the Strategy as a barrier to the integration of female Travellers and ethnic minorities.

The progress made in the Employment Permits Bill, 2005, was welcomed. However, the limitations of the Bill, in restricting the mobility of migrant workers in the first twelve months of their employment were criticised. The vulnerable position of domestic workers was again highlighted; Mr Kjærum noted the CERD Committee's General Recommendation No 30 on Non-Citizens and recalled the Concluding Observations of the Committee, which had called for full implementation of legislation pertaining to migrant workers and the issuing of work permits/authorisations directly to employees.

No progress had been made on the disputed issue of recognition of the Travelling Community as an ethnic minority. Mr Kjærum called for further efforts to arrive at a 'common understanding'. Noting that Travellers have a distinct language, culture and traditions, he called on the Government to take into account the principle of self-identification. The creation of the office of the Garda Ombudsman was welcomed. The need for mandatory human rights training for all Garda cadets and police officers of all levels was identified as was the necessity of ensuring that immigration officers were familiar with international human rights obligations. Commenting on the proposed Immigration Bill, (not yet public at that time) Mr Kjærum expressed the view that the Bill would meet the concerns expressed by CERD. Mr Kjaerum concluded by stressing the importance of continuing the transparency, dialogue and continuous evaluation which, he said, had been the overarching goals of the follow-up process.

[87] The terms of reference for the role of Follow-up Co-ordinator were laid down by the Committee for the Elimination of Racial Discrimination at its 66th Session see CERD/A/60/18 (Annex IV).

[88] The report was submitted to the Committee at its 69th Session. See CERD/C/69/Misc.9 30 July 2006.

[89] Above n 4, at para 3.

REPORTS

Extraordinary Rendition

The continued use of Shannon Airport by the United States in the 'War on Terrorism' generated particular concern in 2006 and is covered further in the *International Law in Ireland Report*.[90] This was particularly so in relation to speculation concerning the suspected use of the airport in the practice of extraordinary rendition, which was the subject of Council of Europe and European Union investigations. The Marty Report (Council of Europe)[91] and the Flava Report (European Union)[92] both suggest (with varying degrees of conviction) that Ireland may have some tangential involvement in extraordinary rendition. According to the Marty Report Ireland is guilty of 'passive collusion' (p 66), while the Flava Report found that there were some 147 suspect stopovers in Ireland and recommended that the Gardaí ought to conduct random searches of American airplanes in Shannon (para 123).

The Government reacted negatively to the conclusions of both reports and asserted that Ireland has fulfilled its positive international obligations in relation to Shannon Airport by virtue of having received diplomatic assurances from the United States that no rendition is carried out through the airport.[93] Thus, while the Irish government accepts that it has a positive obligation in relation to extraordinary rendition[94] and that this practice is illegal in international (and domestic) law,[95] its position is that the receipt of diplomatic assurances from the United States fulfils Ireland's obligations[96] (ie they are adequate promises provided by a credible promisor and that relate to matters within the complete control of the promisor[97]).

Michael D Higgins, Labour TD (Member of Parliament), and Spokesperson on Foreign Affairs, tabled a motion calling on the government to, inter alia, establish a credible independent investigation into the existence of secret and extralegal arrangements between Ireland and any other state regarding the use of Irish territory, and to

[90] Ireland's approach to matters concerning the 'War on Terrorism' and, in particular, extraordinary rendition is considered in full in de Londras, 'International Law in Ireland 2006', this volume of the *Irish Yearbook of International Law*, p 241.

[91] Committee on Legal Affairs and Human Rights (Rapporteur: Dick Marty), *Alleged Secret Detentions and Unlawful Inter-state Transfers Involving Council of Europe Member States*, Draft Report—Part II, 7 June 2006, AS/JUR (2006).

[92] TCIP (Rapporteur: Giovanni Claudio Flava), *Report on the alleged use of European countries by the CIA for the transportation and illegal detention of prisoners*, 30 January 2007, A6-0020/2007.

[93] These positive obligations arise under, inter alia, Art 3 of the European Convention on Human Rights

[94] "Article 52 'Request in Respect of Unacknowledged Deprivation of Liberty: Reply of the Government of Ireland', 21 February 2006, p. 17

[95] See, e.g., 22 February 2006, Minister for Foreign Affairs, *Dáil debates*, col 545; 1 March 206, Minister for Foreign Affairs, *Dáil debates*, col 1809; 29 June 2006, Minister for Foreign Affairs, *Dáil debates*, cols 1690–1691; 20 June 2006, Minister for Foreign Affairs, *Dáil debates*, cols 1770–1771

[96] See, eg, 22 February 2006, Minister for Foreign Affairs, *Dáil debates*, col 685; 1 March 2006, Minister for Foreign Affairs, *Dáil debates*, col 1810; 7 March 2006 Minister for Foreign Affairs, *Dáil debates*, col 290; 29 June 2006 Minister for State for the Department of Foreign Affairs, Deputy Treacy, *Dáil debates*, cols 1578–1579

[97] For a discussion of the compatibility of these diplomatic assurances with international standards see, eg, de Londras, 'Ireland's Potential Liability for Extraordinary Rendition Through Shannon Airport' (2007) 25(7) *Irish Law Times* 106

use the full powers available under domestic law to investigate and inspect planes.[98] The motion, however, was not successful. According to the Government the *Gardaí* (police) have authority to board and inspect planes under the Tokyo Convention, the Air Navigation and Transport Acts 1988 and 1998,[99] and the Criminal Justice (UN Convention against Torture) Act 2000. As a result, a programme of random inspections was unnecessary and, furthermore, would be an unproductive approach to the handling of these matters with the United States government. This call for inspection of planes in Shannon Airport mirrors the position of the Irish Human Rights Commission formulated in 2005[100] and reiterated in 2006.[101]

Irish Human Rights Commission Reports

In November 2006, the Irish Human Rights Commission published a Discussion Document on Economic, Social and Cultural Rights, reflecting the commitment to this area in its Strategic Plan, 2003–6. Irish jurisprudence in this area remains underdeveloped, with, as the Commission notes, a reluctance on the part of the judiciary, in particular, to recognise the justiciability of rights claims. The document aims to map out how a framework for the protection of economic, social and cultural rights might be designed and implemented. The document includes an analysis of the increasingly 'sophisticated and effective' mechanisms for protecting economic social and cultural rights in international law, and draws on models for enforcement from a number of common law jurisdictions, where engagement with rights claims in this field has led to more positive outcomes.

Other publications of note include a *Report on the Determination of Life Sentences* in the light of the ECHR and the jurisprudence of the European Court of Human Rights. The Report's primary conclusion is that Irish law does not, currently, comply with the ECHR.[102] The Commission's *Report on the Rights of De Facto Couples* contributes to the growing body of law reform proposals and policy documents on partnership rights and relationship recognition in Ireland.[103] The Report examines Irish law in the light of international legal standards, concluding that Ireland falls far short of those standards and is also, increasingly, falling behind other European jurisdictions in developing expanded relationship recognition regimes.

[98] 13 June 2006, Michael D Higgins TD, Dáil debates, cols 768–775. This call for inspection of planes in Shannon Airport mirrors the position of the Irish Human Rights Commission formulated in 2005 (IHRC Commission Resolution on 'Rendition') and reiterated in 2006 (see, eg, 28 November 2006, IHRC Submission to the European Parliament's Temporary Committee on Rendition;24 May 2006, IHRC response sent to Minister for Foreign Affairs on 24th May 2006 on the subject of 'rendition')

[99] These Acts empower an authorised person (including a Garda) to board a civilian aircraft where it is suspect that, inter alia, a crime is being committed –Air Navigation and Transport Act 1988, s 33.

[100] IHRC Commission Resolution on 'Rendition'

[101] See, eg, 28 November 2006, IHRC Submission to the European Parliament's Temporary Committee on Rendition; 24 May 2006, IHRC response sent to Minister for Foreign Affairs on 24 May 2006 on the subject of 'rendition'

[102] See McCutcheon and Coffey p 101.

[103] See *Report of the Law Reform Commission on the Rights and Duties of Cohabitants* (2006); *Consultation Paper on the Rights and Rights and Duties of Cohabitees* (2004), the *All Party Oireachtas Committee Tenth Progress Report on the Family, the Civil Partnerships Bill* (2004).

White Paper on Irish Aid

Helen O'Neill

CENTRE FOR DEVELOPMENT STUDIES
UNIVERSITY COLLEGE DUBLIN
MEMBER OF THE IRISH HUMAN RIGHTS COMMISSION

The publication of the first White Paper on Irish Aid in September 2006 represents a major government acknowledgment of the centrality of foreign aid within Ireland's wider foreign policy as well as an expression of Ireland's perception of its place in a still unequal world at the beginning of the 21st century. This publication is a major milestone in the evolution of Ireland's development cooperation policy (including its aid and its trade relations with developing countries). At the same time, it is a reflection of a programme that has displayed a remarkably consistent policy approach since it was established in 1974.

To place the White Paper on Aid in its historical context, it is appropriate to briefly refer to the white paper on broad foreign policy published exactly ten years earlier. Ireland's first white paper on foreign policy, *Challenges and Opportunities Abroad*, was published in 1996.[1] It followed a countrywide consultation process that had been launched in November 1994. The White Paper included a chapter on development co-operation and a chapter on human rights. The former chapter emphasised the centrality of Ireland's relations with developing countries (DCs) within its overall foreign policy, describing Irish aid and development cooperation as 'practical expressions of Ireland's foreign policy commitments to peace and justice in the world'.[2] The primary objective of Ireland's official development co-operation policy—which had been laid down when the programme was established in 1974—was stated to be poverty reduction and the promotion of sustainable development in some of the poorest countries in the world. The other objectives included assisting in establishing and maintaining peace in developing countries by fostering democracy, human rights, gender and social equality and protection of the environment; responding promptly to emergencies and humanitarian disasters; and contributing to building civil society and social solidarity. The geographic focus of the bilateral side of the programme was to remain on sub-Saharan Africa. On the multilateral side, Ireland's long-standing involvement with the United Nations and its development agencies was to be deepened through significantly greater financial contributions and increased participation in their executive committees.

The chapter on human rights stated that the government was convinced of the intrinsic linkage between human rights, democracy and development emphasising that Ireland's commitment to human rights 'has always been a vital part of its expression of

[1] Department of Foreign Affairs (1996), *Challenges and Opportunities Abroad: White Paper on Foreign Policy*.

[2] *Ibid*, at 229.

solidarity with the developing world'.[3] Support from Irish Aid was promised for human rights NGOs in developing countries; assistance to the training of the judiciary, the police and the mass media; and human rights education for police and military personnel. In 1996, Ireland's total official development assistance (ODA) amounted to €142 million or 0.3 per cent of gross national income (GNI).

Ten years after the publication of the White Paper on Ireland's foreign policy came the first white paper focused exclusively on its foreign aid policy. By 2006, ODA had grown to over €800 million or 0.53 per cent of GNI. Ireland was on target to meet its commitment, made by the *Taoiseach*, Mr Bertie Ahern TD, at the UN General Assembly in September 2005, to reach the UN target of 0.7 per cent of GNI by 2012. The government announced at the end of 2004 that it would publish a White Paper on Ireland's aid programme that would set out a roadmap for its development into the medium term

As had been the case in the preparation of *Challenges and Opportunities Abroad*, the production of the White Paper on Irish Aid was preceded by a wide-ranging consultation process involving the Irish public, other government departments, development NGOs, national and international aid agencies and multilateral development organisations. Discussions were also held with the Joint Oireachtas Committee on Foreign Affairs. In response to advertisements placed in the national press seeking written input, 137 submissions were received.[4] A series of public meetings took place at ten locations around the country.[5] The consultation process conducted within Ireland can be seen not just as a means of eliciting views from a wide variety of stakeholders but also as a means of involving those same stakeholders in the outcome itself. In other words, provided the UN target of 0.7 per cent of GNI is reached by 2012—which would put ODA expenditure (at around €1.5 billion) in the second rank of spending by government departments by that date—continued support for the programme by the Irish public would be a necessary condition for its long-term sustainability.

The White Paper was published on 18 September 2006.

THE SUBSTANCE OF THE WHITE PAPER

The White Paper is nearly 130 pages long and divided into ten parts. It begins by asking why Ireland should give aid and answers this question by stating that Irish aid works and that we give aid to help those in greatest need: 'the world's poorest people in the world's poorest countries'.[6] This is consistent with statements made over and over again since the programme was launched in 1974.[7] As regards the growth of Irish ODA, the paper states that the foreign aid budget has been increasing rapidly in recent

[3] Department of Foreign Affairs (1996), *Challenges and Opportunities Abroad: White Paper on Foreign Policy*, at 221.

[4] In the consultation process undertaken in the UK in preparation for the publication of its 2006 white paper on international development, around 600 written submissions were received. (Department for International Development (2006), *Eliminating World Poverty: making governance work for the poor)*.

[5] Athlone, Carrick-on-Shannon, Cork, Dublin, Dundalk, Galway, Letterkenny, Limerick, Tralee and Waterford.

[6] Government of Ireland, *White Paper on Irish Aid*, 2006, p 20.

[7] Helen O'Neill, 'Irish Aid: Policy and Performance' in Olav Stokke (ed), *European Development Assistance, Vol 1, Policies and Performance* (European Association of Development Research and Training Institutes, Tilburg and Norwegian Institute of International Affairs, Oslo, 1984), 239–261.

years, is expected to reach €730 million in 2007 (in fact it exceeded €800 million), and will continue to grow in line with the commitment to reach the UN target of 0.7 per cent of GNI by 2012. In justifying the publication of a White Paper on Aid at this juncture, it is stated that it will provide a framework for expenditure into the future 'and provide a clear benchmark against which our partners in Ireland and internationally can measure our performance'.[8] The White Paper also states that the millennium development goals (MDGs) will guide Ireland's development cooperation policy.[9]

A comment on Ireland's approach to aid giving

A country's foreign aid policy is driven by a mixture of power, interests and values. In the case of large donors, all three motivations are evident in the amounts of aid they provide, the countries to which they provide aid, and the sectors upon which they focus their aid. In the case of small donors like Ireland, power does not figure in its relations with other countries, including developing countries. It does not pursue global strategic interests—although political and economic interests may come into play to a small extent. However, the major determinant of Ireland's aid policy is the values of the Irish people. Irish Aid, in designing and implementing its aid programme, is reflecting the values of the Irish population which have consistently shown, in a series of attitude surveys, a concern for the world's poorest people and with helping to solve problems that affect them such as famine, hunger, ill-health and poor quality of education.[10]

In setting out Ireland's vision for development, the White Paper reiterates the overarching objective of the aid programme as poverty reduction. The main geographic focus will continue to be the poorest countries in sub-Saharan Africa. The traditional focus on health and education is being maintained but is being supplemented by a new focus on governance and human rights as well as support for the private sector.

The bilateral and multilateral sides of the Irish aid programme

Both the bilateral and multilateral sides of the Irish aid programme are examined in detail in Part 3 of the white paper. Individual sections are devoted to country programmes; prevention and response to humanitarian emergencies; spending through NGOs; promotion of human rights and good governance in DCs; investment

[8] *Ibid*, at 23.

[9] The MDGs originated in a set of goals first agreed within the Organisation for Economic Cooperation and Development (OECD) in the early 1990s and published by it in its seminal document *Shaping the 21st Century* in 1996. At the UN Millennium summit held in New York in 2000, the eight goals were accepted by all the member states and then became known as the millennium development goals. The first seven goals are focused on the achievement of objectives within developing countries. They include: eradicating extreme poverty and hunger in DCs; achieving universal primary education; promoting gender equality; reducing child mortality; improving maternal health; combating HIV/AIDS, malaria and other diseases; and ensuring environmental sustainability. Each goal includes a number of quantified targets to be achieved by 2015. The eighth goal, developing a global partnership for development, calls on developing countries to do more to ensure their own development and poverty reduction and calls on industrialised countries to support them through increased aid, debt relief and improved opportunities for trade.

[10] Advisory Council on Development Cooperation (1985 and 1990), *Aid to Third World Countries: attitudes of a national sample of Irish people; DFA (2003), Attitudes towards Development Cooperation in Ireland: the report of a national survey of Irish adults; and various Eurobarometer surveys conducted at regular intervals throughout the EU.*

in education and health; hunger, food security and rural development; gender issues; environment issues; peace and security; and trade and development. In each case, the development challenge is first set in context. Ireland's current approach to addressing it ('Ireland's response') is then described. New initiatives and new areas of activity ('key decisions') designed to improve current responses are highlighted in boxes within each section.

While some of these key decisions reiterate approaches in place since 1974 ('Africa will remain the principal geographic focus for Irish Aid'), most announce major new initiatives. The number of key partner countries in which Irish Aid works (currently Ethiopia, Lesotho, Mozambique, Tanzania, Timor Leste, Uganda, Vietnam and Zambia) is to be increased in the medium term. Malawi, the first country so designated, is a most appropriate choice. Other initiatives at country and regional levels include the decision to deepen Ireland's involvement in fragile states (first focusing on Liberia and Sierra Leone) and building regional programmes in South East Asia (working from Vietnam) and Southern Africa and West Africa. Support will be given to African regional institutions (The African Union (AU), the New Partnership for Africa's Development, the AU Peace and Security Council, the Pan-African Parliament and the African Commission on People's and Human Rights). Working with these institutions is seen as offering an opportunity to address political, development and security issues on a regional basis.

A rapid response initiative (RRI) is to be developed as the centrepiece of a distinctly Irish approach to the prevention and response to humanitarian emergencies. As the White Paper explains, Ireland's traditional response to such emergencies has been through the funding of other actors in the field—UN agencies, NGO humanitarian organisations and the Red Cross family. With an increasing aid budget, there is now an opportunity for Ireland to create its own specific operational capabilities. The RRI will include the pre-positioning and transportation of humanitarian supplies to disaster areas; the availability of a roster of highly-skilled individuals from the public and private sectors, including from the Defence Forces, for deployment at short notice to emergency situations; and enhancing the emergency capacities of international humanitarian response agencies and mechanisms. Irish Aid already supports the Central Emergency Response Fund to enable UN agencies to respond more quickly and better coordinate humanitarian relief.

Other key decisions announced in the White Paper include establishment of a Hunger Task Force to examine the particular contribution Ireland can make toward tackling the root causes of food insecurity, particularly in Africa; an Interdepartmental Committee for Development to ensure that a strong development perspective is integrated into government decision-making across all government departments; and a new Governance Unit within Irish Aid to help combat corruption and ensure that aid is used for the public good in developing countries.

On the multilateral side of the Irish aid programme, the White Paper restates Ireland's commitment to a better trade deal for developing countries in the Doha round of multilateral trade negotiations and to providing assistance to help them to improve their capacity to produce, deliver and sell goods and services on international markets. At the institutional level, the recent growth in contributions to UN development agencies will continue. The criteria guiding future contributions to these agencies will include: coherence with Ireland's overall development objectives; effective and efficient management; commitment to reform; and working in partnership with DC governments and in coordination with the World Bank and other multilateral development institutions and other bilateral donors. At EU level, Ireland will work with like-minded member states to ensure that a greater proportion of EU aid goes to the least-developed countries. It will encourage other EU donors to move toward total untying of their aid and will seek to strengthen coherence at EU level in order that policies in all relevant areas reinforce the Union's development objectives.

Four issues cut across and inform all the work of Irish Aid: gender, environment, HIV/AIDS and governance. The White Paper promised that these will be mainstreamed in the planning, implementation and evaluation of all Irish Aid interventions in future.

One message that emerged clearly during the public meetings that took place during the consultation process was that Irish Aid and its work is not well known among the Irish public. In an attempt to tackle this gap, another key decision in the White Paper is to open a Public Information and Volunteering Centre on Dublin's O'Connell Street. As a first step toward this end, an information booklet on the White Paper was delivered to each home in the country after its release.

DPP v Clancy, Dunlop, Fallon, Moran and O'Reilly (the 'Pitstop Ploughshares' Case)

Joe Noonan

NOONAN LINEHAN ARROLL COFFEY

SOLICITORS, CORK

International law is rarely invoked in the defence of domestic criminal prosecutions. It is rarer still that such a defence succeeds. Yet on 25 July 2006, a jury in Dublin Circuit Criminal Court unanimously acquitted five people of criminal damage who had cited international law as an ingredient of their defence. The alleged offence had taken place at Shannon Airport on 3 February 2003 where the accused had rendered a United States of America Navy aircraft incapable of flight. The five told the Court that they had acted to defend life and/or property at a time when they feared the outbreak of hostilities which would, inter alia, flout international law. The Court, after legal argument, allowed the Jury to hear evidence from Dr. Jean Allain, School of Law, Queens University Belfast, as to the circumstances in which the use of military force by States may be considered lawful. Dr Allain also gave evidence as to the prevailing opinion as of February 2003 among international law experts on the imminent invasion of Iraq. The Court heard about the familiarity or otherwise of frontline Gardai (police) with Irish statutes incorporating the 1984 UN Convention against Torture and the four 1949 Geneva Conventions into domestic law. Evidence was also adduced as to the absence of specific Garda training or instruction with regard to those Irish statutes. At this time Shannon Airport was a major transit point for US Military personnel wherein 89,896 US soldiers had travelled to the Middle East in the lead up to the invasion of Iraq on 20 March 2003.

THE IRISH CONTEXT

> International Law is a primitive discipline. Its unambiguous determination by Courts and its enforcement are not always guaranteed, and it is too dangerously linked to the exercise of political power on the international plane to be left only to the sober consideration of lawyers employed by those in power[1]

[1] Gernot Biehler *International Law in Practice—An Irish Perspective* (Dublin, Thomson-Round Hall, 2005), p 1. Hailsham's view was that international law 'has always been a somewhat sickly patient'—as quoted by Bingham LJ in his Foreword to S Fatima *Using International Law in Domestic Courts* (Oxford, Hart, 2005). Sands, drawing expressive inspiration from Francis Ford Coppola's movie *The Godfather, Part 3*, is more optimistic about the health of the patient: 'The rules of international law will turn out to be more robust than the policies of the Bush administration. In the twenty-first century you need rules, and proper lawyers too' P Sands, *Lawless World* (London, Allen Lane, 2005), p 240.

As Biehler suggests, there is particular merit in examining the practice of international law from an Irish standpoint. This paper discusses an aspect of that practice as it intersected with the defence of five people accused of criminal damage to a US military aircraft: DPP v Clancy, Dunlop, Fallon, Moran and O'Reilly.[2]

The use of military force by a State is rarely uncontroversial even within that State. That internal controversy may lead to civil direct action in an effort to avert, delay or otherwise interrupt the use of force. Such direct action may take lawful or unlawful form. Given the stakes, it can expect to be met with a vigorous response by State authorities. That is evident from the number of people currently serving prison terms in the US for such actions.[3] The US is not unique in that response, nor is its response to internal dissent necessarily at the extreme end of the spectrum. In some States, such actions may be tantamount to suicide, as of torture and indefinite detention await such manifest dissent.

Since independence, Ireland has not used or threatened to use military force against another State. Deployment of Irish troops overseas has normally been for UN sanctioned peace-keeping activities and has enjoyed near universal support at home. The popular sense of Ireland as a small independent nation with a sincere commitment to the rules of law is deep rooted. It finds expression in the Irish Constitution:

> *Bunreacht na hÉireann* Article 29(1–3):
>
> Ireland accepts the generally recognised principles of international law as its rule of conduct in its relations with other States.
>
> Ireland affirms its devotion to the ideal of peace and friendly co-operation amongst nations founded on international justice and morality.
>
> Ireland accepts the generally recognised principles of international law as its rule of conduct in its relations with other States.

It has been suggested that Ireland's commitment to these principles arises from the temporal coincidence between Ireland's emergence as an independent State and the development in the period between 1907 and 1945 of a global international consensus against the use of State violence culminating in the adoption of the UN Charter.[4] The symmetry between the official position of the State and popular sentiment in Ireland fractured in early 2003 when it became apparent that the United States and the United Kingdom, with others, were intent on large scale military intervention in Iraq without United Nations Security Council authorisation.

This fracture was initially difficult to discern as Ireland found itself as a non-permanent member on the UN Security Council, and Government statements insisted that any military intervention in Iraq would need specific UN Security Council authorisation.[5] However, by late January 2003 a public controversy in Ireland emerged with as its focal point the intensive use of Shannon Airport as a key logistic base for transit of US Military personnel to the Middle East. The controversy resulted

[2] Circuit Criminal Court, Dublin, 25 July 2006; unreported.

[3] For an account of how the US courts has deal with direct action dissent in the lead up to the war against Iraq see W Quigley, 'Enforcing International Law through Civil Disobedience' in Brecher (ed) *In the Name of Democracy*, (New York, Metropolitan, 2005).

[4] See J Allain, 'The Use of Force—an Irish Perspective', in Biehler, above, n 1, p 273.

[5] See *Statement by Minister for Foreign Affairs, Mr Brian Cowen TD to Dáil Éireann,* 29 January 2003 http://www.taoiseach.gov.ie/index.asp?locID=379&docID=1416.

from the Government stance that the use of Shannon's facilities would not be withdrawn from the US forces even if those forces entered Iraq in the absence of a further UN Security Council resolution.[6]

Under the 1907 Hague Convention V, neutral States are, as a matter of customary international law, precluded from providing transit facilities to the troops of a belligerent State en route to the battlefield. In the 2003 Horgan v An Taoseach et al,[7] that principle was recognised by the Irish High Court as remaining valid in international law. In his judgment in Horgan, delivered in April 2003, two months after the action taken by the five accused at Shannon, Kearns J concluded that there was:

> [. . .] an identifiable rule of customary law in relation to the status of neutrality whereunder a neutral state may not permit the movement of large numbers of troops or munitions of one belligerent State through its territory en route to a theatre of war with another.

The State as Defendant argued that a more subtle form of neutrality existed. The Court considered this argument but was unimpressed:

> It does not appear to me that even that form of neutrality is to be seen as including the notion that the granting of passage over its territory by a neutral State for large numbers of troops and munitions from one belligerent State only en route to a theatre of war with another is compatible with the status of neutrality in international law.

Despite its conclusions on the duties of neutral States, the High Court declined to grant Mr Horgan a declaration that the Government was acting unconstitutionally in providing these facilities to US Forces. The Court ruled that to make a declaratory order condemning the Government would be to trespass beyond the Court's proper role into the exclusive territory of the Executive. Despite the great historic value attached by Ireland to the concept of neutrality, that status, it said, was 'nowhere reflected in Bunreacht na hEireann, or elsewhere in any domestic legislation'. It was a matter of government policy only, 'albeit a policy to which, traditionally at least, considerable importance was attached'. Ireland was thus, in the High Court's view, in a different position to other States, which have incorporated a permanent status of neutrality into their domestic laws. As to the question of 'participation in a war' and compliance with Article 28 of the Constitution, the Court concluded that it could not 'without proof of quite exceptional circumstances' second-guess the views of the Government on this question. Reflecting its repeated concern to defer to the role of the Executive and the separation of powers, the Court concluded that some 'quite egregious disregard of constitutional duties and obligations' would have to take place before they would intervene under Article 28 of the Constitution: 'This is not a situation where the Court can approach the matter on a "clean sheet" basis, ignoring decisions made by those constitutionally designated to do so within their own special areas of competence'.

[6] See *Statement by Minister for Foreign Affairs, Mr Brian Cowen TD to Dáil Éireann,* 29 January 2003, available at: http://www.dfa.ie/home/index.aspx?id=26129. See also *Statement to the Seanad by Minister Kitt,* 6 February 2003, available at: http://www.dfa.ie/home/index.aspx?id=26123

[7] [2003] 2 *Irish Law Reports Monthly* 357. Mr Horgan was a retired Army Commandant who had also served on UN Peace-keeping mission overseas.

DPP V CLANCY ET AL

Turning to the case at hand. In the early hours of 3 February 2003 three women and two men entered Shannon Airport through a perimeter fence. Once inside, they found a US Navy aircraft parked in a nearby hangar. They had with them several items which, they later testified, illustrated their motivation. These items included information and photographs showing the consequences for Iraqi civilians, particularly children, of the United Nations sanctions and of bombing raids on Iraq in 1996. They had religious symbols, prayer beads, candles, and a copy of the Bible and the Qur'an. They had a statement they had signed describing what they intended to do and setting out their belief that they were obliged to act to save life and property and to prevent violence which would breach international law, the Irish Constitution and religious norms.

They set about the US Navy plane with a range of implements including hammers and a mattock. The plane was rendered incapable of flight. They then laid down the implements, sat in a circle to pray and awaited the response of the authorities which was not long in coming. On entering the hangar, they had seen that the plane was protected by a member of An Garda Siochána (the police). The five were charged with criminal damage contrary to section 2(1) of the Criminal Damage Act 1991. When tried on indictment this offence carries a maximum sentence of 10 years imprisonment.

Initially the five accused were remanded in custody without consent to bail. In the Irish system a custodial remand is relatively rare even for grave offences against the person. An accused person is generally entitled to remain at liberty—on bail—pending trial. In exceptional circumstances, for example if there is evidence that the accused may interfere with witnesses or may not intend to turn up for their trial, bail may be withheld. In this case there seemed to be little risk of interference with witnesses given the open and public nature of the action. As for being a flight risk and not turning up for trial, the nature of the defence to be advanced by the accused depended on the view that would be taken by the judge and jury of their personal integrity and motivation for their actions. That would be destroyed if they, or any one of them, failed to keep their bond to appear for trial. Those arguments did not impress the District Judges and it was only after several weeks in prison that the accused were admitted to bail. Initially bail was granted on stringent terms normally reserved for those accused of murder. These included an obligation to sign daily at a Garda Station, not to travel outside Ireland, to stay out of County Clare, to sign a bail bond, and to stay away from the US Embassy in Dublin. This last condition was waived for one of the five, a US citizen. Two years later, shortly prior to their eventual trial, those conditions were eased to permit foreign travel for the three accused who had family ties overseas.

As a result of a pre-trial discovery motion brought by the defence, the State was required to furnish information on the extent of the US military use of Shannon. Defence Counsel justified the request for disclosure by outlining that the actions of the accused were intended to avert or reduce harm to people in Shannon and Iraq. Prosecuting Counsel argued that Shannon was too remote from Iraq to afford any credibility to this Defence submission. In response, however, the Judge recalled hearing Mr Tony Blair comment that Britain was in 45 minutes peril of attack by Saddam Hussein.

The accused were returned for trial at Dublin Circuit Criminal Court before judge and jury. While the charges of criminal damage preferred against the accused were grounded in a domestic criminal statute, the explanation offered for their actions meant that potentially there would be an international law aspect to the defence. The difficulty in mounting this defence was plain: how could international law find a place for itself in a trial whose purpose was to establish the guilt or innocence of persons accused of seemingly ordinary domestic offences?

The offence of criminal damage is set out the Criminal Damage Act 1991 (as amended by the Non-Fatal Offences against the Person Act 1997).[8] By virtue of the 'lawful excuse' provided for in section 6(2)(c), an accused person will have a good defence to a charge of criminal damage if he/she can establish that the act was carried out for the purpose of protecting another or the property of another and that the action was 'reasonable' in the 'circumstances' as he/she 'believed them to be'. Under section 6(3) it is immaterial whether that belief was justified as long as it is honestly held.[9]

One element of the lawful excuse defence requires to be established to an objective standard—the reasonableness or otherwise of the act. The accused must give subjective evidence of what they believed the circumstances to be. Further, their belief must be shown to have been honestly held. There are therefore three elements to the lawful excuse defence:

1. What did the accused believe the circumstances to be?
2. Was the belief of the accused honestly held?

[8] In edited form the relevant provisions state as follows:

1 (1) In this Act—

'to damage' includes.

(a) in relation to property other than data (but including a storage medium in which data are kept), to destroy, deface, dismantle or, whether temporarily or otherwise, render inoperable or unfit for use or prevent or impair the operation of, [. . .]
'property' means—
(a) property of a tangible nature, whether real or personal, including money and animals that are capable of being stolen, [. . .]

2. (1) A person who without lawful excuse damages any property belonging to another intending to damage any such property or being reckless as to whether any such property would be damaged shall be guilty of an offence.[. . .]

6.—(1) This section applies to—

(a) any offence under Section 2(1) or 5, [. . .]

(2) A person charged with an offence to which this section applies shall, whether or not he would be treated for the purposes of this Act as having a lawful excuse apart from this subsection, be treated for those purposes as having a lawful excuse—[. . .]

(c) if he damaged or threatened to damage the property in question or, [. . .] in order to protect himself or another or property belonging to himself or another or a right or interest in property which was or which he believed to be vested in himself or another and the act or acts alleged to constitute the offence were reasonable in the circumstances as he believed them to be.

(3) For the purposes of this section it is immaterial whether a belief is justified or not if it is honestly held.

[9] The lawful excuse defence was imported into Irish law from the UK Criminal Damage Act 1971—see Charlton *et al Criminal Law* (Dublin, Butterworths, 1999), at 193. Note, however, that that edition of Charlton does not address the amendment made by s 21 of the Non-fatal Offences against the Person Act 1997 to s 6 of the Criminal Damage Act 1991.

3. Was what was done by the accused, holding that belief as to the circumstances, reasonable?[10]

The accused believed that the US planes coming through Shannon were an important part of a build-up to a violent attack breaching international law. Defence Counsel would have to demonstrate among other things that the belief of accused about international law was honestly held.

If the defence succeeded in demonstrating the relevance and admissibility of evidence on the international law issues to the lawful excuse defence, the next issue to be considered would be the division of functions between the trial judge and the jury. The judge in an Irish criminal trial adjudicates on questions of law. The judge directs the jury on the law and the jury accepts the judge's rulings. The jury however, is the sole arbiter of questions of fact. Was the entitlement of the accused to advance a lawful excuse defence not a question of law, and thus within the power of the judge to determine? Prosecuting Counsel invited the Court to find that the defence of lawful excuse should be considered as a question of law to be determined by the judge alone. Depending on the judge's view, the lawful excuse defence should either be ruled out, in which case the jury would not be permitted to consider it, or ruled in, in which case the jury could consider it.

The trial judge rejected the prosecution submission. She held that the availability of the lawful excuse defence was a matter for the jury to decide. The facts and the law were so bound up together that in her view, the availability of the lawful excuse defence was a matter for the Jury as sole arbiter of any factual question. The jury would decide on the evidence whether the lawful excuse defence would avail the accused.

While the ingredients of the lawful excuse defence were multiple, one essential ingredient was the stated belief of the accused that the then-impending military action in Iraq breached international law. The Jury would be entitled to disregard what the accused said on that topic if it did not believe that the stated belief of the accessed was honestly held. It was therefore appropriate to lead defence evidence to demonstrate that stated belief of the accused was soundly based. The Court therefore allowed evidence to be given by the accused themselves about their own understanding of the illegality of the imminent military action. The question then arose as to whether the accused could call any other witnesses on that point.

If a trial judge wishes to hear a potential witness in order to assess the admissibility or relevance of their evidence, the witness may be heard in Court in the absence of the jury in a process known as a voir dire. After a voir dire, the Court decided to allow the jury to hear evidence from Dr Jean Allain, about the circumstances under which a State may lawfully use military force as laid down in the UN Charter. Dr Allain also gave evidence of the views of other international law experts. He testified that, as of February 2003, the prevailing view among international law experts was that military action of the kind then anticipated would contravene the UN Charter and accordingly not be in conformity with international law. This testimony showed that the accused's belief was one which could be honestly held.

[10] There is a detailed analysis of the lawful excuse defence under the equivalent English statute in Ormerod, *Smith & Hogan Criminal Law* (11th edn), 2005, pp 890–911. Following his description at p 911 of an attempt to raise the defence in *Pritchard and others* [2004] EWCA Crim 1981, the author observes: 'This will certainly not be the last the courts hear of this line of defence'.

After another voir dire, the Court allowed the jury to hear evidence from Group Captain Geoffrey Oxlee OBE (Royal Air Force, Retired). Mr Oxlee, giving evidence as an independent expert with a long and distinguished military career, confirmed that interference with a logistics supply plane could have an effect, however limited and unpredictable, on a warring party's ability to implement its military plan. He could not rule out the possibility that such an action might have the effect of saving a life. Nor could he rule it in. He acknowledged that such a plane could be a target, for example, of an opponent State's armed forces.

While the ruling of the final trial judge was consistent with the approach taken by the Judge dealing with the pre-trial discovery motion, not all of the four Circuit Judges involved with the case came to the same view of the issues. This is so, as the accused were subject to three trials before their acquittal. The first two trials failed to survive long enough to allow the issue of guilt or innocence to be put to the jury, as the judges recused themselves. In the first trial it appeared that the judge was not disposed to regard the case as one in which the lawful excuse defence could apply. In the second trial a different Judge formally came to that conclusion. Further illustrating the differing approaches taken, each of the three trial Judges came to a different conclusion about which witnesses presented by the defence should be permitted to testify in front of the jury. The first jury accordingly heard no independent defence witness. The second jury heard former UN Assistant Secretary-General Denis Halliday, retired Staff Sergeant Jimmy Massey of the US Marine Corps, Mr Oxlee, and Kathy Kelly of a US-based NGO Voices in the Wilderness—whose testimony related to the impact of sanctions and bombing on the civilian population and infrastructure in Iraq—and from Dr Allain. The third jury heard from Kathy Kelly, from Mr Oxlee and Dr Allain. This variation is notable given that the same list of defence witnesses was sought to be put forward in each of the three trials.[11]

CONCLUSION

The criminal trial is one whose conclusion admits of no ambiguity. At the end of the trial, the accused will be found guilty or not guilty. Once the process is initiated it must reach one or other of those determinations. The certainty of the outcome and the formality of the process both stand in contrast to the often ambiguous determination of international law questions. The outcome in the DPP v Clancy et al was a unanimous jury acquittal. The trial in a sense was a lightning rod through which international law concepts were brought out of the ether and into a Dublin courtroom. They found their place in a judicial process where the liberty of five individuals was at stake. The jury was given the opportunity, as a result of the judge's ruling that the lawful excuse

[11] It should be noted that between the date of the action of the accused at Shannon in February 2003 and their final trial in July 2006, domestic sensitivity to the use of Shannon intensified with the publicity given to the issue of 'extraordinary rendition'. In December 2005 the Irish Human Rights Commission, a statutory body, publicly expressed concern (see IHRC December 2005 Resolution.) as to the Government's reliance, without more, on US diplomatic assurances, that all relevant legal requirements were being honoured by US aircraft passing through Shannon:

> In view of Ireland's international legal obligation to ensure that no one is sent to a jurisdiction where they may run this risk we call on the Government to seek agreement from the US authorities to inspect the aircraft in question on landing at Shannon or any other Irish airport.

defence was for the jury to determine, to hear evidence about opinions on the lawfulness of the war on Iraq, about the enforceability in Irish courts of the sanctions under the Geneva Conventions, and about the universal jurisdiction principle. That principle would entitle another Irish jury, if given the opportunity, to participate in the legal struggle against torture. The attempt by the prosecution to confine the issue to the relatively simple question as to whether the accused had damaged someone else's property failed on this occasion. The Court, and in turn the jury, took a broader perspective.

International law was not the only factor, and perhaps not even the decisive factor, in the jury's decision to acquit. No outsider is privy to the discussion in the jury room.[12] International law is, however, a systematic effort to bend States to a code of behaviour which is considered to be in some sense 'right'. The success or otherwise of that effort depends in large measure on the willingness of individual states to do what is regarded as 'right' in international law terms. This necessary effort finds an echo in the remark of one juror speaking immediately after the acquittal:

> There are days when you just have to do the right thing. This was one of those days.

[12] Jury acquittals in UK cases sharing some features with *DPP v Clancy et al* case include *Zelter* (1996) and *Boyes* (2001). Zelter and three other women had disabled a Hawk military jet at a site near Liverpool, believing the plane would be used unlawfully by Indonesian forces against civilians in East Timor. The finding of the jury was later the subject of a critical opinion by the Scottish High Court, following a reference by the Lord Advocate General. The Court was not, however, empowered to overturn the acquittal. See Lord Advocate's Reference No 1 of 2000 By Her Majesty's Advocate referring for the Opinion of The High Court on points of law (*R v Angela Zelter and Bodil Ulla Roder and Ellen Moxley* [2001] Scot HC 15 (30 March, 2001). Boyes and her co-accused, dressed in wet-suits and found near the Trident nuclear submarine *HMS Vengeance* carrying hammers and varnish, acknowledged intending to disable the vessel. A Manchester jury acquitted them of conspiracy to cause criminal damage.

The case of Ponting (1985 Crim LR 318) may also be regarded as comparable in some respects. Ponting, an Assistant Secretary in the Ministry of Defence, was acquitted of charges under the Official Secrets Act even though he acknowledged passing official documents on his own initiative to his Member of Parliament. Those documents gave reason to doubt the UK government assertion that the Argentine battleship the *General Belgrano* was steaming into the UK-imposed exclusion zone around the Falkland Islands when it was torpedoed.

Irish Society of International Law

Patrick O'Brien

CHAIRMAN

The Irish Society of International Law was founded in 2002 as a scholarly society dedicated to the promotion of study and debate in the field of international law. It aims, through its events and activities, to increase general awareness of international law and the international legal system, and to stimulate informed debate and scholarship in Ireland about international law and related topics such as international relations and politics. It provides a forum for international legal issues that is of equal value and interest to laypeople, professionals, students and academics alike.

The Irish Society of International Law holds regular discussion groups and lectures, including the annual Seán Lester Lecture; an event dedicated to the Irishman who served as the last Secretary-General of the League of Nations. The annual Seán Lester Lecture is delivered by a high profile person on a topic of international importance. During 2006, the Irish Society of International Law hosted the following events:

EXTRAORDINARY RENDITION-12 APRIL 2006

Dr Gernot Biehler, of Trinity College Dublin, led a discussion group in which the legal basis for the practice of extraordinary rendition was considered. Dr Biehler rejected the legality of the practice and maintained that Ireland could be obliged to prevent acts of rendition by the International Covenant on Civil and Political Rights and the Torture Convention, as well as the common law prohibition on false imprisonment.

THE SADDAM HUSSEIN TRIAL—10 MAY 2006

Prof Mark Drumbl, of Washington and Lee University, put forward the argument that one of the primary functions of criminal tribunals is to create a public narrative of the *ancién regime*. He maintained that the organisation of the prosecutions at the Iraqi High Tribunal into discrete modules, such as that concerning the killings at Dujail in 1982 (for which Saddam Hussein was later executed) in fact frustrated this narrative function.

UN REFORM AND HUMAN RIGHTS—29 SEPTEMBER 2006

Prof Michael O'Flaherty, Member of the United Nations Human Rights Committee and Co-Director of the Human Rights Centre, University of Nottingham, spoke on the topic of 'UN Reform and Human Rights'. He offered an insider's perspective on the negotiations that led up to the creation of the UN Human Rights Council in

March 2006 and discussed some of the problems faced by both the new institution and those it replaces.

THE SECOND ANNUAL SEÁN LESTER LECTURE: BAN KI MOON MAY BE SORRY: THE INTRACTABLE DIFFICULTIES OF UN REFORM—6 DECEMBER 2006

Professsor Ruth Wedgwood, of Johns Hopkins University, delivered the Second Annual Seán Lester Lecture to the Irish Society of International Law. Professor Wedgwood adverted to a number of serious problems with the United Nation's operation and advocated what she termed 'competitive multilateralism' as a means of achieving general reform of the United Nations. Failing action at United Nations level, States should seek to use regional multilateral organisations to resolve international problems. This attitude would force the United Nations to either reform or face increasing irrelevance.

For more information about the Irish Society of International Law, including membership information, and past and future events visit www.isil.ie.

BOOK REVIEWS

Documents on Irish Foreign Policy, 5 vols: I, 1919–22; II, 1923–26; III, 1926–32; IV, 1932–36; V, 1937–39. Edited by Ronan Fanning, Michael Kennedy, Dermot Keogh, Eunan O'Halpin and Catriona Crowe (vols IV and V). Dublin, Royal Irish Academy, 1998 (vols I–II), 2002 (vol III), 2004 (vol IV), 2006 (vol V). Vol I (576 pp, Hbk €38.09, ISBN 1874045631), vol II (596 pp, Hbk €38.09, ISBN 1874045836), vol III (986 pp, Hbk €45, ISBN 1874045968), vol IV (595 pp, Hbk €45, ISBN 1904830038), vol V (554 pp, Hbk €45, ISBN 1-904890-21-0).

In the introduction to her now-classic work, *The Thirty Years' War*, first published in 1938, Veronica Wedgwood observed that 'men follow their own interests for the highest as well as for the lowest causes'. Wedgwood's concern—which is not irrelevant with regard to modern Ireland—was whether the so-called 'wars of religion' of the 17th century were purely the result of 'high' causes, as was constantly asserted by the participants. Her conclusion was that, along with 'high' considerations of religion, eternal salvation, theological concerns and so on, more prosaic and venal interests were involved, such as money, land, political power and influence.

The same can be said of governments publishing documents, which clearly may be done for a combination of legal considerations and high causes. The most enduring series of published diplomatic documents, *Foreign Relations of the United States*, was initiated in 1861 as a more-or-less contemporaneous selection of documents, analogous to the *British and Foreign State Papers* series produced in the United Kingdom from 1831 until 1968. These selections were originally conceived as reference works enabling both governments and other interested parties to keep up-to-date with legislation, treaties and other political and economic documents with an international dimension. But governments have also published selections of documents with quite specific propaganda and foreign policy objectives. Among the most tendentious of these were the collections published by the principal belligerents in the First World War, aiming to seize the moral high ground, justify their own participation and, in turn, cast blame on the enemy. Thus, there were, among others, a British 'Blue Book', a French 'Yellow Book' and a German 'White Book'.

The publication of diplomatic documents was further boosted over the period of the war and its aftermath by three further factors. In the first place, President Woodrow Wilson, determined to base American participation on firm moral principles, announced his famous Fourteen Principles in January 1918, of which the very first was: 'Open covenants of peace, openly arrived at, after which there shall be no private international understandings of any kind but diplomacy shall proceed always frankly and in the public view'. This idealistic aim was not particularly welcome to the worldly diplomats of Europe, who in any case assumed that it would certainly not apply retrospectively. But here a second factor emerged, the decision of the revolutionary new Bolshevik regime in Russia to publish the secret treaties of imperial Russia, which, it was thought, might require other governments to publish their own versions of events. The third, and perhaps most powerful, factor was the determination of the German government after 1918 to challenge the 'war guilt' clause, article 231 of the Treaty of Versailles, with the comprehensive publication of diplomatic documents, in what has been called a kind of 'pre-emptive historiography', designed to demonstrate that (at the very least) 'guilt' for the war was not Germany's alone. Thus, the German Foreign Office produced a magnificent fifty-volume series in the 1920s:

Die Grosse Politik des Europäische Kabinette. This publication was clearly designed to undermine the moral and legal authority of the Versailles Treaty, and indeed, it was quite successful in doing so, certainly influencing much writing on the origins of the war.

The success of the German publication provoked both the British and French governments to commission selections of documents, the former producing eleven volumes of *British Documents on the Origins of the War* by 1938. Apart from their political objective, the British also asserted a more generalised 'public good' reason for the venture. Not only would the British case be properly presented (and independent academic editors were specifically chosen to underpin public confidence in the exercise), but the publication would help to educate both academia and the wider public in the processes and principles of British diplomacy. During the Second World War, by which time *Foreign Relations of the United States* had become a more 'historical' publication, in which the Americans were planning to publish their own inter-war documents, the British decided to embark on another collection, *Documents on British Foreign Policy*, covering the years 1919–39. Although the rationale for this series was essentially political, it had taken on more the air of an exercise in public enlightenment by the time it was published in the 1960s and also appears to have inspired the subsequent (and continuing) *British Documents on British Policy Overseas*, which publishes documents dating from 1945. Indeed, the publication of foreign policy documents has become almost a staple in many countries, always with the aim of informing the public, if not also of advancing less high-minded policy objectives (which in any case are not likely to be indicated quite so explicitly).

So it is with *Documents on Irish Foreign Policy* (*DIFP*). As laid down in 1995, the project's 'basic aim is to make available in an organised and accessible way, to people who may not be in a position easily to consult the National Archives, documents from the files of the Department [of Foreign Affairs] which are considered important or useful for an understanding of Irish foreign policy'. The series was to 'begin at the foundation of the State and publish volumes in chronological order', and 'the basic criterion for the selection of documents' was to be their 'use or importance in understanding the evolution of policies and decisions'. In the 1996 White Paper, *Challenges and Opportunities Abroad*, the project was cast 'as part of the Government's desire to encourage a greater interest in Irish foreign policy'. Indeed, the intention was much more specifically scholarly, as it was hoped that the initiative would 'encourage and assist much greater academic interest in the study of Irish foreign policy' (*DIFP*, I, pp ix–x). The project is a joint venture between the Department of Foreign Affairs and the Royal Irish Academy, and the editors are all independent and highly-respected academics. Although the primary source for the documents selected is the National Archives, other archives (including the United Kingdom National Archives and the University College Dublin Archives) have been used. This is particularly so for the early days, during which secure bureaucratic practices had not yet been established. As the editors wryly observe, 'the nature of the first Dáil Éireann administration meant that some material and information was destroyed, captured in raids or simply not written down'. Editorial standards are high: the documents are reproduced with only minimal intervention, and biographical details of the most important people are mentioned in the text. A few, but by no means all, allusions in the text are explained in footnotes, and this aspect of the editing of the volumes assumes of the reader some existing knowledge of the national and international context. There is a handy 'list of documents reproduced' in all but the first volume, pleasingly suggesting that even the editors were able to learn from history. The volumes are well, though not quite comprehensively, indexed.

Broadly-speaking, the volumes describe a development from confused, ad hoc, early years dominated by status-seeking and assertion to a recognisably mature State with an accepted and respected place within the international states system and a professionalised (if still very small) diplomatic service. As has been noted, the project as a whole was devised to cover Irish foreign relations from 'the foundation of the State', and this itself was, of course, a major preoccupation in the early days. The Editors have dated the foundation of the State to 21 January 1919 and have reproduced as the very first document in volume one the 'Declaration of Independence' passed by the first Dáil. Along with this, as the second document, is the 'Message to the Free Nations of the World' of the same date, calling 'upon every free nation to support the Irish Republic by recognising Ireland's national status and her right to its vindication at the Peace Congress' (*DIFP*, I, pp 1–2). This, however, as with many such acts, was only assertion, and whatever may have been the situation within Ireland itself, Ireland's *international* status actually depended not just on the aspirations and achievements of the revolutionaries themselves but also, crucially, on the formally-expressed views of other sovereign States. Eamon De Valera and his colleagues were very well aware of this, and the earliest Irish diplomatic efforts were devoted towards trying (unsuccessfully, as it turned out) to get Ireland a seat at the Paris peace conference, while simultaneously launching a world-wide propaganda effort and seeking to raise funds (especially in the United States) to support the Irish national endeavour.

If at the beginning Irish nationalists asserted the status of a nation which did not, in international law terms, yet exist, so, too, was the propaganda based on an assertion of support which equally may have been elusive. As Sean T O'Ceallaigh reported home from Paris in May 1919 about the 'Franco-Irish Society', it was a 'body you needn't take too seriously. As far as it exists at all it has been brought into existence by me. . . . I think the total membership of the Society numbers six . . . [but] I thought it well from a propaganda point of view that such a Society should be founded and reports of its meetings be sent to the press from time to time' (*DIFP*, I, p 18). It will be seen, therefore, that even at this early stage, the embryonic Irish foreign service had already grasped the importance of using diplomacy to project a vision of a *desired* world, rather than one which actually existed. In time, the gunmen and politicians back home secured enough concessions from the British to establish at least a proto-State, which was granted by the treaty agreed on 6 December 1921, 'the same constitutional status in the Community of Nations of the British Empire as the Dominion of Canada, the Commonwealth of Australia, the Dominion of New Zealand, and the Union of South Africa' (*DIFP*, I, p 356). Thus, Ireland became a 'dominion' within the British empire for a while.

From the start, what emerged as the twenty-six county 'Irish Free State' sought to establish a position distinct from the other British dominions. In a thoughtful memorandum, George Gavan Duffy, Minister for Foreign Affairs in 1922, argued that the 'ancient Irish nation' should not be compared to those 'new countries—which until recently were mere Colonies of Britain'. A better parallel, he argued, would be a small country like Belgium, which had 'internal difficulties somewhat similar to those in

Ireland' and externally was 'in danger of being absorbed by two constantly warring powers'. Her 'zeal and tenacity in emphasising her sovereignty throughout the World', however, had 'alone prevented this absorption'. He further asserted that 'Ireland's influence in the World' could 'be immeasurably greater than that of Belgium within ten years if our State is conducted on wise national lines at home and on lines of vigorous determination abroad' (*DIFP*, I, p 438). It was an appropriate and uplifting manifesto for the years to come.

Manifestations of independent nationhood come in many guises. In March 1922, Gavan Duffy wrote to Michael Collins (who may at that time have had better things to think about) concerning 'an issue of some importance in connection with our foreign relations'. This was the Postmaster-General's desire that application 'be made for Ireland's admission to the Universal Postal Union' (*DIFP*, I, p 421). Gavan Duffy was not wrong about the importance of the UPU (which, however, does not appear in the otherwise admirable index), for without membership in the Union and formal registration of relevant designs Ireland could not issue postage stamps which would be recognised internationally. The volumes under review do not reveal when Ireland actually joined the UPU, but on 6 December 1922, precisely a year after the Treaty had been signed, the first Irish postage stamp was issued, demonstrating national independence to the humblest letter-writer and, by depicting a map of an unpartitioned Ireland, also asserting sovereignty over the whole island. In similar vein, negotiations about the design and wording of a new Irish passport involved an assertion of sovereignty which affected individual Irish citizens. In January 1924, Michael MacWhite, the Irish representative at the League of Nations, told Dublin that he had been asked 'by several persons here as to how and when they may be able to get *Irish passports*' (*DIFP*, II, p 243). This came just at a moment when the Free State government was arguing with the British government that the technically-correct (in terms of international law) but politically incorrect (from an Irish standpoint) descriptor 'British subject' should be replaced on Irish passports with something more acceptable to Irish nationalist opinion. After some inconclusive exchanges, with London refusing to give ground, Dublin simply acted unilaterally, resolving in March 1924 to describe an Irish passport holder as 'Citizen of the Irish Free State and of the British Commonwealth of Nations' (*DIFP*, II, p 278). Although British consular staff were instructed not to recognise these passports, it does not seem to have caused many practical difficulties, though the matter was not cleared up until the passage of the Irish Nationality and Citizenship Act of 1935.

This legislation was part of De Valera's recasting of the British-Irish constitutional relationship following his coming to power in 1932 and leading a majority government after the general election of January 1933. The impact of this regime change on Irish diplomacy and foreign policy is the main and engrossing theme of *DIFP* volume four. De Valera was determined that Ireland's sovereignty would clearly be established in symbolic terms, as well as through the actual and developing autonomy which had been achieved under the Treaty settlement. He was, for example, resolved to get rid of the Oath of Allegiance to the British Crown, which, although it had had no practical influence on Ireland's status, he extravagantly described to the Irish High Commissioner in London, John W Dulanty, the day after St Patrick's Day 1932 as 'the cause of all the strife and dissension in this country since the signing of the Treaty' (*DIFP*, IV, p 21). We can, too, see De Valera apparently marrying principle with administrative convenience in a February 1934 formal despatch to JH Thomas, the British Secretary for Dominion Affairs, about what was to emerge as the 1935 Nationality Act. The 'necessity for an appropriate code of Irish nationality has long been felt', he declared. In addition, however, he improbably asserted that the legislation was necessary because of 'the pressing need for the conclusion of extradition treaties with a number of countries' (*DIFP*, IV, p 280). It may be that the passage of the Nationality Act was followed by a torrent of extradition treaties, the negotiation of which was surely a task for Irish diplomats, but neither volume four (which runs to December 1936) nor volume five (1937–9) contains any indication of this. The latter, indeed (and perhaps rightly), concentrate more on the resolution of British-Irish differences with the 1938 Anglo-Irish Agreements and Irish responses to the approach of war in Europe.

A constant theme in all these volumes is an understandable Irish determination to carve out an international role sharply distinct from that of the United Kingdom. Volume three, for example, covering 1926–32, includes the 1927 Geneva Naval Conference, when the Irish Free State was for the first time separately represented by its own plenipotentiaries, and Ireland's acceptance in 1929 of compulsory jurisdiction of the Permanent Court of International Justice. But even in this latter development, the importance of asserting Irish sovereignty was as important as any inherent 'rightness' of submitting to the jurisdiction of the Permanent Court, as was made clear by Joseph P Walsh, the long-serving Secretary to the Department of External Affairs (as it was then known) in September 1929. Cabling to Sean Murphy, the Irish representative in Geneva, he said the government would not allow Ireland to agree to any arrangement which prohibited disputes between British dominions from being taken before the Court. 'Circumstances by which Saorstát got her independence vastly different from those of other Commonwealth States', he wrote. 'Right to appeal to International Court as ultimate safeguard of independence must be maintained' (*DIFP*, III, p 367).

The story told in these volumes is not all dry diplomacy. The editors have plundered some private collections to supplement the documents in the National Archives, and in some of these, a pleasing personal note rings through. Thus, we have Sean Nunan in New York complaining to Michael Collins in September 1919 that 'God knows you hardly know who to trust out here. Everyone seems to be out for some game of his own' (*DIFP*, I, p 45). Then there is Ernest Blyth writing to his wife in early September 1926 from Geneva where he was attending the Assembly of the League of Nations. Disastrously, he had gone swimming in Lake Geneva and had sat out in the midday sun in his 'bathing pants', with the result that 'I am sitting in my room writing this with nothing on the upper part of my body but a thick coating of cold cream . . . my shoulders and the upper part of my back have the colour of lobster and the feel of a hot linseed poultice' (*DIFP*, III, p 31). And Michael MacWhite, stranded in Rome in August 1938: 'Nearly all the diplomatic people have been absent since early July and are not expected back before the middle of September or the beginning of October', he wrote, concluding that 'the Italians take their holidays seriously' (*DIFP*, V, p 329).

Clearly, it is hoped that this series of publications will encourage an increased interest in and knowledge of Irish foreign policy-making, a 'high cause' indeed. The overall impression of the selection of documents, however, is that underneath the admirably disinterested educational rationale for the production of the volumes lies a political sub-text. The chief interest of Irish foreign policy in the first two decades of the State, to an at times obsessive degree (and understandably so), concerned relations with the United Kingdom. Nothing mattered more than putting national and diplomatic distance between the new State and its historically dominant neighbour. Generally, however, the selection of documents does not fully reflect this, and one is left with the impression that documents relating to Anglo-Irish matters are somewhat disproportionately leavened with documents dealing with, for example, Ireland's engagement with the League of Nations. To have reflected the intensity of Irish interest as it actually was would have meant downplaying the aspirational involvement with international agencies, which presages Ireland's more substantive diplomatic engagements over the past forty years or so. Thus, the selection of documents in part reflects as much contemporary assumptions and assertions of Ireland's foreign policy as it does historical reality.

These are handsome and impressive volumes, testifying to satisfyingly high production values, but while they are a pleasure to handle and a delight as artefacts, they are also a very old-fashioned mode of publication. Both *Foreign Relations of the United States* and *British Documents on British Policy Overseas* are now published with searchable CD-ROM text, and it is excellent that Ireland's contribution to the gendre is also being published on-line (at www.difp.ie), especially bearing in mind that the entire Oireachtas debates were published electronically, far in advance of the proceedings of the American or British legislatures. Nevertheless, these five volumes will admirably preserve on many a library shelf the textual record of Irish foreign relations over the first two decades of the State and also testify to the commendable commitment of the government in supporting and funding scholarship of a notably high order.

Keith Jeffery
School of History and Anthropology
Queen's University of Belfast

International Law in Practice: An Irish Perspective, by Gernot Biehler, Dublin Thomson, Round Hall, 2005, xli + 474 pp, Pbk 125, ISBN–13: 9781858004051.

As its title indicates, this book places special emphasis on the practice of international law in court and government departments, and it also offers a particularly Irish perspective on its subject. The book emphasises the Irish experience as a small non-aligned State and its contribution to UN peacekeeping and also the jurisprudence of the Irish courts on such issues as neutrality and the relationship between international and national law. International law generally, Gernot Biehler observes in the Preface, is 'a primitive discipline' (vii): he refers to the relative indeterminacy of international law, its irregular enforcement and its strong links to the exercise of political power. He suggests therefore that the subject should be approached in a quasi-jurisprudential manner—drawing on general legal principles—and in a way that takes into particular consideration 'the stances of governments' (vii).

Overall, the book—which is the basic text for the international law course as taught currently at Trinity College Dublin—succeeds in doing what it sets out to do. Its integrated discussions of theory and *realpolitik* as well as its analysis of both Irish and international case law are commendable. The book does not however get off to a good start: while the vast majority of its ten chapters are of a high standard, the opening three chapters are somewhat too idiosyncratic for a textbook introduction.

The first chapter, 'The Features of International Law', begins with a general conception of international law: 'One State's action against or interaction with another State is the main subject of international law' (1). The chapter discusses State sovereignty as well as the 'international unity factor within international law', that is, 'the practical consequence of its reference to a higher legal order' (10). Chapter 2, 'The State in International Law', includes further discussion of sovereignty but argues that the individual is always the ultimate addressee of international law. Taken together, the chapters do not offer a rigorous theoretical framework for the chapters that follow, and there is also too much unnecessary repetition—both chapters include similar references to Jean Bodin and Louis XIV, for example, and both discuss the internal and external aspects of sovereignty and the principle of 'sovereign equality' in the UN Charter. In the eventuality of a second edition—a possibility referred to in the Preface—it would be worth considering fusing and revamping the first two chapters.

The partial account of private international law in Chapter 3, 'Jurisdiction', is also problematic. Although the focus of the chapter and the book is on public international law, if reference to private international law is to be included there should be more explanation of the Brussels I Regulation and similar instruments relating to private law jurisdiction. The nature of the conflict of laws *per se* and of choice-of-law issues also deserves more attention of an introductory kind.

From this point on, however, the book improves greatly. The overview of the sources of international law in Chapter 4 is based on the categorisation contained in Article 38 of the Statute of the ICJ but also on the author's 'personal attitude' (viii) that accords higher significance to customary law than to the law of treaties. All sources of law listed in Article 38, he argues, may be seen as deriving from one common source: 'general practice accepted as law' is 'the prime reason why any action may be held to be internationally legal or not' (82). In line with this perspective, the Vienna Convention on the Law of Treaties is included as one of six Appendices to the book and only those provisions requiring some explanation are dealt with in the text itself, as are the other main sources: general principles; judicial decisions; and the views of 'the most highly qualified publicists of the various nations'. Biehler's argument regarding practice is strong but it could be bolstered further by reference to the idea that, essentially, law is something that is *discovered*—an idea developed most notably in recent times by the French legal philosopher, Michel Villey.

This book is not authored solely by Biehler: two chapters are by Clive Symmons and another is by Jean Allain. In Chapter 5 Symmons addresses the issue of whether monistic-based incorporation theory or dualist-based transformation theory governs Irish practice regarding the relationship between international law and municipal law. Symmons argues that the effect of customary international law on Irish law is much less clear than the treaty law provisions in Article 29 of *Bunreacht na hÉireann* and he advocates an amendment that would indicate in a clear, albeit declaratory, way that the principle of automatic incorporation of customary international law into Irish law pertains, subject to such exceptions as may be laid out. Such an amendment would not only clarify the situation, he suggests, but would also mean that 'only two exceptions would be relevant to defeat a private litigant's claims, whether civil or criminal, based thereon; namely, a clear contrary provision of a constitutional nature (but not including Article 15) or a clearly countervailing statutory provision, so respectively preserving Irish constitutional and parliamentary sovereignty' (151–152).

Symmons also contributes Chapter 6 on Irish practice on recognition of States, governments and illegal acquisition of territory. His analysis emphasises the historical differences—*vis-à-vis* British practice—between Irish practice relating to, on the one hand, recognition of States and illegal territorial acquisitions and, on the other hand, recognition of governments.

The main author deals with international law procedures before the ICJ and in proceedings before Irish courts in Chapter 7. This is a long and comprehensive chapter in which Biehler's experience as a practitioner of international law is evident and which includes discussion of sovereign and diplomatic immunities. Biehler explains that immunities are treated in the context of procedural law in order to strip them of their 'seemingly independent appearance in law and to make clear that inevitably a balance has to be struck between immunities and conflicting rights in the context of legal proceedings before courts of law both national and international' (205–206).

Chapter 8, 'Ireland in International Law', includes an account of Ireland's emergence as an independent state in international law; of the legal basis of Ireland's peace-keeping role and of the State's peace-keeping contributions; and finally of the status of Northern Ireland in international law. This is an informative chapter although it is difficult to see why an overview of the Belfast Agreement is provided before rather than after the outline of Northern Ireland's constitutional history.

Jean Allain's chapter on the Irish approach to *jus ad bellum*—the legality of use of force—traces the history of the United Nations System prohibiting the unilateral use of force and instead vesting that prerogative with States collectively. Allain suggests that, while the system remains intact, and while Ireland has been steadfast in its support for it, its very essence is under attack by States unwilling to accept 'that the consequences of unbridled use of force creates an unstable international system which [. . .] may well lead us down the road towards the scourge of war' (292). Allain considers, however, that the 'true challenge' to the UN System comes from the African Union, which has formally opted-out of it and thereby 'challenged the overall edifice of *jus ad bellum* painstakingly developed over more than half a century' (307).

The final chapter examines neutrality and the Irish perspective on *jus in bello*—the law governing the conduct of war. It includes a thorough and topical overview of international humanitarian law, which, despite its irregular enforcement, the author considers to be 'an exceptional achievement of humanity in all meanings of the word' (310).

While this book is a valuable and interesting contribution to the literature on public international law from the Irish perspective, there is room for improvement in the introductory chapters. This could be remedied in a second edition; indeed it would be essentioal to do so if the intention is to offer a textbook for undergraduate courses other than the one the book was written for originally.

Tim Murphy
University of Akureyri, Iceland

Can Human Rights Survive? by Conor Gearty, Cambridge, Cambridge University Press, 2006, 190 pp, Pbk £12.99, ISBN-10: 0521685524, ISBN-13: 9780521685528.

In these essays delivered as the 2005 Hamlyn Lectures, Professor of Human Rights Law at the London School of Economics and Political Science Conor Gearty leads readers concerned about human rights on a provocative and disturbing tour through its turbulent terrain. His analyses of the three major themes he identifies as threatening the field's survival, or, at best, its 'subver[sion] out of all present recognition', will likely spur very diverse reactions. In the process of making bold arguments, he does not preach a party platform or sketch one grand unifying theory but, rather, raises his own urgent and deep questions. The book stimulates reflection, prompting the reader to ask: do I agree or disagree? and why?

The three themes that Gearty stresses are the field's current crises of authority, legalism, and national security. The first crisis stems from the fact that human rights partisans are lonely 'disciples of an idea rather than a sacred text', indeed an idea without a 'demonstrable foundation' in faith or history. Human rights lie beyond shared values in a post-modern age of doubt. Nonetheless, they now enjoy an uncontested global ideology, almost amounting to a 'bandwagon that looks as though it is here to stay'. But the movement's political activism and legalisation must find or develop a deeper philosophical base. The task, Gearty argues, is demanding since basic conceptions of human rights do not issue from the gut (deep feeling) or from a 'discovery' of 'truth' but from more cerebral argument involving the elaboration of a theory. Recently there has indeed been some movement toward persuasion rather than revelation, as evidenced by theories based on consensus or the ideas of philosophers such as Amartya Sen.

Human rights must go beyond theory to action, to efforts to improve the world and help its dispossessed. This enterprise must be based on a new 'foundationalism', a 'modern form of truth,' something 'universalist' that responds not to the selfish and aggressive side of human nature but to the side of compassion and empathy directed principally to the world's oppressed. The basic ideas informing the human rights movement are radical and transformatory: they give the oppressed 'a language with which to shout for attention'.

A second crisis stems from the progressive legalisation of human rights, as ideas earlier rooted in religion, morals, and politics become embedded in the work of law professionals and in statutes, constitutions, and judicial opinions. 'Which great social movement has ever put the lawyers in its front-line?' Will not human rights lose their energy, their force among the people? In their legal incarnation, human rights impose a barrier between law and politics, pretending to constitute a 'supra-political' force. But rights grow out of and can achieve their goals only through politics. This 'misguided foundationalism' can 'debilitate the political process'.

The trend toward legal and judicial supremacy will also damage the legal system. Judicial review of legislation under human rights criteria arrogates a competence given by the people to their legislative representatives by the vote. As a consequence, law becomes politicized. Ireland, South Africa, and the United States offer prime illustrations of this dangerous trend. The whole legal process assumes the aura of politics—for example, confirmation battles in the United States over Supreme Court justices, amicus briefs from interest groups, failure of the highest courts to follow precedent, and trends in judicial law-making that entrench one or another human right through a process resembling nothing so much as a political campaign. All of this, and more, endangers the Rule of Law, as well as a cardinal principle of democracy: broad political participation by the people. Indeed, the United Kingdom offers a different and preferable approach toward assuring that human rights are 'properly protected and enforced, through the terms of its Human Rights Act that denies supremacy to legal discourse and leaves final power with the people's representatives in Parliament'.

The third crisis of national security addresses current and well-known issues. Gearty fears that anti-terrorism laws lose their character as exceptions to the normal character of law within a democratic society, perhaps necessary exceptions but exceptions nonetheless. Rather, they become mainstays of society, its fundamental assurance of survival. Thus, the course of legislation and judicial opinion in many states does not basically create a gap between older, rooted understandings of human rights and counter-terrorism policies but, rather, redefines the content and reach of human rights to find no gap whatsoever.

In his conclusion, Gearty identifies poverty and environmental damage as the two greatest dangers today and questions not only the capacity of human rights to address them effectively, but whether human rights as we have understood them can survive at all.

There is much to admire in these essays. The book is less a scholarly undertaking drawing on or criticising views of prominent thinkers in the field than an effort to express Gearty's own personal understanding of the field, morally and politically, as well as his acute fears for the survival of the human rights movement. Clearly, Gearty is among the committed. His compassion and empathy for the underbelly of humanity to which he believes the human rights movement should be directed undergird his analysis. The movement is rooted in the 'simple insight that each of us counts, that we are equally worthy of esteem'.

It is, to be sure, an unusual trio of themes to combine within the lecture series; Gearty covers a lot of ground, and at times darts about his subject. Throughout, his critical and provocative spirit, his instinct to explore the large picture rather than deal with concrete issues here and there, his numerous insights, enliven the argument.

There is space only to suggest some of the issues on which I would welcome a spirited conversation (can he engage in any other kind?) with Gearty. Consider his stress on the necessity of a more systematic and elaborated justification, philosophical and moral and universal in its reach, for the human rights corpus. Gearty seems principally to encourage a move from the 'cerebral', such as images like a state of nature or veil of ignorance, to a theory of more intuitive appeal that is more likely to draw a popular response. From this perspective, Sen's focus on freedom in relation to development and on realisation of human capability represents an important step forward, giving prominence to the ethical dimensions of the subject and attention to the world's marginalised. But the human rights beliefs that animate individuals and masses to think, protest, and act in history's great (if sometimes very slow) transformations stem less from popular agreement with reasoned justifications for the movement than from human instincts of justice and injustice, right and wrong, growing perhaps out of a naturalist sense of who humans are and what they owe each other. Those instincts are well captured in the movement's fundamental and unelaborated postulate underlying many treaties and declarations: equal human dignity. Human rights discourse itself is the new universal, here to stay, with great latent power and potential for launching processes of change. This is the triumph of the first six decades of the movement.

Let me also mention the second essay's attack on judicial usurpation. Here my American sensibility may simply clash with that of Europeans who are far readier to assign courts a more humble and restrained role, although the European human rights system and post-war constitutions in many states make the power of judicial review very familiar. Of course, Americans are also engaged in serious debates about the proper domain of courts and about the risk that arrogation of power by them may weaken the democratic spirit. In my view, the contribution of courts to human rights—however striking the opinions of national and regional courts over the last four decades—has not been a dominant factor in the movement's progress, or even an important role in the profound changes seen in parts of the developing world. Courts play their larger role not in human rights revolutions, peaceful or violent, but in new or established orders where the political institutions themselves have made commitments to democracy. Indeed, human rights have enjoyed their greatest successes throughout the world in neither judicial nor legislative fora, but in their capacity to animate repressed peoples to speak up, protest, and move to action in an effort to realise the ideal of being treated consistently with the movement's cardinal principle, equal human dignity.

Henry J Steiner
Harvard Law School

The United Nations, Peace and Security: From Collective Security to the Responsibility to Protect by Ramesh Thakur, Cambridge, Cambridge University Press, 2006, 402 pp, Hbk £47.00, ISBN-13: 9780521855174.

The United Nations was founded as the fruit of aspirations for a new world order free from 'the scourge of war', founded as the preamble of the Charter of the United Nations notes, on a 'faith in fundamental human rights, in the dignity and worth of the human person, in the equal rights of men and women and of nations large and small'. The odd juxtaposition, in a single phrase, of the rights of individuals and of the rights of 'nations' encapsulates a critical, multi-faceted tension at the heart of the organisation: between the right of individuals to protection from the State; the right of peoples to self-determination; the right of States to sovereignty; and the right of States to security. There is now such pressure on the organisation that some commentators see the United Nations as 'a symptom of many of the world's problems' rather than as providing a means to resolve them, whilst others defensively downplay its weaknesses. In his book, *The United Nations, Peace and Security: From Collective Security to the Responsibility to Protect,* Assistant Secretary-General Ramesh Thakur steers a balanced course. He offers an astute analysis of the United Nations that is both unflinching and positive.

Thakur opens his argument with the observation that whilst the United Nations has for most of its existence focused on the security of States now it 'is at long last elevating the doctrine of preventing mass atrocities against people to the same level of collective responsibility as preventing and repelling armed aggression against States' (p 1). This may be putting the case a little too strongly, but General Assembly Resolution

60/1 of 24 October 2005 and Security Council Resolution 1674 of 28 April 2006[1] clearly indicate that the United Nations now considers human security to be an integral aspect of the international peace and security that it is tasked with maintaining. The responsibility for security, whether State or human, entails judgements as to when, how and to what degree force should be used, and it is this that forms the leitmotif of *The United Nations, Peace and Security*. Ramesh Thakur identifies five thematic areas that raise issues relating to the use of force: guidelines on the use of force; the legality-legitimacy gap; the United Nations-United States relationship; the divide between developing and industrial countries; and the rule of law. These provide the lenses through which Thakur examines a range of problems relating to security.

Part I deals with 'soft security perspectives' relating to human security, human rights, international criminal justice and international sanctions. Part II deals with 'hard security issues' relating to the nuclear threat; international terrorism; problem States, such as Iraq; enforcement action pursuant to the collective responsibility to protect; and the erosion of the norm of non-intervention. Normative inconsistency in relation to many of these security 'perspectives' and 'issues' lies at the root of much criticism of the United Nations. The difficulties, Ramesh Thakur argues, are especially acute for developing States. A relatively low priority is given to problems such as disease, poverty, lack of clean water, lack of electricity, and lack of education, all of which are as much a threat to the security of these countries as terrorism is to industrial countries. The people of developing countries have not always benefited as much as they should have from changes in the interpretation of the rules governing the use of force, in particular the international community's increasing express willingness to support enforcement actions where there are serious abuses of human rights (p 1). Such States are also more vulnerable to sanctioned, or tacitly condoned, abuses of the rules on the use of force. The heightened concerns of powerful States as regards international security since 11 September 2001 have added to the anxiety felt by weaker States. It is an anxiety that the industrialised world would be unwise to ignore. Thakur observes that there is a serious 'imbalance of voice in the international discourse' on these issues that 'has built up a dangerous sense of resentment by the silent majority of the world's peoples' (p 22).

The United Nations, Peace and Security is compelling reading for anyone who cares about the future of the United Nations, partly because of the breadth and depth of its analysis but principally because of Thakur's ability not only to understand the organisation's weaknesses but also to see and articulate the means to make it function better. He argues that too often the United Nations has demonstrated a 'failure to tackle urgent collective problems due to institutionalised inability, incapacity, or unwillingness' but that 'the United Nations is the one body that houses the divided fragments of humanity' (p 369) and that it has shown 'a surprising capacity for institutional innovation, conceptual advances, policy adaptation and organisational learning' (p 343). Thakur believes that it is both necessary and possible to make the organisation work or, at any rate, to work better. Giving up is not an option. In his

[1] In Resolution 60/1, the General Assembly undertook 'to take collective action, in a timely and decisive manner, through the Security Council, in accordance with the Charter, including Chapter VII, on a case-by- case basis and in cooperation with relevant regional organizations as appropriate, should peaceful means be inadequate and national authorities are manifestly failing to protect their populations from genocide, war crimes, ethnic cleansing and crimes against humanity'. This undertaking was affirmed by the Security Council in Resolution 1674.

concluding observations, Ramesh Thakur writes '[i]f one has never failed, then one has not tried hard enough: one has not pushed oneself hard enough, not tested the limits of one's potential' (p 368). Quoting Dag Hammarskjöld, he observes that 'the United Nations was not created in order to bring us to heaven, but to save us from hell.'[2] 'Fail better' might well be on its way to becoming the mantra of our time,[3] but in this context it is more than a matter of personal choice: it is a collective imperative.

Siobhán Wills
Faculty of Law, University College Cork

Irish Perspectives on EC Law by Mary Catherine Lucey and Cathrina Keville (eds.), Dublin, Thomson Round Hall, 2003, xxxvi + 396 pp, Pbk €135, ISBN 1-85800-280-X.

This collection of fifteen essays examines the impact of European Community (EC) law on the Irish legal order. It explores selected areas related to the institutional (Chapters One to Three) and substantive law of the European Union (EU) (Chapters Four to Fifteen).

In Chapter One, Cathrina Keville discusses 'The Principle of Effectiveness and the Development of a System of Remedies at European Community Law', focusing on the *Francovich* (Cases C-6 and 9/90 [1991] ECR I-535) and *Brasserie du Pêcheur* (Cases C-46 and 48/93 [1996] ECR I-1029) judgments on state liability for breaches of EC law and the application of this principle by Irish courts. Keville argues that national courts should engage in a balancing exercise between respect for their own procedural autonomy and the need for effective enforcement of rights conferred by EC law when applying principles developed by the European Court of Justice (ECJ). In Chapter Two, 'European Community Judicial Review in the Irish Courts—Scope, Standards and Separation of Powers', Catherine Costello analyses judicial review of national measures in light of EC law, particularly general principles, and discusses the role of national courts where the validity of Community measures is at issue. Costello asserts that the national executive may act either as a double 'agent' of EC and national law, subject to two sets of administrative rules, or as a pure 'agent' of EC law, whereby it may usurp national legislative functions under the guise of implementing Community action. It is suggested that national courts should ensure that the complexities of EC law and the multiple standards governing the legality of such national measures (under national law, EC law or the European Convention on Human Rights) do not undermine the rule of law and the efficacy of national judicial review procedures.

Mary Catherine Lucey's 'Application of European Community Competition Law—Some Implications of Bunreacht na hÉireann' discusses the implications of Council Regulation 1/2003 ([2003] OJ L1/1) for the Irish Competition Authority and explains that the boundaries of the rule of the limited and exceptional nature of judicial powers exercised by bodies other than the judiciary under the Irish Constitution will be tested. In Chapter Five, Barry Doherty provides an overview of 'EC

[2] As quoted in B Uquhart, *Hammarskjöld* (New York, WW Norton, 1994) 48 by Thakur, at 369.
[3] 'Try again. Fail again. Fail better.' S Beckett, *Worstward Ho* (1983).

Telecommunications Law in Ireland'. Máire Ní Shúilleabháin's 'Directive 1999/44 on Certain Aspects of the Sale of Consumer Goods and Associated Guarantees: Improving the Rights of the Irish Consumer?' examines the effect of this Directive on consumer protection in Ireland and highlights problems raised by its domestic implementation. While the distinction that Ní Shúilleabháin draws between consumer and mercantile buyers is welcome, whether the Directive can effectively encourage cross-border shopping is debatable. It is highly likely that market barriers will remain as between Member States opting for the Directive's minimum standards and those retaining higher standards of consumer protection. It should also be pointed out that consumers will probably be highly reluctant to return to a Member State simply to seek a remedy for a defective product that they bought there.

Dermot Cahill discusses the 'Scope and General Principles of the Electronic Commerce Directive' 2000/31 ([2000] OJ L178/1) in Chapter Nine, and in the subsequent Chapter, 'Free Movement of Goods', James McDermott provides an overview of ECJ jurisprudence on the prohibition of discrimination in favour of domestic goods, which may arise either from state-funded promotion campaigns or from national rules on origin-marking or public procurement. Cathy Maguire's 'Transfer of Undertakings' examines how Directive 2001/23 ([2001] OJ L82/16), which safeguards employees' rights in the event of business transfers, has been implemented by the Irish legislature and judiciary.

For his part, James Kingston's 'Human Rights and the European Union—An Evolving System' considers the development of human rights protection within the EU, with emphasis on ECJ case-law and the EU Charter of Fundamental Rights and their interaction with the European Convention on Human Rights and the Strasbourg jurisprudence. In Chapter Thirteen, 'Recent Developments in EC Equality Law', Clíona JM Kimber examines equality issues in the ECJ case law and in Community legislation, including Directive 2000/43 on equal treatment irrespective of racial or ethnic origin ([2000] OJ L 180/22), and Framework Directive 2000/78 on equal treatment in employment ([2000] OJ L 313/16). Bernard Ryans' 'The Free Movement of Persons and Ireland' provides a systematic account of the main principles underlying the free movement of persons, whether economically active or not, as interpreted and applied by the ECJ, and considers their impact on Irish immigration law and rights of equal treatment in economic and social matters. Ryan argues that EU law has called into question important aspects of public policy with regard to the free movement of persons between the United Kingdom and Ireland.

Liz Heffernan's 'Judicial Reform under the Treaty of Nice', Alan Doyle's 'Environmental Law: Integrated Control of Pollution?', Paul Anthony McDermott's 'The Europeanisation of Contract Law', and Gavin Barrett's 'The Rights of Third-Country Family Members under European Community Law' complete the picture of the application of EC law in Ireland.

This book is an important contribution to the ongoing discussion of the interaction between Community and national law and, as such, can only be welcomed. The contributors' critical evaluations of major developments in key areas of EU institutional and substantive law and the impact of such developments on the Irish legal system are strengthened by their ability to highlight deficiencies or points of conflict and to suggest apposite solutions for the Irish legislature and judiciary. As is inevitable with works of this kind, however, the book has been overtaken by recent developments in

EU law, such as recent cases of the ECJ dealing with the free movement of EU citizens and their families and the related Directive 2004/38 ([2004] OJ L158/77). Nonetheless, the collection, which has a foreword by Mr. Justice Nial Fennelly, serves as a valuable reference work not only for legal practitioners and academics in Ireland but also for anyone interested in the interplay between EU and national law.

Dimitrios Doukas
School of Law, Queen's University of Belfast

Defining Terrorism in International Law by Ben Saul, Oxford, Oxford University Press, 2006, 408 pp, Hbk £60.00, ISBN-13: 978-0-19-929597-5.

As its title suggests, this book examines the complex and extremely topical question of defining terrorism in international law. *Defining Terrorism in International Law* looks at both international terrorism and internal terrorism.Ben Saul explores the relevance of the latter in international law in several passages (see Chapter 5) and devotes special attention to international humanitarian law. Overall, the study is well-structured and laid out; the first chapter presents the study's aims and asserts the importance to international criminal law of reaching a comprehensive definition of terrorism. Saul distinguishes between terrorism and traditional crimes in international law and analyses terrorism as a distinct crime. He argues that both international terrorism, affecting as it does more than one State, and internal terrorism, are internationally relevant when they threaten international peace and security (p 47).

The author provides a number of helpful, nuanced, insights as to when acts can and cannot qualify as terrorism. For example, Saul distinguishes between acts committed during peacetime that qualify as terrorism and those that do not and also explores acts that can be variously classified as terrorist or even legitimate acts of belligerency when committed during situations of armed conflict. The author makes considerable use of textual quotations from other scholars which are interesting and informative but are sometimes distracting.

Chapters 3 and 4 form the core of the book and, respectively, critically examine what treaty law and customary international law have to say about the definition of terrorism in international law. In Chapter 3, which considers and compares universal and regional treaties related to terrorism, the author shows that it has been difficult to reach a comprehensive definition of terrorism because of a sectoral approach and the large number of specific treaties that deal with different forms of terrorism in specific contexts or by particular methods (p 135). The author makes important references to the 1937 League of Nations Convention for the Prevention and Punishment of Terrorism (pp 171–173) and the 2000 Draft Comprehensive Convention (p 189) in his consideration of universal instruments and notes that the definitions of terrorism provided in regional instruments can impact upon State practice, though it should be stressed that these instruments do not share a common definition of the phenomenon (p 144), thus make it difficult to drawn overall conclusions.

After an in-depth analysis of practice within the United Nations and other relevant fora, Chapter 4 concludes that there is at present no 'customary international definition or crime of terrorism' (p 270). Customary international law, it is argued, does not support individual criminal responsibility for acts of terrorism as there appears to be a lack of consensus among States. The author stresses the potential impact that emerging norms related to international terrorism may have on customary rules of State responsibility related to attribution. He points out, for example, that there is developing State practice that tends toward holding States responsible for the acts of non-State actors, even when the State does not exercise effective control over the part or the entirety of its territory.

Chapter 4 reviews recent Security Council resolutions that address both specific terrorist acts and terrorism more generally.[1] Particular attention is paid to paragraph three of Resolution 1566 (2004). That paragraph provides a definition of terrorism that could serve as a guide for States and the General Assembly in arriving at a comprehensive definition. It encompasses the acts noted in specific treaties and adds the following elements 'intended to create terror, intimidate a population, or coerce a government or organization' (p 247). This definition is important for several reasons, not the least of which is that it does not require a political motivation. The effect of these Security Council measures has been to harmonise municipal criminal laws and is leading toward a uniform *opinio juris* and State practice.

The author provides a useful examination of municipal laws on terrorism and international as well as municipal jurisprudence on the issue, which is done in great detail and with precision. Among the different regimes at municipal level, Ben Saul argues that there are too few similarities to say that State practice supports a minimum core definition of terrorism. In the majority of cases, States prosecute terrorism as an ordinary crime, without reference to the basic element of the creation of terror that would differentiate it from other ordinary crimes.

Finally, Chapter 5 explores the relationship between terrorism and international humanitarian law. This chapter is particularly interesting because it explores both theoretical and practical issues. According to the author, terrorism has a different meaning in war than it does during peacetime, with international humanitarian law prohibiting the deliberate terrorising of civilians.

To conclude, the book provides a sophisticated study of the definition of terrorism in international law. It is a comprehensive and important contribution to the existing scholarship.

Valeria Eboli
Faculty of Law, University of Pisa

Political Rights Under Stress in 21st Century Europe by Wojciech Sadurski (ed), Oxford, Oxford University Press, 2006, 304 pp, Pbk £40.00, ISBN-13: 978-0-19-929603-3.

Political Rights Under Stress in 21st Century Europe, though not encyclopaedic, charts key issues concerning political rights in today's Europe. The collection of essays appears eclectic at first, yet despite the somewhat scattered nature of the collection, the resulting whole is an intriguing read. The first of the contributions, by Michel

[1] For example, see Security Council Resolutions 1269 (1999), 1377 (2001), and 1456 (2003).

Rosenfeld, alone demands much of the reader's attention. In a broad-ranging survey of theories of political rights, he examines the compatibility of three key schools of thought—liberalism, republicanism and communitarianism—within the idea of pluralism. This theory-laden work, though challenging at times, is nonetheless rewarding for the persevering reader, as it offers a complete theory of rights which deserves engagement. Perhaps the most important lesson from this volume can be captured in Rosenfeld's neat turn of phrase—'arguably when the unity of the polity begins to crack but is in no imminent danger of collapse, it would seem better to enforce rather than weaken political rights'.

Damian Chalmer's piece examines the particular conception of political rights and the political sphere in the EU legal order . He focuses on the 'government of the EU market society'—based in the idea of regulation. Chalmers notes that the EU's response to the New York attacks of 11 September 2001 'should therefore be seen as symptomatic of a more general politics of nervousness', and his essay—found at Chapter Two—is an impressive synthesis of the different strands of this politics. He concludes that government under stress in the EU is concerned with reorientation of norms (rather than temporary deviation from them); centralisation of administrative power; and preservation of the status quo, rather than a return to a pre-existing 'normality'. One of the laudable achievements of Wojciech Sadurski's volume is to address the 'war on terror(ism)' without becoming obsessive. Invoked by both Rosenfeld and Chalmers, and haunting each of the other chapters, the 'war' is perhaps the greatest stress on political rights of our time.

The examination of freedom of expression under the European Convention on Human Rights by Victor Ferreres Comella covers much ground. Taking in most aspects of 'political speech', it is a survey of impressive breadth. Nonetheless, his discussion is wanting in a number of respects. Given that the volume focuses on government under stress, it seems remiss of Comella to omit a discussion of cases that might fall into this category or to examine how speech may be curbed to a possibly greater extent during times of stress. For example, the recent line of 'Turkish cases' should surely have been considered. Another shortcoming concerns Comella's discussion of some aspects of the law—for instance, in respect of the Holocaust or the protection of the judiciary from criticism. It is unclear where the author's restatement of the law ends and where his own argument as to what it should be begins, thus leaving the reader slightly confused as to the current state of the law.

In Chapter Four, Eva Brems' essay picks up on many of the issues mentioned by Rosenfeld and Chalmers. Concerned with freedom of association and its application to 'party closures'—the proscription of political parties—her essay is an enlightened contribution that examines the difficulties of using law to regulate democracy. Important questions are asked, such as *which* parties should be banned?; *when* they should be banned (before they are popular, or when they are at risk of gaining power)?; *who* should make these decisions?; and *what* further action should be taken? Brems draws on the *Refah* and *Batasuna* cases, as well as other rulings of the Vienna Commission, the European Court of Human Rights and United Nations Committees, to enrich the discussion. The sheer depth and breadth of the discussion encourages multiple readings.

The final pair of contributions address matters in Central and Eastern Europe. In the first of these, Jiří Přibáň and Sadurski look at the transition to democracy in the former communist states, and drawing on such examples as the Hungarian constitutional debate regarding incitement to racial hatred, it addresses questions raised by both Comella and Brems. The challenges experienced in the region—lustration, surges in anti-Semitism and racism, militant democracy and the need to craft new constitutional orders—are addressed. Overall, the chapter asks more questions than it can answer and flags a debate of historic importance to the European human rights consciousness—the rights of national minorities.

It is this topic that Gwendolyn Sasse addresses in the final chapter. Noting that 'political rights are inextricably linked to issues of identity and the demos', she analyses the differing approaches to minorities in the developing democracies of Central and Eastern Europe. She compares and contrasts the approaches of the EU and the Council of Europe and, in so doing, gives the reader an understanding of the push and pull factors that have moved Central and Eastern Europe towards plural democracy. In particular, Sasse considers the impact of the conditionality agreements for EU membership embodied in the Copenhagen criteria. If the sheer number of States covered makes for somewhat disjointed reading, the breadth of coverage is nonetheless agreeable. In discussing the reform process in States seeking to 'return to Europe', Sasse reminds the reader of the diverse experiences across the continent. This chapter ties together the various strands of the whole volume, weaving a rich tapestry of 21st century Europe. It is to be commended to any and all with an interest in the subject.

Cian C Murphy
School of Law, King's College London

DOCUMENT SECTION

Department of Foreign Affairs Strategy Statement 2005–2007

MISSION STATEMENT

The Mission of the Department of Foreign Affairs is to advance Ireland's political and economic interests in the European Union and in the wider world, to promote Ireland's contribution to international peace, security and development both through the European Union and through active participation in international organisations, in particular the United Nations, to protect our citizens abroad, and to pursue reconciliation and partnership on the island of Ireland.

Contents

FOREWORD BY THE MINISTER FOR FOREIGN AFFAIRS, MR DERMOT AHERN, TD

This Strategy Statement sets out the foreign policy objectives, as defined by the Government, to be pursued by the Department of Foreign Affairs in the period 2005–2007.

The international climate in which the Department is pursuing these objectives is both complex and volatile. It is essential therefore, that we maintain a clear focus on Ireland's fundamental interests and on the basic principles which underlie our foreign policy.

The full implementation of all aspects of the Good Friday Agreement remains a Government priority and is centrally important to the work of the Department.

In the new context created by the IRA's commitment to end all its activities, which must be verifiably honoured, and by the complete decommissioning of its arms, we will seek the earliest possible restoration of devolved government on an inclusive and sustainable basis. We will also work to develop the full potential of North/South cooperation, and to promote reconciliation and understanding.

We will continue to work within the UN and with our European partners in the building of stability and justice in Iraq, the Middle East, the Balkans, Afghanistan and other areas of tension and conflict, and to address the longer-term issues which fuel such difficulties.

Active involvement in the United Nations has long been a cornerstone of Ireland's foreign policy. It is widely accepted that reform of the UN is necessary in order to make it a more effective instrument of the international community. The Government is strongly supportive of the reforms proposed by UN Secretary General Kofi Annan. I was both delighted and honoured, therefore, to be appointed by the UN Secretary-General as Special Envoy for UN Reform last April. I see my appointment as a measure of Ireland's long-standing commitment to the United Nations and of the esteem it enjoys in all sectors of the membership.

In the European Union, we will continue to promote and protect our national interests in the context of continuing change. We remain committed to the ratification of the European Constitution and we will use the period of reflection and engagement signalled by the European Council in June to develop public understanding of the Union and its continuing importance for Ireland. We will continue to enhance our bilateral relations within the enlarged EU and by the end of 2005 we will have established resident diplomatic Missions in all Member States.

The Department, and our diplomatic missions, will continue to work closely with State agencies and the private sector with a view to bringing real added value to promoting our economic interests overseas. I attach a particular priority to this work.

We will continue to manage the Development Cooperation Ireland programme to the highest standards of international best practice. Our objective is to achieve the goal of making a lasting contribution to poverty reduction and sustainable growth in the world's poorest countries. We have also initiated a broad consultative process in advance of publication by the Department of a White Paper on Development Cooperation policy.

One of the basic tasks of my Department is the protection of Irish citizens abroad. With the greatly increased frequency and range of travel of our citizens and in the volatile international context, this is a growing aspect of work for our missions. The Department will also complete the implementation of our new automated passport issuing system by the end of 2005.

The very demanding and ambitious agenda set out in this Strategy Statement will only be achieved with the continued commitment of the staff at all levels. I would like to pay tribute to the enthusiasm and professionalism shown by them during my tenure to date, as exemplified by their outstanding response to the recent crises caused by the Asian Tsunami and the terrorist attacks in London and Turkey. I am fully confident that the Department will continue to meet the many challenges ahead with sustained commitment and dedication.

MESSAGE FROM THE MINISTER OF STATE, NOEL TREACY TD

As Minister of State at the Department of Foreign Affairs with special responsibility for European Affairs, I am very pleased to welcome the publication of this Strategy Statement. The period covered—2005 to 2007—is likely to be particularly challenging for the European Union.

A number of priority issues will require the attention of Ireland and the other Member States as we move into the second half of the decade: reaching agreement on the Union's future financing; the period for reflection agreed by the European Council in June 2005 which will be used to enable a broad debate on Europe to take place in all of the Member States; the continuing effort to make the EU economy more competitive; the ongoing enlargement process, and the development of the Union's external policy are all crucial to our national well-being and to that of the Union.

Following the defeat of two referenda on the ratification of the EU Constitution, the Member States have agreed on a period of reflection and debate. The Government, which continues strongly to support the Constitution, intends to use the period of reflection to intensify our national engagement on Europe.

The negotiations on the Union's future financing, for the period 2007–2013, will continue during the period of this Strategy Statement. A successful outcome will be crucial in equipping the Union to meet the challenges that lie ahead. Another major challenge will be the effort to achieve the ambitious goals set for the EU economy in the Lisbon Agenda. With concerted effort by Member States at both national and EU levels, the Lisbon Agenda can provide the impetus to complete the implementation of the Single Market and to deliver more growth and jobs.

The enlargement process which took a major and historical step in 2004 with the accession of ten new Member States will continue. Romania and Bulgaria are due to accede in January 2007, if they are ready.

The June 2004 European Council granted candidate status to Croatia and the December 2004 European Council decided that Turkey sufficiently fulfils the Copenhagen political criteria to enable the opening of accession negotiations. The strong desire of so many for EU membership is continuing evidence of the opportunity for peace, progress and prosperity offered by the Union.

It is against the background of these opportunities and challenges that this Strategy Statement is published. The Statement highlights the centrality and importance of Ireland's EU membership to our national interests and values. It also demonstrates that EU membership is a crucial dimension of our place in the wider world. Ireland has always placed a very high value on our membership of the Union. Our experience of EU membership has shown us that small countries can play a very full role and can have their voices heard. In the years ahead, in the new and bigger Union, we will continue to participate fully in the Union's decision-making. In doing so, we can continue to contribute to the development of a better Ireland, to the building of a more cohesive Europe and, by extension, to the building of a fairer and more secure world.

MESSAGE FROM THE MINISTER OF STATE FOR DEVELOPMENT COOPERATION AND HUMAN RIGHTS, CONOR LENIHAN, TD

This Strategy Statement sets out the role Ireland can play within the international community that reflects both our strengths and values as a country.

Over the past two decades Ireland has gained hugely as we have embraced the global economy. According to the latest UN Human Development Report, Ireland is now the tenth most developed country in the world and has the third highest per capita income.

Two thirds of the world is poor with billions of people currently living on less than two dollars a day. The scale of the challenges facing developing countries is truly enormous. While the first world has made great progress in peace and security, economic development, education, disease eradication and health, millions of people still live in countries ravaged by war, famine, disease, poverty, corruption and oppression.

For Ireland, our new found prosperity brings both a responsibility and an opportunity; a responsibility to help reduce vulnerability and foster opportunity not just at home, but also abroad, and an opportunity to develop a set of foreign policy values that reflect our belief in the role of democracy.

In many ways, Ireland has had a stronger voice in international affairs than might be expected for a country of our size. At Government level we have proved that we have the capacity to shape the policies of much larger nations, as demonstrated during our recent term on the UN Security Council and as President of the EU. At an individual and organizational level we have also proved we have the capacity to influence. This is especially true in the areas of conflict resolution, justice, human rights, and development assistance. As Minister of State for Development Cooperation and Human Rights it has been my privilege to witness the large number of Irish people who are working tirelessly in developing countries to improve the lives of less fortunate people. A striking recent example was the urgency to which Irish organizations responded as the awful events were unfolding in South Asia following the Tsunami. On an ongoing basis we are all proud to see how prominent Irish people are using their influence on the international stage to further the cause of development and peace.

The Government's performance in the field of official development assistance has improved dramatically over the last decade. Since the early 1990s the total ODA budget has increased by over 550%.This growth is set to continue following the Government's commitment to spend over 1.8 billion on development assistance between 2005 and 2007.

These additional resources will greatly improve our capacity to reduce poverty and to support the development of poor countries across a whole variety of sectors.

Development assistance does not operate in a vacuum but rather within a broad political and economic environment. The reduction of poverty in developing countries depends not only on aid but also on the trade, investment, environmental and other policies pursued by developed countries. Every country is responsible for its own development and the welfare and the well-being of its own citizens.

Progress can only be made if primary responsibility is assumed by developing countries themselves. Outside assistance can greatly help but only if development is owned, driven and managed by developing country governments and their citizens.

Solutions to the broader challenges of poverty and inequality are increasingly being sought at regional and global levels. It is important that Ireland should not only continue to provide practical support in the form of development assistance but should also strive to influence change across the broader political and economic landscape. It is our collective will that will bring about change.

This strategy is a clear statement of our intent to continue to play our role in helping create a fairer, more equal and more peaceful world. As we look forward our actions and those of the international community in response to these difficult challenges must be comprehensive if poor and vulnerable people everywhere are to share the same hopes for the future that we in Ireland take for granted in our lives today.

INTRODUCTION BY THE SECRETARY GENERAL OF THE DEPARTMENT OF FOREIGN AFFAIRS, DERMOT GALLAGHER

This Strategy Statement is the fifth to be prepared by the Department of Foreign Affairs in accordance with the provisions of the Public Service Management Act 1997.The Statement outlines the framework within which the Department will operate up to the end of 2007. It reflects Government policy as set out in the Programme for Government, and in other relevant agreements, including the current Social Partnership Agreement, Sustaining Progress.

The Strategy Statement provides an overview of the Department and defines the high level goals, objectives and strategies to be pursued in the period ahead. It contains an analysis of both the complex and ever-changing international environment in which the Department operates, and of the main domestic and internal issues it must face in the coming years. The Statement also sets out the indicators which will provide the basis for measuring the effectiveness of the Department's performance.

There are many major challenges facing the Department in the period ahead. The ongoing efforts to advance the peace process in Northern Ireland, the volatile international climate, the debate about the future of the European Union, the proposed reform of the United Nations, the ongoing expansion of our development cooperation programme and the ever increasing demand for consular services all point to the continuing need to develop our capacity to respond quickly and effectively to events as they unfold.

The Department is also facing the organisational challenge arising from the impending decentralisation of our Development Cooperation Directorate to Limerick, which is due to take place in the first half of 2007.The effective management of that process will be one of the main objectives of the Department during the period covered by this Strategy Statement.

The process of preparing this Strategy Statement involved many people throughout the Department. I would like to thank everybody who contributed. I would like also to thank the Department's Partnership Committee for their active support and involvement.

The Department remains fully committed to the partnership process and will continue to maintain and develop it over the period covered by the Statement.

The Department continues to work closely with other Government Departments, State Agencies and the private sector in pursuit of our national political, economic and cultural interests. We will also continue to strengthen our relationships with non-governmental organisations, particularly in regard to our development cooperation programme.

I would like once again to express my thanks to the Department's staff at home and abroad for their continued dedication and professionalism. This was particularly evident during Ireland's very successful Presidency of the European Union in the first half of 2004, where the level of commitment was truly exceptional. I would also like to acknowledge the demands placed on families as a result of the requirements for flexibility and mobility that are a particular feature of the Department's work.

I look forward to working closely with all colleagues in the Department in advancing the agenda set out in this document.

PART 1 HIGH LEVEL GOALS

1: Work to achieve the full implementation of the Good Friday Agreement and the sustained operation of all its institutions, promoting co-operation, mutual understanding and respect between both traditions on the island, between North and South in Ireland and between these islands.
2: Pursue Ireland's foreign policy in accordance with the ideals enshrined in the Constitution and in conformity with the principles of the United Nations Charter, through the development of our bilateral relations with other States, our participation in the European Union's Common Foreign and Security Policy, and our active and principled participation in international organisations.
3: Promote and protect Ireland's interests at the heart of the European Union as it continues to evolve and enlarge, including through the further development of our relations with our current and future EU partners.
4: Promote Ireland's trade, investment and other interests, including its culture, in close co-operation with other Departments, State Agencies and the private sector, ensuring that the State's network of diplomatic and consular missions adds real value to this task.
5: Make a substantive and effective contribution to achieving the Millennium Development Goals, and to poverty reduction and sustainable growth in developing countries, through the policy and programmes of Development Cooperation Ireland, and by working for a just and stable international economic system.
6: Protect and support the interests of Irish citizens abroad, maintain and strengthen links with people of Irish ancestry, and provide a modern and efficient passport and consular service.

PART 2 THE ROLE OF THE DEPARTMENT

The Department of Foreign Affairs advises the Minister for Foreign Affairs, the Ministers of State and the Government on all aspects of foreign policy and coordinates Ireland's response to international developments. It also provides advice and support on all issues relevant to the pursuit of peace, partnership and reconciliation in Northern Ireland, and between North and South of the island, and to deepening Ireland's relationship with Britain.

STRUCTURE OF THE DEPARTMENT

The Department currently comprises twelve units at headquarters (HQ) and a total of 67 diplomatic and consular offices abroad (referred to as "Missions"), as well as the British-Irish Intergovernmental Secretariat in Belfast and the North-South Ministerial Council Joint Secretariat in Armagh. A further six Missions—in Romania, Bulgaria, Latvia, Lithuania, Malta and Vietnam—will be opened later in 2005.

Primary responsibilities:

—*Anglo-Irish Division* deals with Anglo-Irish relations and Northern Ireland.
—*Bilateral Economic Relations Division* coordinates the promotion of Ireland's economic interests abroad.
—*Consular and Passport Division* is responsible for providing consular assistance to Irish citizens abroad and for passport and visa services.
—*Corporate Services Division* is responsible for the day-to-day management of the Department including human resources, change management, training, accommodation, management services, finance and information and communications technology.
—*Cultural Division* has responsibility for cultural relations with other countries.
—*Development Cooperation Directorate* is responsible for the administration of the Irish overseas development programme Development Cooperation Ireland and for the conduct of Irish development policy.
—*European Union Division* coordinates Ireland's approach within the EU.
—*Inspection and Internal Audit Unit* evaluates the performance of Ireland's overseas missions and the adequacy, application and effectiveness of the Department's internal control systems.
—*Legal Division* provides legal information and advice, particularly on matters of public international law, human rights law and EU law.
—*Political Division* is responsible for international political issues, including at the United Nations, and manages Ireland's participation in the EU's Common Foreign and Security Policy.
—*Protocol Division* is responsible for the organisation of State and official visits to and from Ireland, and for liaison with Embassies accredited to Ireland.
—*Press Section* is responsible for informing the domestic and international media about developments in Irish foreign policy.

The Role of Embassies and Other Offices Abroad

Ireland's diplomatic missions and consular offices are dedicated to the pursuit of Ireland's interests abroad and to enhancing Ireland's international profile. They are the external offices of the State, promoting Government policies and participating in the work of international organisations. Ambassadors can also be accredited on a non-resident basis. Diplomatic relations are maintained with 158 countries.

Diplomatic and consular missions perform a range of representational, promotional and reporting functions. They:

—deepen Ireland's relations with host governments and advance our international priorities and objectives.
—report on political, economic, legal, commercial and, as appropriate, EU developments.
—advance Ireland's economic interests through working with others in the public and private sectors to expand trade and tourism, and to highlight the benefits of inward investment in Ireland.
—oversee the implementation of programmes in developing countries funded by the Government's overseas development programme, Development Cooperation Ireland.

—provide assistance to Irish citizens abroad and maintain contact with local Irish communities—promote Irish culture and disseminate information on Ireland.

Missions accredited to multilateral organisations such as the United Nations present Ireland's views in negotiations and debate within these organisations.

The role of the Permanent Representation to the EU in Brussels is to represent the State in its interface with the EU institutions and in negotiations at official level in the Council of Ministers. It also advises on negotiations at political level in the Council of Ministers and at the European Council.

The Department's network of 67 resident diplomatic and consular missions overseas includes 49 Embassies, 6 multilateral missions (to the European Union, to the United Nations in New York and Geneva, to the Organisation for Security and Cooperation in Europe, to the Organisation for Economic Cooperation and Development and UNESCO, and to the Council of Europe) and 12 Consulates-General and other offices. In addition, there are 24 Honorary Consuls General and 62 Honorary Consuls who provide assistance to Irish citizens in 59 countries. Further details are available on the Department's website www.dfa.ie.

At any one time, almost 50% of the Department's staff of approximately 1,400 are serving abroad. This figure includes some 300 locally recruited staff who, through their dedication and local knowledge, make an invaluable contribution to the successful operation of our Missions.

PART 3 ENVIRONMENTAL ANALYSIS

External Environment—Overview

The Department of Foreign Affairs operates in a complex and ever-changing environment shaped by European and wider international influences. The realisation of objectives depends, of course, not just on the efforts of the Department or indeed of the Government as a whole but also on the behaviour of other States and entities.

It is highly desirable for a small State like Ireland that its external environment is governed by norms of international law that provide an effective framework within which to cooperate with other States and within multilateral and regional organisations in the furtherance of our national interests. Participation in a wide range of international organisations, coupled with our membership of the European Union, provides an opportunity to contribute to the achievement and consolidation of an international environment in keeping with the principles set out in Article 29 of the Constitution:

—*the ideal of peace and friendly cooperation amongst nations founded on international justice and morality.*
—*the principle of the pacific settlement of international disputes by international arbitration or judicial determination, and.*
—*the principles of international law as our rule of conduct in our relations with other States.*

Because of the complexity of the external environment it is essential that the limited resources available to the Department are deployed to the optimum, and that it acts in close cooperation with other Government Departments that have external responsibilities, in order to contribute effectively to the attainment of the goals set down in the Programme for Government and in *Sustaining Progress.*

Ireland's national income per head, boosted by exceptional levels of export-led growth, trade liberalisation and the EU Single Market, has reached a level above the EU average. We have also moved from being a country of net emigration to one of net immigration. It is essential for our future economic well-being that Ireland remains at the cutting edge of economic development, through sustained competitiveness and the expansion of new areas for growth such as e-business.

Ireland's foreign policy traditionally benefits from a domestic context marked by significant political consensus on the main external issues. Political debate on foreign policy issues is facilitated by the Oireachtas Committees on Foreign Affairs and on European Affairs and strengthened by the provisions for improved Oireachtas scrutiny of EU legislation. The social partners and non-governmental organisations are also actively engaged on a range of issues central to foreign policy.

Northern Ireland and Anglo-Irish Relations

The continuing implementation of the Good Friday Agreement is central to the Government's pursuit of securing lasting peace in Ireland. The full implementation of the Agreement and the consolidation of its institutions remains the Government's overriding priority. The Department will focus on the challenge of carrying this work to completion, in partnership with other Government Departments, the British Government and the political parties in Northern Ireland.

Considerable progress has been made on the implementation of the Agreement since its overwhelming endorsement by the electorate, North and South, in May 1998. Its institutions were established in 1999 and worked well, developing and underpinning local political accountability. The new beginning promised in the Agreement was taken forward in a broad range of areas ranging from Policing, Security Normalisation and Criminal Justice to Rights, Equality and Community issues.

Since the suspension of the Northern Ireland Assembly and Executive in October 2002, the approach of the two Governments has been directed towards the earliest possible restoration of devolved government, in the context of a complete end to paramilitary activity, and on an inclusive and sustainable basis. The Department will play a full part in that work, including by assisting in the negotiation and achievement of a comprehensive agreement that includes the realisation of these twin objectives. While the political landscape in Northern Ireland is continually evolving, considerable progress towards achieving such a comprehensive agreement has been made, and it will remain a key priority of the Department.

The Department will also continue to support and consolidate the major advances already made in terms of policing and justice. The ongoing implementation of the recommendations of the Patten Report and the Criminal Justice Review is critically important to long-term stability and widespread confidence in the administration of justice. Advancing North/South cooperation in these areas will continue to be a top priority, including in the context of moves to devolve responsibility for policing and justice to a Northern Ireland Executive. The Department will seek to progress the normalisation of security arrangements and to engage in other post-conflict issues, including victims and dealing with the past.

The Government is fully committed to consolidating and protecting the success of the North/South Ministerial Council so as to further develop the spirit of partnership and co-operation between North and South to the mutual benefit of both. The implementation of this commitment will include supporting and promoting the North/South Implementation Bodies, Tourism Ireland and the programme of work under the designated areas of North/South Co-operation. In addition, the advancement of reconciliation and mutual respect between the different traditions will be taken forward on a pro-active basis, including through the Department's Reconciliation Fund.

The establishment of the British-Irish Council and the British-Irish Intergovernmental Conference has enhanced relationships throughout these islands. The Government remains committed to advancing the work of the British-Irish Council as an important institution of the Agreement. The Department will also continue to build on our existing East-West links, including those with the devolved administrations in Cardiff and Edinburgh, to ensure that harmonious and mutually beneficial relationships between Ireland and Britain are fully realised.

Of key importance throughout the development of the peace process has been the continuing political and economic support of the wider international community—including the United States and the European Union—made manifest in particular through the regeneration and reconciliation work assisted by the EU Peace Programme and the International Fund for Ireland. The Department will continue to work proactively to sustain this widespread support and solidarity as we move towards full implementation of the Agreement.

The European Union

EU membership is fundamental to Ireland and shapes the context in which Irish foreign policy operates. The continued development of a coherent and effective Union is a core national interest. The promotion of Ireland's interests within the Union requires coordination and prioritisation within a strategic approach to the EU's wide agenda which embraces many issues of importance and sensitivity for Ireland.

An enlarging and evolving Union presents opportunities and challenges for Ireland. Considerable attention will be devoted in the period ahead to developing relations and alliances with other Member States, including through the opening of Missions in the new Member States and accession countries, with a view to maximizing our ability to shape key Union policies.

The following are some of the important issues which the Union faces in the period ahead:

—The question of the ratification of the European Constitution: The European Council of June 2005, while reaffirming commitment to the EU Constitution, has signalled the launch of a period of reflection and engagement.

—The enlargement process will continue, with Romania and Bulgaria due to accede in January 2007 and negotiations with Croatia and Turkey due to open in 2005. Other Western Balkan countries also have a prospect of becoming candidate countries and the application from the Former Yugoslav Republic of Macedonia is expected to be the subject of a Commission Opinion in 2005—Particular emphasis will be given to the promotion of good relations with Russia, Ukraine and other neighbours of the EU. The European Neighbourhood Policy will need to be effectively implemented to ensure that a commitment to shared values, including respect for human rights, the promotion of good neighbourly relations and the principles of the market economy, will result in closer economic and political cooperation with neighbouring countries.

—The negotiations on the Union's future *Financial Framework* for the period 2007 to 2013, which will determine both the ambition, nature and content of the Union's policies into the next decade and Ireland's contribution to and receipts from the Union, will be a crucial issue in the coming period.

—The Lisbon Agenda, which aims to transform the EU into the most competitive and dynamic knowledge-based economy in the world, remains a priority.

—In November 2004 European Council adopted The Hague Programme for the further development of the area of freedom, security and justice.This has been fleshed out with concrete proposals in an Action Plan presented by the Commission and adopted by the European Council in June 2005.

—The EU's role internationally will continue to develop through the Common Foreign and Security Policy, in accordance with the EU's agreed principles and objectives. In the period ahead, Ireland will continue to pursue and promote its foreign policy goals through active participation in the CFSP.

—The World Trade Organisation (WTO) round of Global Trade Negotiations—*the Doha Development Agenda*—is of particular importance to a country like Ireland, with a small open economy and a high dependence on external trade and investment. Ireland will be working closely with its EU partners to secure a successful and satisfactory outcome.

The Wider International Context

Ireland's foreign policy is shaped by our values and by the external environment to which we relate them.

Enlargement of the European Union has enhanced the stability of our immediate region, but elsewhere in the world regional conflict, failed states and lack of development characterise the daily lives of many of our fellow human beings. In our increasingly interdependent world, instability in one part of the globe can pose a direct threat to international security and stability.

The challenges facing the international community are manifold—regional conflict and failed or failing states, poor governance, the abuse of human rights, environmental degradation and climate change, pandemics such as HIV/AIDS, lack of sustainable development, imbalances in flows of trade, technology and capital and trafficking in human beings and illicit drugs. International terrorism and the proliferation of weapons of mass destruction pose particular problems which require cross-border solutions. Equally, the underlying causes of conflict and instability—poverty, oppression and lack of opportunity—must also be addressed.

These challenges cannot be dealt with within the confines of the traditional nation state alone. They require concerted action by the international community. Global, shared responses are required. The multilateral system of collective security, enshrined in the UN, provides the best way to address the threats to international peace and security and the challenges of poverty and development.

However, recent international divisions, including those over the war in Iraq, have revealed the stresses and tensions within the international system, a situation described by Secretary-General Annan in 2003 as a "fork in the road" for the UN system. The period ahead, therefore, will be a crucial one for the UN.

In September 2005, a High Level Plenary Session of the United Nations General Assembly will bring together Heads of State and Government to review the implementation of the Millennium Summit Declaration and progress towards the Millennium Development Goals. As part of this process, Secretary General Kofi Annan has issued a report (21st March 2005) with recommendations on poverty reduction, human rights and institutional reform of the UN system, including reform of the Security Council and establishment of a new Peace-Building Commission and Human Rights Council. The Minister for Foreign Affairs is acting as one of the five Envoys appointed by the Secretary General to liaise with Governments on UN reform.

The pursuit of Ireland's foreign policy interests is greatly enhanced through our participation in the European Union's Common Foreign and Security Policy. The Union continues to develop the breadth and depth of its international engagement, in accordance with the shared values and objectives of its Member States. The European Security Strategy, adopted in December 2003, provides a coherent framework for the Union's engagement with the wider world, and commits the Union to adopting a holistic approach to security issues. In developing its external relations, the Union is able to draw on the wide range of instruments available to it, including diplomatic and political relations and development cooperation and trade, as well as its developing capabilities for conflict prevention, crisis management and peacekeeping through the European Security and Defence Policy (ESDP).

Ireland's recent Presidency of the EU enabled us to play our part in shaping the development of the Union's external relations and we will continue to contribute constructively to this process in accordance with our foreign policy priorities and traditions.

Peacekeeping, crisis management, conflict prevention and economic and social development remain priorities for Ireland as a concrete expression of our commitment to international peace and security. The complementarity of efforts in the UN and EU to strengthen the international community's capabilities for conflict prevention, humanitarian and crisis management—as for example in the Western Balkans—will be a critical success factor and a continuing objective of Irish foreign policy. The Secretary General of the UN has welcomed the contribution which the EU can make in support of UN crisis management. Nationally, Ireland will continue its traditional commitment to UN peacekeeping, with service in a number of UN peacekeeping operations, most prominently in the UN Mission in Liberia (UNMIL) in which an Irish contingent of 430 serves—the largest such deployment by a Western European country to a UN operation in Africa.

Ireland will play its full part in the effort to defeat the increased menace of international terrorism.

The promotion of human rights is a core principle that informs the formulation and conduct of Ireland's foreign policy. The promotion of human rights is also an integral part of international security. In this context, Irish foreign policy will continue to emphasise the importance of ongoing development of support for and adherence to international human rights standards and the rule of law.

Strategy Statement of the Department of Foreign Affairs 2005–2007 19 Ireland shares the increased international concern about proliferation of weapons of mass destruction and their possible use. Concerted international action is required to address these challenges to our security through efforts towards disarmament and arms control. Ireland is continuing to build on our track record to promote the disarmament and arms control agenda, including at the Review Conference of the Non-Proliferation Treaty in 2005.

Ireland has extensive and valued bilateral relations with an increasing number of countries which have been built up over time, based on historical links, geographical proximity, economic, trade and cultural relations and common pursuit of shared values and objectives. Building on the success of the Presidency and our period on the UN Security Council, the Government will focus on enhancing Ireland's bilateral relations with a broad range of countries. In addition to further developing relations with our current and future partners in the EU, particular emphasis will be placed on enhancing relations with key partners in Asia and Latin America and with the countries to the south and east of the enlarged European Union. Further developing our important relationships with the United States, Russia and China will be a key objective. We will also seek to build our relations with African partners, building on both our bilateral relations and our development cooperation programmes.

On a regional level, we will support the efforts of the international community through the UN, EU, the Organisation for Security and Cooperation in Europe (OSCE) and the Council of Europe to promote a just international environment. We will also support the contribution which regional organisations such as the African Union can make to the promotion of peace and security in their areas.

The external environment in which we determine our foreign policy in the period 2005–2007 will also be affected by developments in other States and regions such as:

—*the development of relations in and between the United States, Russia, China and other major states.*
—*progress achieved in bringing an end to the Arab-Israeli conflict.*
—*efforts to achieve peace and stability in Iraq.*
—*ongoing instability in other areas of the Middle East and in parts of Africa.*
—*efforts to consolidate a stable environment in Afghanistan and.*
—*the threats posed by lack of development, climate change and pandemics such as HIV/AIDS.*

Ireland's Overseas Economic Interests

In an increasingly competitive economic climate Ireland needs to focus on issues of competitiveness and on creating higher value jobs. Speed, creativity, networking and efficiency are vital ingredients for economic success in the information age. These qualities are also key in the Department's role in supporting foreign trade and investment.

The performance of Ireland's exports, including from the indigenous sector, is central to the maintenance of strong growth. The Department will fully leverage the resources of our network of Embassies and Consulates to assist Irish business in gaining and maintaining market access for Irish products. It will work closely with the State

Agencies and other Departments in identifying new market opportunities and in promoting awareness of Ireland as a preferred business partner and as a world-class location for investment and scientific research and development. In particular, it will work to realise the objectives set out in the next phase of the Government's *Asia Strategy.*

Development Cooperation

The environment within which development cooperation operates is changing rapidly. At the international level, it is increasingly recognised that the prospects of developing countries depend not only on Overseas Development Assistance (ODA) but also on the trade, investment, environmental and other policies pursued by developed countries. The gathering pace of globalisation presents both opportunities and threats for developing countries.

In relation to ODA, there is a growing recognition of the need to integrate all external assistance into coherent programmes owned and managed by developing countries themselves, as distinct from supporting stand-alone projects implemented by individual donors. In recognition of the importance of need-based, timely and flexible funding for emergencies, humanitarian assistance will be provided through a broader range of mechanisms including multilateral agencies, the Red Cross and non-Governmental organisations.

A broad consultative process will be put in place on all of these issues, leading to a White Paper on Development Cooperation policy.

The policies of Development Cooperation Ireland will be underpinned by the Millennium Development Goals, a series of internationally agreed targets, which may be summarised as follows:.

—eradicate extreme poverty and hunger—achieve universal primary education.
—promote gender equality and empower women.
—reduce child mortality—improve maternal health.
—combat HIV/AIDS, malaria and other diseases.
—ensure environmental sustainability, and.
—develop a global partnership for development.

In addition, the humanitarian assistance policy will be underpinned by the Good Humanitarian Donorship Initiative, the internationally agreed donor framework on humanitarian action.

A phased three-year package of planned budget increases will enable Ireland to play a greatly enhanced role in development cooperation, both in programme management and advocacy. This new role brings increased opportunities but equally implies increased responsibilities.

In accordance with the Government's decision on the decentralisation programme, arrangements will be made for the smooth transfer of the Development Cooperation Directorate to Limerick in the first phase of decentralisation.

Consular and Passport Services

The number of Irish people travelling abroad has increased very substantially over the last decade and this has been reflected in a rapidly growing demand for passports and consular services. More than twice as many passports were issued in 2003 as in 1996.

The number of non-nationals coming to Ireland who require visas has also risen very significantly. In 2004 the number of visas issued was 113,550 compared with 60,000 in 2000. In the mid-1990s the number of visa applications was around 6,000.

The demand for passport, consular and visa services is expected to continue to grow over the period of the Strategy Statement as the Irish economy continues to flourish. The Department of Foreign Affairs attaches very great importance to providing a first-class service to the public. In this context, the Department is in the final stages of a major project to upgrade its systems and processes for handling passport applications. The outcome will be an improved service to the public, a more secure passport document and a more efficient passport issuing system.

In March 2005 the Government approved the establishment of the Irish Naturalisation and Immigration Service (INIS) as an executive office within the Department of Justice Equality and Law Reform. The new Service will incorporate the Visa Section of the Department of Foreign Affairs but responsibility for the provision of a visa service at diplomatic and consular Missions will remain with the Department.

The provision of consular protection and assistance to Irish citizens abroad is a major priority for the Department.

The growth in international terrorism in recent years has increased the risk for international travellers and this has highlighted the importance of maintaining a vigilant and accessible Consular Service which is capable of responding quickly and flexibly to emergency situations wherever they may arise.

Building Internal Capability

The Department of Foreign Affairs must ensure that, as the external environment changes and becomes more demanding, it maintains and continues to develop the internal capability required to deliver on the foreign policy objectives of the Government. In this context, and in line with commitments in the *Programme for Government* and in *Sustaining Progress,* the Department is committed to aligning its strategies and actions with those of other Government Departments in order to achieve maximum synergy and effectiveness.

The Department recognises that success in achieving its objectives is critically dependent on the effective management of its human resources. This will require the ongoing availability of well trained, experienced and motivated staff and a continuing ability to respond flexibly and effectively to new or changed situations. It also requires the Department to develop its capability to evaluate systems and performance. In this context, the Department will continue to implement an integrated business planning process that links the achievement of the high level goals, objectives and strategies in the Strategy Statement with Divisional and Mission goals set out in annual business plans and with goals in role profiles of individual officers agreed through the Performance Management and Development System (PMDS).The Department has also put in place a comprehensive risk management strategy to ensure that risks are properly assessed and managed as an integral part of its policymaking and administrative processes. Work has also commenced on the development of a data strategy that will identify and prioritise the Department's statistical data needs in order to assist in policy development and other cross cutting issues with which the Department is concerned.

The structure of the Department, with up to 50% of its staff based abroad at any one time, poses particular difficulties both for the development of a coherent and effective business strategy and for staff development. In addition, many areas of the Department's work involve issues and responsibilities that span the work of several Divisions. The operation of a "lead unit" system within the Department, whereby Divisions are assigned lead responsibility for coordination in respect of a particular geographical region or issue, has improved the Department's capability to deal effectively with foreign and domestic policy priorities.

Strategy Statement of the Department of Foreign Affairs 2005–2007. The ongoing implementation of modernisation initiatives on a partnership basis will also be critical to success. The Department will continue to develop the partnership process, which has already contributed to the successful implementation of a number of major change management initiatives. These include the implementation of PMDS and the development of Human Resource Management and Training and Development Strategies. The Department's Partnership Committee has also played a central role in the preparation of both the Department's Modernisation Action Plan and the Progress Reports which have been submitted to the Civil Service Performance Verification Group at regular intervals.

The Department is fully committed to the principles of equality set out in legislation. We will continue to maintain and enhance the range of family-friendly working opportunities and conditions that are currently available to our staff.

The wide geographic spread of the Department's staff also poses challenges for the development of an effective internal communications system. The Department is committed to developing efficient systems for the management, transmission storage and retrieval of its information resources. The development of an intranet is well advanced. A comprehensive internal communications strategy is also being developed.

The Department will support progress under the Government's Quality Customer Service initiative over the period covered by this Strategy Statement, focusing in particular on the commitments contained in our Customer Charter and Customer Action Plan. The commitments include ensuring that our services and facilities are accessible to all our customers, including those with special needs, and meeting the requirements of the Official Languages Act, 2003.

The decentralisation of the Development Cooperation Directorate to Limerick is scheduled to take place within the timeframe covered by this Strategy Statement. The Department will manage this priority project in a manner that will minimise disruption to business continuity. Support services will also be put in place for staff affected by the decentralisation project, whether they are decentralising to Limerick or transferring to another section or Department.

Cross Departmental Issues

The Department recognises the need for better-coordinated and more effective service delivery strategies across Departments with overlapping functions and areas of responsibility. A number of important cross-Departmental issues have been identified and targeted for priority action.

Editors Note: These cross-Departmental issues were not able to be reproduced for technical reasons.

PART 4 OBJECTIVES, STRATEGIES AND PERFORMANCE INDICATORS FOR THE PERIOD 2005–2007

The objectives, strategies and key performance indicators set out in the following sections reflect relevant Government policies in the *Programme for Government* and the current Social Partnership Agreement *Sustaining Progress.* They also take account of relevant crosscutting Government initiatives including *"A Decade of the Asia Strategy 1999—2009"* and *"New Connections"* (the Government's strategy to realise the potential of the Information Society), equality issues as promoted through recent legislation and policies and the National Poverty and Disability Strategies. The analysis of the working environment in Part Three of the Strategy Statement has also guided the Department in identifying its strategic objectives and priorities over the next three years.

NORTHERN IRELAND AND ANGLO-IRISH RELATIONS

The Department advises the Government on all issues relevant to its aim of securing lasting peace in Ireland in particular through the full implementation of the Good Friday Agreement, the consolidation of its institutions, and the development of a spirit of friendship and cooperation between North and South, and throughout these islands.

OBJECTIVE

Assist the Minister for Foreign Affairs in realising the Government's policy goals with regard to Northern Ireland and Anglo-Irish relations, especially the full implementation of the Good Friday Agreement.

STRATEGY

1 Monitor and assess developments within Northern Ireland and maintain a comprehensive network of contacts there in order to achieve a maximum understanding of viewpoints and, in turn, to promote a better appreciation of Government policies.
2 Support and monitor the work of the institutions of the Agreement, including through the work of the Joint Secretariat of the North/South Ministerial Council in Armagh, the Secretariat of the British-Irish Council and the Secretariat of the British-Irish Intergovernmental Conference in Belfast.
3 Co-ordinate policy with the Department of the Taoiseach, the Department of Justice, Equality and Law Reform, and other relevant Departments on Northern Ireland and Anglo-Irish issues.

OBJECTIVE

Promote partnership on the island including through the North- South Ministerial Council and the other institutions of the Agreement, thus deepening economic, social and cultural relations between both parts of the island of Ireland.

STRATEGY

1 Contribute to the development of North/South co-operation and common action, and co-ordinate the input of Government Departments and State Agencies in this area.

OBJECTIVE

Promote peace and stability through the implementation of the policing, justice and security related aspects of the Agreement.

STRATEGY

1: Liaise with relevant parties, including the British Government, to underpin the further implementation of the Agreement in the areas of policing, justice, security normalisation and other confidence-related issues, including parades, inquiries and related post-conflict issues The Department advises the Government on all issues relevant to its aim of securing lasting peace in Ireland in particular through the full implementation of the Good Friday Agreement, the consolidation of its institutions, and the development of a spirit of friendship and cooperation between North and South, and throughout these islands.

OBJECTIVE

Underpin the peace process in Northern Ireland and the border counties by contributing to economic and social development, in particular in the most disadvantaged communities.

STRATEGY

1: Optimise the use of available funding from the International Fund for Ireland and Peace II to encourage economic and social development in marginalised communities.

OBJECTIVE

Stimulate reconciliation between the unionist and nationalist traditions in Ireland.

STRATEGY

1: Encourage internal capacity building within the Unionist and Nationalist communities in Northern Ireland in order to promote and enhance cross-community engagement.
2: Foster and support reconciliation initiatives and cross-community links.

OBJECTIVE

Further develop the close and positive relationship that exists between Britain and Ireland.

STRATEGY

1: Support the effective operation of the British-Irish Intergovernmental Conference and the British-Irish Council.
2: Continue to develop British-Irish relations, including through the work of the British-Irish Inter-Parliamentary Body and through the activities of the Embassy in London and the Consulates in Edinburgh and Cardiff in promoting bilateral contact on all levels.

OBJECTIVE

Develop international support for the Government's policies with regard to Northern Ireland and British-Irish relations.

STRATEGY

1: Continue to develop and co-ordinate relations with the US Government and Congress and actively engage with our EU partners and others in support of the Agreement and the peace process.

KEY PERFORMANCE INDICATORS

1: Extent of implementation of all aspects of the Good Friday Agreement in all its aspects.
2: Effectiveness of arrangements to support the operation of the institutions established under the Good Friday Agreement.
3: Effectiveness of co-ordination arrangements with other Departments with regard to policy development and strategies on Anglo-Irish and Northern Ireland issues.
4: Enhanced relationships with a wide range of representatives from all traditions in Northern Ireland, with a view to broadening and deepening support for the Good Friday Agreement.

5: Ongoing support from the United States, the EU and others for the implementation of the Good Friday Agreement and the peace process.

THE EUROPEAN UNION

EU membership continues to be of fundamental importance to Ireland. The Union provides the context for promoting prosperity, employment, sustainable development, peace and security in Ireland, in Europe and in the wider world. Ireland can best pursue its objectives within Union, as demonstrated by its recent Presidency, by remaining positively engaged at the heart of the Union's activities.

A strategic and coherent approach also requires efficient arrangements for policy coordination within the Irish administration. The Department of Foreign Affairs, working closely with all other Departments and notably with the Department of the Taoiseach, has a particular responsibility to ensure a coordinated response across the range of EU issues. Ireland's Permanent Representation in Brussels plays a central role in advancing Ireland's interests in the EU.

It is important that the Union, as it evolves, continues to be seen as accessible and relevant to the Irish public.

With the accession of ten new Member States and agreement on a European Constitution, the Union finds itself at a time of important change. The enlargement process will continue to move forward. The ratification of the European Constitution will be a major issue for the Union in the period ahead. If ratified, its important and wide-ranging provisions will then fall to be implemented. The outcome of negotiations on the Union's future financing will significantly shape the Union's policy priorities until 2013.The further development of bilateral relations with all our fellow Member States and with the candidate countries will be an increasingly important dimension of Ireland's approach.

The Union's ability to contribute to international peace, security and stability is being enhanced through further improvements in its Common Foreign and Security Policy and through the development of its operational capacity for conflict prevention, humanitarian and crisis management tasks. These and other issues will create major opportunities and challenges for the Union and its Member States and demand a strategic response from the Department of Foreign Affairs and the Irish administration as a whole.

OBJECTIVE

Promote and protect Ireland's interests in the European Union, and to that end develop and pursue a strategic, coordinated and coherent response to its ongoing agenda and its future development.

STRATEGY

1: Provide well focused and timely advice and support to Government, based on Ireland's strategic interests and on developments within the European Union.

2: Develop bilateral relations with other Member States, as well as close contacts with EU institutions, to facilitate greater mutual understanding on EU policy concerns and to encourage joint responses to common problems.
3: Continue to devote attention in particular to enhancing bilateral relations with the new Member States, accession countries and candidate countries through the opening of resident diplomatic Missions, the provision of training and technical assistance and the development of bilateral relations.
4: Seek to ensure close coordination on EU issues within the Department, including with Missions abroad, and between Departments, and keep the coordination function under on-going review with a view to its possible improvement.
5: Work with other Government Departments and the Oireachtas to implement effectively the arrangements for Oireachtas scrutiny of EU matters.
6: Contribute to greater public awareness of, and wider public debate on, developments within the EU and consider how the on-going agenda of the EU can be better communicated to citizens.

OBJECTIVE

Ratification process of the European Constitution.

STRATEGY

1: Advise and inform the Government on all aspects of the ratification process, in Ireland and in other EU Member States.
2: Develop public understanding of the European Constitution, particularly during the period of reflection and engagement signalled in June 2005.
3: Prepare as necessary for implementation of the European Constitution.

OBJECTIVE

Advance Ireland's national position in the negotiations on the Financial Framework for 2007–2013.

STRATEGY

1: Coordinate and develop, in conjunction with the Department of Finance and other Departments, our national approach to the negotiations on the Union's Financial Framework for 2007–2013.
2: Identify, present and promote Ireland's key interests in the negotiations to ensure that our national concerns are fully addressed and protected.

KEY PERFORMANCE INDICATORS

1: Extent to which Ireland's concerns are reflected in the development, implementation and reform of the EU's internal and external policies.
2: Effectiveness of liaison and coordination with other Departments and with our Missions abroad, in particular with the Permanent Representation in Brussels, in the development of Ireland's approach to EU policies and the promotion of Ireland's interests in that regard.
3: Extent to which bilateral relations with other EU Member States are developed and enhanced, notably as a vehicle for advancing priority Irish concerns.
4: Effectiveness of contribution to the success of the further enlargement of the Union and extent of development of our relations with the candidate countries and other neighbours.
5: Quality, timeliness and accuracy of reports and briefing material provided.
6: Increased public awareness and debate on EU issues.

OBJECTIVE

Advance Ireland's national interests and security through our commitment to and pursuit of international peace, security and stability through the rule of law, the peaceful settlement of disputes and the protection of human rights Strengthen the role of the UN as an effective instrument for economic and social development.

STRATEGY

1: Uphold the United Nations Security Council's primary responsibility for maintenance of international peace and security.
2: Support reform of the UN system, including reform of the Security Council and the revitalisation of the UN General Assembly.
3: Contribute to the implementation of the United Nations Millennium Declaration and the achievement of the Millennium Development Goals.
4: Ensure implementation of the UN Security Council and EU sanctions, in conjunction with other Government Departments, the Central Bank and the Financial Services Authority of Ireland.
5: Coordinate with D/Defence and D/Justice, Equality and Law Reform to facilitate Ireland's participation, where appropriate and on a case-by case basis, in humanitarian and crisis management operations in the military and civilian areas, including ESDP operations, subject to the requirements of UN authorisation and Government and Dáil approval.
6: Consider and develop, through the Standing Interdepartmental Committee on peacekeeping, Ireland's policy on peacekeeping.

OBJECTIVE

Organise high-level visits to and from Ireland with a standard of excellence which contributes to the Department's policy objectives.

STRATEGY

1: Coordinate and manage Presidential visits abroad and incoming State visits.

IRELAND'S ROLE IN THE WORLD

Ireland has an abiding interest in a stable, secure, inclusive and cooperative international environment. Through our bilateral relations and through our membership of international organisations and fora, we will continue to pursue Irish interests in this regard in a manner which is fully consistent with Ireland's foreign policy, including our policy of military neutrality.

United Nations

OBJECTIVE

Further develop Ireland's foreign policy in the context of the EU's Common Foreign and Security Policy (CFSP), through which Ireland's voice in the world is significantly enhanced; and continue to play a full part in CSFP development, taking account of our own specific interests and concerns Ensure a leading role for Ireland in conflict prevention and crisis management, including peacekeeping.

STRATEGY

1: Contribute actively to the elaboration of the EU's CFSP and ensure that the further development of the CFSP continues to reflect Ireland's interests and priorities.
2: Contribute to the development of the EU's capabilities for conflict prevention, humanitarian and crisis management tasks through the elaboration of the European Security and Defence Policy (ESDP) in accordance with UN and OSCE principles.
3: Participate actively in international organisations concerned with peace and security, basing our approach on the concept of mutually reinforcing cooperation between the UN, the OSCE and the EU.
4: Engage in activities in the Euro-Atlantic Partnership Council and the Partnership for Peace which promote Ireland's objectives, especially to enhance the capabilities of the Defence Forces for peacekeeping operations authorised by the UN.

Human Rights

OBJECTIVE

Maintain and develop Ireland's contribution to international efforts to ensure respect and protection for human rights and basic freedoms, which are fundamental to international peace and justice.

STRATEGY

1: Ensure that Ireland's commitments in the field of human rights are implemented, including by continuing to ratify key international instruments to which Ireland is not yet a party, working as appropriate with relevant other Government Departments.
2: Participate actively in the work of the UN Commission on Human Rights and of the Third Committee of the UN General Assembly.
3: Work in cooperation with like minded states, including through the Human Security Network, to improve human rights.
4: Contribute to the formulation and implementation of refugee integration and anti-racism policies. In particular, facilitate arrangements for the fulfilment of Ireland's obligations under the UNHCR Resettlement Programme.
5: Develop a Protocol, through the Standing Interdepartmental Committee on Human Rights, to ensure a high level of cooperation between Government Departments and the Human Rights Commission.
6: Continue to develop the relationship between the Department and non-governmental organisations established through the Joint Standing Committee on Human Rights.
7: Contribute to the activities of the Council of Europe and the OSCE in supporting the consolidation of democracy in Europe, and in setting human rights standards.

Disarmament

OBJECTIVE

Pursue the total elimination of nuclear weapons and the prevention of further proliferation of nuclear weapons capability Pursue the implementation and strengthening of treaties banning the use, stockpiling, production and transfer of chemical and biological weapons Pursue the elimination of antipersonnel landmines, the reduction of the threat posed by the use and manufacture of inhumane weapons and the reduction of excessive accumulations of small arms and light weapons and their destabilising effects, inter alia by means of effective controls on the arms trade.

STRATEGY

1: Continue during the Non-Proliferation Treaty review cycles to promote the steps necessary to implement the New Agenda for the Achievement of a Nuclear-free World as adopted in the Final Document of the Non-Proliferation Treaty Review Conference in 2000.
2: Contribute to the implementation of the EU Strategy on the Non- Proliferation of Weapons of Mass Destruction.
3: Contribute to efforts to extend strengthened International Atomic Energy Agency safeguards.
4: Support the efforts of the Organisation for Prohibition of Chemical Weapons to provide an adequate inspection regime for the destruction of chemical weapons stockpiles.

5: Continue to support work within the Biological and Toxin Weapon Convention for the establishment of a verification framework.
6: Contribute to the universalisation of the Mine Ban Convention and its full implementation, including by contributing further support for the rehabilitation of mine victims.
7: Contribute to the development of international controls to reduce the indiscriminate suffering caused by unexploded ordnance and other explosive remnants of war.
8: Support the implementation of the United Nations *Programme of Action (PoA) to Prevent, Combat and Eradicate the Illicit Trade in Small Arms and Light Weapons* in all its aspects.

Terrorism

OBJECTIVE

Promotion of increased international cooperation in the fight against terrorism, both bilaterally and through relevant multilateral organisations, including the UN, EU, OSCE and Council of Europe, emphasising the need to respect human rights at all times in the fight against terrorism and to seek political solutions to international and regional problems which contribute to support for, and recruitment into, terrorism.

STRATEGY

1: Drawing on the special understanding and insights derived from our own national experience, participate fully in the activities of international bodies addressing the problems presented by international terrorism.
2: Maintain our engagement in the work undertaken by the United Nations in combating terrorism, building in particular on the close collaboration which Ireland has developed with the principal committees established under the relevant Security Council resolutions, including the Counter-Terrorism Committee and its Executive Directorate, the Taliban and Al-Qaida Sanctions Committee and subsidiary monitoring groups.
3: Work with our EU partners to ensure that the commitments given in the EU Declaration on Combating Terrorism, adopted under the Irish Presidency in the wake of the Madrid bombings, are met in full. In particular, maintain the momentum towards implementing the detailed provisions of the EU's Revised Plan of Action in the Fight against Terrorism within the agreed time limits.
4: Participate in efforts to fully integrate the fight against terrorism in the external policy of the EU. In particular, through political dialogue with third states, work to achieve the ratification and implementation by all states of the 12 international conventions related to terrorism.
5: Coordinate with other Departments the domestic implementation of measures to combat international terrorism, particularly those relating to the suppression of the financing of terrorism, in accordance with relevant UN Security Council Resolutions and EU Regulations.

6: Contribute to the development of counter-terrorist strategies in the OSCE and the Council of Europe, in the context of the particular orientations and areas of expertise of each organisation.

Africa

OBJECTIVE

Continue to pursue the objectives of peace and stability in Africa, both bilaterally and through our membership of international organisations.

STRATEGY

1: Seek to ensure that the European Union remains actively engaged in the pursuit of peace in the many African countries in conflict, including through partnership with the African Union. Strengthen and expand bilateral relations with individual African countries in which we are represented as well as with those African countries emerging from conflict and to which Ireland has made an active contribution, including during our EU Presidency, in support of peace.
2: Maintain and develop the existing development cooperation programmes with the six programme Countries.

Asia/Oceania

OBJECTIVE

Broaden and strengthen Ireland's political relations with the countries of the Asian region, and contribute to the strengthening of multilateral processes in the Asian region.

STRATEGY

1: Effectively manage bilateral relations, including through increased engagement with the region and ongoing implementation of Ireland's Asia Strategy, and strengthen the level of activity in the EU's relations with Asia, both with third individual countries and through inter-action with regional and inter-regional organisations such as ASEM, ASEAN and SAARC.

Eastern Europe, Southern Caucasus and Central Asia

OBJECTIVE

Develop relations with countries in Eastern Europe, outside the enlarged EU, the Southern Caucasus and Central Asia in order to promote stability, democracy, human rights and economic progress.

STRATEGY

1: Contribute to the evolution of EU relations with these countries, deepen bilateral relations and work to sustain the role of the OSCE, particularly in the human rights, democratisation and conflict prevention areas.

Western Balkans

OBJECTIVE

Contribute to the development of peace, security and stability in the Western Balkans, bilaterally and through our multilateral engagements.

STRATEGY

1: Work with other Government Departments and agencies to strengthen the cohesion and visibility of the various elements of Ireland's presence and activities in the Western Balkans.

Middle East Peace Process

OBJECTIVE

Facilitate the adoption and implementation of the Quartet "roadmap" approach to the Middle East Peace Process.

STRATEGY

1: Work with our partners in the EU and with the international community to renew and accelerate the momentum of the Peace Process Strategy Statement of the Department of Foreign Affairs 2005–2007 36.

Gulf Stability

OBJECTIVE

Contribute to the restoration of peace and security to the Gulf region and encourage the growth of democratic institutions.

STRATEGY

1: Promote efforts to achieve stability and security in the region, building upon the foundations laid during the Irish EU Presidency with the adoption both of the EU

Strategic Partnership for the Mediterranean and Middle East and the EU Medium Term Strategy for Iraq.

North America

OBJECTIVE

Further deepen Ireland's close bilateral relationships with the United States and with Canada and contribute to the development of EU-Transatlantic relations.

STRATEGY

1: Build on the successful EU-US and EU-Canada summits held during the Irish Presidency to deepen our close bilateral relationships with the United States and Canada.
2: Contribute to strengthening and deepening the transatlantic EU-US dialogue on all political and economic issues
3: Contribute to developing further EU-Canada relations.

Latin America and the Caribbean

OBJECTIVE

Further develop Ireland's bilateral relations with the countries of Latin America and the Caribbean Contribute to the development of the EU's relationship with Latin American and Caribbean countries and with regional organisations.

STRATEGY

1: Strengthen our bilateral relations with key Latin American and Caribbean countries.
2: Build on the successful EU-Latin American and Caribbean (EULAC) summit held during the Irish EU Presidency to actively promote a full range of bilateral contacts, including through exchanges of visits at Head of State/Government and Ministerial level and through our Missions.
3: Work for a successful outcome to the next EU-LAC Summit in Vienna in 2006 on the basis of the shared values of democracy and human rights and the objectives of economic development, social cohesion and effective multilateralism.

KEY PERFORMANCE INDICATORS

1: Extent to which Ireland's foreign policy is reflected in the outcomes of our participation in international fora.
2: Implementation of improved liaison and coordination arrangements with our Missions abroad, other Departments, State Agencies and other relevant bodies, to

ensure Ireland's interests are well represented in international bodies and to facilitate implementation of decisions, resolutions and agreements made by these bodies.

3: Quality, timeliness and accuracy of reports and briefing material.

ADVANCING IRELAND'S EXTERNAL ECONOMIC INTERESTS

With one of the most open economies in the world, Ireland is dependent on a liberalised and stable global trading and investment environment. Our future economic growth will be closely linked to growth in the world economy and will hinge on gaining increased access to international markets. Foreign direct investment will continue to play a key role in Ireland's prosperity.

OBJECTIVE

Pursue Ireland's economic and commercial interests abroad by leveraging the resources of our diplomatic network in close cooperation with other Departments, State Agencies and the private sector.

STRATEGY

1: Foster and develop good economic relations with individual countries through Ministerial and official visits and other high level contacts.
2: Facilitate the conclusion of agreements of an economic character such as in double taxation, air transport, science and technology, IT and ecommerce and education.
3: Further strengthen the business support role of the Department and Missions abroad by intensifying cooperation with State Agencies, commercial bodies engaged in export promotion and other Departments.
4: Contribute effectively to the policy review and operational work of the Foreign Earnings Committee and the Trade Advisory Forum.
5: Ensure our Missions are effectively equipped to deliver business support through regular briefings on Ireland's economic interests and priorities and annual trade seminars for overseas staff.
6: Assist our Missions in promoting Science Foundation Ireland and in promoting Ireland as a centre for research and development and high technology.
7: Provide a particular focus on areas of the economy on which the Department can be of greatest assistance, identified in consultation with other Departments, particularly the Department of Enterprise, Trade and Employment and also with the State Agencies.
8: Work to maintain and extend access for exports of Irish manufactured goods, services and food products, including beef, to international markets.

OBJECTIVE

Provide a particular focus on the emerging markets in Asia, Latin America, Eastern Europe and the Middle East for Irish goods and services.

STRATEGY

1: Work with other Government Departments, State Agencies, the private sector and our Mission abroad to ensure that the goals and objectives of the next phase of the Asia Strategy are implemented.
2: Coordinate closely with any other future regional strategy groups.
3: Support awareness-raising programmes also for Eastern Europe.
4: Support the work of the high level oversight group appointed under the next phase of the Asia Strategy to ensure that the strategy continues to respond to the dynamics of the Asian market.

KEY PERFORMANCE INDICATORS

1: Effectiveness of the contribution of the Division to maintaining and extending access for Irish exports, particularly in emerging markets.
2: Successful implementation and effectiveness of coordination structures and processes with other Departments and agencies in further strengthening the business support role of the Department.
3: Number of new economic / trade agreements signed with Ireland's key partners and number of visits abroad with an economic component.
4: Quality and frequency of reports and briefing material prepared.
5: Creation of new organisational arrangements to improve the effectiveness of the operation of the Division
6: Contribution to the opening of additional markets for Irish beef.

DEVELOPMENT COOPERATION

OBJECTIVE

Manage the Development Cooperation Ireland programme to the highest standards of international best practice.

STRATEGY

1: Complete and publish a White Paper on Development Cooperation policy, following a broad consultation process.
2: Cooperate with multilateral organisations and other donors to identify and replicate international best practice in Development Cooperation Ireland activities.
3: Ensure consistency of quality between the diverse elements of the Development Cooperation Ireland programme.

4: Plan and, subject to the necessary approvals, implement the activities required to expand the programme in line with the planned budget increase.
5: Maintain a rigorous evaluation process with a view to searching continuously for improvements to the efficiency and effectiveness of programme implementation.
6: Maintain the highest standards of financial accountability and ensure maximum value for money.

OBJECTIVE

Make an effective contribution to efforts to increase the coherence and impact of international development cooperation.

STRATEGY

1: Ensure maximum coherence within overall foreign policy and close coordination with all partners, domestic and foreign, in the development effort.
2: Ensure that external aid fits coherently within the strategies and programmes of developing countries Development cooperation policy has as its absolute priority the reduction of poverty, inequality and exclusion in developing countries. It embraces the broad range of trade, investment and other issues which affect developing countries. Development assistance refers to support provided by developed to developing countries. Ireland is committed to achieving the UN target for official development assistance (ODA) of 0.7% of GNP. The budget for 2005 is 545m and 1.8 billion will be spent on ODA in the three years 2005–2007.This will ensure that further progress is made towards reaching the UN target.

OBJECTIVE

Work closely with and support Irish NGOs and missionary organisations in pursuit of their critically important roles in development assistance.

STRATEGY

1: Build on the long-standing tradition of working in partnership with NGOs—Irish, international and indigenous—as well as individuals and groups interested in development.
2: Contribute to the strengthening of the role of civil society in developing countries.
3: Monitor the multi-annual programmatic funding for NGOs and support for missionary development work.
4: Strengthen public awareness and ownership of the Development Cooperation Programme, through the development of an appropriate communications policy for the ODA programme to ensure that the public fully understands both the scale of the commitment and the way in which the fund is being spent.

KEY PERFORMANCE INDICATORS

1: Effectiveness of arrangements for implementing the Development Cooperation Ireland programme.
2: Publication of the White Paper on Development Cooperation policy following a broad consultative process.
3: Quality and effectiveness of monitoring and evaluation processes.
4: Use of international fora to advance Ireland's Development Cooperation policy.
5: Inclusion of additional countries in Development Cooperation Ireland's Bilateral Programme.
6: Implementation of improved coordination arrangements with other Departments and with development agencies.
7: Increased awareness and support in Ireland for the Development Cooperation Ireland Programme.

CONSULAR AND PASSPORT SERVICES

OBJECTIVE

Deliver a high quality Passport Service to the public.

STRATEGY

1: Complete the implementation of the new automated passport issuing system by the end of 2005.
2: Work with the REACH project and other agencies to provide on-line access to passport services.
3: Pursue work on the development of biometric passports In response to increasing demand for passports in recent years, as well as requirements for higher security standards and our obligation to provide a Quality Customer Service, the Passport Office is in the process of modernising the passport issuing system. This is being done in the context of the Civil Service wide programme for e-Government, ultimately, to support the provision of on-line passport services. The implementation of the new system commenced on 29 November 2004 and the roll-out is expected to be completed by the end of 2005.

Consideration is also being given to the requirements for introducing biometric passports, in order to comply with the requirements of U.S. and emerging EU legislation. Further progress on this is planned for 2005.

Consular Services, through Irish Missions abroad, provide a range of services relating to the legal rights and physical welfare of Irish citizens visiting or resident in other countries. They also process applications for Irish citizenship based on marriage or descent, and legalise documents. The demand for consular services continues to increase as more Irish people travel abroad.

Consular Services also issue visas to foreign nationals wishing to visit Ireland. The number of nationals of other countries travelling to Ireland for employment, business, study or holidays continues to increase rapidly. We are committed, with the Department of Justice, Equality and Law Reform, to providing an efficient and user friendly visa-issuing service. We also work closely with the Department of Enterprise, Trade and Employment to issue work visas and work authorisations to non-nationals coming to work in Ireland in certain specified categories of employment.

OBJECTIVE

Provide a high quality consular service to Irish citizens.

STRATEGY

1: Work closely with Irish Missions abroad and, where appropriate, with Missions of other EU Member States, to ensure a fully effective response to the needs of Irish citizens abroad.
2: Provide more comprehensive and up-to-date information on consular services, including travel advice.
3: Advance the conclusion of bilateral prisoner transfer agreements with selected countries, in consultation with Missions abroad and the Department of Justice, Equality and Law Reform.

OBJECTIVE

Provide an effective visa service for people travelling to Ireland, in cooperation with the Department of Justice, Equality and Law Reform.

STRATEGY

1: Implement, in conjunction with the Department of Justice, Equality and Law Reform a project to modernize and upgrade the visa issuing service in order to provide a faster and more effective response to visa applicants.

KEY PERFORMANCE INDICATORS

1: Meet the targets and maintain the service standards set out in the Department's Customer Charter.
2: Complete implementation of the passport project by end 2005.
3: Complete implementation of visa project by mid 2006.
4: Positive feedback from customers of passport, consular and visa services Strategy Statement of the Department of Foreign Affairs 2005–2007 44.

PROTOCOL SERVICES

OBJECTIVE

Organise high-level and high quality visits to and from Ireland.

STRATEGY

1: Coordinate and manage Presidential visits abroad.
2: Manage key visits abroad by the Taoiseach, in support of specific Government strategies, such as the Asia Strategy.
3: Plan and manage incoming visits by Heads of State and Government, Foreign Ministers and other high-level visitors.
4: Assist in the preparation of official visits abroad by members of the Government and the Oireachtas.
5: Procure quality goods and services for State and Official visits, including accommodation, transport, gifts and catering.
6: Ensure effective communication with relevant third parties—Diplomatic Missions, Áras an Uachtaráin, Department of the Taoiseach, Garda Siochána, Airport Authorities, State Bodies etc. in the context of planning and coordination of visits, with a view to enhanced coordination of effort and maximising results.

OBJECTIVE

Maintain the necessary network of relationships to facilitate achievement of the Department's overall strategies.

STRATEGY

1: Facilitate the operation of, and maintain good relations with, foreign diplomatic and consular missions in Ireland through the provision of appropriate privileges and immunities.
2: Ensure prompt and effective processing of permissions for foreign military aircraft to overfly or land in Ireland and for naval vessels to visit Irish ports Protocol work is focused on the organisation of State and official visits to and from Ireland and liaison with Embassies in relation to the operation of their Missions and Consulates in Ireland. The organisation of visits, provision of hospitality and the development of relationships with Embassies in and accredited to Ireland enhances Ireland's reputation abroad and adds value to our efforts to create the conditions for the promotion of foreign trade and inward investment.

OBJECTIVE

Provide a high-quality, value-for-money hospitality service which contributes to the achievement of these objectives.

STRATEGY

1: Continue to provide an hospitality service to the highest possible standards, catering for the full range of events from State Dinners and Government lunches to meetings, receptions, seminars and other lunches and dinners associated with the work of the Department and the Government.
2: Continue to streamline all aspects of work procedures and processes to ensure quality service for our rapidly increasing number of external customers, maximising the use of information technology in order to achieve this.

KEY PERFORMANCE INDICATORS

1: State and Official visits are organised in a timely, efficient and effective manner.
2: Positive feedback received from relevant third parties on the quality of service provided.
3: Timely and efficient processing of requests relating to immunities and privileges .

CULTURE

OBJECTIVE

Raise the profile of Ireland by promoting its arts, literature and design.

STRATEGY

1: Promote Irish culture abroad by initiating and developing projects and by encouraging and supporting Missions in also doing so, maximising the advantages provided by their local expertise.

OBJECTIVE

Strengthen bilateral relations with other countries through cultural links.

STRATEGY

1: Continue support for Missions abroad in organising cultural events that increase knowledge and appreciation of Irish culture.

OBJECTIVE

Promote greater mutual understanding through culture.

STRATEGY

1: Implement bilateral cultural agreements with other countries, in association with the Department of Arts, Sport and Tourism Cultural diplomacy is an important aspect of the promotion of Ireland abroad. Against the backdrop of Ireland's rich heritage in the arts, literature and design, the Cultural Division works primarily through the Department's network of Embassies abroad and in co-operation with Government Departments, State bodies and individuals. In particular, the Division works closely with the Department of Arts, Sport and Tourism and with Culture Ireland on cultural projects and on the operation of cultural agreements with several foreign countries. It also works with the Department of Education and Science to promote educational exchanges and liaises with the Fulbright Commission on the administration of the Commission's programme of scholarly exchanges with the United States. The Division also supports Embassy initiatives in regard to the holding of Irish cultural events, including exhibitions, concerts, readings and lectures.

KEY PERFORMANCE INDICATORS

1: Qualitative evaluation of events.
2: Audiences reached, and their response
3: Positive feedback from other Government Departments, State Bodies and individuals Strategy Statement of the Department of Foreign Affairs 2005–2007 47.

LEGAL SERVICES

OBJECTIVE

Ensure an appropriate legal input into the formulation and implementation of Ireland's foreign policy.

STRATEGY

1: Liaise closely with officers of the Department and provide legal advice, as appropriate, thus contributing to effective risk management.
2: Liaise, as appropriate, with other Departments and the Law Offices of the State on international legal matters
3: Participate actively in preparations to enable Ireland to ratify the Treaty establishing a Constitution for Europe.

OBJECTIVE

Contribute to effective Irish participation in international legal fora.

STRATEGY

1: Represent Ireland in international bodies such as the UN, the Assembly of States parties to the Rome Statute of the International Criminal Court, the bodies established under the UN Convention on the Law of the Sea and relevant Council of Europe and EU bodies.
2: Represent Ireland in proceedings before the European Court of Human Rights and other international courts, tribunals and bodies.

OBJECTIVE

Publicise information on all international agreements to which Ireland is party.

STRATEGY

1: Lay before Dáil Éireann those international agreements to which Ireland becomes party.
2: Publicise appropriately, using up to date information technology methodologies, those international agreements to which Ireland becomes party.
3: Where appropriate, register with the UN those international agreements to which Ireland becomes a party The Department's Legal Division provides legal information and advice to the Minister for Foreign Affairs, particularly on matters of public international law, human rights law and EU law, and represents Ireland in international legal proceedings and in international fora and negotiations concerned with international legal matters. The Division is also responsible for laying before the Dáil international agreements to which the State has become a party, for making available to the public details of such agreements and for registering them with the UN Secretariat.

KEY PERFORMANCE INDICATORS

1: Timely provision of legal advice / assistance as required.
2: Effective representation of Ireland's position and interests in relevant fora.
3: Timely compliance with obligations / commitments in regard to publication of agreements.

CORPORATE SERVICES: HUMAN RESOURCE MANAGEMENT, CHANGE MANAGEMENT AND TRAINING

The Department's approach to human resource management (HRM) is informed generally by the ongoing Civil Service modernisation process and in particular by the HRM provisions in *Sustaining Progress*. The Department's current HRM Strategy, which covers the period 2002–2004, provides for the development of a more strategic and focused approach to human resource issues. The Strategy will be reviewed and updated in consultation with the Department's Partnership Committee to encompass our ongoing and new HRM priorities over the period covered by this Strategy Statement. New priorities will include management of the human resources aspects of the project to decentralise the Development Cooperation Directorate to Limerick.

OBJECTIVE

Continue to implement the changes in HRM policy and practice set out in the HRM Strategy so as to ensure that the Department has the quality and level of resources necessary to enable it to provide a service of excellence.

STRATEGY

1: Continue the development of a more strategic approach to human resource planning, through:.

—working with the Public Appointments Service to ensure that the Third Secretary recruitment process meets the Department's needs in terms of the quality and suitability of new recruits.
—devolving HRM functions to line Divisions and Missions.
—improving the HRM services provided to staff, supported by the development of improved ICT systems.
—ensuring that our obligations under relevant equality and other workplace legislation and guidelines are fulfilled.
—maintaining and enhancing family-friendly working opportunities and conditions.
—implementing the new internal Promotion Policy, agreed at Departmental Council in 2004, which provides for a greater number of posts to be filled through merit-based promotion competitions.

2: Implement the Department's HRM policy at Mission level by.

—providing support to staff in relation to issues arising from service abroad.
—providing support for Missions on issues relating to the employment of local staff abroad.
—providing a mechanism to address grievances for locally employed staff in our Missions abroad.

3: Review and update the Department's current HRM Strategy in 2005, to encompass ongoing and new HRM priorities over the period covered by this Strategy Statement, including revising HR procedures, as necessary, to take account of legislative changes due to come into effect with in the Civil Service Regulation (Amendment) Act 2005.

4: Manage the human resources aspects of the decentralisation of the Development Cooperation Directorate to Limerick in a manner that both minimises disruption to business continuity and recognises that staff-related issues are central to the success of the project.

5: Manage the human resources impact on the Department of the wider Civil Service decentralisation programme.

OBJECTIVE

Support the achievement of the Department's business strategies and objectives through the provision of high quality training and development programmes.

STRATEGY

1: Implement the Department's Training and Development Strategy, 2004–2008.
2: Develop specific policies in 2005 on induction, language training (including Irish), pre-posting preparation and management development and on training for professional and technical staff.

OBJECTIVE

Continue to implement the change / modernisation programme set out in the Department's Action Plan in order to develop a more open, collaborative and performance driven culture.

STRATEGY

1: Further develop and integrate the Department's business planning process, particularly in relation to reporting and monitoring of progress.
2: Continue to implement and enhance the Performance Management and Development System (PMDS) within the Department by—progressing the integration of PMDS with other HRM policies and practices—incorporating upward feedback into the 2005 PMDS cycle—developing a quality assurance system during 2005 to ensure that PMDS is being implemented consistently across the Department.
3: Develop an internal communications strategy in 2005 that will provide a framework for structured communication and consultation within the Department on business and performance issues.
4: Continue to implement "A Positive Working Environment—the Civil Service Code on Bullying and Harassment" Strategy Statement of the Department of Foreign Affairs 2005–2007 50.

OBJECTIVE

Progress the Quality Customer Service (QCS) initiative in the Department.

STRATEGY

1: Coordinate the formulation, development and implementation of QCS policy in the Department.
2: Prepare a new Customer Service Action Plan in 2005, in consultation with the Partnership Committee.

3: Develop an internal customer charter / guide to best practice by the end of 2005.
4: Monitor the implementation of commitments contained in the Customer Service Action Plan and Internal Customer Charter.
5: Provide for the development of the Department's capability to offer services to customers through Irish, in order to meet the requirements of the Official Languages Act, 2003.

OBJECTIVE

Further develop and deepen the Partnership process within the Department.

STRATEGY

1: Continue to develop the role of Partnership, particularly in relation to the formulation and implementation of modernisation initiatives
2: Review and update, through Partnership, the Department's Modernisation Action Plan by end September 2005.
3: Continue to support the operation of local partnership committees within the Department and examine the feasibility of establishing further local committees.

KEY PERFORMANCE INDICATORS

1: Effective implementation of the policies and undertakings in the Department's HRM Strategy.
2: Meet targets dates specified.
3: Effective management of the human resources aspects of the decentralisation of the Development Cooperation Directorate to Limerick; completion of the project on time and with minimal disruption to the Department's business processes.
4: Improved range and quality of services provided to the Department's internal and external customers through both official languages.
5: Improved range and quality of training and development programmes, focused on meeting the Department's business objectives and on improving staff performance.
6: Range of issues progressed through the Partnership process, and extent of progress achieved Strategy Statement of the Department of Foreign Affairs 2005–2007 51.

CORPORATE SERVICES: FINANCIAL AND MANAGEMENT SERVICES, INFORMATION TECHNOLOGY AND ACCOMMODATION

Managing the Department's expenditure in the most economic, efficient and effective manner is critical to internal resource management. Implementing the Management Information Framework, as part of the civil service modernisation programme, is a key element in the drive for greater efficiency and effectiveness in the management and use of resources.

Ensuring the efficient management, transmission, storage and retrieval of information resources underpins the Department's work to achieve its strategic goals. The integrated Freedom of Information/Coordination Unit, Registry, Archives, Library, Website and Information Units will continue to ensure that the Department's legislative requirements and information needs are met.

The continuing implementation of the Department's ICT Strategy Plan over the coming years will be a critical element in achieving the Department's policy objectives and in progressing the Information Society Action Plan.

The provision of a good working environment for staff continues to be a priority. The overall objective is to bring all accommodation at HQ and abroad up to the highest standards possible taking into account the safety and needs of staff and visitors, including those with disabilities.

OBJECTIVE

Plan, budget, control and account for the financial resources required to achieve the Department's organisational objectives, to manage its business functions and to attain best value for money.

STRATEGY

1: Manage the Department's budgeting and accounting system, in line with Government financial procedures and best practice, to ensure adequate controls on the use of financial resources and in order to achieve maximum value for money.
2: Implement the remaining elements of the Management Information Framework.
3: Ongoing review and enhancement of the Department's system of internal financial controls in order to ensure a strong framework for accountability.
4: Undertake expenditure reviews of key programme and other areas to provide assurance that key objectives have been achieved and value for money has been obtained.
5: Ongoing review and implementation of the Department's Risk Management Programme.

OBJECTIVE

Develop and implement systems for the ongoing effective management, storage, retrieval and transmission of information in order to meet the business needs of the Department.

STRATEGY

1: Maintain a coherent and secure information/document management system that enables the Department to meet its legislative requirements and to acquire, organize, store and retrieve information efficiently and effectively.

2: Maintain and develop the Department's website and develop Mission websites.

OBJECTIVE

Provide for the Health and Safety of all staff in accordance with the Safety, Health and Welfare At Work Act, 1989.

STRATEGY

1: Update the Department's Safety Statement and maintain close liaison with the Department's Health and Safety Committee.
2: Ensure appropriate training for staff on Health and Safety issues.
3: Assist and advise missions abroad in drawing up Contingency Plans for dealing with emergency situations, including terrorist attacks.

OBJECTIVE

Provide well focused and timely advice and support in relation to the Department's activities under the Freedom of Information Acts 1997 and 2003 (FOI Acts).

STRATEGY

1: Participate effectively in internal training and induction courses.
2: Attend interdepartmental meetings on an ongoing basis to ensure up to date knowledge of developments.
3: Revise and update the Department's Sections 15 and 16 Manual and the Department's Freedom of Information Procedures Manual.

OBJECTIVE

Promote Ireland overseas.

STRATEGY

1: Publish and disseminate information on aspects of Ireland (e.g. Information Sheets, Facts about Ireland, Ireland in brief).
2: Make better use of the Departmental and Mission websites for the dissemination of information on Ireland.

OBJECTIVE

Implement the Department's ICT Strategy Plan to support the business needs of the Department.

STRATEGY

1: Implement the projects identified in the Department's ICT Strategy Plan in collaboration with Sections, Divisions and Missions, as internal customers.
2: Support, maintain and develop the existing ICT infrastructure at HQ and Missions.
3: Monitor the effectiveness and efficiency of the Department's telephony systems.
4: Work with Sections and Missions to provide business focussed ICT applications.
5: Provide advice on Information Society and e-Government initiatives.
6: Support, maintain and develop communications systems with international organisations.
7: Ensure staff have the necessary skills to take advantage of the IT and communications facilities available.

OBJECTIVE

Provide a good working environment for staff, and meet the commitments in the Department's Customer Service Action Plan, in particular in relation to the needs of those with disabilities.

STRATEGY

1: Plan and implement, with the Office of Public Works, a programme of refurbishment and upgrading of Iveagh House and other buildings; and source adequate office space to meet the Department's needs at HQ.
2: Provide and maintain suitable and secure accommodation for our Missions abroad.
3: Continue the search for suitable accommodation in Limerick for the Development Cooperation Directorate, in cooperation with the Office of Public Works, with a view to meeting the target of decentralising the Directorate in the first quarter of 2007.
4: Investigate, with relevant State Departments and Agencies, the purchase of properties on a cost benefit basis.

KEY PERFORMANCE INDICATORS

1: Meet the targets dates for completion of reviews and projects.
2: Ongoing upgrade of Departmental e-mail systems at Missions.
3: Extension of the Department's Wide Area Network (WAN) to all Missions.
4: Ongoing implementation of change to Management Information System for Departmental accounting practices.
5: Ensure ongoing compliance with the Freedom of Information Acts, 1997 and 2003 and other relevant legislation.
6: Maintain sufficient stocks of information materials to meet demand.
7: Maintain a functional website which adheres to international standards of accessibility.

INSPECTION AND INTERNAL AUDIT

The Inspection and Internal Audit Unit examines, in a systematic way, the operation of Missions abroad with a view to ensuring resources are deployed as effectively and as productively as possible in line with overall Departmental strategy.

The Unit also performs an independent internal audit function. This function will shortly be merged with the Evaluation and Audit Unit in the Development Cooperation Directorate to make one Audit Unit for the Department, as recommended by the external Audit Committee.

OBJECTIVE

Ensure that Headquarters and overseas Missions function in accordance with the requirements of the Department and that they are pursuing policy objectives in an efficient and effective manner and in line with the Departmental Strategy Statement.

STRATEGY

1: Carry out visits of inspection and support to Missions, and monitor the implementation of recommendations of inspection reports at six monthly intervals, engaging specialists as required.

OBJECTIVE

Ensure the efficiency and effectiveness of the internal control systems within the Department.

STRATEGY

1: Undertake an internal audit programme in consultation with the Department's Audit Committee including, where necessary, with specialist assistance.

OBJECTIVE

Ensure adherence to the audit objectives of the Mullarkey report on the Accountability of Secretaries General.

STRATEGY

1: Review as necessary the implementation of the Mullarkey recommendations, including those concerning the Department's risk strategy, in consultation with the Department's Audit Committee.

KEY PERFORMANCE INDICATORS

1: Number of inspection visits and audits completed.
2: Quality of reports.
3: Effective and prompt implementation of recommendations.
4: Improved internal controls put in place to reduce business risks.

PRESS

Press Section ensures that the domestic and international media are informed about developments in Irish foreign policy.

OBJECTIVE

Work with the domestic and international media to enhance their understanding of Irish foreign policy and of the Government's approach to Northern Ireland.

STRATEGY

1: Communicate the Government's foreign policy to the media.
2: Arrange media press briefings / press opportunities for the Minister and Ministers of State on matters of policy.
3: Respond to media inquiries relating to Irish foreign policy and to other aspects of the Department's work, and correct errors when they occur.

OBJECTIVE

Promote awareness overseas of Ireland and its achievements, in particular building on the success of the EU Presidency.

STRATEGY

1: On the recommendation of Missions and in cooperation with other Government Departments and State Agencies, organize familiarization visits of foreign media personnel to Ireland.
2: Facilitate media arrangements for outgoing official and State visits, as appropriate.
3: Monitor international media coverage of Ireland and coordinate any response required.
4: Maximise positive international media coverage of major events and public policy developments in Ireland
5: Maximise the efficient use by media of the Department's website.

KEY PERFORMANCE INDICATORS

1: Quality, accuracy and timeliness of information provided.
2: Effective management of press opportunities and quality of coverage achieved.
3: Positive international media coverage following incoming visits and positive feedback from visiting media.

SUPPORTING IRISH EMIGRANTS

The Irish Abroad Unit is responsible for promoting progress on initiatives which build on the Report of the Task Force on Policy regarding Emigrants. The Unit works to encourage greater collaboration between all of the partners, in Government and voluntary sectors, in Ireland and abroad, so as to enhance the coherence and effectiveness of activities. The Unit is responsible for managing the financial support that the Department directs to the voluntary organisations that are engaged in the delivery of services to Irish emigrants, particularly the more vulnerable and marginalised. Also included in its remit is strengthening links with Irish people and people of Irish ancestry living abroad.

OBJECTIVE

Coordinate the provision of Government support to Irish emigrants, those considering emigration and those who wish to return to Ireland.

STRATEGY

1: Ongoing review of progress in the implementation of the recommendations of the Task Force on Policy regarding Emigrants
2: Close liaison and regular meetings with Government Departments providing services which impact on emigrants.

OBJECTIVE

Work closely with and support the voluntary agencies that assist Irish emigrants, those considering emigration and those who wish to return to Ireland.

STRATEGY

1: Promote closer cooperation between statutory and voluntary agencies in Ireland and abroad and provide Voluntary agencies with an effective channel of communication to the Government.
2: Enhance the capacity of voluntary agencies to engage effectively with the statutory authorities of their host country.

3: Ensure that funding is directed to the organisations that assist vulnerable Irish people abroad.
4: Review grant application procedures with a view to identifying and implementing improvements; and ensure a rigorous evaluation process.

OBJECTIVE

Strengthen links with Irish people and people of Irish ancestry living abroad.

STRATEGY

1: Deepen the relationship between Ireland and its community abroad.
2: Develop initiatives which enhance the special affinity of Ireland with people of Irish ancestry living abroad.

KEY PERFORMANCE INDICATORS

1: Improved coordination arrangements with other Government Departments.
2: Frequency of meetings at home and abroad with partners in the Voluntary sector.
3: Number of evaluations carried out.
4: Financial systems reviewed and revised to take account of increased allocations.
5: Review of grant applications process completed
6: Increased range of contacts, including with stakeholders in the private, public, voluntary and education sectors.
7: Elaboration of policy on interaction with Irish people and those of Irish ancestry abroad.

Department of Foreign Affairs Annual Report 2006

MISSION STATEMENT

The Mission of the Department of Foreign Affairs is to advance Ireland's political and economic interests in the European Union and in the wider world, to promote Ireland's contribution to international peace, security and development both through the European Union and through active participation in international organisations, in particular the United Nations, to protect our citizens abroad, and to pursue reconciliation and partnership on the island of Ireland.

FOREWORD BY THE MINISTER FOR FOREIGN AFFAIRS

I am very pleased to accept the Annual Report for 2006, which has been prepared in accordance with the provisions of the Public Service Management Act, 1997.

As Minister for Foreign Affairs, I welcome a heightened awareness and public interest in international relations. Throughout 2006, my colleagues and I at the Department of Foreign Affairs, Minister of State Noel Treacy, T.D., and Minister of State Conor Lenihan, T.D., sought to promote and enhance public engagement across the whole spectrum of issues dealt with by the Department. Its newly-designed and user-friendly website now provides people with greater access to information on my work and that of the Ministers of State and the Department as a whole, as well as providing up to date information on Ireland's policy on the main international issues.

The number and complexity of challenges facing the Department of Foreign Affairs grows with each year that passes. 2006 was no exception. The continued stalemate in the Middle East and the humanitarian and political crises in Iraq and Darfur dominated the European and international political agenda. Ireland's constructive engagement within the European Union ensured an increase in the level of EU financial assistance to the Palestinians, including increased Irish assistance. During my visit to Darfur, I urged the Government in Sudan to redouble efforts to urgently resolve the crisis and facilitate vital access for humanitarian workers. Our work on these and other issues will continue. However, challenges notwithstanding, 2006 was a year of significant progress and achievement for the Department.

The St. Andrews Agreement, published in October, was a significant step forward towards the full implementation of the Good Friday Agreement. Political progress was accompanied by significant steps towards recognition of our shared history on this island and dynamic North/South economic and trade cooperation of practical benefit to all of the people on this island.

Active involvement in the UN remains a cornerstone of Ireland's foreign policy. Building on my previous experience as an Envoy of the UN Secretary General, I remain strongly committed to the continued reform of the UN. This reform is essential to secure and enhance the primacy of the UN in the 21st century for dealing with issues of international peace and security, and inter-related global challenges including development, human rights and climate change. Ireland's ability to make an even greater contribution to the peaceful resolution of conflict was further enhanced by the establishment of a Conflict Resolution Unit in the Department.

Launched by the Taoiseach in September, the Government's White Paper on Aid was the result of an innovative process of consultation with the public, the Irish development community, partner countries, UN agencies, and other government departments. It sets out for the first time as Government policy Ireland's approach to development assistance and underlines the leading role that Ireland will continue to play in the fight against poverty and underdevelopment.

Throughout the year, the Department of Foreign Affairs continued to work to modernise and enhance the consular and passport services provided to Irish citizens. The first mass evacuation of Irish citizens took place, organised by the Department, in response to events in Lebanon. The introduction of the ePassport in October

provides Irish citizens with a world-class secure and modern travel document and ensures that Irish citizens will continue to have the facility to travel visa free to the US. Our support to vulnerable and isolated Irish citizens abroad was enhanced with increased funding amounting to €12 million.

I would like to pay tribute to my colleagues at the Department of Foreign Affairs, Minister of State Treacy and Minister of State Lenihan for their continued work, support and commitment on European Affairs and Overseas Development Assistance respectively. Equally, I must acknowledge the hard work of the staff of the Department who support me and my Ministers of State in delivering on the Department's key strategic priorities.

Foreign policy must continue to develop and foreign policy makers must continue to adapt to respond efficiently and effectively to the challenging international environment. I am confident that our innovations and achievements in 2006 have further enhanced the capability of the Department of Foreign Affairs to anticipate and respond to these challenges, both globally and closer to home, and to protect and support Irish citizens abroad.

Dermot Ahern TD.
Minister for Foreign Affairs

INTRODUCTION

Introduction by the Secretary General

I am very pleased to present the Minister with this Annual Report of the Department of Foreign Affairs for 2006.

It was another challenging but productive year for the Department. Working under the direction of the Minister for Foreign Affairs and Ministers of State Treacy and Lenihan, some impressive achievements and advances were made across a number of important policy and service areas.

Looking back on 2006, the highlights for me would include:

—The Department's work supporting the achievement of the St. Andrews Agreement and the deepening of North/South co-operation and reconciliation on the island;
—The establishment of the Conflict Resolution Unit, which aims to make a positive contribution in specific areas of conflict around the world;
—The Minister's visit to Darfur and his work through the year to assist in addressing this tragic situation;

—The Department's ongoing support for the process of reform and renewal within the UN, building on the Minister's work in 2005 as Special Envoy to the UN Secretary General
—Our contribution to the ongoing debates about the Future of Europe and its Enlargement, including the sponsorship of the legislation for the recent accession of Bulgaria and Romania to the European Union; and
—The work done on the preparation and launch of the first ever Government White Paper on Development Aid and the successful delivery of a quality Aid Programme that exceeded €600M in 2006.

While the Department's achievements in policy terms were significant, I am very conscious that we are also judged by the quality of day to day service given to our citizens. In terms of services, 2006 was also a significant year:

—Over 630,000 passports were issued to Irish citizens—in other words, over 12,000 every week of the year;
—The on-time and cost-efficient introduction of the e-passport in October means that Ireland has one of the most secure passports in the world and that our citizens continue to benefit from the US visa waiver programme;
—The allocation of €12M to support emigrant services in Britain, the US and elsewhere meant that thousands of vulnerable and isolated Irish citizens were given real assistance on the ground;
—Practically every day of the year, an Irish citizen experiencing distress in some part of the world was being assisted by a consular officer of the Department—either from HQ or in a Mission abroad; and
—In July, the Department, through its Crisis Response arrangements, arranged for the safe evacuation of some 200 citizens from Lebanon.

The Department of Foreign Affairs has a staff of over 1,500 people. It operates across 13 Divisions at Headquarters and 76 Missions outside of the State. The effectiveness of its policy formulation and the quality of its service delivery are dependent on the Department being fully joined up in its operations. This coherence is achieved through the hard work and efficiency of all of our staff, including those in the "back-office" areas.

I wish to express my appreciation to the Minister and Ministers of State for their leadership and direction through 2006. The success achieved is also due to the quality and commitment of the staff that the Department is fortunate to have at its disposal. I am proud of the work done by all of my colleagues in the Department, particularly of their high level of professional commitment and dedication to service. Their dedication, and indeed the contribution made by the support and solidarity of their partners and family members, is hugely appreciated.

Dermot Gallagher
Secretary General

OUR STRATEGY

Ireland's foreign policy is shaped by our values and by the external environment to which we relate them. The Department of Foreign Affairs' Strategy Statement

2005–2007 defines the Department's high level goals, strategic objectives and priorities for this period. It is these objectives which form the basis for the work of the Department over this period and on which this Annual Report is based.

In December 2006, the Minister for Foreign Affairs, Dermot Ahern, T.D., launched the Department's newly-designed, user-friendly website: www.dfa.ie. The website provides detailed and up-to-date information on the full range of services provided by the Department, from the latest press releases to an online tracking facility for passport applications. Documents referenced in this Annual Report such as the Strategy Statement for 2005–2007, the White Paper on Irish Aid and the St. Andrews Agreement are all available on the website.

STRUCTURE OF THE DEPARTMENT

Under the political direction of the Minister for Foreign Affairs, the Department is managed by the Secretary General, who is also the accounting officer for its two Votes—Vote 28 (Foreign Affairs) and Vote 29 (Development Cooperation). The Secretary General is supported by a Management Advisory Committee (MAC) comprising the Heads of the main Divisions in the Department.

The work of the Department is divided between thirteen divisions at headquarters (HQ) and a total of 74 diplomatic and consular offices abroad (referred to as "Missions"), as well as the British-Irish Intergovernmental Secretariat in Belfast and the North-South Ministerial Council Joint Secretariat in Armagh.

HQ Divisions:

Anglo-Irish Division
Bilateral Economic Relations Division (BERD)
Corporate Services Division
Cultural Division
Development Cooperation Directorate
European Union Division
Inspection Division
Irish Abroad Unit
Legal Division
Consular and Passport Division
Political Division
Press Section
Protocol Division

EXTERNAL ENVIRONMENT

The Department of Foreign Affairs operates in a complex and ever-changing environment shaped by European and wider international influences. The realisation of objectives depends, therefore, not just on the efforts of the Department but also on the behaviour of other States and entities.

Because of the complexity of the external environment, it is essential that the resources available to the Department are deployed to the optimum effect. We cannot and do not work in isolation. The Department acts in close cooperation with other Government Departments that have external responsibilities, in order to contribute effectively to the attainment of the goals set down in the Programme for Government and in successive Partnership Agreements.

HIGH LEVEL GOALS, 2005–2007

The Department's high level goals for the period 2005–2007, on which this report is largely based, are:

Northern Ireland and Anglo-Irish Relations	Work to achieve the full implementation of the Good Friday Agreement and the sustained operation of all its institutions, promoting co-operation, mutual understanding and respect between both traditions on the island, between North and South in Ireland and between these islands.
Ireland's Role in the World	Pursue Ireland's foreign policy in accordance with the ideals enshrined in the Constitution and in conformity with the principles of the United Nations Charter, through the development of our bilateral relations with other States, our participation in the European Union's Common Foreign and Security Policy, and our active and principled participation in international organisations.
The European Union	Promote and protect Ireland's interests at the heart of the European Union as it continues to evolve and enlarge, including through the further development of our relations with our current and future EU partners.
Advancing Ireland's	Promote Ireland's trade, investment and other interests, includ-
Economic Interests	ing its culture, in close co-operation with other Departments, State Agencies and the private sector, ensuring that the State's network of diplomatic and consular missions adds real value to this task.
Irish Aid	Make a substantive and effective contribution to achieving the Millennium Development Goals, and to poverty reduction and sustainable growth in developing countries, through the policy and programmes of Development Cooperation Ireland, and by working for a just and stable international economic system.
Consular and Passport Services	Protect and support the interests of Irish citizens abroad, maintain and strengthen links with people of Irish ancestry, and provide a modern and efficient passport and consular service.

2006: SUMMARY OF DEVELOPMENTS AND ACHIEVEMENTS

Northern Ireland and Anglo-Irish Relations	Publication of the St. Andrews Agreement
	Rapid progress in ending paramilitary and criminal activities
	Significant improvement in the overall security situation
	Minister hosted first Reconciliation Networking Forum
	Inaugural meeting of the Forum to discuss a Bill of Rights for Northern Ireland
	Launch of a Comprehensive Study on the all-island economy
	Signing of Memorandum of Understanding on the creation of a Single Electricity Market
	Increased co-operation on North/South trade promotion and infrastructure development
	Minister co-chaired five meetings of the British-Irish Intergovernmental Conference
	British-Irish Council Summit and five Ministerial meetings
Ireland's Role in the World	Establishment of Conflict Resolution Unit (CRU)
	Deployment of 150 Defence Forces personnel to UNIFIL mission in southern Lebanon
	Minister Ahern visited Darfur to deliver key messages to the Government in Sudan
	Provision of political and financial support for the electoral process in the Democratic Republic of Congo
	Decision in favour of participation in the Swedish-led Nordic Battlegroup
	Inauguration of the new UN Human Rights Council
	Agreement on a UN Convention on the Rights of People with Disabilities
	Support for new UN Peace Building Commission and major donation to the Peace Building Fund
The European Union	Taoiseach's visit to European Commission and European Parliament
	President of European Parliament visited Ireland
	EU's Budget for 2007–2013 agreed
	European Communities (Amendment) Act 2006 enabling the accession of Bulgaria and Romania to the EU
	EU Leaders engaged in an in-depth debate on the enlargement process
	The European Council reaffirmed the EU's broad commitment to the enlargement process
	Period of reflection on Constitutional Treaty extended

Advancing Ireland's Economic and Cultural Interests	Taoiseach led trade mission to India Minister visited Japan and China Promotion of Ireland's world-class research and development facilities Beckett Centenary Exhibition
Irish Aid	Ireland's first ever White Paper on Irish Aid published Minister of State Lenihan signed agreement with the World Food Programme for the pre-positioning and transportation of humanitarian supplies to disaster areas (Rapid Response Initiative) Work advanced on Hunger Task Force Planning commenced on Irish Aid Information and Volunteering Centre President McAleese made State visits to three Irish Aid programme countries in Africa Work advanced on decentralisation of Development Cooperation Directorate to Limerick
Consular and Passport Services	Mass evacuation of Irish citizens from Lebanon Establishment of Crisis Centre Successful completion—on time and well within budget—of project to include biometric features in Irish passports. ePassport launched Increase in passport applications and increased use of Northern Ireland Passport Express (NIPX) service Online passport application tracking facility introduced Increased funding for emigrant services for vulnerable citizens

NORTHERN IRELAND AND ANGLO-IRISH RELATIONS

High Level Goal, 2005–2007:

Work to achieve the full implementation of the Good Friday Agreement and the sustained operation of all its institutions, promoting co-operation, mutual understanding and respect between both traditions on the island, between North and South in Ireland and between these islands.

2006 in Review

2006 was an important year for the peace process. It saw a renewed push by the Governments on the political front, culminating in the publication of the St. Andrews Agreement in October 2006.

Government efforts to rebuild trust and confidence between the parties and restore political momentum took place against the backdrop of an ever-improving security context, dynamic North/South co-operation and respectful acknowledgement of the shared history of the people of the island through official commemorations marking the Easter Rising and honouring all who died at the Battle of the Somme.

Throughout 2006, our international partners, in particular the United States, continued to provide valuable practical and political support for the Government's ongoing efforts to secure full implementation of the Good Friday Agreement.

As the year drew to a close, both Governments were working intensively with the political parties in Northern Ireland to secure implementation of the St. Andrews Agreement.

2006: Developments and Achievements

St. Andrews Agreement

The St. Andrews Agreement (October 2006) underpins the Good Friday Agreement. It outlines a clear way forward for all parties to commit to the full operation of stable power-sharing government and to full support for policing and the criminal justice institutions.

The St. Andrews text also set out important commitments in the area of human rights and equality. A notable step forward on the human rights agenda of the Good Friday Agreement took place on 18 December 2006, with the inaugural meeting of the Forum to discuss a Bill of Rights for Northern Ireland.

Improved Security

2006 saw rapid progress in ending paramilitary and criminal activities and significant further improvement in the overall security situation.

In its October 2006 assessment, the Independent Monitoring Commission confirmed that the Provisional IRA remained committed to following an exclusively peaceful and political path, was not engaged in terrorist or paramilitary activity, and had neither the capacity nor intent to re-start its paramilitary campaign.

The British Army's comprehensive security normalisation programme also proceeded rapidly and is on schedule for completion by July 2007.

The 2006 parading season was the most peaceful in years, achieved through the collective efforts of the Parades Commission, and political and community representatives throughout the summer period.

There were also positive developments within loyalism during the year, with the main paramilitary groupings currently engaged in community transformation processes.

Addressing the legacy of the conflict

During 2006, the Minister and officials met with victims and survivors groups, and other key stakeholders, and closely followed the work of the PSNI Historical Enquiries Team and the Police Ombudsman in this area.

Concerns regarding the British proposal to hold an inquiry into the murder of Patrick Finucane under the UK Inquiries Act 2005 were raised with the British Government, the US Government and at the Council of Europe.

In December 2006, the Minister raised the Government's serious concerns in relation to the findings of the reports of the Oireachtas Joint Committee on the Barron Inquiry with the British Government and stressed the need for these to be addressed.

2006—An active year for Reconciliation work

The Department continued to support the valuable reconciliation work of cross-community groups and organisations. In 2006, this assistance amounted to over €3 million in grants from the Department's Reconciliation Fund awarded to 140 groups involved in reconciliation work.

In July 2006, Minister Ahern hosted the first Reconciliation Networking Forum for groups from all over the island under the auspices of the Fund.

The International Fund for Ireland (IFI) continued to provide much needed financial support to reconciliation activities and its work continued to benefit from strong international support. In December 2006, an EU Regulation committed €60 million to the work of the Fund for the period 2007—2010. The US Administration announced a commitment of $10.8 million for 2007 and Canada affirmed that it would continue to support the Fund's work to 2009.

In 2006, the Fund committed €33.6 million to reconciliation work benefiting the most disadvantaged areas and communities of Northern Ireland and across the six southern border counties.

Our Shared History

In November 2006 Minister Ahern welcomed the enactment of legislation by the British Government pardoning all soldiers executed for military offences during the First World War, including 26 Irish volunteers. The Government had raised this issue formally with the British Government through a comprehensive report in 2004.

2006 saw significant steps towards recognition of the shared history of people on the island from every tradition—in particular the marking of the ninetieth anniversary of the Easter Rising and the Government's official commemoration to honour those from the island, North and South, who died at the Battle of the Somme.

North/South Cooperation—practical delivery

2006 saw a further increase in momentum behind North/South cooperation for the benefit of all of the people on the island. This included several practical developments:

1) The launch of the Comprehensive Study on the All-Island Economy.
2) Considerable progress was made towards the creation of a Single Electricity Market on the island.
3) Co-operation on trade promotion intensified, with businesses from both parts of the island taking part in successful trade missions to India and Canada.
4) Initiatives in the area of health saw the commencement of radiotherapy services in Belfast for patients from Donegal.
5) A number of major mobile phone operators introduced all-island tariff options in response to pressure from the two Governments.

In addition to these specific developments, there was an increased emphasis in 2006 on co-operation in the planning and delivery of infrastructure development North and South, in order to maximise returns on major capital investments.

In that context too, work progressed with the British Government in scoping out a possible North/South dimension to any financial support package for a restored devolved Executive.

The British-Irish Intergovernmental Conference

The British-Irish Intergovernmental Conference (BIIGC) was established under the Good Friday Agreement to promote bilateral co-operation between the Irish and British Governments and, in recognition of the Government's particular involvement in Northern Ireland, to enable it to "put forward views and proposals" on non-devolved Northern Ireland matters.

It also brings the two Governments together to promote bilateral cooperation at all levels on matters of mutual interest, particularly important in the absence of fully-functioning devolved institutions in Northern Ireland.

In 2006, Minister Ahern jointly chaired (with Secretary of State for Northern Ireland, Peter Hain, MP) five meetings of the BIIGC—the most to date in any one year.

The British-Irish Council (BIC)

The Department continued to support and develop the work of the British-Irish Council (BIC) throughout 2006.

A meeting at Summit level in June 2006 focussed specifically on the challenges of climate change. Five Ministerial meetings took place during the year to:

—address transport issues;
—share best practice on social inclusion and tackling drug misuse;
—assess environmental challenges; and,
—look at cultural co-operation in the area of minority languages.

The BIC also formally adopted a new area of work in 2006—meeting the challenges of changing demographics for the economies and societies of its member administrations.

IRELAND'S ROLE IN THE WORLD

High Level Goal, 2005–2007:

> Pursue Ireland's foreign policy in accordance with the ideals enshrined in the Constitution and in conformity with the principles of the United Nations Charter, through the development of our bilateral relations with other States, our participation in the European Union's Common Foreign and Security Policy, and our active and principled participation in international organisations.

2006 in Review

Ireland remains committed to promoting a more secure and just international environment. Our foreign policy is guided by the ideals enshrined in the Constitution and the principles of the United Nations Charter.

The Department continued to work in support of the Government's efforts to achieve these goals, through active participation in all aspects of the EU's Common

Foreign and Security Policy (CFSP), our committed membership of the United Nations and other international organisations, and through the development of our bilateral political relations with other States.

This work, led by the Political Division of the Department, provided the basis for active Irish input on a full range of international issues throughout the year, including:

—political aspects of the EU enlargement process;
—the question of final status for Kosovo;
—Ireland's rapidly developing relationships with China and India;
—the complex relationship between the EU and Russia;
—EU and UN efforts to tackle international terrorism; and,
—efforts to bring about change in states where international norms of human rights and democracy are not observed, such as Burma, Zimbabwe and Belarus.

The European and international political agenda in 2006 were, however, dominated by the interlinked crises in the Middle East and the complex political and humanitarian crisis in Darfur. Ireland actively engaged on both of these issues, including through the deployment of Defence Forces personnel to the UNIFIL peace-keeping mission in southern Lebanon and a visit by the Minister for Foreign Affairs to Darfur, as well as on-going diplomatic activities by him in relation to this tragic situation.

2006: Developments and Achievements

Middle East

2006 saw conflict between Israel and Hezbollah in Lebanon, violence in the Gaza Strip, and a political crisis in Palestine following the election of a Hamas government. Ireland actively responded to these events in a constructive and practical manner by: Arguing strongly within the EU and the broader international community for dialogue and a return to the so-called Quartet Roadmap which provides for negotiations leading to a two-State solution.

Working to ensure that the EU maintained its financial support for the Palestinian people. Through our efforts and those of like-minded partners, Irish and EU financial assistance to the Palestinians rose during 2006 in spite of the difficult situation.

Deploying 150 Defence Forces personnel to join the new UNIFIL mission in southern Lebanon charged with keeping the peace in the aftermath of the Israel-Hezbollah conflict.

Conflict Resolution Unit

2006 saw the establishment of a new Conflict Resolution Unit (CRU), as provided for in the Government's White Paper on Irish Aid. The Unit is located within the Political Division and works closely with Irish Aid.

The decision to establish the CRU stems from the positive evolution of our own peace process, the increase in our overseas development aid and our foreign policy support for multilateralism, disarmament, peacekeeping and decolonisation. Ireland is well-placed to play a more active role in international conflict prevention and resolution.

The establishment of the new Unit accords with the strategic vision of the United Nations, as stated by then Secretary General Annan and endorsed at the 2005 World Summit, which is based on an acknowledgement of the inextricable links between development, collective security and human rights.

Africa

We continued to play an active role in international efforts to tackle the political and humanitarian crises faced by other countries in Africa. Unfortunately, 2006 saw a continuation of the political and humanitarian crisis in Darfur. Ireland remained closely involved in international efforts to deal with the crisis.

This proactive engagement included a visit by Minister Ahern to Darfur in July 2006. The Minister used his visit to deliver clear messages to the Government in Sudan on the need to accept a robust international peacekeeping force in Darfur, and to work for a sustainable political settlement. The Minister also emphasised the importance of ensuring vital access for humanitarian workers, who are striving to deal with human tragedy on an enormous scale.

Throughout the year, the Minister and Department took every opportunity in multilateral fora and through bilateral contacts to maintain the maximum pressure on the Sudanese Government and other parties to resolve the Darfur crisis without delay.

On a more positive note, we provided strong political and financial support for the successful electoral process in the Democratic Republic of Congo, the first for over forty years.

United Nations

Ireland engaged closely with the full range of UN issues in 2006. Building on the Minister's earlier role as an Envoy for the UN Secretary General, we continued in particular to pursue our commitment to UN reform.

Our support for the newly established Peace Building Commission was underlined through a major donation to the related Peace Building Fund.

In July 2006, our commitment to UN reform was further acknowledged when Jan Eliasson, President of the UN General Assembly appointed Ambassador David Cooney, Permanent Representative of Ireland to the UN, as Co-Chair of the General Assembly Working Group on Management Reform and Mandate Review.

International Security and Defence

The Department continued to play an active and constructive role in the development of policy on international security and defence matters, in close coordination with the Department of Defence. This work included coordination of Irish participation in, and support for, missions in the framework of the European Security and Defence Policy (ESDP).

2006 also involved close co-operation with the Department of Defence and with a number of EU partners on preparatory work in relation to possible Irish participation in EU Battlegroups. This led to a Government decision in November 2006 in favour of participation in the Swedish-led Nordic Battlegroup.

Human Rights

Ireland welcomed the 2006 inauguration of the new UN Human Rights Council, part of the reforms agreed by world leaders at the UN Summit of September 2005. Since its inauguration, we have played an active role in discussions there, in coordination with other EU Member States.

Ireland was closely engaged in the detailed discussions at the UN in New York which led in November 2006 to the landmark agreement on a UN Convention on the Rights of People with Disabilities.

International Disarmament and Non-proliferation

Ireland remained an active and leading advocate of international disarmament and non-proliferation, operating within a range of international fora including the EU, the New Agenda Coalition and the G10.

The year saw the intensification of several major threats to the non-proliferation regime; notably the continuing international crisis over Iran's decision to resume uranium enrichment, and North Korea's nuclear testing.

We remained closely involved in international discussions and assessment of the proposed US-India nuclear deal, which was discussed at the Nuclear Suppliers Group on a number of occasions. The issue was also the subject of bilateral exchanges during the Taoiseach's visit to India in January 2006 and the visit to Dublin in October 2006 of Shyam Saran, Indian Prime Minister Singh's Special Envoy.

Extraordinary Rendition was the subject of extensive Oireachtas, international and media interest during 2006. The Minister for Foreign Affairs comprehensively addressed this issue on a considerable number of occasions, both in the Dáil and elsewhere. He made clear the Government's complete opposition to the practice and set out the steps taken by the Government.

The Government's approach to this sensitive issue was co-ordinated by the Department which was also involved in preparing Ireland's detailed response to a questionnaire on this and related issues from the Secretary General of the Council of Europe. In November 2006 the Minister appeared before a European Parliament Committee to discuss these issues.

THE EUROPEAN UNION

High Level Goal, 2005–2007:

> Promote and protect Ireland's interests at the heart of the European Union as it continues to evolve and enlarge, including through the further development of our relations with our current and future EU partners.

2006 in Review

The Department's European Union (EU) Division continued to work closely with other Government Department's to ensure a strategic and coordinated response across a wide range of EU issues in pursuit of Ireland's objectives.

The enlargement process and the "future of Europe" remained at the top of the European agenda throughout 2006 which also saw a series of high level visits to Brussels and Dublin.

In October 2006, EU Foreign Ministers welcomed a report from the Commission confirming that Bulgaria and Romania would be in a position to accede to the EU on 1 January 2007. The accession of Bulgaria and Romania marks the successful completion of the fifth enlargement of the EU.

EU leaders engaged in an in-depth debate on the enlargement process going forward and in December 2006 the European Council reaffirmed its broad commitment to the process.

EU Foreign Ministers welcomed the continued progress made by Turkey in the reform process and urged Turkey to undertake determined efforts to intensify the reform process and its implementation. However, due to a lack of progress by Turkey in other areas, it was agreed to partially suspend enlargement negotiations.

In June 2006, the period of reflection on the Constitutional Treaty was extended until 2008. The Department continued to use this period to explain and advance Ireland's views on the Constitutional Treaty to key partners.

2006: Developments and Achievements

Visits

2006 saw a series of high-level visits to Brussels and Dublin which strengthened and enhanced Ireland's relations with the European institutions:

> The Taoiseach visited both the European Commission and the European Parliament. The President of the European Parliament, Mr. Josep Borrell, paid a return visit to Ireland during which the Minister for Foreign Affairs hosted a series of briefings, including on the ongoing EU support for the peace process.

A Budget for the Union

The Inter-Institutional Agreement on the Union's budget for 2007–2013 was signed in May 2006. The Agreement was the result of intensive negotiations involving the Council, European Commission and European Parliament in follow-up to the agreement reached by EU leaders in December 2005. Our active participation in the negotiations ensured a positive outcome for Ireland.

Preparation for a new language

The Department, in close cooperation with the Department of Community, Rural and Gaeltacht Affairs, continued to work throughout 2006 with the European Institutions on the preparation for the introduction of the Irish language as an official and working language of the EU on 1 January 2007.

Regular Briefings to Oireachtas

Throughout the year, the Minister for Foreign Affairs and the Minister of State for European Affairs briefed the Oireachtas Joint Committee on European Affairs prior to meetings of the General Affairs and External Relations Council (GAERC) and submitted regular reports on EU business.

Enlargement—the work continues

In October 2006, EU Foreign Ministers welcomed a report from the Commission concluding that Bulgaria and Romania, based on the progress made, would be in a position to take on the rights and obligations of EU membership on 1 January 2007.

The European Communities (Amendment) Bill 2006 enabling the accession of Bulgaria and Romania to the EU on 1 January 2007 passed through the Oireachtas and the Instrument of Ratification of the Accession Treaty was deposited in Rome in October 2006.

In December 2006, EU Foreign Ministers welcomed the continued progress made by Turkey in the reform process. However, due to a lack of progress by Turkey in fulfilling its obligations under the Ankara Protocol (which requires Turkey to normalise relations with all EU Member States, including Cyprus), it was agreed to suspend enlargement negotiations in certain areas. Negotiations in these areas will not be reopened until the Commission verifies that Turkey has fulfilled its commitments related to the Ankara Protocol.

EU leaders conducted an in-depth debate on the enlargement process and in December 2006, the European Council reaffirmed the EU's broad commitment to the enlargement process, based on the ability of acceding countries to assume fully the obligations of EU membership and the capacity of the Union to function effectively with an increased membership.

As well as supporting the Government's involvement in this Enlargement debate, the Department continued to provide technical assistance to the new Member States of the EU and to the Accession States through its Bilateral Assistance Programme. In 2006, this included pre-Presidency training for Slovene officials, in anticipation of the Slovenian Presidency in 2008.

Constitutional Treaty—active reflection

In June 2006, the European Council extended the period of reflection on the Constitutional Treaty and decided that the necessary steps to advance the ratification of the Treaty should be taken by 2008.

The Department actively used this period of reflection in 2006 to engage in intensive contacts and consultations with key partners to explain and advance Ireland's views on the Constitutional Treaty. As part of this work, we held bilateral consultations with the Finnish Presidency and had extensive contact with Germany in advance of its Presidency in 2007, an important stage in the debate about the future of Europe. In June, the Department also submitted a report on activities in Ireland during the 'period of reflection' on the future of Europe and, in October, we prepared the official Irish response to the Commission's White Paper on EU Communications Policy.

Enhanced Public Engagement

2006 was a year of close cooperation with the National Forum on Europe, which continued to play a major role in promoting public engagement with the EU.

The Department's Communicating Europe Initiative funded a range of projects designed to inform the Irish public about the EU.

May 2006 saw the Minister of State for European Affairs, Mr. Noel Treacy, T.D., participating in "Europe Day", a day devoted to EU business by the Oireachtas. The Minister took a leading role in the debates and answered questions submitted by the general public.

ADVANCING IRELAND'S ECONOMIC INTERESTS AND CULTURE

High Level Goal, 2005–2007:

> Promote Ireland's trade, investment and other interests, including its culture, in close co-operation with other Departments, State Agencies and the private sector, ensuring that the State's network of diplomatic and consular missions adds real value to this task.

2006 in Review

The Department's Bilateral Economic Relations Division (BERD) worked closely with other Departments and State agencies in identifying new market opportunities and in promoting awareness of Ireland as a preferred business partner and as a world-class location for educational services, investment and scientific research and development. The Division also ensured that the resources of Ireland's diplomatic and consular network abroad were effectively leveraged to promote and protect Ireland's economic interests.

2006 provided significant opportunities to boost Ireland's economic interests. The Department maximised the economic and trade potential of visits abroad by the President, the Taoiseach, the Minister for Foreign Affairs and other Ministers, as well as inward high-level visits.

The Government's Asia Strategy continued to be a priority for the Department which coordinated a significant number of high-level visits to and from Asia in 2006. 2006 was also a significant year for the Department in promoting Ireland's rich cultural heritage overseas.

2006: Developments and Achievements

The Government's Asia Strategy continued to be a priority for the Department. This Strategy seeks to intensify the levels of political, business and other forms of interaction with the priority Asian countries. It was in this context that the Department successfully coordinated a significant number of high-level visits to and from Asia in 2006, including:

—The Taoiseach's successful visit to India, accompanied by one of the largest Irish trade delegations ever.
—Visits by the Minister for Foreign Affairs to Japan and China.
—Several high-level visitors to Ireland from the Asia/Pacific region including the Chinese Vice-Premier, the Australian Prime Minister and the Governor General of New Zealand.

Our focus was, of course, wider than Asia. During 2006, the President visited Saudi Arabia and Jordan and the South African Deputy President made a visit to Ireland.

The Department also initiated a visit to Ireland by the founder and Executive Chairman of the Davos World Economic Forum, Professor Schwab.

Ireland: world-class research and development facilities

The programme of St Patrick's Day promotional visits overseas by Government Ministers, coordinated by the Department, provides a unique annual opportunity to showcase Ireland and advance our economic interests.

In 2006 the visits were used to highlight Ireland's development as a knowledge economy with world-class research and development facilities.

Irish Beef

Efforts to re-open international markets to Irish beef continued in 2006. The Department, in cooperation with the Department of Agriculture and Food, maintained close contact with key decision makers in important markets to ensure that they were kept fully up to date on developments regarding the safety of Irish beef.

Added Value

During the year the Department initiated a comprehensive review of the economic work of Irish diplomatic Missions abroad, with a view to enhancing the capacity of our Missions to contribute to the Government's economic objectives in foreign markets.

Cultural Promotion

2006 was another productive year for the Department in promoting Irish culture overseas. The Department, working in close association with *Culture Ireland/ Cultúr Éireann*, continued to promote Ireland's rich cultural heritage using the network of Irish diplomatic Missions by providing funding for events including exhibitions, concerts, readings and performances.

A Well-Travelled Centenary Celebration

2006 year marked the centenary of the birth in Dublin of Nobel Laureate Samuel Beckett. To mark the occasion, the Department commissioned a travelling exhibition *Beckett: A Centenary Celebration* based on the author's life and literary work. This exhibition was made available in English, French and Spanish to facilitate access across cultures.

To date, the exhibition has been on display in more than 50 locations abroad.

It was also used in Ireland, in collaboration with the Dublin City Library and Archive, as part of the Beckett Festival agenda of events.

IRISH AID

High Level Goal, 2005–2007:

> Make a substantive and effective contribution to achieving the Millennium Development Goals, and to poverty reduction and sustainable growth in developing countries, through the policy and programmes of Development Cooperation Ireland, and by working for a just and stable international economic system.

2006 in Review

In 2006, the total Official Development Assistance (ODA) budget, across different Departments, amounted to €734 million, €600 million of which was allocated to the Department of Foreign Affairs and managed by Irish Aid.

This total ODA figure brought spending to 0.5% of GNP in 2006. This is one year ahead of the schedule for reaching the UN aid spending target of 0.7% GNP by 2012, pledged by the Taoiseach in New York in September 2005.

2006 saw the publication of Ireland's first ever White Paper on Irish Aid, the culmination of an extensive and inclusive consultation process.

President McAleese undertook successful State visits to three Irish Aid programme countries in Africa where she visited several projects and programmes funded by Irish Aid.

Work advanced on the decentralisation of the Development Cooperation Directorate of the Department, which manages Irish Aid, to Limerick.

2006: Developments and Achievements

In June 2006, the Department coordinated a successful two-week programme of State visits by President and Dr Martin McAleese to three Irish Aid Programme countries in Africa—Lesotho, Mozambique and Tanzania. The President visited many projects and programmes funded by Irish Aid.

President McAleese's visit to Tanzania also included a visit to the International Criminal Tribunal for Rwanda (ICTR) where the President sat in on the court proceedings and discussed the work of the court with the President of the ICTR, Judge Erik Mose.

White Paper on Irish Aid

Ireland's first ever White Paper on Aid was published in September 2006 and is available on the Department's website (www.dfa.ie). The White Paper was widely welcomed by the Oireachtas, the Irish development community and our partners in the developing world. Since its launch in September 2006, over 4000 copies of the document has been distributed and over 40,000 people in Ireland and across the world have downloaded the document from the Irish Aid website.

The White Paper sets out for the first time as Government policy Ireland's approach to development assistance. It was the result of a broad and inclusive consultation process with the public, the Irish development community, other government departments, our partner countries and UN agencies, as well as the experience of over 32 years.

Much of the White Paper builds on changes that have happened in the aid programme over the past ten years. Over that time, the way Irish Aid works has changed significantly, moving away from individual projects towards programmes that are based on partnership, where developing countries themselves lead the development process.

These changes are reflected in the White Paper's guiding principles. Our aid will remain untied, we will retain a clear focus on the poorest countries, particularly in Africa, and partnership will be central to all Irish Aid programmes.

The White Paper reinforces Ireland's longstanding commitment to the key areas of education and health, ensuring that these social areas will remain at the very core of the Irish Aid programme.

Ireland will continue to take a lead in the fight against the scourge of HIV/AIDS. Spending on HIV/AIDS and other communicable diseases will continue to exceed €100 million a year; over 10% of the total Irish Aid budget.

The White Paper also outlined how Irish Aid will both deepen and broaden its engagements as the programme grows financially. In the medium term, Irish Aid will increase the number of its bilateral partner countries from eight to ten. Malawi will be the first country so designated.

Irish Aid will also deepen its focus on working in fragile states. Building on existing activities, including Ireland's role in UN peacekeeping operations, the initial focus will be on both Sierra Leone and Liberia. Irish Aid will also increase its responses to humanitarian emergencies, wherever they occur.

2006 saw work advance on a number of new initiatives launched in the White Paper:

—In the context of the Rapid Response Initiative, which will enable Ireland to respond more effectively to sudden-onset emergencies, Minister of State, Mr. Conor Lenihan TD, signed an agreement in November 2006 with the World Food Programme for the pre-positioning and transportation of humanitarian supplies to disaster areas. Supplies of shelter and housing, water and sanitation equipment will be pre-positioned from early 2007 at the UN Humanitarian Response Depot in Brindisi, Italy, and at the Curragh Camp.

—Early in 2007 the Department will put in place a roster of skilled and experienced individuals from the public and private sectors, including from the Defence Forces, for deployment at short notice to emergency situations.

—Work advanced on the establishment of a Hunger Task Force to examine the particular contribution Ireland can make to address the root causes of food insecurity, particularly in Africa. The Task Force will be established in early 2007.

—Planning commenced for the opening of an Irish Aid Information and Volunteering Centre in 2007 which will make more and better information available to the public about volunteering opportunities for individuals, institutions and communities.

CONSULAR AND PASSPORT SERVICES

High Level Goal, 2005–2007:

Protect and support the interests of Irish citizens abroad, maintain and strengthen links with people of Irish ancestry, and provide a modern and efficient passport and consular service.

2006 in Review

The Department's Consular Section in Dublin coordinates the actions of Irish Missions abroad on behalf of Irish citizens and liaises with family members in Ireland. Throughout the year, the Department provided support in a wide range of areas, including advice about the safety of travel to particular countries or regions, guidance about aspects of living and working conditions in other countries, and assistance in situations of difficulty or distress.

2006 saw the first mass evacuation of Irish citizens organised by the Department in response to the outbreak of conflict in southern Lebanon. It also saw the establishment of a dedicated Crisis Centre to respond to major emergencies overseas involving Irish citizens.

The Department successfully completed—on time and well within budget—the project to include biometric features in Irish Passports. The new ePassport was launched by the Minister in October 2006.

630,000 passports were issued in 2006. Use of the Passport Express Service and the Northern Ireland Passport Express (NIPX) service increased. An online tracking facility for passport applications was introduced as part of the Department's newly-designed website.

The Department's Irish Abroad Unit continued to strengthen links with Irish communities abroad. In 2006, an allocation of €12 million was made available for emigrant services, in particular for the most vulnerable of our citizens, an increase of 45% from 2005.

2006: Developments and Achievements

Protecting and Supporting Irish citizens

2006 saw the first ever mass evacuation of Irish citizens by the Department in response to the outbreak of hostilities between Israel and Hezbollah in southern Lebanon in July.

In all, approximately 200 Irish citizens were evacuated by land, air and sea from Lebanon. The evacuation process and the provision of information to Irish citizens in the region and their families in Ireland were run from the Department's Crisis Centre. The Crisis Centre, staffed by volunteers from throughout the Department, was activated following the outbreak of conflict and operated from 9am until 10pm during the peak of the crisis.

During 2006, we also successfully provided effective assistance to our citizens in other difficult situations, including kidnappings in Iraq, Nigeria and Ethiopia.

A Modern and Efficient Passport Service

2006 recorded a 2% increase in passport applications over 2005 with a total of approximately 630,000 passports issued.

Over half of the applications were received through the An Post Passport Express Service. Three-quarters of the approximately 40,000 passport applications received from citizens in Northern Ireland used Northern Ireland Passport Express (NIPX). The number of post offices in Northern Ireland, which operate this special service for Irish passports, increased from 40 in 2004 to over 70 in 2006.

As a result of the major investment in passport development in recent years, the Irish passport now contains a range of sophisticated anti-fraud elements and is widely regarded as among the best and most secure in the world.

In 2006, the Department successfully completed—on time and well within budget—the project to include biometric features in Irish Passports. This has facilitated Ireland's continued participation in the US Visa Waiver Scheme.

ePassport

The new ePassport was launched by Minister Ahern on 16 October 2006.

While it looks much the same as its predecessor, it has a microchip embedded in the data page and an international ePassport symbol embossed in gold on the front cover. The microchip contains the digitised facial image and the personal details of the passport holder, as they appear on the data page, and can be read electronically at border controls.

This project was the first to be assessed by the Government's new Peer Review Process for monitoring IT Projects across the Public Service, which welcomed the budgetary savings on the project and future savings to Irish citizens on US visa fees.

On-line Services

The Department's newly designed website, launched by the Minister in December 2006, provides an on-line service to the public that allows passport applicants to track the progress of their applications over the internet.

To avail of this service, an applicant simply needs to enter his/her application number and the service informs the applicant of the stage that his/her application has reached.

A Modern and Efficient Consular Service

The Department's newly-designed website provides up to date and comprehensive travel advice for Irish citizens intending to travel abroad.

Dedicated Crisis Centre

Work on a dedicated Crisis Centre in Dublin was successfully completed in 2006 and the Centre was officially opened on 9 January 2007.

Of international standard, the Crisis Centre is fully equipped to provide an emergency response service to deal with large-scale emergencies, crises and disasters, whether natural or man made, involving Irish citizens abroad. The Centre will be capable of linking up with Crisis Centres in other EU capitals, to share information and risk assessments.

Strengthening Links with people of Irish Ancestry

The needs of the Irish community in Britain, in particular older people and those who are vulnerable or isolated, remain a key Government priority. Most of the available funding is directed to Irish community organisations there who are working at the coalface with our vulnerable citizens.

In 2006, an allocation of €12 million was available for emigrant services, an increase of 45% on the 2005 figure.

The Minister for Foreign Affairs also approved grants to organisations in the United States that provide information and support services to Irish immigrants there, particularly to the undocumented Irish.

Funding was provided to Irish emigrant groups in Australia, Canada and, for the first time, to groups in Argentina, South Africa and Zimbabwe.

Support was in addition directed to organisations in Ireland engaged in pre-departure information for intending emigrants, as well as providing assistance to emigrants returning home.

SUPPORT SERVICES

Building Internal Capability:

> The Department of Foreign Affairs must ensure that it maintains and continues to develop the internal capability required to deliver on the foreign policy objectives of the Government.

2006 in Review

The work of the Department's officials at home and abroad towards achieving our high-level goals was further supported and facilitated by the Department's corporate and support services. These provide an essential platform upon which the Department's policy formulation and service delivery functions can be effectively discharged.

Protocol Services

Throughout 2006, Protocol Division organised State and official visits by the President abroad and official visits to Ireland by Heads of State, Prime Ministers, Foreign Ministers and other distinguished guests of the Government.

Visits during 2006

The Division organised visits abroad by President McAleese to:

Saudi Arabia	Lesotho
Cyprus	Hungary
Jordan	Mozambique
Malta	USA (Montana, Colorado and Indiana)
Austria	Tanzania
UK (Edinburgh, Lancashire, Yorkshire and London)	

In January 2006, the Division co-ordinated the arrangements for the Taoiseach's visit to India (New Delhi, Mumbai and Bangalore).

During the course of 2006, the Division organised High Level Visits to Ireland by:

The King and Queen of Norway
The Governor General of New Zealand
The President of Croatia
The President of Egypt
The Prime Minister of Australia
The Prime Minister of Croatia
The Prime Minister of the Slovak Republic
The Vice Premier of the People's Republic of China
The President of the European Parliament.

Protocol Division also worked with the resident and non-resident diplomatic corps accredited to Ireland. This currently comprises 54 Embassies and 4 other diplomatic representations in Dublin, as well as 61 countries accredited to Ireland on a non-resident basis. The Division organised the credential ceremonies for new Ambassadors as well as annual events attended by the Diplomatic Corps.

Press Office

The Press Office provides an effective media service to the Minister and the Department, including Divisions at HQ and Missions abroad.

During 2006, the Press Office dealt efficiently and effectively with an increased number of press queries covering the entire range of issues handled by the Department, from national and local newspapers, from the broadcast media, and from representatives of wire agencies based in Ireland.

The Department's Press Office also worked closely with other Government Departments, Missions abroad and State Agencies to organise visits to Ireland by members of the foreign media.

The Press Office published all speeches/press releases by the Minister for Foreign Affairs and the Ministers of State at the Department on the Departmental website and distributed them directly to the media. The Department's Press Office also handled press arrangements for several incoming high-level visits in 2006.

Legal Services

Legal Division assisted and advised the Department on various issues relating to each of the Department's High Level Goals:

Northern Ireland: Advised on the full implementation of the Good Friday Agreement, including in relation to the St Andrews Agreement and the North-South Implementation Bodies.

Foreign Policy: Ensured an integrated legal and policy approach to foreign relations in accordance with the Constitution and UN Charter, including in relation to drafting a UN Comprehensive Terrorism Convention and two human rights conventions, both adopted by the General Assembly in 2006, enforcement of UN and EU sanctions, enactment of the International Criminal Court Act

	2006 and further development of good working relationships with states seeking extradition of suspects from Ireland.
European Union:	Advised on EU legal matters, including in preparation for the accession of Bulgaria and Romania.
Trade and culture:	Advised on international agreements on bilateral economic relations and cultural matters.
Irish Aid:	Advised Irish Aid on its work.
Consular, Passport:	Advised on drafting Passports Bill 2006 and on consular protection of the rights of Irish citizens abroad.

Inspection Unit

The Inspection Unit supports the Department's Missions abroad by examining the contribution they make to the achievement of the Department's High Level Goals and how they manage their resources. In this way, the Unit helps to enhance the effectiveness of Missions and to strengthen the overall governance and performance of the Department.

During 2006, the Inspection Unit increased significantly the number of inspections carried out. A total of 14 Missions were visited, representing almost 20% of the Mission network. Reports were prepared on each visit for discussion by the Department's senior management. The implementation of the recommendations made in the inspection reports is proceeding and is being monitored by the Inspection Unit.

Corporate Services

Corporate Services Division is responsible for the overall management of the financial and human resources of the Department, ensuring coherent operation across its various Divisions at Headquarters and its 76 Missions outside of the State.

In discharging its human resource management responsibilities, the Department recognises that the quality of its staff represents a major asset. It seeks to fully comply with the obligations from successive Partnership Agreements, with the commitments arising from the various initiatives under Strategic Management Initiative and with the best practice employment standards across the Civil Service. With over 1,500 staff distributed across the world, the Department constantly reviews its policies and practices to optimise the performance and professional fulfilment of its human resources. The Department remains committed to providing the highest standard of service to all our customers, at home and abroad, in accordance with the principles of Quality Customer Service approved by Government. The publication in March of the Department's Customer Service Action Plan underlines our ongoing and practical commitment to fulfilling the obligations of the Department's Customer Charter. The First Language Scheme, which came into effect on 1 December, sets out the level of services that are currently available through Irish.

The Department recognises the importance of ensuring that its financial resources are used efficiently and effectively. The details of the Department's expenditure in 2006 under both of its Votes and penalty interest on late payments are contained in Appendices 1, 2 and 3. The Department is also very conscious of the need to secure good value for money for the expenditure it incurs. Appendix 4 outlines the various reviews being undertaken by the Department under the Government's Value for Money and Policy Review Initiative.

Significant achievements and developments during 2006 included:

—Continued implementation of the modernisation and flexibility changes mandated under *Sustaining Progress* and *Towards 2016* Partnership Agreements;
—Substantial progress in preparing for the decentralisation of the Development Cooperation Directorate to Limerick. By the end of 2006, the construction of a permanent HQ was well under way, an advance party move was actively being progressed and 70% of the Directorate staff to be decentralised had been designated;
—The establishment of a dedicated Procurement Management Unit, the preparation of a corporate procurement plan for the Department and the successful execution of a number of significant tendering exercises, including for a biometric feature in passports; and
—The purchase of four Mission properties abroad—Ankara, the Hague, Ljubljana and Strasbourg—and the completion of refurbishment projects in a number of other Embassies owned by the State, including Paris and the Holy See.

APPENDICES

Appendix 1

Vote 28 (Foreign Affairs) Estimates and Outturn for 2006

Appendix 2

Vote 29 (International Cooperation) Estimates and Outturn for 2006

Appendix 3

Prompt Payment of Accounts Act, 1997

Appendix 4

Status Report on Value for Money Reviews (2006–2008 Programme)

APPENDIX I

VOTE 28 (FOREIGN AFFAIRS) ESTIMATES AND OUTTURN FOR 2006

	Service	Estimate Provision €000	Outturn €000
	ADMINISTRATION		
A.1.	SALARIES, WAGES AND ALLOWANCES	91,619	90,281
A.2.	TRAVEL AND SUBSISTENCE	8,187	7,812
A.3.	INCIDENTAL EXPENSES	6,707	6,033
A.4.	POSTAL AND TELECOMMUNICATIONS SERVICES	8,811	8,033
A.5.	OFFICE MACHINERY AND OTHER OFFICE SUPPLIES	37,030	32,514
A.6.	OFFICE PREMISES EXPENSES	41,764	36,188
A.7.	CONSULTANCY SERVICES	1,074	641
	OTHER SERVICES		
B.1.	REPATRIATION AND MAINTENANCE OF DISTRESSED IRISH PERSONS ABROAD	27	160
C.1.	SUPPORT FOR IRISH IMMIGRANT GROUPS	12,000	11,701
D.1.	INFORMATION SERVICES	564	480
E.1.	CONTRIBUTIONS TO BODIES IN IRELAND FOR THE FURTHERANCE OF INTERNATIONAL RELATIONS (GRANTS-IN-AID)	288	288
F.1	NORTH-SOUTH AND ANGLO-IRISH COOPERATION	2,697	3,397
F.2.	INTERNATIONAL FUND FOR IRELAND	195	195
G.1	CULTURAL RELATIONS WITH OTHER COUNTRIES	981	862
H.1	IRISH-AMERICAN ECONOMIC ADVISORY BOARD	28	22
I.1	CONTRIBUTIONS TO INTERNATIONAL ORGANISATIONS	26,361	26,711
J.1	TITLE V OF THE TREATY ON EUROPEAN UNION	516	422
K.1	ASSISTANCE TO EU CANDIDATE COUNTRIES	2,847	2,072
L.1	ATLANTIC CORRIDOR PROJECT	250	250
M.1	MILLENIUM PROJECTS	1,200	0
N.2	ASIA STRATEGY	200	96
	Gross Total	243,346	228,158
Deduct:—			
O.	APPROPRIATIONS-IN-AID	39,000	39,490
	Net Total	204,346	188,668

APPENDIX 2

VOTE 29 (INTERNATIONAL COOPERATION) ESTIMATES AND OUTTURN FOR 2006

	Service	Estimate Provision €000	Outturn €000
	ADMINISTRATION		
A.1.	SALARIES, WAGES AND ALLOWANCES	15,744	14,899
A.2.	TRAVEL AND SUBSISTENCE	2,660	2,470
A.3.	INCIDENTAL EXPENSES	3,531	3,095
A.4.	POSTAL AND TELECOMMUNICATIONS SERVICES	1,500	1,112
A.5.	OFFICE MACHINERY AND OTHER OFFICE SUPPLIES	1,020	959
A.6.	OFFICE PREMISES EXPENSES	2,099	2,352
A.7.	CONSULTANCY SERVICES	2,000	2,237
	OTHER SERVICES		
B.	PAYMENT TO GRANT-IN-AID FUND FOR BILATERAL AID AND OTHER COOPERATION (GRANT-IN-AID)	426,510	426,510
C.	EMERGENCY HUMANITARIAN ASSISTANCE	60,000	60,000
D.	PAYMENTS TO INTERNATIONAL FUNDS FOR THE BENEFIT OF DEVELOPING COUNTRIES	22,650	22,637
E.	CONTRIBUTIONS TO UNITED NATIONS AND OTHER DEVELOPMENT AGENCIES	62,900	62,900
	Gross Total	600,614	599,171
Deduct:—			
F.	APPROPRIATIONS-IN-AID	135	656
Net Total		600,479	598,515

APPENDIX 3

PROMPT PAYMENT OF ACCOUNTS ACT, 1997

Payment of invoices by the Department is governed by the provisions of the Prompt Payment of Accounts Act, 1997 as amended by the European Communities (Late Payment in Commercial Transactions) Regulations, 2002. The Department endeavours to pay all invoices as soon as possible after the satisfactory delivery of the goods and services.

The total amount of penalty interest on late payments on the Department's Vote in 2006 (Vote 28) was €478.77 in respect of 18 cases. In addition, a total of €382.19 was paid in penalty interest on late payments under Vote 29 (International Cooperation) in respect of 6 cases.

APPENDIX 4

STATUS REPORT ON VALUE FOR MONEY REVIEWS (2006–2008 PROGRAMME)

Vote 28—Foreign Affairs

Value of Money Review	Purpose of Review	Target Date	Current Status
Support for Irish Emigrant Groups	To evaluate the value for money achieved with the Department's support for Irish Emigrant Groups Abroad	12/2006	Work in progress; draft report will be completed shortly
Automated Passport Project	Specific focus of the review to be decided	12/2007	Work yet to commence

Vote 29—Development Cooperation

Value of Money Review	Purpose of Review	Target Date	Current Status
Development Cooperation Ireland's Emergency Humanitarian Assistance for a specific disaster (Tsunami)	To analyse what has been achieved with Irish Aid support for the Tsunami-affected countries. To evaluate the relevance, effectiveness, efficiency, sustainability, attentiveness to cross-cutting issues and management of Irish Aid's Tsunami response programme.	12/2006	Draft Report completed; awaiting independent expert review.
Development Aid to Mozambique	To evaluate the implementation of the Mozambique Country Programme, funded by Irish Aid	12/2007	Draft Report completed; awaiting independent expert review.
HIV/Aids Budget Line	Specific focus of the review to be decided	12/2008	Consideration of the focus of the review has commenced.

Address to the Annual Royal Irish Academy Conference on International Affairs[1]

THE MINISTER FOR FOREIGN AFFAIRS

MR DERMOT AHERN TD

NOVEMBER 2005

President
Members of the Royal Irish Academy,
Ladies and Gentlemen,

As Minister for Foreign Affairs, I wish to place on record my deep appreciation of the Royal Irish Academy's role in the study of international affairs and Ireland's role in the world.

The Academy, through its Committee for the Study of International Affairs, now chaired by Dr John Doyle, provides a forum for informed debate on contemporary international developments. And its exceptionally high-quality publication of the Documents on Irish Foreign Policy series is providing an absolute treasure trove of material for academics and the interested public. I am pleased and proud that my Department is closely associated with, and supports, the endeavours of the Academy.

Given the central place that the United Nations holds in Ireland's foreign policy, it is fitting that this Conference commemorates the fiftieth anniversary of our membership. The theme is "Looking Forward". I will in a moment offer some reflections on the role that the United Nations should play in the twenty-first century, and how Ireland can best support it in that role.

I would like first, however, to look back and reflect briefly on what membership of the United Nations meant for Ireland when it joined the Organisation.

IRELAND'S MEMBERSHIP OF THE UNITED NATIONS

Ireland had been a vigorous and committed member of the League of Nations. A distinguished Irish diplomat, Seán Lester, was its last Secretary-General. And Éamon de Valera, as President of its Assembly, was a passionate advocate of its noble principles. But as these principles were first betrayed and then swept aside altogether in the march to war, for fifteen years Ireland found itself at the very margins of international events.

In particular, we were largely cut off from the great and dynamic upsurge of international co-operation and economic growth which followed the end of the Second World War. Our economy and society were introspective and sclerotic, and were failing many thousands of our people, who left in search for a better life abroad. By the mid-fifties some few even questioned the very viability of our State. In such a context, entry to the United Nations was like pulling back the curtains and letting the sunlight pour in. We are used to thinking of the United Nations as the universal organisation.

[1] The Address by the Foreign Minister to the Annual Royal Irish Academy Conference on International Affairs also appears in the Royal Irish Academy's publication: *Irish Studies in International Affairs*.

After all, according to UN Charter, membership is open to all peace-loving states. In its early years, however, the members of the UN controlled entry to what was an exclusive club. The original membership was determined by the wartime Allies and further membership was closely controlled along Cold War lines.

Eventually these barriers were swept away by the great tide of decolonisation, with which Ireland so strongly empathised, and which we partly inspired. Membership of the United Nations became the prime symbol, and guarantee, of sovereignty. But before this new era dawned, Ireland and other countries were obliged to sit in the waiting room, while the permanent members of the Security Council negotiated a balanced package of new members

This was a frustrating period for those knocking at the UN's door. It was especially frustrating for a state like Ireland that belonged to no military alliance, and lacked a wider arena in which to advance its interests and values.

When we did join, we lost no time in making it clear that we were bringing to the United Nations an approach to world issues that was determined, not by alliances, but by our own values and our own historical experience.

The first of my predecessors as Minister to address the General Assembly, following our accession, was Liam Cosgrave, who is happily still with us. There were two major events that he had to deal with in his address: the Suez invasion and the invasion of Hungary. The former demonstrated that old empires could no longer expect to ride roughshod over the interests of sovereign states: the latter exposed the ruthless brutality of a new form of tyranny. Over thirty years were to pass before Hungary fully regained its freedom.

Liam Cosgrave made it crystal clear how Ireland felt about these actions, both of which underlined the volatility of international relations at the time.

A year later, Frank Aiken—my predecessor both as Minister and as TD for Louth—reminded the General Assembly that another world war, whatever its cause, would neither democratise nor communise the world, but annihilate it.

Ireland became dedicated to the reduction of international tensions and in particular to arms control; our efforts bore fruit eventually in the Nuclear Non-proliferation Treaty.

And Ireland was not long a member of the Organisation when it answered the call of the UN to send military observers into the Middle East and a Defence Forces contingent into the Congo. Since then, members of the Defence Forces and the Garda Síochána have served under the UN flag across the globe.

Nothing embodies Ireland's commitment to the United Nations more tangibly and nothing has brought greater honour to this State than the service and sacrifice of the Irish men and Irish women who have worn the light blue beret with such distinction.

This special contribution to the cause of peace, which was commemorated by veterans of the Congo and other missions last weekend, continues today in Liberia and elsewhere.

Foreign policy is set by Governments and Ministers, but is carried out by diplomats. I would like to pay tribute to the outstanding diplomatic officers who have represented Ireland with loyalty and distinction at the United Nations. I trust I will be forgiven if I single out for mention two in particular from the era of our accession—Freddie Boland, who served as President of the General Assembly, and—if he will forgive the coloration—the evergreen Conor Cruise O'Brien.

A modern historian has concluded that Ireland's independent role at the United Nations in that era was "planned far in advance, thoroughly reviewed by Irish diplomats, professionally implemented and ardently defended".

Government and diplomatic service, therefore, worked together closely in establishing a tradition of well-considered support for effective multilateralism, which has been a central feature of Ireland's foreign policy under successive governments ever since.

ROLE AS ENVOY

President,

It was in the spirit of this tradition that I accepted a mandate from Kofi Annan to act as one of his Envoys in promoting his recommendations for United Nations reform, aimed at enhancing its effectiveness in addressing the threats and challenges of today.

And I should say that in acting as Envoy, I was very pleased to work closely with the Secretary-General's Chief of Staff, Mark Malloch Brown, from whom this Conference will hear shortly.

One of the things that struck me forcibly, as I went about my advocacy, was the sheer strength and durability of the sixty-year-old UN Charter. It may need updating in a couple of places—the structure of the Security Council, for instance, is seriously outdated. But otherwise it contains everything that we need as a framework for common action for common purposes, and it should continue to serve us far into the twenty-first century.

The challenges, on the other hand, have changed. It is common ground that the effectiveness of the United Nations following the end of the Cold War was mixed. There were successes, but there were also failures.

The fault lay not in the Charter, but in the failure of the international community to recognise the extent of certain threats, and the need for prompt and determined action to meet them. We are all familiar with the tragedies that took place as a result.

Both the failures and the successes demonstrated more than ever the need for an effective and efficient United Nations. The international community acts most effectively when it acts together. This was Ireland's experience as a member of the Security Council during 2001 and 2002, when in the great majority of cases the Council acted unanimously and often successfully, particularly on African issues.

But it was clear nonetheless that change was needed. When the Security Council subsequently failed to remain united on Iraq, the crisis of confidence that ensued gave the Secretary-General the opportunity to set in motion a process for wide-ranging reforms. These, in turn, were placed before world leaders at last September's UN Summit.

It fell to Ireland, during its EU Presidency in 2004, to draft and secure agreement on the European Union's contribution to the work of the Secretary-General's High-Level Panel. We brought to the task not only our long record of activism in the United Nations, but also our recent Security Council experience.

Many elements of the EU Contribution were taken up by the Panel, and emerged in the Secretary-General's recommendations.

The recommendations were based on the now familiar premise that without development there can be no security, without security there can be no development, and without respect for human rights there can be neither. The recent Summit fully acknowledged that these issues are interlinked.

Of course, the outcome of the Summit was far from fully satisfactory. Commitments in many areas were less ambitious or precise than one would have wished.

And there was at least one major gap—the absence of any reference to nuclear disarmament and non-proliferation. But I think the Summit achieved enough to be seen as a success, provided, and it is an important provision, that the impetus for change is not lost.

MILLENNIUM DEVELOPMENT GOALS

The Summit unanimously endorsed the Millennium Development Goals as the benchmarks of progress towards the ending of extreme poverty—an outcome that was by no means assured in the run-up.

The MDGs are in no way utopian. They are eminently achievable with political will. But it would be foolish to underestimate the challenge. Achieving them requires a partnership: the developing countries must adopt appropriate national strategies and reform their institutions, while adequate financial resources must be made available in a stable and predictable fashion.

Trade and private investment also have a vital role. I believe we can achieve a very substantial degree of trade liberalisation for development, while preserving the essential interests of all.

The Taoiseach at the Summit committed Ireland to reaching the ODA target of 0.7% by 2012 and, in doing so, heralded a new and very exciting time for our aid programme.

Details of new record levels of expenditure were announced yesterday. Similar increases will follow each year from now until 2012. The challenge of the current expansion is to continue to deliver assistance to the high standards for which Ireland has become known around the world.

NEW INITIATIVES

The expansion of our programme will enable us to consolidate those areas where we are already active.

It also provides us with the opportunity for new areas of cooperation.

Next year's White Paper on Development, Ireland's first ever, will set out our plan of expansion over the coming years.

The Taoiseach has already announced a doubling of our financial commitment to funding for HIV/AIDS and other communicable diseases. We will participate in the replenishment of the Global Fund to Fight AIDS, Tuberculosis and Malaria by contributing €30 million over the years 2006–2007.

Having recently reviewed our programme in depth with my colleague Minister of State Conor Lenihan, today I am announcing details of just four elements of that plan.

1. A Rapid Response Corps
2. A Volunteer Corps
3. A More Visible Aid Programme
4. Clear Commitment to UN Peace Building

1. RAPID RESPONSE CORPS

The events of the past twelve months—the Tsunami, Niger, Pakistan—have proven beyond all doubt that the developed world lacks the mechanisms to respond rapidly to humanitarian crises in the field.

At EU level, Ireland has pushed for greater emphasis on building up the Union's humanitarian response capability.

At a national level, we are determined to push ahead now with the establishment of an Irish Rapid Response Corps.

This Corps will comprise individuals with relevant and specialist skills and experience in niche areas who will be available to travel at short notice to situations of great need.

All such individuals in the State will be invited to register with a national rapid response register.

We will ensure the necessary specialised training for these key personnel.

We will also pre-position humanitarian supplies, including tents and ready to eat meals—again, all ready to be deployed at short notice. This will result in the immediate saving of lives.

In addition, we will ramp up support to the UN Joint Logistics Centre—the Centre which provides the logistic framework for the World Food Programme and other agencies.

2. VOLUNTEER CORPS

Ireland already has a dedicated, professional and world-class corps of volunteers in the Developing World.

We plan to augment their efforts now and bring this volunteering tradition into the mainstream.

To that end Minister of State Lenihan and I are establishing a Volunteer Corps Unit within my Department with a clear and straightforward mandate—to harness the strong volunteer spirit which exists across the country.

We will facilitate development partnerships between Irish companies and State agencies across all sectors with their counterparts in the Developing World.

We will harness the skills of Irish workers in industry, in education, in the health sector, and across the public and private sectors—and facilitate matching their skills with needs in the developing world.

We will provide greater assistance to existing volunteering and development agencies, and identify opportunities for more Irish individuals to work with groups such as the United Nations Volunteers Organisation.

However, it's not just about matching Irish skills with developing world needs.

We will increase funding for development immersion-type visits by young people and secondary schools—building a new generation of advocates for the developing world.

In addition, we will establishing a "Shop Front" where members of the public can access all information available on volunteering opportunities—and an outreach programme whereby we will bring this information to communities throughout Ireland.

3. MORE VISIBLE AID PROGRAMME

Ireland's Aid Programme belongs not to Government or their Aid Agencies but to the Irish people who fund it through their taxes and support.

Irish aid is making a real difference to the lives of many thousands of people every day. While this work is carried out on behalf of the Irish public, and with their money, there is little awareness of the scale and nature of the programme.

This must change if we are to ensure that there is full public knowledge of, and support for, our work.

Meeting the needs of the world's poorest and most vulnerable people is one of the great challenges of our time. There is a moral imperative to act. In a world that sometimes seems increasingly insecure, it is also in our own interests to act.

The Millennium Development Goals provide a yardstick against which we can measure our efforts. To achieve the Goals on target, Kofi Annan has said that we must "break with business as usual and dramatically accelerate and scale up action until 2015". Ireland is stepping up to the mark.

4. UN PEACE-BUILDING

Sustainable development can only be achieved in an environment of peace and stability. The preservation of international peace and security is a central purpose of the United Nations.

We know from our own long experience in peacekeeping and our recent term on the Security Council that where there is conflict, especially internal conflict, it is not enough to end the fighting. Preventing a return to conflict requires the strengthening of institutions, the reintegration of fighters into society, and a reasonable prospect of social and economic progress.

Yet the countries in question, with weak institutions or none, are those least likely to attract development funding and are the most likely to once again fall into conflict.

We therefore agreed with our EU partners early last year, at the start of our Presidency, that this gap in the UN system should be filled, and that the EU should propose to the High-Level Panel the creation of a political body that would mobilise and coordinate resources to keep fragile states from reverting to conflict, or from falling into it in the first place.

I am therefore glad to report that the UN General Assembly is well on the way to establishing a Peacebuilding Commission, along with a Peacebuilding Fund, by the end of the year, as decided at the Summit.

The Commission will be an advisory body, bringing together the authorities of the country in question, with representatives of the Security Council, the Economic and

Social Council, the UN Secretariat and other relevant agencies, major donors and contributors to the relevant peace-keeping mission, as well as the Bretton Woods institutions. It will aim to ensure a coordinated approach to the rehabilitation of countries emerging from conflict that places them firmly on the road to lasting stability and development.

It is essential, if the Peacebuilding Commission is to succeed, that the countries which it aims to assist feel the fullest possible ownership of the process.

The Government is committed to working closely with the Peacebuilding Commission, as an essential bridge between peacekeeping and long term development cooperation.

As part of our increased development budget and in line with the best traditions of Irish foreign policy, we intend to make a very substantial contribution to the Peacebuilding Fund. And, while the modalities of the Peacebuilding Commission's operation are not yet clear, we are going to explore very actively indeed how Irish personnel, either seconded to the Commission or working alongside it, can contribute to its work.

CONFLICT PREVENTION/ROLE OF REGIONAL ORGANISATIONS

It is much better, of course, if conflict is avoided in the first place. And the remarkable thing—contrary to what most people may think—is that it is increasingly being avoided. One of the most interesting documents I have seen recently is the Human Security Report 2005, which documents a quite striking decline in the number of wars, genocides and human rights abuses over the past decade.

To take one statistic: since the early 1990s, there has been an 80% decrease in the number of conflicts producing at least 1000 deaths in battle a year.

The report, which is not a United Nations document, but is produced for the Canadian Human Security Centre by a very experienced team of specialists, convincingly ascribes the decline to the UN-led post-Cold War upsurge in peacekeeping, peace building and conflict prevention.

Despite the huge problems which still exist, this is deeply encouraging. It shows that concerted international activity, led by and under the umbrella of the UN, can and does make a real difference. It gives the lie to many of the assertions made by the critics of the UN and of the multilateral approach. Indeed leaders at the Summit fully recognised the role played in conflict prevention by the UN Secretary-General through the exercise of his good offices, and indicated their support for efforts to strengthen the Organisation's capacity in this area.

The UN cannot, nonetheless, do everything, and should not have to act on its own in every crisis.

When Kofi Annan was here in Ireland a year ago, he made it clear how much the UN needed and appreciated the cooperation of regional organisations. He thanked Ireland for the work done during its Presidency to enhance EU cooperation with the UN. The Summit Outcome Document specifically mentions the importance of the EU's security and defence policy, including the development of its rapid response capacity.

EU-UN cooperation has now been developed further, and a number of EU-led peace support operations have taken place, and are taking place. The African Union is carrying the major share of the burden in Western Sudan, with the cooperation of the EU and others, and with the authorisation of the UN Security Council. NATO and the EU, mandated by the UN Security Council, are carrying out similar tasks in Kosovo, Bosnia and Afghanistan, and Ireland is making an active contribution to these missions.

Ireland and other developed countries have military capacities and assets that are as yet unavailable in many developing countries, and they must remain at the disposal of the United Nations.

The highly successful joint Irish-Swedish Quick Reaction Force in Liberia is an example of the kind of element—what Kofi Annan has called a "force multiplier"—that makes the rest of the peacekeeping force effective. I want to make it clear, therefore, that it is the Government's view that peacekeeping in Africa or elsewhere should not be left solely to the countries of the region.

RESPONSIBILITY TO PROTECT

A key outcome of the Summit was the acceptance that, notwithstanding Article 2.7 of the UN Charter, which excludes intervention in matters falling within the domestic jurisdiction of any state, the international community has a responsibility to protect populations against genocide, war crimes, ethnic cleansing and crimes against humanity.

This is, in effect, a commitment made at the highest level to ensure that events such as those in Rwanda and Srebrenica never happen again.

As the Taoiseach told the Summit, threats to peace nowadays arise chiefly from internal strife, and these threats do not stop at national borders. Peace and security requires the exercise by national governments of their sovereign responsibility to protect their citizens and, where they do not, the international community has a right, indeed a duty, to step in. This includes, should it prove necessary, by coercive measures, although military force must always be a last resort.

I hope that the terms of the commitment made by leaders at the Summit will effectively overcome one major problem that has stood in the way of effective action up to now.

The international community has, since the 1948 Convention on Genocide, long accepted a responsibility to prevent genocide. Sadly, but perhaps inevitably when populations were threatened and efforts were made to invoke this Convention, the question was asked: "But is this genocide?"

From now we should not any more have to witness grotesque efforts to calculate just how many murders add up to genocide. The principle of the responsibility to protect suffering populations, irrespective of the precise definition of the nature of their agony, has been firmly established. I hope it will never be necessary to act on the principle but, if it is necessary, there can be simply no excuse not to act.

TERRORISM

The Security Council, even before September 11th, identified terrorism as a threat to international peace and security.

As we have seen again in recent weeks, terrorists threaten all states, rich and poor, of all religious and ethnic characters. Ireland and its EU partners are working inside and outside the EU to develop policies and actions that would make it more difficult for terrorists to operate.

The EU Action Plan was first established under the Irish Presidency in response to the Madrid bombings, and has been developed and refined since then, with a review every six months by the European Council.

At the UN we are, I hope, close to agreeing a comprehensive Convention against terrorism, following the establishment of thirteen previous Conventions addressing various aspects of terrorism. However, Conventions on their own are not enough. I hope that, once the new Convention is agreed, we will quickly begin negotiations on a global counter-terrorism strategy, agreed and implemented by all states.

The fight against terrorism must, of course, be carried out in full respect for human rights norms.

The violation of such norms is not only wrong in itself but it is also counter-productive as it can be used to justify further atrocities. It moreover undermines the authority of states and leaders who seek to promote respect for human rights and the rule of law.

HUMAN RIGHTS

Human rights will remain a central focus of Ireland's foreign policy. A key part of this will be to continue to work for a strengthening of the machinery of the United Nations in this area.

I think it is fair to say that the human rights work of the United Nations, and of its Commission on Human Rights, has fluctuated in its effectiveness. It did outstanding work in creating the Universal Declaration on Human Rights, and in establishing a range of human rights norms.

In recent years, however, the CHR, while continuing to do indispensable work, has increasingly become a theatre for sterile battles between those who wish to extend human rights and those who have, with increasing effectiveness, been resisting efforts to call violators to account. It also has many practical deficiencies.

The Secretary-General recommended a new departure, in the form of a Human Rights Council meeting regularly through the year and dealing with human rights situation as they arose. The Summit agreed in principle but, I am afraid, left the detail to be worked out. The EU, for its part, is firmly committed to working for the establishment of the new Human Rights Council by the end of this year; however, the issues are complex and the negotiations intense. Ireland, in this regard, is placing particular emphasis on ensuring that the very positive involvement of civil society in the work of the CHR will be carried forward in the new body.

Good human rights practices and the rule of law do not emerge by themselves in developing countries and in countries in transition. Laws must be adopted and the capacity to observe them must be developed. I would like to pay tribute to the work of Mary Robinson in raising the profile of the Office of the UN High Commissioner for Human Rights, and developing its role in this crucial area.

This helped lay the groundwork for the agreement at the Summit to double the resources of the Office to help in capacity-building and technical assistance. This work is necessarily slow, and requires patience, but it will be a critical part of the UN's work for human security in the years ahead.

I would like to emphasise one final point in this area—exhortation and condemnation, while important and necessary, are simply not enough. Ultimately, the effectiveness of any action must be judged by whether it serves to promote and protect the observance of human rights on the ground.

DISARMAMENT AND NON-PROLIFERATION

Unfortunately, there are threats which the Summit did not properly address. The Taoiseach and I made clear our dismay at the inability to reach agreement on disarmament and non-proliferation, especially following the failure earlier this year of the NPT Review Conference. There remains an obscene contrast between spending on arms and spending on development.

I am appalled at the evident weakening of international commitment to the Nuclear Non-Proliferation Treaty, and indeed other disarmament treaties, and at the failure of some countries to assure the world of the peaceful nature of their nuclear programmes. I am also deeply troubled by the resistance of some countries to enter into a binding agreement on illicit trafficking in small arms and light weapons: these, as we all know, have caused vast devastation, particularly in Africa.

Everything points more and more to the validity of Ireland's long-held position that disarmament and non-proliferation, while one should never be a precondition for the other, are mutually reinforcing.

We must continue to insist that countries comply with their non-proliferation obligations, but the prospects of success would be very much greater in the context of a convincing commitment to disarmament. And in this regard the greatest onus, in my view, rests on nuclear weapons states to take the lead and show by force of example that further progress is possible.

Instead we have witnessed a depressing and deeply short-sighted retreat from the positive developments of the 1990s and of the commitments freely undertaken at the 2000 NPT Review Conference, in particular.

SECURITY COUNCIL REFORM

The Summit reaffirmed the authority of the Security Council to mandate coercive action, and its primary responsibility for the maintenance of international peace and security. But no agreement was reached on the reform of the Security Council's composition. This is, of course, a highly complex and divisive issue. As Envoy, I sought to avoid comment on it, because I thought this would detract from my effectiveness in focussing attention on the other significant issues on the agenda.

That said, it is clear, as the Secretary General himself has said, that the Security Council does not adequately reflect the world as it now is. Ireland will approach future work on its reform on the basis of a number of key principles.

First, we wish to see an increase in the size of the Council to reflect the realities of the twenty-first century.

Secondly, that increase should be regionally balanced, including enhancing the role of Africa.

Thirdly, any change should not lessen the capacity of smaller Member States, like Ireland, to continue to aspire to membership from time to time.

Fourthly, while we would ideally wish to see the complete removal of the veto, there should be no conferral of new veto powers.

Fifthly, an expanded Security Council should accommodate member states that play a particularly significant role in the UN system, for instance financially, in peace-keeping or through their capacity for regional leadership.

MANAGEMENT REFORM

The members of the United Nations deserve a Secretariat that operates to the highest standards of efficiency, effectiveness and accountability. This is not something of interest merely to the major contributors, but to all the member states, so that the Organisation can work for them in the best way possible. The Secretary-General has long been committed to applying such standards.

Change and modernisation are sensitive matters in any organisation. They are particularly sensitive in an international organisation, as all of its member states have a stake in what it does.

In discussing UN reform, I believe it is important to distinguish between what the Secretariat does, which is the province of the member states, and how it does it, where the Secretary-General should have the lead role. It is obvious from the report on the administration of the Oil for Food Programme that both the Member States and the Secretariat have lessons to learn.

I welcome the measures that the Secretary-General has already taken, and look forward to working with our EU partners on the further proposals that the Summit has invited him to make to enhance the effective management of the UN and to update the Organisation. I can only hope that Member States will be as diligent in examining their own failings.

CONCLUSION

We will never reach a moment when we will finally be able to announce that the United Nations is now reformed, and therefore perfect. This is not how the world is. The world moves on, and the UN must move with it.

Reform will always be a work in progress. New challenges will emerge, some threats will fade, others will arise, nations will lose or gain power and influence, and the UN must adapt.

The Organisation has passed through a period of unprecedented challenge, which left it struggling to catch up.

Despite this, it remains the essential source of legitimacy for our common action in support of international peace and security, and an indispensable framework for universal action on the wide range of economic and social problems that confront us.

I passionately believe that the United Nations, for all its flaws and failures, remains indispensable and irreplaceable. Of course the real too often diverges from the ideal. The work of the United Nations can be messy and inadequate. To the dismay of its friends, its procedures can too easily be exploited by those who ignore and pervert its core values, and who wish to block the efforts of those who try to act on those values. It can be sluggish and inefficient.

But it, and it alone, is based on a recognition of the essential equality of all of the peoples of the world and of the states in which they are organised. It, and it alone, seeks to take a fully holistic view of all the challenges and threats faced by humanity.

The experience of our fifty years of membership is that the United Nations can be a powerful force for good, and it can truly be said that if it did not exist, we would surely seek to invent it.

The United Nations can only be as effective as its Member States together allow it to be. Ireland will continue to work with its international partners to ensure that we implement what we have agreed, try to achieve consensus on what remains to be done, and above all collectively commit ourselves to the United Nations as the central, pivotal organisation that will nobly and effectively serve the people of the world long into the future.

Thank you, President.

The International Law Commission's Draft Articles on the Responsibility of International Organisations

STATEMENT BY MS PATRICIA O'BRIEN, LEGAL ADVISER,
DEPARTMENT OF FOREIGN AFFAIRS OF IRELAND
TO THE UNITED NATIONS GENERAL ASSEMBLY
61ST SESSION, SIXTH COMMITTEE
AGENDA ITEM 78

REPORT OF THE INTERNATIONAL LAW COMMISSION
ON THE WORK OF ITS 58TH SESSION

NEW YORK,
27 OCTOBER 2006

Mr. Chairman,

On behalf of Ireland, I wish to thank the Commission for undertaking the important and difficult task of formulating a regime of responsibility for international organisations. I would also like to congratulate the Special Rapporteur on his fourth report and commend him for his work so far.

Having considered draft articles 17 to 30, together with the Commission's comprehensive commentary and the reports of the Special Rapporteur, we would like to offer comments on two draft provisions, namely draft article 22 on necessity and draft article 28 on international responsibility in the case of provision of competence to an international organisation.

DRAFT ARTICLE 22—NECESSITY

Mr. Chairman, Ireland welcomes draft articles 17 to 24 on circumstances precluding wrongfulness. We also support the inclusion of a draft article on necessity[1], while remaining conscious of the need to limit the scope of this exception within defined boundaries.

[1] Draft article 22:

1. Necessity may not be invoked by an international organization as a ground for precluding the wrongfulness of an act not in conformity with an international obligation of that organization unless the act:

   Is the only means for the organization to safeguard against a grave and imminent peril an essential interest of the international community as a whole when the organization has, in accordance with international law, the function to protect that interest; and

   Does not seriously impair an essential interest of the State or States towards which the obligation exists, or of the international community as a whole.

2. In any case, necessity may not be invoked by an international organization as a ground for precluding wrongfulness if:

   (a) The international obligation in question excludes the possibility of invoking necessity; or
   (b) The organization has contributed to the situation of necessity.

Protection of member states' interests

It is our concern that draft article 22, in its current form, fails to adequately protect member states' essential interests.

A state may choose to entrust certain functions to an international organisation. However, simply because a state has transferred functions does not mean that it no longer retains essential interests in relation to those functions. These essential interests of the state may be imperilled by an act or omission of the organisation, even if the organisation's conduct is consistent with, and indeed required by, its own legal obligations.

However, according to the wording of the most recent draft article 22 adopted by the Commission, unless a member state's essential interest coincides with an essential interest of the international community as whole, the international organisation is unable to invoke necessity.

Obviously, states may be reluctant to transfer powers to an international organisation if their essential interests are not afforded sufficient protection. We therefore support the view held by some members of the Commission that an international organisation should be entitled to invoke an essential interest of its member states when claiming necessity.

Nexus between the imperilled essential interest and an organisation's functions

Mr. Chairman, a second point which we would like to raise in relation to draft article 22 is our concern that it may not reflect the present reality of movement towards international integration. Under the present formulation, in order to have recourse to the claim of necessity, an organisation must have as one of its functions the protection of the essential interest under threat. In other words, draft article 22 makes an organisation's ability to invoke necessity dependant on its functions.

While, in the modern era, international integration has led to states granting international organisations more and more functions, most of these organisations deal individually with discrete issues and are entrusted with a narrow range of functions. Draft article 22, in its present form, may fail to adequately accommodate this state of affairs. After all, it is quite plausible that the actions of an international organisation might imperil an essential interest of a member state, or indeed of the international community as a whole, without that organisation having as one of its functions the protection of that interest. In such circumstances, the current wording of draft article 22 would leave the organisation without recourse to the claim of necessity in order to safeguard the imperilled essential interest.

Reference to the constituent instrument in determining the essential interests

Thirdly, Mr. Chairman, in relation to draft article 22 we welcome the observation of the Special Rapporteur that in determining the essential interests which an international organisation has the function to protect, reference only to the constituent instrument may be too restrictive. Conversely, not *all* the functions which an organisation is conferred with in its constituent instrument are to be regarded as essential interests.

For these reasons we urge the Commission to review the formulation of this article.

Draft article 28—International responsibility in case of provisions of competence to an international organisation

We now turn our attention to draft article 28, concerning international responsibility in case of provision of competence to an international organisation. Recalling our comments in relation to draft article 15 at the 60th Session of the General Assembly, we would like to express our support for the efforts of the Special Rapporteur to make provision for member states to incur responsibility for acts of international organisations in certain circumstances. We express reservations, however, as to the wording of draft article 28.[2]

The scope of the draft article in its present form is inadequately defined. The draft article's insistence on the provision of competence in relation to the circumvented obligation may unduly narrow the scope of the article where a restrictive understanding of this requirement is employed. In such circumstances, the member state may not have provided the organisation with competence in relation to the

Specific obligation being circumvented but may nevertheless, in the knowledge that the organisation had a general competence that could impinge upon the obligation, have intended that it be breached by the organisation.

Conversely, a broad understanding of the provision of competence requirement could result in state responsibility where an international organisation acts upon a general competence which may affect the obligation in question but without any intent on the part of the member state that the obligation be breached. In this regard, we welcome the Commission's commentary on draft article 28, which provides that the use of the term "circumvention" is intended to exclude that international responsibility arises when the act of the organisation, which would constitute a breach of international organisation if taken by the state, has to be regarded as an unwitting result of providing the international organisation with competence.

On a practical level, we believe that the determination of whether or not a state has provided and organisation with competence in relation to an obligation could prove problematic. Our primary concern, however, is in the absence of any requirement of intent in draft article 28 which would limit the potential scope of the draft article.

CONCLUSION

In closing, Mr. Chairman, Ireland reiterates its appreciation for the important work of the Commission on this challenging topic and looks forward to its next report.

[2] 2 Draft articles 28:

1. A State member of an international organization incurs international responsibility if it circumvents one of its international obligations by providing the organization with competence in relation to that obligation, and the organization commits an act that, if committed by that State, would have constituted a breach of that obligation.
2. Paragraph 1 applies to whether or not the act in question is internationally wrongful for the international organization.

Irish Submission to the Comission on the Limits of the Continental Shelf

EXECUTIVE SUMMARY OF PARTIAL SUBMISSION

TABLE OF CONTENTS

APPENDICES

LIST OF FIGURES

1. Introduction

Ireland first formally claimed a limited area of continental shelf in 1968 by means of designation by statutory order made pursuant to the Continental Shelf Act 1968. This was followed by a series of westward-progressing continental shelf designations during the 1970s, culminating in the 1976 designation (yellow on map) which reached 25∞W. This was subsequently modified by the 1989 designation (Statutory Instrument No. 141 of 1989—grey on map) which gave effect to the Agreement of 7 November 1988 between Ireland and the UK on delimitation of areas of the continental shelf between the two countries. (*See* plate section.)

Work on preparing Ireland's submission to the United Nations Commission on the Limits of the Continental Shelf (CLCS) began in 1994 with budget sanction given for a Continental Margin seismic survey in 1995 and a Continental Margin bathymetric survey in 1996.

Ireland ratified the 1982 United Nations Convention on the Law of the Sea (UNCLOS) on 21 June 1996 and it entered into force with respect to Ireland on 21 July 1996.

Data processing, analysis, interpretation and compilation have continued until 2005, in parallel with two sets of quadrilateral discussions with neighbouring States to the NW (Faroe Islands/Denmark, Iceland, Ireland and the UK) and to the SW (France, Ireland, Spain and the UK).

2. Outer limits of Ireland's extended continental shelf in the area abutting the Porcupine Abyssal Plain (See plate section)

The present submission deals only with the outer limits of the continental shelf in the area abutting the Porcupine Abyssal Plain, from foot of slope (FOS) profile 46 to FOS profile 60.

3. Specific provisions of Article 76 invoked to support the submission

The outer limits contained in this submission are based on the provisions of both Article 76.4 (a)(i) and 76.4 (a)(ii) of UNCLOS.

4. Names of Commission Members who provided advice during the preparation of the submission

Ireland was assisted in the preparation of this submission by Mr. Peter F. Croker, member of the Commission on the Limits of the Continental Shelf (1997-present). No advice was provided by any other members of the Commission.

5. Endpoints of the outer limit, overlapping claims and unresolved maritime boundaries (See plate section)

Due to ongoing discussions with neighbouring States with regard to portions of the Irish Designated Continental Shelf Area to the northwest and the southwest, Ireland has elected to split its submission. The partial submission is made in respect of the area abutting the Porcupine Abyssal Plain (marked as Zone B in Figure 1.3 above). It constitutes the first part of Ireland's complete submission of information on the limits of its continental shelf beyond 200 nautical miles from the baselines from which the breadth of the territorial sea is measured.

Having regard to Article 76, paragraph 10 and Article 9 of Annex II of UNCLOS, and in accordance with paragraph 3 of Annex I to the Rules of Procedure of the

Commission, in order not to prejudice unresolved questions relating to the delimitation of boundaries between Ireland and some of its neighbours in other portions of the extended continental shelf claimed by Ireland, submissions in respect of those other portions (Zone A and Zone C) will be made at a later date.

Details of the most northerly and southerly points (endpoints) of the outer limit in respect of which this submission is made, and the corresponding foot of slope points from which they are measured (FOS46 & FOS60), have been communicated to the governments of the Faroe Islands/Denmark, France, Iceland, Spain and the UK. It is the view of Ireland that the consideration of this partial submission by the CLCS will not prejudice the question of delimitation of boundaries in either Zones A or C.

6. Detailed description of the outer limits of Ireland's extended continental shelf in the area abutting the Porcupine Abyssal Plain (See plate section)

A total of 15 foot of slope points (FOS 46 to FOS 60) have been picked along the Porcupine Ridge-Goban Spur margin. From these FOS points an outer limit based on the FOS+60 nautical miles (M) formula (Hedberg formula) has been generated. On seismic lines PAD95-12 and PAD95-13 (corresponding to FOS profiles 46 and 50 respectively), sufficient sediment thickness has been demonstrated to allow the application of the 1% sediment thickness formula (Gardiner or Irish formula). The final outer limits consist of a series of straight lines, as provided for in the Convention being not more than 60M long, which join points along the Gardiner or Hedberg lines. The coordinates of these points and the lengths of the connecting straight lines are listed in Appendix 1.1.

7. State Bodies Responsible for the Preparation of the Continental Shelf Submission of Ireland

This submission, together with all maps, figures, enclosures, appendices and databases were prepared by the Petroleum Affairs Division of the Department of Communications, Marine and Natural Resources of Ireland, which has statutory responsibility for Ireland's Continental Shelf.

Appendix 1.1: List of coordinates defining the outer limits of Ireland's extended continental shelf in the area abutting the Porcupine Abyssal Plain

All coordinates relate to the WGS 84 geodetic reference system.

ID	Latitude (°N)	Longitude (°W)	Method	From ID	To ID	Distance (m)	Distance (M)
1	51.0376718	-17.4926083	1% Sediment Thickness				
2	50.2478896	-16.7035439	1% Sediment Thickness	1	2	104085.29	56.20
3	50.0691902	-16.5126452	FOS + 60M	2	3	24107.91	13.02
4	50.0554937	-16.4979397	FOS + 60M	3	4	1851.94	1.00
5	50.0419552	-16.4828907	FOS + 60M	4	5	1851.88	1.00
6	50.0285778	-16.4675026	FOS + 60M	5	6	1851.88	1.00
7	50.0153645	-16.4517798	FOS + 60M	6	7	1851.91	1.00

Table continued

ID	Latitude (ºN)	Longitude (ºW)	Method	From ID	To ID	Distance (m)	Distance (M)
8	50.0023213	-16.4357247	FOS + 60M	7	8	1851.84	1.00
9	49.9894483	-16.4193439	FOS + 60M	8	9	1851.95	1.00
10	49.9767514	-16.4026397	FOS + 60M	9	10	1851.97	1.00
11	49.2097194	-15.4275948	FOS + 60M	10	11	110665.59	59.75
12	49.1932741	-15.4236130	FOS + 60M	11	12	1851.83	1.00
13	49.1768732	-15.4192158	FOS + 60M	12	13	1851.94	1.00
14	49.1605229	-15.4144053	FOS + 60M	13	14	1851.90	1.00
15	49.1442276	-15.4091816	FOS + 60M	14	15	1851.88	1.00
16	49.1279917	-15.4035514	FOS + 60M	15	16	1851.78	1.00
17	49.1118183	-15.3975125	FOS + 60M	16	17	1851.91	1.00
18	49.0957133	-15.3910671	FOS + 60M	17	18	1851.87	1.00
19	49.0796798	-15.3842174	FOS + 60M	18	19	1851.97	1.00
20	49.0637237	-15.3769680	FOS + 60M	19	20	1851.86	1.00
21	49.0478481	-15.3693211	FOS + 60M	20	21	1851.90	1.00
22	49.0320589	-15.3612745	FOS + 60M	21	22	1851.86	1.00
23	49.0163592	-15.3528370	FOS + 60M	22	23	1851.80	1.00
24	49.0007521	-15.3440066	FOS + 60M	23	24	1852.00	1.00
25	48.9852450	-15.3347876	FOS + 60M	24	25	1851.81	1.00
26	48.9698395	-15.3251846	FOS + 60M	25	26	1851.85	1.00
27	48.9545401	-15.3151976	FOS + 60M	26	27	1851.94	1.00
28	48.9393514	-15.3048333	FOS + 60M	27	28	1851.88	1.00
29	48.9242780	-15.2940895	FOS + 60M	28	29	1851.94	1.00
30	48.9093243	-15.2829750	FOS + 60M	29	30	1851.78	1.00
31	48.8944919	-15.2714901	FOS + 60M	30	31	1851.96	1.00
32	48.8797885	-15.2596368	FOS + 60M	31	32	1851.84	1.00
33	48.0979064	-14.6273868	FOS + 60M	32	33	98708.61	53.30
34	48.0833284	-14.6153696	FOS + 60M	33	34	1851.74	1.00
35	48.0688832	-14.6029975	FOS + 60M	34	35	1851.96	1.00
36	48.0545769	-14.5902751	FOS + 60M	35	36	1851.94	1.00
37	48.0404143	-14.5772069	FOS + 60M	36	37	1851.81	1.00
38	48.0263984	-14.5637951	FOS + 60M	37	38	1851.80	1.00
39	48.0170407	-14.5545155	FOS + 60M	38	39	1249.70	0.67

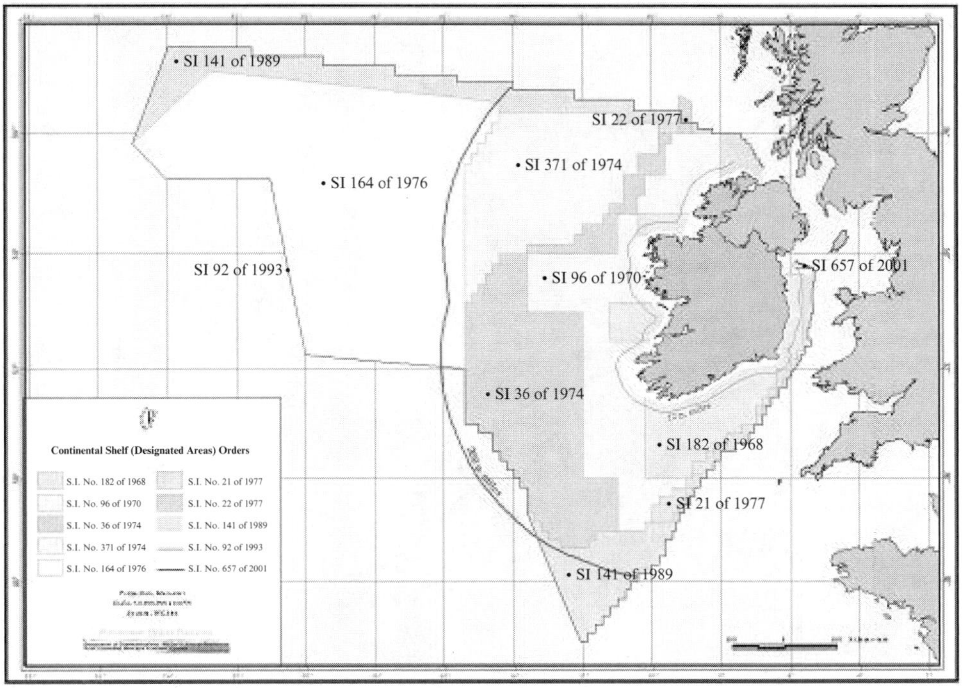

Figure 1.1: History of Continental Shelf Designations by Ireland 1968-1989

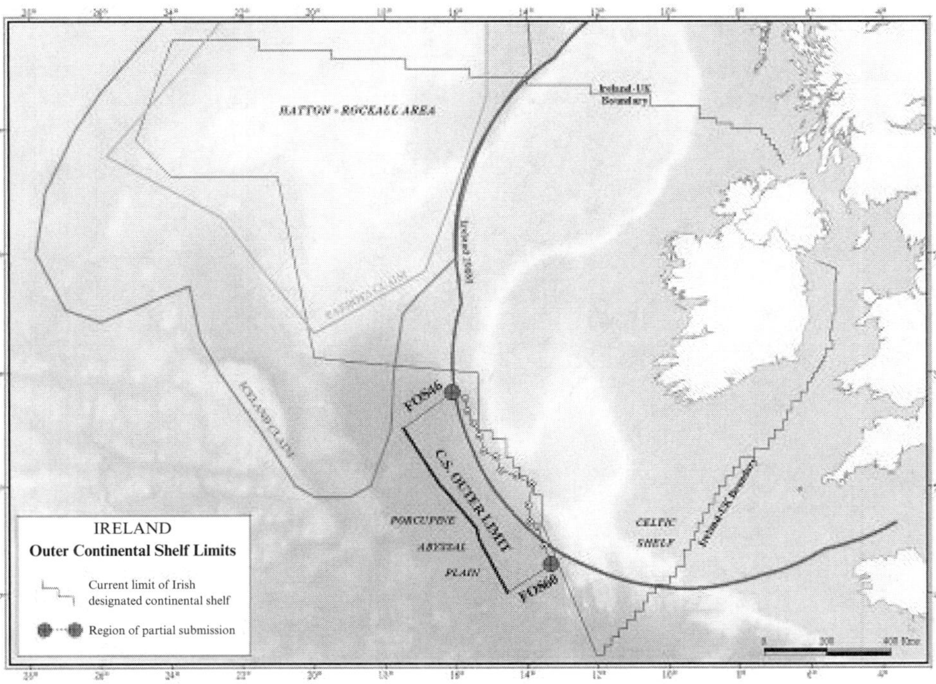

Figure 1.2: The outer limits of Ireland's extended continental shelf in the area abutting the Porcupine Abyssal Plain (bathymetry from GEBCO 2003)

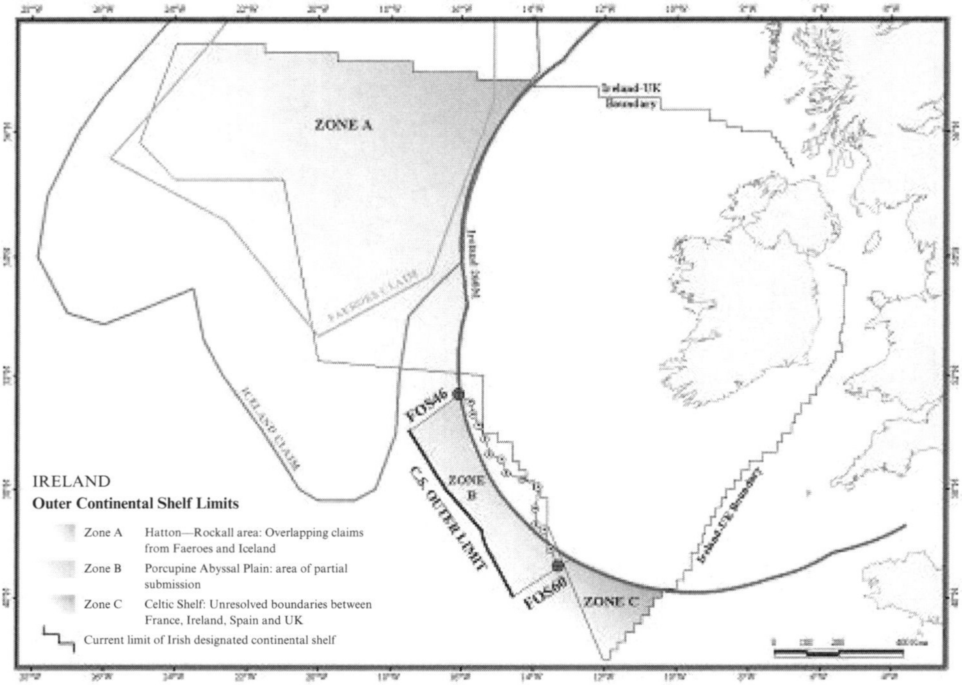

Figure 1.3: Zonation of Ireland's extended continental shelf

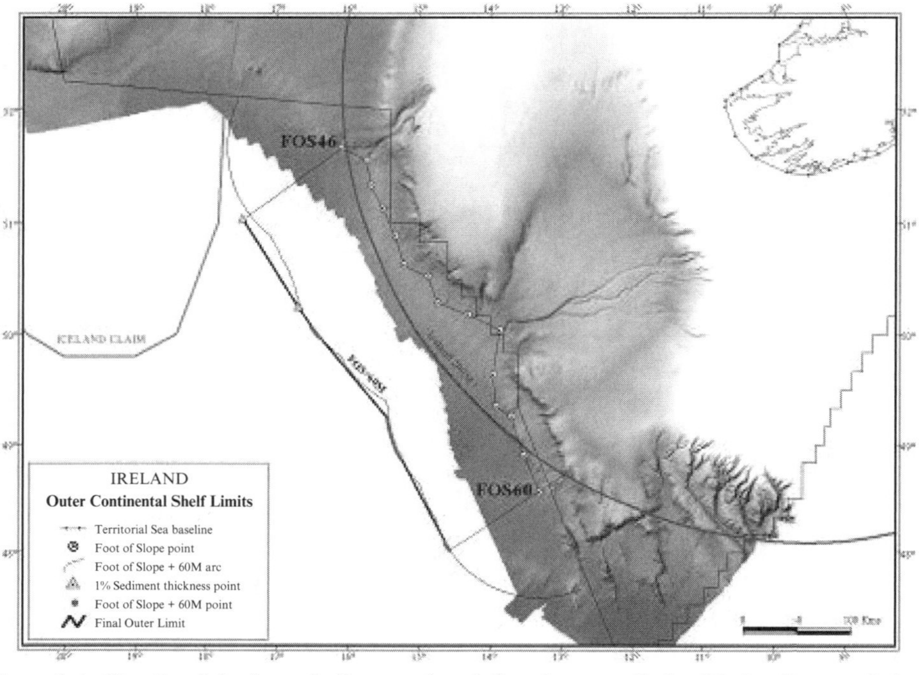

Figure 1.4: Details of the formula lines used to define the outer limit of Ireland's extended continental shelf in the area abutting the Porcupine Abyssal Plain (bathymetry from PAD 1996 and INSS 2000-2003 bathymetric surveys)

EXECUTIVE SUMMARY: JOINT SUBMISSION (WITH FRANCE, SPAIN AND UNITED KINGDOM)

TABLE OF CONTENTS

APPENDIX

LIST OF FIGURES

1. Introduction

This submission to the Commission is made by France, Ireland, Spain and the United Kingdom of Great Britain and Northern Ireland (hereinafter referred to as the 'four coastal States') pursuant to Article 76, paragraph 8, of the Convention in support of the establishment by these four coastal States of the outer limits of their continental shelf in the area of the Celtic Sea and the Bay of Biscay that lies beyond 200 nautical miles from the baselines of each State from which the breadths of their respective territorial seas are measured. This submission is, therefore, of a joint nature, and comprises a single document prepared collectively and collaboratively by the four coastal States concerned. (*See* plate section.)

2. Outer limit of the extended continental shelf in the Celtic Sea and Bay of Biscay area

The present joint submission deals only with the outer limit of the continental shelf in the Celtic Sea and Bay of Biscay area. It extends from the southern limit of the Partial Submission of Ireland to a point on the Spanish 200M continental shelf limit (Fig. 1).

3. Specific provisions of Article 76 invoked to support the submission

The outer limits contained in this submission are based on the provisions of Articles 76.4 (a)(i) and 76.4 (a)(ii) and 76.4 (b) of UNCLOS.

4. Names of Commission Members who provided advice during the preparation of the submission

The four coastal States were assisted in the preparation of this submission by Mr. Peter F. Croker, member of the Commission on the Limits of the Continental Shelf (1997-present). No advice was provided by any other member of the Commission.

5. Absence of Disputes

In accordance with paragraph 2(a) of Annex I to the Commission's Rules of Procedures, the four coastal States wish to inform the Commission that the area of continental shelf that is the subject of this joint partial submission is not the subject of any dispute between them and any other State(s).

6. Detailed description of the outer limit of the extended continental shelf in the Celtic Sea and Bay of Biscay area (See plate section)

The four coastal States have used both of the formulae lines (i.e. both Hedberg and Gardiner) in this joint submission. A limit based on the Hedberg formula (60 nautical miles from the foot of the continental slope) has been generated from all of the 8 foot of slope points (FOS 1 to FOS 8). On the seismic data submitted, sufficient sediment thickness has, in the view of the four coastal States, been demonstrated to allow the application of the 1% sediment thickness formula (the Gardiner or Irish formula) from FOS 5. Therefore, FOS 5 generates fixed points from the application of both the Hedberg and Gardiner formulae and the Gardiner point has been selected. Only the fixed points generated from FOS 1, 4 and 5 actually contribute to establishing the final outer limit of the area that is the subject of this joint submission (Fig. 2).

7. State Bodies Responsible for the Preparation of the Joint Continental Shelf Submission

This submission, together with all maps, figures, enclosures, appendices and databases, was prepared jointly by EXTRAPLAC of France, a consortium composed of Ifremer, SHOM, IFP and IPEV under the auspices of the General Secretariat of the Sea; the Petroleum Affairs Division of the Department of Communications, Marine and Natural Resources of Ireland; the IGME Marine Geology Division of the Geological Survey of Spain and the Hydrographic and Oceanographic Services of Spain; the National Oceanography Centre and the United Kingdom Hydrographic Office of the United Kingdom.

Appendix 1: List of coordinates defining the outer limit of the extended continental shelf in the Celtic Sea and Bay of Biscay area

All coordinates relate to the WGS 84 geodetic reference system.

FP	Latitude (°N)	Longitude (°W)	Method	From FP	To FP	Distance (m)	Distance (M)
1	48.0170407	14.5545155	Fixed point from FOS1+60M arc terminated at southern limit of Ireland's partial submission to the CLCS				
2	47.3821081	14.3248005	Fixed point at 60M from FOS point 4	1	2	72669.59	39.24
3	47.3659249	14.3189907	Fixed point at 60M from FOS point 4	2	3	1851.96	1.00
4	47.3498099	14.3127878	Fixed point at 60M from FOS point 4	3	4	1851.90	1.00
5	47.3337678	14.3061964	Fixed point at 60M from FOS point 4	4	5	1851.77	1.00
6	47.3178003	14.2992165	Fixed point at 60M from FOS point 4	5	6	1851.97	1.00
7	47.3019149	14.2918503	Fixed point at 60M from FOS point 4	6	7	1851.84	1.00
8	47.2861149	14.2841001	Fixed point at 60M from FOS point 4	7	8	1851.82	1.00
9	47.2704034	14.2759681	Fixed point at 60M from FOS point 4	8	9	1851.93	1.00
10	47.2547851	14.2674588	Fixed point at 60M from FOS point 4	9	10	1851.97	1.00
11	47.2392662	14.2585722	Fixed point at 60M from FOS point 4	10	11	1851.85	1.00
12	47.0037342	14.1227919	Fixed point at 60M from FOS point 5	11	12	28139.07	15.19
13	46.9883165	14.1135774	Fixed point at 60M from FOS point 5	12	13	1851.76	1.00
14	46.9730036	14.1039924	Fixed point at 60M from FOS point 5	13	14	1851.97	1.00
15	46.9578015	14.0940435	Fixed point at 60M from FOS point 5	14	15	1851.88	1.00
16	46.9427151	14.0837309	Fixed point at 60M from FOS point 5	15	16	1851.80	1.00
17	46.9277459	14.0730589	Fixed point at 60M from FOS point 5	16	17	1851.94	1.00
18	46.9129002	14.0620298	Fixed point at 60M from FOS point 5	17	18	1851.89	1.00
19	46.8981813	14.0506482	Fixed point at 60M from FOS point 5	18	19	1851.86	1.00
20	46.8835937	14.0389139	Fixed point at 60M from FOS point 5	19	20	1851.91	1.00
21	46.8691393	14.0268361	Fixed point at 60M from FOS point 5	20	21	1851.97	1.00
22	46.8548258	14.0144146	Fixed point at 60M from FOS point 5	21	22	1851.77	1.00
23	46.8406533	14.0016541	Fixed point at 60M from FOS point 5	22	23	1851.90	1.00
24	46.8266281	13.9885566	Fixed point at 60M from FOS point 5	23	24	1851.87	1.00
25	46.8127518	13.9751291	Fixed point at 60M from FOS point 5	24	25	1851.90	1.00
26	46.7990308	13.9613714	Fixed point at 60M from FOS point 5	25	26	1851.85	1.00
27	46.7854652	13.9472903	Fixed point at 60M from FOS point 5	26	27	1852.03	1.00
28	46.7720627	13.9328903	Fixed point at 60M from FOS point 5	27	28	1851.81	1.00
29	46.7656604	13.9257734	Fixed point at 60M from FOS point 5	28	29	895.53	0.48
30	45.8277417	13.4627682	Fixed point from sediment thickness at 1% distance to FOS point 5	29	30	110190.16	59.50
31	44.8516616	13.2160010	Fixed point on Spanish 200M continental shelf limit	30	31	110190.59	59.50

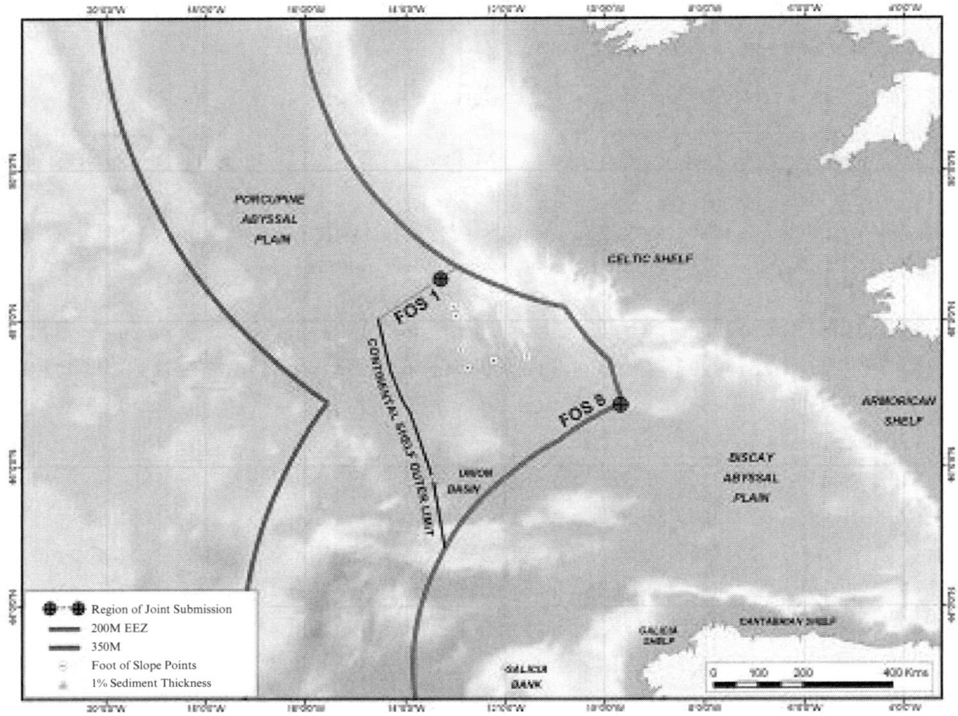

Figure 1: Outer continental shelf limit in the Celtic Sea and Bay of Biscay area

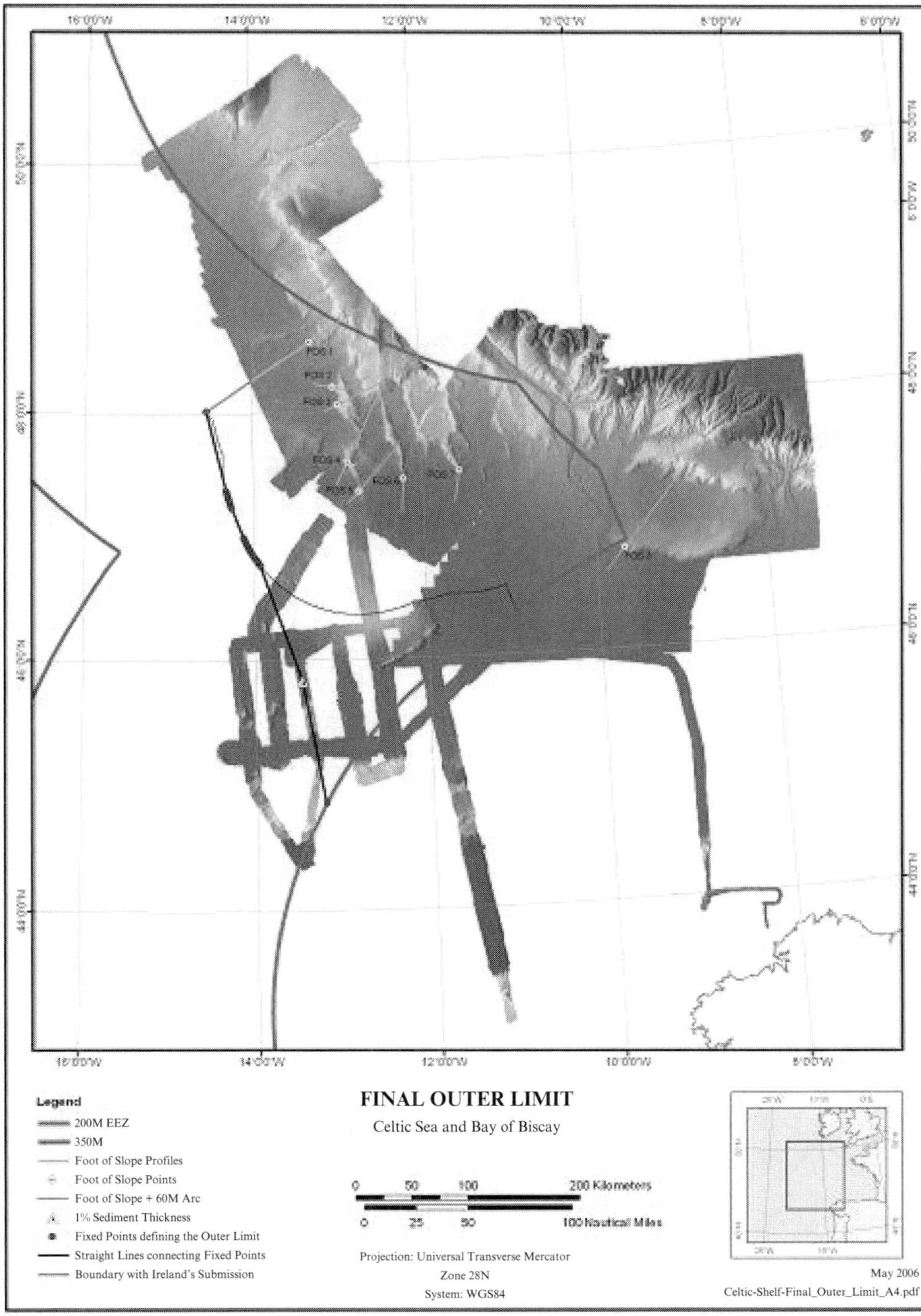

Figure 2: Details of the formulae lines used to define the outer limit of the extended continental shelf in the Celtic Sea and Bay of Biscay area

Agreement at St Andrews

SINN FEIN, GERRY ADAMS

IRISH TAOISEACH, BERTIE AHERN

BRITISH PRIME MINISTER, TONY BLAIR

DEMOCRATIC UNIONIST PARTY, IAN PAISLEY

13 October 2006

Over the past three days in St Andrews we have engaged intensively with the Northern Ireland political parties with a view to achieving the goal we set in Armagh in April, which is shared by all the parties and the overwhelming majority of people in Northern Ireland: the restoration of the political institutions. We believe that the transformation brought about by the ending of the IRA's campaign provides the basis for a political settlement.

Our discussions have been focused on achieving full and effective operation of the political institutions. When we arrived in Scotland a limited number of outstanding issues remained to be resolved, including support for and devolution of policing and the criminal justice system, changes to the operation of the Agreement institutions, and certain other matters raised by the parties or flowing from the Preparation for Government Committee. The two Governments now believe that the agreement we are publishing today clears the way to restoration.

POWER SHARING AND THE POLITICAL INSTITUTIONS

Both Governments remain fully committed to the fundamental principles of the Agreement: consent for constitutional change, commitment to exclusively peaceful and democratic means, stable inclusive partnership government, a balanced institutional accommodation of the key relationships within Northern Ireland, between North and South and within these islands, and for equality and human rights at the heart of the new dispensation in Northern Ireland. All parties to this agreement need to be wholeheartedly and publicly committed, in good faith and in a spirit of genuine partnership, to the full operation of stable power-sharing Government and the North-South and East-West arrangements.

Following discussion with all the parties, we have made an assessment of practical changes to the operation of the institutions and we are publishing today a clear outline of these. The British Government will introduce legislation in Parliament before the statutory November deadline to enact these changes, once parties have endorsed the agreement and agreed definitively to restore the power sharing institutions. Details of these changes are set out in Annex A.

POLICING AND THE RULE OF LAW

We have consistently said that support for policing and the rule of law should be extended to every part of the community. We believe that all the parties share this objective. Notwithstanding the right of every political party to hold the police to account, we believe that there are fundamental principles of support for the police and the courts which underpin any democratic society.

We believe that the essential elements of support for law and order include endorsing fully the Police Service of Northern Ireland and the criminal justice system, actively encouraging everyone in the community to co-operate fully with the PSNI in tackling crime in all areas and actively supporting all the policing and criminal justice institutions, including the Policing Board.

Discussions on the devolution of policing and justice have progressed well in the Preparation for Government Committee. The Governments have requested the parties to continue these discussions so as to agree the necessary administrative arrangements to create a new policing and justice department. It is our view that implementation of the agreement published today should be sufficient to build the community confidence necessary for the Assembly to request the devolution of criminal justice and policing from the British Government by May 2008.

HUMAN RIGHTS, EQUALITY, VICTIMS AND OTHER ISSUES

Both Governments have also discussed other matters raised by the parties. Some of these relate to the final implementation of the Agreement and others have been raised in the context of the Preparation for Government Committee. The British Government has also agreed to take forward a number of measures to build confidence in both communities and to pursue a shared future for Northern Ireland in which the culture, rights and aspirations of all are respected and valued, free from sectarianism, racism and intolerance. Details of all these issues are set out in Annex B.

FINANCIAL PACKAGE FOR THE NEWLY RESTORED EXECUTIVE

The Governments are also committed to working with the parties to establish the most favourable possible financial climate for a newly restored Executive. The Chancellor of the Exchequer and the Minister for Finance will meet delegations from the First and Deputy First Minister to take this forward. Details of how this might be achieved are set out in Annex C.

CONCLUSION

We believe that all parties should be able to endorse this agreement and to implement it in good faith, building the trust and confidence necessary for a stable and lasting settlement. We have set out a fixed timetable for the implementation of this agreement in Annex D and have asked parties, having consulted their members, to confirm their acceptance by 10 November. Following endorsement of the St Andrews agreement by the parties the Assembly will meet to nominate the First and Deputy First Minister on 24 November. Between that date and restoration of the Executive on 26 March the new Programme for Government Committee will agree all the necessary arrangements relating to ministerial responsibilities, ensuring that d'Hondt can be run and the Executive can operate immediately.

Verification and compliance mechanisms relating to the Assembly already exist, as set out in the agreement between the Governments published in May 2003 and in the Belfast Agreement. The Prime Minister and the *Taoiseach* are determined that default by any one of the parties following restoration of the Executive should not be allowed to delay or hinder political progress in Northern Ireland.

The Governments have made clear that in the event of failure to reach agreement by the 24 November we will proceed on the basis of the new British Irish partnership arrangements to implement the Belfast Agreement.

It is clear to us that all the parties wish to see devolution restored. It is also clear to us that all parties wish to support policing and the rule of law. We hope they will seize this opportunity for bringing the political process in Northern Ireland to completion and establishing power-sharing government for the benefit of the whole community.

ANNEX A

PRACTICAL CHANGES TO THE OPERATION OF THE INSTITUTIONS

Following discussion with all the parties in the Preparation for Government Committee and here at St Andrews, we are proposing practical changes to the operation of the institutions of the Agreement in the interests of efficiency and fairness, as envisaged by the Agreement itself. We believe the changes will enable all the institutions to operate in an effective and stable manner, with all parties engaging in good faith and in a spirit of genuine partnership.

Strand 1 Issues

A statutory ministerial Code. An amendment to the Northern Ireland Act 1998 would provide for a statutory ministerial Code, and place a duty upon Ministers (including junior Ministers), notwithstanding their executive authority in their areas of responsibility as defined in the Agreement, to act in accordance with the provisions on ministerial accountability of the Code. The Code would reflect a requirement for safeguards to ensure that all sections of the community could participate and work together successfully in the operation of these institutions and that all sections of the community were protected. There would be arrangements to ensure that, where a decision of the Executive could not be achieved by consensus and a vote was required, any three members of the Executive could require it to be taken on a cross-community basis.

The 1998 Act would be amended to require inclusion in the Code of agreed provisions in relation to ministerial accountability. Consistent with paragraphs 19 and 20 of the Agreement, this would provide for the Executive to be the forum for:

(i) the discussion of, and agreement on, issues which cut across the responsibilities of two or more Ministers, including in particular those that are the responsibility of the Minister of Finance and Personnel.

(ii) prioritising executive proposals;
(iii) prioritising legislative proposals;
(iv) recommending a common position where necessary—for instance, on matters which concern the response of the Northern Ireland administration to external relationships;
(v) agreement each year on (and review as necessary of) a programme incorporating an agreed budget linked to policies and programmes (Programme for Government).

The Code will also provide for the discussion of and agreement on any issue which is significant or controversial and:

(a) clearly outside the scope of the agreed Programme for Government or
(b) which the First Minister and Deputy First Minister agree should be brought to the Executive.

The new Code would be discussed by the parties and agreed by the Executive when formed. The First Minister and Deputy First Minister would propose the Code to the Assembly. It would have effect once endorsed by cross-community support there. Any amendments to the Code would require cross-community support in the Assembly.

Assembly referrals for Executive review. An amendment to the 1998 Act would provide for referrals from the Assembly to the Executive of important ministerial decisions. Thirty members of the Assembly might initiate such a referral, within seven days of a ministerial decision or notification of the decision where appropriate. Before he could pass the referral to the Executive, the Presiding Officer, following consultation with the parties in the Assembly, would be required to certify that it concerned an issue of public importance. The Executive would consider the issue within seven days. A second referral could not be made by the Assembly in respect of the same matter. Only matters covered by the Ministerial Code, as set out above, would require a collective decision by the Executive.

Reflecting the Pledge of Office, Ministers would be required to act in accordance with any relevant decisions of the Executive and/or Assembly.

Amendments to the Pledge of Office. The Pledge of Office would require that Ministers would participate fully in the Executive and NSMC/BIC, and would observe the joint nature of the office of First Minister and Deputy First Minister. Before the Government legislates on the pledge of office it will consider the outcome of further Preparation for Government Committee discussions on policing and the rule of law.

Appointment of Ministers in the Executive. An amendment would be made to the 1998 Act on appointment of Ministers in the Executive. The Nominating Officer of the largest party in the largest designation in the Assembly shall make a nomination to the Assembly Presiding Officer for the post of First Minister. The Nominating Officer of the largest party in the second largest designation in the Assembly shall similarly nominate for the post of Deputy First Minister. The d'Hondt procedure will then run, as already set out in the 1998 Act, to fill the Ministerial posts in the Executive. Where a vacancy arose later in the office of the FM or DFM, the nominating officer(s) of the party(ies) entitled to nominate as above for the office(s) would do so and the nominee would take up office once he had taken the pledge of office. Where a vacancy arose in another ministerial office, it would be filled as at present. It will be a matter for the standing Institutional Review Committee referred to in paragraph 12 to consider whether the new procedures should continue beyond the life of the present Assembly.

Functions of Office of First Minister and Deputy First Minister. The First Minister and Deputy First Minister would reach agreement as to whether any functions of the current OFMDFM should be transferred to other departments, and would put proposals to the Executive and Assembly accordingly.

Committee of the Centre. An amendment to the 1998 Act would provide for the existing Assembly Committee of the Centre to be placed on a statutory footing like that of other departmental scrutiny committees.

Reviews. An amendment to the 1998 Act would provide for the Assembly to appoint a standing Institutional Review Committee, to examine the operational aspects of the Strand One institutions. Matters to be reviewed in this way would be agreed among the parties. The Committee's reports would be considered by the Executive and Assembly, and, where agreed changes required legislative steps outside the scope of the devolved institutions, by the British Government in consultation as appropriate with the Irish Government.

The First Minister and Deputy First Minister would appoint an Efficiency Review Panel, to examine efficiency and value for money of aspects of the Strand One institutions. The FM/DFM would put to the Assembly for approval proposals for the panel's remit, which might include the size of the Assembly and the departmental structure. The Panel would take into account as appropriate the work of the Review of Public Administration. The Panel's report would be considered by the Executive and Assembly, and, where agreed changes required legislative steps outside the scope of the devolved institutions, by the British Government in consultation as appropriate with the Irish Government.

Repeal of the Northern Ireland Act 2000. The Northern Ireland Act 2006 provides for the automatic repeal of the Northern Ireland Act 2000 if the Assembly is restored by the date set out in that Act. The Government remains committed to the repeal of the Northern Ireland Act 2000 on the restoration of devolved government in Northern Ireland.

Community designation. An amendment to the 1998 Act would provide that an Assembly Member would not be able to change community designation for the whole of an Assembly term except in the case of a change of membership of political party.

Strands Two and Three issues

Executive role in preparation for NSMC and BIC meetings. The amendment to the Northern Ireland Act 1998 on a ministerial Code, described in the British Government's Strand One proposals, would bear on Executive proceedings relating to the North-South Ministerial Council and British-Irish Council.

The Code would provide that draft NSMC and BIC decision papers would be circulated to all Executive members within a period (to be decided by the Executive) in advance of a scheduled NSMC or BIC meeting. Any member of the Executive would have the right to seek an Executive discussion on such a paper. Notwithstanding the lead Minister's executive authority in his/her area of responsibility as defined in the Agreement, where the Code provided that certain matters should be considered/

agreed in the Executive Committee (see paragraphs 3 to 5 of the British Government's Strand One proposals), this would apply to any draft NSMC/BIC decision papers falling within those agreed provisions.

Attendance at NSMC and BIC. Amendments to the 1998 Act would provide for a minister with lead departmental interest in an issue under consideration at an NSMC/BIC meeting to be entitled to attend (with a power for a minister so entitled, by consent, to arrange for another minister attending to discharge his/her responsibilities), and a power for the FM/DFM to adjudicate where a Minister's lead departmental interest was disputed. In the circumstances where a lead Minister was not proposing to attend the meeting in question, and had not arranged for a replacement Minister to discharge his/her responsibilities, there would also be a statutory obligation on FM/DFM to nominate a replacement for a lead Minister to attend the NSMC/BIC and discharge his/her responsibilities. There would be a statutory power for the FM/DFM to require such relevant information from the lead department as would be necessary for the NSMC/BIC meeting in question. Finally, reflecting the existing requirement for representation of the Executive on a cross-community basis at meetings of the NSMC/BIC, there would be a statutory obligation on the FM/DFM to nominate the other Minister whose presence is necessary to fulfil that requirement.

Review. The Northern Ireland Executive and Irish Government, under the auspices of the NSMC, would appoint a Review Group to examine objectively (1) the efficiency and value for money of existing implementation bodies and (2) the case for additional bodies and areas of co-operation within the NSMC where mutual benefit would be derived. The Group would also input into the work commissioned by the NSMC in June 2002 on the identification of a suitable substitute for the proposed Lights Agency of the Foyle, Carlingford and Irish Lights Commission. The Group would report with recommendations to the NSMC. Any changes to the existing arrangements would require the specific endorsement of the Assembly and Oireachtas. In the meantime, the NSMC would continue to oversee the ongoing work of the Implementation Bodies and work in the areas of co-operation.

Assembly/Oireachtas scrutiny of implementation bodies. Chairs and Chief Executives of North/South bodies, when called upon and at least yearly, would appear before relevant Assembly Committees. There is provision in the South for similar arrangements in relation to the Oireachtas.

North-South Parliamentary Forum. The Northern Ireland Executive would encourage the parties in the Assembly to establish a North-South parliamentary forum bringing together equal numbers from the Oireachtas and the Assembly, and operating on an inclusive basis.

Independent Consultative Forum. The Northern Ireland Executive would support the establishment of an independent North/South consultative forum appointed by the two Administrations and representative of civil society.

Secretariat of British-Irish Council. Following consultation with its other members, and with a view to giving further impetus to its work, the two Governments would facilitate the establishment of a standing secretariat for the British-Irish Council, if members agree.

East-West Inter-parliamentary Framework. Following appropriate consultation with the British-Irish Inter-parliamentary Body, the two Governments would encourage the Oireachtas, the British Parliament and the relevant elected institutions to approve an East-West Inter-parliamentary Framework which would embrace all their interests. The framework would operate on an inclusive basis.

If the Preparation for Government Committee wishes to reconvene to discuss further changes and reaches agreement by 31 October, the Governments stand ready to implement any such agreed changes

ANNEX B

HUMAN RIGHTS, EQUALITY, VICTIMS AND OTHER ISSUES

The Government will continue to actively promote the advancement of human rights, equality and mutual respect. In the pursuit of which we commit to the following:

- In early November, we will publish an Anti-Poverty and Social Exclusion strategy to tackle deprivation in both rural and urban communities based on objective need and to remedy patterns of deprivation. The strategy will build on the good work of the 'Neighbourhood Renewal' and 'Renewing Communities' initiatives. This can be taken forward by an incoming Executive.
- The Government will introduce legislation this autumn to establish a Victims' Commissioner for Northern Ireland.
- We will establish a forum on a Bill of Rights and convene its inaugural meeting in December 2006.
- The Government believes in a Single Equality Bill and will work rapidly to make the necessary preparations so that legislation can be taken forward by an incoming Executive at an early date.
- The Government will introduce an Irish Language Act reflecting on the experience of Wales and Ireland and work with the incoming Executive to enhance and protect the development of the Irish language.
- The Government firmly believes in the need to enhance and develop the Ulster Scots language, heritage and culture and will support the incoming Executive in taking this forward.
- We have begun consulting with the Parties on terms of reference for a review which will examine all the issues around parading in Northern Ireland with a view to developing an agreed long term strategy.
- The Government will work with business, trade unions and ex-prisoner groups to produce guidance for employers which will reduce barriers to employment and enhance re-integration of former prisoners.
- The 50/50 recruitment arrangements to the PSNI will lapse when the Patten target for Catholic officers has been achieved.
- We will bring forward in the next parliamentary session legislation to give the Northern Ireland Human Rights Commission additional powers. These will include the power to compel evidence, access places of detention and rely on the Human Rights Act when bringing judicial proceedings in its own name. We will publish the Government's response to the consultation carried out on these matters last year, before 24 November.

- We will bring forward separate legislation before the end of 2006 to reform entry requirements to ensure access for EU nationals to posts in the Civil Service.
- During the autumn we will facilitate a meeting of the Northern Ireland Grand Committee in Northern Ireland.

ANNEX C

FINANCIAL PACKAGE FOR THE NEWLY RESTORED EXECUTIVE

All of the parties have raised the question of the future economic progress of Northern Ireland. The Governments are committed to working with all the parties to establish a platform for long-term economic stability and reform necessary for a newly restored Executive. In the context of restoration of the institutions, the Governments remain committed to ensuring the Executive has the capacity to provide quality public services, to continue the process of necessary reform, to plan for the future, to make the long-term capital investments to underpin the economic transformation of Northern Ireland, as well as bringing long-term benefits for the island as a whole.

In the context of the forthcoming Comprehensive Spending Review, the Chancellor agrees to meet all parties to consider proposals—including those from the Assembly subgroup on economic challenges facing Northern Ireland—that make the most of new opportunities arising from greater peace and stability. We will also consider the potential for further North/South economic cooperation including proposals for joint investment initiatives. In the context of preparations for restoration, both Governments will work with the parties on these issues.

In response to the strongly expressed views of many in the NI community, the British Government will introduce a cap on domestic rates under the new capital values system and will examine the possibility of further rate reliefs for pensioners on lower incomes.

ANNEX D

TIMETABLE FOR IMPLEMENTATION OF THE ST ANDREWS AGREEMENT

13 October:	Governments publish St Andrews agreement. Parties consult, including through the DUP Assembly group, the Sinn Fein Ard Comhairle and other appropriate party bodies, on the St Andrews agreement, and respond by 10 November.
17 October:	New Programme for Government Committee begins regular meetings to agree priorities for new Executive, with parties represented at leadership level.
20/21 November:	Legislation at Westminster to give effect to the St Andrews agreement, including practical changes to the institutions (Annex A).
24 November:	Assembly meets to nominate FM/DFM.
January:	IMC Report.
March:	Endorsement by the electorate of the St Andrews agreement.
14 March:	Members of the Executive nominated by party leaders.
26 March:	Power devolved and d'Hondt run.

Failure to agree to establish the Executive will lead to immediate dissolution of the Assembly, as will failure to agree at any stage, and the Governments will take forward new partnership arrangements on the basis previously announced.

ANNEX E

FUTURE NATIONAL SECURITY ARRANGEMENTS IN NORTHERN IRELAND: PAPER BY THE BRITISH GOVERNMENT

Building on the useful discussions that have already taken place with the parties on the issue, this paper outlines the arrangements that are being put in place for the handling of national security intelligence in Northern Ireland and the accountability measures that will be in place, once lead responsibility passes to the Security Service in late 2007. The change will bring Northern Ireland into line with the rest of the UK, to provide a consistent and co-ordinated response to the threat from terrorism, including from international terrorist groups such as Al Quaeda. It also, since national security is an excepted matter, prepares the way for devolution.

The British Government is confident the new arrangements will bring real benefits to both the Security Service and the PSNI. A key driver behind the practical arrangements currently being devised and tested is the unique interface in NI between national security and serious/organised crime. The new arrangements preserve and build upon the Patten reforms: that is a fundamental principle of these changes.

New integrated working arrangements—the first such approach in the UK—will strengthen the PSNI's criminal intelligence capability. This is because PSNI officers will be co-located with Security Service personnel and will work in a variety of roles including as intelligence analysts/advisors and for the purpose of translating intelligence into executive action. These arrangements are designed precisely for the purpose of ensuring that intelligence is shared and properly directed within the PSNI. Integration of personnel in this way is an essential protection against concerns that some intelligence would not be visible to the PSNI.

The Security Service has no executive policing responsibilities, even in countering threats to national security. While the Security Service will provide the strategic direction, the PSNI's contribution to countering terrorism will remain absolutely central. In all circumstances, including where the interest is national security related it will be the role of the PSNI to mount executive policing operations, make arrests and take forward prosecutions under the direction of the Public Prosecution Service.

There will be no diminution in police accountability. The role and responsibilities of the Policing Board and the Police Ombudsman vis a vis the Police will not change. Police officers working with the Security Service in whatever capacity will remain accountable to the Chief Constable and under the oversight of the Police Ombudsman. The Security Service and the Ombudsman's office have been working together to agree arrangements for the Ombudsman's access to sensitive information held by the Service, where this becomes necessary for the discharge of the Ombudsman's statutory duties. The Service has already disclosed sensitive information to the Ombudsman's office in a number of cases. It is important to ensure that comprehensive accountability mechanisms are in place for all aspects of policing in Northern Ireland, and we will continue to discuss these matters with the parties.

The Government will publish in due course high level versions of the MoUs currently being developed between the Security Service and the PSNI and others, as appropriate

The great majority of national security agents will be run by the PSNI, under the strategic direction of the Service, mirroring the arrangements the Service has with the police in GB. This makes sense in NI in particular because of the interface between serious crime and national security; the police also have the advantage of local knowledge. The Security Service will continue to run directly a small number of agents who are authorised to obtain information in the interests of national security as distinct from countering criminality, where the circumstances make that appropriate. The principles observed by the PSNI and the Security Service in running agents are the same, and are enshrined in the Regulation of Investigatory Powers Act 2000.

The Policing Board will, as now, have the power to require the Chief Constable to report on any issue pertaining to his functions or those of the police service. All aspects of policing will continue to be subject to the same scrutiny as now. To ensure the Chief Constable can be fully accountable for the PSNI's policing operations, the Security Service will participate in briefings to closed sessions of the Policing Board to provide appropriate intelligence background about national security related policing operations.

On policing that touches on national security the Chief Constable's main accountability will be to the Secretary of State, as it is now. The Security Service is fully accountable through existing statutory arrangements and the due processes of Parliament. In addition, three separate Commissioners oversee different elements of covert work in NI: the Intelligence Services Commissioner; the Interception of Communications Commissioner; and the Surveillance Commissioner. Relevant complaints relating to the actions of the intelligence agencies are investigated by the Investigatory Powers Tribunal, a panel comprising senior members of the legal profession. There is also the Parliamentary Intelligence and Security Committee whose remit is to examine the expenditure, administration and policy of the security and intelligence agencies and whose reports are placed before Parliament; the Government has already indicated that it is prepared to consider how the Northern Ireland focus of the Committee might be strengthened.

In summary, a whole range of safeguards will continue in place: the Policing Board's continuing role in ensuring efficient policing; the safeguards embodied in RIPA; the Ombudsman's role in investigating complaints against police officers; Parliament's scrutiny of intelligence matters through the Intelligence and Security Committee; the various Commissioners' oversight of particular types of covert operations; and the Investigatory Powers Tribunal's remit to deal with complaints. Not only are these arrangements comprehensive, they are as transparent as the sensitivity of the issues allows.

Further to reinforce this comprehensive set of safeguards, the Government confirms that it accepts and will ensure that effect is given to the five key principles which the Chief Constable has identified as crucial to the effective operation of the new arrangements, viz:

a. All Security Service intelligence relating to terrorism in Northern Ireland will be visible to the PSNI.

b. PSNI will be informed of all Security Service counter terrorist investigations and operations relating to Northern Ireland.
c. Security Service intelligence will be disseminated within PSNI according to the current PSNI dissemination policy, and using police procedures.
d. The great majority of national security CHISs in Northern Ireland will continue to be run by PSNI officers under existing police handling protocols.
e. There will be no diminution of the PSNI's ability to comply with the HRA or the Policing Board's ability to monitor said compliance.

In that connection, the Government believes that the Policing Board's Human Rights advisers should have a role in human rights proofing the relevant protocols that will underpin the Chief Constable's five key principles, and also in confirming that satisfactory arrangements are in place to implement the principles. The detailed operation of this safeguard will require further consideration.

As far as the employment of former police officers by the Security Service under these new arrangements is concerned, there will be no bar on former officers serving in the new organisation, but for operational reasons there will be a need for such individuals to have working experience of the arrangements under which the PSNI currently operate. The same rigorous vetting procedures will apply to them as they do to all new staff joining the service.

Irish Republican Army Statement of 28 July 2005

The leadership of *Oglaigh na hEireann* has formally ordered an end to the armed campaign.

This will take effect from 4pm this afternoon.

All IRA units have been ordered to dump arms.

All Volunteers have been instructed to assist the development of purely political and democratic programmes through exclusively peaceful means.

Volunteers must not engage in any other activities whatsoever.

The IRA leadership has also authorised our representative to engage with the IICD [Independent International Commission on Decommissioning] to complete the process to verifiably put its arms beyond use in a way which will further enhance public confidence and to conclude this as quickly as possible.

We have invited two independent witnesses, from the Protestant and Catholic churches, to testify to this.

The Army Council took these decisions following an unprecedented internal discussion and consultation process with IRA units and Volunteers.

We appreciate the honest and forthright way in which the consultation process was carried out and the depth and content of the submissions.

We are proud of the comradely way in which this truly historic discussion was conducted. The outcome of our consultations show very strong support among IRA Volunteers for the Sinn Fein peace strategy.

There is also widespread concern about the failure of the two governments and the unionists to fully engage in the peace process.

This has created real difficulties. The overwhelming majority of people in Ireland fully support this process.

They and friends of Irish unity throughout the world want to see the full implementation of the Good Friday Agreement.

Notwithstanding these difficulties our decisions have been taken to advance our republican and democratic objectives, including our goal of a united Ireland.

We believe there is now an alternative way to achieve this and to end British rule in our country. It is the responsibility of all Volunteers to show leadership, determination and courage.

We are very mindful of the sacrifices of our patriot dead, those who went to jail, Volunteers, their families and the wider republican base.

We reiterate our view that the armed struggle was entirely legitimate. We are conscious that many people suffered in the conflict.

There is a compelling imperative on all sides to build a just and lasting peace. The issue of the defence of nationalist and republican communities has been raised with us.

There is a responsibility on society to ensure that there is no re-occurrence of the pogroms of 1969 and the early 1970s.

There is also a universal responsibility to tackle sectarianism in all its forms.

The IRA is fully committed to the goals of Irish unity and independence and to building the Republic outlined in the 1916 Proclamation.

We call for maximum unity and effort by Irish republicans everywhere. We are confident that by working together Irish republicans can achieve our objectives.

Every Volunteer is aware of the import of the decisions we have taken and all *Oglaigh* are compelled to fully comply with these orders.

There is now an unprecedented opportunity to utilise the considerable energy and goodwill which there is for the peace process.

This comprehensive series of unparalleled initiatives is our contribution to this and to the continued endeavours to bring about independence and unity for the people of Ireland.

Index